Organic Chemistry

HARPERCOLLINS COLLEGE OUTLINE

Organic Chemistry

Michael Smith, Ph.D.
University of Connecticut

HarperPerennial
A Division of HarperCollins*Publishers*

An American BookWorks Corporation Production
Project Manager: William Hamill
Editor: Swayze Editorial

Library of Congress Cataloging-in-Publication Data

Smith, Michael.   1946 Oct. 17-
  Organic chemistry / Michael Smith.
    p.   cm.   —   (HarperCollins college outline)
  Includes index.
  ISBN: 0-06-467126-7 (pbk.)   :
  1. Chemistry, Organic.   I. Title.   II. Series.
QD251.2.S56   1993
547—dc20   92-53293
                                                              CIP

96 97 ABW/RRD 10 9 8 7 6 5

Contents

Preface

Although organic chemistry is defined as the chemistry of carbon, a typical two semester course focuses on the bonding of carbon compounds as well as functional group manipulation and formation of carbon-carbon bonds for those molecules. Perhaps the most difficult part of an Organic Chemistry course is discovering what one does not know, before the exam. The only way to do this is to use study problems (homework) to test yourself. For any given textbook, there are only so many problems of a given type for a given subject. The purpose of this Organic Chemistry review book is to provide a "book of questions" which can be used as an adjunct to most currently used Organic Chemistry textbooks. It is filled with both discussion type questions and short answer questions. There are many examples of directly worded "reaction questions" where the student must give the specific structure to a specific reaction. There are also several synthesis type problems.

The book is organized in a manner that roughly parallels the three most popular books currently in use. Rather than using a lengthy discussion followed by some questions, as in other books of this type, the material is taught totally in the form of questions. Several leading, discussion type questions are asked to give the necessary information for any given subject. Other questions build upon this and short answer questions punctuate the information. The book is oriented towards a mechanistic rationale for reactions. Where possible, complete mechanisms are included for pertinent and important reactions, again in the form of discussion type questions.

It is hoped that this book will prove useful to students taking Organic Chemistry for the first time who need practice. It should also be useful for those students who need to "bone up" on Organic Chemistry for pre-medical or pre-pharmacy exams. Graduate students who are studying for preliminary or orientation exams in a chemistry graduate program should also find this book useful. This all-question format should facilitate a "self-guided" tour through or a review of Organic Chemistry and is offered with that goal in mind.

I must thank Fred N. Grayson and Tom Dembofsky of American Book-Works, who initiated this project and who have seen it through to completion. Mr. Bill Hamill is responsible for actually putting the manuscript into book form and deserves many thanks for that, as does Ms. Jennifer Dowling for translating manuscript drawings into book form.

The manuscript for this book was typed on a MacIntosh IIci® computer using MicroSoft Word 5.1™ (registry number 00-034-0510-96113129). All manuscript structures were drawn using CSC ChemDraw Plus™ (Serial Number 40413) and the proton NMR structures in Chapter 17 were generated using Beaker 2.1™ (ISBN 0-534-15973-7). The infrared diagrams were taken from the Sadtler Indices. The picture of the Dean-Stark apparatus in the end-of-chapter problems was drawn with Canvas 3.1™ (User Number 4032160730).

Finally, I must thank my wife Sarah and my son Steven for their patience, understanding and support during the preparation of this manuscript.

Michael B. Smith
Storrs, Connecticut
October, 1992

1

Structure and Bonding

This chapter will introduce the carbon atom and the covalent bonds that join carbon atoms together in organic molecules. The most fundamental properties of atoms and of covalent bonds will be introduced, including hybridization, electronic structure, molecular orbital theory and the shape of organic molecules. The fundamental causes of the physical properties exhibited by organic molecules will also be introduced.

1.1. ATOMIC ORBITALS

WHAT IS THE WORKING STRUCTURE OF AN ATOM?

Each atom of a given element possesses a fixed number of protons, neutrons and electrons. The protons and neutrons comprise the nucleus and the electrons are located in discreet energy levels (quanta) from the nucleus. The nucleus is electrically positive and electrons are negatively charged. When carbon forms a covalent bond (two electrons are in each bond, represented by C-X, where X is any atom; see section 2.3), it uses electrons from the outermost shell. These electrons are conveniently described by their "shape" and distance relative to the nucleus.

WHAT ARE ATOMIC ORBITALS AND WHAT ARE MOLECULAR ORBITALS?

The space occupied by electrons is described by the term orbital. Different orbitals are described by their distance from the nucleus (the energy required to 'hold' the electron) as well as the three-dimensional configuration of their electrons. If the electrons are associated with the atom of a free element, they are said to be in *atomic orbitals*. Once bonds have been formed, the atomic elements become part of molecules, and the electronic positions are described by *molecular orbitals*.

s and p Orbitals

WHAT IS AN S-ORBITAL?

For the elements hydrogen (H) and Helium (He), electrons reside in a *spherically symmetrical orbital* at a discreet distance from the nucleus. This corresponds to the first quantum level. *All spherically symmetrical orbitals are referred to as s-orbitals* and have the general shape of *1.1*. The 1s-orbital represents the first energetically favorable level where electrons can be held by the nucleus. This results from the electrostatic attraction of the positive nucleus and the negatively charged electron(s).

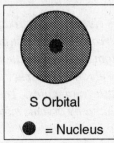

S Orbital

● = Nucleus

Fig. 1.1

WHAT IS A P ORBITAL?

Beginning in the second row, there is a second energy level for elements. First there is a 2s orbital, but there is also a 2p level composed of three identical p orbitals. A p-orbital is 'dumbbell' shaped (as in *1.2*) with electron density on either side of the nucleus (the point of zero electron density is between the electron lobes).

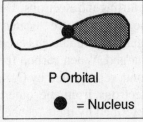

P Orbital

● = Nucleus

Fig. 1.2

WHAT IS A NODE?

A node is a point of zero electron density.

HOW MANY ORBITALS ARE THERE IN EACH VALENCE SHELL?

Each orbital can hold two electrons. For the first valence shell containing H and He, there is one s-orbital. For the next valence shell (containing B, C, N, O, F), there is one 2s orbital, but three 2p orbitals. The 2p orbitals have different spatial orientations, correlated with the x, y and z axes of a three dimensional coordinate system. The three p orbitals are, therefore, p_x, p_y and p_z.

Electron Configuration

WHAT IS ELECTRONIC CONFIGURATION?

As each orbital (energy level) occurs further from the nucleus, the electrons are held less tightly. Each orbital can hold a maximum of two electrons (as in *1.3*) and each energy level will contain different numbers of electrons (two electrons for s orbitals, six electrons for p orbitals and ten electrons for d orbitals). Orbitals will fill from lowest energy to highest energy orbital, according to the order shown in *1.4*.

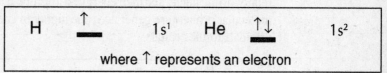

Fig. 1.3

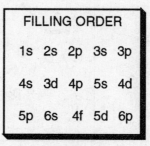

Fig. 1.4

HOW ARE THE ORBITALS FILLED WITH ELECTRONS?

Orbitals 'fill' according to the Aufbau Principle: each orbital in a sublevel s, p or d will contain one electron before any contains two, as with H and He in 1.3. Orbitals containing two electrons they will have opposite spin quantum numbers (they are said to be spin paired, $\uparrow\downarrow$).

DESCRIBE THE ORDER IN WHICH ORBITALS WILL BE FILLED WITH ELECTRONS THROUGH THE 2P LEVEL.

The order for the 2p orbitals will be $2p_x \rightarrow 2p_y \rightarrow 2p_z \rightarrow 2p_x \rightarrow 2p_y \rightarrow 2p_z$:

$$\underline{\uparrow}\ \_ \quad \rightarrow \underline{\uparrow}\underline{\uparrow}\ \_ \quad \rightarrow \underline{\uparrow}\underline{\uparrow}\underline{\uparrow} \quad \rightarrow \underline{\uparrow\downarrow}\underline{\uparrow}\underline{\uparrow} \quad \rightarrow \underline{\uparrow\downarrow}\underline{\uparrow\downarrow}\underline{\uparrow} \quad \rightarrow \underline{\uparrow\downarrow}\underline{\uparrow\downarrow}\underline{\uparrow\downarrow}$$

Molecular Orbitals

WHAT IS THE DIFFERENCE BETWEEN A MOLECULAR ORBITAL AND AN ATOMIC ORBITAL?

Once two atoms are joined in a covalent bond, their electrons are in a different position relative to the nuclei of the two atoms. This energy level is different from that in the atom, and the pertinent orbitals are referred to as molecular orbitals rather than atomic orbitals.

Linear Combination of Atomic Orbitals

HOW ARE MOLECULAR ORBITALS FORMED FROM ATOMIC ORBITALS?

To form a molecular orbital, a mathematical device known as LCAO (Linear Combination of Atomic Orbitals) is used. Taking diatomic hydrogen (H_2) as an example, the atomic orbitals of two hydrogen atoms are 'mixed' to form the molecular orbitals of H_2 (*1.5*). Each hydrogen atomic orbital (H A.O.) contains one electron in the 1s orbital. Each of these orbitals is at the same energy. When they mix to form the molecular orbital, the electrons are in a 'different' position relative to the nuclei and their energy is different. If two atomic orbitals mix, two molecular orbitals are generated, one higher in energy and one lower than the original atomic orbitals.

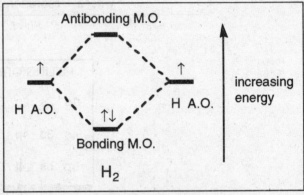

Fig. 1.5

DESCRIBE BONDING AND ANTIBONDING MOLECULAR ORBITALS.

When two molecular orbitals (M.O.) are formed by mixing the atomic orbitals, they are split symmetrically as in *1.5*. The two electrons will go into the lowest available energy level and this will fill before the higher level orbital is filled. The two electrons will be spin paired to minimize energy. A bond requires two electrons, and if the electrons in the lowest molecular orbital are used to form the covalent bond, it is called the *bonding molecular orbital*. The higher orbital does not contain electrons but is the next available quantum level if extra electrons are added to the system, or if a lower energy electron is energetically 'promoted' to the higher level. This potential site of electron density is called the *anti-bonding molecular orbital*. In the ground state (normal energies) the bonding M.O. is filled and the antibonding M.O. is empty.

1.2 BONDING

Ionic Bonding

WHAT IS AN IONIC BOND?

An ionic bond occurs when two atoms are held together by electrostatic forces. Sodium chloride (NaCl), for example, exists in the solid state as Na^+Cl^-.

WHY DOES Na IN NaCl ASSUME A POSITIVE CHARGE?

If the valence electrons for each atom are represented as dots (one dot for each electron), the picture of NaCl will be as that shown below.

$$Na^{+} \quad :\overset{\displaystyle ..}{\underset{\displaystyle ..}{Cl}}:^{-}$$

All the electrons are on chlorine and more are on sodium. There is special stability associated with a filled row (note the Noble gases: He, Ne, etc.). In order for sodium (Na: $1s^2 2s^1$) to achieve a 'filled' shell, it can either lose one electron (Ionization Potential) to mimic the He atom or gain seven electrons (the ability to gain one electron is called Electron Affinity) to mimic the Ne atom. The loss of one electron is much lower in energy than gaining seven. Loss of the negative electron leads to a positive charge (see Formal Charge in section 1.5).

WHY DOES Cl ASSUME A NEGATIVE CHANGE IN NaCl?

Chlorine (Cl: $1s^2 2s^2 2p^6 3s^2 3p^5$) can either gain one electron to mimic the Ne atom or lose seven electrons to mimic the He atom. Clearly, the loss of seven electrons will be very high in energy. For this reason, Cl will gain an electron, leading to a negatively charged atom. The strong electrostatic attraction between the positive sodium and the negatively charged chlorine binds the two atoms together in an ionic bond. The chlorine will be the negative 'pole' since it is the most electronegative atom.

Covalent Bonding — DEFINE A COVALENT BOND.

A covalent bond is usually composed of two electrons that are shared between two atoms. In the case of hydrogen (H_2), this is represented as H:H, where the (:) indicates the presence of two electrons shared between the hydrogen nuclei. This type of bond occurs when the atom cannot easily gain or lose electrons (there is a small electronegativity difference between atoms).

WHAT IS VALENCE?

Valence is usually defined as the number of bonds an atom can form to satisfy the octet rule and remain electrically neutral. This is not to be confused with valence electrons, which are the number of electrons in the outermost shell. In the second row, the valence is the same as 8—the group number (4 for carbon, 3 for nitrogen, 2 for oxygen and 1 for fluorine). Boron is an exception. There are only three electrons and, therefore, the possibility of forming only 3 covalent bonds to remain neutral. The valence of boron is 3 but it is electron deficient and this makes it a Lewis acid.

WHY DOES CARBON HAVE A VALENCE OF FOUR?

With carbon (C $1s^2 2s^2 2p^2$), there are four electrons in the highest valence shell (n=2). The gain of four electrons or the loss of four electrons is prohibitively high in energy. Carbon readily forms bonds with many other atoms, however, including another carbon atom. These bonds are formed by sharing the electrons, as shown by the figures. Each carbon of the structure *1.6* has eight electrons. It brings four from atomic carbon and shares four more (three from three hydrogens and one from another carbon). The second carbon also has eight electron (four from the atom, three shared with hydrogen and one shared with carbon). In a covalent bond, the electrons are mutually shared between the nuclei so each nucleus has eight electrons (a filled shell) around it. This mutual sharing of electrons is also shown for two carbon atoms, where the bond is represented as a line (C-C). The two electrons are equally distributed between the two carbon atoms, as shown in *1.7*. This is shown generically for two atomic nuclei, with the electrons distributed between the nuclei (*1.8*).

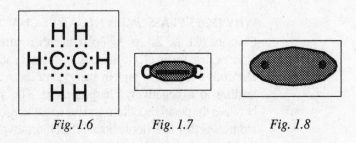

Fig. 1.6   Fig. 1.7   Fig. 1.8

Lewis Electron Dot Formulas

WHAT IS A LEWIS ELECTRON DOT STRUCTURE?

In section 1.2, electrons are shown as dots. When molecules are drawn with all atoms represented as dots (two dots represent a bond), the structure is called a Lewis Electron Dot Formula. In structure *1.6*, the molecule ethane (C_2H_6 = CH_3CH_3) was drawn as its Lewis dot formula.

Polar Covalent Bonds

WHAT IS A POLARIZED COVALENT BOND?

When a bond is formed between two atoms that are not identical, the electrons do not have to be equally shared. If one atom is more electronegative (electronegativity is the ability of an atom to attract electrons to itself), it will pull a greater share of electrons from the bond. The higher the propensity of that atom to hold electrons results in a 'polarized' covalent bond. As shown in *1.9*, the electron density is distorted towards one of the atoms, always the most electronegative. Since one atom has more electron density, it will have a greater 'negative charge'. The molecule is neutral so there are no ionic charges, but the distortion of electron density leads to a 'partial charge' represented by δ^+ at the atom with the least electron density and δ^- at the atom with the most electron density.

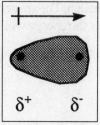

Fig. 1.9

WHAT SYMBOLS ARE USED TO REPRESENT THE DIPOLE OF A POLARIZED COVALENT BOND?

One way to represent this distortion of electrons is with the symbol +→, with the + representing the positive atom and → the negative. The covalent bond is polarized, leading to a dipole moment. Any bond between a less electronegative atom and a more electronegative atom will lead to a polar covalent bond.

WHICH OF THE FOLLOWING ARE POLAR COVALENT BONDS? FOR THE POLARIZED BONDS, IDENTIFY THE NEGATIVE AND POSITIVE POLES.

(a) C-O (b) C-C (c) O-H (d) H-H (e) Br-Br (f) C-N (g) N-N (h) C-Li (i) O-O (j) H-Br (k) Na-Cl

Only those bonds between dissimilar atoms will be polarized, therefore (a), (c), (f), (h) and (j) are polarized covalent. NaCl (k) is an ionic bond because the electronegativity difference is very large. The negative poles will be oxygen in (a) and (c), nitrogen in (f), carbon in (h) [carbon is more electronegative than lithium] and bromine in (j). Note that the positive pole can be a variety of atoms (C, H, Li).

Dipole-Dipole Interactions

WHAT IS VAN DER WAAL'S ATTRACTION?

When there are no polarizing atoms in the molecules, the only attraction between molecules results from the electrons of one molecule being attracted to the positive nuclei of atoms in another molecule. This is known as *Van der Waal's attraction* (sometimes called *London forces*).

WHAT CAUSES TWO MOLECULES WITH C-O OR C=O BONDS TO ASSOCIATE TOGETHER IN THE LIQUID PHASE?

When two molecules, each with a polarized covalent bond, come into close proximity, the charges for one bond will be influenced by the charge on the adjacent molecule. In the example shown (*1.10*), the negative oxygen of one molecule is attracted to the positive carbon of the second molecule. Likewise, the positive carbon of that molecule is attracted to the negative oxygen of the other. This intermolecular electrostatic interaction is referred to as a *dipole-dipole interaction*. The net result of this interaction is that these molecules will be associated together and some energy will be required to disrupt this association. The greater the dipole moment, the stronger the interaction and the greater the energy will be required to disrupt the molecules.

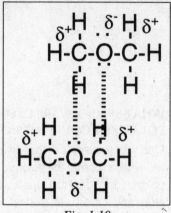

Fig. 1.10

WHAT IS A HETEROATOM?

A heteroatom is defined as any atom other than carbon or hydrogen. Examples are O, N, S, P, Cl, Br, F, Mg, Na, etc.

HOW DOES THE PHYSICAL SIZE OF THE GROUPS ATTACHED TO THE HETEROATOM INFLUENCE DIPOLE-DIPOLE INTERACTIONS?

The electrostatic interaction of the two dipolar molecules is diminished by the physical size imposed by the carbon groups. The groups compete for the same space (*steric hindrance*) and repel each other, counteracting the electrostatic attraction to some extent.

Hydrogen Bonds

WHY IS THE ATTRACTION BETWEEN TWO GROUPS BEARING AN O-H GROUP STRONGER THAN BETWEEN TWO GROUPS BEARING A C=O GROUP?

When hydrogen forms a polar covalent bond with heteroatoms (atoms other than carbon or hydrogen, the most common are O–H, N–H, S–H), the hydrogen takes the δ^+ charge of the dipole. Since the classical Brønsted acid is H^+, a polarized hydrogen in O–H can be considered somewhat acidic since it has some positive character. This will be discussed in sections 11.4 and 14.3. The increased acidity and bond polarity leads to a stronger interaction with a negative heteroatom when brought into close proximity to a positive polarized hydrogen. This interaction is significantly stronger than a normal dipole-dipole interaction, and is referred to as a *hydrogen bond, 1.11*. The space occupied by an oxygen and an hydrogen is significantly less than that observed with the carbon groups (see structure *1.10*). Since the steric hindrance is less, the electrostatic interaction dominates, and is much stronger, and thus the hydrogen bond is stronger.

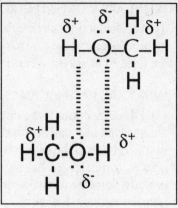

Fig. 1.11

1.3 HYBRIDIZATION

Molecular Orbital Theory

GIVE A BRIEF WORKING DEFINITION OF MOLECULAR ORBITAL THEORY AS IT IS APPLIED TO SIMPLE COVALENT BONDS.

When two atoms combine to form a covalent bond, the atomic orbitals of each atom are combined to form a molecular orbital. The electrons in each atomic orbital are transferred from energy levels near the atom to the space between the nuclei of the bonded atoms. A useful device for tracing this process is called Molecular Orbital Theory. In its simplest version, the atomic orbitals of each 'free' atom are mixed to form molecular orbitals. This was mentioned in section 1.1 using the Linear Combination of Molecular Orbitals with H_2 given as an example. For molecules containing more electrons than hydrogen, and for those containing electrons in other than s orbitals, the diagram is more complex.

GIVE THE MOLECULAR ORBITAL DIAGRAM FOR DIATOMIC CARBON (C-C).

Atomic carbon has an electronic configuration $1s^2 2s^2 2p^2$. The molecular orbital diagram is shown in *1.12*.

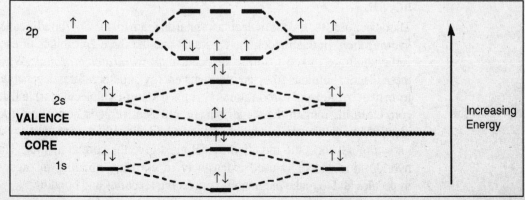

Fig. 1.12

WHAT ARE 'CORE' ELECTRONS?

The molecular orbitals resulting from combining the 1s electrons are so close to the nucleus that they are too tightly bound to share in a covalent bond. These are referred to as *core electrons* and *are not involved in covalent bonding*.

WHAT ARE VALENCE ELECTRONS?

Only those electrons in the outermost electronic shells (*the valence electrons*) are involved in covalent bonds. In the case of carbon-carbon single bonds, the two 2s orbitals combine to give two molecular orbitals. The three identical p orbitals (orbitals that have the same energy are referred to as *degenerate orbitals*) combine to give six molecular orbitals. The total number of orbitals remains constant, but the molecular orbitals are split into high energy and low energy components. The electrons cannot occupy the same energy in the molecule as they do in the atom. Since the energies must be different and since each orbital set cannot be of the same energy, one is higher and one is lower in energy relative to the original atomic orbitals. The orbitals are symmetrically split, as shown.

sp³ Hybridization

EXPLAIN WHY THE MOLECULAR ORBITAL DIAGRAM FOR DIATOMIC CARBON IS INCORRECT.

The molecular orbital diagram for carbon (C–C bond) given above suggests that bonding should be of several types. The 2s molecular orbitals combine to form one type of bond; the p orbitals combine to form another type of bond, and there appear to be unshared electrons in the orbitals. *This is not correct*. In fact, each carbon atom forms four identical bonds to other carbon atoms or to hydrogen atoms. The molecular orbital diagram does *not* predict the correct bonding. A new model is required. In this new model, it is recognized that all the bonds are equal in the final molecule. This requires four identical bonds in the valence shell of carbon.

WHAT IS THE HYBRIDIZATION MODEL FOR A CARBON–CARBON BOND?

The device used to 'fix' the molecular orbital diagram for the C–C bond is called *hybridization*. In this model, the 2s orbital and the three 2p orbitals of each carbon atom are 'mixed' to form four identical *sp³ hybrid atomic orbitals*. When these identical orbitals (they are the same energy and, therefore, degenerate) from two 'hybridized' carbon atoms are mixed to form a molecular orbital, the core electrons remain the same, but the covalent orbitals now show four identical bonds (two electrons per bond) as in *1.13*. Since the correct answer was known in advance, the modified model must give the correct answer. This hybridization model is used extensively to correlate bonding in organic molecules and to make predictions concerning reactions and bonding.

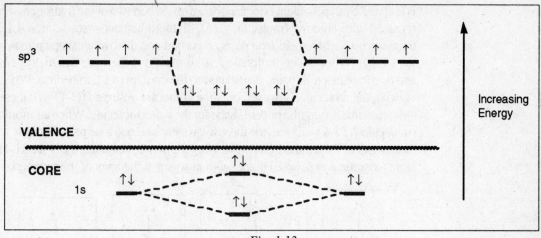

Fig. 1.13

1.4. VSEPR MODEL AND MOLECULAR GEOMETRY

Unshared Electrons ## WHAT IS THE VSEPR MODEL?

All molecules are three dimensional, of course, and a useful model that will predict the general shape of a given molecule is the *Valence Shell Electron Pair Repulsion* (*VSEPR*) model. In this model there are two key components: (1) the geometry around molecules bonded to carbon, oxygen and nitrogen are assumed to be tetrahedral (carbon forms a tetrahedral array of atoms around each carbon) and (2) electron pairs occupy space and are counted as 'groups'.

USE THE VSEPR MODEL TO PREDICT THE SHAPE OF COVALENT MOLECULES.

The electrons in each bond around carbon will repel (like charges repel), but the bonds are connected to a central loci (the carbon atom) and the four atoms or groups attached to carbon cannot separate. The most efficient spatial arrangement that minimizes electronic repulsion is to put each atom or group at the corner of a regular tetrahedron (bond angles are 109°28').

USE THE VSEPR MODEL TO PREDICT THE THREE-DIMENSIONAL SHAPE OF CH_4, CH_2Cl_2, H_2O AND NH_3.

In structure *1.14*(this molecule is named methane—see section 2.1) the four hydrogen atoms are distributed to the corners of a regular tetrahedron. There are no unshared electron pairs on the carbon and the 'shape' of the entire molecule is dictated by the covalent bonds, *tetrahedral*. When two of the hydrogens are replaced with chlorine (molecule *1.15*), dichloromethane—see section 4.1), there are no unshared electron pairs on carbon and the overall shape remains tetrahedral. When water (molecule *1.16*) is analyzed, there are two hydrogens and two lone electron pairs, distributed to the corners of a tetrahedron. When viewing the molecule, however, only the atoms are observed (H–O–H); these atoms assume an angular or *bent* shape for the water molecule. When ammonia (molecule *1.17* is analyzed, the three hydrogens and one lone pair distribute to the corners of the tetrahedron. On viewing the *atoms*, however, the N–H–H–H atoms assume a *pyramidal* shape, with nitrogen at the apex of the pyramid.

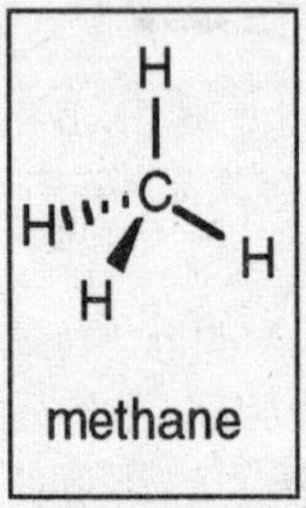

| methane | dichloromethane | water | ammonia |
| *Fig. 1.14* | *Fig. 1.15* | *Fig. 1.16* | *Fig. 1.17* |

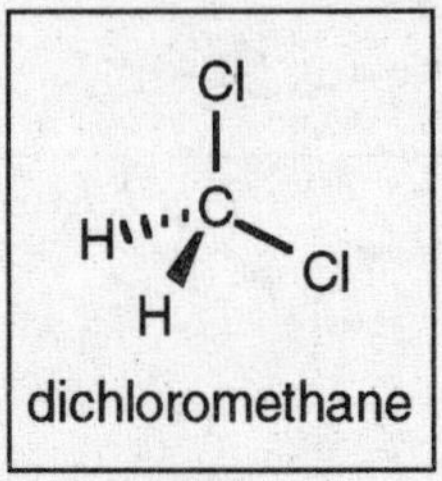

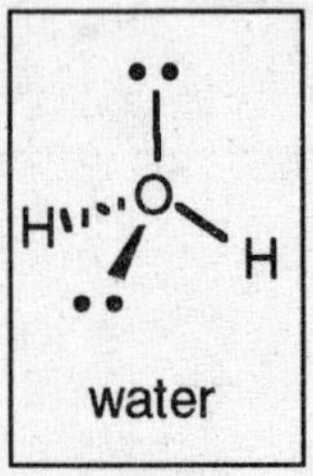

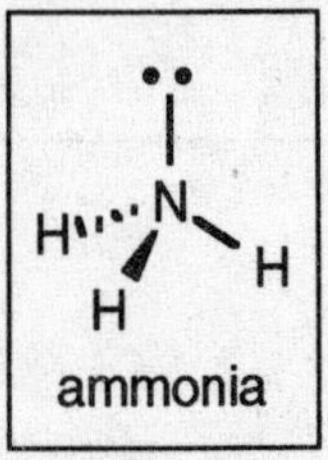

WHAT ARE THE MAIN SHORTCOMINGS OF THE VSEPR MODEL?

This VSEPR model is flawed in some cases since it does not predict differences in shape due to the size of the various atoms and ignores attractive and repulsive forces that are present in some molecules. It does a reasonable job for simple molecules, however, and it usually invoked as the 'first guess' of the shape of a molecule.

Dipole Moment

The VSEPR model can be used to predict the three-dimensional shape of molecules. If the individual dipole moment of each bond in that molecule is superimposed on the VSEPR model, the dipole moment for the molecule can be estimated. The relative polarity (polar vs. non-polar) of the molecule can also be estimated.

HOW CAN THE VSEPR MODEL BE USED TO PREDICT THE DIPOLE MOMENT?

In a molecule such as methane (*1.14*), the C–H bond is not considered to be polarized (the electronegativity of C and H are assumed to be the same, although they are not the same in reality). Since there is no dipole moment for any bond, the dipole moment for the molecule (the sum of all bond dipole moments $= \Sigma$ μ) where μ is the bond moment. For dibromomethane (*1.18*), there are two bond moments, along the C–Cl bonds. The negative pole of each bond is the bromine. Since dipole moments are directional, the dipole moment for the *molecule* is the vector sum of all the individual bond moments. The direction of the dipole moment for dibromomethane is, therefore, along a line that bisects the Br–C–

Br angle and will be equal in magnitude to the vectorial sum of the two individual bond moments.

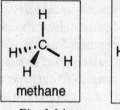

methane

Fig. 1.14

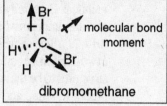

molecular bond moment

dibromomethane

Fig. 1.18

1.5. ISOMERS

Isomerism

One of the important features of carbon that distinguishes it from most other atoms in the Periodic Table is its ability to form covalent bonds to itself, as well as to other carbon atoms. With a valence of four (4), each carbon will form four other bonds. This leads to a very large number of molecules that contain carbon. It also leads to an interesting phenomenon called isomerism.

DEFINE ISOMERS.

Isomers refers to two or more molecules that have the same empirical formula but the individual atoms are connected in different ways, leading to *different molecules*.

Structural Isomers WHAT ARE THE ISOMERS FOR THE FORMULA C_6H_{14}?

Structural isomerism can be illustrated by a molecule with the empirical formula C_6H_{14}. Each carbon will have four bonds and each hydrogen will have one bond. There are, however, four (4) different ways to assemble molecules such that these criteria are satisfied. Some symbolism must be explained. In *1.19*, the six carbons are connected in a linear manner, and adding the hydrogens leads to a molecule that satisfies the empirical formula. A more expedient way to represent this formula is also shown, the *condensed* structure ($CH_3CH_2CH_2CH_2CH_2CH_3$). In this notation, the carbon indicated is connected to two other carbons (one to the right and one to the left) and the two hydrogen atoms to the *right* of that carbon are connected directly to it. All atoms other than carbon that are connected to a given carbon are shown to the right (for *1.21* one of the carbons is to the right but the other is to the left).

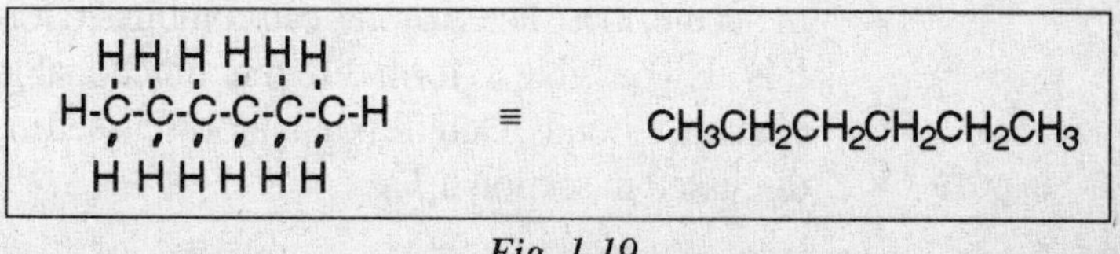

$$H-\underset{H}{\overset{H}{C}}-\underset{H}{\overset{H}{C}}-\underset{H}{\overset{H}{C}}-\underset{H}{\overset{H}{C}}-\underset{H}{\overset{H}{C}}-\underset{H}{\overset{H}{C}}-H \equiv CH_3CH_2CH_2CH_2CH_2CH_3$$

Fig. 1.19

A different structure can also be drawn (*1.20*) where there are five linear carbons with a one-carbon fragment attached at the next-to-last carbon. That single carbon can be connected to the 'right' or to the 'left' but the two structures are identical *since they can be completely superimposed one on the other.* A third structure appears when the single carbon fragment is placed on the 'middle' carbon (in *1.21*). The same structure appears when four carbons are placed in a line and a two-carbon fragment is attached. Examining the five encircled carbons shows the structures to be the same. A fourth molecule (*1.22*) occurs when four carbons are placed in a line and two one-carbon fragments are added. These four different molecules are called *isomers (molecules with the same empirical formula but different points of attachment for the individual atoms).*

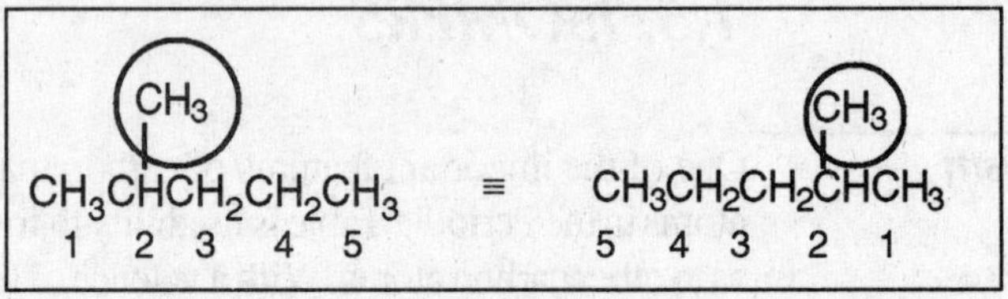
CH3
CH3CHCH2CH2CH3
1 2 3 4 5
≡
CH3
CH3CH2CH2CHCH3
5 4 3 2 1

Fig. 1.20

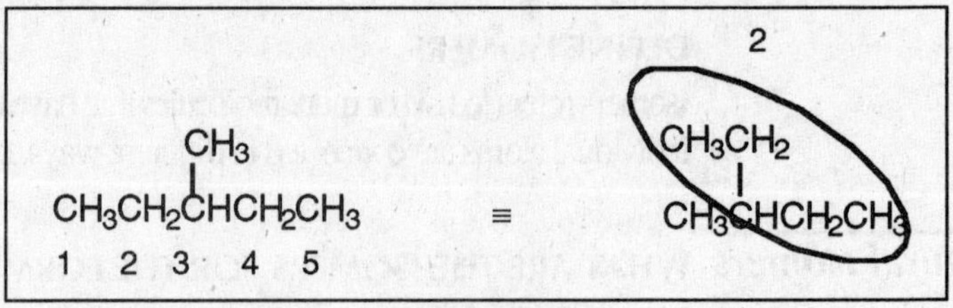
CH3
CH3CH2CHCH2CH3
1 2 3 4 5
≡
2
CH3CH2
CH3CHCH2CH3

Fig. 1.21

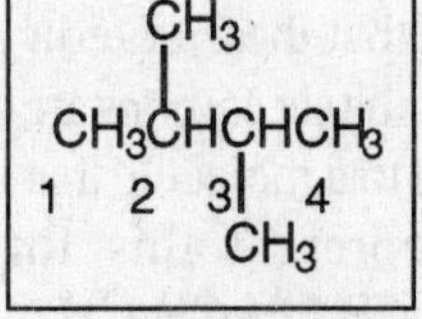
CH3
CH3CHCHCH3
1 2 3 4
CH3

Fig. 1.22

Functional Groups WHAT IS A FUNCTIONAL GROUP?

When atoms other than carbon or hydrogen are incorporated into an organic molecule, these heteroatoms can combine to form different *functional groups.* It is also possible to form different functional groups from carbon atoms that contain pi-bonds. Double bonds are discussed in section 5.1 and triple bonds are discussed in section 6.1.

SHOW THE FUNCTIONAL GROUP FOR THE FOLLOWING: HYDROXYL, THIOL, CARBONYL, CARBOXYL, AMINO, CYANO, ALKENE, ALKYNE AND ETHER.

When these functional groups are incorporated into a molecule they usually form a *class* of molecules that tend to have unique chemical and physical properties. Examples of each type of functional group are obtained by attaching one or more *R* group to each functional group, where R is a generic carbon group. The key functional groups are:

O-H	hydroxyl	S-H	thiol	C = O	carbonyl
H-O-C = O	carboxyl	C-N	amino	C ≡ N	cyano (nitrile)
C = C	alkene	C ≡ C	alkyne	C-O-C	ether

SHOW A GENERIC FORMULA FOR EACH OF THE FOLLOWING: ALCOHOL, THIOL, ALDEHYDE, KETONE, CARBOXYLIC ACID, AMINE, NITRILE, ALKENE, ALKYNE AND ETHER.

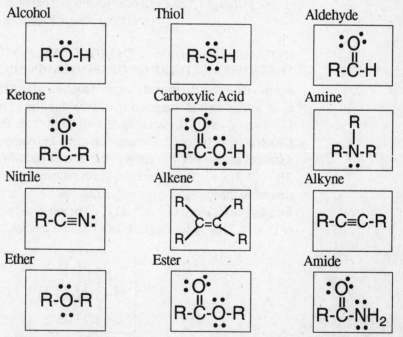

When the functional group OH (hydroxyl) is in a molecule, the class is called *alcohols*. When the carbonyl (C=O) is incorporated, there are two structural variations. The carbonyl can be connected to an hydrogen (H) and a carbon group (R) to give an *aldehyde* or the carbonyl can be connected to two carbon groups (R) to give a *ketone*. If the carbonyl also contains an hydroxyl (–COOH), the molecule is called a *carboxylic acid*. If a trisubstituted nitrogen is in the molecule, the class is called an *amine*. If there is one R group and two hydrogens it is a primary amine (1° = primary). If there are two R groups and one H, it is a secondary (2°) amine and three R groups give a tertiary (3°) amine. The class of compounds that contains a nitrile group (C≡N) is called a *nitrile*. If the molecule contains a carbon-carbon double bond (C=C), it is an *alkene* and if it contains a carbon-carbon triple bond (C≡C) it is an *alkyne*. The class of compounds characterized by a C–O–C bond is the *ether*. These are the major functional groups that will be discussed in this book (a few others will be added later, as the body of information increases and the applications of these groups arise).

Formal Charge

How does one know if a structure is real? Does it have positive or negative charges? These questions can be answered by a technique known as *Formal Charge*. It is based on the number of valence electrons, the number of electrons used to form covalent bonds and the number of unshared electrons.

WHAT IS THE FORMULA FOR DETERMINING FORMAL CHARGE?

The formula is:

$$\text{Formal Charge} = \Omega = (\text{Valence Number}) - (\text{Number Unshared Electrons}) - (\tfrac{1}{2})(\text{Number Shared Electrons})$$

DETERMINE THE FORMAL CHARGE OF EACH ATOM AND ALSO FOR THE ENTIRE MOLECULE OF DIMETHYLAMINE ([CH$_3$]$_2$NH), *1.23*.

For this molecule the formal charge of each atom must be determined. The sum of all atomic formal charge will be the formal charge for the molecule. For C^1, $\Omega = 4 - 0 - (\tfrac{1}{2})(8) = 0$. For C^2, Ω also $= 0$. In all cases, the valence number is the Group number (4 for C). There are no unshared electrons and eight covalently shared electrons. For the nitrogen, the valence (group) number is 5 and Ω is $5 - (0) - (\tfrac{1}{2})(8) = +1$. The formal charge for each hydrogen is $0 [1 - 0 - (\tfrac{1}{2})(2)]$. To determine the formal charge for the molecule Ω_{mol}, the sum of the formal charge for all atoms is used: $\Omega_{mol} = \Sigma (\Omega_{atom})$. For this example, $\Omega_{mol} = 0 + 0 + [8x0] + (+1) = +1$. This molecule exists as a cationic species.

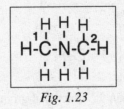

Fig. 1.23

WHAT IS THE CRITERION FOR A 'REAL' MOLECULE BASED ON FORMAL CHARGE?

If a structure is drawn and has a charge of greater than +2 or less than -2, that structure is likely to be very high in energy and should be questioned. For the molecules encountered in the first organic course, it is very unusual for a molecule to exist as anything but a neutral compound (formal charge = 0), a mono-cation (formal charge of +1) or a mono-anion (formal charge of –1).

1.6. PHYSICAL PROPERTIES

WHAT IS A PHYSICAL PROPERTY?

A physical property is a parameter associated with a pure molecule that is unique and assists in the identification of that molecule. Examples are dipole moment, polarity, boiling point, melting point, adsorbtivity, refractive index and solubility. While some of these physical properties may overlap with other similar or related molecules, it is highly unusual for *all* of the physical properties to overlap. This set of physical properties allows each molecule to be identified as an individual.

Boiling Point

WHAT IS THE DEFINITION OF BOILING POINT?

Boiling point is formally defined as the temperature at which the molecules in the gas phase over a liquid phase are at equilibrium.

WHAT ARE THE FACTORS THAT INFLUENCE BOILING POINT?

To get molecules into the gas phase, the intermolecular forces holding them together in the liquid phase must be disrupted. This requires heat. In general, the greater the mass of the molecule, the higher the boiling point but the intermolecular interactions of the molecule are very important. Three examples will illustrate this statement: (a) $CH_3CH_2CH_3$ (propane), (b) $CH_3(C=O)H$ (acetaldehyde) and (c) CH_3OH (methanol). In case (a) there are no dipole interactions and the only intermolecular forces are Van der Waal's forces (sometimes called London forces). These are quite weak and the boiling point of propane is –42.1°C for a molecular weight of 44.10. For case (b), the polarized C=O bond leads to a much stronger intermolecular interaction where the dipole-dipole interactions bind the molecules together. It takes more energy to disrupt these interactions and the boiling point is 20.2°C for a molecular weight of 44.05. There is no increase in weight to account for the 62.3°C increase in temperature required to boil acetaldehyde. When methanol in case (c) is examined, the boiling point of 64.7°C for a molecular weight of 32.04 is far higher than expected. This is due to the hydrogen bonding interactions that are possible, which are stronger than the dipole interactions found in acetaldehyde.

Melting Point

WHAT IS THE DEFINITION OF MELTING POINT?

Melting point is defined as the temperature at which the molecules in the solid phase are in equilibrium with those in the liquid phase.

WHAT FACTORS INFLUENCE MELTING POINT?

An increase in molecular weight often leads to an increase in melting point. The most important feature of a molecule, however, is more difficult to describe. The more symmetrical a molecule, the higher the melting point. Conversely, the more amorphous a molecule, the lower the melting point. If we compare pentane ($CH_3CH_2CH_2CH_2CH_3$) with 2,2-dimethylpropane (see section 2.4—$(CH_3)_4C$), the melting points are $-129.7°C$ for pentane and $-16.6°C$ for dimethylpropane. The latter molecule is more compact and will 'fit' into a crystal structure better than the 'floppy' linear molecule pentane. This enhanced 'packing' leads to a higher melting point.

Solubility

WHAT IS SOLUBILITY?

Solubility is the ability of one molecule (a solid, a liquid or a gas) to dissolve into another molecule that is in the liquid state.

HOW DOES SOLUBILITY GIVE INFORMATION ABOUT THE STRUCTURE OF A MOLECULE?

The old axiom 'like dissolves like' can be used with remarkable accuracy. In general, non-polar molecules will dissolve well in non-polar liquids such as hydrocarbons but not in polar liquids such as water. Conversely, a polar molecule will not dissolve in a non-polar liquid but will dissolve in a polar liquid. If a molecule contains one or more C–heteroatom bonds (and the net dipole moment is not zero) it is considered to be polar. If it contains no polarized bonds it is considered to be non-polar. There are exceptions to this latter statement that use the qualifying statement for the heteroatom case. A molecule such as CCl_4 has a net dipole moment of zero for the molecule and is non-polar. The actual test of polarity (and usually solubility) is, therefore, the dipole moment for the molecule. There are degrees of polarity and degrees of solubility. Molecules that undergo extensive hydrogen bonding are very polar and very soluble in polar liquids such as water. A molecule with a small dipole (CH_3Cl) will be less polar than one with more dipole interactions ($CHCl_3$) and this will be reflected in partial solubilities in polar solvents but some solubility in non-polar solvents. This is a difficult property to quantify.

*T*his chapter has provided the most fundamental tools of Organic Chemistry. In the following chapters these tools will be applied to the many functional groups that comprise organic molecules and their reactions.

END OF CHAPTER PROBLEMS

1. Describe a 3s orbital and a 3p orbital.
2. What is the difference between a $2p_x$ and a $2p_y$ orbital?
3. Give the electronic configuration for each of the following: O, F, Cl, S, Si.

4. Identify each of the following as having an ionic bond or a covalent bond. (a) K–Cl (b) Na-C$\equiv$N (c) H_3C–Br (d) H_2N–H (e) H_2N–Na (f) HO-Na (g) HO-H.

5. Give the number of covalent bonds each atom can form an remain electrically neutral. (a) C (b) N (c) F (d) B (e) O.

6. Why is BF_3 considered to be a Lewis acid?

7. Which of the following bonds has the greatest δ^- charge? C–C, C–N, C–O, C–F.

8. Which of the following has the highest boiling point? Explain.

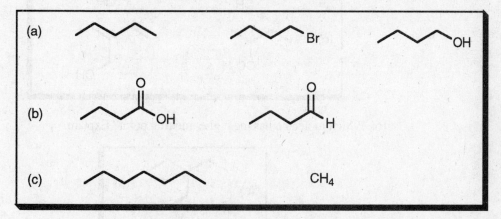

9. Identify the valence electrons in each of the following (also identify the atom involved). (a) $1s^2 2s^2 2p^3$ (b) $1s^2 2s^2 2p^6 3s^1$ (c) $1s^2$ (d) $1s^2 2s^2 2p^6 3s^2 3p^3$

10. Predict the shape of each of the following: (a) CH_3OCH_3 (b) Cl_2CH c) CH_3OH (d) $NH(CH_3)_2$.

11. Indicate the direction of the dipole moment on the VSEPR model for each of the following: (a) CH_3OCH_3 (b) Cl_2CH (c) CH_3OH (d) NH_3 (e) CHBrCl.

12. Draw eight different isomers for each of the following, using condensed structures: (a) C_8H_{18} (b) C_7H_{16}.

13. What is the functional group identified with each of the following?: (a) alcohol (b) ketone (c) alkyne (d) aldehyde.

14. Determine the formal charge for all atoms in each molecule. Calculate the formal charge for each *molecule*.

15. Indicate which molecule has the higher boiling point in each of the following pairs. In each case explain your answer.

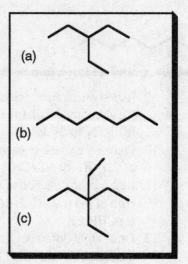

16. Which molecule has the higher melting point? Explain.

2

Alkanes

In this chapter the most basic of organic molecules, the alkanes, will be discussed. Alkanes are molecules that contain only carbon and hydrogen connected by single covalent bonds. The method for naming alkanes will be introduced, as well as their chemical and physical properties.

2.1. DEFINITION AND BASIC NOMENCLATURE

WHAT IS THE DEFINITION OF AN ALKANE?

An alkane is a hydrocarbon (composed of only carbon and hydrogen) that possesses the most simple empirical formula for organic molecules that do not contain a functional group. All alkanes have the general formula C_nH_{2n+2}.

WHAT IS THE GENERAL APPROACH TO NAMING ALKANES?

C_1	CH_4	*methane*	C_{11}	$CH_3(CH_2)_9CH_3$	*undecane*
C_2	CH_3CH_3	*ethane*	C_{12}	$CH_3(CH_2)_{10}CH_3$	*dodecane*
C_3	$CH_3CH_2CH_3$	*propane*	C_{13}	$CH_3(CH_2)_{11}CH_3$	*tridecane*
C_4	$CH_3(CH_2)_2CH_3$	*butane*	C_{14}	$CH_3(CH_2)_{12}CH_3$	*tetradecane*
C_5	$CH_3(CH_2)_3CH_3$	*pentane*	C_{15}	$CH_3(CH_2)_{13}CH_3$	*pentadecane*
C_6	$CH_3(CH_2)_4CH_3$	*hexane*	C_{16}	$CH_3(CH_2)_{14}CH_3$	*hexadecane*
C_7	$CH_3(CH_2)_5CH_3$	*heptane*	C_{17}	$CH_3(CH_2)_{15}CH_3$	*heptadecane*
C_8	$CH_3(CH_2)_6CH_3$	*octane*	C_{18}	$CH_3(CH_2)_{16}CH_3$	*octadecane*
C_9	$CH_3(CH_2)_7CH_3$	*nonane*	C_{19}	$CH_3(CH_2)_{17}CH_3$	*nonadecane*
C_{10}	$CH_3(CH_2)_8CH_3$	*decane*	C_{20}	$CH_3(CH_2)_{18}CH_3$	*icosane*

Alkanes are named according to a set of rules established by the International Union of Pure and Applied Chemistry, IUPAC). The rules define a prefix that shows the number of carbon atoms and a suffix that defines the functional group. In this case, there is no functional group and the suffix is -ane. The prefixes are based on the Latin numbers for 1–20 that correspond to the number of carbon atoms. In each case, the hydrogens are added to satisfy the valence of four and the C_nH_{2n+2} formula.

WHAT ARE THE GENERAL PHYSICAL PROPERTIES OF ALKANES?

Alkanes are very non-polar molecules and generally insoluble in water or other highly polarized liquids. They have no functional group and, therefore, associate in the liquid phase only by Van der Waal's forces, leading to low boiling points. Once the mass of the alkane is sufficiently large, however, the boiling point also becomes rather high and very large alkanes are solids. In the following list, the first number is the boiling point and that in brackets [ ] is the melting point: propane = -42.1°C [-187.7°C]; pentane = +36.1°C [-129.7°C]; decane = +174.1°C [-29.7°C]; icosane = +343.8°C [+36.4°C].

2.2. STRUCTURAL ISOMERS

WHY IS THE CONCEPT OF ISOMERISM IMPORTANT FOR ALKANES?

Due to the ability to form isomers, there are literally millions of possible alkanes. In section 1.5, the four different isomers of hexane were shown. As the number of carbons increase, the number of constitutional isomers increases dramatically: 9 for C_7H_{16}, 4347 for $C_{15}H_{32}$ and greater than 62×10^9 for $C_{40}H_{82}$.

Since isomers will all be different molecules (4347 for $C_{15}H_{32}$) with different physical properties (boiling points, melting points, solubility, etc.), a system is required to identify (name) each individual molecule and distinguish it from all other isomers. The two rules listed above based on the number of carbons and the suffix defining the alkane group are insufficient. Additional rules must be added.

2.3. IUPAC NOMENCLATURE

WHAT ARE THE IUPAC RULES PERTINENT TO ALKANE NOMENCLATURE?

The following section describes the basic rules of nomenclature for organic molecules. In this chapter, the main focus will be on alkanes. Additional rules will be introduced as each new functional group is discussed.

Basic Rules

The first rule must identify the length of the carbon chain, but a rule must be added to locate the number and type of carbon groups attached to that initial carbon chain. To do this, the carbon chain must be numbered. If we take the four isomers of hexane from section 1.5, the necessity for these rules becomes apparent. In one of these cases, there was a five carbon linear chain with a one carbon group attached to it. The rules required to distinguish this molecule are:

1. Determine the longest continuous chain of carbon atoms and assign the alkane base name (methane → icosane).
2. Number the longest chain such that the substituent (atom or groups attached to the longest chain) receives the lowest possible number.
3. Determine the number of carbon atoms in the substituent and assign a name based on the alkane names, but *drop the -ane ending and add -yl.* A one-carbon substituent is meth*yl*, a two-carbon substituent is eth*yl*, etc.

Always place the substituent in front of the base name (alkane *1.20* is methylpentane, for example) and indicate the position of the substituent with a number. The longest chain is five, which is a pentane. The substituent is a one-carbon fragment (circled), therefore = methyl. Number the pentane chain to give the methyl group the lowest number (2 rather than 4) and this is named 2-methylpentane. With this numbering system, it is now obvious why we labeled these two structures as identical. They not only superimpose, they receive the same name.

WHY IS AN ISOMER OF HEXANE (*1.20*) NAMED AS A PENTANE?

Although there are six carbons, the longest continuous carbon chain is only five carbons and it is, therefore, named as a pentane. Another isomer of hexane (*1.21*) illustrates the versatility of this nomenclature system. This is also a pentane (5 carbons) and the substituent is also a methyl group. The position of the methyl substituent in *1.21* is now different than in *1.20* and it is named 3-methylpentane— a different isomer. The next isomer of hexane raises a slightly different problem. There are two methyl substituents in *1.22* with a four carbon chain.

WHAT HAPPENS WHERE THERE ARE SEVERAL OF THE SAME GROUPS IN THE SAME MOLECULE?

A new rule must be added to deal with this situation.

4. When there are two or more identical substituents, assign each one a number according to its position on the carbon chain and use the prefix di- (two), tri- (three), tetra- (four), penta- (five), etc.

If there are two methyl groups the name will be dimethyl. Four ethyl groups will be tetraethyl. A corollary is necessary for this rule when the substituents are not the same.

(Corollary to Rule 4) When the substituents are different, assign each a number according to its position on the carbon chain and arrange the substituents alphabetically in the final name.

If a methyl and an ethyl group are substituents, the name will be ethylmethyl, as in 6-ethyl-3-methyldecane (draw this structure as a useful exercise). For the hexane isomer *1.22*: The longest continuous chain is four (a butane). The substituents are both one carbon fragments (methyl groups). There are two methyls, therefore it is a dimethylbutane. The lowest *combination* of numbers is 2,3, therefore *1.22* is named 2,3-dimethylbutane.

As noted in this example, the *lowest combination of numbers* is used.

NAME THE SPECIFIC SUBSTITUTED DIHEPTANE (*2.1*) SHOWN.

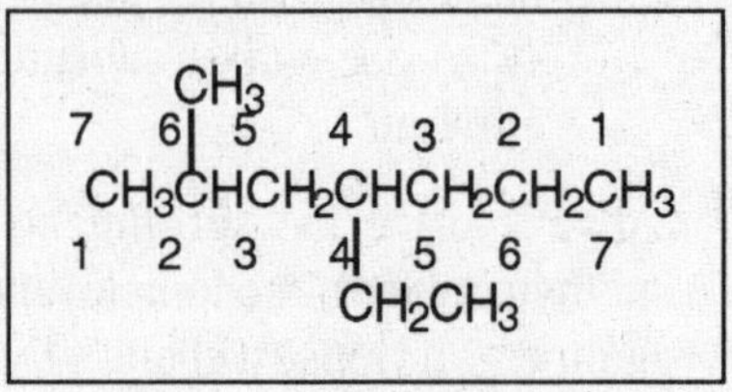

Fig. 2.1

The longest continuous chain is seven (a heptane). There is a one-carbon substituent (methyl) and a two-carbon substituent (ethyl) and this is an ethylmethylheptane. It could be named as a 2, 4 derivative or a 4,6 derivative. The 4, 2 combination is smaller than the 6, 4 combination and *2.1* is named 4-ethyl 2-methylheptane.

There is one case where the heteroatom is treated as a substituent, the halogens.

5. If a halogen is present in the molecule, treat it as a substituent, dropping its -ine ending and adding -o. Fluorine becomes fluoro, chlorine becomes chloro, bromine becomes bromo and iodine becomes iodo.

In many isomeric alkanes, the substituent is much more complex than a simple linear fragment such as methyl, ethyl, etc. The substituent can also be a group or atom other than a carbon group. In general, if a functional group is present, that group dominates the name (*see nomenclature sections in later chapters*)

For carbon substituents containing complex structures, the rule is more complex.

6. If the carbon substituent is complex (not linear), identify the longest continuous chain of the substituent and use rules 1 and 3 from above to determine if it is an ethyl, butyl, hexyl group, etc. Determine the substituents on the substituent chain, number the substituent chain such that the point of attachment to the main chain is always 1, and assign a number to the secondary substituent. Set apart the complex substituent in brackets.

NAME THE MOLECULE 2.2.

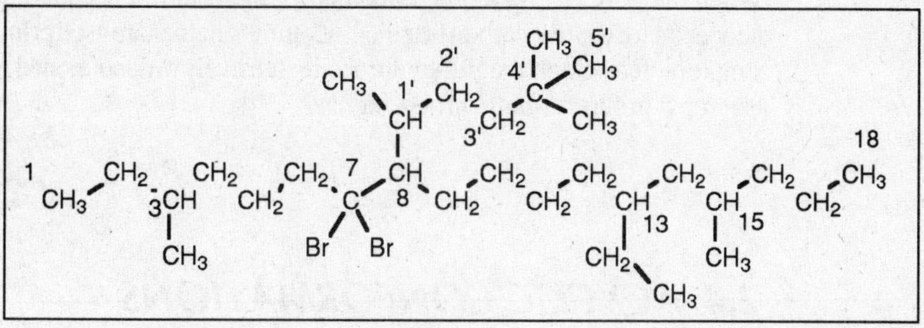

Fig. 2.2

This specific example illustrates both of these last rules. The longest chain is 18 and this is an octadecane. There are two methyl groups at C_3 and C_{15}, two bromines at C_7 and an ethyl (two-carbon fragment) at C_{13}. At C_8, there is a complex substituent that has five carbons from the point of attachment to the octadecane chain ($1' \rightarrow 5'$, and is therefore a pentyl side chain). Substituents are on the side chain (three methyls are at $C_{1'}$ and at $C_{4'}$. This side chain is, therefore (1,4,4-trimethylpentyl), where the primes are dropped for the actual name. The name of this molecule is, therefore, 7,7-dibromo-13-ethyl-3,15-dimethyl-8-(1,4,4-trimethylpentyl)octadecane.

Common Names

WHAT ARE COMMON NAMES?

Since the IUPAC rules are relatively recent, a system of naming organic molecules developed over many years that persists today for some molecular fragments and small molecules. This system of common names is based on the number of methyl groups on a fragment and their relative position.

GIVE THE STRUCTURE FOR ISOPROPYL, ISOBUTYL, ISOPENTYL, SECONDARY BUTYL, SECONDARY PENTYL, TERTIARY BUTYL, TERTIARY PENTYL AND NEOPENTYL.

$-CH(CH_3)_2$	isopropyl	$-CH_2CH(CH_3)_2$	isobutyl
$-CH_2CH_2CH(CH_3)_2$	isopentyl	$-CH(CH_3)CH_2CH_3$	secondary (sec-)butyl
$-CH(CH_3)CH_2CH_2CH_3$	sec-pentyl	$-C(CH_3)_3$	tertiary (tert-, t-) butyl
$-C(CH_3)_2CH_2CH_3$	tert-pentyl	$-CH_2C(CH_3)_3$	neopentyl

DISCUSS THE STRUCTURAL BASIS FOR COMMON NAMES.

The iso- group is used when one carbon at the end of the chain bears a CH and two methyl groups. The total number of carbon atoms dictates the name (isopropyl for three carbons, isobutyl for four carbons, etc.). The *secondary* (or *sec-*) group has a CH, one methyl and an alkyl group (not methyl). This leads to *sec*-butyl for four carbons and *sec*-pentyl for five carbons. The tertiary (*tert-* or just *t-*) group is a carbon with two methyls and one alkyl (which may be methyl). This leads to *t*-butyl for four carbons, *t*-pentyl for five carbons, etc. When the -$C(CH_3)_3$ group is at the end of the chain, it is called neo-, as in neopentyl for the five carbon fragment. Common names are used primarily with simple molecules, although they are used extensively to denote small groups (an isopropyl group, a *t*-butyl group, etc.).

2.4. ACYCLIC CONFORMATIONS

WHAT IS THE RESULT OF A MOLECULE DISSIPATING EXCESS ENERGY BY ROTATION ABOUT A SINGLE COVALENT BOND?

The atoms in a covalent bond can rotate around that bond. This occurs because the molecule must dissipate excess energy (heat) and molecular motion (vibration, rotation, etc) is one way the molecule can do this. When the atoms or groups on a carbon-carbon single bond rotate, the spatial arrangement of the atoms or groups changes with the rotations. These are called *rotamers*.

Rotation Around Carbon Bonds (Ethane)

DISCUSS WHAT OCCURS IF THERE IS ROTATION ABOUT THE CARBON–CARBON BOND OF ETHANE.

If the carbon–carbon bond in ethane is examined for rotamers, it is clear there are virtually an infinite number of possibilities. We will focus attention on two rotamers, the highest energy and the lowest energy, since these will determine the barriers to overall rotational motion of the molecule. In one of these (*2.3*) it appears that one hydrogen on the 'back' carbon bisects the angle formed by H–C–H on the 'front' carbon. The other (*2.4*) is shown at the right and the two hydrogen atoms 'eclipse' each other.

WHY IS *2.3* THE LOWEST ENERGY CONFORMATION?

Structure *2.3* is the lowest energy since the hydrogens are further apart. As the molecule rotates about the carbon-carbon bond, the hydrogen atoms come into close proximity and compete for the same space. They repel and this leads to a high energy interaction that is called a *steric interaction*. These different rotamers are called *conformations*. The low energy structure (*2.3*) is called the *anti* conformation and the high energy structure (*2.4*) is called the *eclipsed* or *syn* conformation.

DRAW THE ANTI- AND ECLIPSED CONFORMATIONS IN NEWMAN PROJECTION.

If these two conformations are turned so that one 'sights' down the carbon–carbon bond, one carbon atom is in front and the other is behind it. The so-called

Newman Projection makes the rear atom a *circle* and the front atom a *dot*, with the three other bonds radiating from these atoms. This view allows the steric interactions and especially the high/low energy conformations to be seen more clearly. The anti conformation is *2.5* with the syn conformation being *2.6*. If the rear carbon of the anti conformation is fixed and the front carbon is rotated 60° clockwise, the syn conformation results. In these Newman projections, the anti conformation clearly shows the hydrogens to be as far apart as possible. Conversely, the hydrogens are very close together in the syn conformation, illustrating the higher energy of this rotamer.

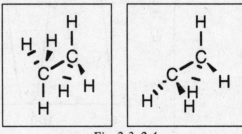

Fig. 2.3, 2.4

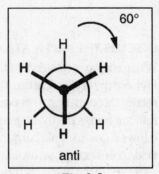

Fig. 2.5

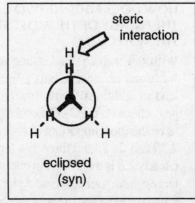

Fig. 2.6

DRAW THE ENERGY DIAGRAM FOR ROTATION OF THE CARBON–CARBON BOND OF ETHANE THROUGH 360°.

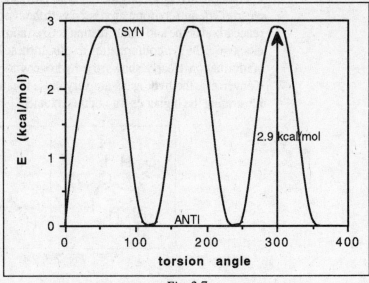

Fig. 2.7

DISCUSS THE IMPLICATIONS OF THIS DIAGRAM.

When ethane is rotated by 60° about the carbon-carbon bond, a series of three high energy (syn) and three low energy (anti) conformations appear as the bond rotates through 360°. This defines the 'free' rotation of ethane. Each time the rotation brings the hydrogens together, an *energy barrier* hinders the rotation (slows it down). This barrier is measured to be 2.9 kcal/mol. Since at least 23 kcal/mol of energy are usually available at ambient temperatures, ethane rotates as shown in the graph and one can *not* isolate or 'freeze' the different rotamers.

Gauche Conformations

HOW DOES ADDING TWO CARBONS (TO GIVE BUTANE) CHANGE THE ENERGY OF THE MOST STERICALLY HINDERED ROTAMER IN THE MOLECULE?

With longer chain alkanes such as butane, the *anti* and *syn* conformations noted for ethane also appear, but the increased steric interactions of the methyl groups lead to additional conformations that must be considered. If the Newman projections for the C_2–C_3 bond are examined, six conformations are considered to be the most important (*2.8–2.13*). There are three *anti* conformations (*2.8, 2.10* and *2.12*) and three *syn* (eclipsed) conformations (*2.9, 2.11* and *2.13*). Clearly *2.8* is the lowest in energy since the methyl groups are *anti* and these largest groups are responsible for the greatest steric interaction. Similarly, *2.11* must be the highest in energy since the methyl-methyl interaction is maximized (this energy barrier was measured to be 6.0 kcal/mole). There are two additional *syn* conformations that are equal in energy (3.4 kcal/mole), *2.9* and *2.13*. These are lower in energy than *2.11* but higher in energy than any of the *anti* conformations. There are two *anti* conformations where the methyl groups are closer together than in *2.8* (*2.10* and *2.12*). These two conformations are referred to as *gauche* conformations and are higher in energy (measured to be 0.8 kcal/mol) than *2.8* but lower in energy than any *syn* conformation. Clearly, the rotation of the C_2–C_3 bond of butane is complex as it rotates 360° but the maximum barrier to rotation is 6 kcal/mole, significantly higher than the 2.9 kcal/mol encountered in ethane. This reflects the greater steric interaction of methyl–methyl vs. hydrogen–hydrogen.

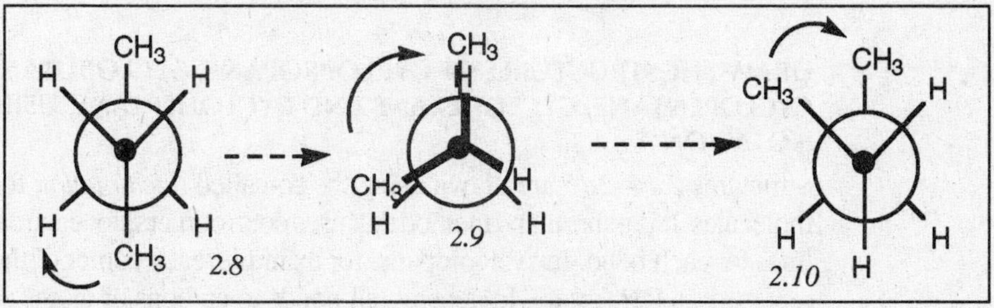

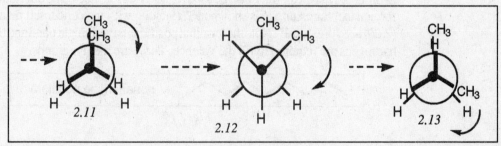

Fig. 2.8–2.10

Fig. 2.11–2.13

2.5. CYCLIC ALKANES

WHAT IS THE GENERAL FORMULA FOR A CYCLIC ALKANE?

There is a class of alkanes that exist with the two terminal carbons tied together into a ring (a cyclic alkane). Forming this bond changes the general formula from C_nH_{2n+2} for an acyclic alkane to C_nH_{2n} for a cyclic alkane.

Nomenclature

WHAT IS THE GENERAL RULE FOR NAMING CYCLIC ALKANES?

The nomenclature for cyclic alkanes is similar to that for acyclic alkanes. The total number of carbons dictates the alkane name (propane, butane, pentane, etc.) but the word cyclo- is added to show that it is a ring. This leads to cyclopropane (*2.14*), cyclobutane (*2.15*), cyclopentane (*2.16*), cyclohexane (*2.17*) and cycloheptane (*2.18*), etc.

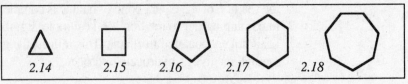

Fig. 2.14–2.18

DRAW THE STRUCTURES OF CYCLOPROPANE, CYCLOBUTANE, CYCLOPENTANE, CYCLOHEXANE AND CYCLOHEPTANE. USING LINE NOTATION.

Structures *2.14–2.18* are drawn using the so-called *line notation* for organic molecules. It is a shorthand method that uses dots (corners) for each carbon and lines for each bond. In cyclopropane, for example, each corner of the triangle represents a CH_2 group. In general, all bonds to carbons or atoms other than hydrogen are shown. The remaining valences of each carbon are assumed to be hydrogen. This method can also be used for acyclic molecules. The line notation for nonane, for example, is shown as *2.19* along with the condensed notation (*2.20*) used previously. Note the terminal positions have a single bond and three hydrogens are required to fill the valence. These are methyl groups.

nonane (line notation)

Fig. 2.19

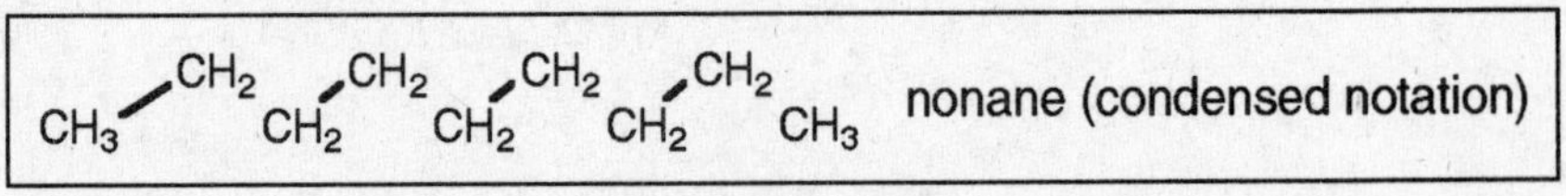

CH_3 — CH_2 — CH_2 — CH_2 — CH_2 — CH_2 — CH_2 — CH_2 — CH_3 nonane (condensed notation)

Fig. 2.20

Structure

IS 'FREE ROTATION' POSSIBLE AROUND CARBON–CARBON BONDS IN CYCLIC MOLECULES? WHY OR WHY NOT?

Each of the carbons in the cyclic alkanes is, of course, three dimensional with the usual tetrahedral geometry. Cyclic molecules can *not* undergo the 'free' rotation observed with acyclic alkanes since the bonds are connected in a ring. In order to dissipate excess energy, however, the molecules distort by partial-rotation of the carbon–carbon bonds, leading to unique conformations for cyclic alkanes.

Baeyer and Torsion Strain

WHAT IS TORSION STRAIN AND ANGLE STRAIN?

The Newman projections for planar cyclopentane (*2.21*) and planar cyclohexane (*2.22*) show a severe interaction of the eclipsing hydrogens which destabilizes both planar structures. This interaction is referred to as *torsion strain* or *Pitzer strain*. In addition, there is something called *angle strain* or *Baeyer strain*. This arises when the bond angles in the ring are distorted from the 'ideal' tetrahedron of 109°28'.

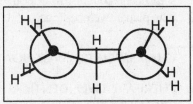

Fig. 2.21

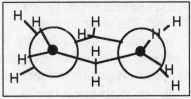

Fig. 2.22

HOW DO CYCLIC MOLECULES RELIEVE TORSION STRAIN AND ANGLE STRAIN IN C₃, C₄ AND C₅ CYCLIC ALKANES?

In cyclopropane the angle strain is severe (bond angles of 60°) as it is in cyclobutane (bond angles of 90°). In planar cyclopentane, the bond angles of 108° show little angle strain but significant torsion strain (see *2.21*). In planar cyclohexane, the bond angles are 120° and there is also great torsion strain (see *2.22*). In order to relieve the steric and electronic interactions, the molecule partially rotates, giving the lowest average conformation to be *2.23* for cyclopentane, *2.24* for cyclohexane and *2.25* for cyclobutane. In other words, *cyclic alkanes are not planar*, with the exception of cyclopropane. Conformation *2.23* (cyclopentane) is referred to as the *envelope* conformation, conformation *2.24* (cyclohexane) is referred to as the *chair* conformation and *2.25* is a *bent* conformation. The Newman projections for envelope cyclopentane (*2.26*) and chair cyclohexane (*2.27*) show that the torsion strain has been relieved and in *2.27* each H–C–C bond resembles the gauche conformation of butane.

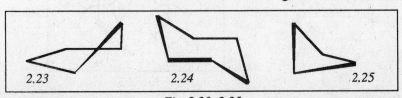

Fig. 2.23–2.25

WHAT ARE THE BOND ANGLES IN CHAIR CYCLOHEXANE?

In cyclohexane, the bond angles are 120°28' (there is no angle strain) and there is minimal torsion strain.

IN THE ENVELOPE FORM OF CYCLOPENTANE THE ANGLE STRAIN IS INCREASED RELATIVE TO THE PLANAR FORM. WHY THEN IS THE ENVELOPE FORM OF CYCLOPENTANE THE LOWEST ENERGY FORM?

In cyclopentane, the angle strain is increased (bond angles of 105°) but the significant reduction in torsion strain makes the envelope much lower in energy than planar cyclopentane.

Cyclohexane   CHAIRS, BOATS, TWIST-BOATS AND HALF-CHAIRS

THERE ARE TWO IDENTICAL CHAIR CONFORMATIONS OF CYCLOHEXANE. DISCUSS HOW ONE IS CONVERTED INTO THE OTHER BY PARTIAL ROTATION ABOUT CARBON–CARBON BONDS.

Cyclohexane is particularly flexible, leading to several different conformations. The most important conformation is the *chair*, but there are two energetically identical chair conformations for cyclohexane. The pseudo rotation of chair *2.28* leads to a *twist-boat* conformation (*2.29*) which then contorts to give a *boat* conformation (*2.30*). Twisting the other side of the boat leads to another twist-boat (*2.31*) which then leads to the other chair conformation (*2.32*). There are also two significantly higher energy conformations, the two *half-chair* conformations, (*2.33*) and (*2.34*). Twist boat (*2.29*) is about 5.5 kcal/mol higher in energy than the chair (*2.28*) but must go through the half chair (*2.33*). The activation energy for this transition is about 10.8 kcal/mol. The boat conformation (*2.30*) is about 5.7 kcal/mol higher in energy than chair (*2.28*). Twist boat *2.31* and half chair *2.34* have the same energy as the other identical conformations.

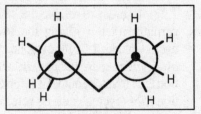

Fig. 2.26

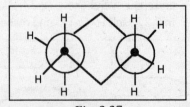

Fig. 2.27

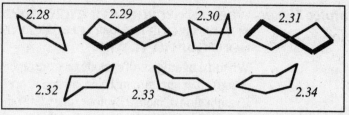

Fig. 2.28–2.34

Axial and Equatorial Positions In Chair Conformations

DRAW CHAIR CYCLOHEXANE SUCH THAT THE AXIAL AND EQUATORIAL BONDS ARE CLEARLY SHOWN.

The chair conformation can be viewed as having a 'top' and a 'bottom' (see hydrogens [H*] in planar cyclohexane (*2.35*). When planar cyclohexane is distorted into a chair (see *2.36*), the H* are in different relative positions. All six H* are on 'top' of the molecule, but three of them are 'vertical' and three are 'horizontal' relative to the plane of the four ring carbons. The 'vertical' H* are called *axial* hydrogens and those bonds connected to H* are called axial bonds. The 'horizontal' H* are called *equatorial* hydrogens and the bonds connected to those hydrogens are called equatorial bonds. The 'top' of the molecule has three axial positions and three equatorial positions. Likewise, the 'bottom' of the molecule has three axial and three equatorial bonds. Note that if the 'top' has an axial bond, that carbon will have an equatorial bond on the 'bottom'.

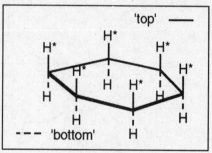

Fig. 2.35

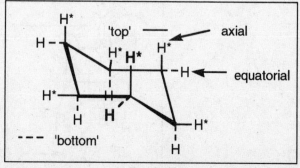

Fig. 2.36

Substituted Cyclic Alkanes

WHEN AN HYDROGEN OF CYCLOHEXANE IS REPLACED WITH A METHYL GROUP THE TWO CHAIR CONFORMATIONS BECOME NON-EQUIVALENT. WHY?

When the hydrogens of cyclohexane are replaced with alkyl groups (or another group), that group can be in an axial position or an equatorial position. Examination of methyl cyclohexane (*2.37*) shows that the methyl is in an axial position in one chair conformation (*2.38*) and in the equatorial position in the other (*2.39*). These two chairs are in equilibrium with each other. As shown in structure *2.40*, the presence of a methyl group in the axial position leads to a significant steric interaction with the other axial hydrogens (a 1,3-diaxial interaction, often called *A-strain*). The three axial hydrogens on the 'bottom' of structure *2.40* also show this A strain. The greater size of the methyl, however, dictates that the A-strain of the axial methyl with the axial hydrogens is greater than the A-strain for the three axial hydrogens on the 'bottom'. The larger the group in the axial position (and the larger number of groups in the axial position), the larger the A-strain and the higher energy will be that structure. Examination of *2.38* and *2.39*, therefore, suggests that *2.38* is higher in energy than *2.39*, creating an energy difference (ΔE) for the two chair conformations.

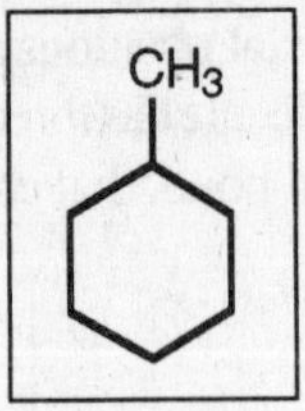

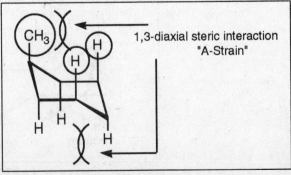

Fig. 2.37

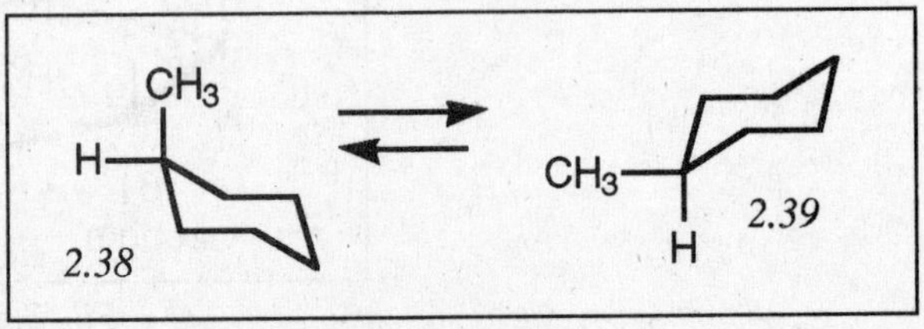

Fig. 2.38, 2.39

Fig. 2.40

WHY IS THERE ONE LOW ENERGY CONFORMATION IN SUBSTITUTED CYCLOHEXANE DERIVATIVES SUCH AS METHYLCYCLOHEXANE, *t*-BUTYLCYCLOHEXANE AND BROMOCYCLOHEXANE?

The ΔE between *2.38* and *2.39* (see above) leads to a conformational bias for *2.39* over *2.38*. That is, at equilibrium there will be a higher percentage of *2.39* since it is lower in energy than *2.38*. In general, the lowest energy conformation will predominate for any given cyclic alkane. For this reason, chair cyclohexane predominates as the major conformation of cyclohexane because the boat, half-chair and twist boat conformations are much higher in energy. The envelope form of cyclopentane predominates over the planar form because it is lower in energy. Likewise, methylcyclohexane exists largely in the chair form with the methyl group equatorial. It is therefore reasonable to draw *t*-butylcyclohexane (*2.41*) and bromocyclohexane (*2.42*) with those groups in the equatorial position and to assume that the A strain present when those groups are axial will make those conformations very high in energy, destabilizing them. In short, *2.41* and *2.42* represent the low energy conformations and will be present in the greatest percentage of any conformation available to those molecules.

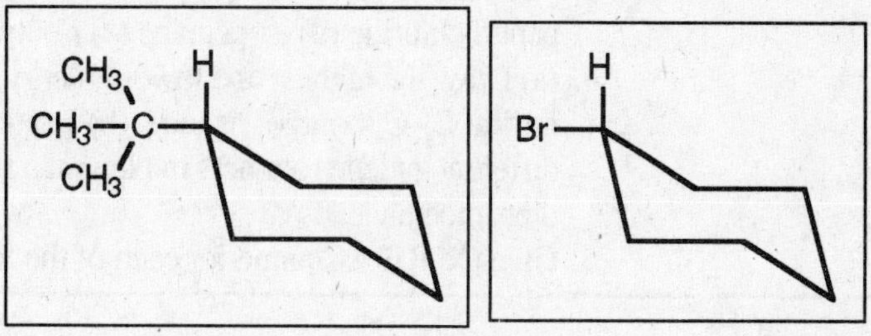

Fig. 2.41, 2.42

This chapter introduced alkanes. The fundamental system of nomenclature used for alkanes applies to most of the organic molecules that will appear in this book. The concept of conformations and conformational analysis is also fundamental to most organic molecules. The steric interactions that led to a preference for one or a few conformations will be important in many of the reactions discussed in later chapters.

END OF CHAPTER PROBLEMS

1. Give the IUPAC name for each of the following.

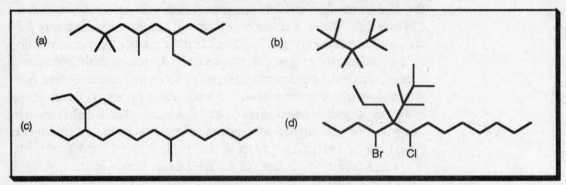

2. Give the structures in line formulae for each of the following IUPAC names: (a) 3,3,6,6-tetramethylpentadecane (b) 1-bromo-4-(2,2-dimethylbutyl)dodecane (c) 5,7,8-tetramethylicosane (d) 3,3,4,4-tetraethyloctane (e) 7-(3,3-dimethylpentyl)hexadecane.

3. Draw the structures of (a) neopentyl bromide (b) isobutane (c) *tert*-pentyl chloride (d) isopentane (e) *t*-butyl iodide.

4. (a) Draw the highest and lowest energy rotamer in Newman projection for the C_3–C_4 bond of hexane. (b) Draw the highest, lowest and two different gauche rotamers in Newman projection for 1,2-dibromoethane.

5. Give the IUPAC name for each of the following.

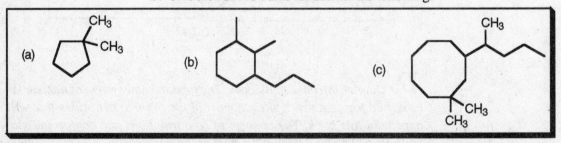

6. Which of the following molecules has the smallest angle strain? Which has the greatest torsion strain? Which has the angle strain greater than the torsion strain?

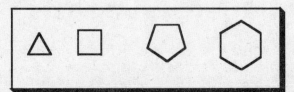

7. Draw both chair conformations for each of the following. Label the highest and lowest energy chair conformation in each case.

3

Stereochemistry

*O*rganic molecules are three dimensional; this gives special properties to molecules that possess chiral atoms (an atom that possess four different groups or atoms). This chapter will introduce the concept of chirality, including enantiomers, diastereomers, meso compounds and absolute configuration. The Cahn-Prelog-Ingold selection rules will be given in order to determine the absolute configuration of a chiral center. The optical properties of chiral molecules will also be discussed, including the highly important physical property, specific rotation.

3.1. CHIRALITY

GIVE A WORKING DEFINITION OF CHIRALITY.

Chirality is a property of molecules whose spatial arrangement of atoms leads to asymmetry; a mirror image of that molecule will be a different molecule. This difference in three dimensional structure leads to a new type of isomer called a *stereoisomer*. Stereoisomers differ only in the spatial position of their groups. A molecule with this property is said to be *chiral*. Many natural substances are chiral and this is a key factor in their reactivity, particularly with amino acids and enzymes, saccharides, DNA and RNA in mammalian systems. Chiral molecules are also produced by plants and these substances have a variety of properties, including those which behave as defensive substances or attractive substances. Chiral molecules are also responsible for the chemicals that trigger odor responses in humans when released into the air from plants or animals.

Defining A Chiral Center

WHAT IS A CHIRAL CENTER?

A chiral center (also called an asymmetric center) is defined as an atom (usually carbon but it does not have to be carbon) that has four *different* atoms or groups attached to it and possesses no symmetry. An example is 2-hexanol: $CH_3CH_2CH_2CH_2CH_2CH(OH)CH_3$ where *C* is the chiral center.

Enantiomers

WHAT IS AN ENANTIOMER?

When a mirror is held up to a molecule possessing a chiral center, its *mirror image* is observed. If one tries to superimpose (match every atom in both molecules by laying one on the other), the chiral molecule and its mirror image are *not superimposable*. They are, therefore, *different molecules. Enantiomers* are defined as isomers that are non-superimposable mirror images.

DRAW THE ENANTIOMERS FOR 2-BROMOBUTANE.

In 2-bromobutane (*3.1*), C_2 is chiral (a bromine, a methyl, an ethyl and an hydrogen are attached to it). The mirror image of *3.1* is structure *3.2*. If *3.2* is rotated by 180°, the second structure (also labeled *3.2*) shown below *3.1* results. If one tries to superimpose these molecules, the methyl and hydrogen do not match and they are different molecules. This attempt to superimpose the molecules is shown in *3.3*. Two non-superimposable mirror images of molecules that contain a chiral center are called *enantiomers*. Therefore, *3.1* is the enantiomer of *3.2* and *3.2* is the enantiomer of *3.1*.

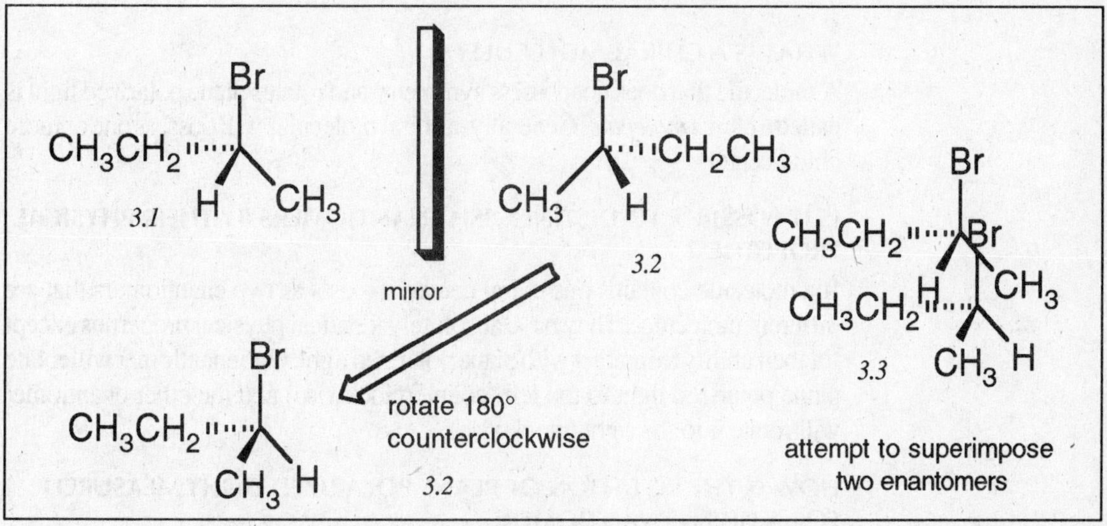

Fig. 3.1–3.3

Fischer Projections

WHAT IS A FISHER PROJECTION?

A convenient notation for molecules containing a chiral center involves crossed lines. The horizontal line represents the bonds (and the attached atoms) projected out of the plane of the paper *towards you*. The vertical line represents bonds projected behind the plane of the paper, *away from you*. This representation is called a *Fisher Projection*. Structure *3.4* is the Fisher projection of one of the 2-bromobutane enantiomers from above (*3.1*). If *3.5* is the Fisher projection of enantiomer *3.2* (from above) then its mirror image (*3.4*) is the same structure as *3.1* from above.

DRAW THE FISHER PROJECTIONS FOR THE ENANTIOMERS OF 2-BROMOBUTANE.

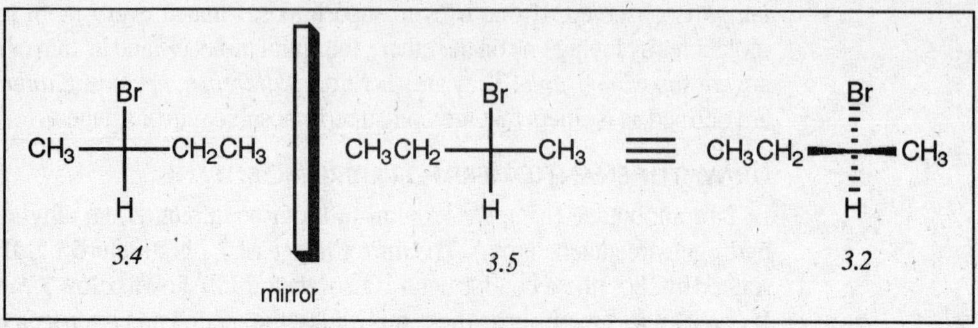

Fig. 3.2, 3.4, 3.5

3.2. SPECIFIC ROTATION

WHAT IS A CHIRAL MOLECULE?

A molecule that does not possess symmetry and rotates plane polarized light is called a *chiral molecule*. Generally, a chiral molecules will possess one or more chiral centers.

IS IT POSSIBLE TO DISTINGUISH ENANTIOMERS BY THEIR PHYSICAL PROPERTIES?

If a molecule contains one chiral center, it exists as two enantiomers that are different molecules. They have absolutely identical physical properties except for their ability to interact with plane polarized light. One enantiomer will rotate plane polarized light to the left (counterclockwise) and the other enantiomer will rotate it to the right (clockwise).

HOW IS THE ROTATION OF PLANE POLARIZED LIGHT MEASURED FOR A GIVEN ENANTIOMER?

The instrument used to measure this property is called a *polarimeter*. A polarimeter consists of a light source with a polarizing filter. The resulting polarized light is confined to a single plane and is directed *through* a chamber containing a *solution* of the chiral molecule in an appropriate solvent (one that dissolves the chiral molecule and does not itself have a chiral center). One sights through the tube containing the sample and when compared to a blank (a tube containing only solvent) the angle of the plane polarized light changes as it passes through the sample. This is measured in degrees (°) and is defined as the *observed rotation*, α. For example, if α for a molecule is measured to be +60° for one enantiomer, α for the other enantiomer will be a -60°. The rotation is of the same magnitude but opposite is sign (+ denotes clockwise rotation of the light and – denotes counterclockwise rotation of the light). The temperature of the experiment (25°C in this case) and the type of light used (sodium D line) are usually included: α_D^{25} .

WHAT IS SPECIFIC ROTATION?

Since the length of the polarimeter tube and the concentration and solvent used may vary, some standardization is required. If the tube is longer, there are more molecules present to interact with plane polarized light for a given concentration and the observed rotation will be larger. As the concentration increases, there are also more molecules interacting with the light and α increaeses. A parameter called *specific rotation* was defined and given the symbol: $[\alpha]_D^{25}$ measured in degrees. The parameters that determine this physical property are path length (l) recorded in decimeters (dm), concentration (c) in g/mL and the observed rotation, α. Specific rotation is then given by the expression:

$$[\alpha]_D^{25} = \frac{\alpha}{(1)(c)}$$

IF α = +60°, l = 5 dm AND c = 1.25 g/mL WHAT IS $[\alpha]_D^{25}$ = ?

Using the formula given above, $[\alpha]_D^{25} = +9.6°$.

IF THE SPECIFIC ROTATION OF ONE ENANTIOMER OF 2-BUTANOL IS +13.5° WHAT IS THE SPECIFIC ROTATION OF THE OTHER ENANTIOMER?

The magnitude of the specific rotation is the same for both enantiomers. This parameter differs only in sign. If one enantiomer of 2-butanol has a specific rotation of +13.5°, the other enantiomer must have a specific rotation of -13.5°.

WHAT IS A RACEMIC MIXTURE?

A special case arises when there is an equal mixture of the two enantiomers (50:50 mixture of the + and - enantiomer). The specific rotation of this mixture is zero (0) and the mixture is called a *racemic mixture* (sometimes called a *racemic modification*). This implies that the specific rotation of enantiomeric mixtures are *additive*. Therefore if one enantiomer has a specific rotation of +60° and its enantiomer is -60°, a 70:30 mixture (+ : -) would show a specific rotation reflecting this mixture: $[\alpha]_D^{25} = (+60°)(0.7) + (-60°)(0.3) = +42° + (-18°) = +24°$.

3.3. SEQUENCE RULES

FOR ENANTIOMER *3.1* OF 2-BROMOBUTANE (SEE ABOVE), IS THE SPECIFIC ROTATION + OR –?

The specific rotation data for 2-bromobutane raises an interesting question, is the specific rotation of enantiomer *3.1* + or -? There is *no way* to tell from the structure and specific rotation tells nothing about the relative positions of the groups on the chiral carbon. There is an experiment in which the specific rotation is determined over a range of concentrations and temperatures that does give information about the relative positions of groups on a chiral center. This phenomenon is called circular dichroism but will not be discussed in this review.

Specific Rotation vs. Absolute Configuration

WHAT IS THE DISTINCTION BETWEEN SPECIFIC ROTATION AND ABSOLUTE CONFIGURATION?

Specific rotation is a physical property of a molecule that is determined from the interaction of the enantiomers with plane polarized light. Absolute configuration is the natural spatial arrangement of atoms around a chiral center and is an interpretive property, not a physical property. An enantiomer with a specified absolute configuration could have either a (+) or a (-) specific rotation.

Cahn-Prelog-Ingold Sequencing Rules

WHAT ARE THE SEQUENCE RULES USED TO DETERMINE ABSOLUTE CONFIGURATION?

A set of rules are used to determine absolute configuration called the *Cahn-Prelog-Ingold Selection Rules*. The rules are used to assign a designator (*R* or *S*) to each enantiomer. The rules assign a priority (a = highest and d = lowest priority) to each *group* on the chiral center based on the *atoms* attached to the chiral center. These sequencing rules are as follows:

1. Working from the point of attachment to the chiral center, the first atom encountered is prioritized according to its *atomic number*. Therefore, F > O > N > C > H. [Corollary: If the atoms are the same, higher mass isotopes take the higher priority: therefore, $^3H > ^2H > ^1H$ and $^{18}O > ^{16}O$].
2. If the atoms are identical (two carbons for example), proceed outward from the chiral center *to the first point of difference*, based on the atoms, not the entire group. Then use rule (1) to determine the priority
3. If the atoms at the first point of difference are identical but the number of substituents on those atoms are different, use the *number* of groups on each atom to determine the priority. (a) Three carbons > two carbons > one carbon, for example. (b) This rule is used *only* if the two atoms at the first point of difference are identical and priority cannot be otherwise determined.

With these three rules, many molecules can be assigned the R or S configuration using the so-called 'steering wheel' model (*3.6* and *3.7*). In this model, the molecule is rotated to place the lowest priority group away from the viewer. If a line drawn from the highest group (a)→ (b) and then to (c) rotates clockwise, the molecules is assigned the *R configuration*. If that line rotates from (a)→(b)→(c) but is counterclockwise, the molecule is assigned the *S configuration*.

WHAT IS THE 'STEERING WHEEL' MODEL?

The *'Steering Wheel' Model* essentially sights down the base of a tetrahedron which 'surrounds' the chiral carbon. The lowest priority group (d) is *always* to the rear of the model. If a line is drawn from a→b→c is clockwise, the molecule is assigned the R configuration (*3.6*). If that line is counterclockwise, the molecule is assigned the S configuration (*3.7*).

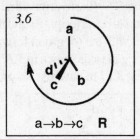
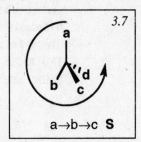

Fig. 3.6, 3.7

DETERMINE THE ABSOLUTE CONFIGURATION OF THE ENANTIOMER OF 1-CHLORO-1-FLUOROETHANE (*3.8*).

In this example, the atom with the highest atomic mass is chlorine (a), followed by fluorine (b), the carbon of the methyl (c) and, finally, hydrogen (d). This assignment gives a model with the low priority group (d) pointed towards the viewer. To make the (d) group point to the rear in the steering wheel model, the (c) group is rotated to the left by about 120° (see *3.9*). This motion *does not break any bonds* and moving (c) moves (a) to the right and (b) rotates to the right (see *3.10*). The a→b→c priority is then clockwise and A has the R configuration. *This illustrates Rule 1.*

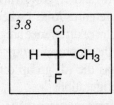
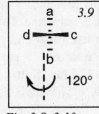
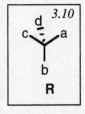

Fig. 3.8–3.10

DETERMINE THE ABSOLUTE CONFIGURATION OF THE ENANTIOMER OF 1,3-HEXANEDIOL (*3.11*).

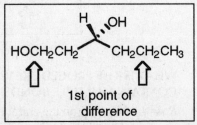

Fig. 3.11

In this example, the highest priority atom is the oxygen of the hydroxyl group (a), and the lowest priority group (d) is the hydrogen. The next atoms are both carbon and Rule 1 does not allow the priority to be assigned. By *Rule 2*, the first point of difference is the second carbon from the chiral center. The first carbons both have one carbon and two hydrogens attached [C^{CHH}] but the next carbons are different (the first point of difference) with one having a C^{CHH} (the propyl) and the other having C^{OCH} (the hydroxyethyl). Since O takes priority over C, the hydroxyethyl group takes priority (b) and the propyl group takes priority (c). This gives a model with the (d) group forward. The model must be rotated by 180° to the left, along the axis shown in *3.12*, to give a model with the (d) group to the rear, showing *3.11* to have the R configuration (see *3.13*).

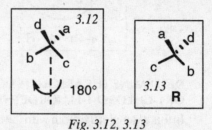

Fig. 3.12, 3.13

DETERMINE THE ABSOLUTE CONFIGURATION OF *3.14*.

In this example (2-amino-3-ethyl-3-methyl-1-butanol), the nitrogen is the highest priority (a) with the next three atoms all being carbon. At the first point of difference, the 'hydroxymethyl' carbon has two hydrogens and an oxygen [C^{OHH}], the isopropyl group is C^{CCH} and the ethyl group is C^{CHH}. The C^{OHH} is clearly higher in priority and takes (b). Using Rules 1 and 2, however, the only atoms available for the (c) and (d) groups and carbon and hydrogen, which are indistinguishable. This requires *Rule 3* where the number of similar atoms on the carbon at the first point of difference are counted. The C^{CCH} has two carbons to one for the C^{CHH} and the isopropyl group becomes (c) and the ethyl group is (d). The model now has the (d) group directed to the rear (*3.15*) and this molecule has the S configuration.

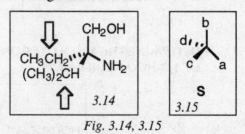

Fig. 3.14, 3.15

WHAT IS THE PROCEDURE WHEN GROUPS ON THE CHIRAL CENTER CONTAIN MULTIPLE BONDS (DOUBLE OR TRIPLE)?

Rule 4. If a group on the chiral center contains a double or a triple bond, the number of bonds to that atom is taken as the total number of atoms. In other words, a C–C=O is taken to be C^{COO}, where the itallicized carbon is attached to one carbon and *two* oxygens (one O for each bond of the double bond).

WHAT IS THE ABSOLUTE CONFIGURATION OF THE ENANTIOMER OF *3.16*?

The multiple bond rule is illustrated by molecule *3.16* where the O is the highest priority (a) and the hydrogen is the lowest priority (d). The first carbon of the C=C group is C^{HCC} due to the double bond but the ethyl group is C^{CHH}. Rule 3 must be invoked since only carbon and hydrogen are present. In this case, C^{CCH} takes priority (b) over the C^{CHH} which takes priority (c). Tilting the model forward slightly from *3.17* puts the (d) group to the rear (*3.18*) and molecule D has the S configuration.

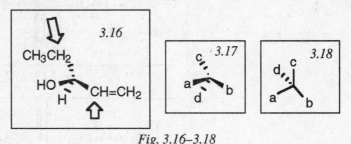

Fig. 3.16–3.18

3.4. DIASTEREOMERS

WHAT IS THE MAXIMUM NUMBER OF STEREOISOMERS FOR A MOLECULE CONTAINING *n* CHIRAL CENTERS?

When a molecule has two or more chiral centers there are many more possibilities for stereoisomers. In general, for a chiral molecule with n chiral centers, there will be a *maximum* of 2^n stereoisomers.

Two Chiral Centers   **DRAW ALL STEREOISOMERS FOR 2-BROMO-3-PENTANOL.**

When a molecule has two chiral centers, the 2^n rule predicts 2^2 or four stereoisomers. Molecule *3.19* (2-bromo-3-pentanol), is drawn as a Fisher projection but two other representations (*3.20* and *3.21*) are also given to show the stereochemical relationship. Molecule *3.19* has an enantiomer, *3.22*. This only constitutes two stereoisomers, however. Molecule *3.19* has the RS configuration and its enantiomer (*3.22*) has the SR configuration. If one of the chiral centers is *inverted* from R to S (molecule *3.23*) it has the SS configuration. Molecule *3.23* also has an enantiomer (*3.24*) with the RR configuration. Structures *3.19*, *3.22*, *3.23* and *3.24* are the four stereoisomers that were predicted. Structures *3.19* and *3.22* are enantiomers but structures *3.23* and *3.24* are also enantiomers.

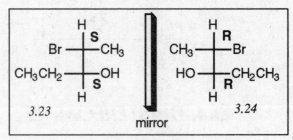

Fig. 3.19–3.21

Fig. 3.19, 3.22

Fig. 3.23, 3.24

DEFINE DIASTEREOMERS.

What is the relationship of *3.19* and *3.23* or *3.22* and *3.24*? They are clearly stereoisomers with the same empirical formula. They are, however, non-superimposable, non-mirror images. In other words, they are *different compounds*. The term for stereoisomers that are not superimposable and not mirror images is *diastereomer*. Compounds *3.19* and *3.22*, *3.19* and *3.24*, *3.22* and *3.23* and *3.22* and *3.24* are diastereomers.

Meso Compounds IS IT POSSIBLE TO HAVE FEWER THAN THE NUMBER OF STEREOISOMERS PREDICTED BY THE 2^N RULE?

Yes. In some cases, a molecule with two or more chiral centers will give two stereoisomers that are enantiomers but the other stereoisomer will have a *superimposable* mirror image (that is, the two structures are the same molecule). Such a molecule is termed a *meso compound*. This gives a total of three different stereoisomers, not the predicted four.

DISCUSS WHY 2,3-DIBROMOBUTANE HAS ONLY THREE STEREOISOMERS.

A simple example of a *meso compound* is 2,3-dibromobutane. Structure *3.25* has a non-superimposable mirror image (*3.26*) and *3.25/3.26* are enantiomers. Structure *3.27* also has a mirror image (*3.28*) but it is superimposable so there are only *three stereoisomers*, not four. In other words, *3.27* and *3.28* represent only one structure since they are superimposable. A diminished number of stereoisomers is the result of having a meso compound. Closer inspection of *3.27* (see *3.30*) shows that there is a plane of symmetry that bisects the molecule (the 'top' half of the molecule is identical with the 'bottom' half) when drawn as the eclipsed rotamer. This *symmetry* is characteristic of meso compounds. If a rotamer can be found where every atom matches as in *3.30* (Br matches Br, methyl matches methyl and H matches H), this will be a meso compound. Analysis of *3.29* (which correlates with *3.25*) shows that there is no symmetry in this plane (the Br and H do not match). This lack of symmetry leads to the presence of enantiomers.

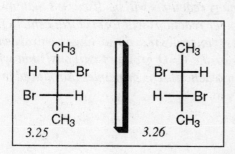
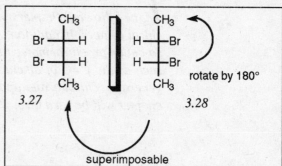

Fig. 3.25–3.26 and 3.27–3.28

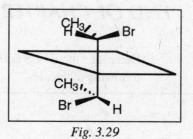

Fig. 3.29

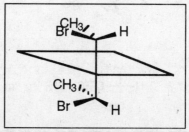

Fig. 3.30

3.5. OPTICAL RESOLUTION

IS IT POSSIBLE TO SEPARATE ENANTIOMERS?

Since enantiomers have the same physical properties of boiling point, melting point, solubility, adsorbtivity, etc., it is virtually impossible to physically separate them. Occasionally, the crystal structure of one solid enantiomer is noticeably different enough that it can be selectively removed (as in Pasteur's separation of tartaric acid by physically picking out the different crystals under a microscope). More commonly, the only way to separate enantiomers is by a method called optical resolution. In this technique, the enantiomeric mixture (usually a racemic mixture) is reacted with another chiral molecule to produce diastereomers. Diastereomers are different compounds, with different physical properties. They can, therefore, be physically separated. Once separated, another chemical reaction cleaves the bond between the enantiomer of interest and the second chiral molecule, *resolving* the individual enantiomers.

In the following chapters, many reactions will be discussed that involve chiral centers. In addition, other reactions will form chiral centers from so-called prochiral molecules (molecules that do not have a chiral center, such as the C=C of alkenes or the C=O group of carbonyls but which generate a chiral center upon reaction). The principles introduced in this chapter will be used throughout.

END OF CHAPTER PROBLEMS

1. Determine the R or S configuration for each chiral center in the following molecules.

2. Which of the following are not suitable for use as a solvent in determining the specific rotation of a chiral unknown? Explain.

CH₃OH   H₂O   CH₂Cl₂

3. For a polarimeter with a path length of 10 dm, determine the specific rotation for each of the following (concentration is given in brackets with each observed rotation value. (a) -24.6° (c = 0.47 g/mL) (b) +143.4° (c = 1.31 g/mL) (c) +0.8° (c = 0.65 g/mL) (d) -83.5° (c = 5.0 g/mL)

4. Calculate the % of R and S enantiomers present in the following *mixtures* of R + S enantiomers. In each case the specific rotation value for the R enantiomer is +120°. (a) [α] = -14.8° (b) [α] = +109.2° (c) [α] = +4.6° (d) [α] = -18.3°

5. Draw all diastereomers for (a) 2-bromo-3-heptanol and (b) 4-methyl-3-octanol in Fisher projection. Which of the stereoisomers are diastereomers?

6. Discuss the number of stereoisomers possible for 2,3-butanediol and for 2,3-cyclopentanediol.

4

Alkyl Halides

*A*lkyl halides are molecules in which a hydrogen atom has been replaced with fluorine (alkyl fluorides), chlorine (alkyl chlorides), bromine (alkyl bromides) or iodine (alkyl iodides). The presence of the halogen leads to a polarized C–X bond which is capable of reacting with a variety of reagents (usually called nucleophiles) to generate other types of functional groups. Reactions that generate halides will be discussed, as well as the reactions of halides to form other compounds.

4.1. PROPERTIES

The Polarized C–X Bond

DESCRIBE IN A GENERAL WAY THE PHYSICAL PROPERTIES OF ALKYL HALIDES.

ALKYL HALIDES are characterized by a C–X bond, where X = F, Cl, Br or I. The C–X bond is highly polarized with a $\delta+$ carbon and a $\delta-$ halogen. Fluorine is the most electronegative element and the C–F bond is the most polarized. Fluorine is a small atom, however, and that bond is relatively strong. Although less polarized, the C–I bond is relatively weak due to the long bond length dictated by the large iodine atom when bonded to carbon.

Nomenclature

WHAT IS THE IUPAC NAME OF COMPOUND 4.1?

The halogen atoms in alkyl halides are *not* treated as functional groups and, therefore, do not have a specific ending. Halide nomenclature treats the halogen as a *substituent* where the -ine ending is dropped and replaced with -o. Fluorine becomes fluoro-, chlorine becomes chloro-, bromine is bromo- and iodine is iodo-. A typical example is 5-bromo-3-chloro-2,5-dimethyloctane (*4.1*).

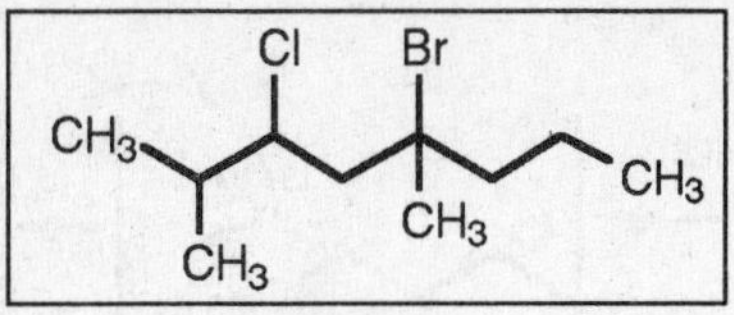

Fig. 4.1

4.2. PREPARATION FROM ALCOHOLS

LIST SEVERAL REAGENTS THAT TRANSFORM ALCOHOLS INTO ALKYL HALIDES.

A standard method for the preparation of alkyl halides involves treating alcohols (R–OH, see chapter 11) with a reagent that contains excess halogen. Typical chlorination reagents are thionyl chloride ($SOCl_2$), phosphorous trichloride (PCl_3), phosphorus oxychloride ($POCl_3$), phosgene ($Cl_2C=O$) and phosphorus pentachloride (PCl_5). The usual brominating agents are phosphorous tribromide (PBr_3) and thionyl bromide ($SOBr_2$). Reagents to make the iodide are often unstable and are prepared as needed by reaction of red phosphorus and iodine. Both HCl and HBr can be used in many cases to prepare the chloride or bromide, respectively.

Alcohols and Acids (HX)

TERTIARY ALCOHOLS

WHAT IS THE MECHANISM FOR THE CONVERSION OF 2-METHYL-2-PENTANOL INTO 2-CHLORO-2-METHYLPENTANE?

Alcohols function as a *base* in the presence of strong acids such as HCl or HBr. The alcohol (2-methyl-2-pentanol, *4.2*, for example) is protonated by HCl to form an *oxonium salt* (*4.3*). This cation loses water (H_2O) to form a *carbocation* (*4.4*). A carbocation is a tricoordinated carbon that is *planar* and obviously electron deficient. The cation will react with any species that can donate an electron pair. In this solution both water and chloride ion (Cl⁻) can provide electrons to the carbon. A species that *donates an electron pair to carbon* is called a *nucleophile*. A nucleophile literally means "nucleus loving,' where the nucleus is a positive species. In general, charged nucleophiles are stronger than neutral nucleophiles and the *nucleophilic strength* of an atom *increases* to the *left* and *down* the Periodic Table. Cation *4.4* therefore reacts preferentially with chloride to give 2-chloro-2-methylpentane (*4.5*). The molecules in brackets are called *intermediates* and are *transient products* that are not isolated. The alcohol and the alkyl chloride are the *starting material* and the *product*, respectively. When the starting material(s), product(s) and all intermediates are shown, as above, this is called the *mechanism* of the reaction.

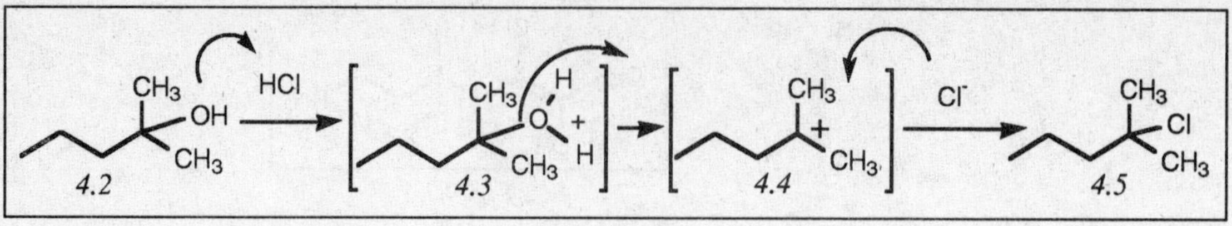

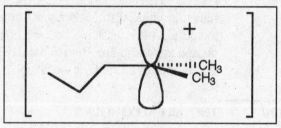

Fig. 4.2–4.5

Carbocations

WHAT IS A CARBOCATION?

The cation intermediate (*4.4*) is reproduced as *4.6*, where its planar nature is seen. In essence, a carbocation is an *empty p orbital* (cationic, therefore no electrons). The nucleophilic chloride can attack from either the bottom or top of the planar cation to give *4.5*. Carbocations are high energy species, making them unstable to isolation. The electropositive carbon of the cation will draw electrons from any available source to diminish the net charge and thereby increase its stability (less charge = more stable = lower energy). Carbon groups are capable of releasing electrons to an electropositive center. *Alkyl groups are electron releasing.*

Fig. 4.6

WHY DOES THE CATION PRODUCED FROM A CHIRAL ALCOHOL LEAD TO A RACEMIC PRODUCT?

If chiral alcohol *4.7* is treated with HCl, the cation that is produced (*4.8*) is planar and the chiral center has been lost. The nucleophilic chloride ion can attack the cation from either the 'top' or the 'bottom', as shown, to produce a mixture of two chlorides, *4.9* and *4.10* (a racemic mixture).

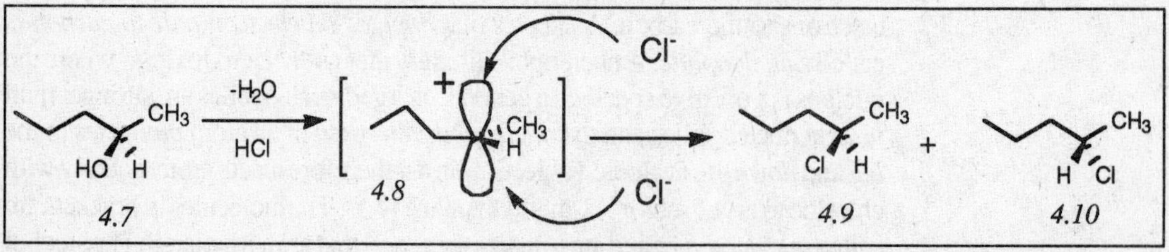

Fig. 4.7–4.10

DETERMINE THE MOST STABLE CARBOCATION (METHYL, 1°, 2° OR 3°).

There are four types of cation, tertiary (three carbon groups [R = alkyl carbon group] on the positive carbon as in *4.11*), secondary (two carbon group on the carbon as in *4.12*), primary (one carbon group on the carbon as in *4.13*) and methyl (three hydrogens on the carbon, as in *4.14*). Three carbons will release more electron density to the electropositive center, providing more stabilization that the electron density released by one carbon group in the primary cation. A tertiary cation will, therefore, *be more stable than either a secondary or a primary cation*. The order of cation stability is: tertiary > secondary > primary > methyl.

$$\left[R-\overset{\oplus}{C}\overset{R}{\underset{R}{|}} \right] \qquad \left[R-\overset{\oplus}{C}\overset{R}{\underset{H}{|}} \right] \qquad \left[R-\overset{\oplus}{C}\overset{H}{\underset{H}{|}} \right] \qquad \left[H-\overset{\oplus}{C}\overset{H}{\underset{H}{|}} \right]$$

4.11   *4.14*

most stable   *4.12*   *4.13*   least stable

least reactive   most reactive

easiest to form   most difficutl to form

Fig. 4.11–4.14

WHAT IS THE LEAST REACTIVE CARBOCATION: METHYL, 1°, 2° OR 3°?

Since the tertiary cation is the most stable, it will be the least reactive with the nucleophile. Conversely, the high energy (less stable) methyl cation will be the most reactive. This is misleading, however, in terms of the actual reactivity since formation of a methyl cation requires significantly more energy than the tertiary (higher activation barrier) and is very difficult. The tertiary reacts better because it is relatively easy to form whereas the primary cation does not react because it does not form. *If* a primary cation could form, however, it would be extremely reactive.

Primary Alcohols

PRIMARY ALCOHOLS ARE CONVERTED TO HALIDES UPON TREATMENT WITH HX; IS THE MECHANISM OF THIS REACTION THE SAME AS OBSERVED WITH TERTIARY ALCOHOLS?

No. The difference in energy between primary and tertiary cations is evident in the reaction of the primary alcohol 1-butanol, (*4.15*) with HCl. The initial reaction to form the oxonium salt (*4.16*) is the same as above. Loss of water to form a primary cation, however, requires too much energy and does not occur. The chloride will instead attack the *carbon* connected to the OH_2 species to form a new C–Cl bond and breaking the C–O bond. This is an S_N^2 reaction (see section 4.4). Polarization of the C–O bond shows the carbon to be electropositive, *but not cationic*. Such a carbon is termed *electrophilic* (literally 'electron loving') and will be attacked by nucleophiles. Displacement by chloride leads to the product, 1-chlorobutane, *4.17*. The difficulty in forming a primary cation leads to a different mechanism for this reaction when compared to the tertiary alcohol. It is noted that methanol (CH_3OH) reacts with HCl to give chloromethane ($ClCH_3$) by an identical mechanism and that secondary alcohols will give products resulting from *both* mechanisms (cationic and direct displacement at carbon).

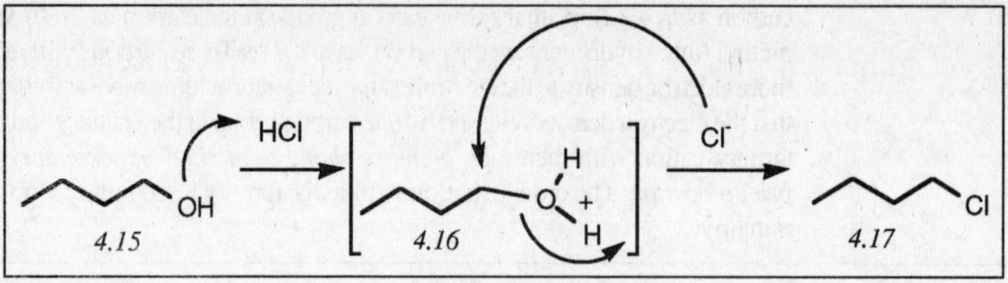

Fig. 4.15–4.17

Both HBr and HI react by a similar mechanism to give alkyl bromides and alkyl iodides. The reaction with HI is not as efficient, however. Substitution of OH with Cl via a cation ($4.2 \rightarrow 4.5$) is called *Nucleophilic Substitution, Unimolecular* (S_N^1), and direct substitution by Cl ($4.15 \rightarrow 4.17$) is called *Nucleophilic Substitution, Bimolecular* (S_N^2). These reactions will be discussed further in sections 4.5 and 4.4, respectively.

Reaction with Thionyl Chloride

EXPLAIN HOW THIONYL CHLORIDE CONVERTS S-2-PENTANOL INTO S-2-CHLOROPENTANE.

Thionyl chloride ($SOCl_2$) reacts with primary, secondary and tertiary alcohols to give the corresponding chloride. Thionyl bromide ($SOBr_2$) reacts similarly to give the primary, secondary or tertiary bromide. There are two versions of the reaction with thionyl chloride (but *not* with thionyl bromide), with and without base. When an amine (such as triethylamine) is added, it functions as the base (see section 16.1) and the mechanism is different from the reaction without a base. In the first versions, S-2-pentanol (*4.18*) reacts with thionyl chloride, as shown, to give *4.20*. The alcohol oxygen attacks the sulfur, displacing a chloride, forming as sulfinate ester (*4.19*) and HCl. This molecule decomposes by losing SO_2 (sulfur dioxide) and the Cl is delivered to the carbon bearing the oxygen, *intramolecularly*, to gives 2-chloropentane (*4.10*). Note that the Cl in *4.10 is on the same side as the OH in 4.18*. This will take on added significance in section 4.4, which deals with stereochemical inversion or retention of configuration.

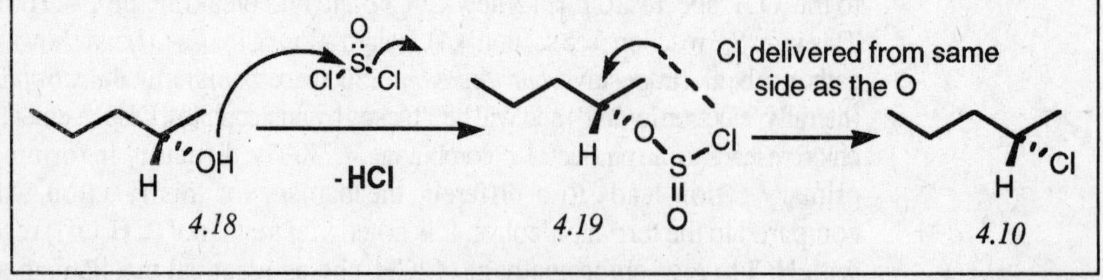

Fig. 4.18–4.10

WHEN TRIETHYLAMINE IS ADDED TO THE REACTION OF S-2-PENTANOL AND THIONYL CHLORIDE, THE PRODUCT IS R-2-CHLOROPENTANE. WHY?

When an amine base (triethylamine, NEt$_3$) is added to this reaction, *4.18* reacts as before to give *4.19* and HCl. The amine reacts with HCl, however, to form the ammonium chloride, *4.20*. This generates a nucleophilic chloride in the reaction medium. Rather than an intra-molecular decomposition, *4.19* reacts with the chloride ion *intermolecularly* to give 2-chloro-pentane (*4.9*) but the chloride is on the opposite side of the molecule from the OH in *4.18*. They are *different* molecules and this inversion of configuration will be explained in section 4.4.

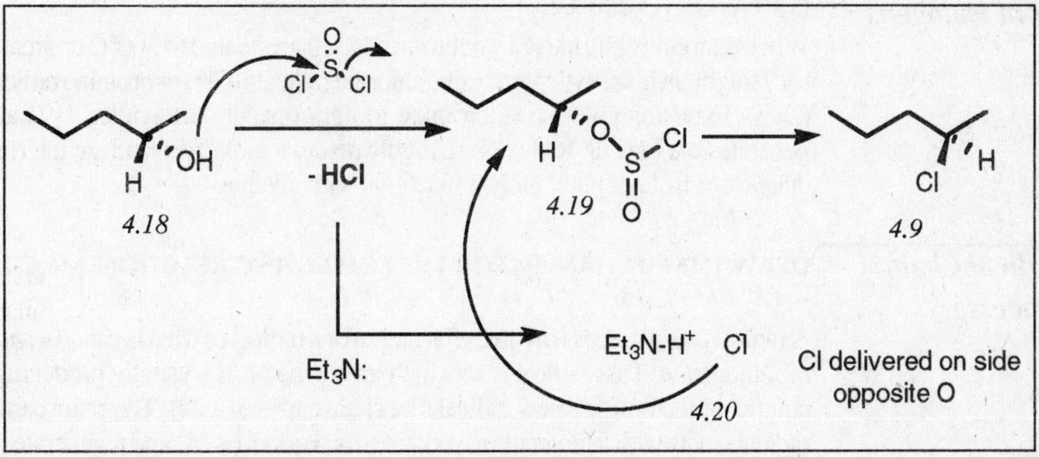

Fig. 4.18–4.9

Phosphorous Halides

LIST OTHER INORGANIC REAGENTS THAT CONVERT ALCOHOLS TO ALKYL HALIDES.

The other phosphorus halides (PCl$_3$, PCl$_5$, PBr$_3$ and POCl$_3$) react similarly to thionyl chloride and bromide. Treatment of primary, secondary or tertiary halides with these reagents give the respective chloride or bromide.

4.3. RADICAL HALOGENATION OF ALKANES

WHAT IS THE TERM FOR BREAKING A BOND SUCH THAT EACH ATOM RECEIVES ONE ELECTRON? WHAT IS THE NAME OF THE RESULTING INTERMEDIATE?

Certain molecules are characterized by breaking a bond in an homolytic manner (each atom of the covalent bond receives one electron), and the resulting products have a single electron. These intermediates are called *free radicals* and are capable of reacting with alkanes (and other molecules) to remove a hydrogen, generating a carbon radical. Such radicals then react with other radicals to give a *coupling reaction* where the radical species replaces a hydrogen of the alkane precursor. This is called a *radical substitution reaction*. In general, this is a poor reaction unless the radical reacts faster with one type of hydrogen rather than another. This means that the rate of reaction of the radical with a primary hydrogen may be slower than the rate of reaction for a tertiary hydrogen.

Free Radicals From Halogens

WHAT IS THE PRODUCT WHEN DIATOMIC CHLORINE OR BROMINE IS HEATED TO 300°C?

When diatomic chlorine (Cl_2) or bromine (Br_2) are heated to 300°C or greater, they fragment homolytically to give chlorine radicals (Cl •) or bromine radicals (Br •). Exposing chlorine or bromine to light (usually ultraviolet, UV) also generates the radical. Radicals are highly reactive molecules and are intermediates (not isolated) that initiate reactions with alkanes.

Radical Chain Processes

DRAW THE MECHANISM FOR THE FOLLOWING REACTION: Me_3C-H + $Cl_2 \overset{h\nu}{\rightarrow} Me_3C$-Cl.

A radical chain process involves formation of a radical in what is called a *chain initiation step*. That radical reacts with an alkane (*4.21*), usually producing a neutral molecule and a new radical (the chain carrier) (*4.22*). The chain carrier radical reacts with a molecule to produce the product (*4.23*) and regenerate the chain carrying radical. These are called *chain propagation steps*. If two of the radicals collide, they form a neutral molecule but do not produce a new radical chain carrier. This stops the radical process and is called a *chain termination step*. To begin the process again, a new chain initiation step is necessary.

Bromine/Chlorine Selectivity

DISCUSS WHY 2,4-DIMETHYLPENTANE REACTS WITH CHLORINE TO GIVE THREE DIFFERENT CHLORINATED PRODUCTS. DRAW THEM.

In reactions with alkanes, halogen radicals abstract one of the hydrogens from the alkane to produce H-X and a carbon radical such as *4.22* from 2-methylpropane (*4.21*). That radical then reacts with additional halogen to produce an alkyl halide (2-chloro-2-methylpropane, *4.23* and the chain carrying radical such as Cl•). *Every* hydrogen atom in the alkane can be removed and replaced with an halogen. 2,4-Dimethylpentane (*4.24*), for example, can react with chlorine gas at 300°C to give three different products, *4.25*, *4.26* and *4.27*. These three products arise by removal of three different kinds of hydrogen, H_a, H_b and H_c. Replacement of H_a gives *4.25*; replacement of H_b gives *4.26* and replacement of H_c gives *4.27*. If each hydrogen is replaced at a given rate (see below) then the relative amounts of *4.25*, *4.26* and *4.27* can be predicted based on the number of each kind of hydrogen. If the rates are different, this must be factored in.

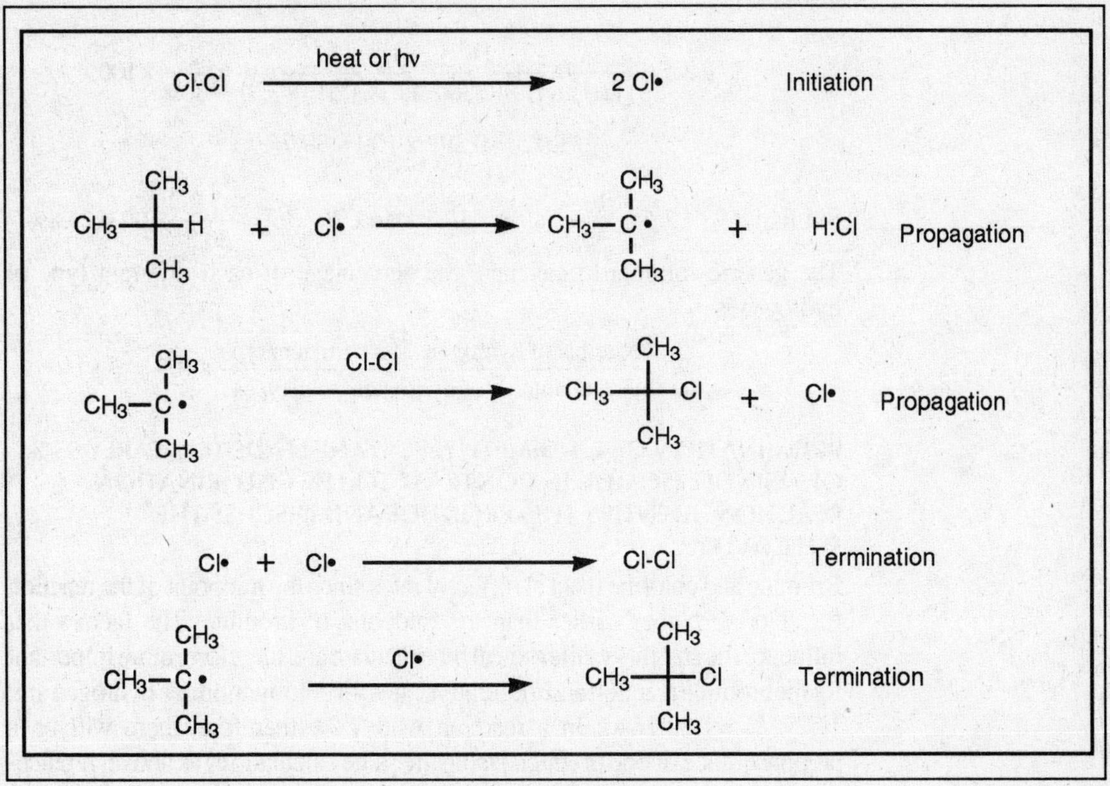

Fig. 4.21–4.23

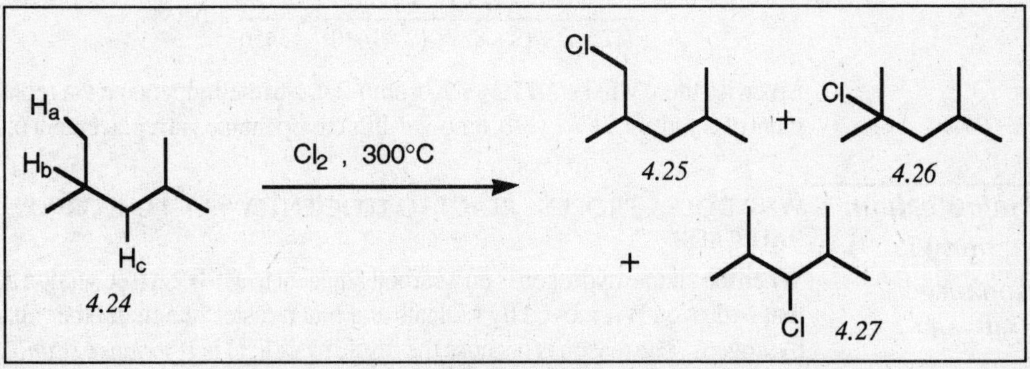

Fig. 4.24–4.27

PREDICT THE RELATIVE PERCENTAGES OF *4.25*, *4.26* AND *4.27* FROM THE CHLORINATION OF 2,4-DIMETHYL-PENTANE.

For alkanes, a chlorine radical removes primary hydrogens with a relative rate of 1, secondary hydrogens with a relative rate of 3.9 and tertiary hydrogens with a relative rate of 5.2 [3°:2°:1° = 5.2:3.9:1]. For *4.24*, there are 12 primary H_a's (all identical hydrogens), 2 tertiary H_b's and 2 secondary H_c's. The relative amount is then:

$$\% \ 4.3.5 = \frac{(12H_a \times 1)}{(12H_a \times 1) + (2H_b \times 5.2) + (2H_c \times 3.9)} = \frac{12}{30.2} \times 100$$

$$\%4.3.5 = 0.397 \times 100 = 39.7\%.$$

Similarly, $\% \ 4.3.6 = \dfrac{10.4}{30.2} \times 100 = 34.5\%$ and $\% \ 4.3.7 = \dfrac{7.8}{30.2} \times 100 = 25.8\%.$

The generic formula to calculate the percentage of each different type of hydrogen is

$$\% = \frac{\text{Number of hydrogens of a particular type}}{\text{Total number of hydrogens of all types}} \times 100$$

BROMINATION OF 2,4-DIMETHYLPENTANE LEADS TO NEARLY 95% OF A SINGLE ISOMER, IN CONTRAST TO THE CHLORINATION REACTION. IDENTIFY THIS PRODUCT AND DISCUSS THE SELECTIVITY.

Bromine and chlorine react at different rates since the midpoint of the reaction for chlorine comes earlier than the midpoint of bromine. The factors that influence the stability of the radical intermediate are, therefore, more important for the bromine reaction and the relative rates for chlorination of a hydrogen are: 1°:2°:3° = 1:82:1640. In a reaction with *4.24*, therefore, there will be a preponderance of one product. Using the same calculations as above, replacement of Ha will give 1-bromo-2,4,4-trimethylpentane,

$$\frac{(12 \times 1)}{(12 \times 1) + (2 \times 82) + (2 \times 1640)} = \frac{12}{3456} = 0.35\%.$$

Likewise there will be 4.75% of 2-bromo-2,4,4-trimethylpentane via replacement of H_b but 94.91% of 3-bromo-2,4-dimethylpentane via replacement of H_c.

α-Halogenation: Reaction Via Resonance Stabilized Intermediates

WHY DOES 1-PROPENE REACT SO EFFICIENTLY WITH CHLORINE RADICALS?

When the alkane hydrogen is on a carbon adjacent to a π-bond (see section 5.1), that hydrogen is removed by radicals at a much faster rate than other alkane hydrogens. The reason is because the resulting radical is *resonance stabilized*. This means that the radical is *delocalized* over several atoms rather than localized on a single atom. If 1-propene (*4.28*) is reacted with chlorine, the chlorine radical (Cl•) reacts with *4.28* to produce the so-called allyl radical, *4.29*. The radical is in a p-orbital, as shown in *4.30* which is parallel to the p-orbitals of the π-bond. These orbitals can overlap in a manner that transfers the radical to the 'end' carbon, as shown in *4.31*, and also transfers the position of the π-bond. The radical is said to be delocalized over all the carbons and *both* structures (*4.31* and *4.32*) are necessary to represent the actual structure of *4.29*. This phenomenon is called *resonance*. A resonance stabilized structure is more stable and lower in energy. In the radical reaction, this extra stability means the radical is formed *faster*, allowing reaction with more chlorine to give the allyl chloride (3-chloro-1-propene, *4.30*).

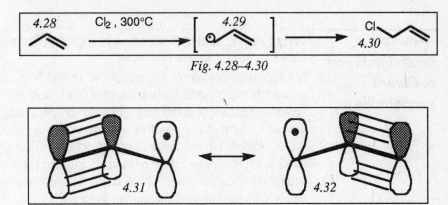

Fig. 4.28–4.30

Fig. 4.31, 4.32

DRAW THE PRODUCTS FROM THE REACTION OF 2-BUTENE WITH CHLORINE AND SHOW ALL RESONANCE STRUCTURES FOR THE RADICAL INTERMEDIATES. DO THE SAME FOR THE REACTION OF TOLUENE WITH CHLORINE.

If 2-butene (*4.33*) is reacted with chlorine, the implications of the resonance intermediate can be seen in the two products, *4.34* and *4.35*. A chlorine radical attaches to both of the radical site in the allylic intermediate. Similarly, if toluene (*4.36*) reacts with chlorine, a resonance stabilized radical is formed (*4.37*), leading to chloromethylbenzene, *4.38*. For reasons to be discussed in chapter eight, the 'intact' benzene ring in *4.38* is more stable than any of the resonance contributors where that ring does not contain the full complement of six pi-electrons. The chlorine in the final product will therefore be attached *only* to the benzylic carbon as shown in *4.38*. In both of these reactions, photochemical energy (provided by a sunlamp) was used to break diatomic chlorine into chlorine radicals.

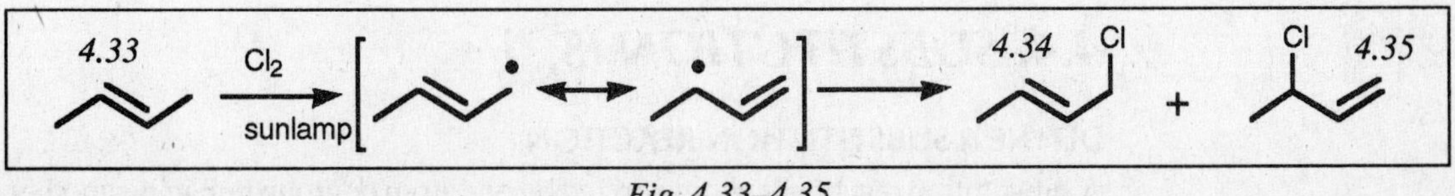

Fig. 4.33–4.35

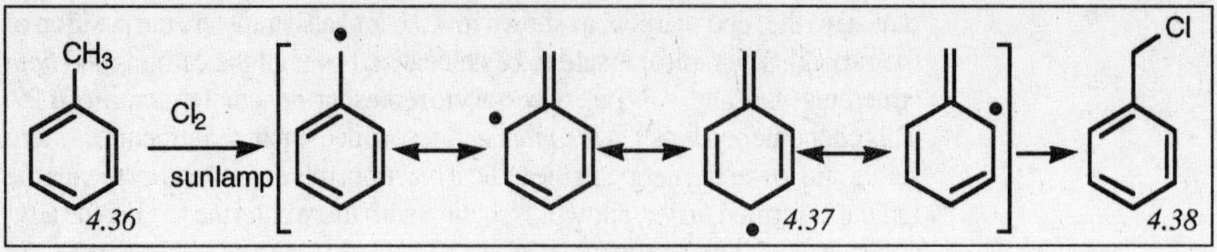

Fig. 4.36–4.38

N-Bromo-succinimide and N-Chloro-succinimide

WHAT IS THE STRUCTURE OF N-CHLOROSUCCINIMIDE AND HOW DOES IT REACT WITH TOLUENE?

N-Chlorosuccinimide (*4.39*, called NCS) and N-bromosuccinimide (*4.40*, called NBS) are cyclic derivatives of succinic acid (see section 14.6). When heated in benzene or carbon tetrachloride with an alkane (particularly alkanes with an allylic hydrogen such as 2-butene or alkanes with a benzylic hydrogen such as toluene) in the presence of photochemical energy (a sunlamp) *4.39* is a source of chlorine and chlorine radicals. Similarly, *4.40* is a source of bromine and bromine radicals. When NCS is reacted with toluene, *4.38* is formed, and when NBS reacts with toluene, *4.41* is formed.

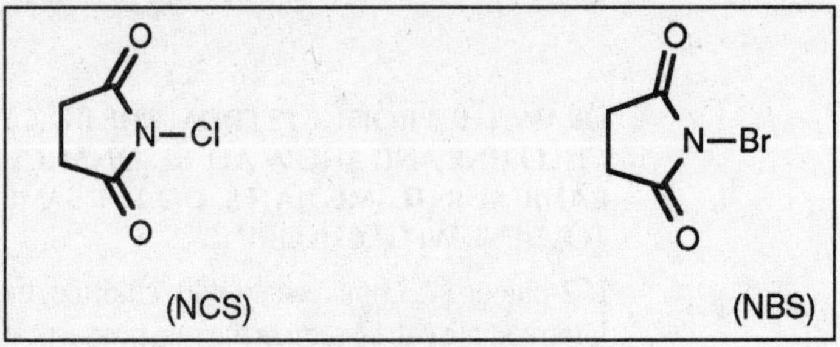

(NCS)   (NBS)

Fig. 4.39, 4.40

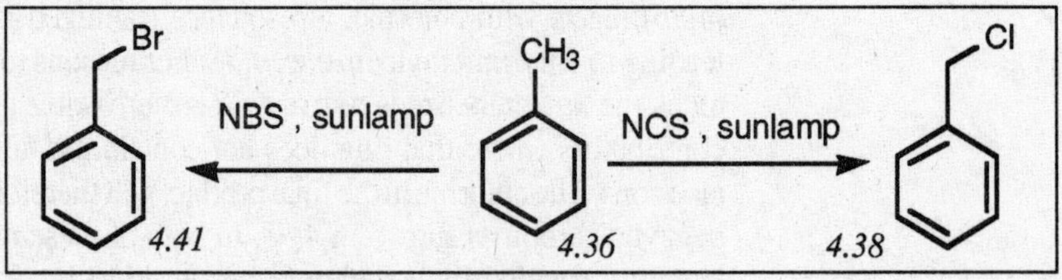

Fig. 4.41

4.4. SUBSTITUTION (S_N^2)

DEFINE A SUBSTITUTION REACTION.

A substitution reaction is characterized by one atom or group replacing another atom or group at an sp^3 atom (usually carbon). This is made possible by the polarized bond of an alkyl halide (C–Cl, C–Br or C–I) where the carbon is electron deficient and its polarity is $\delta^{\oplus}$. That carbon is most likely to react with an electron rich species. If an electron rich species donates its electron to a carbon, it is called a *nucleophile*, and the positive carbon is an *electrophile*.

GIVE A SIMPLE EXAMPLE OF A NUCLEOPHILIC SUBSTITUTION INVOLVING MOLECULES WITH NO MORE THAN ONE CARBON.

A simple example of a substitution is the reaction of a nucleophile (iodide) with bromomethane (*4.42*, the electrophile) to give iodomethane (*4.43*).

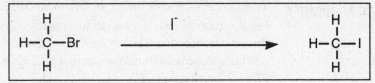

Fig. 4.42, 4.43

Walden Inversion

WHAT IS THE TRANSITION STATE FOR NUCLEOPHILIC BIMOLECULAR SUBSTITUTION AT CARBON?

The incoming nucleophile must *collide* with the electrophile (the $\delta^{\oplus}$ carbon) for this substitution reaction to occur. The iodide is negatively charged and will be repelled by the $\delta^{\ominus}$ bromine in *4.42*. If iodide approaches the carbon over one of the hydrogens (remember *4.42* is three-dimensional and tetrahedral, as in *4.44*), the iodide and hydrogen repel (*steric repulsion*) as they attempt to occupy the same space. The path of least resistance is, therefore, *backside attack*, where iodide approaches the carbon 180° away from the bromine. As iodide approaches carbon, the hydrogen atoms are pushed away until a five-coordinate *transition state* is formed (*4.45*) where the three hydrogens and the carbon are coplanar, the C–I bond is beginning to form and the C–Br bond is beginning to break. This transition state is the logical mid-point of the reaction and is *not* a product that can be isolated or even observed. As the C–I bond is formed, the hydrogens are pushed further away and the C–Br bond is broken, to form *4.43*. The net result of this collision via backside attack is *inversion of configuration at the electrophilic carbon*.

Kinetics

HOW CAN ONE DETERMINE HOW FAST A REACTION OCCURS RELATIVE TO ANOTHER ONE?

The conversion of *4.44* into *4.46* is a collision process (involves two molecules —second order) which makes it a *bimolecular reaction*. It is a bimolecular substitution, is second order and is termed a S_N^2 reaction. The rate of the reaction (rate = disappearance of the starting material in moles/sec or appearance of product in moles/sec—usually measured as disappearance of starting material) is given by the expression: rate = k [nucleophile] [halide], where [] represents the concentration in moles/liter of each molecule. For a S_N^2 reaction, increasing the concentration of either nucleophile or halide will increase the rate of the reaction. The parameter (k) is called the rate constant. Larger rate constants are associated with faster reactions.

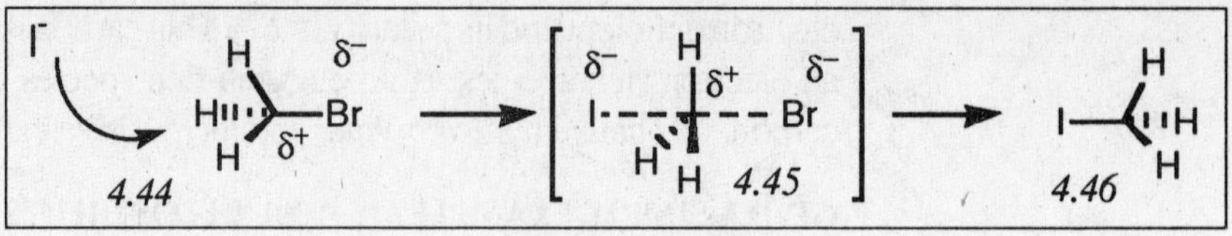

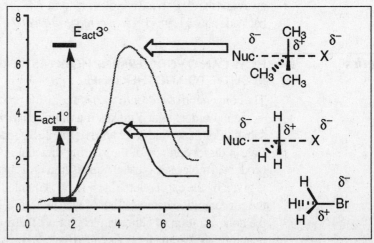

Fig. 4.44–4.46

Influence of Steric Hindrance

EXPLAIN WHY BROMOMETHANE REACTS MUCH FASTER THAN 2-BROMOPROPANE WITH SODIUM IODIDE.

For S_N^2 reactions, primary halides react much faster than secondary halides with the same nucleophile. Tertiary halides are essentially unreactive under the same conditions. The *relative rate constants* are: $CH_3X = 1.0$; 1° (such as $CH_3CH_2X = 0.033$; 2° (such as $Me_2CHX = 8.3 \times 10^{-4}$; and, 3° (such as $Me_3CX) = 5.5 \times 10^{-5}$. The S_N^2 reaction with methyl, primary and secondary halides is useful with a variety of nucleophiles, but S_N^2 reactions with 3° halides give no substitution. The reason is steric hindrance in the transition state. As seen in *4.47*, when the alkyl group (R) is small the four co-planar atoms (C,R,R,R) are easily accommodated in the five-center transition state. When the R groups are large (R=R=R=methyl) the steric crowding is too great, leading to a very high activation energy for formation of that transition state (see *4.48*). For primary and secondary systems, the activation energy is low enough that a reasonable rate is observed.

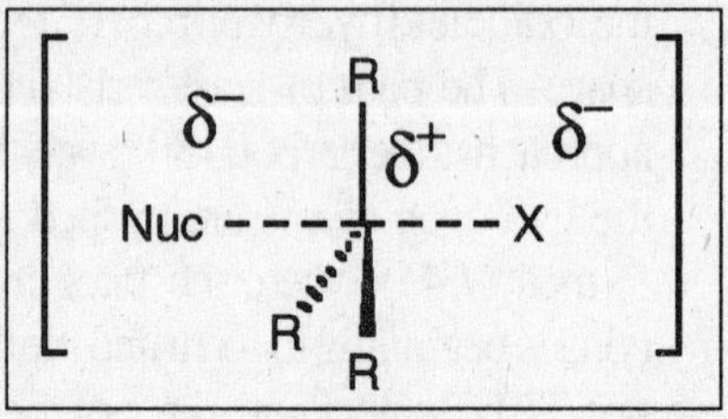

Fig. 4.47

Fig. 4.48

Polar vs. Non-Polar Solvents

DISTINGUISH POLAR AND NON-POLAR SOLVENTS.

There are two major classifications for solvents: polar (these contain highly polarizable atoms and bonds and usually have a high dipole moment) and non-polar (they have a low or zero dipole moment and generally contain no heteroatoms or heteroatoms whose individual bond moments cancel).

DISTINGUISH PROTIC AND APROTIC SOLVENTS.

Each solvent can also be characterized as protic (these contain an acidic hydrogen—X–H where X = O, S or N) or aprotic (these contain no acidic hydrogens—or very weakly acidic hydrogens such as C–H). Common protic solvents are: H_2O, CH_3OH (MeOH), CH_3CH_2OH (EtOH), NH_3, CH_3COOH. Common aprotic solvents are pentane, diethyl ether, tetrahydrofuran (THF), dichloromethane, dimethyl sulfoxide (DMSO) and dimethylformamide (DMF). Water is the most polar of the protic solvents listed. DMSO followed by DMF are the most polar of the aprotic solvents listed. Pentane (a hydrocarbon with no heteroatoms) is the least polar of the solvents listed. In general, polar protic solvents are water soluble and non-polar aprotic solvents are water insoluble. The S_N^2 reaction proceeds best in polar aprotic solvents and is slowest in polar protic solvents.

4.5. SUBSTITUTION (S_N^1)

EXPLAIN WHY 3-BROMO-3-METHYLPENTANE REACTS WITH POTASSIUM IODIDE IN AQUEOUS ETHANOL TO GIVE 3-METHYL-3-IODOPENTANE WHEN THE SAME REACTION IN ANHYDROUS DMF GAVE NO REACTION.

In aqueous media, the carbon-bromine bond of 3-methyl-3-bromopentane (*4.49*) can be broken and loss of bromine gives a carbocation, *4.50*. The water 'pulls' the bromine atom off the carbon by hydrogen bonding. As the bond begins to weaken, the charge increases and water begins to solvate the developing charges until the ionic intermediates (cation *4.50* and bromide ion) are separated and completely solvated by the water. The water, therefore, not only assists in pulling off the bromine but also solvates the charges as they form. This carbocation is quickly attacked by the nucleophilic iodide to give the product, 3-iodo-3-methylpentane, *4.51*. This process involves a completely different mechanism than the S_N^2 reaction discussed above.

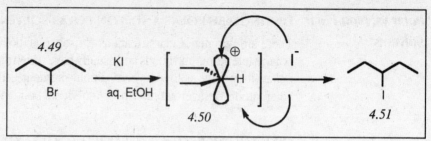

Fig. 4.49–4.51

Kinetics

WHICH HALIDE REACTS FASTER WITH KI IN AQUEOUS ETHANOL, 2-BROMO-2-METHYLPROPANE OR 1-BROMO-ETHANE?

The tertiary halide reacts much faster under S_N^1 conditions. The relative rate of reaction for tertiary, secondary and primary halides that react with KI in aqueous acetone is:

$$CH_3Br = 1.0; \ CH_3CH_2Br = 1.0; \ (CH_3)_2CHBr = 11.6; \ (CH_3)_3CBr = 1.2 \times 10^6$$

This data reflects the energy required to form the intermediate cation (high energy for the slow reactions of bromomethane and bromoethane and low energy for the faster reactions of 2-bromo-propane and 2-bromo-2-methylpropane. The general reaction rate for halides in the S_N^1 reaction is: $3° > 2° >> 1° >>> X\text{-}CH_3$.

Carbocations

WHAT IS THE NATURE OF A CARBOCATION?

Inspection of *4.50* shows that the carbocation is tricoordinate (three substituents) and is electron deficient (see section 4.2). The cation is *planar* around the electron deficient carbon (the two ethyl groups and the hydrogen are *coplanar*. The cation is thought of as an sp^2 hybridized carbon bearing an *empty p orbital*.

WHICH IS THE MORE STABLE CATION, THAT DERIVED FROM IONIZATION OF 2-BROMO-2-METHYLPROPANE OR THAT FROM IONIZATION OF BROMOETHANE?

The rate data shown above clearly suggests that the tertiary halide ionizes (reacts) faster than the primary. This is correlated with the relative stability of the intermediate cations. The tertiary cation is more stable than the secondary, which is more stable than the primary: i.e. $3° > 2° > 1° \oplus CH_3$.

The reason for this order of stability is the presence of carbon groups on the cationic carbon. Carbon groups are *electron releasing*. If electron density is pushed towards the empty p orbital (the cationic center) the net formal charge of the cation is diminished. Lower charge is associated with greater stability and the more carbon groups attached to the cationic center, the more stable will be that cation. The tertiary cation has three carbon groups, the secondary has two and the primary has one (methyl has no carbon groups).

Solvent Effects

WHY DOES 2-BROMO-2-METHYLPROPANE IONIZE TO A CATION WHEN IT IS A PERFECTLY STABLE MOLECULE?

The bromine (called a *leaving group*) does not 'fly off' the molecule. Two things must happen. First there must be something to help 'pull' it off. This is the protic solvent water ($^{\delta\oplus}H-O^{\delta\ominus}-H^{\delta\oplus}$) where the electropositive hydrogen coordinates to the electronegative bromine and 'pulls' it. This pulling lengthens the C–Br bond, making it weaker, which increases the $\delta\oplus$ charge on the C_2 carbon of 2-bromo-2-methylpropane. The water therefore assists removal of the leaving group and this is essential to a S_N^1 reaction.

The second important consideration is stability of the ion being formed (3° cations are stable and relatively easy to form; 1° cations are relatively unstable and difficult to form). The cation product is stabilized by the aqueous solvent where the $^{\delta\ominus}O$ of water donates electron density to the positive center of the cation, further stabilizing it by *solvation*. A solvent that can solvate the cation product is essential.

Solvation of the cation is important for another reason. Water solvates both cations and anions, solvent separating them (as with NaCl). Coordination of water to the $\delta\oplus$ carbon of the halide and to the $Br^{\delta\ominus}$ will help separate them by solvation. This accelerates the rate of ionization.

Rearrangements

DISCUSS THE OUTCOME OF THE REACTION OF *4.52* WITH KI IN AQUEOUS ETHANOL.

Comparing starting material (*4.52*) and the product (*4.53*) clearly reveals that there has been a *skeletal rearrangement* since the bromine in *4.52* is on C_3 and the iodide of *4.53* is on C_2. This rearrangement occurs in the intermediate cation, a common occurrence in carbocations. Ionization of *4.52* generates a secondary cation (*4.54*). The adjacent C–H bond on the tertiary center can be parallel to the p orbital of the cation in one rotamer and the electron density of that bond can migrate towards the electron deficient center. If the bond (carrying the hydrogen) moves to that carbon (C_3 from C_2) a more stable tertiary cation will be formed (*4.56*). Since *4.56* is lower in energy than *4.54*, this process is *exothermic* (by about 15 kcal/mol). The mid-point of this rearrangement is represented as *4.55*, where the hydrogen migrates from C_2 to C_3. This hydrogen migration is called a *1,2-hydride shift*.

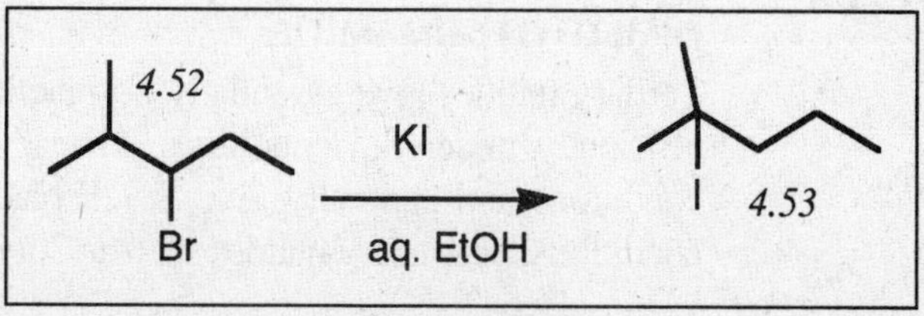

Fig. 4.52, 4.53

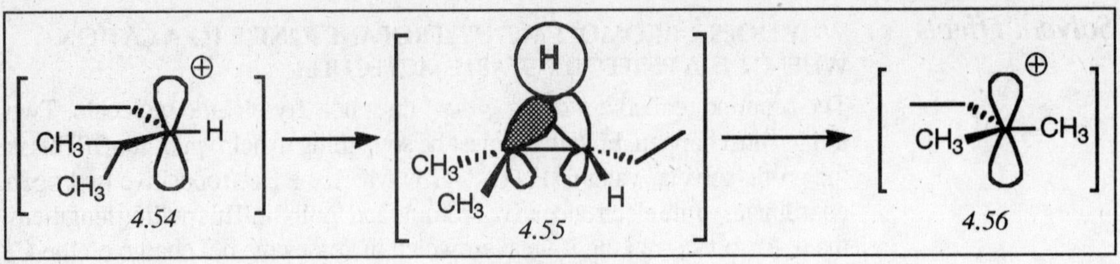

Fig. 4.54–4.56

4.6. S_N^2 VS. S_N^1

There are many reactions where the S_N^2 and S_N^1 process compete with each other, resulting in mixtures of products.

Protic vs. Aprotic Solvents

IS THE REACTION OF BROMOMETHANE WITH KI FASTER IN AQUE-OUS ETHANOL OR IN TETRAHYDROFURAN?

In general, protic solvents such as water and ethanol solvate both cations and anions, separating those charges. The more polar solvent (water) efficiently separates and solvates ions. Aprotic solvents solvate cations but not anions, and separation of ions is not possible. The unimolecular process (S_N^1) requires separation of both cations and anions and, therefore, is efficient only in protic solvents. Bimolecular process demand a collision. If the nucleophile and/or halide is solvated, the solvent molecules 'get in the way' of the collision, slowing it down. Aprotic solvents only solvate cations. The nucleophile (which is usually anionic) is not solvated and can approach the electrophilic center of the halide much easier, facilitating collision and reaction. For this reason, bromoethane reacts with KI (by an S_N^2 process) faster in tetrahydrofuran (an aprotic solvent) than in the protic solvent, aqueous ethanol.

Structural Features of the Halide

EXPLAIN WHY 2-IODOBUTANE USUALLY REACTS WITH KOH TO GIVE 2-BUTANOL AS A MAJOR PRODUCT IN AQUEOUS DIMETHYLFORMAMIDE.

Tertiary halides give essentially no reaction under S_N^2 conditions but react efficiently under S_N^1 conditions. Primary halides react rapidly under S_N^2 conditions and generally give S_N^2 displace-ment or no reaction under S_N^1 conditions. Secondary halides such as 2-iodobutane are midway in reactivity and secondary cations are midway in stability. The conditions described in this question are S_N^1 conditions but the S_N^2 process can compete. In a polar aprotic solvent such as dimethylformamide (DMF), the S_N^2 product (the alcohol) is predicted to be the major product. In water, solvation inhibits the S_N^2 reaction, but ionization to a cation and trapping water also leads to the alcohol via a S_N^1 reaction.

In general, primary halides give exclusively S_N^2 reactions in protic and aprotic solvents, including water. Tertiary halides give no reaction under S_N^2 conditions and ionization followed by substitution under S_N^1 conditions. The product formed from secondary halides depends upon the nucleophile and the reaction conditions. In polar, aprotic solvents, S_N^2 reactions dominate. In water, S_N^1 competes with S_N^2. In polar, protic solvents, elimination dominates if the nucleophile is also a base (see section 5.4).

Stereochemical Features

PREDICT THE PRODUCT WHEN *4.57* REACTS WITH KCN IN DMF AND EXPLAIN THE STEREOCHEMISTRY.

The product of the reaction of S-2-iodoheptane (*4.57*) and potassium cyanide is R-2-cyano-heptane, *4.58*. This S_N^2 reaction proceeds with complete inversion of configuration at the chiral center.

Fig. 4.57, 4.58

PREDICT THE PRODUCT WHEN *4.57* REACTS WITH KCN IN AQUEOUS ETHANOL AND EXPLAIN THE STEREOCHEMISTRY.

The presence of water makes the S_N^1 reaction competitive and it proceeds by a *planar* carbocation. Formation of a carbocation from *4.57* via loss of iodide results in a planar, achiral carbon. This cationic carbon can be attacked by cyanide from either the top or the bottom. Attack from one face generates the S-enantiomer (*4.58*) with net inversion. Attack from the other face generates the R-enantiomer (*4.59*) with net retention. The planar nature of the cation therefore leads to a racemic mixture. It is noted that the S_N^2 reaction can also occur in this medium, leading to more *4.58*.

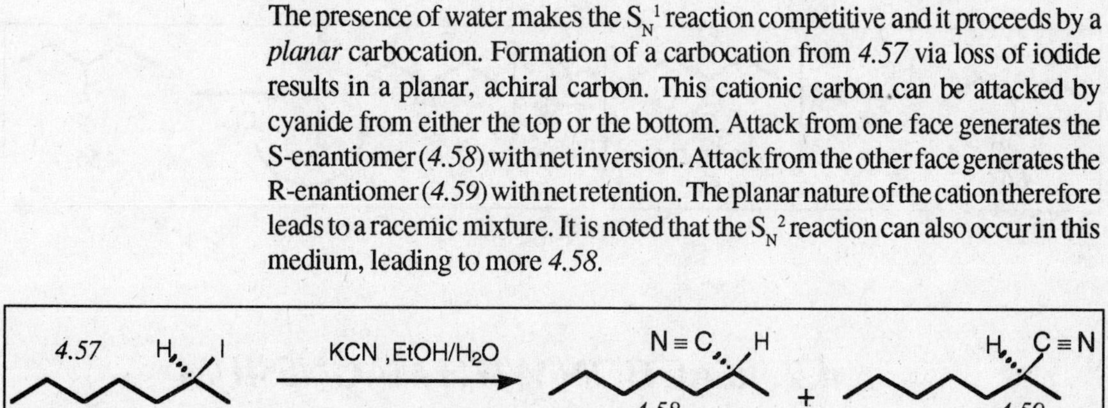

Fig. 4.57–4.59

Alcohols and HX   PRIMARY ALCOHOLS

WHAT IS THE INTERMEDIATE, IF ANY, WHEN 1-PENTANOL IS TREATED WITH HCL UNDER ANHYDROUS CONDITIONS? WHAT IS THE PRODUCT, IF ANY?

The basic oxygen of the alcohol (*4.60*) reaction with the acidic hydrogen of HCl to form an *oxonium* ion (*4.61*). The energy required for this cation to ionize (by losing water) to form a primary cation is too high. The nucleophilic chloride displaces H_2O, which is a good leaving group, in a S_N^2 reaction, giving 1-chloropentane (*4.62*) as the product.

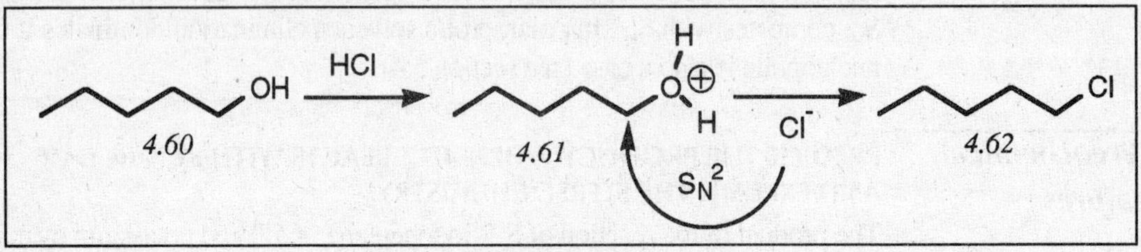

Fig. 4.60–4.62

TERTIARY ALCOHOLS

WHAT IS THE INTERMEDIATE, IF ANY, WHEN 3-PENTANOL IS TREATED WITH HCL UNDER ANHYDROUS CONDITIONS? WHAT IS THE PRODUCT, IF ANY?

As with the primary alcohol, tertiary alcohol *4.63* reacts with HCl to form an oxonium ion, *4.64*. Ionization of water to form a secondary cation (*4.65*) is possible and chloride can attack *4.65* to form the chloride, *4.66*. It is also possible for chloride to attack *4.64* in an S_N^2 reaction, also giving *4.66*. The products probably result from a mixture of these two mechanistic processes.

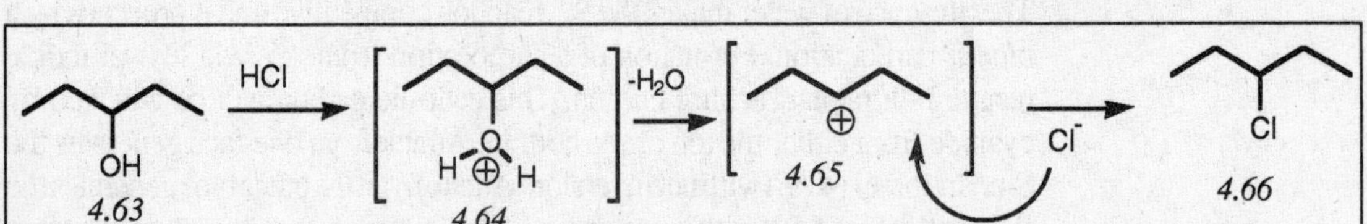

Fig. 4.63–4.66

4.7. REACTION WITH MAGNESIUM

Magnesium metal reacts with alkyl halides to form an organic molecule that contains magnesium, an *organometallic* compound. First exploited by Victor

Grignard in the early 1900's, this type of compound is known as a Grignard reagent and its reactions with ketones and aldehydes are known as Grignard reactions (see section 13.4).

The Grignard Reagent

WHAT IS THE PRODUCT WHEN IODOMETHANE REACTS WITH MAGNESIUM METAL IN DIETHYL ETHER?

The product is H_3C–Mg–I (methylmagnesium iodide), a *Grignard reagent*. In ether, magnesium inserts between the C–I bond. This is a relatively unstable molecule and the ether is necessary to stabilize it by coordination of ether (via the oxygen) with the magnesium. The oxygen is a Lewis base and Mg is a Lewis acid.

WHAT IS THE BOND POLARIZATION OF THE C–Mg BOND?

Since Mg lies to the left of carbon in the Periodic Table, carbon is the most electronegative atom. The bond polarity is: $^{\delta\ominus}C - Mg^{\delta\oplus}$ and the carbon of the Grignard reagent behaves as a *carbanion* (nucleophilic carbon) in most of its reactions.

GIVE THE MAJOR PRODUCTS OF THE REACTIONS. OF 4.67–4.69.

In all three cases, the product is the corresponding Grignard reagent. 2-Bromocyclopentane (*4.67*) gives *4.70*, E–2-chloro-2-hexene (*4.68*) gives *4.71* and bromobenzene (*4.69*) gives *4.72*. In the latter two cases (the vinyl halide and the benzene derivative), THF is used rather than diethyl ether. THF is a stronger Lewis base than diethyl ether and the extra coordination with Mg is required to stabilize these Grignard reagents.

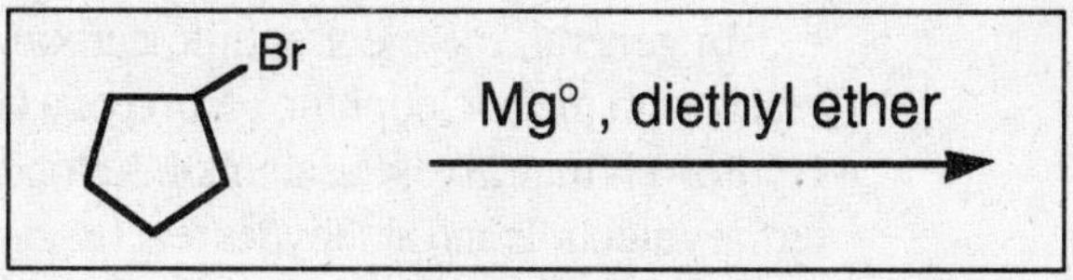

Fig. 4.67

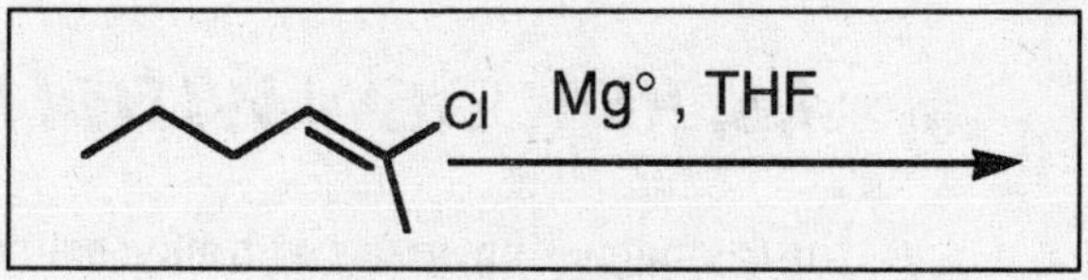

Fig. 4.68

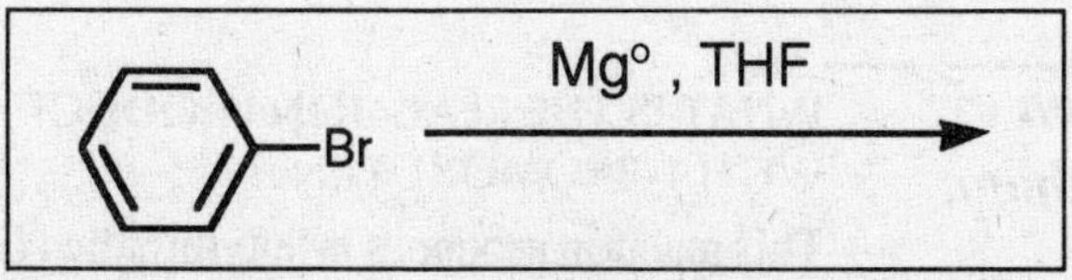

Fig. 4.69

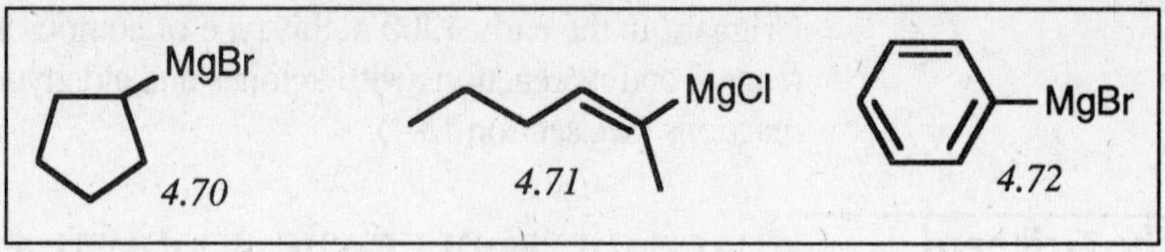

Fig. 4.70–4.72

Reaction with Carbonyls

WHAT IS THE PRODUCT THAT RESULTS FROM THE REACTION OF METHYLMAGNESIUM BROMIDE AND ACETONE (THE IUPAC NAME IS 2-PROPANONE)?

The reaction product is 2-methyl-2-propanol in a two-step reaction. In the first step, the nucleophilic carbon of the Grignard reagent behaves as a nucleophile and attacks the $\delta\oplus$ carbon of the ketone (acetone). When the $C^{\delta\ominus}$ and $C^{\delta\oplus}$ collide, the π-bond of the carbonyl (see section 5.1 and chapter 13) is broken and those two electrons are transferred to the more electronegative oxygen, making the anion (*4.73*). A second step (*hydrolysis*) is required in which aqueous acid is added to *4.73* to protonate the alkoxide and generate the alcohol product (*4.74*).

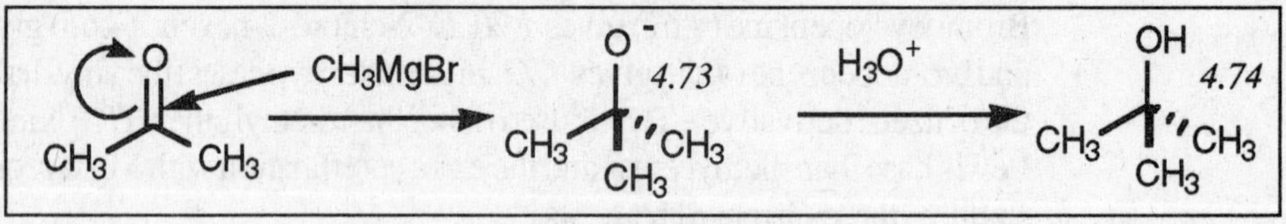

Fig. 4.73, 4.74

In general, the electrophilic carbon of a carbonyl (aldehyde or ketone) reacts with the nucleophilic carbon of a Grignard reagent to form an alkoxide. Hydrolysis then gives the alcohol. Ketones react with Grignard reagents to give tertiary alcohols and aldehydes react to give secondary alcohols. Formaldehyde is the only aldehyde that reacts to give a primary alcohol.

4.8. REACTION WITH LITHIUM

Just as magnesium reacts with alkyl halides to form Grignard reagents, lithium reacts with alkyl halides to form organolithium reagents. This is another example of an organometallic compound.

Preparation of Organolithium Reagents

WHAT IS THE REACTION PRODUCT WHEN LITHIUM METAL REACTS WITH 1-BROMOBUTANE?

This reaction produces *n*-butyllithium ($CH_3CH_2CH_2CH_2Li$). Unlike Grignard reagents, lithium is monovalent, forming C–Li. The generic reaction is: R–X + Li°→R-Li + Li–X, where Li° actually exits as Li–Li.

WHAT IS THE PREDICTED REACTIVITY OF AN ORGANOLITHIUM REAGENT SUCH AS BUTYLLITHIUM.

Organolithium reagents are characterized by a C–Li bond, which is polarized similarly to the C–Mg bond of a Grignard reagent (the C–Li has the polarization $^{\delta\ominus}C-Li^{\delta\oplus}$). Organolithium reagents will, therefore, function as nucleophiles in the presence of an electrophilic species such as acetone or other ketones and aldehydes.

Reaction with Carbonyls

WHAT IS THE MAJOR PRODUCT OF THE REACTION OF *4.75* AFTER THE THREE REACTIONS SHOWN?

Initial reaction of 1-bromohexane (*4.75*) and lithium produces 1-lithiohexane (hexyllithium). This nucleophilic species reacts with cyclohexanone to give the alkoxide, and hydrolysis will generate the alcohol, *4.76*. This is exactly analogous to the reaction of a Grignard reagent with a ketone or aldehyde.

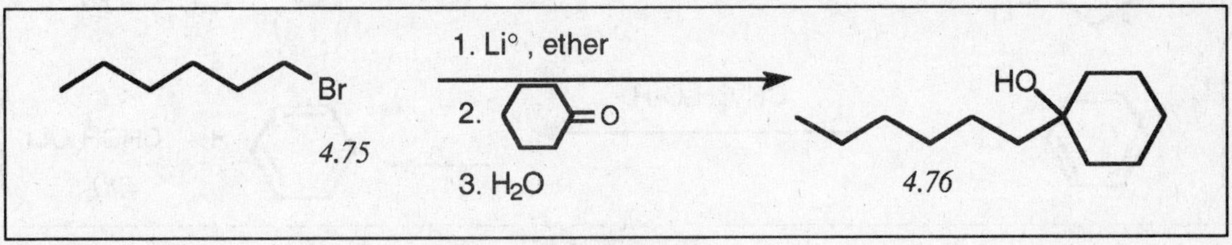

Fig. 4.75, 4.76

Basicity

EXPLAIN WHY BUTYLLITHIUM IS A STRONGER BASE THAN BUTYLMAGNESIUM BROMIDE.

The C–Li bond is more highly polarized than the C–Mg bond. Therefore, the $\delta\ominus$ charge on the carbon of the organolithium reagent is greater (more carbanionic). One must also focus on the conjugate acid by-product (acid + base → conjugate acid + conjugate base). The conjugate acid of the organolithium (and also of the Grignard reagents) is an alkane, a very weak acid ($pK_a > 40$): R–Li+H$^+$X$^-$→R–H+LiX. When comparing butyllithium and butylmagnesium bromide, the acids (R–H) are the same for both (butane), and the greater bond polarity of C–Li is usually the dominant factor which makes butyllithium the stronger base.

WHAT IS THE MAJOR PRODUCT OF THE REACTIONS OF *4.77–4.79*?

Each of these reactions is an acid-base reaction where the organolithium is the base. In the first reaction, 1-lithiopentane (*4.77*) reacts with water (the acid) to give pentane and LiOH. In the second case, lithiocyclopentane (*4.78*) reacts with dimethylamine to produce cyclopentane and lithium dimethylamide (*4.80*). Amines are usually basic due to the lone electron pair on nitrogen. In this case, the organolithium is a much more powerful base than the amine, making the N–H bond an acid (pK_a 25). Phenyllithium (*4.79*) reacts with ethanol to form benzene and lithium ethoxide (*4.81*). Alcohols are amphoteric and in the presence of the powerful base (*4.79*), ethanol is an acid.

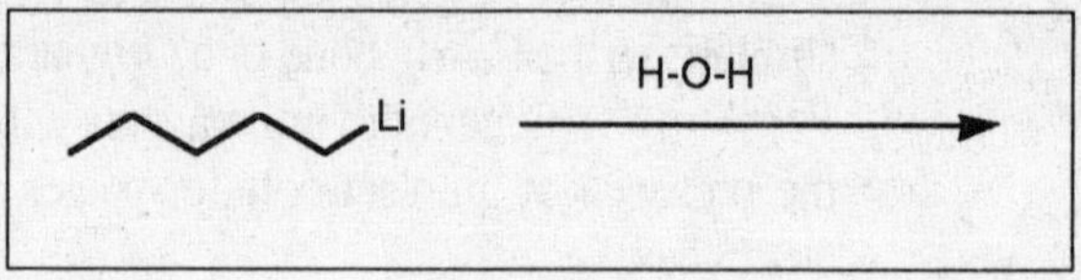

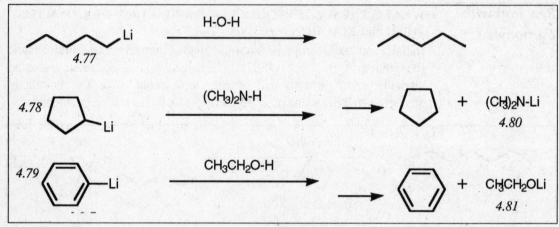

Fig. 4.77

Fig. 4.77–4.81

Organocuprates

WHAT IS THE PRODUCT WHEN A GRIGNARD REAGENT OR AN ORGANOLITHIUM REAGENT REACTS WITH 1-BROMO-PENTANE?

Grignard reagents and organolithium reagents give very poor yields of substitution products when they react with alkyl halides. *n*-Butyllithium, for example, reacts with 1-bromobutane but very little, or no octane (Bu–Bu, the substitution product) is produced. Elimination (see chapter five) and *disproportionation* (self oxidation-reduction) products predominate. In this case butene and butane are the major products.

In general, alkyl halides do not give god yields of substitution products with Grignard reagents or organolithium reagents, *unless a transition metal is added to the reaction.*

PREPARATION

WHAT IS THE STRUCTURE OF LITHIUM DI-N-BUTYLCUPRATE?

When two equivalents of 1-lithiobutane (butyllithium) react with cuprous iodide (CuI), which is Cu(I), the copper forms an *'ate' complex*, which occurs when a metal expands its valence and assume a negative charge. In this case, R_2Cu^- forms, with Li^+ as the counterion. Dibutylcuprate is, therefore, [Bu–Cu–Bu]$^\ominus$ and lithium di-*n*-butylcuprate is $LiBu_2Cu$.

REACTION WITH ALKYL HALIDES

HOW DOES AN ORGANOCUPRATE REACT WITH ALKYL HALIDES?

Dialkylcuprates are carbanion-like reagents that react with carbonyls, to a limited extent, but react rapidly and in high yield with alkyl halides. In this reaction, one of the alkyl groups displaces the halogen of the alkyl halide to give the substitution product (a coupling product). 1-iodoethane, for example, reacts with lithium dibutylcuprate to give hexane: $LiBu_2Cu+CH_3CH_2-I \rightarrow Bu-CH_2CH_3$.

Alkyl halides are important building blocks in organic chemistry. Once they are formed, they can be converted into a variety of other functional groups by relatively straightforward chemical reactions. The nucleophilic and electrophilic centers present in molecules introduced in this chapter will also appear throughout the book. The fundamental principles of reactions and reactivity were also introduced and these basic concepts are key to understanding virtually all organic reactions.

END OF CHAPTER PROBLEMS

1. Give the IUPAC name for each of the following.

2. Draw Lewis dot formulas for (a) phosgene (b) thionyl bromide.
3. Give the complete mechanism for each of the following.

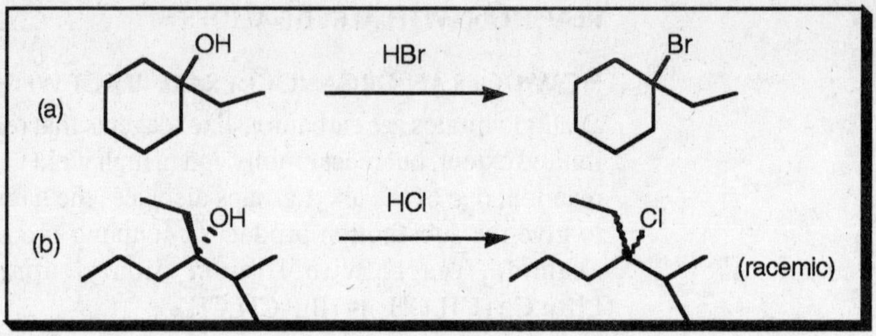

4. Explain why cation A is less stable than cation B.

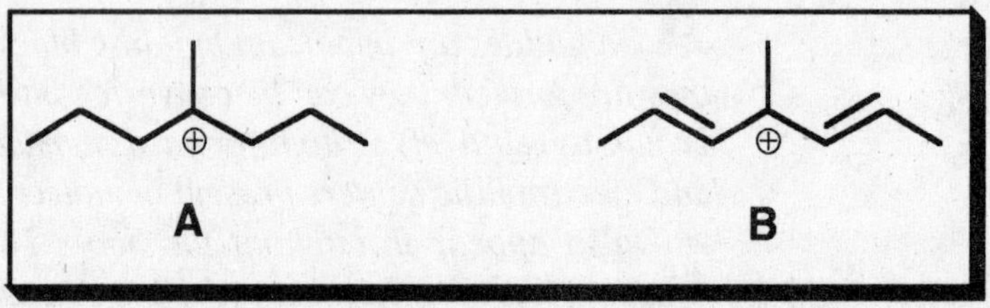

5. Show all products and the relative % of each product for the following reaction.

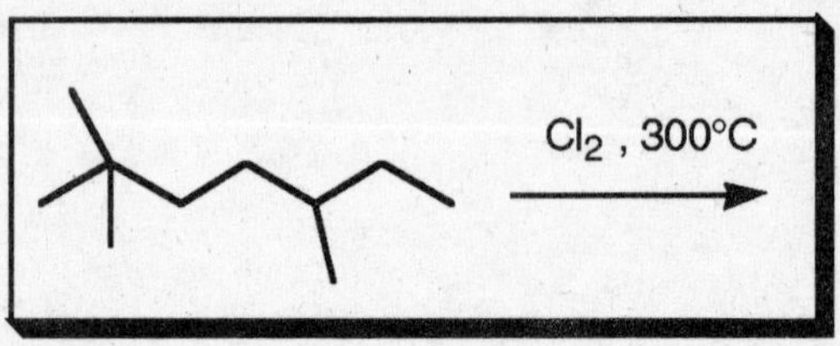

6. If the concentration of KI in the reaction of KI and 1-bromopentane is increased to 10 equivalents, what is the effect on the rate of that reaction? Explain.

7. Explain why the rate of reaction of 1-bromo-2,2-dimethylpropane in a S_N^2 reaction is 3.3×10^{-7} relative to the rate of reaction of bromomethane under the same conditions, although the former is a primary halide.

8. Explain why the rate of reaction of allyl bromide in an S_N^2 reaction is 1.3 times faster than the rate of reaction of bromomethane, under the same conditions.

9. Draw the structures of THF, DMF, DMSO and dichloromethane.

10. Write the rate expression for a S_N^1 reaction. What is the effect on the rate if 10 equivalents of 2-bromo-2-methylpropane are added to 1 equivalent of KI when compared to the reaction when one equivalent of both reagents is used?

11. Explain why the hydrogen migrates in this reaction rather than the methyl and provide the complete mechanism.

12. Explain why this reaction gives a mixture of enantiomeric chlorides but there is a slight preponderance of the inversion product.

13. Explain why ethanol cannot be used as a solvent for the reaction of ethylmagnesium bromide and 2-butanone.

14. Amines (R_2NH) are usually viewed as bases due to the presence of the lone electron pair. Explain why Et_2NH (diethylamine) behaves as an acid in the presence of butyllithium.

15. In each case that follows, give the major product of the reaction. Remember stereochemistry and if there is no reaction indicate that by N.R.

(a) [structure] OH → HBr

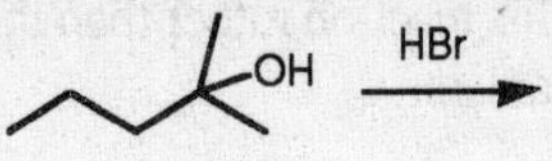

(b) [structure] OH → HCl

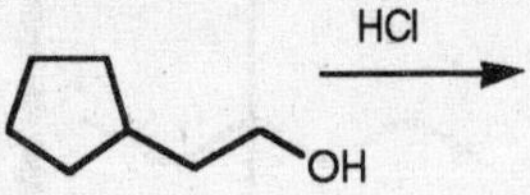

(c) [structure] OH → SOCl₂ / pyridine

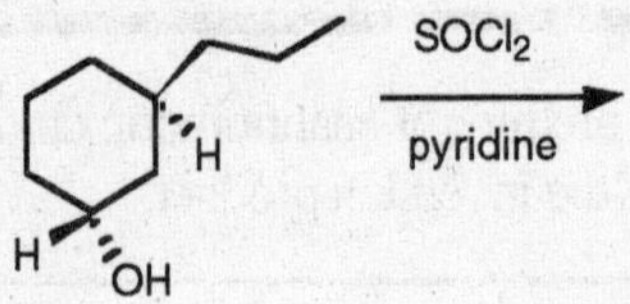

(d) [structure] OH → PBr₃

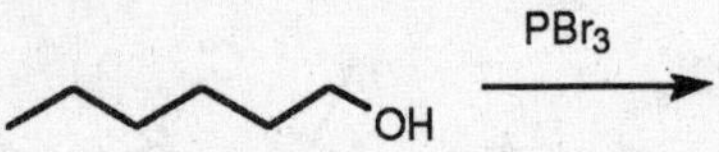

(e) [structure] → Br₂, hν

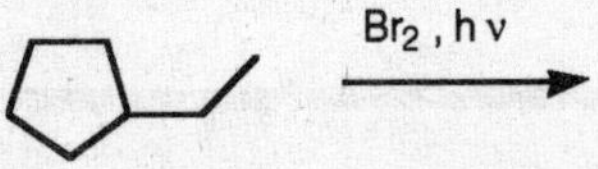

(f) [structure] → Cl₂, 300°C

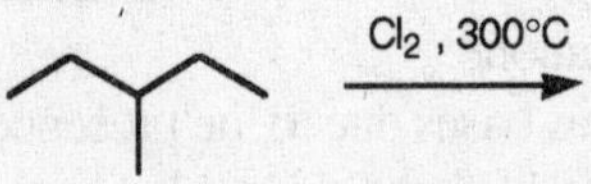

(g) [structure] → Br₂, hν

(h) [structure] → NBS, hν

(i) [structure] Me H I → KCN, DMF

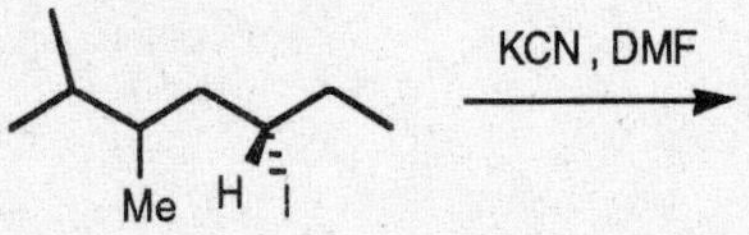

(j) [structure] Me Br → KI, THF

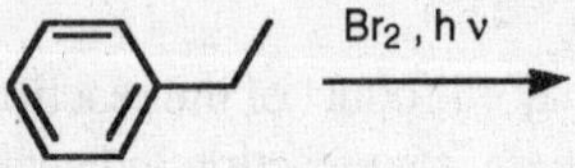

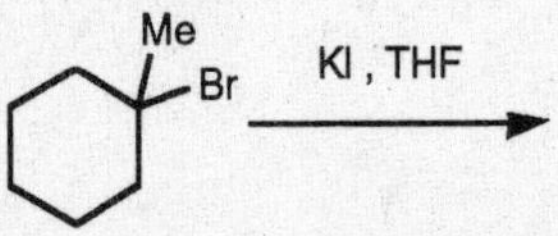

(k) [structure] H Br → KI, THF

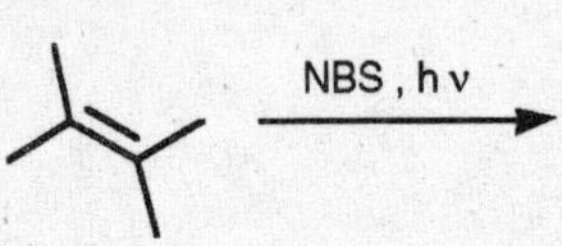

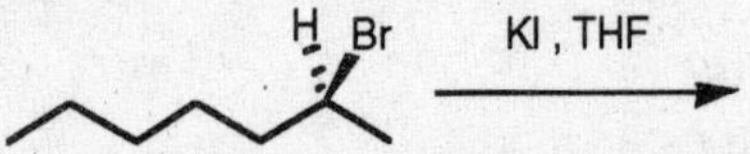

(l) C₅H₁₁—C≡C:⁻ Na⁺ → 1-iodobutane / DMF

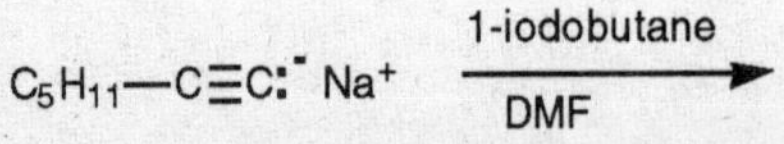

(m) [structure] I → KCN, DMF, 50°C

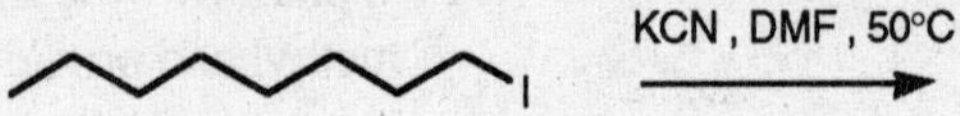

(n) [structure] Br → KCN, aq. EtOH

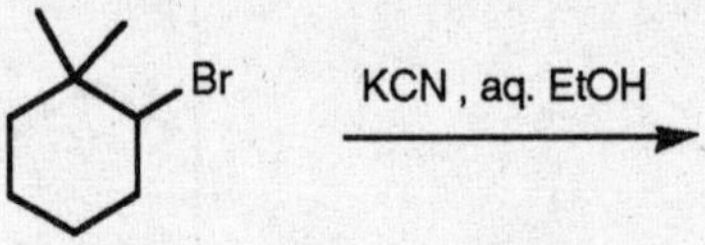

(o) [structure] Br → KCN, aq. EtOH

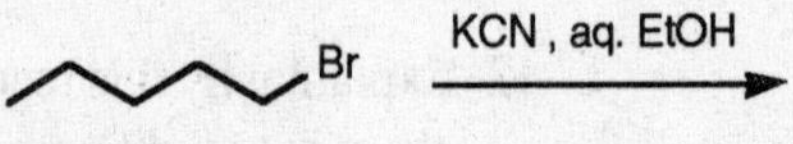

(p) [structure] OH → HBr

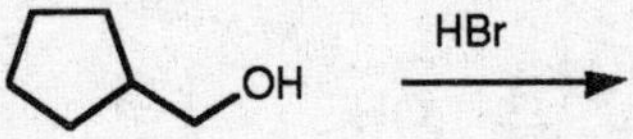

(q) [structure] Cl → 1. Mg°, ether 2. 2-butanone 3. H₃O⁺

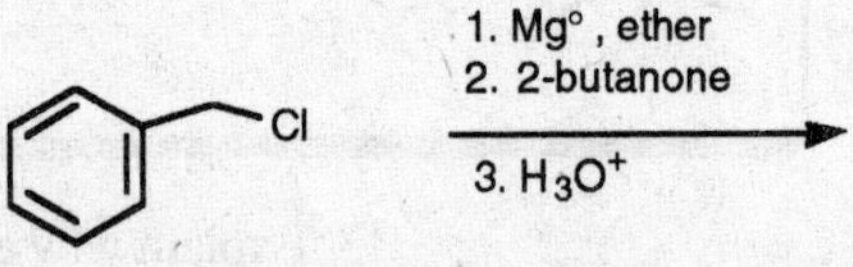

(r) [structure] O → 1. PhMgBr, THF 2. H₃O⁺

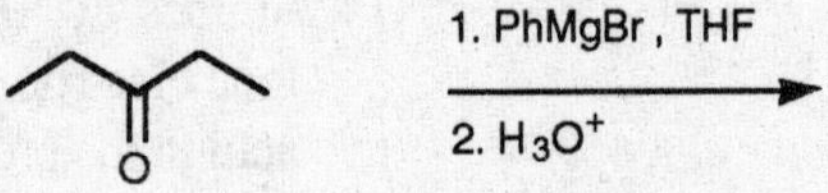

(s) [structure] H → 1. [structure]MgCl, ether 2. H₃O⁺

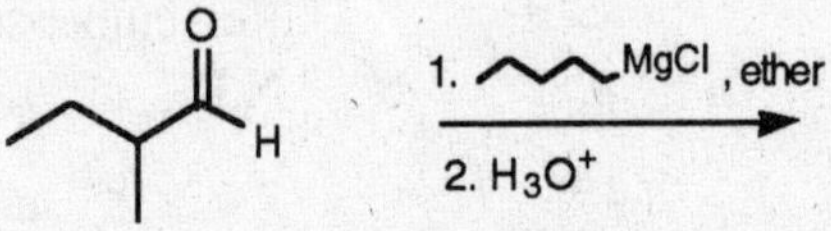

(t) [structure] I → 1. Li°, ether 2. propanal 3. H₃O⁺

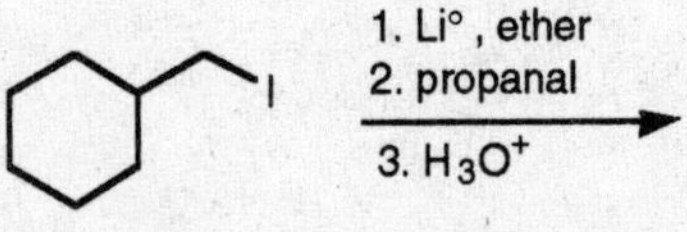

(u) [structure] OH → [structure]Li

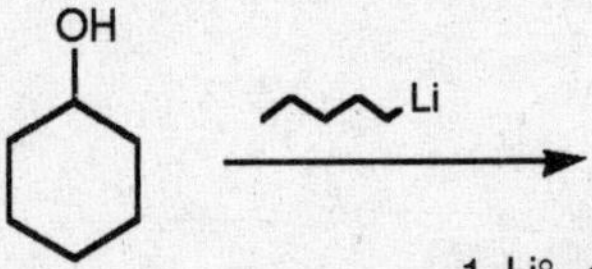

(v) [structure] I → 1. Li°, ether 2. CuI, -10°C 3. PhCH₂Br 4. H₂O

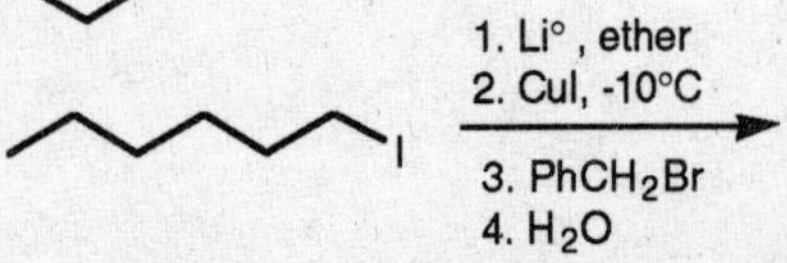

(w) [structure] I → 1. Bu₂CuLi, ether 2. H₃O⁺

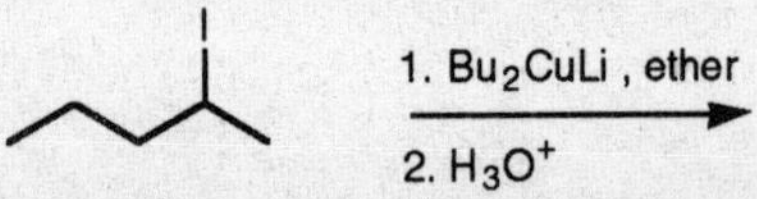

5

Alkenes

Alkenes are a class of compounds characterized by a carbon-carbon double bond (a π-bond), which is highly reactive with a variety of reagents. This π-bond can function as a base in the presence of a suitable acid or as a nucleophile with a sufficiently strong electrophile. Reaction of the π-bond with acid generates cations, which can then react with nucleophiles. Alkenes are among the most important of all functional groups due to the versatility of their chemistry. This chapter will also introduce the important class of reactions called addition reactions, which are characteristic of alkenes.

5.1. STRUCTURE

Bonding

THE π BOND AND SP² HYBRIDIZATION

DESCRIBE THE BONDING IN ETHENE.

Ethene (C_2H_4 or $CH_2=CH_2$) is the simplest member of the alkene family. It is a planar molecule and has two different kinds of bonds between the carbon atoms: a C-C single bond (called a sigma [σ] bond) and a weaker bond called a π-bond. This is usually drawn as *5.1*. The σ-bond is a strong bond directed along the line between the two carbon nuclei (see *5.2* and C–C in *5.3*). The π-bond is formed by overlap of the two parallel p-orbitals on the sp² carbons. This bond is formed by sharing a portion of the electron density of the p-orbitals (see *5.2* and *5.3*), with electron density above and below the plane of the carbons and hydrogens. This 'sideways overlap' is characteristic of a π-bond. It is important to emphasize that in *5.2* and *5.3*, there is only one π-bond, with lobes above and below the plane of the carbon atoms.

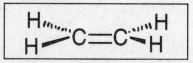

Fig. 5.1

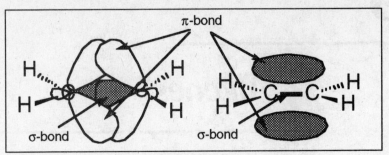

Fig. 5.2, 5.3

WHICH IS THE STRONGER BOND IN ETHENE, THE σ-BOND OR THE π-BOND?

Since the σ-bond has electron density concentrated in a line between the two carbon nuclei, it is very strong. The π-bond has much less electron density concentrated between the carbon nuclei due to the 'sideways overlap' of the p-orbitals. Since it has less electron density between the carbon atoms, the π-bond is a weaker bond (more easily broken).

WHAT IS THE HYBRIDIZATION OF THE CARBON ATOMS IN ETHENE?

Each carbon of ethene is sp² hybridized. Each is trigonal planar, attached to three other atoms and possesses a p-orbital (as part of the π-bond). This sp² hybridization is characteristic of the carbon-carbon double bonds of all alkenes.

DRAW THE MOLECULAR ORBITAL DIAGRAM FOR THE C=C BOND OF ETHENE.

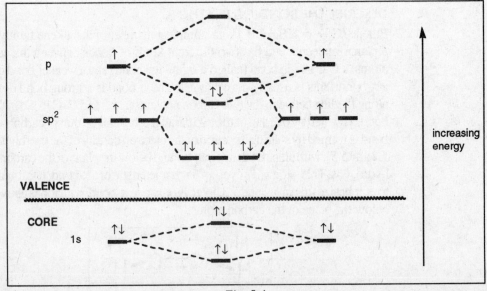

Fig. 5.4

The molecular orbital diagram for ethene (*5.4*) uses three degenerate sp² hybridized orbitals from each carbon to form three identical molecular orbitals. The extra p-electron resides in an higher energy orbital and mixes with the other p-orbital to form the bonding molecular orbital, which represents the π-bond. The molecular orbital for the π-bond is lower in energy than the unfilled anti-bonding orbital from the sp² hybrids.

STABILITY OF ALKENES

WHICH ALKENE IS THE MOST THERMODYNAMICALLY STABLE, 2-METHYL-2-BUTENE OR 3-METHYL-1-BUTENE?

In general, alkyl groups release electron density to the π-bond of the alkene. This extra electron density strengthens the π-bond, making it more stable. A tetrasubstituted alkene is, therefore, more stable than a trisubstituted alkene, which is more stable than a disubstituted alkene. In this example, 2-methyl-2-butene (a trisubstituted alkene) is more stable than 3-methyl-1-butene (a monosubstituted alkene).

LEWIS BASICITY OF THE Π-BOND

GIVE A MECHANISTIC RATIONALE FOR THE REACTION OF 1-PROPENE WITH HCl.

The π-bond of the alkene behaves as a base, donating two electrons to the acidic H⁺ of HCl. This forms a new C–H bond and generates a carbocation (*5.5*). The chloride ion attacks the cationic center to give the final product, 2-chloropropane (*5.6*). The H⁺ could reside on either carbon of the double bond, but *5.5* is the major product. This will be explained in section 5.5.

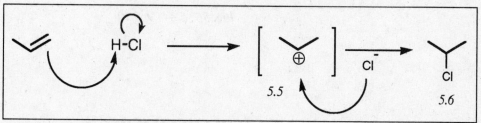

Fig. 5.5, 5.6

5.2. NOMENCLATURE

WHAT IS THE IUPAC ENDING USED OF ALKENES?

The -ane ending is dropped from the alkane name and replaced with -*ene*. The only rule change that is important involves the C=C unit. The double bond *must* be part of the longest continuous chain and the first carbon of C=C that is encountered must receive the lowest possible number, regardless of the substitution pattern (assuming that C=C is the highest priority functional group).

GIVE THE CORRECT IUPAC NAME FOR 5.7–5.10.

Alkene *5.7* has an 8-carbon chain containing the double bond with an ethyl substituent. The name is, therefore, 3-ethyl-3-octene. Alkene *5.8* is a cyclic 6-carbon alkene and is called cyclohexene. Numbering to give the geminal dimethyls (both methyl groups on the same carbon) the lowest number, this becomes 4,4-dimethylcyclohexene (remembering that C_1 and C_2 of cyclohexene must contain C=C). Alkene *5.9* is a 7-carbon chain containing one Br, two methyls and one ethyl. The name is 2-bromo-3-ethyl-4,6-dimethyl-1-heptene. Alkene *5.10* is a cyclooctene with a methyl and an ethyl group. Since the groups are named alphabetically, this is 1-ethyl-2-methylcyclooctene.

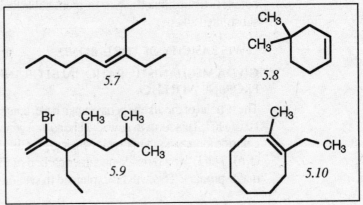

Fig. 5.7, 5.8, 5.9, 5.10

5.3. ALKENE STEREOISOMERS

AN ALKENE IS NAMED 3-HEXENE, BUT THERE ARE TWO DIFFERENT 3-HEXENES. EXPLAIN.

The two different isomers of 3-hexene are *5.11* and *5.12*. The π-bond prevents rotation about the C=C double bond. The two ethyl substituents are, therefore, *locked* in place and cannot be interchanged without breaking and making bonds. These two compounds differ only in the relative spatial position of the groups and are called *stereoisomers*. Since they are different compounds, they require different names to properly identify them.

Definition of cis and trans Isomers

WHAT IS A TRANS- ISOMER?

Alkene *5.11* has both substituents (ethyl) *on opposite sides of the molecule.* When two like groups are on opposite sides of an alkene, the name applied is *-trans*. Alkene *5.11* is, therefore, *trans*-3-hexene.

WHAT IS A CIS- ISOMER?

Examination of *5.12* shows that both carbon substituents (CH_2CH_3) are *on the same side of the molecule.* When two like groups are on the same side of an alkene, the name applied is *-cis*. Alkene *5.12* is, therefore, *cis*-3-hexene.

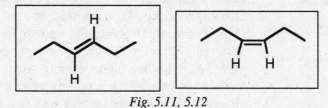

Fig. 5.11, 5.12

GIVE THE IUPAC NAMES FOR *5.13* AND *5.14.*

In *5.13*, the two like groups are methyl. Since the methyl on C_1 and that on C_2 are on opposite sides of the double bond, this is a *trans* alkene (*trans*-2,3-dimethyl-2-heptene). In *5.14*, the two like groups are the ethyl groups and they are on the same side of the double bond. This is a *cis*- alkene (*cis*-4-ethyl-3-heptene).

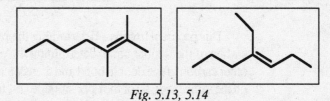

Fig. 5.13, 5.14

WHEN THE NAME OF 2-METHYL-2-OCTENE (*5.15*) IS GIVEN, THERE IS NO CIS- OR TRANS- DESIGNATOR. EXPLAIN.

The two like groups are methyl, but they are both on C_1. The *cis*- and *trans*-nomenclature is used only when one of the like groups is on C_1 and the other is on C_2 of the C=C unit. Since the like groups are on the same carbon in *5.15*, there are no *cis*-/*trans*- isomers and the name is simply 2-methyl-2-octene.

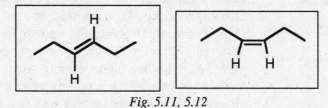

Fig. 5.15

Determination of Substituent Priorities—E/Z Nomenclature

EXPLAIN WHY THE CIS- AND TRANS- NAMES DO NOT APPLY TO 2-CHLORO-3-ETHYL-5-METHYL-2-HEXENE (5.16).

There are no like groups and the *cis-/trans-* nomenclature does not apply. Is the Cl *cis-* to the ethyl or the 2-methylpropyl group? A different nomenclature system is required to properly name compounds such as this.

DESCRIBE THE E-/Z- NOMENCLATURE SYSTEM.

This system is based on a comparison of the substituents on C_1 and C_2 of the double bond. The substituents are assigned a priority based on the Cahn-Prelog-Ingold selection rules introduced in section 3.4. Using *5.16* as an example, one carbon of the double bond has a chlorine and a methyl substituent. Since Cl > C, the chorine is the highest priority group. The other carbon of the double bond has an ethyl group and a 2-methylpropyl group. Using the sequence rules, 2-methyl-propyl is the higher priority group. Comparing the Cl and the 2-methylpropyl shows these priority groups to be on the same side of the molecule. They are given the notation Z (for *zusammen* = together). The name of *5.16*, therefore, is Z-2-chloro-3-ethyl-5-methyl-2-hexene.

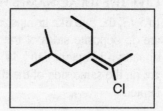

Fig. 5.16

This protocol involves determining the priority of the two groups on one carbon of the double bond, determining the priority of the two groups on the other carbon of the double bond and then determining if the priority groups are on the same side (Z-) or the opposite side (E-, for *entgegen* = apart or opposite).

Alkene *5.17* is an example of an E- alkene. The first carbon has a methyl group and a 1-bromoethyl group, with the latter having the higher priority. The other carbon has a methyl and a hydrogen, with the ethyl being the higher priority. The ethyl group and the 1-bromoethyl group are on opposite sides of the double bond, making this an E- alkene. The name is E-2-bromo-3-methyl-3-hexene.

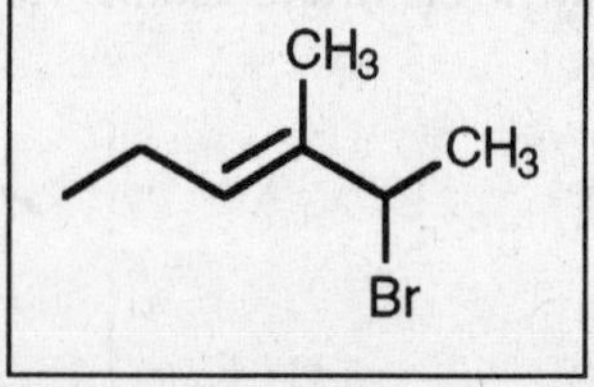

CH_3

CH_3

Br

Fig. 5.17

5.4. PREPARATION OF ALKENES

There are several important methods for the preparation of alkenes. This section will focus on one of the most important methods, elimination from alkyl halides.

The E² Reaction

WHEN 2-BROMO-2-METHYLPROPANE (*5.18*) IS MIXED WITH KOH IN ETHANOL, A S_N^2 REACTION IS NOT POSSIBLE BUT A RAPID REACTION TAKES PLACE GIVING 2-METHYLPROPENE (*5.19*) AS THE PRODUCT. EXPLAIN THIS PROCESS.

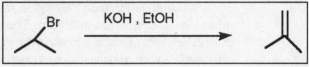

Fig. 5.18, 5.19

The OH⁻ reagent is nucleophilic and will be attracted to the carbon bearing the bromine. The energy required for this S_N^2 reaction is too high (see section 4.4) and the substitution reaction will not occur. Bond polarization makes the β-hydrogen (the hydrogen attached to the second carbon away from the bromine, the β-carbon) electropositive. The hydroxide attacks the β-hydrogen in an acid-base reaction, as shown in *5.20*. Removal of this hydrogen leads to a transition state such as *5.21* where water (H–OH) is being formed, the bromine is being displaced and a carbon-carbon double bond is beginning to form. The final product is *5.19*.

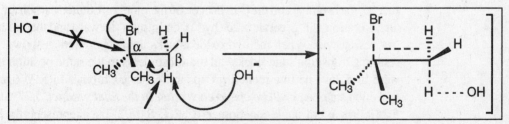

Fig. 5.20, 5.21

The reaction is bimolecular (requires a collision of OH and the β-hydrogen) and is, therefore, second order in its kinetics (rate = k [RX] [OH⁻]). Since the bromine in *5.20* is displaced by the electrons in the C–H$_\beta$ moiety, those electrons should displace Br from the rear (backside attack). This requires that the β-hydrogen be oriented at an angle of 180° relative to the leaving group (Br). This requires an *anti*-attack (OH⁻ attacks the β-hydrogen only when the leaving group and β-hydrogen have an *anti* conformation). The reaction is an *elimination reaction* since the elements of Br and H are *eliminated* from *5.18*. This bimolecular elimination is termed *E²*.

WHY DOESN'T THE E² REACTION OCCUR WHEN *5.18* IS REACTED WITH POTASSIUM IODIDE IN ETHANOL?

Potassium iodide is not very basic (the conjugate acid is HI, strong acid → weak base) and cannot remove the β-hydrogen in *5.18*. If there is no base to remove this hydrogen, the E² reaction is not possible.

WHY DOES THE E² REACTION OF *5.22* GIVE *5.23* AS THE MAJOR PRODUCT RATHER THAN *5.24*?

There are two β-hydrogens, H_a and H_b in *5.22*. Removal of H_a generates *5.23* and removal of H_b generates *5.24*. It was previously established (section 5.1) that the more highly substituted alkene is the more thermodynamically stable. The E² reaction is under thermodynamic control (it is an acid-base reactions and, therefore, an equilibrium reaction). The product will always be the more thermodynamically stable alkene, in this case *5.23*. The more thermodynamically stable alkene, and the major product of the E² reaction, will *always be the most highly substituted alkene*.

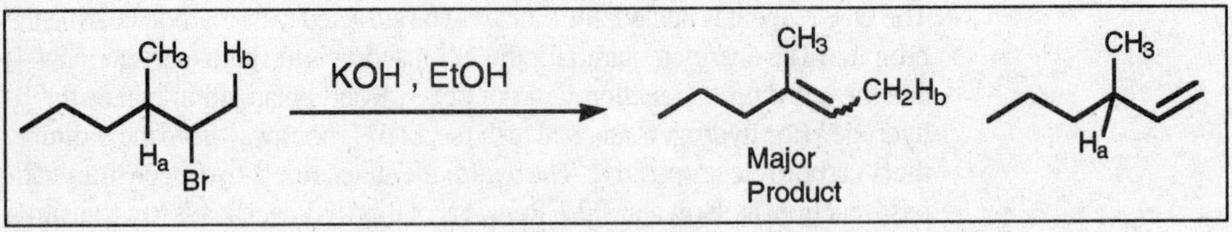

Fig. 5.22–5.24

THE E² REACTION OF *5.25* GIVES EXCLUSIVELY ONE ISOMER, *5.27*. EXPLAIN WHY THE OTHER STEREOISOMER IS NOT FORMED.

In *5.25*, the bromine and the β-hydrogen on the more substituted carbon are *not* anti. Rotation will generate *5.26* (hydrogen 'moves' forward and the bromine 'moves' down). When the hydroxide attacks the β-hydrogen as shown, the resulting transition state 'locks' all the substituents in the same position they were in *5.26*. The two methyl groups are *cis*-to each other in *5.26* (the E² transition state) and *will be cis- to each other in the final product, 5.27*. Since *5.25* is drawn as a single enantiomer ([C_2R, C_3R], *5.27* but it represents the RR/SS diastereomer since it is racemic. Reaction of the C_2R/C_3S of the C_2S/C_3R diastereomer of *5.25* will lead to the *trans*-alkene. The E² reaction is, therefore, *stereospecific*.

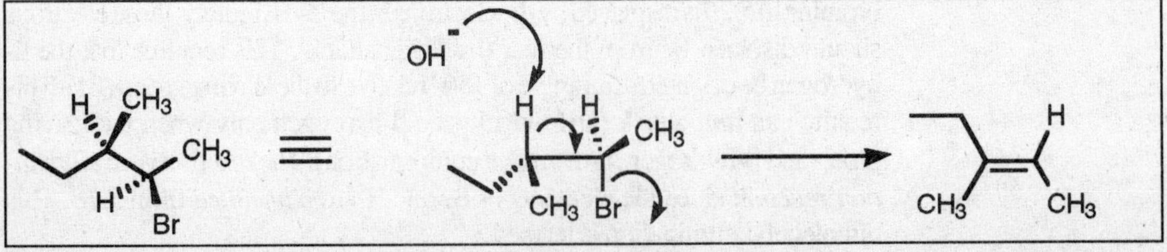

Fig. 5.25–5.27

CYCLOHEXANE DERIVATIVE *5.28* GIVES *5.29* AS THE ALKENE PRODUCT OF THE E^2 REACTION BUT *5.30* GIVES NO ELIMINATION PRODUCTS AT ALL. EXPLAIN THIS OBSERVATION.

This question cannot be answered using the two-dimensional drawing shown. Cyclohexane derivatives exist primarily as chair conformations (section 2.5) where *5.31* and *5.32* represent *5.28*. There are two β-hydrogens, but only in *5.31* are H$_a$ and Br *anti-* (*trans*-diaxial). The other β-hydrogen is equatorial and at right angles to Br—it cannot be removed to give the E^2 reaction. Only removal of H$_a$ can give the E^2 product. Because of this, the alkene is formed *only* towards the methyl (Me) and not towards the ethyl (Et) (see *5.32*). The chair conformations for *5.30* are *5.33* and *5.34*. The Br is axial *only* in *5.33*, but both β-hydrogens are equatorial. In *5.34* both β-hydrogens are axial but the Br is equatorial. An E^2 reaction is *not* possible from either *5.33* or from *5.34* and treatment with hydroxide gives no reaction (N.R.). The bromine-bearing carbon is probably too sterically hindered to give a S$_N$^{2} reaction.

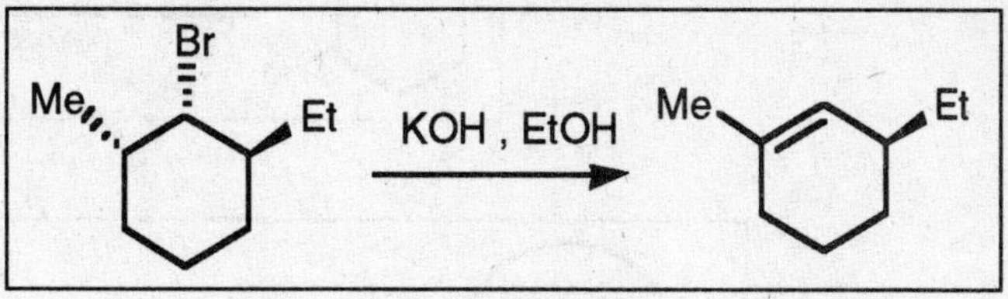

Fig. 5.28, 5.29

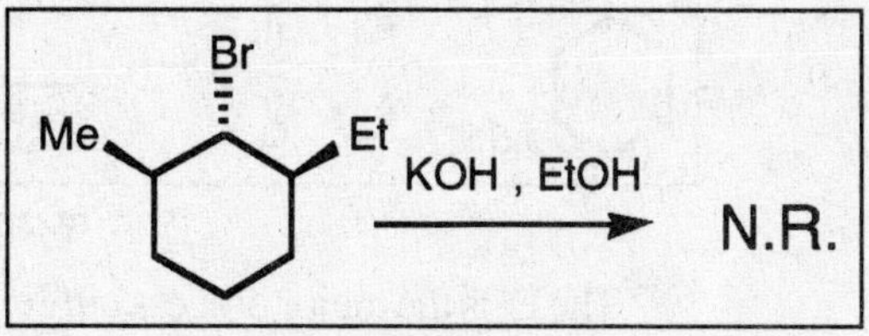

Fig. 5.30

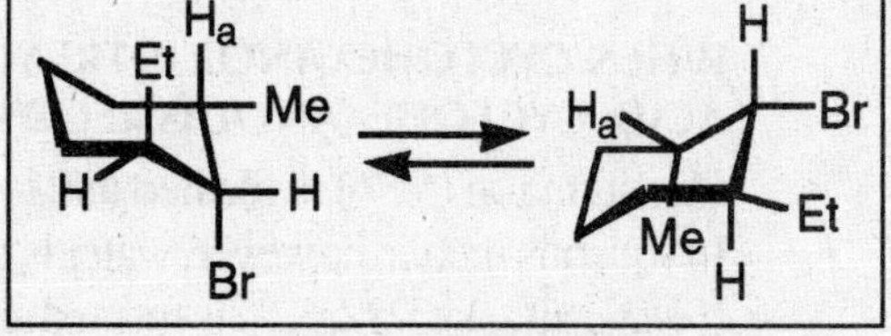

Fig. 5.31, 5.32

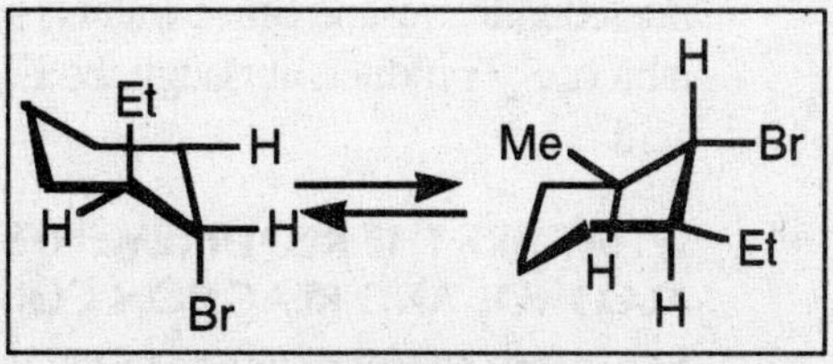

Fig. 5.33, 5.34

The E¹ Reaction

TREATMENT OF CYCLOHEXANOL (*5.35*) WITH CONCENTRATED SULFURIC ACID GENERATES CYCLOHEXENE. EXPLAIN THIS REACTION WITH AN APPROPRIATE MECHANISM.

As in sections 4.2 and 4.6, the oxygen of *5.35* reacts with the acidic hydrogen to form an oxonium salt, *5.36*. The by-product of losing H^+ from H_2SO_4 is the bisulfate anion, $HSO_4^{\ominus}$, which is a very poor nucleophile. This makes both an S_N^2 displacement or a S_N^1 reaction unlikely. Since bisulfate is a weak base, the β-hydrogen (which is acidic due to its proximity to the cation center in *5.37*) can be removed to form the alkene, cyclohexene. This is a unimolecular process (ionization to the cation *5.36*) and is an elimination, therefore it is called an *E¹ reaction*.

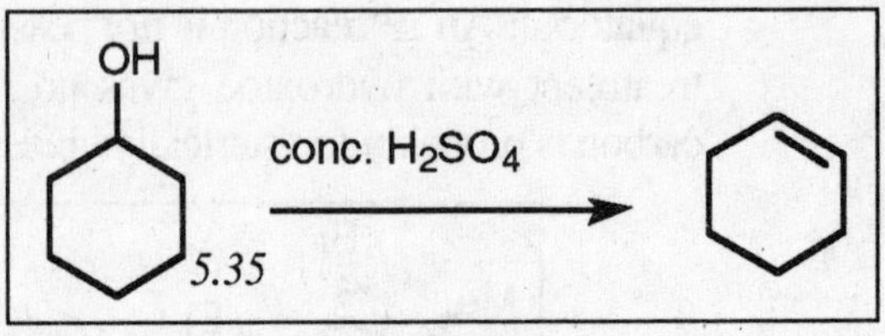

Fig. 5.35

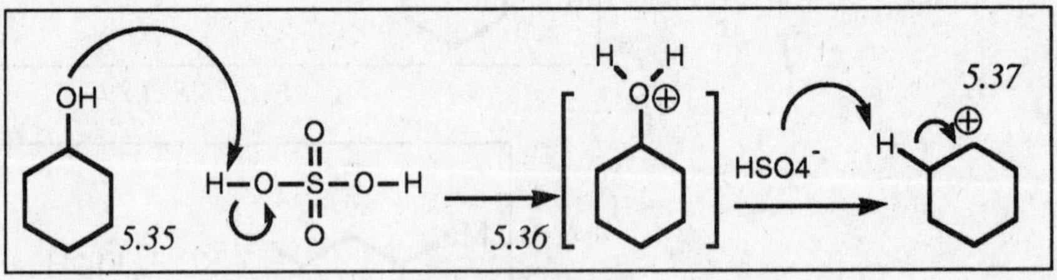

Fig. 5.35–5.37

The E^1 is the major process *only* when a cation is formed in the presence of a base but there is not a nucleophile in the medium that can react via the S_N^1 process.

WHEN CYCLOHEXANOL IS TREATED WITH AQUEOUS SULFURIC ACID, CYCLOHEXANOL IS RECOVERED. EXPLAIN THIS REACTION.

Oxonium ion (*5.36*) is formed and ionization to the cation (*5.37*) also occurs. In aqueous media, however, water is present and can function as a nucleophile. If water attacks *5.37*, *5.36* is formed and loss of a proton regenerates the starting alcohol. The E^1 reaction occurs as the major process only when there is no nucleophile present. Since water is a nucleophile, aqueous H_2SO_4 leads to quite a bit of S_N^1 product, although the E^1 reaction dominates in anhydrous sulfuric acid.

WHAT ARE THE REQUIREMENTS (STRUCTURE OF THE HALIDE OR ALCOHOL AND REACTION CONDITIONS) FOR AN E¹ REACTION?

In general, a tertiary halide or alcohol precursor must be used since they will generate a relatively stable tertiary cation. Primary substrates do not give the cation and secondary substrates give relatively stable secondary cations. The secondary cation may give this reaction but other reactions often compete. With halides, water is usually necessary to help form and stabilize the cation, but water will be a nucleophile and give the S_N^1 reaction as the major process. In such cases, E^1 is usually a minor process. With alcohols, anhydrous acids can be used to generate the cation, but the conjugate base of that acid must not be nucleophilic. This restricts the acid to molecules such as sulfuric acid, perchloric acid ($HClO_4$) and tetrafluoroboric acid (HBF_4).

Competition Between Elimination and Substitution

GIVE THE MAJOR PRODUCT(S) FOR THE REACTIONS OF *5.38–5.41* AND OFFER AN EXPLANATION FOR YOUR CHOICE.

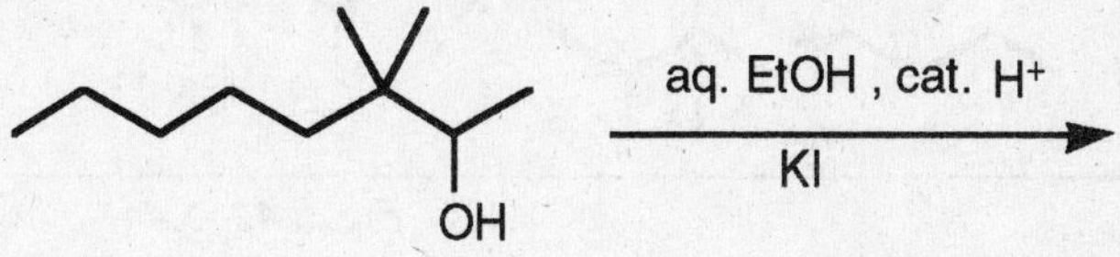

Fig. 5.38

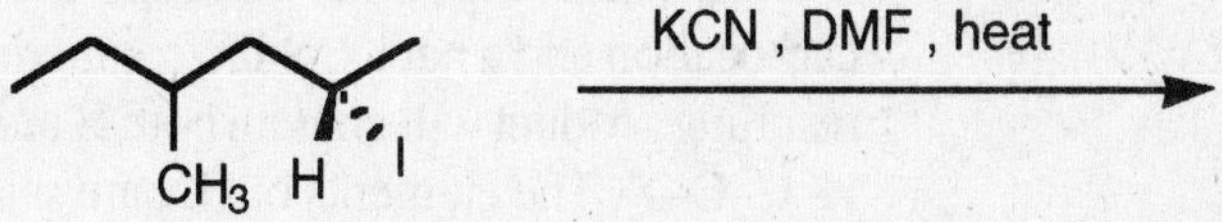

Fig. 5.39

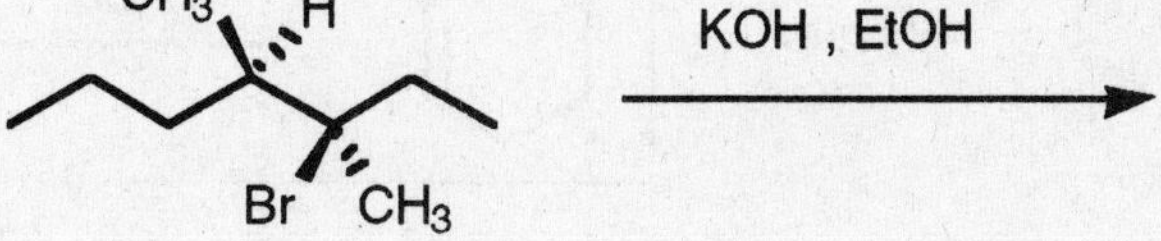

Fig. 5.40

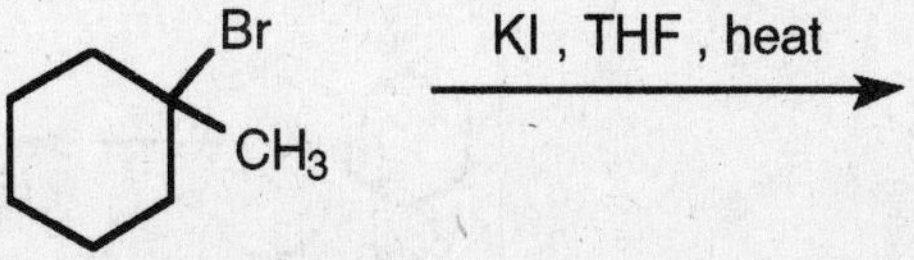

Fig. 5.41

In reaction (a), the aqueous solvent and acid catalyst suggest an S_N^1 reaction. Ionization to a cation is followed by rearrangement (the methyl group migrates to give a more stable tertiary cation) and iodide attacks the cation to give the product, *5.42*. Reaction (b) is an S_N^2 reaction and proceeds with 100% inversion of configuration at the chiral center. The nucleophile (C≡N) displaces the leaving group (I) at the S- chiral center to give the R-nitrile, *5.43*. Reaction (c) suggests an E^2 reaction (tertiary halide—KOH) and elimination of the hydrogen will give a tetrasubstituted alkene as the more stable product. Since *5.40* represents one diastereomer, a single alkene product will be formed, *5.43*. In reaction (d), the tertiary halide cannot react with KI under these S_N^2 conditions, and the correct answer is no reaction.

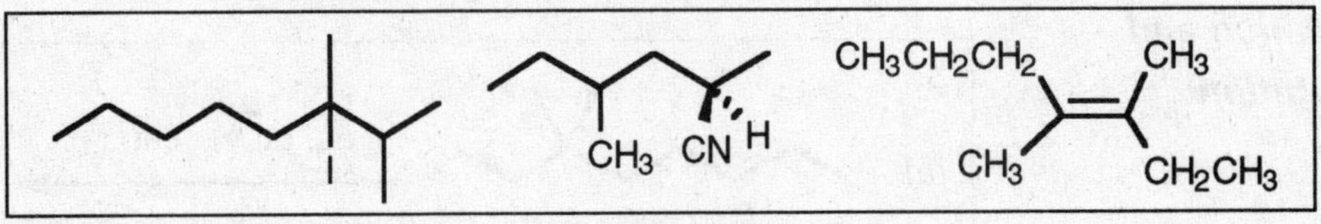

Fig. 5.42–5.44

5.5. REACTIONS OF ALKENES

In the presence of an acid such as H–X, the π-bond of an alkene will function as a base, donating two electrons to H⁺. This will generate a new C–H bond, a carbocation and a nucleophilic counterion, X⁻. If X⁻ reacts with the cation, the resulting product will contain both H and X to give the transformation C=C → H–C–C–X. The elements of HX are said to have *added* to the alkene and this is an *addition reaction*.

Addition of HX   GIVE THE MECHANISM FOR THE TRANSFORMATION OF *5.44* INTO *5.45*.

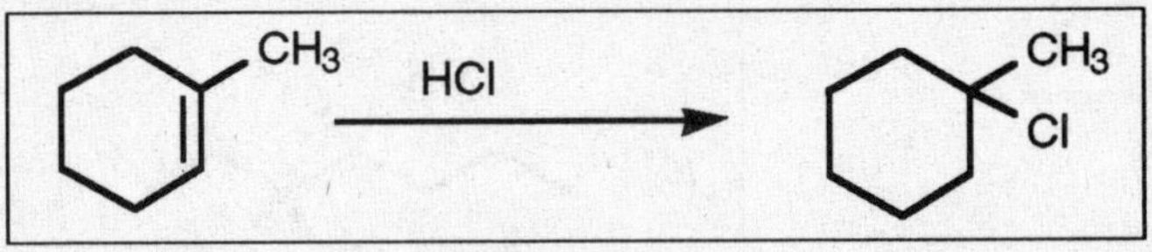

Fig. 5.44, 5.45

The π-bond in *5.44* behaves as a base and attacks H⁺ of HCl, giving a carbocation intermediate, *5.46*. The nucleophilic by-product (Cl⁻) attacks the electrophilic carbon of *5.46* to give the final product, chloride *5.45*.

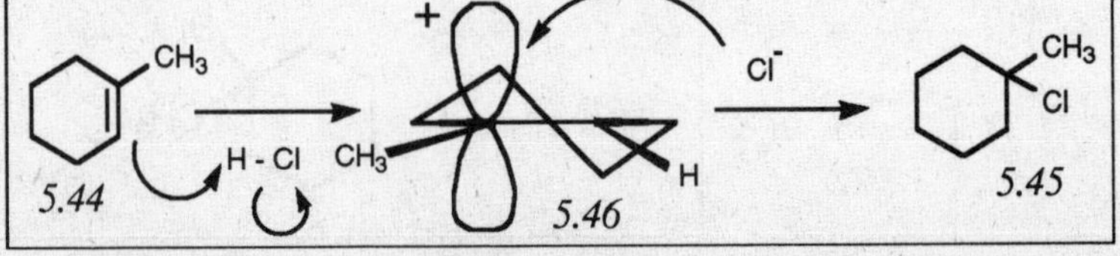

Fig. 5.44–5.46

Markovnikov Addition

WHEN 2-METHYL-2-PENTENE (*5.5.4*) REACTS WITH HCl, THE H⁺ CAN BE TRANSFERRED TO TWO DIFFERENT CARBONS. DRAW BOTH POSSIBLE CATIONIC INTERMEDIATES.

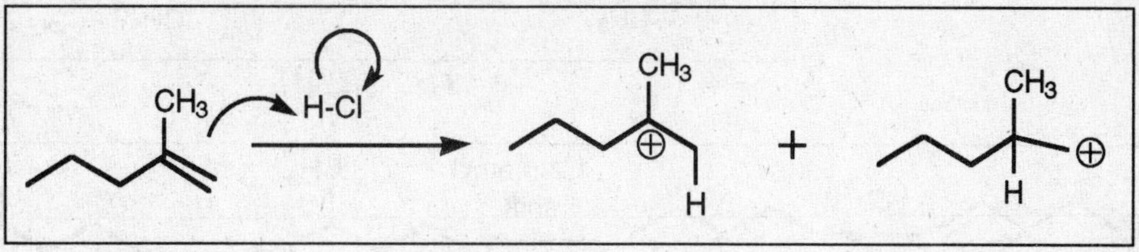

Fig. 5.47–5.49

Cation Stability

WHICH IS THE MORE STABLE CATION DERIVED FROM *5.47*, *5.48* OR *5.49*? EXPLAIN.

Intermediate *5.48* is a tertiary cation and is more stable than the primary cation (*5.49*) derived from the reaction of HCl and *5.47*. Alkyl groups are electron releasing and *5.48* has three alkyl groups attached to the cationic center. Cation *5.49* has only one alkyl group attached to the cationic center. The greater release of electrons stabilizes *5.48* much more than is possible in *5.49* and the energy required for its formation is much lower.

WHAT IS THE MAJOR PRODUCT WHEN *5.47* REACTS WITH HCl?

The major product of the reaction of *5.48* and HCl is 2-chloro-2-methylpentane, derived from the cationic intermediate *5.48*.

EXPLAIN WHY TERTIARY CATIONS ARE MORE STABLE THAN SECONDARY CATIONS. (SEE SECTION 4.5)

As noted in section 4.5, tertiary cations have more electron releasing carbon groups attached to the electropositive carbon than the secondary cation. Electron release diminishes the formal charge on the cation and greater stability is associated with less change.

Rearrangements

Cation rearrangements were introduced in section 4.5.

GIVE THE MECHANISM OF THE TRANSFORMATION OF *5.50* INTO *5.51*.

3,3-Dimethyl-1-pentene (*5.50*) initially reacts with the H⁺ of HBr to give a secondary cation, *5.52*. No hydrogen is available for rearrangement, but if an adjacent methyl group migrates via a 1,2-methyl shift, the more stable tertiary cation (*5.53*) will be formed. Cation *5.53* then reacts with bromide to give the major product, *5.51*.

Since addition of HX reagents to alkenes generates a carbocation, these reactions are subject to both the loss of stereochemistry and the rearrangement noted in S_N^1 reactions (see section 4.5).

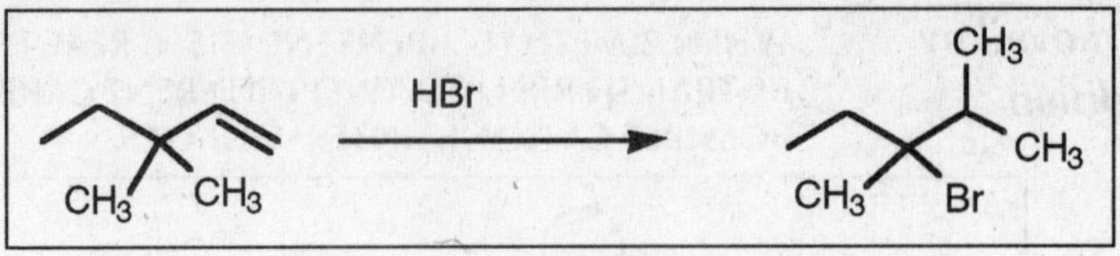

Fig. 5.50, 5.51

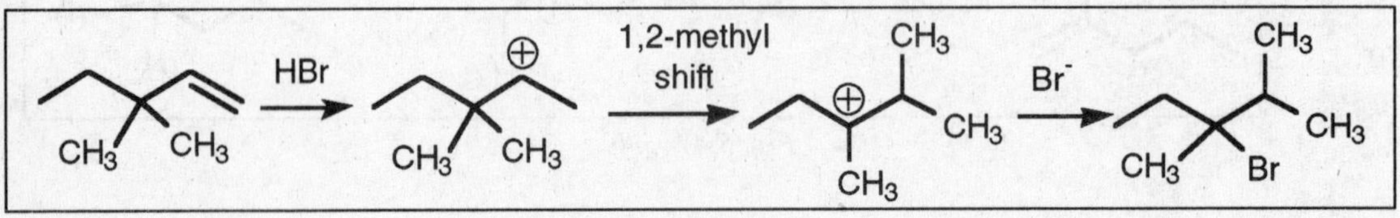

Fig. 5.50–5.53

Anti-Markovnikov Addition

WHAT IS THE MAJOR PRODUCT FROM THE REACTIONS OF *5.54* AND HBr, THE PRESENCE OF DI-*TERT*-BUTYLPEROXIDE?

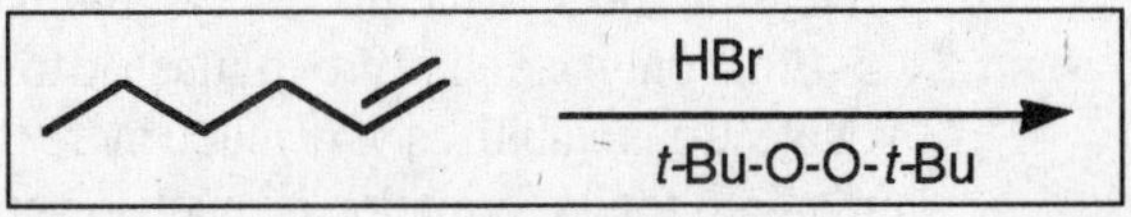

Fig. 5.54

The reaction of alkene *5.54* does not give the 2-bromo-hexane expected from the reaction with HBr via a cation. The major product is *1-bromohexane* (*5.57*), where the presence of the peroxide changes the mechanistic course of the reaction to one involving a radical intermediate.

Alkenes and HBr in the Presence of Peroxides

WHAT IS THE PRODUCT WHEN HBr REACTS WITH DI-*t*-BUTYLPEROXIDE?

Di-*t*-butylperoxide is $Me_3C-O-O-CMe_3$ and easily cleaves upon heating to give radicals such as $Me_3C\bullet$. When this radical reacts with HBr, $Me_3C–O–H$ (2-methyl-2-butanol = *t*-butanol) is formed along with a bromine radical, Br•.

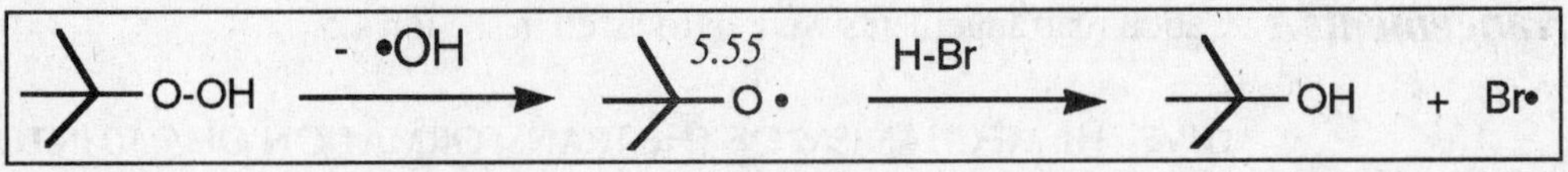

Fig. 5.55

EXPLAIN WHY BROMINE RESIDES ON THE LESS SUBSTITUTED CARBON WHEN HBr REACTS WITH 1-HEXENE (*5.54*) IN THE PRESENCE OF *t*-BUOOH (*5.55*).

In the reaction of *5.54*, the π-bond of the alkene reacts with Br• (produced by cleavage of hydroperoxide *5.55* to give *t*-butanol and Br˙) rather than with H+ and the initial product is a carbon radical, *5.56*. This radical intermediate reacts with additional HBr to produce the product (1-bromohexane, *5.57*) and a bromine radical (Br•) which can continue the radical chain reaction. The bromine ends up on the less substituted carbon because Br• reacts with the alkene to form the more stable radical, in this case a secondary radical rather than a primary radical.

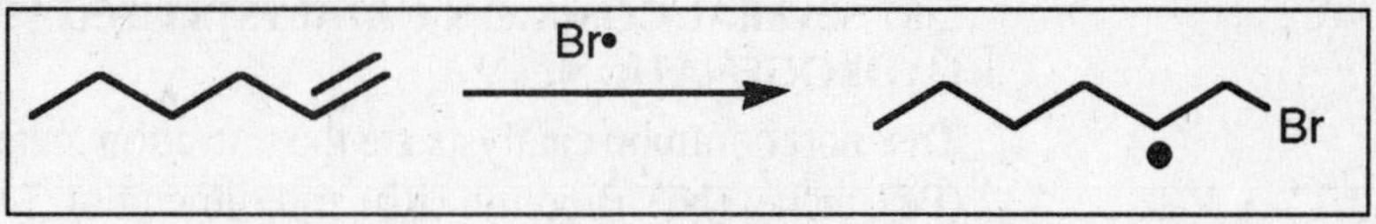

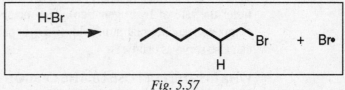

Fig. 5.54, 5.56

Fig. 5.57

Stability of Alkyl Radicals

GIVE THE RELATIVE ORDER OF STABILITY OF ALKYL RADICALS.

Carbon radicals can be considered as electron deficient species for this purpose. Just as with cations, carbon groups are electron releasing and stabilize the radical. Therefore, a tertiary radical is more stable than a secondary, which is more stable than a primary. $3° > 2° > 1° > •CH_3$.

An important difference in radical chemistry is the observation that carbon radicals do *not* rearrange as carbocations do. Another important consideration is that the reaction shown for HBr is not general. It works with HBr and a peroxide, but not with HCl or HI.

Catalytic Hydrogenation

EXPLAIN WHY 1-HEXENE (*5.54*) DOES NOT REACT WITH HYDROGEN GAS WHEN NO OTHER REAGENTS ARE PRESENT.

Diatomic hydrogen gas (H–H) is not polarized and is not very polarizable. When the alkene comes into close proximity to H_2, there is no "H⁺" or "H•" for the alkene to react with. The only way H_2 can react with an alkene is when another reagent is present than can react with H_2 to break the H-H bond.

THE CATALYST

WHAT IS THE MAJOR PRODUCT WHEN E-3-METHYL-3-HEPTENE (*5.58*) REACTS WITH HYDROGEN GAS IN THE PRESENCE OF A CATALYTIC AMOUNT OF PLATINUM OXIDE (PtO₂)?

The platinum oxide is a *catalyst* for the addition reaction of hydrogen gas to the alkene, converting *5.58* to the alkane (3-methylheptane, *5.59*). Only a catalytic amount of PtO_2 is required to promote this reaction, which is known as *catalytic hydrogenation*.

$$ \text{H}_2 \text{ , PtO}_2 \text{ , MeOH} $$

Fig. 5.58, 5.59

LIST SEVERAL COMMON CATALYSTS USED FOR CATALYTIC HYDROGENATION.

The most common catalysts are the transition metals platinum (Pt), palladium (Pd), nickel (Ni), rhodium (Rh) and ruthenium (Ru). These expensive metals must be finely divided since catalytic hydrogenation occurs in heterogeneous systems as a surface reaction (the higher the surface area of the catalyst, the faster the rate of hydrogenation). The metals are often converted to metal compounds such as platinum oxide (PtO_2) or palladium chloride ($PdCl_2$), which can also serve as catalysts.

WHAT IS THE PURPOSE OF THE CARBON IN THE CATALYST PALLADIUM ON CARBON (PD/C)?

Since palladium and platinum are very expensive, the finely divided metal is often mixed with inert materials that have a high surface area, such as carbon black. The carbon is called a *solid support* and 'dilutes' the catalyst as well as increasing the relative surface area. Metals can also be adsorbed or mixed with calcium carbonate ($CaCO_3$), barium carbonate ($BaCO_3$), alumina (Al_2O_3) or Kieselguhr (a form of diatomaceous earth).

GIVE A MECHANISTIC RATIONALE FOR THE CATALYTIC HYDROGENATION OF 2-BUTENE WITH PALLADIUM ON CARBON.

If the catalyst is treated as a surface (as in *5.60*), hydrogen approaches the metal. The metal transfers electrons to hydrogen and a homolytic cleavage leads to hydrogen atoms which bind to the metal (as in *5.61*). When the alkene approaches the metal, the π-bond binds to the surface of the metal and a hydrogen atom is transferred to the alkene, generating a carbon radical (which is also bound to the metal as in *5.62*). Transfer of a second hydrogen liberates the alkane product (here, butane) and regenerates the catalyst, which can react with more hydrogen.

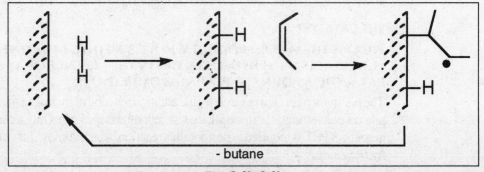

- butane

Fig. 5.60–5.62

GIVE THE MAJOR PRODUCT OF THE REACTIONS OF *5.63–5.66.*

Reaction (a) generates cyclopentane. Reaction (b) gives 2,5-dimethylhexane. Reaction (c) has two equivalents of hydrogen and two double bonds. Both are hydrogenated and the product is 2-methylheptane. In reaction (d), there is no metal catalyst and this gives no reaction.

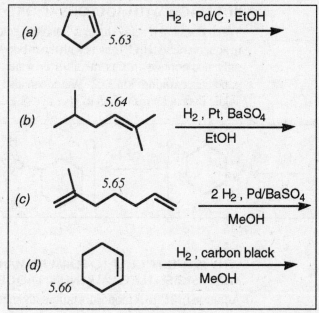

Fig. 5.63–5.66

HEAT OF HYDROGENATION

WHAT IS HEAT OF HYDROGENATION?

Each covalent bond requires that a certain amount of energy be added to break it. That same amount of energy is inherent to the bond and is called the *bond dissociation energy*. When a carbon-carbon double bond is broken during catalytic hydrogenation, the bond dissociation energy for that bond is released and is called *heat of hydrogenation* (alternatively, the amount of heat that must be added to disrupt the C=C bond).

WHAT INFORMATION DOES HEAT OF HYDROGENATION PROVIDE ABOUT ALKENES?

The stronger a C=C bond, the more energy is required to break it. Conversely, for a weaker bond, less energy is required. If the C=C bond of an alkene is stronger than another C=C bond (tetrasubstituted vs. monosubstituted for example) the heat of hydrogenation will be higher for the stronger alkene bond. Heat of hydrogenation therefore gives information concerning the inherent strength of different alkenes.

Hydration

It is possible to add the elements of water (H–O–H) to an alkene, but only if another reagent is added to initiate the reaction. Water is inert to alkenes under neutral conditions.

AQUEOUS ACID

EXPLAIN THE FACT THAT CYCLOHEXENE IS INSOLUBLE IN WATER, BUT REACTS WITH AQUEOUS ACID TO GIVE CYCLOHEXANOL.

Water does not react with the π-bond of cyclohexene (*5.66*) but the H$^+$ present in aqueous acid (H$_3$O$^+$) reacts with the π-bond to form a carbocation (*5.67*). The only nucleophile in this medium is water and reaction of H$_2$O with *5.67* generates oxonium ion *5.68*. Water can also function as a base, removing the acidic hydrogen from *5.68* to give cyclohexanol (*5.69*) as the product.

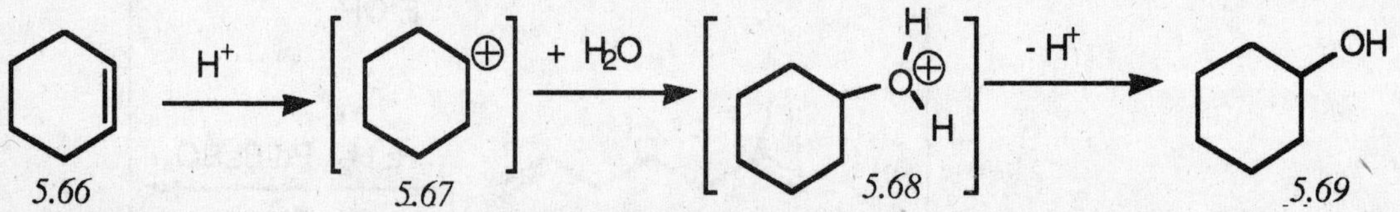

Fig. 5.66–5.69

WHY IS IT DIFFICULT TO FORM PRIMARY ALCOHOLS FROM MONOSUBSTITUTED ALKENES IN AQUEOUS ACID?

Addition of H$^+$ to a monosubstituted alkene will always give the more stable secondary cation as the major product, leading to a secondary alcohol in aqueous acid (see section 5.5). Formation of a primary cation (in order to form a primary alcohol) requires too much energy to be formed preferentially under these conditions.

OXYMERCURATION-DEMERCURATION

WHAT IS THE INITIAL PRODUCT IN THE REACTION OF CYCLOHEXENE AND MERCURIC ACETATE?

Mercuric acetate Hg[OAc]$_2$ (OAc = acetyl, see *5.70*) contains mercury, which functions as a Lewis acid. Reaction with the basic π-bond of *5.66* generates a mercury-stabilized cation (*5.71*) which reacts with the best nucleophile available in the medium (water is a better nucleophile than the acetate anion) to give the mercuric alcohol product (*5.73*) via *5.72*.

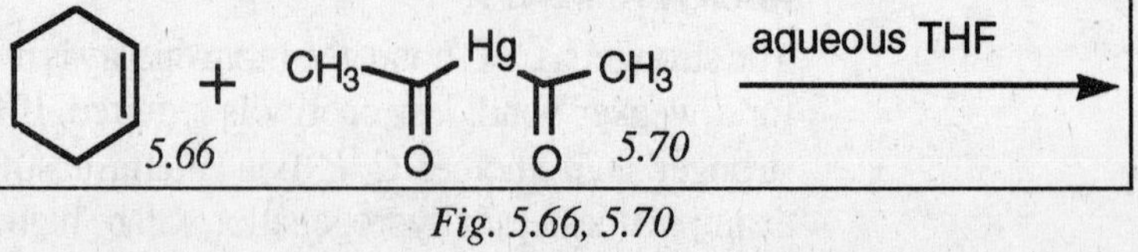

Fig. 5.66, 5.70

HOW IS THE MERCURY REMOVED FROM *5.73*?

A reagent must be added to break the C–Hg bond and replace it with hydrogen (generating C–H). This is called a hydrogenolysis reaction. The best reagent for doing this is sodium borohydride (NaBH$_4$—see section 11.3). If *5.73* is treated with NaBH$_4$, the product is cyclohexanol, *5.69*.

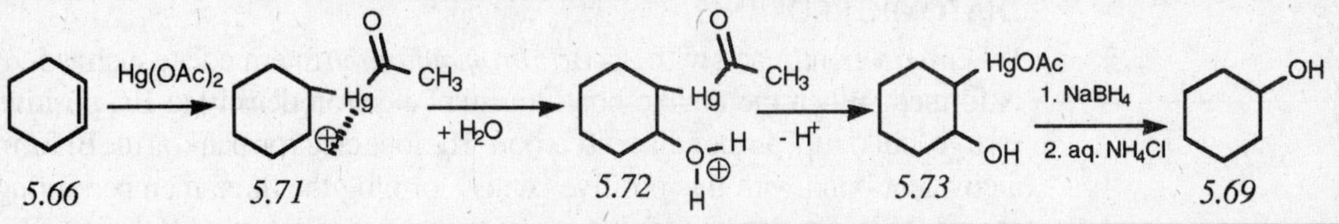

Fig. 5.66, 5.71, 5.72, 5.73, 5.69

EXPLAIN WHY THE REACTION OF MERCURIC ACETATE AND 3-METHYL-1-HEXENE (*5.74*) LEADS TO 3-METHYL-2-HEXANOL (*5.77*), WITHOUT REARRANGEMENT.

Inspection of the mercury stabilized cation derived form cyclohexene (*5.71*) provides the answer. The mercury donates electron density back to the cationic center, providing some stabilization. Sufficient stabilization is provided that the rearrangement reaction is much slower, so slow that addition of water to the cation is faster. 3-Methyl-1-hexene (*5.74*) initially generates the mercury stabilized cation *5.75*, which adds water to give *5.76*. 'Back-donation' by mercury inhibits the expected rearrangement. Reduction with NaBH$_4$ gives the final alcohol product, *5.77* (3-methyl-2-hexanol). *Note that the mercury adds to give the more stable secondary cation (5.75), just as in the reactions of alkenes with HX.*

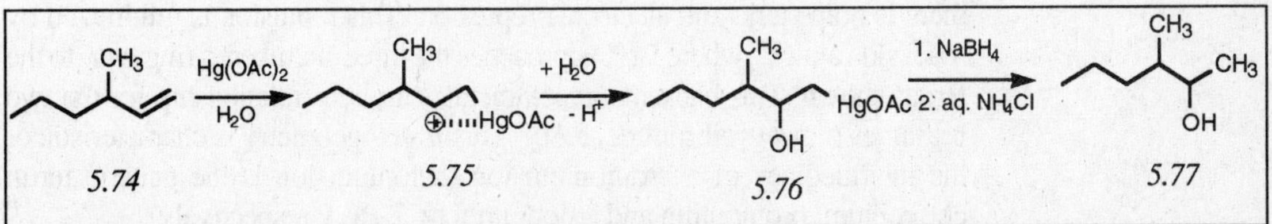

Fig. 5.74–5.77

Addition of Halogens

Alkenes react with halogens such as diatomic chlorine, bromine or iodine to give *vicinal* dihalides. A vicinal halide has two halogen atoms on *adjacent* atoms (X–C–C–X). The mechanism of this addition is different from the reactions with HX and leads to *trans*-dihalides.

HALONIUM IONS

WHY DOES AN ALKENE REACT WITH DIATOMIC BROMINE (Br$_2$)?

The Br–Br bond is polarizable and in the presence of the alkene (the alkene comes in to close proximity to one of the bromines), the closest Br becomes $\delta_\oplus$ by *induced polarization*. In the presence of the alkene, therefore, Br–Br becomes $^{\delta\oplus}Br$–$Br^{\delta\ominus}$. With this induced dipole, the π-bond can transfer two electrons to $Br^{\delta\oplus}$ and generate $Br^\ominus$ as a leaving group.

WHAT IS THE INTERMEDIATE WHEN CYCLOHEXENE REACTS WITH DIATOMIC BROMINE?

When the π-bond reacts with Br–Br, a *bromonium ion* intermediate such as *5.78* is formed. When the double bond transfers electron density to Br, positive charge 'builds up' on the adjacent carbon. The lone electron pairs on the Br form a covalent bond with this positive center, forming the three-membered ring shown. This is re-drawn as *5.79* to show the proper perspective of the ion. The bromide counterion acts as a nucleophile, opening the three-membered ring to give the *trans*-dibromide product, *5.80*.

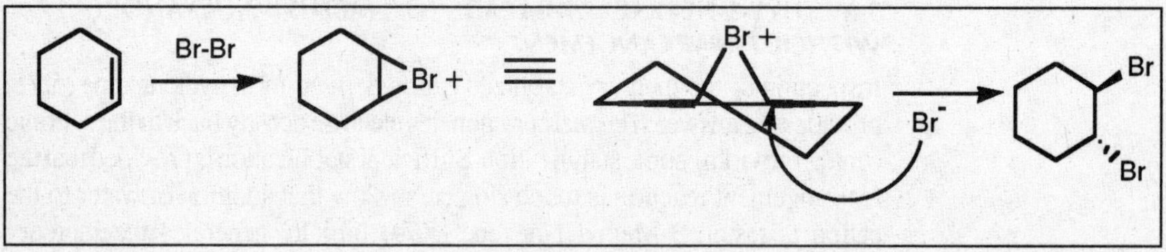

Fig. 5.66, 5.78, 5.79, 5.80

WHEN INTERMEDIATE 5.78 REACTS WITH BROMIDE (Br⊖), FROM WHICH FACE WILL IT APPROACH, FROM THE SAME SIDE AS THE BROMINE, OR FROM THE OPPOSITE SIDE? JUSTIFY YOUR ANSWER.

This is best answered by inspection of *5.79*. If $Br^\ominus$ approached from the 'top', there is both steric and electronic repulsion. This repulsion is minimized by 'backside attack', where $Br^\ominus$ approaches the three-membered ring *anti-* to the Br, as shown. This backside attack dictates an *anti-* relationship for the two bromines (a *trans*-dibromide, *5.80*). This *trans-* geometry is characteristic of the intermediacy of a bromonium ion (halonium ion is the generic term: chloronium, bromonium and iodonium for Cl, Br, I, respectively).

STEREOCHEMISTRY

WHAT IS THE PRODUCT WHEN E-4-ETHYL-3-OCTENE (5.81) REACTS WITH Br₂ IN CCl₄?

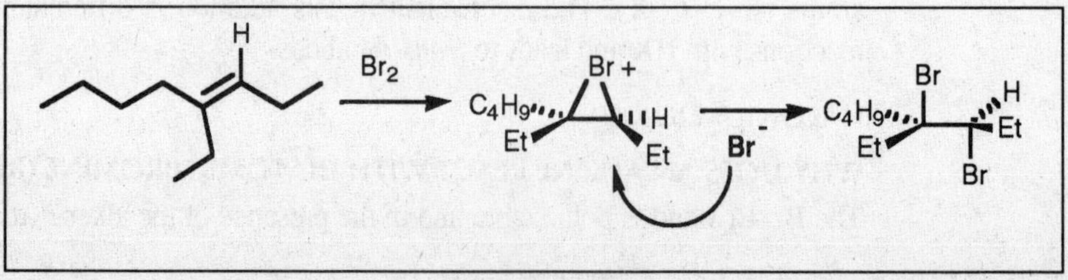

Fig. 5.81–5.83

This reaction also proceeds by a bromonium ion intermediate (*5.82*). *Anti-* attack is also required, which dictates an *'anti-'* relationship for the bromines in the product, *5.83*. Since this is an acyclic molecule, *cis-/trans-* isomers are not possible. Diastereomers are possible, however. *Anti-* attack dictates that a single diastereomer is formed (*5.83*). Since the bromine can form the bromonium ion on either the 'top' or the 'bottom' of the alkene, diastereomer *5.83* is *racemic*. Formation of a racemic diastereomer is the norm for this reaction, which is diastereospecific but shows no enantioselectivity at all. Note that Br$^\ominus$ attacks *5.82* at the less sterically hindered carbon. Attack at the other carbon of the bromonium ion would generate the enantiomer.

HOW MANY STEREOISOMERS ARE PRODUCED WHEN CIS-2-BUTENE REACTS WITH Br$_2$?

cis-2-Butene (*5.84*) reacts with Br$_2$ to give bromonium ion *5.85*. *Anti-* attack by Br$^\ominus$ leads to *5.86* as the only diastereomer (but it is racemic). If the 'bottom' carbon is rotated by 180°, rotamer *5.87* results. The mirror image of *5.87* is not superimposable and since this *diastereomer* is racemic, two stereoisomers result from this reaction.

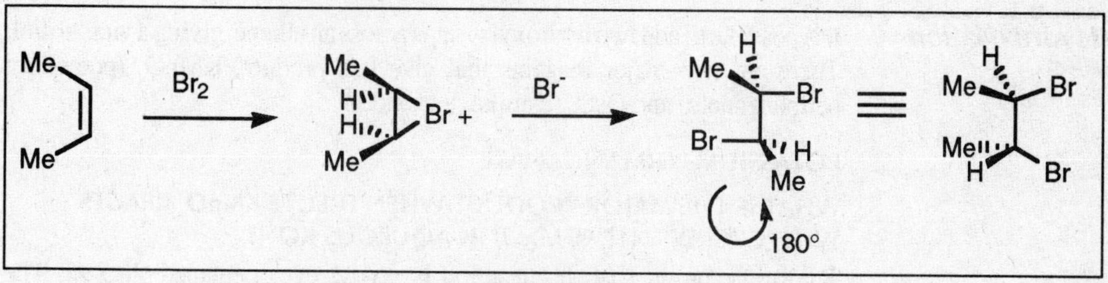

Fig. 5.84–5.87

If *trans*-2-butene were reacted with Br$_2$, only one diastereomer would result, meso 2,3-dibromobutane.

HYPOHALOUS ACIDS

WHAT IS THE PRODUCT WHEN CHLORINE IS DISSOLVED IN WATER?

When chlorine (Cl$_2$) is dissolved in water, hypochlorous acid (HOCl) is formed. This molecule is polarized as Cl$^\oplus$ OH$^\ominus$. Similarly, HOBr is formed when bromine (Br$_2$) is dissolved in water.

WHAT IS THE PRODUCT OF THE REACTION BETWEEN 3-METHYLCYCLOPENTENE (*5.88*) AND HOCl?

The product is a *vicinal* (on adjacent carbons) chlorohydrin (chlorine and OH in the same molecule), *5.90*. Initial reaction of *5.88* with Cl$^\oplus$ from the HOCl generates a chloronium ion, *5.89*. Although water is present, the three-membered ring remains largely intact and the nucleophile (OH⁻) attacks carbon (from the face opposite the Cl in *5.89*) to give the racemic diastereomer, *5.90*.

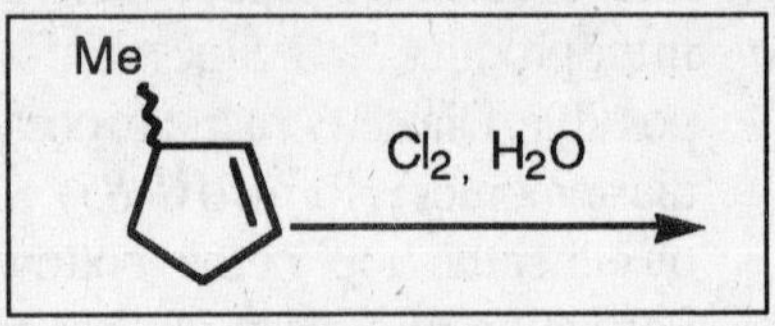

Me

Cl$_2$, H$_2$O

Fig. 5.88

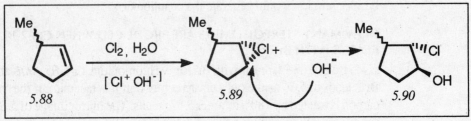

Me   Me   Me

Cl$_2$, H$_2$O   ''/Cl +   ''/Cl

[Cl$^+$ OH$^-$]   OH$^-$ OH

5.88   *5.89*   *5.90*

Fig. 5.88–5.90

Hydroxylation

It is possible to add two hydroxyl groups across an alkene, giving a vicinal diol. There are two major reagents that give this product, KMnO$_4$ (potassium permanganate) and OsO$_4$ (osmium tetroxide).

POTASSIUM PERMANGANATE

WHAT IS THE MAJOR PRODUCT WHEN DILUTE KMnO$_4$ REACTS WITH CYCLOPENTENE (*5.63*) IN AQUEOUS KOH?

The major product of this reaction is *cis*-1,2-cyclopentanediol, *5.92*. The reaction proceeds by initial formation of a cyclic manganese compound (*5.91*) which is decomposed by hydroxide to give the diol.

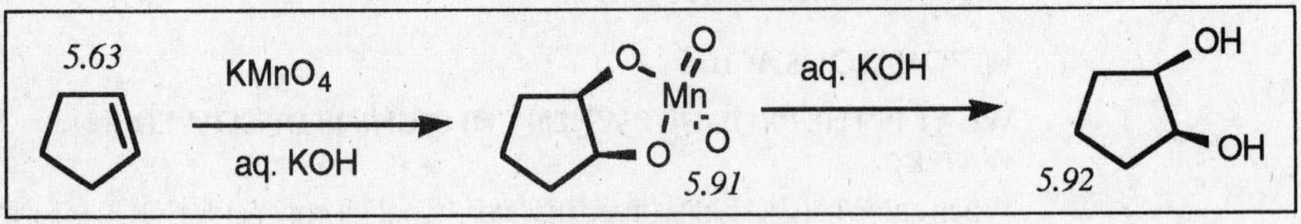

5.63   OH

KMnO$_4$ O   O   aq. KOH

Mn   OH

aq. KOH   O   O   *5.91*   *5.92*

Fig. 5.63, 5.91, 5.92

WHAT IS THE PURPOSE OF THE KOH IN THIS REACTION?

Intermediate *5.91* is the initial product of the reaction of cyclopentene and permanganate (see *5.93*) and a second chemical reaction (with hydroxide) is required to convert *5.91* into the diol product (*5.92*). Hydroxide attacks the Mn in *5.91* and breaks the Mn–O–C bond between Mn and O (see *5.94*). Two attacks by hydroxide and proton transfer to the O$^-$ species gives the diol.

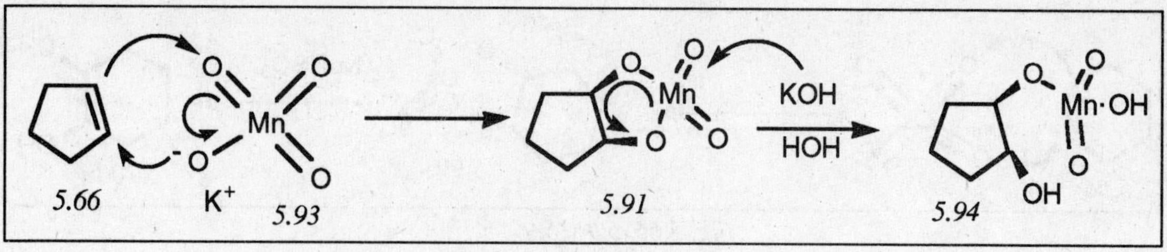

Fig. 5.66, 5.93, 5.91, 5.94

WHY DOES THIS REACTION PRODUCE THE *CIS-* DIOL?

As seen in *5.93*, the alkene reacts with two of the oxygens on MnO_4^-. The two bonds are formed close together in time (possibly in a concerted manner) generating the *cis-* stereochemistry in *5.91*. The *trans-* compound could form only if there were a bond rotation prior to formation of the second C–O bond. The bond making process is too fast to allow this, and the *cis*-stereochemistry is characteristic of this reaction. Since hydroxide attacks Mn and not carbon, the stereochemistry at the carbon is retained.

WHAT IS THE MAJOR PRODUCT WHEN TRANS-3-HEXENE REACTS WITH KMnO₄ AND AQUEOUS KOH?

Since the *cis*-diol is formed without formation of the *trans*-diastereomer, the reaction is diastereospecific (it will form the racemic *cis*-diol). In acyclic molecules such as *trans*-3-hexene (*5.95*), the terms *cis-/trans-* do not apply to the acyclic diol product, but the cyclic manganese intermediate will 'lock' the *cis*-stereochemistry of the ethyl groups into place. Hydroxide opens *5.96* to give *5.97* as the only diastereomeric product, as a racemic mixture.

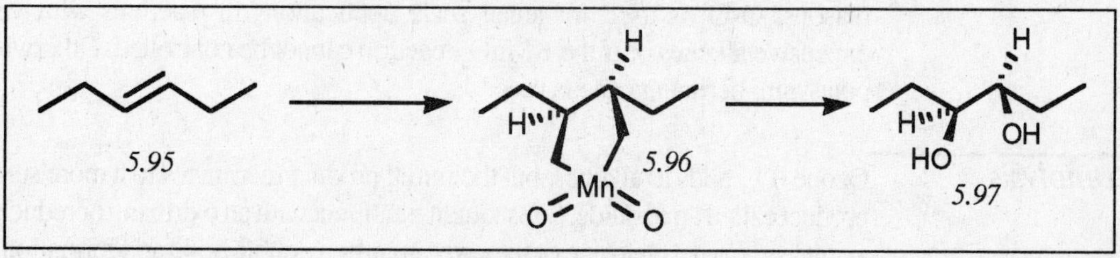

Fig. 5.95–5.97

OSMIUM TETROXIDE

HOW DOES OsO₄ REACT WITH CYCLOHEXENE?

Osmium tetroxide (OsO_4, *5.98*) reacts very similarly to KMnO₄. The alkene reacts with the oxygens of OsO_4 to form an osmate ester (*5.99*). A reagent other than KOH is required to decompose this osmate and generate the diol (*5.100*). The usual reagent is sodium thiosulfite ($NaHSO_3$), which is added in an aqueous solution *in a second* chemical step. The combination of OsO_4 and aqueous $NaHSO_3$ converts alkenes to vicinal *cis-* diols.

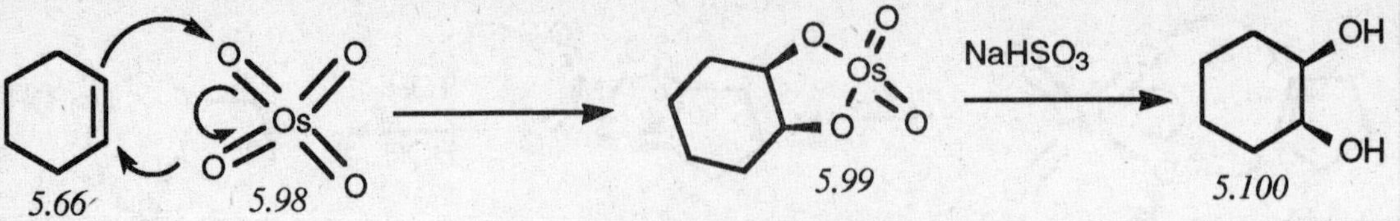

Fig. 5.66, 5.98, 5.99, 5.100

WHAT IS THE MAJOR PRODUCT OF THE REACTION OF E-2-HEXENE AND OSMIUM TETROXIDE?

Hydroxylation with OsO_4 is also diastereospecific, as with the permanganate hydroxylation. In this case, *E*-2-hexene is converted to the racemic diastereomer *5.101* because of the *cis*- addition of osmium tetroxide.

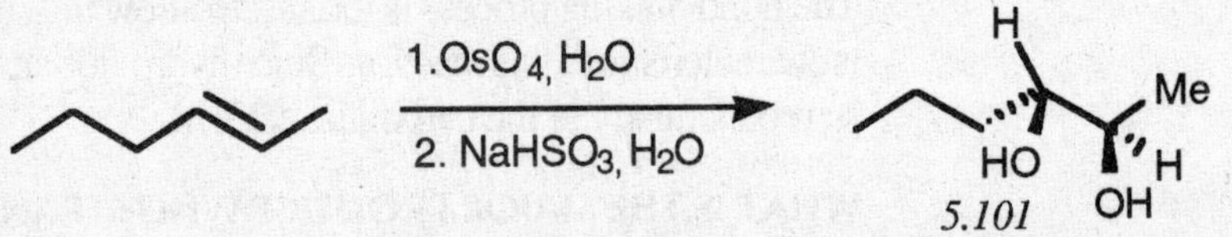

Fig. 5.101

IF KMnO₄ AND OsO₄ LEAD TO THE SAME PRODUCTS, WHY USE OsO₄?

The yields of *cis*-diol tend to higher with OsO_4 and there are fewer side reactions. If permanganate reactions become too hot or too concentrated, oxidative cleavage of the alkene can result. This is rarely a problem with OsO_4. There are drawbacks, however, since OsO_4 is expensive and toxic. For these two reasons, OsO_4 is used for small scale applications in reactions with very expensive alkenes or if the $KMnO_4$ reaction cannot be controlled. Otherwise, potassium permanganate is used.

Ozonolysis

Ozone (O_3) adds to alkenes, but the initial product rearranges to a more stable product called an ozonide. Subsequent treatment with an oxidizing or reducing agent leads to net cleavage of the carbon-carbon double bond and formation of aldehydes, ketones or carboxylic acids.

OZONE AND RESONANCE

DRAW ALL THE RESONANCE FORMS OF OZONE.

There are four resonance forms that bear positive and negative charges, *5.102–5.105*.

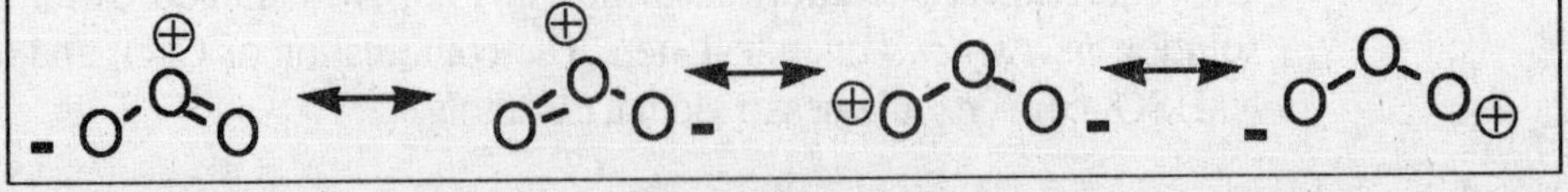

Fig. 5.102–5.105

WHICH RESONANCE FORM(S) IS(ARE) MOST LIKELY TO PREDICT THE REACTIVITY OF OZONE WITH THE Π-BOND OF AN ALKENE?

As with to OsO_4 and MnO_4^-, ozone reacts with alkenes such as cyclohexene via *5.104* or *5.105*, where the π-bond of an alkene attacks the positive oxygen and the negatively charged oxygen of ozone in turn attacks the developing positive charge on the carbon (see *5.106*) to form a cyclic species, *5.107* (a 1,2,3-trioxolane).

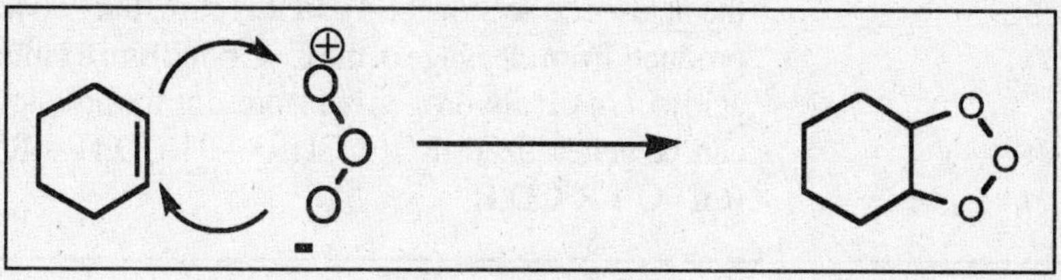

Fig. 5.106, 5.107

OZONIDE FORMATION

WHEN OZONE REACTS WITH 2-BUTENE THE OBSERVED PRODUCT IS NOT THE INITIAL 1,2,3-TRIOXOLANE. EXPLAIN.

The initially formed 1,2,3-trioxolane (*5.108*) is unstable and rearranges to the more stable 1,2,4-trioxolane, *5.109*. This final product is called an *ozonide*.

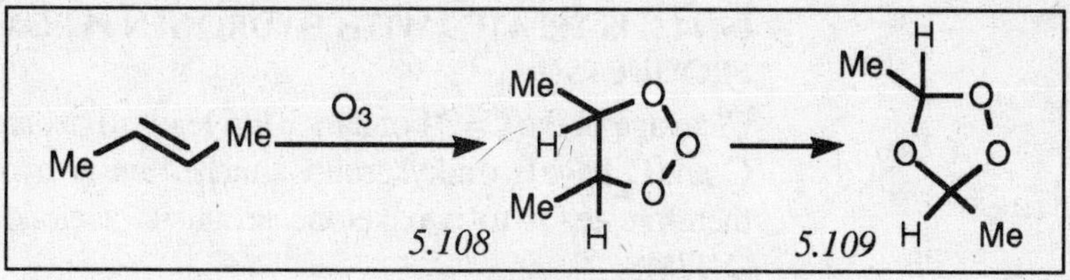

Fig. 5.108, 5.109

WHAT IS THE MECHANISM FOR TRANSFORMATION OF 1,2,3-TRIOXOLANE *5.108* TO 1,2,4-TRIOXOLANE *5.109*?

In this mechanism, ozonide *5.108* cleaves at the O–O bond to give a zwitterion (a dipolar ion), *5.110*. The O^- moiety transfers electrons to form a carbonyl (ethanal) and *5.111*. The O^- of *5.111* attacks the carbonyl of ethanal and the oxygen of ethanal in turn attacks the C=O moiety of *5.111* to give the ozonide, *5.109*. This latter reaction occurs before the two molecules shown in *5.111* can 'drift apart'.

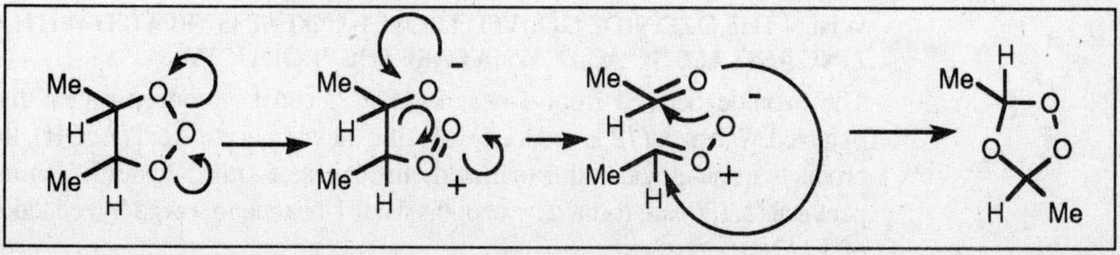

Fig. 5.108, 5.110, 5.111, 5.109

OXIDATION TO ACIDS AND KETONES

WHEN THE OZONIDE DERIVED FROM 1-HEXENE IS TREATED WITH HYDROGEN PEROXIDE, WHAT ARE THE PRODUCTS?

Both C_1 and C_2 in *5.112* (the ozonide of 1-hexene) have at least one hydrogen attached (these carbons are derived from the C=C bond). With an oxidizing agent such as hydrogen peroxide, both C_1 and C_2 are converted to a carboxylic acid (initial oxidation to an aldehyde is followed by rapid oxidation, *in situ*, to the acid—see section 11.4). In this case, the two acid products (two carbonyl products from cleavage of the C=C bond) are formic acid (*5.113*) and pentanoic acid (*5.114*). If a hydrogen is not present, the product is a ketone. These reactions can be generalized: $RCH=CHR^1 \rightarrow RCO_2H + R^1CO_2H$ and $R_2C=CHR^1 \rightarrow R_2C=O + R^1CO_2H$.

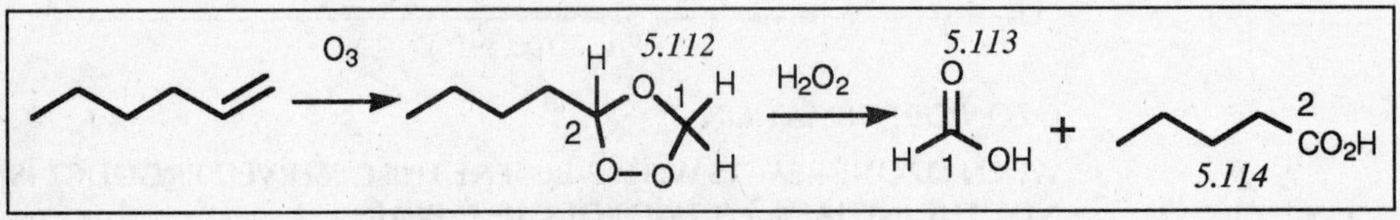

Fig. 5.112–5.114

WHEN THE OZONIDE DERIVED FROM 2,3-DIMETHYL-2-PENTENE (*5.115*) IS TREATED WITH HYDROGEN PEROXIDE, WHAT ARE THE PRODUCTS?

Cleavage of the C=C bond in *5.115* leads to ozonide *5.116*. In this case, both C_1 and C_2 have two alkyl groups attached and no hydrogens. Oxidation of *5.116* therefore leads to two ketone products, acetone (*5.117*) and 2-pentanone (*5.118*).

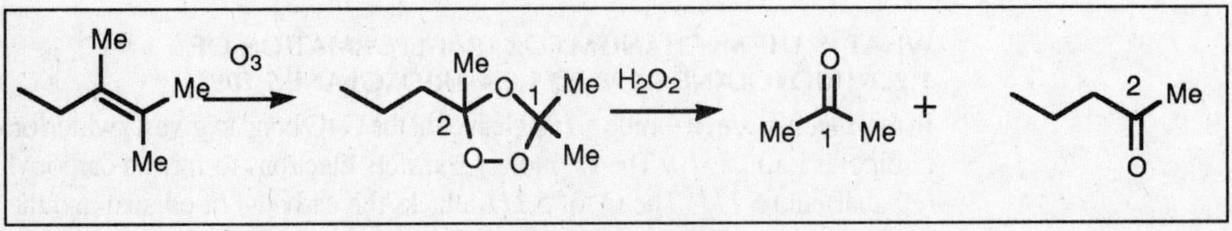

Fig. 5.115–5.118

REDUCTION TO ALDEHYDES AND KETONES

WHEN THE OZONIDE DERIVED FROM 1-HEXENE IS TREATED WITH ZINC AND ACETIC ACID, WHAT ARE THE PRODUCTS?

The ozonide derived from 1-hexene (*5.112*) can be reduced rather than oxidized. When *5.112* is reduced with zinc metal in acetic acid (AcOH), the products are aldehydes rather than acids. In this case, formaldehyde (*5.119*) and pentanal (*5.120*) are formed by ozonolysis of 1-hexene followed by reduction of *5.112*.

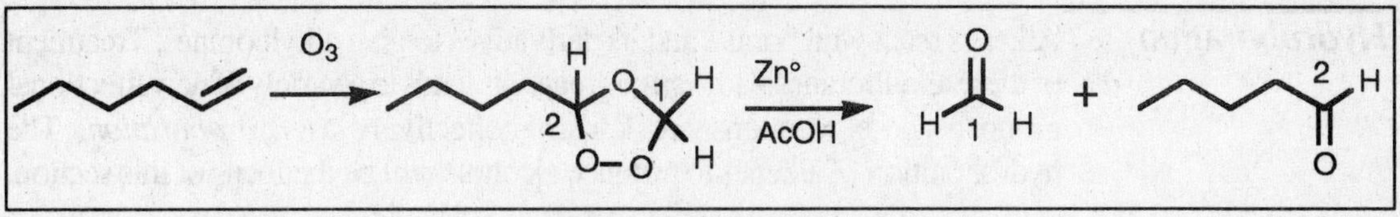

Fig. 5.112, 5.119, 5.120

GIVE THE PRODUCT(S) OF THE REACTIONS OF *5.121–5.124.*

In reaction (a), *5.121* is cleaved (Me$_2$S reduces the ozonide) into two aldehydes: benzaldehyde and 4-methylpentanal. In reaction (b) the two double bonds in diene *5.122* are cleaved (an oxidative workup of the ozonide) and there are three products: propionic acid + 5-keto-heptanoic acid (*5.125*) + ethanoic acid. Cleavage of the double bond in *5.123*, in reaction (c), gives a single molecule with two functional groups, keto-aldehyde *5.126*. Finally, diene *5.124* in reaction (d) is cleaved to two products, ethanoic acid and keto-acid *5.127*.

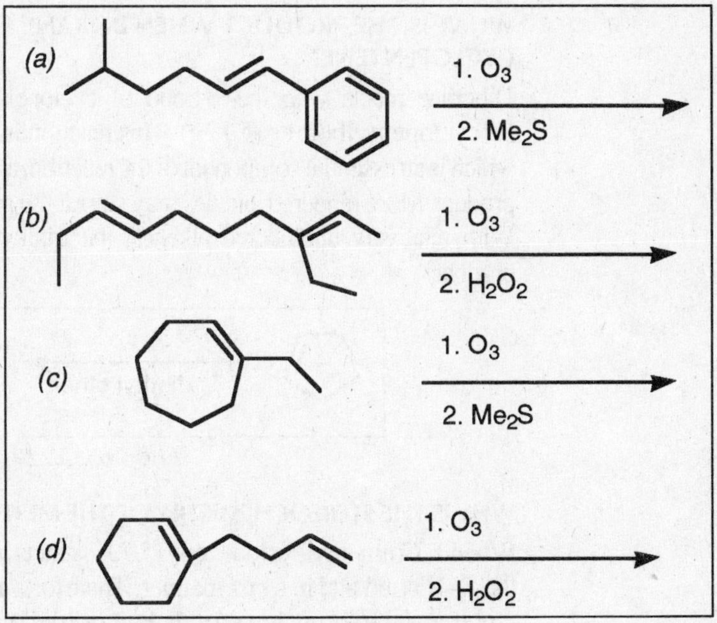

Fig. 5.121–5.124

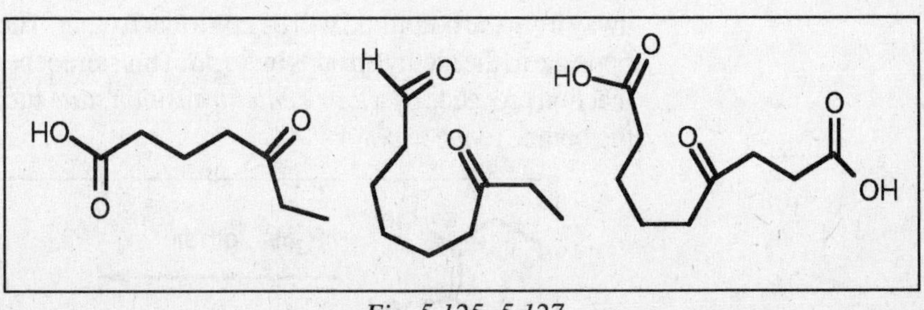

Fig. 5.125–5.127

Hydroboration

Alkenes react with borane and its derivatives to give alkylboranes. Treatment of these alkylboranes with various reagents leads to a variety of new functional groups. These reactions are known collectively as *hydroboration*. The hydroboration of alkenes to produce alcohols will be the focus of this section.

STRUCTURE OF BORANE

GIVE THE STRUCTURE OF BORANE.

Borane is BH_3, but it exists primarily as a hydrogen bridged dimer, *5.128*.

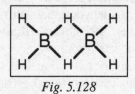

Fig. 5.128

SYN ADDITION TO ALKENES

WHAT IS THE PRODUCT WHEN BORANE REACTS WITH CYCLOPENTENE?

Diborane reacts with the π-bond of cyclopentene to give a trialkylborane (tricyclopentylborane, *5.129*). This reaction is catalyzed by the ether solvent, which is an essential component of the reaction, although it does not appear in the product. More hindered alkenes may stop at the monoalkyl or the dialkylborane. With relatively unhindered alkenes, the trialkylborane is the most common product.

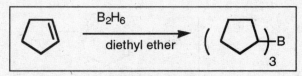

Fig. 5.63, 5.129

WHY IS THE STEREOCHEMISTRY OF THE METHYL GROUPS IN *5.131* *CIS-*?

When 1,2-dimethylcyclohexene (*5.130*) reacts with borane, the B and the H of the B–H bond add in a *cis-* manner. Therefore, B and H in *5.131* are *cis-* (BR_2 represents the formation of a dialkyl or trialkylborane where R = dimethyl-cyclohexyl and/or hydrogen). The two methyl groups in *5.130* will be pushed away from the boron and will be *cis-* to each other. The boron and hydrogen are opposite to the methyl groups in *5.130*. This stereochemistry arises because the reaction proceeds by a *four-center transition state* such as *5.132* for addition of the borane to the π-bond.

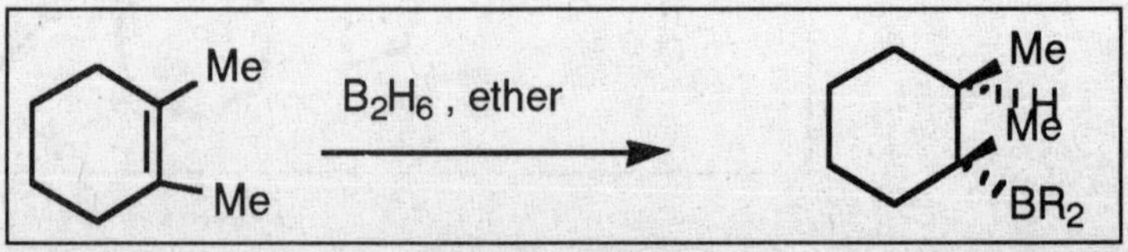

Fig. 5.130, 5.131

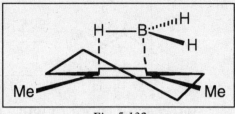

Fig. 5.132

THE REACTION OF BORANE AND 1-PENTENE CAN GIVE TWO POSSIBLE PRODUCTS BUT ONE IS FORMED IN 80–90% YIELD. EXPLAIN.

The boron can attach to either the first carbon (path a) or the second (path b). The two products are *5.134* (via path a) and *5.135* (via path b). The major product is *5.134* and monosubstituted alkenes such as *5.133* *always* give attachment at the less sterically hindered carbon as the major product. Comparison of transition state *5.136* with *5.137* reveals that the BH_2 moiety interacts sterically with the propyl group of *5.133* in transition state *5.137*. In *5.136*, however, the bulky BH_2 group interacts only with hydrogens. Since transition state *5.136* is less sterically hindered than *5.137* it is lower in energy and leads to the major product.

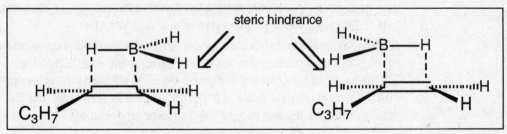

Fig. 5.133–5.135

Fig. 5.136, 5.137

HIGHER ORDER BORANES

WHAT IS THE PRODUCT WHEN BORANE REACTS WITH 2-METHYL-2-BUTENE?

The product of this reaction is dialkylborane *5.138*, which has been given the common name of disiamylborane (disiamyl = diisoamyl).

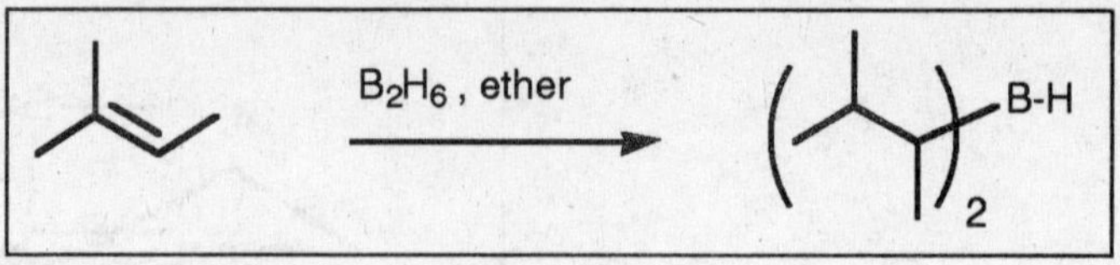

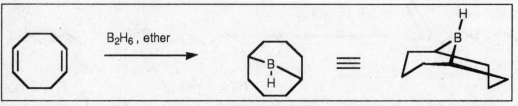

Fig. 5.138

WHAT IS THE PRODUCT WHEN BORANE REACTS WITH 2,3-DIMETHYL-2-BUTENE?

The product of this reaction is monoalkylborane *5.139*, which has been given the common name of thexylborane (thexyl = *tertiary*-hexyl).

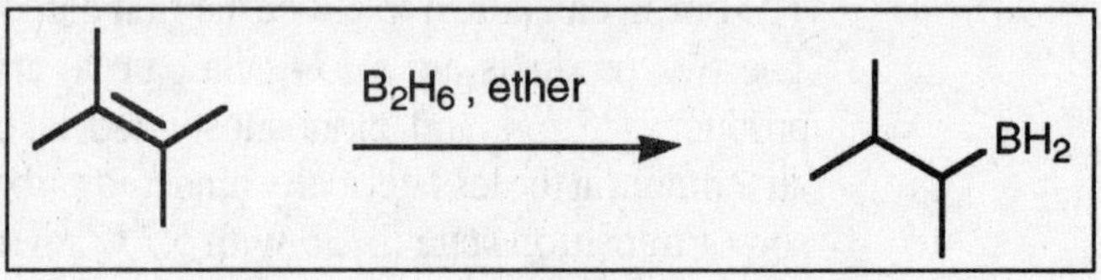

Fig. 5.139

WHAT IS THE PRODUCT WHEN BORANE REACTS WITH 1,5-CYLCOOCTADIENE?

The product is a dialkylborane where the borane has 'bridged' the two alkenes on opposite sides of the ring. The product (*5.140*) is named 9-borabicyclo[3.3.1]nonane, or 9-BBN.

Fig. 5.140

THE REACTION OF 1-PENTENE AND 9-BBN IS MORE SELECTIVE THAN THE IDENTICAL REACTION WITH BORANE. EXPLAIN.

Inspection of transition state *5.141* shows that the steric hindrance imposed by the bicyclononyl system is very severe when interacting with the hydrogens, but it is far worse in *5.142* where that group interacts with the propyl group. The difference in energy for these two transition states is very great and *5.141* is greatly preferred, leading to *5.143* as the major product (>99%).

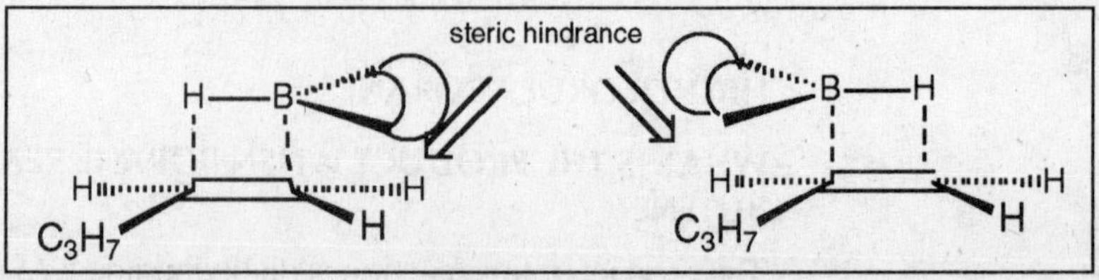

Fig. 5.141, 5.142

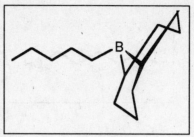

Fig. 5.143

Oxidation to Alcohols

The main application of hydroboration is the ability to convert the monoalkyl, dialkyl and trialkylborane products into alcohols by treatment with basic hydrogen peroxide in an oxidation step. Many other transformations of organoboranes are also possible but this section will focus only on the conversion to alcohols.

WHAT IS THE MAJOR PRODUCT OF EACH OF THE REACTIONS OF 5.144–5.146?

Hydroboration of 1-hexene (*5.144*) in reaction (a) followed by oxidation leads to 1-hexanol (*5.147*). In reaction (b), 1-methylcyclopentene (*5.145*) is converted to *trans*-2-methylcyclopentanol (*5.148*). cis-Addition of borane leaves the boron and methyl group on opposite faces, leading to the *trans*-geometry (remember the *cis*-addition refers to the B and the H of the borane). In reaction (c), alkene *5.146* is converted to secondary alcohol *5.149*.

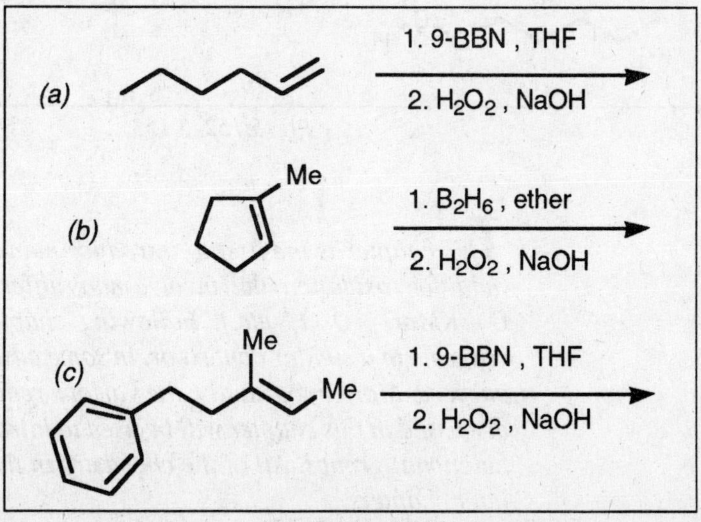

(a) 1. 9-BBN , THF
     2. H_2O_2 , NaOH

(b) Me
     1. B_2H_6 , ether
     2. H_2O_2 , NaOH

(c) Me
     Me
     1. 9-BBN , THF
     2. H_2O_2 , NaOH

Fig. 5.144–5.146

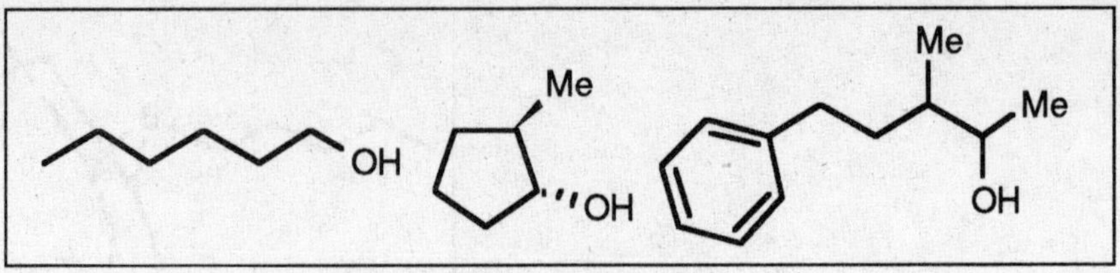

Fig. 5.147–5.149

GIVE THE MECHANISM FOR THE CONVERSION OF AN ALKYLBORANE (*5.150*) TO THE ALCOHOL, *5.153*.

In the presence of hydroxide, hydrogen peroxide is deprotonated to give the hydroperoxide anion ($^{\ominus}$OOH). This anion attacks the boron of *5.150* to form an 'ate' complex, *5.151*. A boron → oxygen alkyl shift (a 1,2 shift) leads to formation of a B–O bond in *5.152*. Sequential reactions of $^{\ominus}$OOH with boron leads to the alcohol product, *5.153* (1-pentanol) and boric acid [B(OH)$_3$].

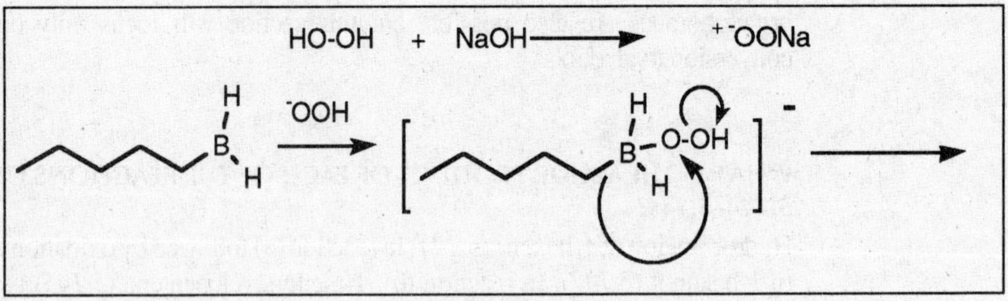

Fig. 5.150, 5.151

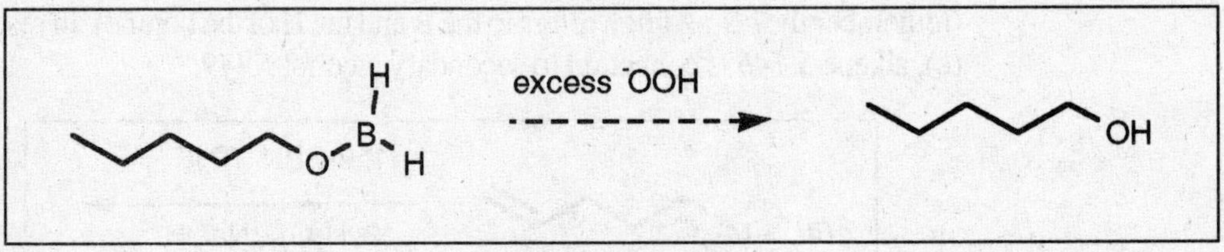

Fig. 5.152, 5.153

*T*his chapter is the first to introduce many different types of reactions (addition, oxidation) that involve many different types of reagents (HX, X$_2$, O$_3$, KMnO$_4$, OsO$_4$ etc.). Following chapters will use many of these reagents in a similar context or, in some cases, for a completely different purpose. More importantly, the various reactions and functional groups discussed in this chapter will be used to introduce new reactions and new functional groups. All of the chemistry in this chapter will be applied in later chapters.

END OF CHAPTER PROBLEMS

1. What is the geometry of the atoms in 2,3-dimethyl-2-butene?
2. Discuss why alkene A is more stable than alkene B.

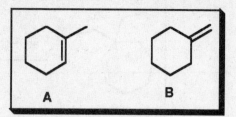

A   **B**

3. Give the mechanism for the following reaction.

$$\text{HCl}$$

4. Why does 2-methyl-2-butene react faster with HCl than does 1-butene?
5. Give the IUPAC name for each of the following.

(a)

(b)

(c)

(d)

(e)

(f)

6. Explain how Z-3-chloro-3-hexene is also properly labeled as a *trans*-alkene (i.e., why does Z *not* translate directly to *cis*).
7. Explain why the H⁺ of HBr adds to C_1 rather than C_2 to give the major product.

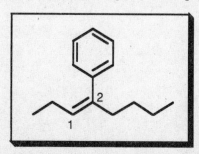

8. Give at least our *different* transition metals that can be used in hydrogenation reactions.

9. Give the mechanism for the following reaction.

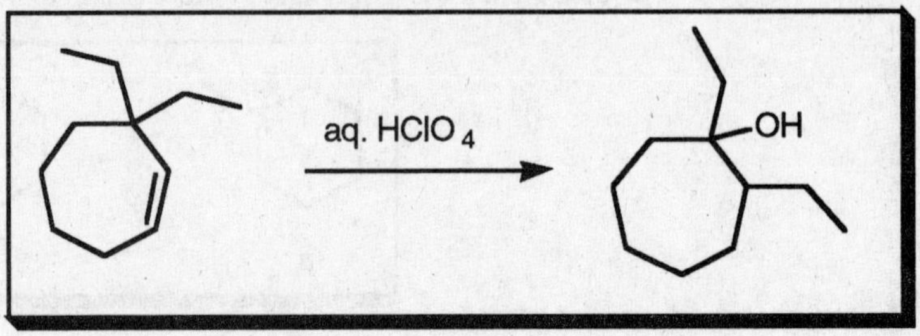

10. What is an induced dipole?

11. Does *trans*-2-butene react with iodine to give a meso compound or the d,l-pair?

12. In the reaction of 2-methyl-1-pentene and bromine, which carbon is attacked by bromide ion? Explain.

13. In each of the following reactions give the major product. Remember stereochemistry, and if there is no reaction indicate by N.R.

(a) 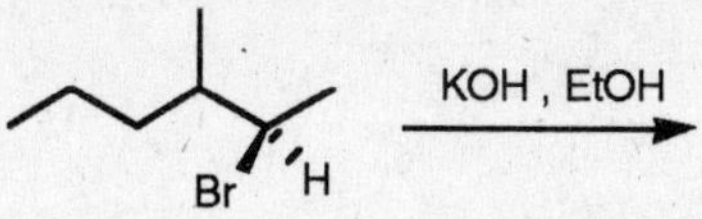 KOH , EtOH

(b) 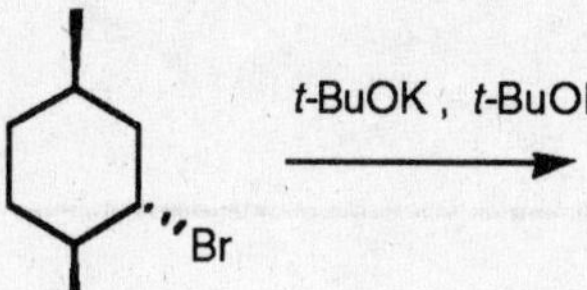 t-BuOK , t-BuOH

(c) 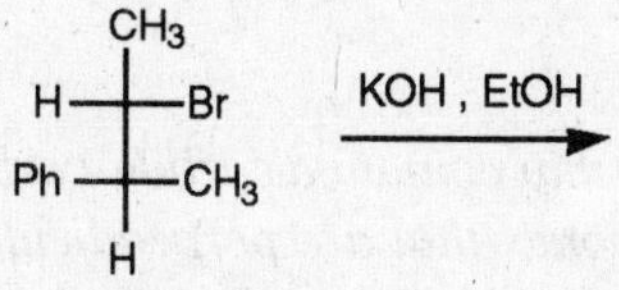 KOH , EtOH

(d) 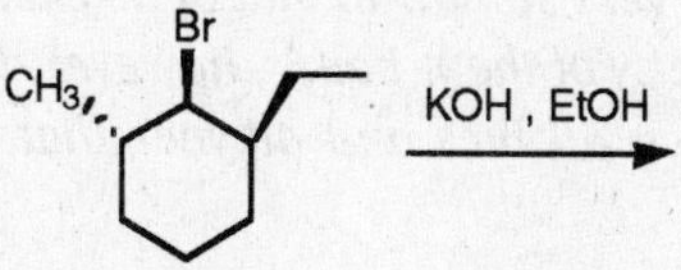 KOH , EtOH

(e) 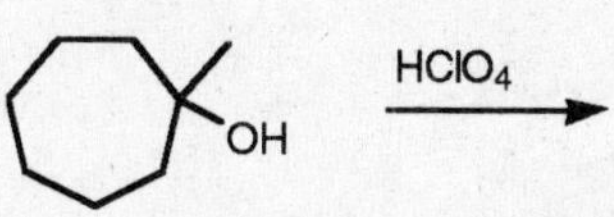 HClO₄

(f) 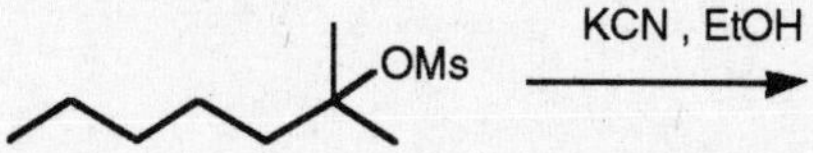 KCN , EtOH

(g) 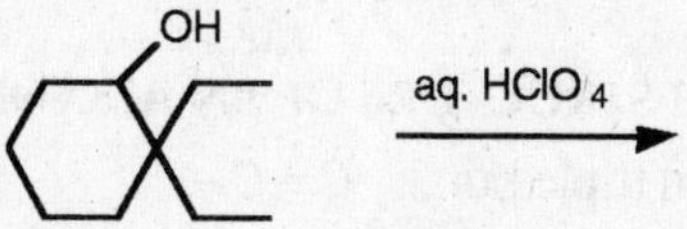 aq. HClO₄

(h) 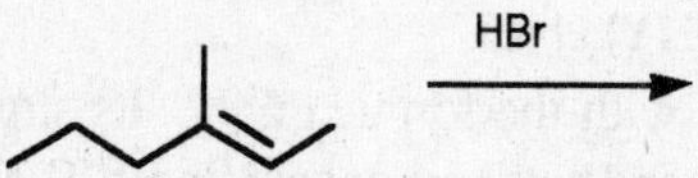 HBr

(i) 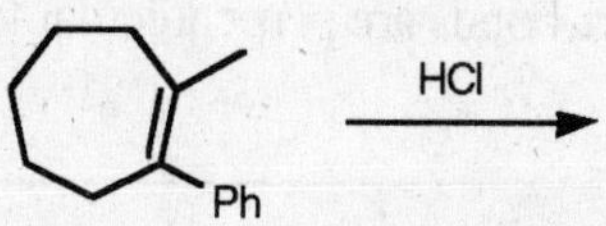 HCl

(j) 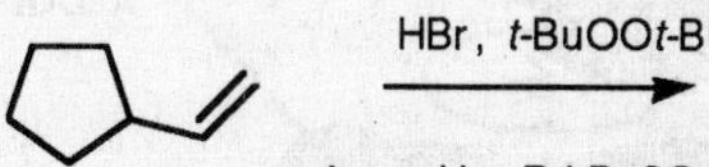 HBr , t-BuOOt-Bu

(k) 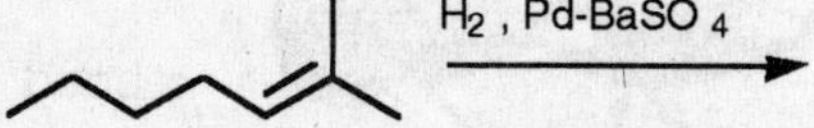 H₂ , Pd-BaSO₄

(l) 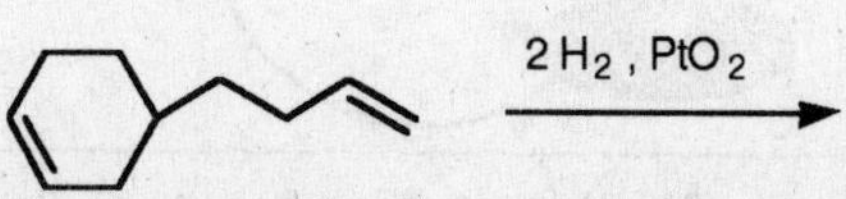 2 H₂ , PtO₂

(m) 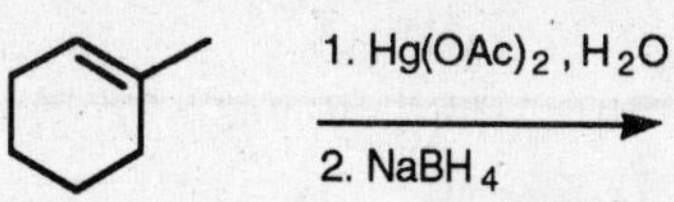 1. Hg(OAc)₂ , H₂O 2. NaBH₄

(n) 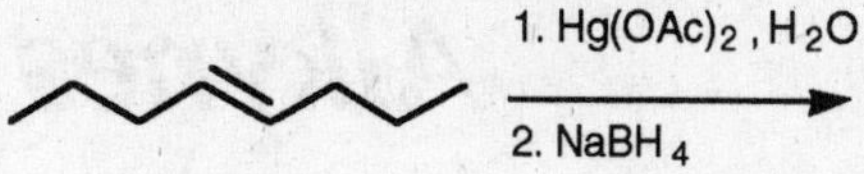 1. Hg(OAc)₂ , H₂O 2. NaBH₄

(o) 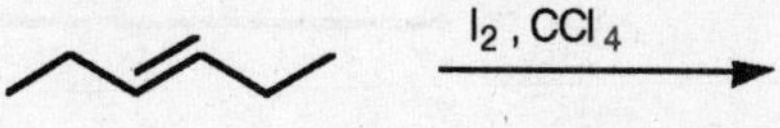 I₂ , CCl₄

(p) 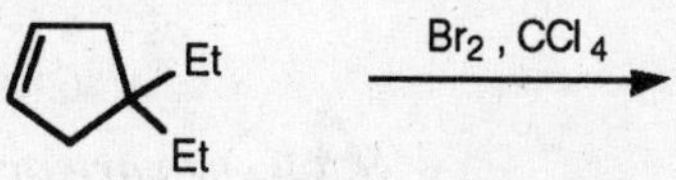 Br₂ , CCl₄

(q) 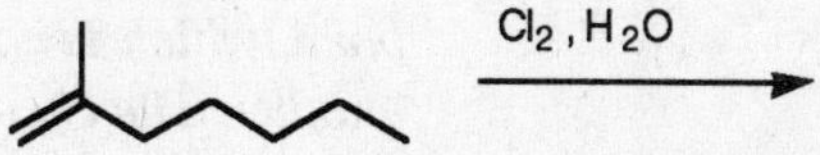 Cl₂ , H₂O

(r) 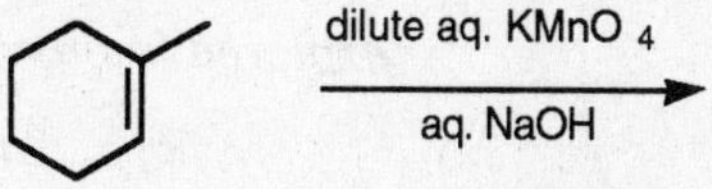 dilute aq. KMnO₄ aq. NaOH

(s) 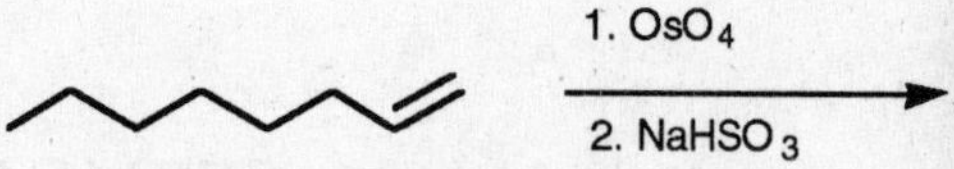 1. OsO₄ 2. NaHSO₃

(t) 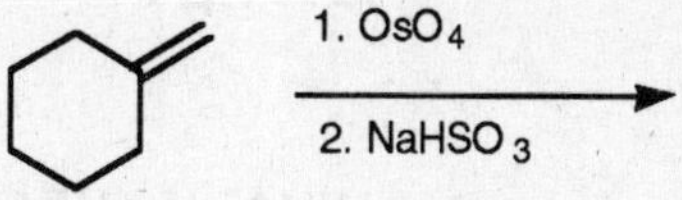 1. OsO₄ 2. NaHSO₃

(u) 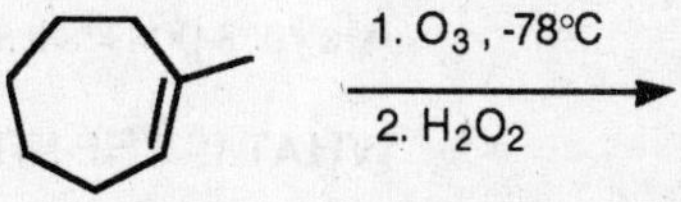 1. O₃ , -78°C 2. H₂O₂

(v) 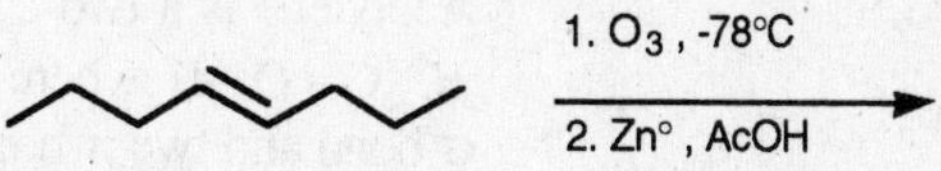 1. O₃ , -78°C 2. Zn° , AcOH

(w) 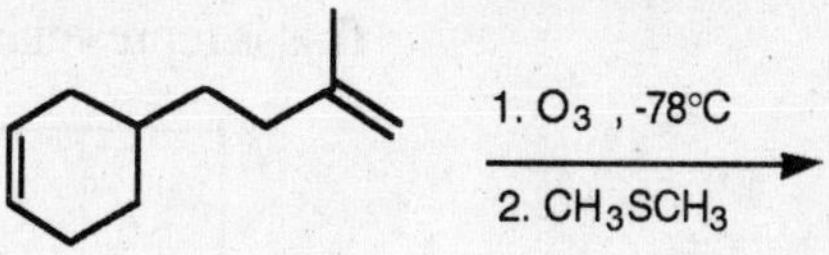 1. O₃ , -78°C 2. CH₃SCH₃

(x) 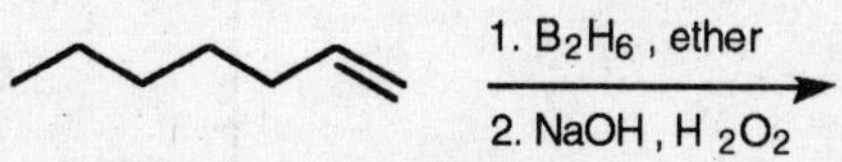 1. B₂H₆ , ether 2. NaOH , H₂O₂

(y) 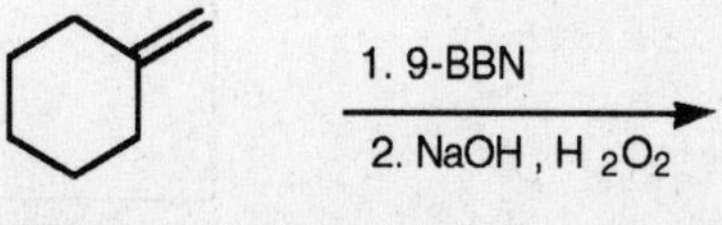 1. 9-BBN 2. NaOH , H₂O₂

6

Alkynes

*A*lkynes are organic hydrocarbons that contain a carbon-carbon triple bond, which is composed of two π-bonds that are perpendicular to one another. The chemistry of alkynes is very similar to that of alkenes due to the presence of π-bonds. The proximity of the π-bonds, however, leads to some interesting differences between alkenes and alkynes that will be explored in this chapter.

6.1. STRUCTURE

WHAT IS THE CHARACTERISTIC STRUCTURE OF AN ALKYNE?

Alkynes possesses a carbon-carbon triple bond: $-C \equiv C-$

WHAT IS THE STRUCTURE OF ACETYLENE?

Acetylene is a two-carbon molecule with the formula C_2H_2. Its structure is $H-C \equiv C-H$, where both hydrogens and both carbons are linear. There is one σ-bond and two π-bonds. The two π-bonds are perpendicular to one another. This is represented in *6.1*.

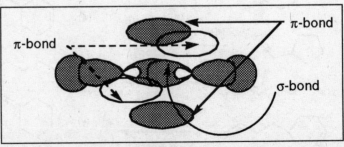

Fig. 6.1

The Triple Bond and sp Hybridization

GIVE THE MOLECULAR ORBITAL DIAGRAM FOR THE CARBON-CARBON TRIPLE BOND OF ETHYNE.

The molecular orbital diagram is shown in *6.2*. There are two electrons in sp hybrid orbitals (for the sp σ-bonds) and two electrons in p orbitals (for the two π-bonds).

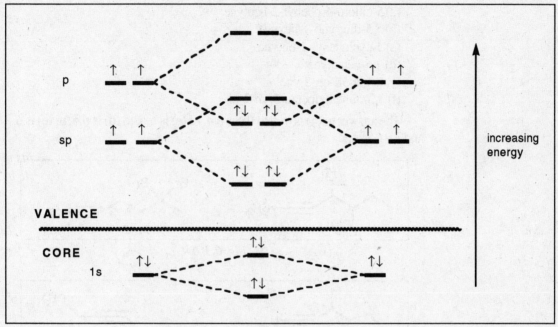

Fig. 6.2

Isomers

NAME THE TWO DIFFERENT STRUCTURAL TYPES OF ALKYNES.

Monosubstituted alkynes and disubstituted alkynes (terminal and internal, respectively).

GIVE A GENERIC STRUCTURE FOR EACH TYPE OF ALKYNE.

Monosubstituted (terminal) = $R - C \equiv C - H$
Disubstituted (internal) = $R - C \equiv C - R$

6.2. NOMENCLATURE

WHAT IS THE IUPAC ENDING FOR ALKYNES?

The -ane ending of an alkane is dropped and replace with the alkyne ending,

-yne. A four carbon alkyne is, therefore, butyne. The position of the first carbon of the triple bond is given the lowest number and the $C \equiv C$ unit must be in the longest continuous chain. The IUPAC name for $CH_3CH_2CH_2C \equiv CCH_3$ is 2-hexyne and $CH_3CH_2C \equiv CH$ is 1-butyne.

GIVE THE CORRECT STRUCTURE FOR EACH OF THE FOLLOWING.

(a) 5-chloro-4-phenyl-2-heptyne
(b) 5,5-dibromo-1-hexyne
(c) 3-cyclohexyl-1-butyne
(d) 3,6-octadiyne
(e) hepta-5E-en-2-yne
(f) 3,3-dimethyloctan-5-yn-2-ol

The answer to (a) is *6.3*, to (b) is *6.4*, to (c) is *6.5*, to (d) is *6.6*, to (e) is *6.7* and to (f) is *6.8*.

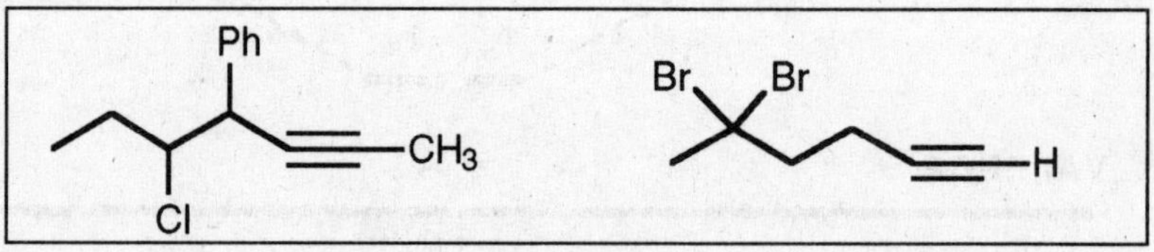

Fig. 6.3, 6.4

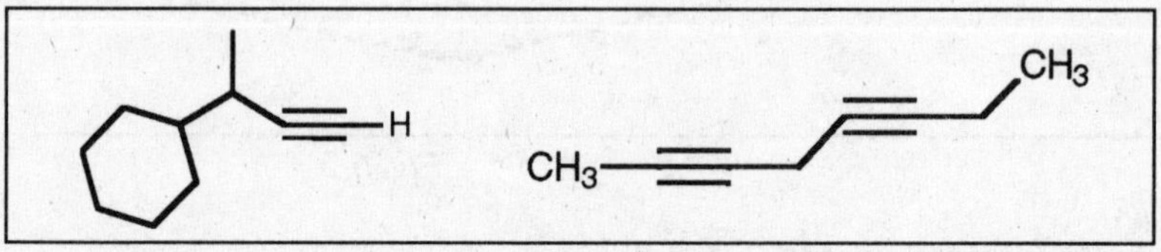

Fig. 6.5, 6.6

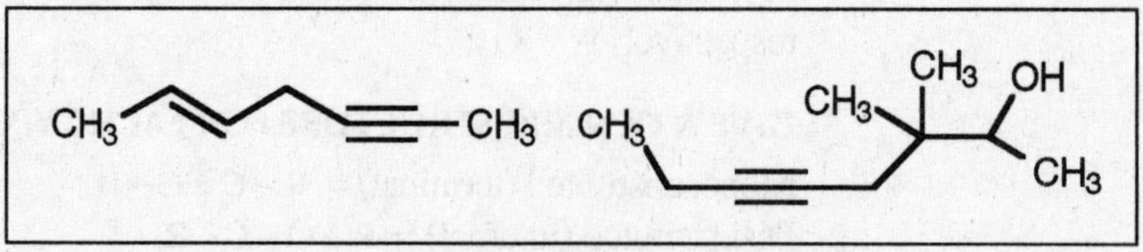

Fig. 6.7, 6.8

6.3. PREPARATION AND REACTIONS

Most alkynes are prepared in one of two ways: elimination of geminal dihalides with strong base or by alkylation of acetylene or monosubstituted alkynes.

Preparation From Geminal Dihalides

HOW ARE GEMINAL DIHALIDES PREPARED?

Geminal dihalides (both halogens on the same carbon) are prepared from alkynes. Sequential addition of HBr or HCl to an alkyne gives the geminal dihalide (see section 6.3 below).

IF 1,2-DIBROMOPENTANE (*6.9*) IS TREATED WITH ONE EQUIVALENT OF NaNH₂, WHAT IS THE PRODUCT?

The initial product of the reaction of 1,2-dibromopentane and sodium amide in ammonium is a vinyl halide (*6.10*) which is derived from an E^2 reaction to produce the more stable alkene.

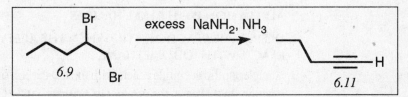

Fig. 6.9, 6.10

WHAT IS THE PRODUCT WHEN 1,2-DIBROMOPENTANE IS TREATED WITH AN EXCESS OF SODIUM AMIDE IN LIQUID AMMONIA?

In the presence of at least two equivalents of sodium amide (NaNH₂), *6.9* is first converted to *6.10*. Sodium amide is a sufficiently strong base to remove the hydrogen on the carbon-carbon double bond, generating the alkyne, *6.11* (1-pentyne).

Fig. 6.9, 6.11

WHY IS SODIUM AMIDE COMMONLY USED FOR THE 'SECOND' ELIMINATION REACTION RATHER THAN AN ALKOXIDE BASE?

Removal of an alkene hydrogen (C=C–H) is more difficult since it is much less acidic than hydrogen on an sp carbon in *6.10*. For this reason a significantly stronger base is required, and NaNH₂ is much more powerful than *t*-BuO⁻K⁺.

Preparation From Other Alkynes

ACIDITY OF ALKYNE HYDROGENS

WHAT IS THE pKₐ OF THE C–H BOND OF ACETYLENE (ETHYNE)?

The pKₐ of the hydrogen in acetylene (H–C ≡ C–*H*) is about 25. Compared to water (pKₐ of 15.8) and acetic acid (pKₐ of 4.7), acetylene is a *very* weak acid and requires a strong base to remove the acidic hydrogen. The product of the acid/base reaction is called an *acetylide*, with a negative charge residing on carbon: $H-C \equiv C-H + BASE \rightarrow H-C \equiv C : ^{\ominus}$

WHAT BASES CAN BE USED TO REMOVE THE HYDROGEN OF AN ALKYNE?

As just mentioned, a powerful base is required to remove the weakly acidic alkyne hydrogen. The most common bases used are sodium amide ($NaNH_2$ in liquid ammonia), *n*-butyllithium in ether solvents or sodium hydride (NaH) in anhydrous solvents. Sodium hydride is very attractive since the by-product of the acid/base reaction is hydrogen gas $\left(\frac{1}{2}H_2\right)$ and the sodium salt of the alkyne (a sodium acetylide, $R-C \equiv C : ^{\ominus} Na^{\oplus}$).

WHAT IS THE CHEMICAL REACTIVITY OF AN ACETYLIDE?

Since the negative charge resides on carbon, acetylides are powerful *nucleophiles* and acetylides behave as *carbanions*.

WHY IS THE HYDROGEN OF AN ALKYNE MORE ACIDIC THAN THE HYDROGEN OF AN ALKENE OR AN ALKANE?

This is related to the hybridization of the C–H bond. In general, acidity increases with increased 's character' of the bond: $sp > sp^2 > sp^3$. An alkyne is, therefore, more acidic than an alkene, which is more acidic than an alkane. An s-orbital is generally better able to stabilize a negative charge than a p-orbital and an sp orbital has 50% s character. An sp^3 orbital has only 25% s-character and an sp^2 orbital has 33% s character.

ALKYLATION WITH ALKYL HALIDES

DEFINE THE REACTION TYPE WHEN THE ACETYLIDE OF 1-BUTYNE REACTS WITH IODOMETHANE.

A nucleophilic acetylide reacts with the $\delta\oplus$ carbon of an alkyl halide in an S_N2 reaction. In this case, the product is 2-pentyne ($CH_3CH_2C \equiv C:^-Na^+ + MeI \rightarrow CH_3CH_2C \equiv CCH_3$).

WHAT SOLVENTS ARE APPROPRIATE FOR THE REACTION OF ACETYLIDES AND ALKYL HALIDES?

Since this is an S_N2 reaction, a polar aprotic solvent should be used, such as THF, DMF or DMSO.

GIVE THE MAJOR PRODUCT OF EACH OF THE REACTIONS OF *6.12–6.15*.

In reaction (a), alkyne *6.12* is treated with base to generate the acetylide. Subsequent treatment with methanol, which is an acid in the presence of the basic acetylide, protonates the acetylide and the product of the reaction is *6.12*. In reaction (b) alkene *6.13* is first converted to the geminal dibromide with HBr and treatment with excess $NaNH_2$ generates *6.16*. The first elimination gives the more stable trisubstituted vinyl bromide and the second elimination gives *6.16*. In reaction (c), alkyne *6.14* is converted to the acetylide with base and alkylation with benzyl bromide gives the disubstituted alkyne product, *6.17*. In reaction (d), acetylene (*6.15*) is deprotonated and reacted with iodomethane to give 1-propyne. A second deprotonation-alkylation sequence (with iodopentane) gives the final product, 2-octyne, *6.18*.

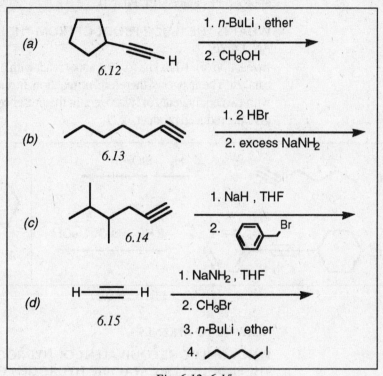

Fig. 6.12–6.15

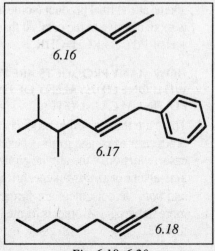

Fig. 6.18–6.20

Reaction with Hydrogen (Catalytic Hydrogenation)

ALKYNES TO ALKANES

HOW MANY EQUIVALENTS OF HYDROGEN ARE REQUIRED TO CONVERT AN ALKYNE TO AN ALKANE?

The conversion of an alkyne to an alkane is $R-C \equiv C-R \rightarrow RCH_2CH_2R$ and requires a minimum of two equivalents of hydrogen gas, along with an appropriate catalyst (Pt, Pd, Ni).

WHAT IS THE MAJOR PRODUCT FROM THE REACTIONS OF 6.19 AND 6.20?

In reaction (a), 1-hexyne (*6.19*) cannot react with hydrogen because there is no catalyst. The answer is, therefore, no reaction. In reaction (b), alkyne *6.20* reacts with two equivalents of hydrogen, in the presence of a palladium catalyst, to give the reduced product, *6.21*.

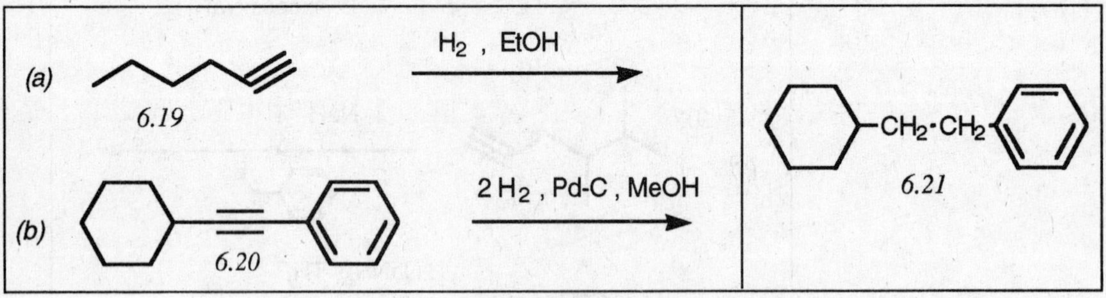

Fig. 6.19–6.21

ALKYNES TO ALKENES

WHEN ONLY ONE EQUIVALENT OF HYDROGEN IS USED, WHAT IS THE PRODUCT OF CATALYTIC HYDROGENATION OF AN ALKYNE?

A single equivalent of hydrogen, with an appropriate catalyst, will give an alkene as the final product (some alkane may be formed if the alkene product is more reactive to the catalyst than is the alkyne). The reaction is: $R-C \equiv C-R + H_2 + Pd/C \rightarrow RCH=CHR$.

HOW MANY PRODUCTS ARE POSSIBLE WHEN 3-HEXYNE IS TREATED WITH ONE EQUIVALENT OF HYDROGEN IN THE PRESENCE OF A PLATINUM CATALYST?

There are three possible products, two major and one minor. The two major products are *cis-* and *trans-*3-hexene and the minor product is hexane. In this case, reduction of the alkyne group in 3-hexyne to the alkene gave give either a *cis-*alkene or a *trans-*alkene. In this case, there is no way to control the reaction and *both* stereoisomers are formed. In many cases, the thermodynamically more stable *trans-*isomer is formed in greater amount than the *cis-*, but both are formed.

CONTROLLING OVER-REDUCTION

WHY IS IT IMPORTANT TO CAREFULLY CONTROL THE NUMBER OF EQUIVALENTS OF HYDROGEN ADDED TO AN ALKYNE WHEN THE ALKENE IS THE DESIRED PRODUCT?

If too much hydrogen gas is used, the alkene product of the reduction can be further reduced to give the alkane (as in 6.3). Another problem is that the alkene product may be more reactive to the catalyst (or to hydrogen after being bound to the catalyst) and react faster than unreacted alkyne. For this reason, the alkane often accompanies the alkene as a minor product.

IF ONE EQUIVALENT OF HYDROGEN GAS IS USED BUT THE REACTION CONDITIONS ARE VIGOROUS (HEAT, PRESSURE), WHAT TYPES OF PRODUCTS ARE POSSIBLE?

Since the alkene product may be more reactive than the alkyne starting material, vigorous conditions (heat and pressure) may cause overreaction. To minimize this, both the temperature and the pressure of the reaction are controlled, along with the number of equivalents of hydrogen gas. Another important factor in this reaction is the nature of the catalyst. In general, palladium catalysts are used to reduce alkynes to alkenes, although rhodium and ruthenium catalysts are also very useful.

THE LINDLAR CATALYST AND CIS ALKENES

WHAT IS THE LINDLAR CATALYST?

The original Lindlar catalyst was a mixture of palladium chloride ($PdCl_2$), which was precipitated on calcium carbonate ($CaCO_3$) in acidic media and deactivated with lead tetraacetate [$Pb(OAc)_4$] to give the named Pd–$CaCO_3$–PbO catalyst. Later, palladium on barium carbonate ($BaCO_3$) or calcium carbonate ($CaCO_3$) was deactivated with quinoline (6.22) and found to give similar reactivity. This latter catalyst is now known as the Lindlar catalyst.

The importance of the Lindlar catalyst is shown by the conversion of alkyne 6.20 to 6.23. The Lindlar catalyst gives almost exclusively the cis-alkene from the alkyne, with little or no contamination by the trans-alkene or from the over-reduction product (in this case 6.21). *The preferred use of the Lindlar catalyst is, therefore, formation of cis-alkenes from alkynes.*

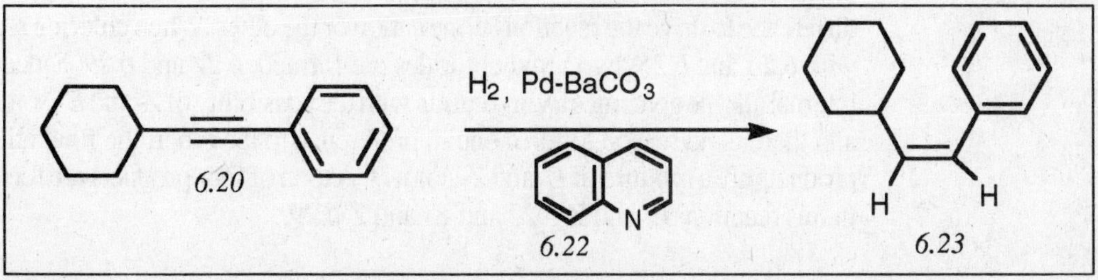

Fig. 6.20, 6.22, 6.23

Addition Reactions

Just as alkenes react with HX reagents and X_2 reagents to give the 1,2-addition products, alkynes react with these reagents. The final products usually contain a double bond since only one of the two π-bonds react with the reagent. In some cases, the initially formed vinyl compound reacts further to give a product that does not contain a carbon-carbon π-bond.

ADDITION OF ACIDS (HX)

WHEN 1-PENTYNE REACTS WITH HBr, TO WHICH CARBON OF THE TRIPLE BOND IS THE BROMINE ATTACHED?

The bromine is attached to the more highly substituted carbon. One of the π-bonds of the alkyne donates an electron pair to H^+ generating a 'vinyl cation', in this case 6.24. The addition of HBr can generate a less stable primary vinyl cation or a more stable secondary vinyl cation. The more stable cation forms and reaction with Br leads to the final product, 6.25 (2-bromo-1-pentene).

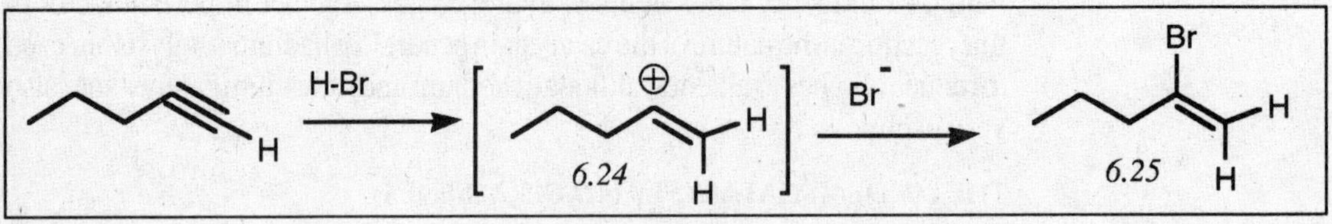

Fig. 6.24, 6.25

WHAT IS THE RELATIVE STABILITY OF A 'VINYL CATION'?

A secondary vinyl cation is much less stable than a normal secondary cation, but once formed it is more reactive with a nucleophile. Vinyl cations do not rearrange and react very quickly. In general, alkyl cations are more stable than vinyl cations and a 3° vinyl cation is more stable than a 2° vinyl cation, which is more stable than a 1° vinyl cation.

WHAT ARE THE PRODUCTS WHEN HCl REACTS WITH 2-HEXYNE?

The H^+ can add to either carbon of the triple bond to give a vinyl cation, 6.26 or 6.28. Both are secondary vinyl cations and both will form. There is no energy difference to drive the reaction to one cation or the other. When chloride reacts with 6.26 and 6.28, two vinyl chlorides are formed, 6.27 and 6.29. Since the internal alkyne generates a vinyl cation with the possibility of Z- and E-isomers, and there is no reason to form one in preference to the other, the final alkene products are a mixture of E- and Z-isomers. A total of four products are formed in this reaction, E- and Z-6.27 and E- and Z-6.29.

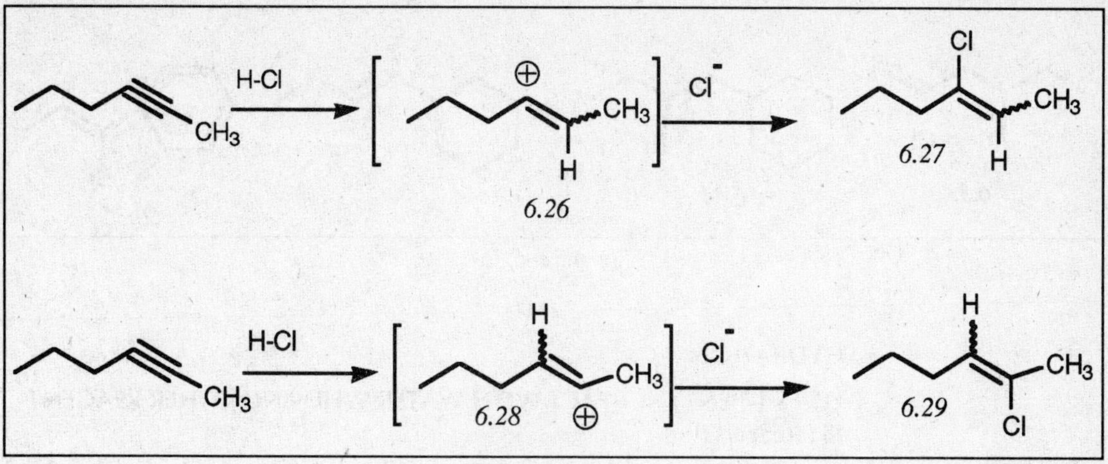

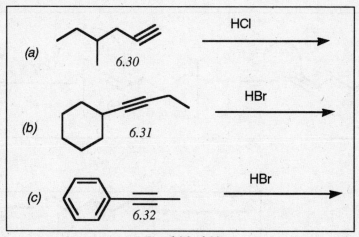

Fig. 6.28–6.31

GIVE THE MAJOR PRODUCTS FROM THE REACTIONS OF *6.30–6.32*.

In reaction (a) the more stable 2° vinyl cation is formed from alkyne *6.30* and the final product is *6.33*. In reaction (b), two 2° vinyl cations of essentially equal stability are formed from *6.31* and two products are formed, *E-* and *Z-6.34* and *E-* and *Z-6.35*. Alkyne *6.32* possesses a phenyl group and the 2° vinyl cation resulting from addition of H⁺ can be stabilized by delocalization of the charge into the phenyl ring. For this reason, the cationic center next to the phenyl ring is more stable than the cation with the charge next to the methyl group. There is one major product, *6.36*.

Fig. 6.30–6.32

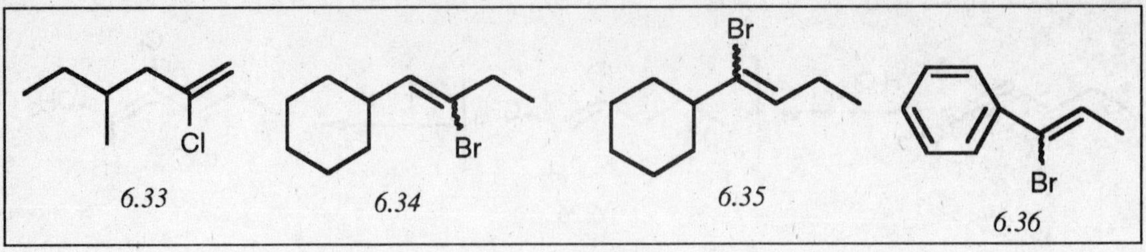

6.33 6.34 6.35 6.36

Fig. 6.33–6.36

HYDRATION

DOES 1-PENTYNE REACT WITH WATER WHEN NO OTHER REAGENT IS PRESENT?

No. Water is too weak an acid to react with the very weakly basic π-bonds of an alkyne. A reaction can only occur if a strong acid is added to the alkyne, to generate a vinyl cation, allowing water to behave as a nucleophile.

WHAT IS THE INITIAL PRODUCT WHEN 2-PENTYNE REACTS WITH AQUEOUS ACID?

The initial reaction of 2-pentyne and H^+ generates vinyl cation *6.37*. Water attacks the cation to form an oxonium ion (*6.38*), which loses a proton to form an *enol* (*6.39*). Enols are relatively unstable and transfer a hydrogen (from the O–H) to the adjacent carbon of the carbon-carbon double bond to generate a carbonyl, in this case ketone *6.40* (2-pentanone). The *initial product* is, however, enol *6.41*.

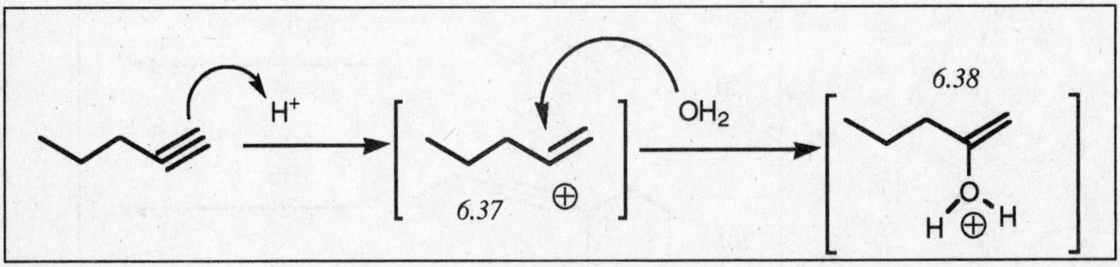

6.37 6.38

Fig. 6.37, 6.38

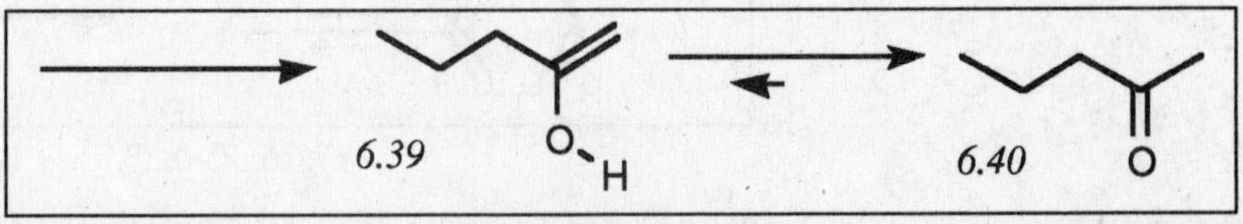

6.39 6.40

Fig. 6.39, 6.40

WHAT IS KETO-ENOL TAUTOMERISM?

Keto-Enol tautomerism is the equilibrium reaction between an enol and its carbonyl partner (as with *6.39* and *6.40*). If the π-bond of the carbon-carbon double bond in the enol (see *6.41*) donates electrons to the acidic O–H bond, a new C–H bond is formed and a new π-bond is formed between carbon and oxygen (a carbonyl—see *6.42*). This equilibrium almost always favors the keto form over the enol form. One should assume that if an enol is formed, it will not be stable to isolation and the final product will be the carbonyl (ketone or aldehyde in these cases).

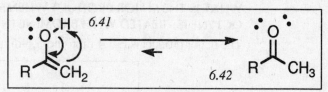

Fig. 6.41, 6.42

WHAT IS THE PRODUCT WHEN 1-HEXYNE IS TREATED WITH A MIXTURE OF MERCURIC ACETATE AND MERCURIC SULFATE IN AQUEOUS MEDIA?

Just as in oxymercuration reaction of alkenes, the mercuric salts stabilize a vinyl cation (the more stable secondary) and addition of water leads to an enol which tautomerizes to 2-hexanone as the major product. The difference between alkynes and alkenes is that the vinyl mercury compound is unstable and rapidly loses mercury from the enol intermediate to form the ketone directly.

ADDITION OF HALOGENS

WHAT IS THE TRANSIENT INTERMEDIATE IN THE REACTION OF BROMINE TO 2-BUTYNE AND WHAT IS THE PRODUCT?

Just as bromine adds to an alkene to form a bromonium ion (see section 5.5), bromine adds to one π-bond of 2-butyne to form *6.43*. The bromide in attacks this ion, opening it to form the vicinal vinyl dibromide, in this case 2,3-dibromo-2-butene, *6.44*. In general, the *trans-* isomer predominates since the ring opening requires *anti*-attack, as with reactions of alkenes.

Fig. 6.43, 6.44

WHY DO THE BROMINES IN THE PRODUCT OF A REACTION BETWEEN 3-HEXYNE AND BROMINE HAVE A *TRANS*- RELATIONSHIP?

As noted in *6.43*, a 'vinyl bromonium ion' is formed and the nucleophilic bromide ion that opens this intermediate will attack on the face opposite the bromine (*anti*- attack) due to steric and electronic repulsive forces.

IF TWO EQUIVALENTS OF CHLORINE ARE ADDED TO 3-HEXYNE, WHAT IS THE FINAL PRODUCT?

The product is 3,3,4,4-tetrachlorohexane.

WHAT IS THE MAJOR PRODUCT WHEN 5,6-DIMETHYL-1-PHENYL-3-OCTYNE IS TREATED WITH BROMINE IN CCl₄?

The major product is E-3,4-dibromo-5,6-dimethyl-1-phenyl-3-octene, *6.45*.

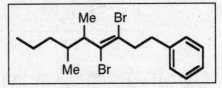

Fig. 6.45

HYDROBORATION AND OXIDATION

GIVE THE INITIAL PRODUCT WHEN 2-PENTYNE IS TREATED WITH DIBORANE.

The product is a vinylborane, *6.46*. Oxidation generates an enol (*6.47*) which tautomerizes to pentanal.

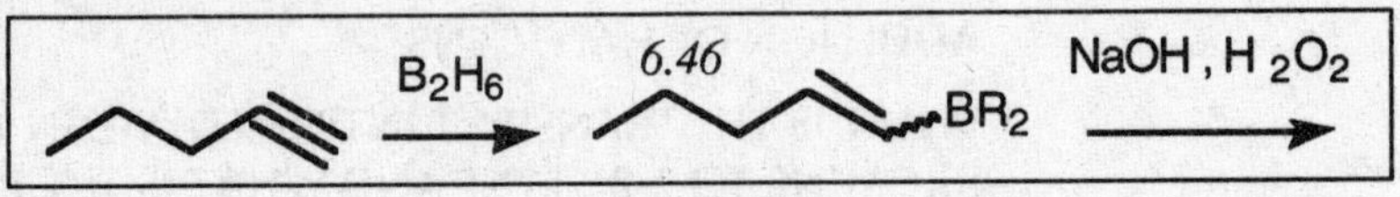

Fig. 6.46

Fig. 6.47

WHAT IS THE FINAL PRODUCT OF THE HYDROBORATION (i. DIBORANE ii. NaOH, H_2O_2) OF 2-BUTYNE?

The final product is 2-butanone, via tautomerization of the initially formed enol (*6.48*).

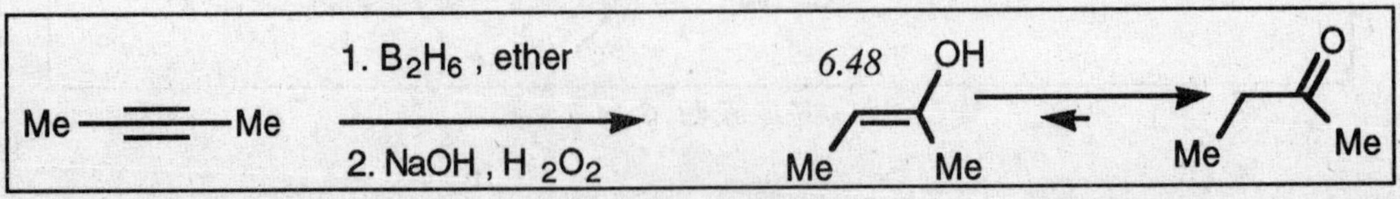

Fig. 6.48

WHAT IS THE FINAL PRODUCT OF THE HYDROBORATION (i. DIBORANE ii. NaOH, H₂O₂) OF 2-HEXYNE?

Since this is not a symmetrical alkyne, two vinylboranes (*6.49* and *6.50*) are formed. Oxidation converts them to the enol, and tautomerization leads to two products, 2-hexanone and 3-hexanone.

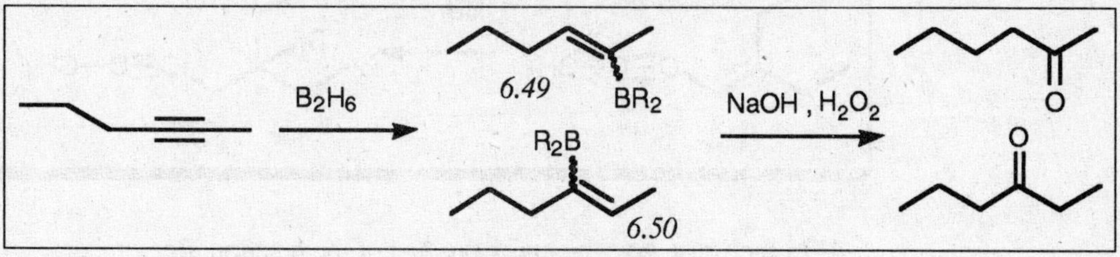

Fig. 6.49, 6.50

This chapter showed that the chemistry of alkynes and alkenes is similar but that the differences are predictable based on a few simple concepts. Apart from the new chemical reactions and new functional groups introduced, the idea of predicting differences in reactivity of similar functional groups is probably the most important concept to be gleaned from this chapter.

END OF CHAPTER PROBLEMS

1. Give the correct IUPAC names for each of the following.

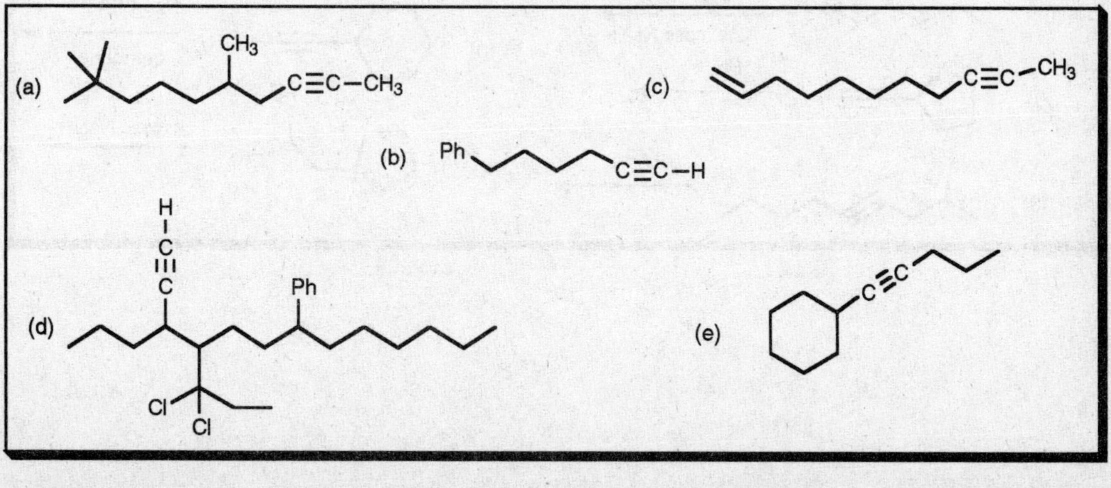

2. Which hydrogen is removed first when $HC \equiv C-CO_2H$ is treated with one equivalent of n-butyllithium? Explain.

3. Explain the result of this reaction.

4. In each case give the major product of the reaction. Remember stereochemistry and if there is no reaction, indicate by N.R.

7

Conjugation

*W*hen a π-bond is directly attached to another π-bond, one influences
the reactivity and properties of the other. One π-bond can be part of an
alkene and the other can be part of an alkene (forming a diene), a carbonyl
(giving α,β-unsaturated ketones, aldehydes and acid derivatives) or part
of other functional groups such as imines, nitro compounds or nitriles. This
special arrangement of π-bonds is called **conjugation**. The important
properties of conjugation include the interaction of these molecules with
ultraviolet light (and other light such as infrared light) and the changes in
chemical reactivity that are induced, relative to unconjugated molecules.
The concept of resonance will be introduced and also the idea of competing
reactions, 1,2- vs. 1,4-addition with conjugated π-bonds.

7.1. RESONANCE

Charge Dispersal Through π-Bonds

**DESCRIBE THE ELECTRON DISTRIBUTION WHEN A π-BOND IS
ADJACENT TO A P ORBITAL.**

When a π-bond is adjacent to a p-orbital, as in a cation, the three p-orbitals (two
from the π-bond and the other one (see *7.1*)) will share electron density. The
electrons are, therefore, distributed over all three orbitals and the positive charge
will be dispersed to the two termini (shown by δ⊕). This is represented as two
structures (see *7.2*) and is called *resonance*. The species represented by *7.1* is
said to be *resonance stabilized*.

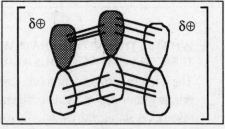

Fig. 7.1

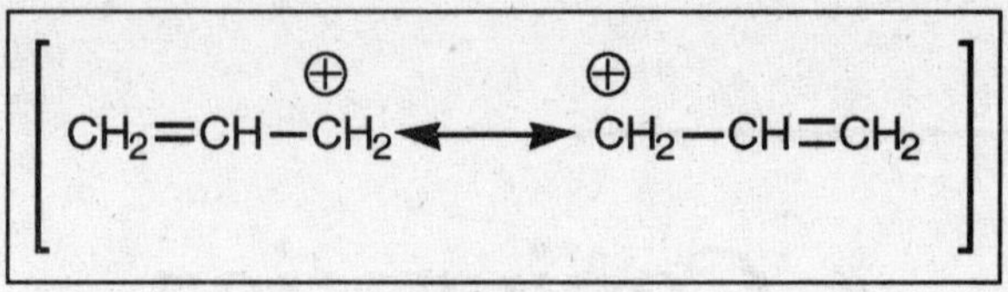

Fig. 7.2

EXPLAIN WHY THE RESONANCE SHOWN FOR CH$_2$=CH–CH$_2\oplus$ DOES NOT OCCUR IN CH$_2$=CHCH$_2$CH$_2$CH$_2\oplus$.

In CH$_2$=CHCH$_2$CH$_2$CH$_2\oplus$ the p-orbitals of the π-bond are too far away from the p-orbital containing the positive charge to share electron density. It is, therefore, impossible to disperse the charge, and it is localized on a single carbon.

Allylic and Benzylic Cations

The resonance stabilized cation illustrated by *7.1* and *7.2* is referred to as an allylic cation. The resonance (delocalization of the charge) makes the allylic cation significantly more stable than a simple alkyl cation. The cation is conjugate to the π-bond.

FORMATION

WHAT IS THE INTERMEDIATE FOR THE REACTION OF 2-PROPEN-1-OL WITH H$^+$?

When 2-propen-1-ol (CH$_2$=CHCH$_2$OH) reacts with an acid, an oxonium salt is formed (CH$_2$=CHCH$_2$OH$_2^+$), which loses water to form the allyl cation, *7.2*.

WHAT IS THE INTERMEDIATE FOR THE REACTION OF 3-PENTEN-2-OL WITH H$^+$?

This alcohol (*7.3*) is considered to be an *allylic* alcohol and will form an allylic cation. Initial reaction with acid generates *7.4* and loss of water gives the resonance stabilized cation *7.5*.

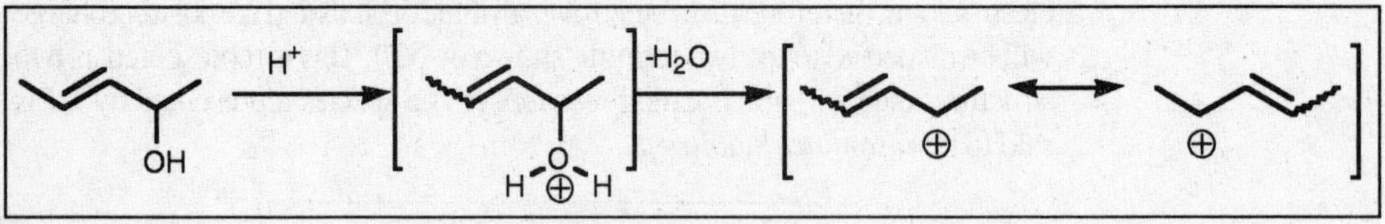

Fig. 7.3–7.5

WHAT IS THE INTERMEDIATE WHEN 1-PHENYL-1-ETHANOL (*7.6*) IS TREATED WITH AQUEOUS ACID?

The initially formed cation (via loss of water from the oxonium ion, *7.7*) is a primary cation, *7.8*. A rearrangement (1,2-hydrogen shift) will generate a resonance stabilized cation, *7.9*, where the charge is delocalized into the benzene ring, as shown. The final product is benzylic alcohol *7.10*.

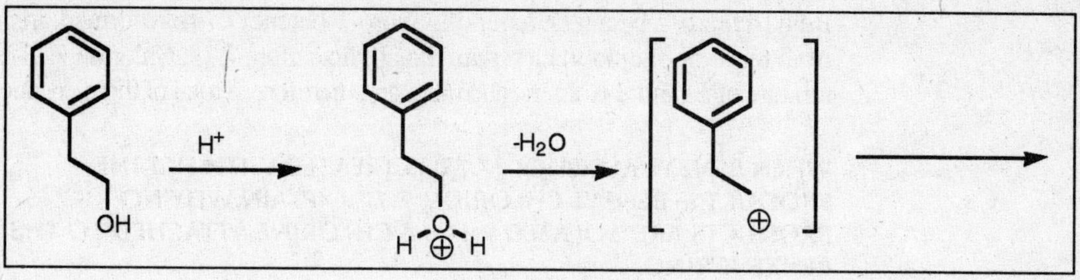

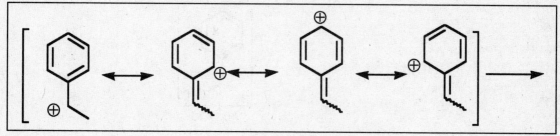

Fig. 7.6–7.8

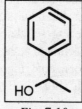

Fig. 7.9

Fig. 7.10

RESONANCE AND REACTIONS

DRAW ALL RESONANCE STRUCTURES FOR THE ALLYL CATION.

The resonance structures for the allyl cation are shown in *7.2*.

WHAT IS (ARE) THE MAJOR PRODUCT(S) WHEN 2-BUTEN-1-OL (*7.11*) IS TREATED WITH HCl?

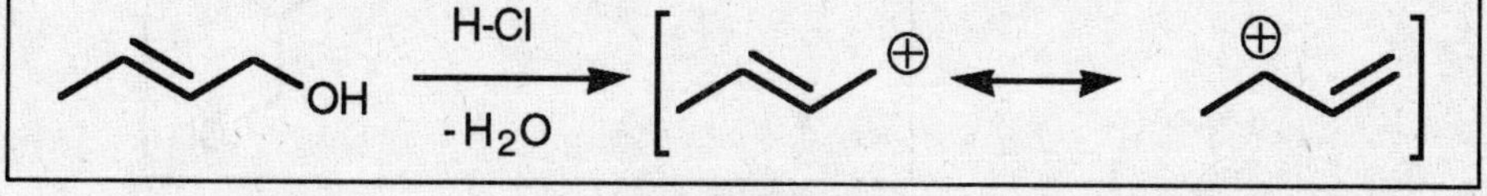

Fig. 7.11, 7.12

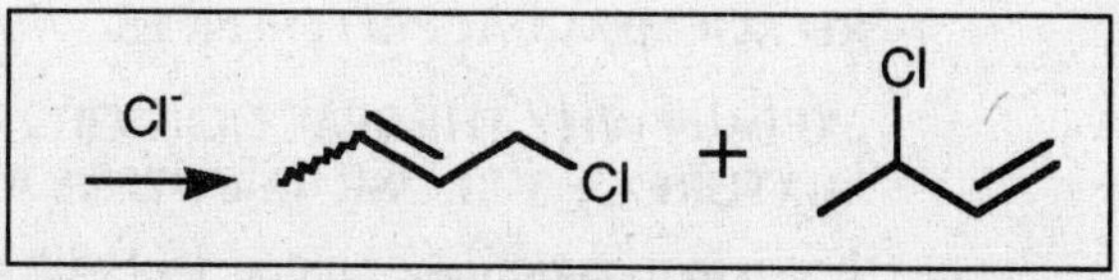

Fig. 7.13, 7.14

Both 1-chloro-2-butene (*7.13*) and 3-chloro-1-butene (*7.14*) are formed, arising from reaction of chloride ion with the allylic cation, *7.12*. Chloride *7.13* is a mixture of *E*- and *Z*-isomers, and there are, therefore, a total of three products.

WHEN BENZYL ALCOHOL (*7.15*) IS TREATED WITH HCl THE PRODUCT IS BENZYL CHLORIDE, *7.17* EXPLAIN WHY NO PRODUCTS ARE ISOLATED WITH A CHLORINE ATTACHED TO THE BENZENE RING.

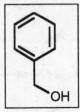

Fig. 7.15

The resonance stabilized intermediate for this reaction (*7.16*) has the charge delocalized on the benzene ring. If chlorine were to attach to the benzene ring, however, the final product would lose the resonance stability inherent to the benzene ring (see chapter 8), making that reaction too high in energy to compete with attachment at the benzylic position. In addition, if the chlorine attached to the benzene ring, elimination of HCl is very facile, regenerating the aromatic ring.

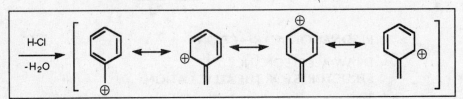

Fig. 7.16

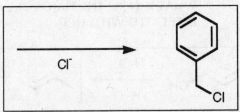

Fig. 7.17

REGIOCHEMICAL PREFERENCES

EXPLAIN WHY THE REACTION OF 2-BUTEN-1-OL AND HBr GIVES A MIXTURE OF 3-BROMO-2-BUTENE AND 1-BROMO-2-BUTENE.

Just as the reaction of 2-butene-1-ol with HCl gave *7.13* and *7.14* via cation *7.12*, reaction of HBr gives the analogous bromides.

WHAT IS THE MAJOR PRODUCT WHEN 5-HEXEN-1-OL (*7.18*) REACTS WITH HCl?

The product is *7.19*. No resonance stabilized intermediate is possible for reaction with the alkene, and the hydroxy oxygen is more basic than the π-bond. Formation of the oxonium ion and displacement by chloride gives the product in an S_N^2 reaction (see section 4.6).

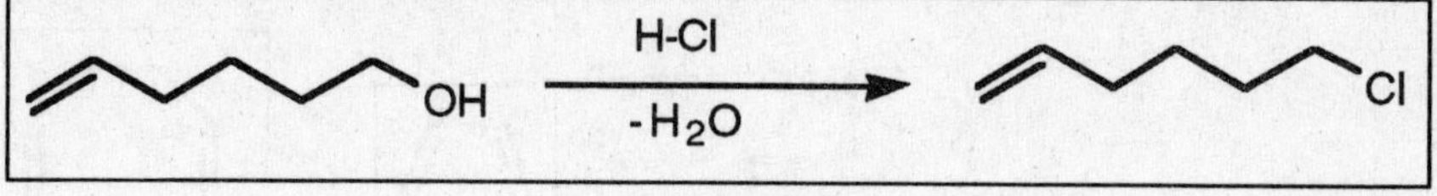

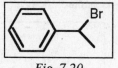

Fig. 7.18, 7.19

WHAT IS THE PRODUCT WHEN 2-PHENYL-1-ETHANOL REACTS WITH HBr?

The product is 1-bromo-1-phenylethane (*7.20*), via cation *7.9*.

Fig. 7.20

7.2. DIENES

Structure

WHAT IS THE STRUCTURE OF 1,3-BUTADIENE?

The structure of 1,3-butadiene is $CH_2=CH-CH=CH_2$.

IS 1,3-BUTADIENE RESONANCE STABILIZED?

1,3-Butadiene is *not* resonance stabilized. Each double bond has the π-bond localized between the two carbons.

IS THE C_2–C_3 BOND LENGTH OF 1,3-BUTADIENE SHORTER OR LONGER THAN THE C_2–C_3 BOND OF 1-BUTENE? EXPLAIN.

There is some overlap of the p-orbitals on the C_2 and C_3 carbons of 1,3-butadiene. For this reason, the bond length is somewhat shorter than the normal C–C single bond found between C_2 and C_3 in 1-butene. This overlap does not constitute resonance, however.

Nomenclature

WHEN TWO DOUBLE BONDS ARE PRESENT IN A MOLECULE, WHAT IS THE IUPAC RULE FOR NAMING SUCH COMPOUNDS?

The prefix *di-* is used for two functional groups of the same kind (diene). Tri- is used for three groups (triene) and tetra- is used for four groups (tetraene). A molecule with two carbon-carbon double bonds is, therefore a *diene* and numbers are used to denote the first carbon of each double bond. The double bonds should be given the lowest possible numbers and *both* double bonds must be part of the longest continuous chain.

WHAT IS THE STRUCTURE OF (A) CYCLOPENTADIENE (B) 1,5-CYCLOOCTADIENE?

(a) The structure is *7.21*; (b) The structure is *7.22*.

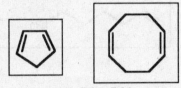

Fig. 7.21, 7.22

Give the structure for (a) E-3-bromo-4,5-dimethyl-1,6-octadiene (*7.23*) (b) 1,4-diethyl-1,3-cyclohexadiene (*7.24*) (c) 5,5-dimethylcyclopentadiene (*7.25*) (d) 2E,4E-heptadiene (*7.26*) (e) 2E, 4Z-heptadiene (*7.27*).

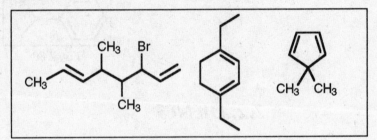

Fig. 7.23–7.25

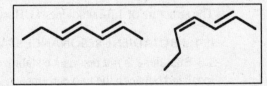

Fig. 7.26, 7.27

IS 1,5-HEXADIENE CONSIDERED TO HAVE A CONJUGATED DOUBLE BOND?

No. The double bonds are separated by two $-CH_2$ groups and they are not conjugated.

Conformation

DRAW THE CISOID AND TRANSOID CONFORMATIONS OF 1,3-BUTADIENE.

The *cisoid* conformation has the two C=C groups on the same side of the molecule (as in *7.28*), whereas the *transoid* conformation has the C=C groups on opposite sides (as in *7.29*). These are rotamers generated by rotation around the C_2–C_3 bond of the diene.

WHICH IS MORE STABLE, CISOID 1,3-BUTADIENE OR TRANSOID 1,3-BUTADIENE?

The transoid form (*7.29*) is more stable because the hydrogens on the C=CH$_2$ groups sterically interact in *7.28*. This interaction disappears in *7.29*.

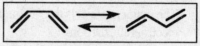

Fig. 7.28, 7.29

WHAT IS THE MORE STABLE ROTAMER OF 2Z,4Z-HEXADIENE?

The *transoid* rotamer (*7.30*) is more stable than the *cisoid* rotamer (*7.31*). In *7.31* the two methyl groups on the C=C groups come close together (steric hindrance), destabilizing that rotamer relative to the transoid form.

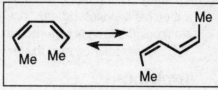

Fig. 7.30, 7.31

Addition Reactions

ADDITION OF HX

WHAT IS THE INTERMEDIATE WHEN HCl REACTS WITH 1,3-BUTADIENE?

The intermediate in this reaction is an allylic cation, *7.32*. When chloride ion reacts with this cation, chlorine is delivered to *both* cationic carbons, generating two products (*7.33* and *7.34*).

Fig. 7.32

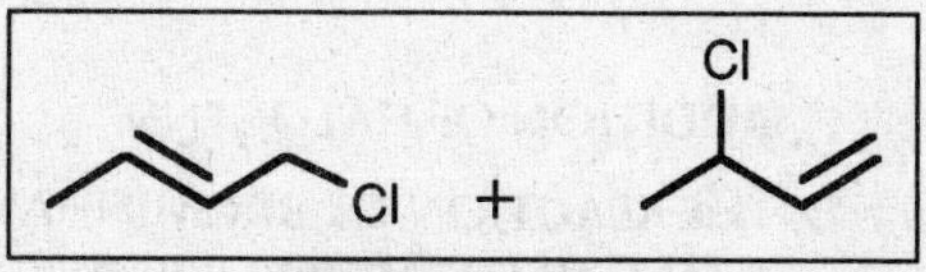

Fig. 7.33, 7.34

WHAT IS THE PRODUCT WHEN HCl REACTS WITH 1,3-PENTADIENE?

There are three products: *E*- and *Z*-1-chloro-2-pentene (*7.35*) and 3-chloro-1-pentene (*7.36*).

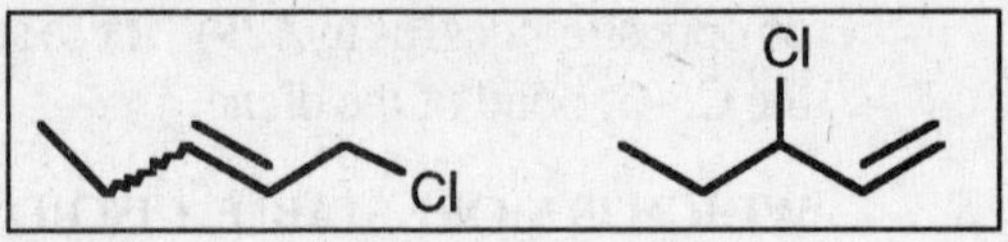

Fig. 7.35, 7.36

WHEN 1,3-BUTADIENE REACTS WITH HCl AT -78°C, WHAT IS THE MAJOR PRODUCT? EXPLAIN.

The major product is the "1,2-addition" product, *7.34*. At low temperature the electrophilic carbon of *7.32* with the secondary cationic position is more stable than the one with the positive charge on the primary carbon. Reaction with $Cl^{\ominus}$ generates *7.34* as the major product. This is referred to as the *kinetic product*.

WHEN 1,3-BUTADIENE REACTS WITH HCl AT 30°C, WHAT IS THE MAJOR PRODUCT? EXPLAIN.

At higher temperatures, both canonical forms of *7.32* are present but the "primary" cation has a disubstituted double bond, whereas the "secondary" cation has a monosubstituted double bond. Under thermodynamic equilibration conditions (higher temperature) the more stable alkene product is favored, *7.33*. This is referred to as the *thermodynamic product*.

HYDRATION

WHAT ARE THE PRODUCTS WHEN 2E,4E-HEXADIENE REACTS WITH AQUEOUS ACID?

The products are a mixture of *E*- and *Z*-4-hexen-3-ol (*7.38*) and *E*- and *Z*-3-hexen-2-ol (*7.39*), both derived from the allylic cation, *7.37*.

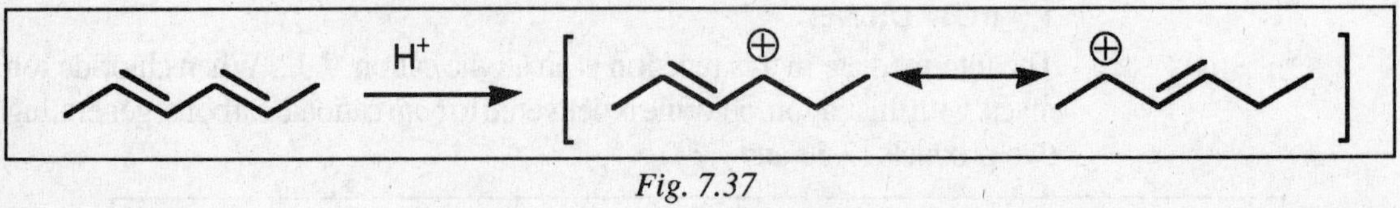

Fig. 7.37

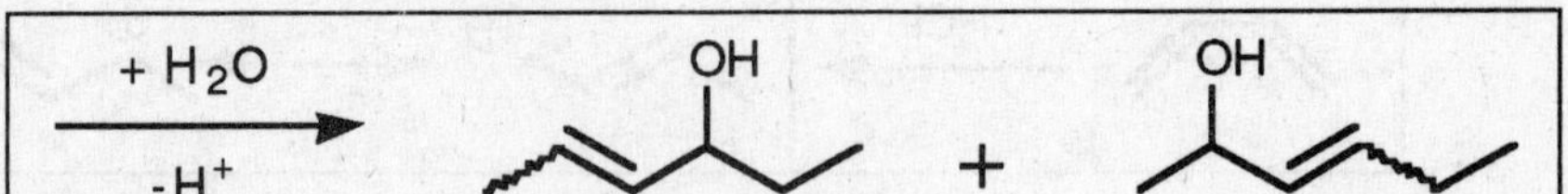

Fig. 7.38, 7.39

ADDITION OF HALOGENS

THE REACTION OF BROMINE AND 1,3-BUTADIENE AT -40°C GIVES WHAT AS THE MAJOR PRODUCT? EXPLAIN.

The major product is the "1,2-addition" product, 3,4-dibromo-1-butene, *7.40*. The "1,4-addition" product (*7.41*) arises by $Br^{\ominus}$ attacking the C–C moiety and opening the bromonium ion (see below) but this is a higher energy process that is very slow at this low temperature.

WHAT IS THE PRODUCT WHEN BROMINE AND 1,3-BUTADIENE REACT AT 30°C?

At higher temperatures, the thermodynamic product (the "1,4-addition product, *7.41*) predominates but there is a mixture of *7.40* and *7.41*.

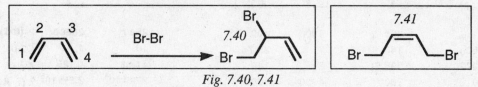

Fig. 7.40, 7.41

IF A BROMONIUM ION IS THE INTERMEDIATE IN REACTIONS OF BROMINE AND A CONJUGATED DIENE, EXPLAIN HOW 1,4-ADDITION CAN OCCUR.

The bromonium ion formed in this reaction is *7.42*. Rather than attack the C–C of the bromonium ion, Br⁻ can attack the remaining π-bond, transferring electron density towards Br⁺, opening the three-membered ring. This is labeled an S_N2' reaction (nucleophilic substitution with allylic rearrangement) and generates *7.41* directly.

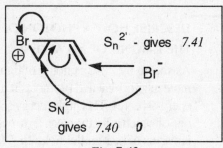

Fig. 7.42

EXPLAIN WHY LOWER REACTION TEMPERATURES FAVORS 1,2-ADDITION.

As mentioned above, attacking the C=C that is not part of the bromonium ion requires more energy. When the reaction is kept cold, this higher energy process is slower than direct opening of the bromonium ion to give *7.40*.

7.3. ULTRAVIOLET SPECTROSCOPY

The Electromagnetic Spectrum

WHAT IS THE RELATIVE POSITION (RELATIVE ENERGY) OF ULTRAVIOLET LIGHT IN THE ELECTROMAGNETIC SPECTRUM?

From *7.43* it is apparent that ultraviolet (UV) light is *higher* in energy than visible light or infrared light ($\approx$ 71-143 kcal/mol for UV vs. 35-71.5 kcal/mol for visible).

U.V.	near U.V.	Vis.		I.R.		
		violet	red			
10	200	400	800	2860	28600	ν (mμ) (nm)
2860	143	71.5	35.75	10	1	kcal
11972	598.6	299.3	149.7	41.86	4.186	KJ
100	2000	4000	8000	2.86×10^4	2.86×10^5	λ (Å)
1000×10^3	50×10^3	25×10^3	12.5×10^3	3530	353	ν (cm^{-1})

Fig. 7.43

WHAT FUNCTIONAL GROUPS ABSORB ULTRAVIOLET LIGHT?

The functional groups that best accept a photon of UV light are those that contain a conjugated π-bond or a polarized π-bond. Simple alkenes do not absorb UV light effectively but conjugated dienes and conjugated carbonyls give strong absorbtion bands. The carbonyl group of ketones and aldehydes also absorbs UV light, as does benzene.

UV and π-Bonds

DESCRIBE HOW A PHOTON OF ULTRAVIOLET LIGHT REACTS WITH THE π-BOND OF AN ALKENE.

As shown by *7.44*, a photon of light excites an electron in a valence, bonding molecular orbital and promotes it to an antibonding orbital, generating a high energy species. This high energy species can dissipate energy in several ways, one of which is for the electron to cascade back to the lower energy orbital, with emission of heat and/or light. In *7.44*, the electron is promoted from one of the vibrational levels ($v_o \rightarrow v_3$) to a higher energy antibonding orbital. The energy difference between these energy levels (ΔE) is the energy quoted in the previous figure (in kcal/mol) for that absorption.

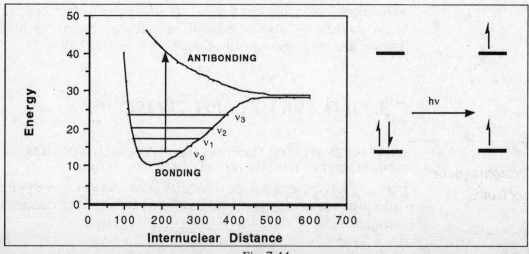

Fig. 7.44

WHY IS THE UV ABSORPTION MAXIMUM FOR 1,3-BUTADIENE SHIFTED RELATIVE TO THAT OF AN ALKENE SUCH AS 1-BUTENE?

For 1,3-butadiene (see following table), the most intense absorption in the UV appears at 217 nm (131.8 kcal/mol where 1 kcal = 28600 nm). For a simple alkene this signal appears at about 165 nm (173.3 kcal/mol). It takes more energy for the simple alkene to absorb the light than it does the conjugated diene. The interaction of the π-bonds in the conjugated diene makes absorption of the light easier (lower in energy), accounting for the difference in absorption maxima (see following question).

For both alkenes and conjugated dienes, the orbital that accepts the photon is a π orbital and the orbital that receives the electron after promotion is a high energy π-orbital, a π^* orbital. The ΔE is, therefore due to a $\pi \rightarrow \pi^*$ transition.

WHY IS THE ABSORPTION FOR A CONJUGATED DIENE MORE INTENSE THAN THAT OF AN ALKENE?

Absorbance is the amount of light absorption and is calculated by *Beer's Law:*

$$A = \varepsilon\, l\, c$$

where ε is the molar extinction coefficient, a physical constant for each compound, and l is the length of the sample cell in cm. The parameter c is the concentration in mols/liter. For both alkenes and conjugated dienes, there is a $\pi \rightarrow \pi^*$ transition but conjugated dienes have a *smaller* ΔE than simple alkenes. For this reason, it takes less energy for the absorption.

It is beyond the scope of most undergraduate organic books, but $\pi \rightarrow \pi^*$ transitions can be classified as spin-*allowed* and spin-*forbidden*. Multiplicity is the sum of the spin quantum numbers of all the electrons in a species. If the multiplicity of the excited state is different from the multiplicity of ground state, the transition is spin-forbidden. If they are the same, it is spin-allowed. In general, allowed transitions have larger extinction coefficients (more intense peaks) than forbidden processes. An overly simplistic way to give the answer to this question is, therefore, that conjugation leads to a lower energy spin-allowed transition that is more intense. This is also very dependent upon the solvent and the wavelength of light that is used.

WHAT ARE THE COMMON EXTINCT COEFFICIENTS AND STRONGEST ABSORPTION BANDS FOR SOME COMMON MOLECULES?

All values from this table are taken from *Practical Handbook of Spectroscopy*, Robinson, J.W. (Ed.), CRC Press, Boca Raton, 1991, pp. 566–630.

Molecule	Molar Extinction Coefficient	Strongest Band (nm)
1-butyne	4467	172
2-butanol	316	174
1-butene	15849	175

Molecule	Molar Extinction Coefficient	Strongest Band (nm)
trans-2-butene	12589	177
2,3-dimethyl-2-butene	13813	198
2-methyl-1-butene	2754	200
cis-2-butenoic acid	11482	204
trans-2-butenoic acid	15849	205
cyclohexene	447	207
acrolein	11221	207
3-buten-2-one	6457	210
1,3-butadiene	20893	217
2-methyl-1,3-butadiene	21379	224
1,3-pentadiene	22908	224
cyclohex-2-enone	8230	225
2,3-dimethyl-1,3-butadiene	21379	226
benzaldehyde	14125	241
2,5-dimethyl-2,4-hexadiene	13100	242
acetophenone	18600	252
2-nitrotoluene	4330	254
benzene	212	254
1,3-cyclohexadiene	10000	259
nitrobenzene	7180	259
toluene	238	261
3-nitrotoluene	7700	264
1,4-dinitrotoluene	14454	266
4-nitrotoluene	11700	274
cyclohexanone	27	280
2-butanone	21	280
1-phenyl-1,3-butadiene	22387	280
pentanal	13	283
1,4-diphenyl-1,3-butadiene	30199	313

(continued)

Characteristics of an Ultraviolet Spectrum

WHAT IS λ_{MAX}?

The wavelength at which the maximum absorbance occurs is called $\lambda_{max.}$. It is used to help identify certain functional groups in a molecule.

WHAT IS THE EXTINCTION COEFFICIENT?

This question was answered in section 7.3.

HOW CAN UV SPECTROSCOPY DISTINGUISH BETWEEN 1,3-BUTA-DIENE AND 1,5-HEXADIENE?

Since 1,3-butadiene contains conjugated π-bonds it will have a λ_{max} at about 217 nm whereas 1,5-hexadiene (with only simple alkene units) will have a λ_{max} between 160-190 nm. In addition, the extinction coefficient for the conjugated diene will be much larger (more intense signal at the same concentration) than the unconjugated diene.

WHAT IS THE λ_{MAX} FOR THE CARBONYL OF ACETONE?

This can be answered by the table of absorption spectra presented here.

Molecule	Transition	λmax (nm)	E (kcal) (KJ)
C_4H_9–I	$n \rightarrow \sigma^*$	224	127.7 (534.6)
$CH_2=CH_2$	$\pi \rightarrow \pi^*$	165	173.3 (725.4)
$HC \equiv CH$	$\pi \rightarrow \pi^*$	173	165.3 (691.9)
acetone	$\pi \rightarrow \pi^*$	150	190.7 (798.3)
	$n \rightarrow \sigma^*$	188	152.1 (636.7)
	$n \rightarrow \pi^*$	279	102.5 (429.1)
$CH_2=CHCH=CH_2$	$\pi \rightarrow \pi^*$	217	131.8 (551.7)
$CH_2=CHCHO$	$\pi \rightarrow \pi^*$	210	136.2 (570.1)
	$n \rightarrow \pi^*$	315	90.8 (380.1)
benzene	$\pi \rightarrow \pi^*$	180	158.9 (665.2)

Note that acetone has several absorption maxima and each different type of transition ($\pi \rightarrow \pi^*$ or $n \rightarrow \pi^*$, where n is an unshared electron) will have its own λ_{max}.

WHAT IS THE λ_{MAX} FOR METHYL VINYL KETONE (3-BUTEN-2-ONE)?

The $\pi \rightarrow \pi^*$ maxima for this conjugated ketone is similar to that of the conjugated aldehyde (acrolein) shown: 210 nm. The $n \rightarrow \pi^*$ maxima is 315 nm.

*U*ltraviolet spectroscopy was introduced in this chapter. It is only one of several methods used to identify organic molecules. The others will be discussed in later chapters. Resonance is an important concept for stabilizing reactive intermediates in organic reactions. Understanding this concept will allow the reader to make predictions of product distribution and rates of reaction in many organic reactions.

END OF CHAPTER PROBLEMS

1. Draw all resonance forms for each of the following.

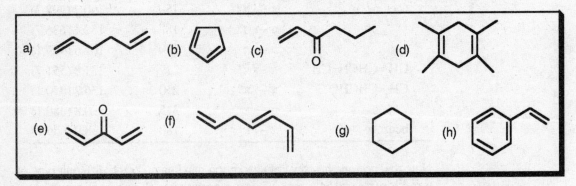

(a) ⊕CH₂

(b) ⊕

(c) ⊕

(d) ⊕

2. Which of the following contain a conjugated C=C bond?

a)

(b)

(c) O

(d)

(e) O

(f)

(g)

(h)

3. Give the IUPAC name for all molecules in question 2. Give the structure of 3E,5E-octadiene and 3-methyl-1,3Z-pentadiene.

4. Identify each of the following as having a 'transoid' conformation or a 'cisoid' conformation and indicate for which molecules the transoid and cisoid rotamers are in equilibrium.

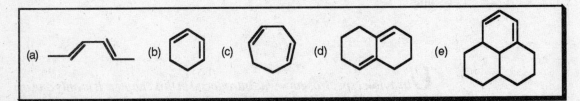

(a)

(b)

(c)

(d)

(e)

5. What are the products when HBr reacts with 1,3-pentadiene at -78°C?
6. Correlate each of the following:

83 kcal = _____ KJ = _____ cm^{-1} = _____ nm
132 KJ = _____ nm = _____ Å = _____ kcal
0.45 nm = _____ kcal = _____ cm^{-1}
2.4 kcal = _____ nm = _____ Å = _____ cm^{-1}

7. Which of the following are expected to give strong absorption bands in the UV?

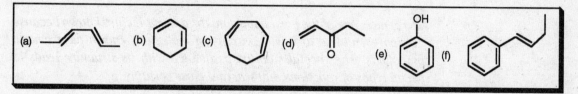

8. If the extinction coefficient of 3-buten-2-one is 6457 and the extinction coefficient of 2-butanone is 17, what is the absorbance of each one if the concentration is 0.3 M in a 5 cm cell?
9. Explain why the extinction coefficient of 1,4-diphenyl-1,3-butadiene is large than the extinction coefficient for 1,3-butadiene.
10. For each reaction give the major product. If there is no reaction, indicate by N.R.

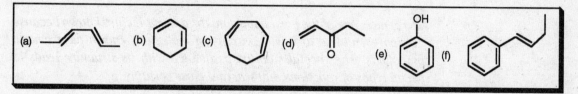

8

Benzene

Benzene is one of the most important organic molecules known because it is representative to a wide variety of molecules known as aromatic compounds. The special stability associated with its structure leads to special types of reactions that warrant close scrutiny.

8.1. STRUCTURE

WHAT IS THE EMPIRICAL FORMULA OF BENZENE?

The formula is C_6H_6.

Cycloheptatriene vs. Benzene

HYDROGENATION OF CYCLOHEXENE IS A PROCESS THAT RELEASES 28.6 KCAL/MOL OF ENERGY. FOR TWO DOUBLE BONDS IN CYCLOHEXADIENE, 55.4 KCAL/MOL IS RELEASED (ROUGHLY TWICE THE VALUE OF 28.6). WHEN BENZENE IS HYDROGENATED, HOWEVER, ONLY 49.8 KCAL/MOL IS RELEASED, NOT THE 3X28.6 KCAL EXPECTED FOR "CYCLOHEPTATRIENE". EXPLAIN.

If the C=C units in benzene were the same as in cyclohexene and cyclohexadiene, 3x28.6 kcal would be expected. The fact that less energy is liberated suggests that benzene is inherently more stable than either the alkene or the diene. This 'extra stability' is about 36 kcal/mol and is due to the special lowering of energy that occurs when the p-orbitals are parallel, contiguous (every p-orbital has a p-orbital neighbor on every adjacent carbon) and able to share electron density with their neighboring p-orbitals. In other words, benzene is stabilized by resonance.

The Kekulé Structure

DRAW A PICTURE THAT REPRESENTS THE ELECTRON DELOCALIZATION IN BENZENE DUE TO RESONANCE.

Benzene is a planar molecule consisting of six sp^2 hybridized carbons connected in a ring, with six p-orbitals perpendicular to the plane of the carbons (see *8.1*).

There are six p-electrons in the six contiguous orbitals that are delocalized over all six orbitals.

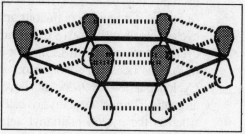

Fig. 8.1

WHAT ARE THE KEKULÉ STRUCTURES?

Kekulé structures are representations of benzene where the bonds are localized and different structures are used to show that the bond positions "change". These structures (*8.2*) are meant to represent delocalization of the electrons and to represent the fact that the structure does not have true double or single bonds, but rather a bond that is 'in between' (shorter than a normal single bond but longer than a normal double bond).

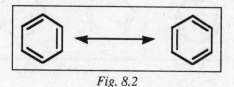

Fig. 8.2

WHAT ARE THE NECESSARY STRUCTURAL FEATURES REQUIRED FOR RESONANCE?

A continuous and contiguous array of p-orbitals are required for resonance.

Aromaticity

WHAT ARE THE STRUCTURAL FEATURES REQUIRED FOR AROMATICITY?

Several criteria are required for aromaticity: a *continuous* and contiguous *array of p-orbitals* in a *cyclic* system are required (every carbon must be sp^2 hybridized). A total of *$4n+2$ π-electrons* (where n is a series 0,1,2,3,... generating a new series $4n+2 = 2,6,10,14,18,22,...$). If the number of π-electrons is equal to one of the numbers in this series, the compound may be aromatic. All of the italicized criteria are *required* for aromaticity. If one of them is missing, the compound is not aromatic.

CAN A CATION OR ANION BE AROMATIC?

Yes. As long as the criteria given above are met, a cation or anion can be aromatic.

CLASSIFY *8.3–8.15* AS AROMATIC OR NON-AROMATIC.

Cyclobutadiene (*8.3*) has only 4 π-electrons and is not aromatic. The cyclopropenyl cation (*8.4*) has 2 π-electrons and is aromatic. Cyclopentadiene (*8.5*) does not have a continuous array of p-orbitals and is not aromatic. The cyclopentadienyl cation (*8.6*) has only 4 π-electrons and is not aromatic. The cyclopentadienyl anion (*8.7*) has 6 π-electrons and is aromatic. Cyclohexadiene (*8.8*) does not have a continuous array of p-orbitals and is not aromatic. Cycloheptatriene (*8.9*) does not have a continuous array of p-orbitals and is not aromatic. The cycloheptatrienyl cation (*8.10*) has 6 π-electrons and is aromatic whereas the cycloheptatrienyl anion (*8.11*) has 8 π-electrons and is not aromatic. Likewise, cylooctatetraene (*8.12*) has 8 π-electrons and is not aromatic.

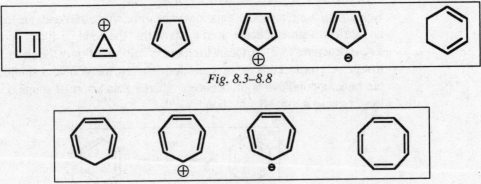

Fig. 8.3–8.8

Fig. 8.9–8.12

ARE MOLECULES OTHER THAN BENZENE CONSIDERED TO BE AROMATIC?

Yes. As illustrated by the previous question, there are many examples of polycyclic molecules that are aromatic. As long as the criteria listed above are met, a molecule may be aromatic. Typical examples are naphthalene (*8.13*), anthracene (*8.14*) and phenanthrene (*8.15*).

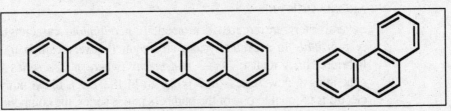

Fig. 8.13–8.15

UV Spectrum   **WHAT IS THE λ_{max} FOR BENZENE?**

One absorption signal for benzene occurs at 254 nm (112.6 kcal/mol) in the UV and another appears at 204 nm (140.2 kcal/mol).

IS THE UV ABSORPTION FOR BENZENE A STRONG SIGNAL OR A WEAK SIGNAL?

The UV band at 254 nm is relatively weak (an extinction coefficient of only 212) but the signal at 204 nm is relatively strong (extinction coefficient of 7900).

8.2. AROMATIC DERIVATIVES

As mentioned above, there are a multitude of aromatic compounds—some benzene derivatives, some not. In this particular section, only derivatives of benzene will be considered.

Structures

GIVE A LIST OF FUNCTIONAL GROUPS THAT CAN BE ATTACHED TO A BENZENE RING.

Several of the functional groups are halogen (as in *8.16*), hydroxyl (*8.17*), amino (*8.18*), cyano (*8.19*), carboxylic acid (*8.20*), ester (*8.21*), aldehyde (*8.22*), ketone (as in *8.23*), methoxy (*8.24*), ethoxy (*8.25*), methyl (*8.26*), ethyl (*8.27*), sulfonic acid (*8.28*), alkene (*8.29*) and nitro (*8.30*).

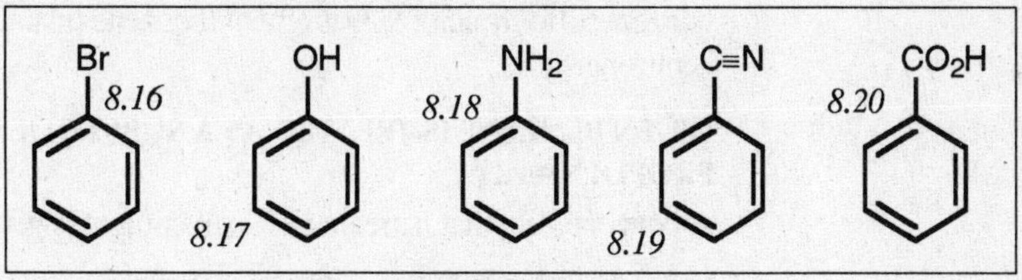

Fig. 8.16–8.20

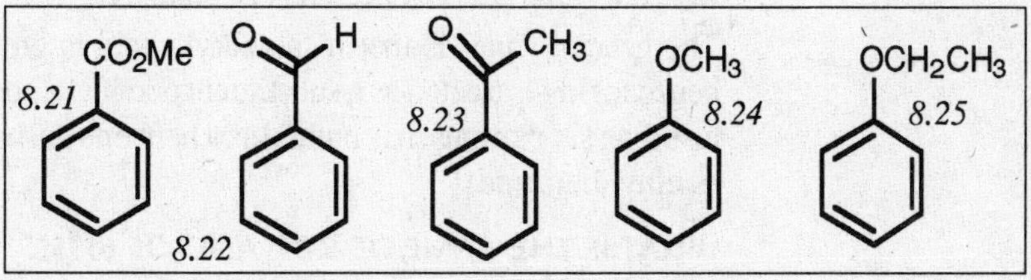

Fig. 8.21–8.25

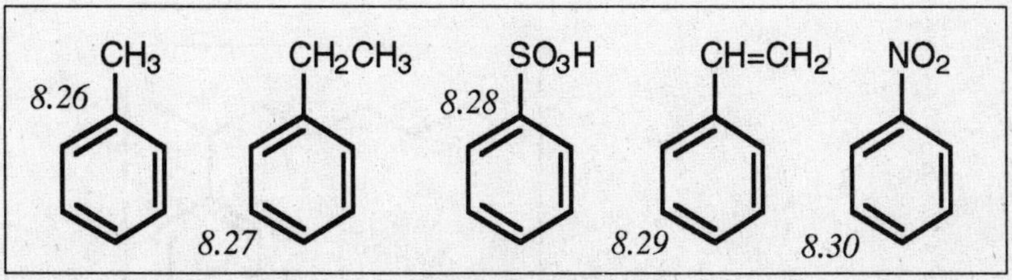

Fig. 8.26–8.30

HOW MANY ISOMERS ARE POSSIBLE IF TWO METHYL GROUPS ARE ATTACHED TO A BENZENE RING?

A total of three different isomers are possible, 1,2-dimethylbenzene (*8.31*), 1,3-dimethylbenzene (*8.32*) and 1,4-dimethylbenzene (*8.33*).

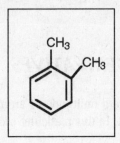
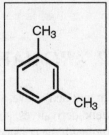
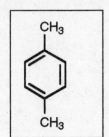

Fig. 8.31–8.33

Nomenclature

FOR THE LIST OF FUNCTIONAL GROUPS ATTACHED TO BENZENE IN STRUCTURES *8.16–8.30*, PROVIDE THE CORRECT IUPAC NAME.

Derivative *8.16* is bromobenzene, *8.17* is phenol, *8.18* is aniline, *8.19* is benzonitrile, *8.20* is benzoic acid, *8.21* is methyl benzoate (see section 15.1), *8.22* is benzaldehyde, *8.23* is acetophenone, *8.24* is anisole, *8.25* is phenetole, *8.26* is methylbenzene (usually called toluene), *8.27* is ethylbenzene , *8.28* is benzenesulfonic acid, *8.29* is ethenylbenzene (usually called styrene) and *8.30* is nitrobenzene.

WHEN BENZENE IS TREATED AS A SUBSTITUENT, WHAT IS THE PROPER NAME?

A benzene ring that is treated as a substituent is given the name *phenyl*.

IF A BENZENE RING IS ATTACHED TO A LONG CHAIN ALKANE, IS IT AN ALKYLBENZENE OR PHENYL ALKANE?

The general 'rule' is that if the alkyl chain is greater than six carbons, the benzene ring is treated as a substituent and it is a phenylalkane. If the chain is less than six carbons, it is named as a benzene derivative (alkyl benzene such as ethyl benzene).

WHAT IS THE NAME OF *8.34* AND OF *8.35*?

Benzene derivative *8.34* is 3-phenyloctane and *8.35* is (2-methylpropyl)-benzene.

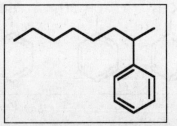
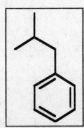

Fig. 8.34, 8.35

*B*enzene is but one example of the vast area of aromatic organic chemistry which includes derivatives of benzene as well as molecules that 'look like benzene' but where one or more carbons have been replaced by heteroatoms such as nitrogen, oxygen or sulfur. These are called heteroaromatic compounds and their chemistry is referred to as heterocyclic chemistry. The fundamental concepts of aromatic stability and the special reactivity of benzene is characteristic or most aromatic compounds.

END OF CHAPTER PROBLEMS

1. Which of the following are aromatic?

2. Draw all Kekulé structures for the following molecules.

3. Give the correct IUPAC name for each of the following.

9

Electrophilic Aromatic Substitution

*When benzene reacts with a suitable electrophilic species (X) that group replaces a hydrogen on the benzene ring (Ph–H → Ph–X). In this chapter, the X group will be cationic, replacement of H by X is a substitution and benzene is aromatic. This process is called **electrophilic aromatic substitution**. This chapter will introduce many derivatives of benzene, along with a new nomenclature system. The concept of resonance stabilized intermediates will be much more important for predicting stability of intermediates and distribution of products in this chapter. Several new types of molecules will also be introduced, along with their special chemistry.*

9.1. REACTION OF BENZENE WITH CATIONS

EXPLAIN WHY BENZENE DOES NOT REACT WITH HBr OR Br_2 IN THE ABSENCE OF OTHER ADDED REAGENTS.

Benzene is a very weak Lewis base. To function as a Lewis base benzene must donate the π-electrons, but these are 'tied up' in the aromatic cloud that gives benzene its special stability. Both HBr and Br–Br are insufficiently strong Lewis acids to react. The loss of resonance energy associated with donation of electrons by benzene precludes its reaction.

Benzene as a Lewis Base

GIVE A MECHANISTIC RATIONALE FOR THE REACTION OF BENZENE WITH A CATION, $X^{\oplus}$.

Benzene donates a pair of electrons to $X^{\oplus}$, forming a C–X bond and leaving a positive charge on the ring, as in *9.1*. This carbocation intermediate is resonance stabilized since the positive charge can be delocalized by the adjacent π-bonds.

A total of three resonance forms can be drawn, representing the relative stability of the cationic intermediate. A proton is lost from *9.1* to regenerate the aromatic ring in the final product, *9.2*. This overall process involves cationic intermediates and leads to substitution of the hydrogen by X. It is therefore called electrophilic aromatic substitution.

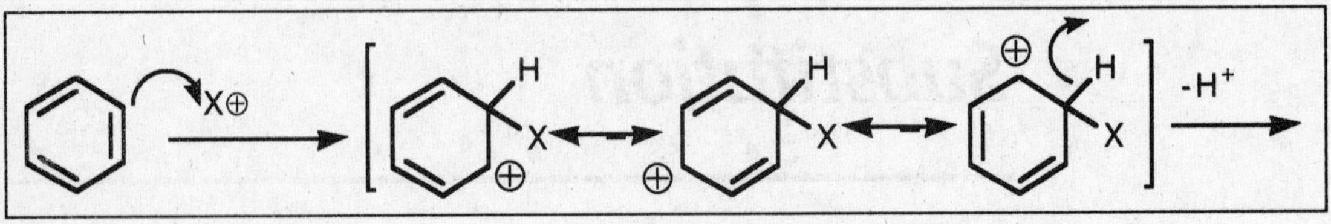

Fig. 9.1

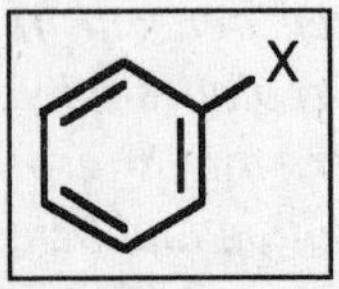

Fig. 9.2

WHAT IS THE NAME GIVEN TO THE RESONANCE STABILIZED INTERMEDIATE (*9.1*) IN THIS REACTION?

This intermediate is sometimes referred to as a *Wheland intermediate*.

Aromatic Substitution

WHY DOES THE RESONANCE STABILIZED INTERMEDIATE LOSE A PROTON TO GIVE THE SUBSTITUTION PRODUCT?

To form *9.1* the aromatic character of benzene has been disrupted. The hydrogen is easily lost from *9.1* because reformation of the aromatic ring is an exothermic process.

WHAT IS THE NAME GIVEN TO THIS ENTIRE PROCESS?

As mentioned earlier, this process is called *Electrophilic Aromatic Substitution*.

9.2. HALOGENATION

Benzene reacts with halogens, in the presence of a suitable Lewis acid, to give a halobenzene (chlorobenzene, bromobenzene or iodobenzene).

Halogens and Lewis Acids

WHAT IS THE PRODUCT WHEN DIATOMIC BROMINE REACTS WITH FERRIC BROMIDE (FeBr$_3$)? WITH ALUMINUM CHLORIDE (AlCl$_3$)?

When FeBr$_3$ comes in close proximity to diatomic bromine, the closest bromine takes on a negative charge (an induced dipole), inducing a positive charge on the other bromine (see *9.3*). Bromine is very polarizable and induced polarity is relatively facile in the presence of a suitable Lewis acid. The bromine (behaving as a Lewis base) attacks the iron, which is a Lewis acid, generating the usual complex. This Lewis acid-Lewis base complex, *9.4*, contains an electrophilic bromine, $Br^{\oplus}$.

Fig. 9.3, 9.4

Similar reaction with $AlCl_3$ generates the aluminum complex, *9.5*, also containing $Br^{\oplus}$.

$$Br_2 \ + \ AlCl_3 \longrightarrow Br^{\oplus} \ BrAlCl_3^{-}$$
$$9.5$$

Fig. 9.5

Aryl Halides

NOMENCLATURE

HOW ARE ARYL HALIDES NAMED BY THE IUPAC SYSTEM?

They are named as benzene derivatives using the chloro, bromo, iodo, fluoro prefixes (see sections 2.4 and 8.2). The names are, therefore, fluorobenzene, chlorobenzene, bromobenzene and iodobenzene.

GIVE THE STRUCTURE OF 1,4-DIBROMO-3-CHLOROBENZENE.

The structure is *9.6 but this is an incorrect name.* The substituents are numbered to give the smallest numbers. Derivative *9.6* is, therefore, 1,4-dibromo-2-chlorobenzene.

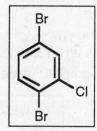

Fig. 9.6

AROMATIC SUBSTITUTION

GIVE THE MECHANISM FOR THE CONVERSION OF BENZENE TO BROMOBENZENE BY REACTION WITH BROMINE AND FeBr₃.

The intermediate *9.1* leads to *9.2* as the product (bromobenzene, X = Br) and this is the mechanism for all such reactions. The specific mechanism involves intermediate *9.7* and formation of bromobenzene, *9.8*.

WHY DOES THE REACTION OF BROMINE AND AlCl₃ WITH BENZENE GIVE BROMOBENZENE AND NOT CHLOROBENZENE?

The initial product of the reaction between bromine and aluminum chloride is 9.5, where the electrophilic species is $Br^{\oplus}$. Since $Br^{\oplus}$ is the species that reacts with benzene (to form 9.7), the final product is bromobenzene (9.8).

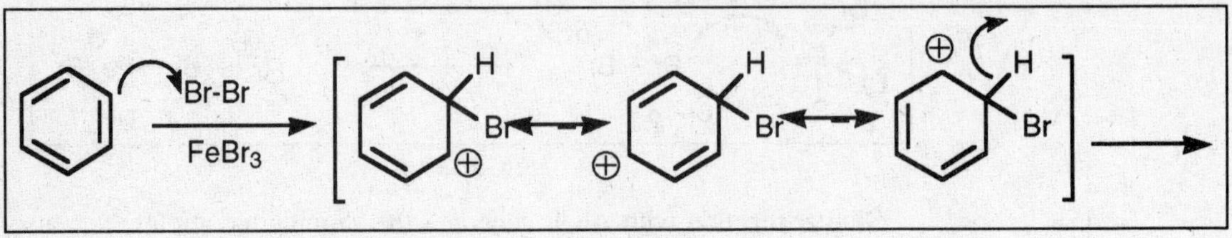

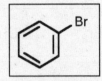

Fig. 9.7

Fig. 9.8

IS THIS REACTION RESTRICTED TO BROMINE?

No. Chlorine is converted to $Cl^{\oplus}$ in the presence of a Lewis acid and generates chlorobenzene. Formation of fluorobenzene and iodobenzene are also possible by this method with a suitable Lewis acid.

9.3. NITRATION

A mixture of nitric acid and sulfuric acid converts benzene to nitrobenzene.

Nitric Acid and Sulfuric Acid

WHAT IS THE ELECTROPHILIC SPECIES FORMED WHEN NITRIC ACID REACTS WITH SULFURIC ACID?

The electrophilic species is the nitronium ion, $NO_2^{\oplus}$ (9.9).

$$HNO_3 + H_2SO_4 \rightleftharpoons H_2NO_3^{\oplus} + HSO_4^{\ominus}$$
$$H_2NO_3^{\oplus} + H_2SO_4 \rightleftharpoons NO_2^{\oplus} + H_3O^{\oplus} + HSO_4^{\ominus}$$

Fig. 9.9

IN THE REACTION OF NITRIC ACID AND SULFURIC ACID, WHICH IS THE ACID AND WHICH IS THE BASE?

Since nitric acid accepts the proton from sulfuric acid, an oxygen of nitric acid functions as a base and sulfuric acid is the acid (sulfuric acid is the stronger acid).

Nitrobenzene From Benzene

DRAW THE RESONANCE INTERMEDIATES FOR THE REACTION OF BENZENE WITH HNO_3/H_2SO_4.

Initial reaction with $NO_2^{\oplus}$ generates the Wheland intermediate, *9.10*. Loss of a proton generates the final substitution product, nitrobenzene (*9.11*).

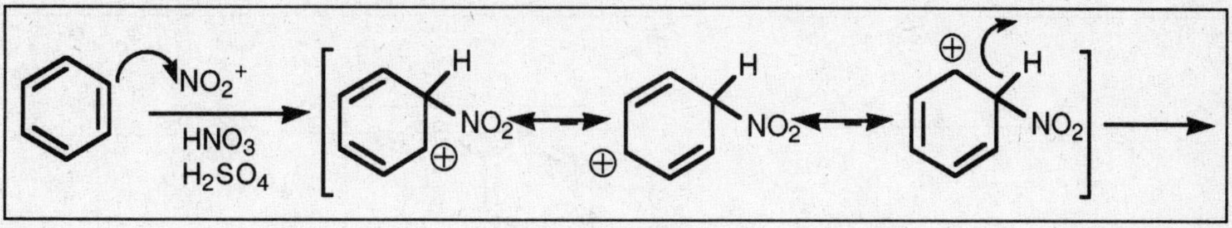

Fig. 9.10

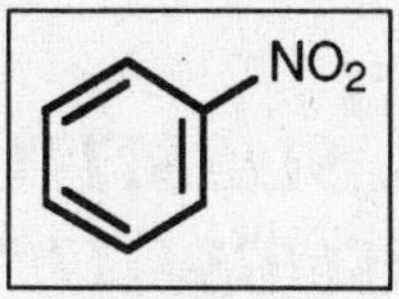

Fig. 9.11

9.4. SULFONATION

Benzenesulfonic acid is produced when benzene reacts with fuming sulfuric acid.

Fuming Sulfuric

WHAT IS FUMING SULFURIC ACID?

Fuming sulfuric acid is sulfuric acid that is saturated with sulfur trioxide, SO_3.

WHAT IS THE ELECTROPHILIC SPECIES IN FUMING SULFURIC ACID?

Both SO_3 and $HSO_3^{\oplus}$ are electrophilic species in this medium but SO_3 is taken to be the reactive entity.

Benzenesulfonic Acid From Benzene

DRAW THE RESONANCE INTERMEDIATES IN THE REACTION OF BENZENE WITH FUMING SULFURIC ACID.

The benzene ring attacks the sulfur of SO_3 to generate a dipolar ion such as *9.12*. Loss of hydrogen in the usual manner regenerates the aromatic ring with transfer of a hydrogen to the oxygen of the SO_3^- moiety, forming benzenesulfonic acid, *9.13*.

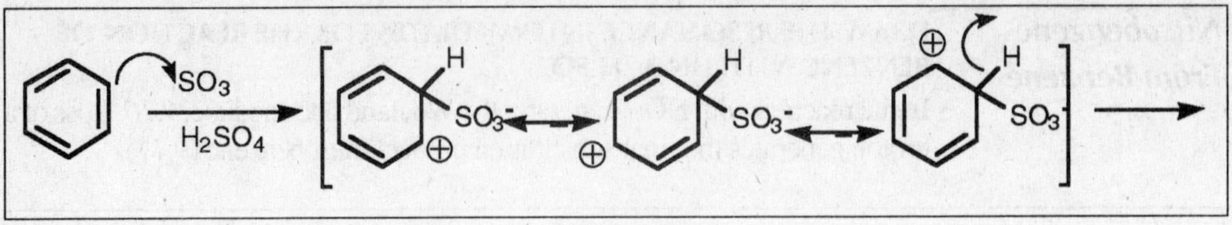

Fig. 9.12

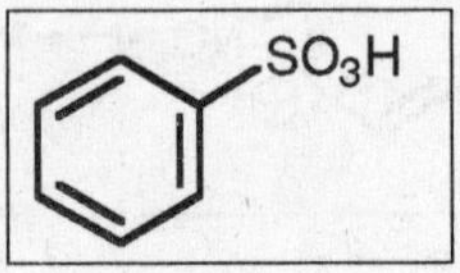

Fig. 9.13

9.5. SUBSTITUTED BENZENE DERIVATIVES (DISUBSTITUTION)

Ortho, Meta and Para Nomenclature

WHAT IS THE COMMON NAME OF TWO SUBSTITUENTS THAT ARE SITUATED ON A BENZENE RING IN A: (A) 1,2 FASHION (B) 1,3-FASHION (C) 1,4-FASHION?

The common name for (a) 1,2-substitution is *ortho* (b) for 1,3-substitution is *meta* and (c) for 1,4-substitution is *para*.

WHAT IS THE IUPAC METHOD FOR NAMING 9.14–9.18?

The numbers are used with the highest priority functional group being assigned to C_1. The ring is numbered to give the substituents the lowest possible number. This will lead to 1,3-dichlorobenzene for *9.14*, 1,4-dimethylbenzene for *9.15*, 2-chlorophenol for *9.16*, 1,2-diethylbenzene for *9.17* and 1,4-difluorobenzene for *9.18*.

USING THE ORTHO, META AND PARA NOMENCLATURE GIVE THE NAME OF 9.14–9.18.

Compound *9.14* is *ortho*-dichlorobenzene; *9.15* is *para*-xylene; *9.16* could be called *ortho*-chlorophenol but if the two groups are not the same, the *ortho/meta/para* nomenclature is not used very often. In this case, 2-chlorophenol, is the better name. Compound *9.17* is *ortho*-diethylbenzene and *9.18* is *para*-difluorobenzene.

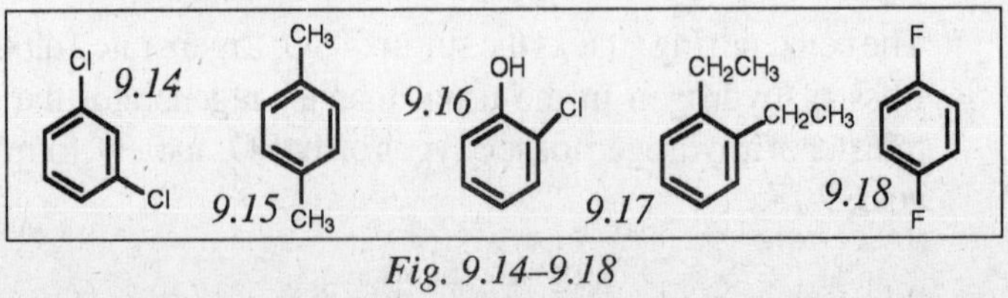

Fig. 9.14–9.18

USING THE IUPAC NOMENCLATURE GIVE THE NAME OF *9.19–9.26.*

Compound *9.19* is 3-chloroanisole; *9.20* is 3-methylbenzoic acid; *9.21* is 2-chloroaniline; *9.22* is 4-bromotoluene (or 4-bromomethylbenzene); *9.23* is 4-ethylpentylbenzene (1-[4-ethyl-phenyl]pentane could also be used); *9.14* is 1,3-dichlorobenzene; *9.15* is 1,4-dimethylbenzene; *9.24* is 2-methylphenol; *9.25* is 3-fluorobenzonitrile and *9.26* is 3-bromoiodobenzene.

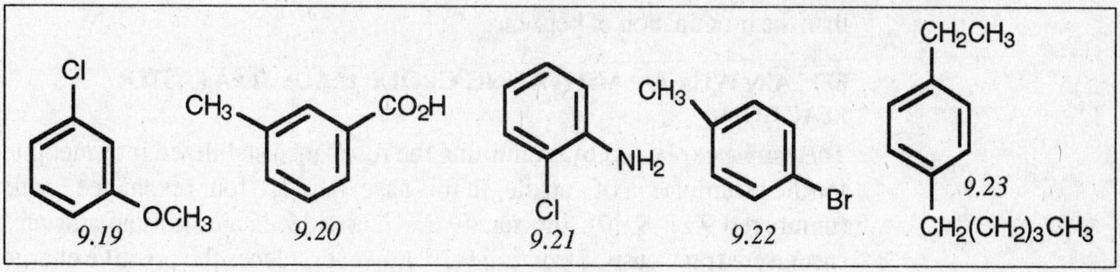

Fig. 9.19–9.23

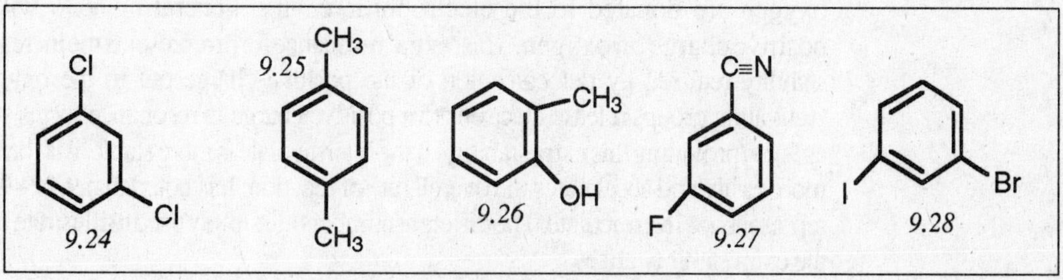

Fig. 9.14, 9.15, 9.24–9.26

Electron Releasing Groups

An electron releasing group is one that has a negative charge or a $\delta\ominus$ charge directly attached to a benzene ring.

ACTIVATING GROUPS

GIVE A LIST OF ACTIVATING GROUPS IN THE ORDER OF THEIR ACTIVATING POWER.

most activating   OH, NH$_2$, NR$_2$
                            N(C=O) [an amide], R, O(C=O)R [an ester], OR
least activating   R, Ar (R = alkyl, Ar = aromatic)

Alkyl groups are considered to be electron releasing.

REACTION KINETICS

WHY ARE ELECTRON RELEASING GROUPS REFERRED TO AS ACTIVATING GROUPS?

When an electron releasing group is attached to a benzene ring, the rate of electrophilic aromatic substitution is greatly increased. Phenol, for example, undergoes bromination about 6×10^{11} times faster than benzene and toluene undergoes chlorination about 340 times faster than benzene. The fact that the methyl group in toluene increases the rate of the reaction relative to benzene and causes it to be placed among the activating substituents.

WHICH MOLECULE REACTS FASTER WITH BROMINE/FeBr$_3$, ANISOLE OR BENZENE?

As mentioned, anisole reacts much faster because it contains a strongly electron releasing group. Bromination of anisole, for example is 1.79×10^5 times faster than the bromination of benzene.

EXPLAIN WHY AN ACTIVATING GROUP LEADS TO A FASTER REACTION.

The can be explained by examining the resonance stabilized intermediate for the bromination of anisole. In this case there are four resonance forms (numbered *9.27–9.30*). Structures *9.27, 9.28* and *9.29* are the usual structures encountered previously. Structure *9.29*, however, places the positive charge immediately adjacent to the oxygen of OMe and the unshared electrons on oxygen are donated to the electrophilic center, generating *9.30* with a positive charge on oxygen. This 'extra' resonance form represents the increased stability realized by delocalization of the positive charge out to the oxygen. Activating groups release electrons to a positive charge in resonance forms such as *9.29*, providing this extra stability. If the intermediate is more stable, it is formed more easily and accelerates the overall rate of reaction. It is noted that *9.27–9.30* represent *one* intermediate. The different numbers are simply used to illustrate how the extra stability arises.

ORDER OF ACTIVATING STRENGTH

WHY IS OCH$_3$ A MORE POWERFUL ACTIVATING GROUP THAN CH$_3$?

The OMe group has unshared electrons on oxygen that can stabilize an intermediate such as *9.29* to a greater extent (release more electron density) than CH$_3$, which has no unshared electrons. The OMe group leads to four resonance contributors (*9.27–9.30*) whereas a methyl substituent leads to only three since the charge cannot be delocalized onto the methyl as it can onto OMe.

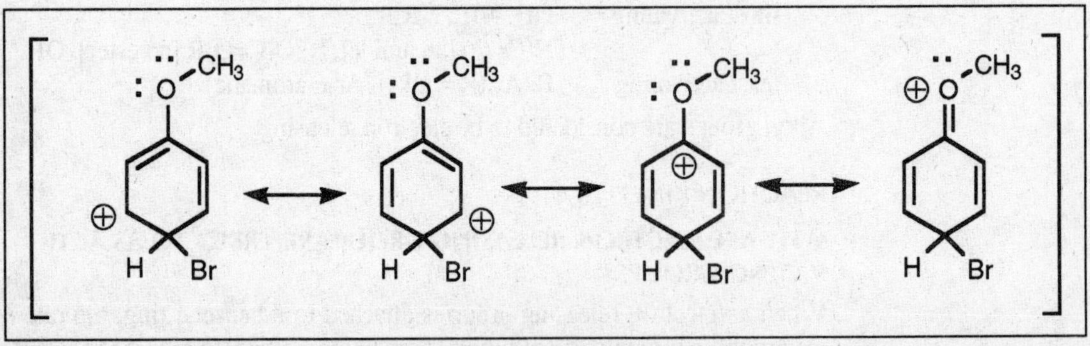

Fig. 9.27–9.30

ALTHOUGH NH₂ IS AN ACTIVATING GROUP, THE REACTION OF BROMINE/AlCl₃ AND ANILINE DOES NOT GIVE A BROMOANILINE DERIVATIVE. EXPLAIN.

The NH_2 group functions as a strong Lewis base and reacts with $AlCl_3$ to form *9.31 before* $AlCl_3$ can react with bromine, which is a weaker Lewis base than aniline.

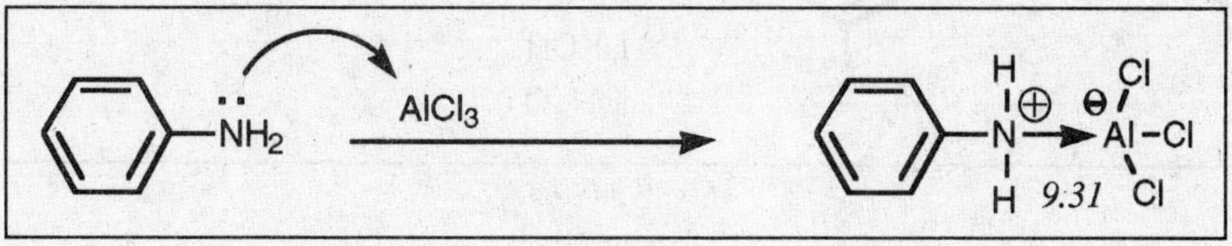

Fig. 9.31

HOW CAN ANILINE BE CHEMICALLY CHANGED TO ALLOW REACTION WITH Br⊕?

If the lone electron pair on nitrogen is somehow 'delocalized' the basicity is diminished. The most common method for doing this is to *protect* the nitrogen as an amide (see sections 15.2 and 16.5). If aniline is reacted with acetyl chloride (*9.32*), the acetamide derivative (N-acetyl aniline, *9.33*) is formed. If *9.33* is reacted with bromine and $AlCl_3$, a mixture of *ortho*- and *para*- bromo derivatives (*9.34* and *9.35*, respectively) is formed. Treatment with aqueous acid (or i. NaOH ii. H_3O^+) will remove the acetyl group, regenerating the NH_2 group, giving *9.40* and *9.37*.

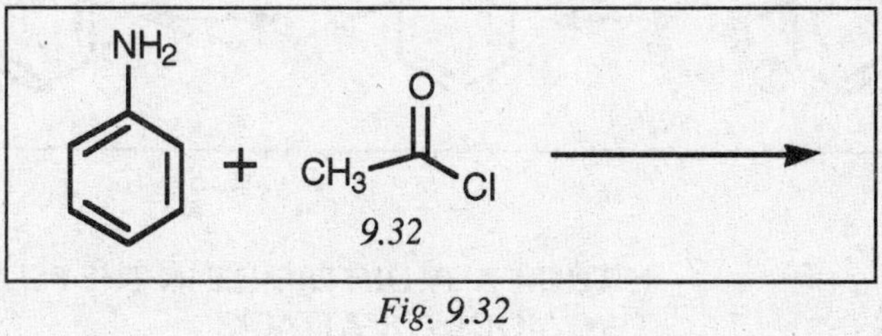

Fig. 9.32

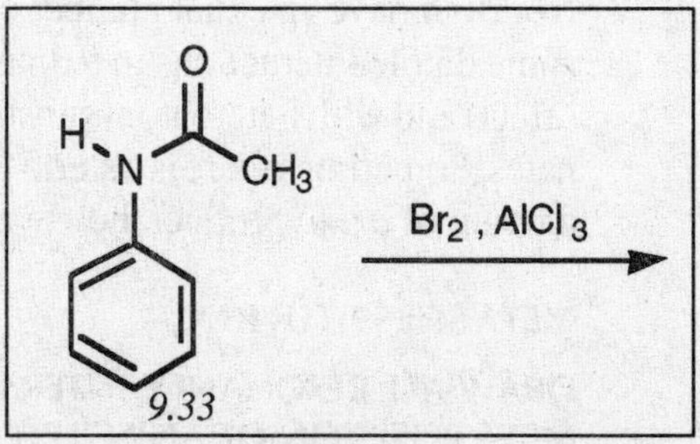

Fig. 9.33

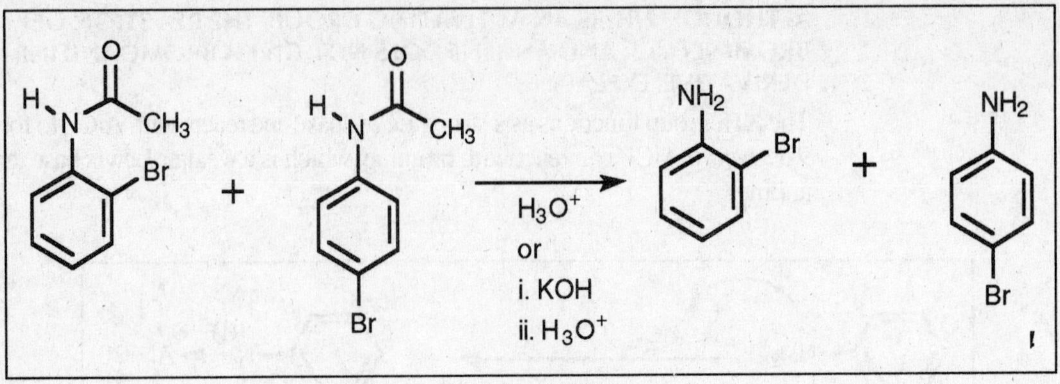

Fig. 9.34–9.37

INFLUENCE OF RESONANCE INTERMEDIATES ON ORTHO/PARA SUBSTITUTION

DRAW ALL RESONANCE INTERMEDIATES WHEN Br$^{\oplus}$ REACTS WITH ANISOLE AT THE ORTHO POSITION AND THEN AT THE PARA POSITION.

Attack at the *ortho* position generates a resonance stabilized intermediate (*9.38*) with four contributors. Attack at the *para* position also generates an intermediate with four resonance contributors (see *9.27–9.30*).

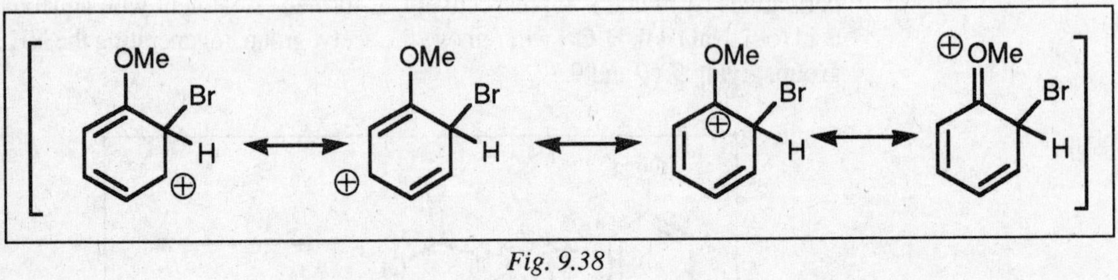

Fig. 9.38

IS THERE ANY DIFFERENCE IN THE RELATIVE STABILITY FOR THESE TWO MODES OF ATTACK?

No. Both have an equal number of resonance contributors. There may be some dipole interactions in *9.38* that stabilize this intermediate (the ortho effect) and with heteroatom substituents the *ortho* product often predominates. Sometimes there is a steric factor for *ortho* attack that diminishes the amount of *ortho* product, however.

META SUBSTITUTION

DRAW ALL RESONANCE INTERMEDIATES FOR ATTACK OF Br$^{\oplus}$ AT THE META POSITION OF ANISOLE.

Resonance intermediate *9.39* is formed, with three resonance contributors.

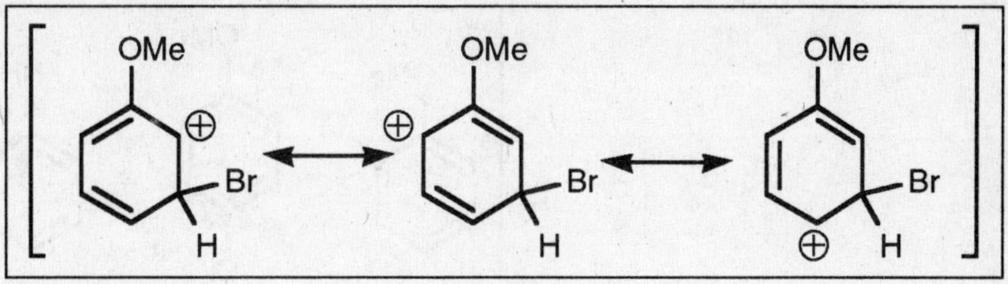

Fig. 9.39

DOES 'META ATTACK' LEAD TO A MORE STABLE OR LESS STABLE INTERMEDIATE? EXPLAIN.

It leads to a less stable intermediate. The positive charge on the ring in *9.39* is never positioned on the carbon bearing the OMe and delocalization of electron on the oxygen is not possible. With fewer resonance contributors, the intermediate is less stable and the reaction is slower.

WHAT ARE THE MAJOR PRODUCTS WHEN ANISOLE REACTS WITH Br_2/$FeBr_3$? EXPLAIN.

The two major products are 2-bromoanisole and 4-bromoanisole. Loss of H^+ from the more stable intermediates *9.38* and *9.27–9.30* (which is one intermediate, the four numbers are arbitrary) leads to the two major products.

GIVE THE MAJOR PRODUCT(S) FOR THE REACTIONS OF *9.40–9.42*.

The reaction of anisole (*9.40*) and Cl_2/$AlCl_3$ generates a mixture of 2-chloroanisole (*9.43*) and 4-chloroanisole (*9.44*). N-acetyl aniline (*9.41*) undergoes nitration to give a mixture 2-nitro-N-acetyl aniline (*9.45*) and 4-nitro-N-acetyl aniline (*9.46*). Sulfonation of ethylbenzene (*9.42*) generates a mixture of 2-ethylbenzenesulfonic acid (*9.47*) and 4-ethylbenzene-sulfonic acid (*9.48*). In all cases the *meta* product is a minor product.

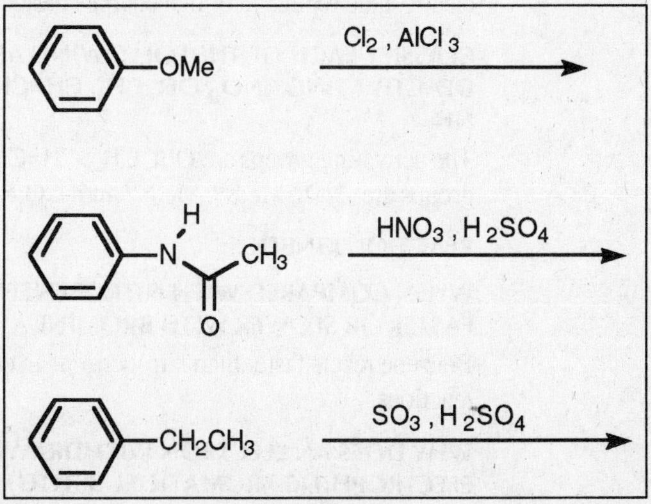

Fig. 9.40–9.42

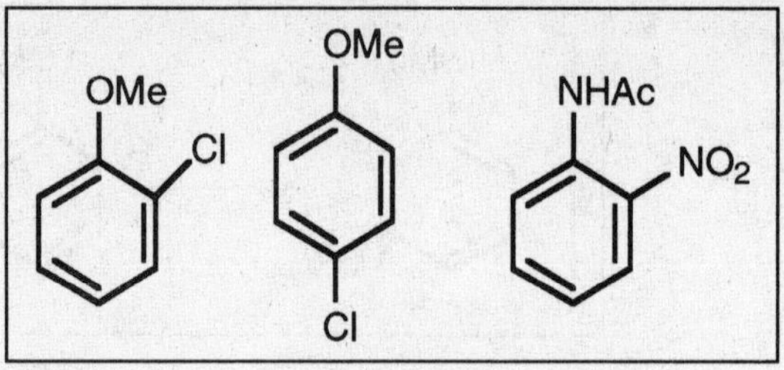

Fig. 9.43–9.45

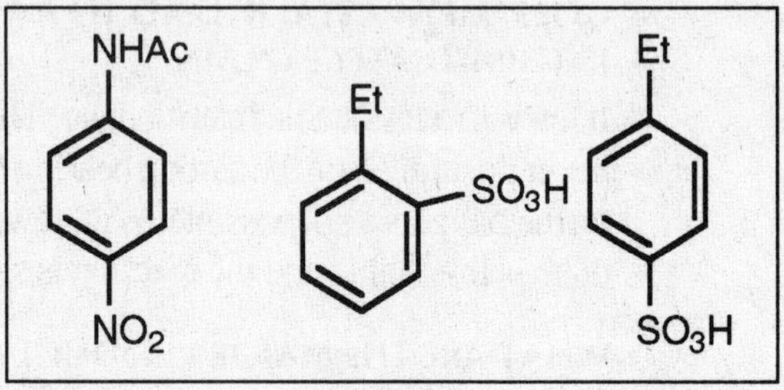

Fig. 9.46–9.48

Electron Withdrawing Groups

An electron withdrawing group is one that has a positive or $\delta^{\oplus}$ charge directly attached to the benzene ring.

DEACTIVATING GROUPS

WHY ARE ELECTRON WITHDRAWING GROUPS REFERRED TO AS DEACTIVATING GROUPS?

When the benzene ring attacks an electrophilic species ($X^{\oplus}$), the resonance stabilized intermediate has a positive charge in the ring. If this positive charge is adjacent to a $\oplus$ or $\delta^{\oplus}$ charge on an electron withdrawing group substituent, the electrostatic repulsion of like charges destabilizes the intermediate.

CLASSIFY EACH OF THE FOLLOWING AS ACTIVATING OR DEACTIVATING. $-NO_2$, OEt, CH_3, $CH=CH_2$, $Me_2S^{\oplus}$, $Me_3N^{\oplus}$, $-CO_2Et$, Ph, NH_2.

The activating groups are OEt, CH_3, $CH=CH_2$, Ph and NH_2. The deactivating groups are $-NO_2$, $Me_2S^{\oplus}$, $Me_3N^{\oplus}$ and $-CO_2Et$.

REACTION KINETICS

WHEN COMPARED WITH NITROBENZENE, DOES BENZENE REACT FASTER OR SLOWER WITH BROMINE AND ALUMINUM CHLORIDE?

Benzene reacts faster than nitrobenzene in electrophilic aromatic substitution reactions.

WHY DOES AN ELECTRON WITHDRAWING GROUP SLOW ELECTROPHILIC AROMATIC SUBSTITUTION?

The nitro group is an example of an electron withdrawing group and it has a positive charge on the nitrogen. Repulsion of this charge with the positive charge of the intermediate derived from attack of an electrophile raises the energy of that intermediate and slows the overall reaction.

ORDER OF DEACTIVATING ACTIVITY

GIVE A LIST OF DEACTIVATING GROUP IN RELATIVE ORDER OF THEIR ABILITY TO DEACTIVATE A BENZENE RING.

$-CN$, $-^{\oplus}NR_3$, $-^{\oplus}SR_2$, $CF_3 > -NO_2$, $-SO_3H$, $R_2C=O > X$ (Cl, Br, F, I), $-CH_2X$

WHY IS NITRO (NO_2) A MORE POWERFUL DEACTIVATING GROUP THAN THE CARBONYL OF A KETONE (AS IN ACETOPHENONE)?

The nitrogen of nitro has a formal charge of $+1$ [$O=N^{\oplus}-O^{\ominus}$] whereas the carbon of a carbonyl is part of polarized bond and has a $\delta^{\oplus}$ charge. The greater the electrophilic character of the atom (the larger the positive charge), the greater will be its deactivating ability.

Influence on Resonance Intermediates

ORTHO/PARA SUBSTITUTION

DRAW ALL RESONANCE INTERMEDIATES WHEN Br$^{\oplus}$ REACTS AT THE ORTHO POSITION OF NITROBENZENE AT THE PARA POSITION.

There is one intermediate for *ortho* attack, with three resonance contributors, *9.49–9.51*. There is also one intermediate for *para* attack, with three resonance contributors, *9.52–9.54*.

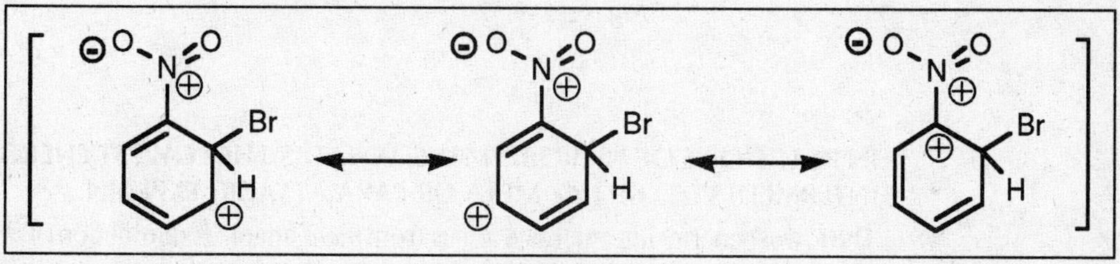

Fig. 9.49–9.51

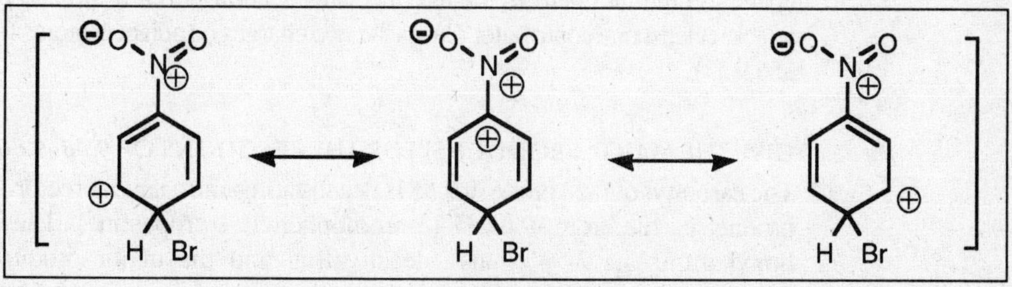

Fig. 9.52–9.54

WHICH IS THE HIGHEST ENERGY RESONANCE FORM FOR ORTHO ATTACK?

For *para* attack the highest energy contributor is *9.51* where the two positive charges are on adjacent atoms. In this contributor, repulsion by the like charges is maximized. Similarly, contributor *9.53* has two like charges on adjacent atoms and is the highest energy contributor. These two resonance contributors greatly destabilize the intermediate, making it more difficult to form (this slows the overall rate of reaction).

META SUBSTITUTION

DRAW ALL RESONANCE INTERMEDIATES WHEN Br⊕ REACTS AT THE META POSITION OF NITROBENZENE.

Attack at the *meta* position generates one intermediate with three resonance contributors (*9.55–9.57*).

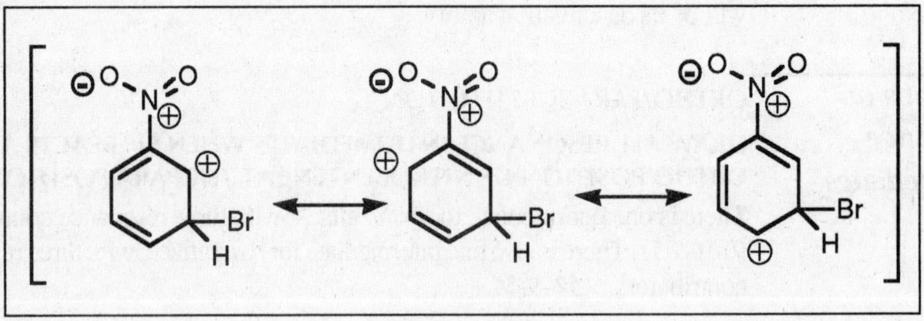

Fig. 9.55–9.57

IN REACTIONS OF NITROBENZENE, WHAT IS THE LOWEST ENERGY INTERMEDIATE: ORTHO, META OR PARA ATTACK? EXPLAIN.

The lowest energy intermediate arises from *meta* attack. Examination of *9.55–9.57* reveals that the positive charge on the ring is never adjacent to the positive charge on the nitrogen. In the intermediates resulting from *ortho* and *para* attack, at least one contributor places the two charges on adjacent atoms (*9.51* and *9.53*).

GIVE THE MAJOR PRODUCT(S) FOR THE REACTIONS OF *9.58–9.60*.

The carbonyl of the ketone in *9.58* is deactivating and a *meta* director. The product is, therefore, *9.61* [1-(3-bromophenyl)-1-propanone]. The carboxyl group in *9.59* is also deactivating and the major product is benzenesulfonic acid-3-carboxylate (*9.62*). Initial reaction of *9.60* with iodomethane generates a dimethylsulfonium ion (a deactivating group whereas -SMe is activating). The product of nitration is, therefore, 3-(dimethylsulfonium)nitrobenzene, *9.63*.

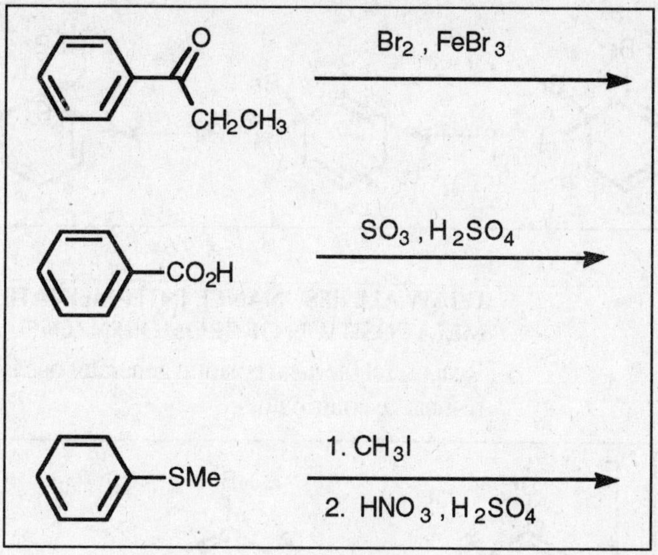

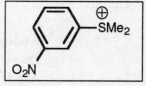

Fig. 9.58–9.60

Fig. 9.61–9.63

Halobenzenes

DOES BROMOBENZENE REACT FASTER OR SLOWER THAN BENZENE IN ELECTROPHILIC AROMATIC SUBSTITUTION REACTIONS?

Bromobenzene reacts *slower* than benzene in electrophilic aromatic substitution. Other aryl halides (fluorobenzene, chlorobenzene and iodobenzene) also react slower than benzene.

IS Br AN ACTIVATING OR A DEACTIVATING GROUP?

Bromine is a deactivating group. The other halogens (F, Cl, I) are also deactivating.

DRAW ALL RESONANCE INTERMEDIATES WHEN Br⊕ REACTS AT THE ORTHO POSITION OF BROMOBENZENE.

There are a total of four resonance contributors to the intermediate resulting from *ortho* attack. Similarly, *para* attack leads to four resonance contributors. In *9.64* the positive charge on the ring is adjacent to the bromine atom. The charge can be delocalized onto bromine (which contains electrons that can be donated to the positive center), leading to an additional resonance forms.

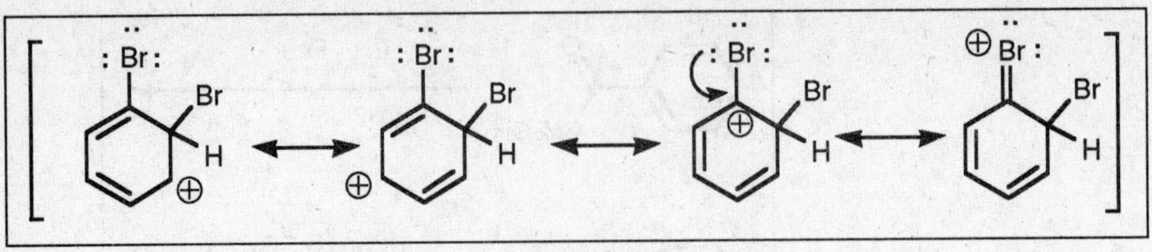

Fig. 9.64

DRAW ALL RESONANCE INTERMEDIATES WHEN Br⊕ REACTS AT THE META POSITION OF BROMOBENZENE?

Reaction at the *meta* position generates one intermediate (*9.65*) with only three resonance contributors.

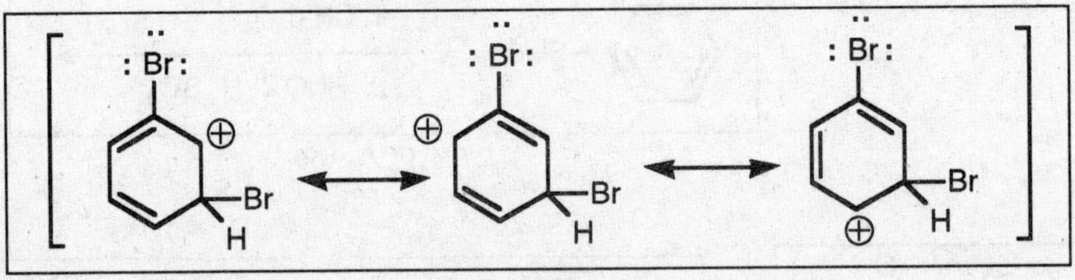

Fig. 9.65

WHICH GIVES THE MORE STABLE INTERMEDIATE, ORTHO ATTACK OR META ATTACK?

Attack at the *ortho* and *para* positions generate an intermediate with four resonance contributors whereas *meta* attack generates an intermediate with only three resonance contributors. The intermediates arising from *ortho* and *para* attack are, therefore, more stable. Halogens on a benzene ring are *ortho/para* directors although they are deactivating.

WHAT IS THE MAJOR PRODUCT(S) WHEN BROMOBENZENE REACTS WITH Cl$_2$ AND AlCl$_3$?

When bromobenzene reacts with chlorine and AlCl$_3$, the major products are a roughly equal mixture of 2-chlorobromobenzene and 4-chlorobromobenzene.

Arenes

WHAT IS AN ARENE?

An arene is an allyl benzene (a benzene with an alkyl substituent).

WHAT IS THE COMMON NAME OF 1,2-DIMETHYLBENZENE? OF 1,3-DIMETHYLBENZENE? OF 1,4-DIMETHYLBENZENE?

Common names are often used for these compounds. A dimethylbenzene is referred to as a *xylene*. 1,2-Dimethylbenzene is called *ortho*-xylene. 1,3-Dimethylbenzene is called *meta*-xylene and 1,4-dimethylbenzene is called *para*-xylene.

WHAT IS THE IUPAC NAME OF EACH OF THE FOLLOWING COMPOUNDS?

The IUPAC name of *9.66* is ethylbenzene. Arene *9.67* is 1,2,5-trimethylbenzene; *9.68* is 3-ethylpropylbenzene and *9.69* is 1,2-(di-1-methylethyl)benzene, although it is most commonly referred to as 1,2-diisopropylbenzene.

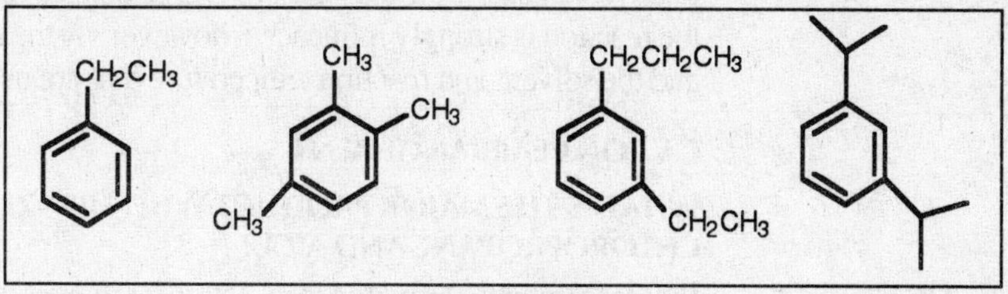

Fig. 9.66–9.69

9.6. FRIEDEL-CRAFTS ALKYLATION

Alkyl Halides and Lewis Acids

WHAT IS THE INTERMEDIATE PRODUCT WHEN AN ALKYL HALIDE REACTS WITH $AlCl_3$?

The intermediate of this reaction is a carbocation. When 2-bromopropane reacts with $AlCl_3$ the product is $Me_2CH^{\oplus} \, AlCl_4^{\ominus}$.

CATION STABILITY

WHAT IS THE PRODUCT WHEN 1-CHLORO-2,2-DIMETHYLPROPANE REACTS WITH $AlCl_3$?

The product is the tertiary cation, *9.70*.

Fig. 9.70

WHAT IS THE INITIAL PRODUCT WHEN 1-CHLOROBUTANE REACTS WITH $AlCl_3$?

The initial product of this reaction is a primary cation (*9.71*), but this rearranges to the more stable secondary cation (*9.72*), as expected with any carbocation.

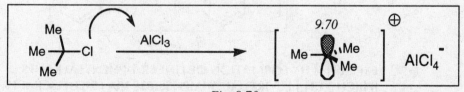

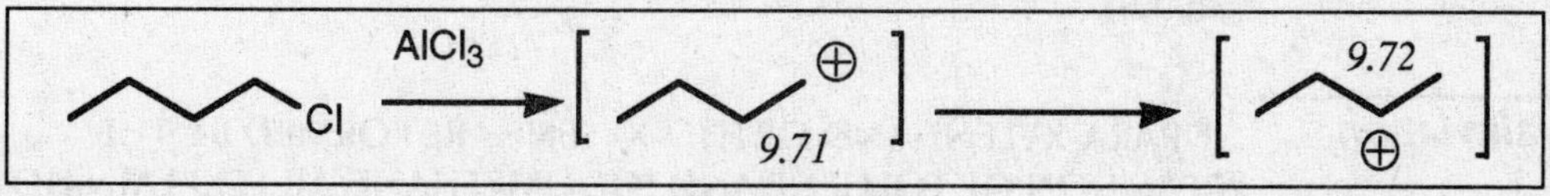

Fig. 9.71, 9.72

EXPLAIN WHY BENZENE REACTS FASTER WITH TERTIARY HALIDES THAN WITH PRIMARY HALIDES.

The energy required to form a tertiary cation is relatively low and $AlCl_3$ (or another Lewis acid) easily removes the halide to generate the cation. With primary halides, the activation energy for removing the halide (to generate a relatively unstable primary cation) is high and the reaction is slow. The rate of the reaction is strongly influenced, however, by the strength of the Lewis acid and the solvent and reaction temperature that are used.

CATION REARRANGEMENT

WHAT IS THE MAJOR PRODUCT WHEN BENZENE REACTS WITH 1-CHLOROPROPANE AND $AlCl_3$?

Since the initially formed primary cation rearranges to *9.73*, benzene reacts with *9.73* to give (1-methylethyl)benzene [isopropylbenzene, *9.75*] via the usual cationic intermediate, *9.74*.

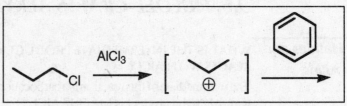

Fig. 9.73

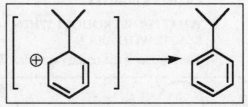

Fig. 9.74, 9.75

EXPLAIN WHY FORMATION OF LINEAR 1-PHENYLALKANES [Ph(CH_2)_nCH_3] IS VIRTUALLY IMPOSSIBLE VIA FRIEDEL-CRAFTS ALKYLATION.

Virtually all primary halides will react with the Lewis acid to give a primary cation but this unstable intermediate almost always rearranges to a more stable secondary or tertiary cation. Since the relative population of primary cation is very low, substitution products arising from that species are rare (no linear arenes).

Polyalkylation

IF PARA-XYLENE AND ORTHO-XYLENE ARE FORMED BY THE REACTION OF TOLUENE AND IODOMETHANE/AlI_3, EXPLAIN HOW 1,2,4-TRIMETHYLBENZENE IS ALSO FORMED IN THE REACTION.

Toluene reacts with iodomethane to give a new methyl group at the ortho and para positions, as with para-xylene (9.76). Since xylene has two alkyl groups, the benzene ring is more activated than in toluene, and xylene reacts faster with the MeI, AlCl₃ reagent than does toluene. The third methyl group will be incorporated ortho to the methyls (as in 9.77), which are both ortho/para directors.

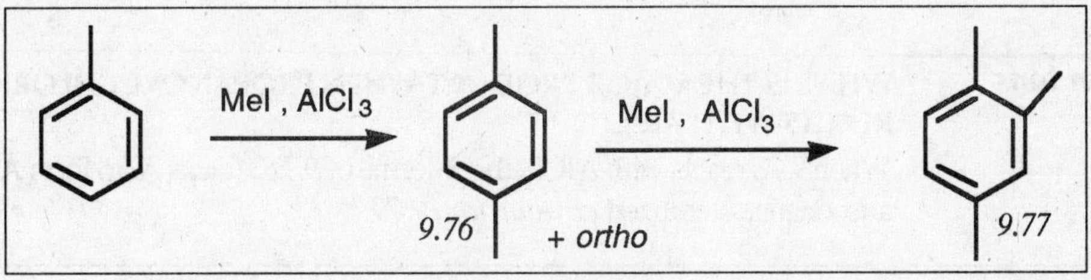

Fig. 9.76, 9.77

WHICH IS THE MORE REACTIVE BENZENE DERIVATIVE, 1,2-DIETHYLBENZENE OR TOLUENE?

As in the formation of 9.77, 1,2-diethylbenzene is more activated than toluene and will react faster in electrophilic aromatic substitution reactions.

HOW CAN POLYALKYLATION BE SUPPRESSED IN ELECTROPHILIC AROMATIC SUBSTITUTION?

If a large excess of the initial aromatic substrate is used (a large excess of toluene in the examples cited), the mono-alkylation product (xylene) will usually predominate. Alternatively, although it is usually impractical, the initial substitution product can be removed from the reaction medium as it is formed.

9.7. FRIEDEL-CRAFTS ACYLATION

Just as benzene derivatives react with alkyl halides, they also react with acid chlorides (see sections 14.5 and 15.2).

Acid Chlorides

WHAT IS THE STRUCTURE OF AN ACID CHLORIDE?

A acid chloride is a derivative of carboxylic acids where the –OH group has been replaced with Cl, as in 9.78 (see section 15.1).

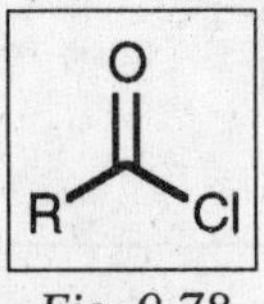

Fig. 9.78

HOW ARE ACID CHLORIDES PREPARED?

Acid chlorides are prepared by treating a carboxylic acid with a halogenating reagent such as $SOCl_2$, PCl_3, PCl_5 or $POCl_3$ (see section 15.2).

HOW ARE ACID CHLORIDES NAMED?

The -oic acid ending for carboxylic acids is replaced with -oyl chloride. The acid chloride of propionic acid is, therefore, propanoyl chloride.

Acylium Ions

WHAT IS THE MAJOR PRODUCT WHEN PROPANOYL CHLORIDE REACTS WITH AlCl₃?

When *9.78* reacts with $AlCl_3$, the chlorine of *9.78* attacks Al to form $AlCl_4^-$ and a resonance stabilized *acylium ion*, *9.79*.

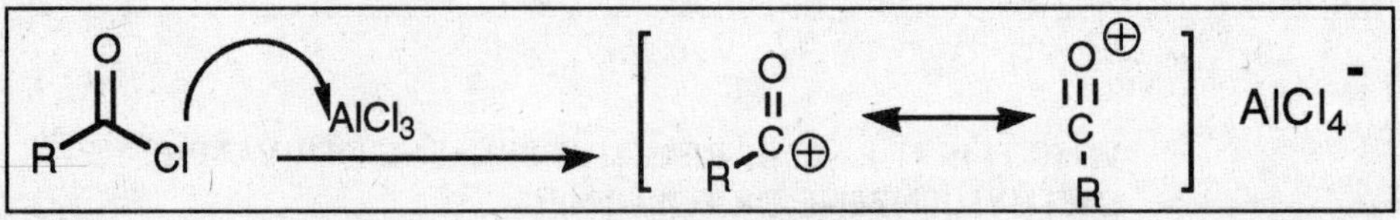

Fig. 9.78, 9.79

DOES AN ACYLIUM ION REARRANGE AS A NORMAL CARBOCATION DOES?

No. An acylium ion is stabilized by the oxygen atom to give the resonance contributors shown in *9.79*. This additional stability essentially stops cationic rearrangement.

Resonance Stabilized Intermediates

WHEN BENZENE REACTS WITH AN ACYLIUM ION, WHAT ARE THE RESONANCE INTERMEDIATES?

The initial reaction produces the usual cation *9.80*, with the carbonyl attached to the ring. Loss of a proton generates the phenyl ketone product, *9.81*.

WHAT IS THE PRODUCT WHEN PROPANOYL CHLORIDE REACTS WITH AlCl₃ AND BENZENE?

When propanoyl chloride (*9.78*, R = Et) reacts with benzene and $AlCl_3$, the product is 1-phenyl-1-propanone (*9.81*, R = Et).

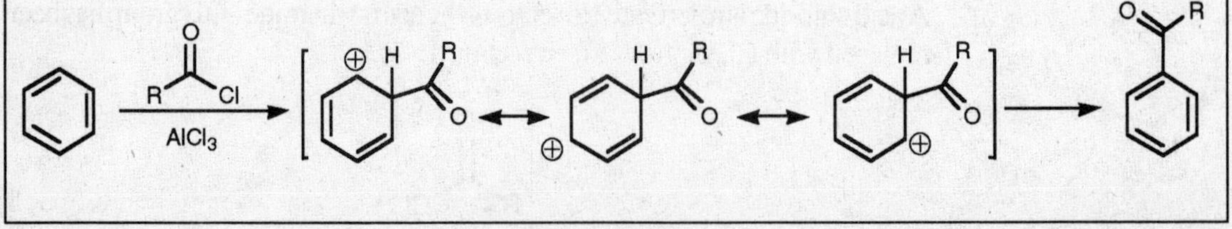

Fig. 9.80, 9.81

WHAT IS THE PRODUCT WHEN ANISOLE REACTS WITH PROPANOYL CHLORIDE AND AlCl₃?

The OMe group of anisole is strongly activating and an *ortho/para* director. The products are, therefore, a mixture of (2-methoxyphenyl)-1-propanone (*9.82*) and (4-methoxyphenyl)-1-propanone (*9.83*).

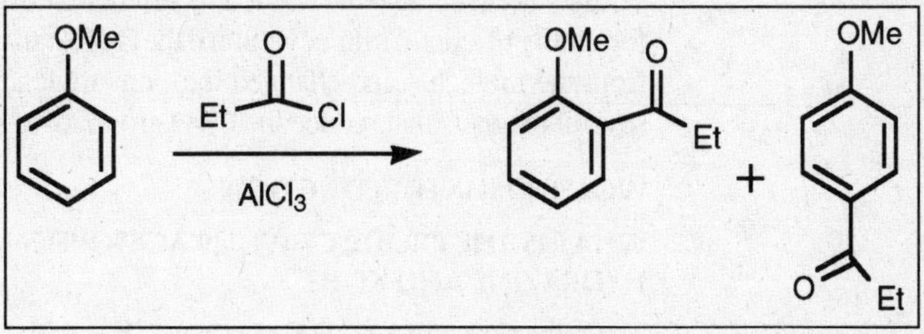

Fig. 9.82, 9.83

WHAT IS THE PRODUCT WHEN NITROBENZENE REACTS WITH PROPANOYL CHLORIDE AND AlCl₃?

In this case the NO_2 group strongly deactivates the ring and Friedel-Crafts acylation does *not* occur. The correct answer is no reaction.

WHAT IS THE PRODUCT WHEN ANILINE REACTS WITH PROPANOYL CHLORIDE AND AlCl₃?

Since the nitrogen of aniline can function as a Lewis base, the first reaction with $AlCl_3$, generates *9.84*. No further reaction will occur since the ring is now deactivated. This problem can be solved by *protecting* the nitrogen as an amide. Initial reaction of aniline with acetic anhydride (*9.85*) gives the acetamide derivative (*9.86*, see section 14.5). The amide is less basic than the amine and reacts with an acid chloride to give the ketone product (*9.87*). The acetamide is removed by acid hydrolysis followed by neutralization with acid to give the amine, *9.88*.

Ketone Formation PRODUCT STABILITY

IS THE PRODUCT OF A FRIEDEL-CRAFTS ACYLATION MORE REACTIVE OR LESS REACTIVE THAN BENZENE?

The product is a ketone and the C=O group is deactivating (due to the $\delta^\oplus$ charge on the carbonyl carbon). This makes the ketone product *less* reactive than benzene.

IS REARRANGEMENT A PROBLEM IN FRIEDEL-CRAFTS ACYLATION?

The acylium ion (*9.79*) is stabilized by the oxygen, leading to the resonance forms shown previously. This stability makes rearrangement very unlikely.

IS POLYACYLATION A PROBLEM IN FRIEDEL-CRAFTS ACYLATION?

No. Since the carbonyl is a deactivating group, the product is generally less reactive than the starting material. Further acylation is not, therefore, a problem.

PRIMARY ARENE FORMATION

Primary arenes cannot be formed by Friedel-Crafts alkylation, but they can be formed by Friedel-Crafts acylation if the C=O (carbonyl) group can be removed from the molecule and changed into a methylene ($-CH_2-$) group. There are several reagents that reduce the C=O group to $-CH_2-$.

WOLFF-KISHNER REDUCTION

WHAT IS THE PRODUCT WHEN ACETOPHENONE IS TREATED WITH HYDRAZINE AND KOH?

The reduction of a ketone C=O to a $-CH_2-$ with hydrazine (NH_2NH_2) under basic conditions is called the *Wolff-Kishner Reduction*. When acetophenone (*9.89*) is treated with KOH and NH_2NH_2, the product is ethylbenzene, *9.90*.

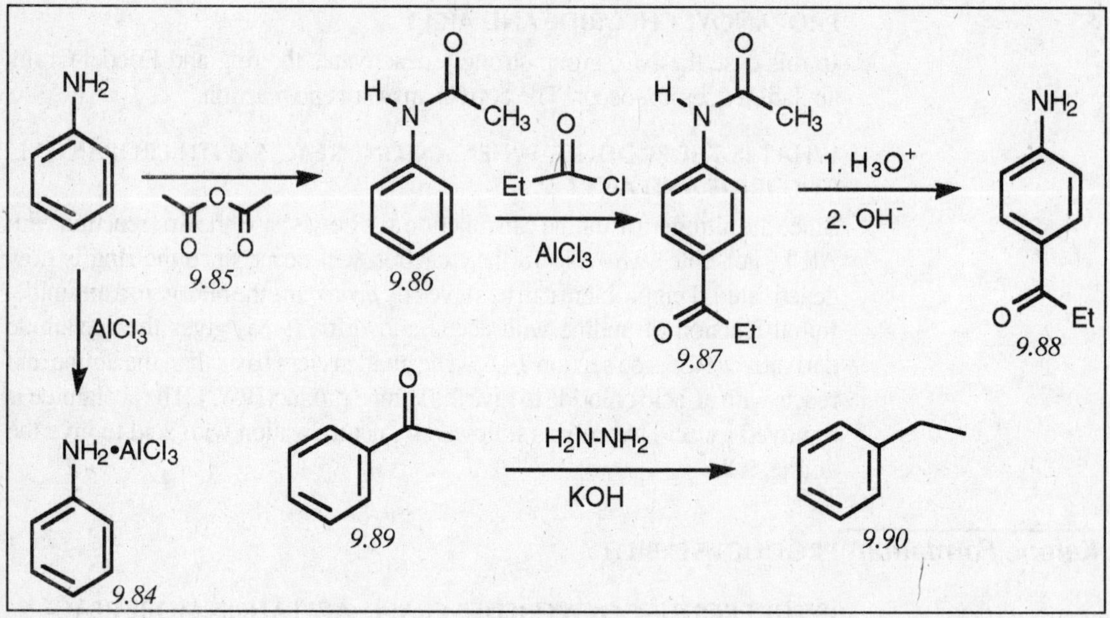

Fig. 9.84–9.90

GIVE THE MECHANISM OF THE WOLFF-KISHNER REDUCTION OF ACETOPHENONE.

Initial reaction of the NH_2 group and the carbonyl leads to a hydrazone (*9.91*), a type of *Schiff Base* (see section 16.5). The hydroxide removes a proton from the NH_2 group to give the resonance stabilized anion, *9.92*. The 'carbanion form' of *9.92* reacts with water (which is an acid in this system) to form *9.93*. Loss of diatomic nitrogen ($N \equiv N$) forms the carbanion intermediate (*9.94*), which reacts with water to complete the reduction, producing *9.90*.

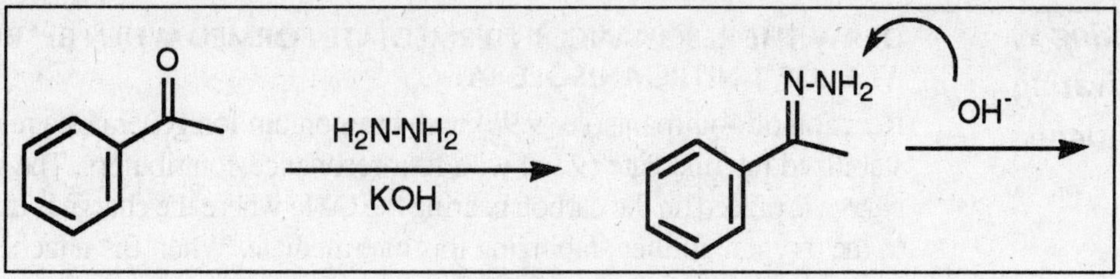

Fig. 9.89, 9.91

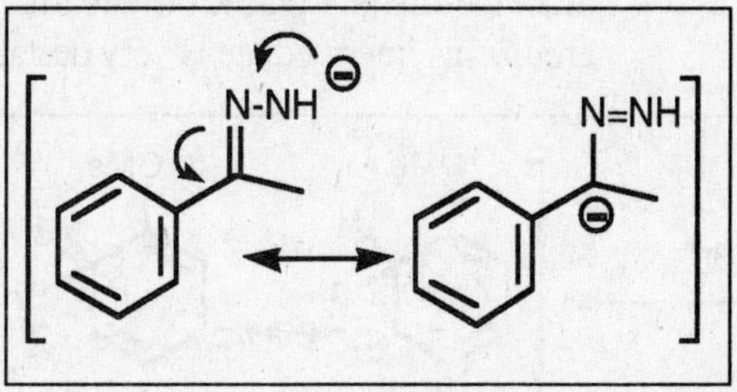

Fig. 9.92

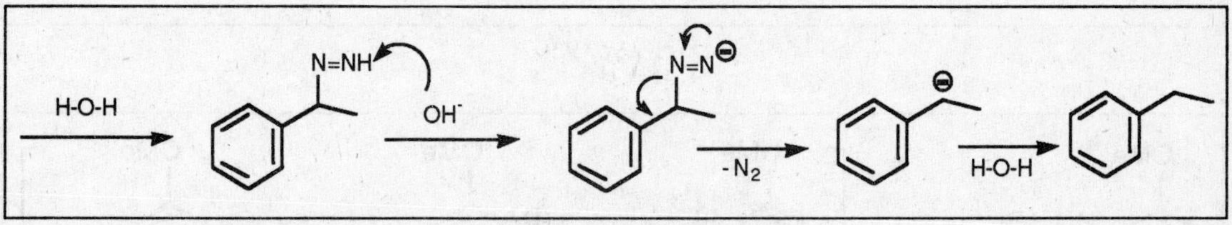

Fig. 9.93–9.95, 9.90

CLEMMENSON REDUCTION

WHAT IS THE PRODUCT WHEN ACETOPHENONE (*9.89*) IS TREATED WITH ZINC AMALGAM AND HCl?

When acetophenone is treated with HCl an zinc amalgam the product is ethylbenzene (*9.90*). This reduction process is called *Clemmenson Reduction* and is the acid medium compliment of the basic medium Wolff-Kishner Reduction. Ethanol is often used as a solvent in this reaction.

WHAT IS ZINC AMALGAM?

An amalgam is an element compounded with mercury. Zinc amalgam is, therefore, written as Zn/Hg or Zn(Hg).

9.8. TRISUBSTITUTION

When two substituents are attached to a benzene ring, electrophilic aromatic substitution will give a trisubstituted derivative. All of the 'rules' described for mono-substitution apply to this reaction.

Activating vs. Deactivating Substituents

DRAW THE RESONANCE INTERMEDIATE FORMED WHEN Br$^\oplus$ REACTS AT C$_2$ OF 4-NITROANISOLE. AT C$_3$.

Reaction of 4-nitroanisole (*9.96*) with bromonium ion generates a resonance stabilized intermediate (*9.97*) with four resonance contributors. The positive charge is placed on the carbon bearing the OMe where the charge is dispersed to the oxygen, further stabilizing this intermediate. When Br$^+$ attaches to C$_3$, resonance intermediate *9.98* is formed, with three resonance contributors. Since the charge is placed on the carbon bearing the positive nitrogen of the nitro group, this intermediate is very destabilized.

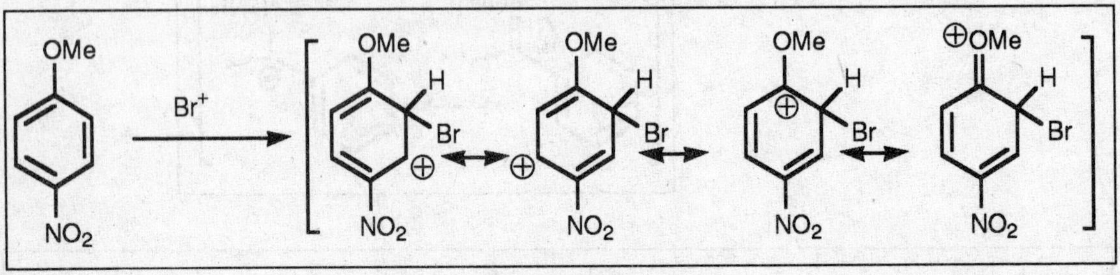

Fig. 9.96, 9.97

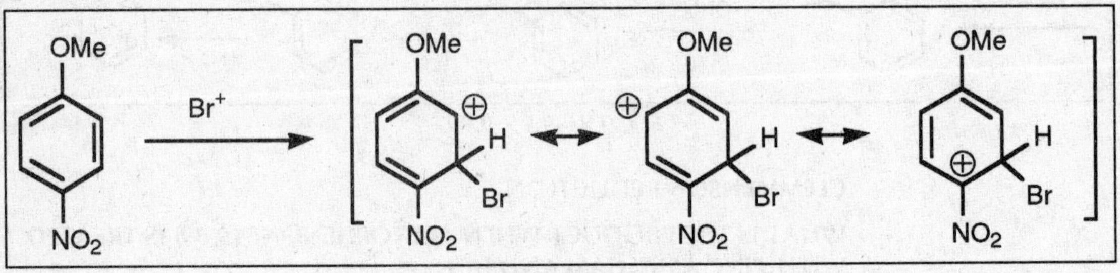

Fig. 9.96, 9.98

WHICH IS PREFERRED, ATTACK AT C$_2$ OR C$_3$? EXPLAIN.

The comparison of *9.97* with *9.98* clearly shows that attack at C$_2$ generates a more stable intermediate. Attack at C$_3$ places the positive charge adjacent to the positive nitrogen and leads to a very unstable intermediate, compared with the highly stabilized *9.97* resulting from attachment of Br to C$_2$. Therefore, attack at C$_2$ is preferred.

WHAT IS THE MAJOR PRODUCT OF THIS REACTION?

The major product of this reaction is 2-bromo-4-nitroanisole.

INFLUENCE OF SUBSTITUENTS ON THE RATE

IF AN ACTIVATING AND A DEACTIVATING GROUP ARE IN A MOLECULE, WHICH DOMINATES THE ELECTROPHILIC SUBSTITUTION REACTION? EXPLAIN.

By definition, an activating group increases the rate of electrophilic aromatic substitution whereas a deactivating group diminishes the rate of the reaction. If both are in the same molecule, electrophilic aromatic substitution will be directed by the reaction with the faster rate, dictated by the activating group.

STERIC HINDRANCE IN THE PRODUCTS

THE REACTION OF 3-NITROANISOLE AND BROMINE/AlCl₃ CAN GENERATE THREE ISOMERIC PRODUCTS, ASSUMING OME IS THE DIRECTING GROUP. DRAW THEIR STRUCTURES.

When 3-nitroanisole (*9.99*) reacts with Br_2/$AlCl_3$ the bromine will attach at the *ortho* and *para* positions, relative to OMe. This leads to three different products, 2-bromo-3-nitroanisole (*9.100*), 4-bromo-3-nitroanisole (*9.101*) and 5-bromo-3-nitroanisole (*9.102*).

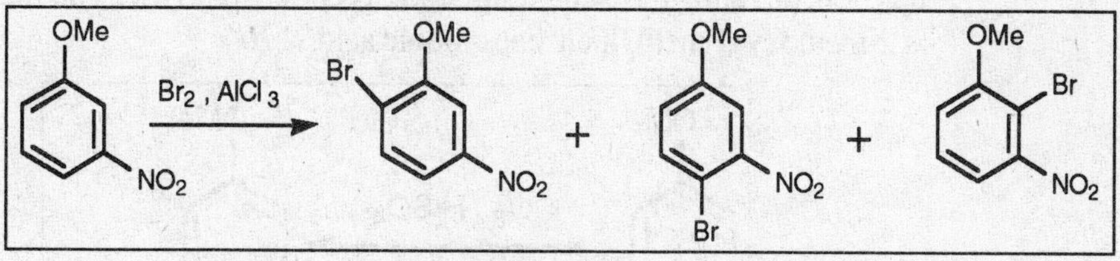

Fig. 9.99–9.102

OF THE THREE PRODUCTS DRAWN, TWO ARE FORMED IN NEAR EQUAL AMOUNTS BUT 2-BROMO-3-NITROANISOLE IS A MINOR PRODUCT IN THIS MIXTURE. EXPLAIN.

Both *9.100* and *9.101* are formed without problem. In order to form *9.102* the bromine, which is relatively large, must be inserted between the OMe and NO_2 groups. There is considerable steric hindrance as the bromine approaches this position (and in the cation intermediate where that carbon is sp^3 hybridized and tetrahedral), raising the energy required for its formation and leading to diminished yields of this isomer.

IN THIS REACTION, 5-BROMO-3-NITROANISOLE IS THE MAJOR PRODUCT. EXPLAIN.

As the bromine approaches the aromatic ring, there is some coordination of Br⊕ with the electron pairs on the methoxy oxygen. This coordination leads to a greater preference for attack at the *ortho* position and a greater percentage of that isomer. This is known as the *ortho effect*.

Two or More Activating Groups

WHAT IS THE PRODUCT WHEN 4-METHOXYANISOLE REACTS WITH NITRIC AND SULFURIC ACID?

4-Methoxyanisole (*9.103*) has two identical *ortho/para* directing groups and the only available position is *ortho*. The sole product is, therefore, 2-nitro-4-methoxyanisole, *9.104*.

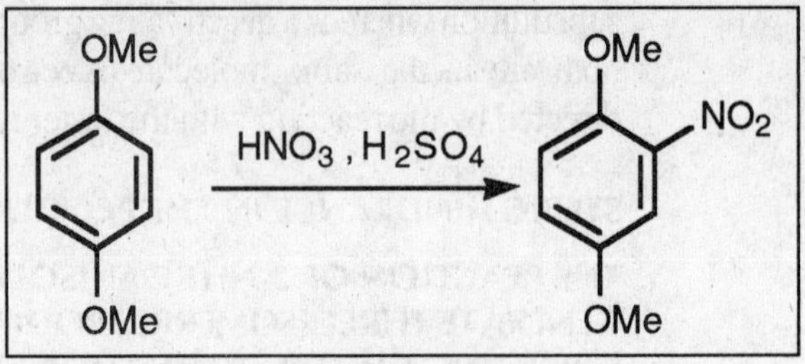

Fig. 9.103, 9.104

WHAT IS THE PRODUCT WHEN 4-METHYLANISOLE REACTS WITH FUMING SULFURIC ACID?

There are two *ortho/para* directors in 4-methylanisole (*9.105*), but the OMe group is more powerful than the methyl group (Me). The OMe dominates the reaction, directing the SO_3 group *ortho* to OMe, not to Me. The final product is 2-methoxy-4-methylbenzenesulfonic acid, *9.106*.

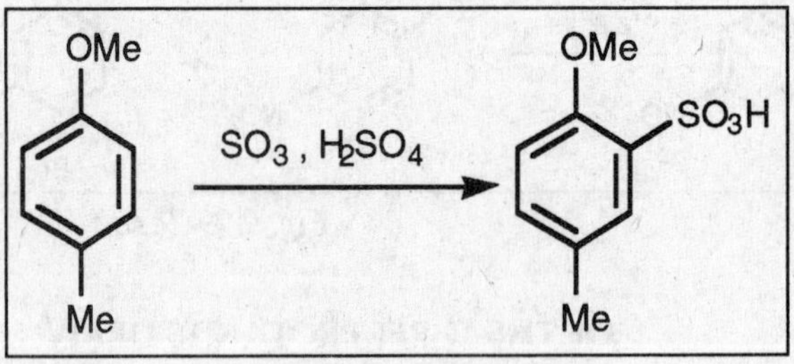

Fig. 9.105, 9.106

WHAT IS THE PRODUCT(OR PRODUCTS) WHEN 2-METHYLANISOLE REACTS WITH CHLORINE/AlCl₃?

2-Methylanisole (*9.107*) reacts with chlorine to form 4-chloro-2-methylanisole (*9.108*), where the more powerful activator OMe directs the reaction. Obviously, 6-chloro-2-nitroanisole is also formed in the reaction.

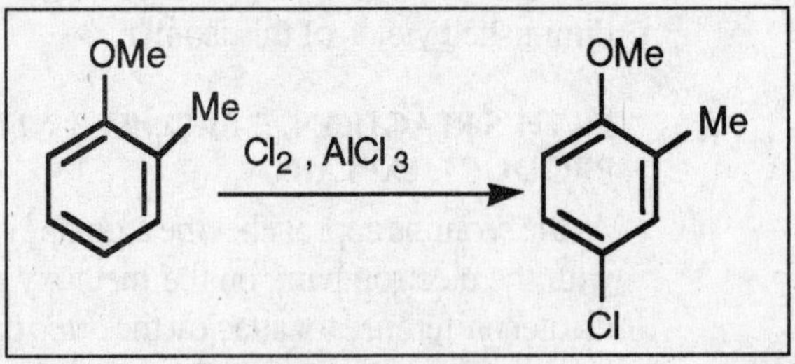

Fig. 9.107, 9.108

Two or More Deactivating groups

WHAT IS THE PRODUCT WHEN 4-NITROACETOPHENONE REACTS WITH Cl₂/AlCl₃?

4-Nitroacetophenone (*9.109*) reacts with chlorine to give 3-chloro-4-nitroacetophenone, *9.110*. Both the carbonyl and the nitro groups are *meta* directors and deactivating groups. The nitro group *is more deactivating*, however, and a nitro directed reaction will be *slower* than a carbonyl directed reaction. For this reason, the product will have the chlorine *meta* to the carbonyl, which is the *less deactivating* group.

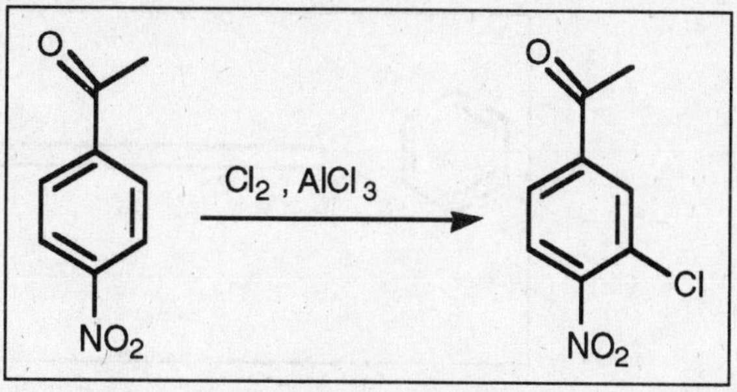

Fig. 9.109, 9.110

WHAT IS THE PRODUCT WHEN NITRIC ACID AND SULFURIC ACID REACT WITH 1,3-DINITROBENZENE?

Both of the nitro groups in 1,3-dinitrobenzene (*9.111*) are deactivating and *meta* directors. The product will form with difficulty and the yield may be low, but it will be 1,3,5-trinitrobenzene, (*9.112*).

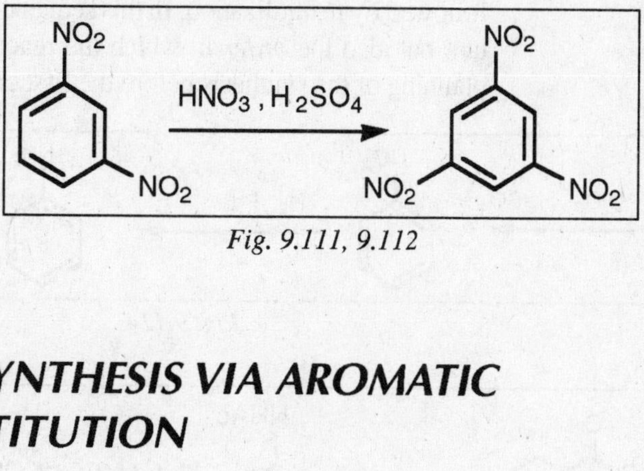

Fig. 9.111, 9.112

9.9. SYNTHESIS VIA AROMATIC SUBSTITUTION

WHAT IS SYNTHESIS?

Synthesis is a progression of chemical steps that begins with a molecule (the starting material) and adds functional groups or carbon-carbon bonds via chemical reactions until a new molecule (the target or product) is constructed.

A Multi-step Reaction Sequence

PROVIDE A SUITABLE SYNTHESIS FOR THE CONVERSION OF BENZENE INTO 1-(4-AMINOPHENYL) BUTANONE.

The first step is to choose whether the NH$_2$ group is incorporated first or the carbonyl. Since the carbonyl is a *meta* director and deactivating, *9.113* is most likely formed by first incorporating the amine unit, an *ortho/para* director. To incorporate nitrogen, the first reaction is a nitration to give nitrobenzene. The nitro group is *reduced* with hydrogen and a palladium catalyst (see section 5.5) to give aniline.

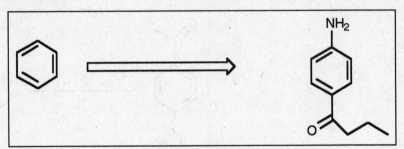

Fig. 9.113

Before a Friedel-Crafts reaction can be done, the basic amino group must be protected as the amide. Treatment of aniline with acetic anhydride leads to N-acetyl aniline (*9.114*) and subsequent reaction with butanoyl chloride and AlCl$_3$ leads to the ketone, *9.115* (along with the expected *ortho* substituted ketone). To complete the synthesis of *9.113*, the *ortho* and *para* ketones are separated and the amide group is removed from *9.115* with aqueous acid followed by neutralization. In this sequence, not only the reactions are important but also the *order* in which the reactions are performed. This requires planning of the synthesis before the first chemical step is performed.

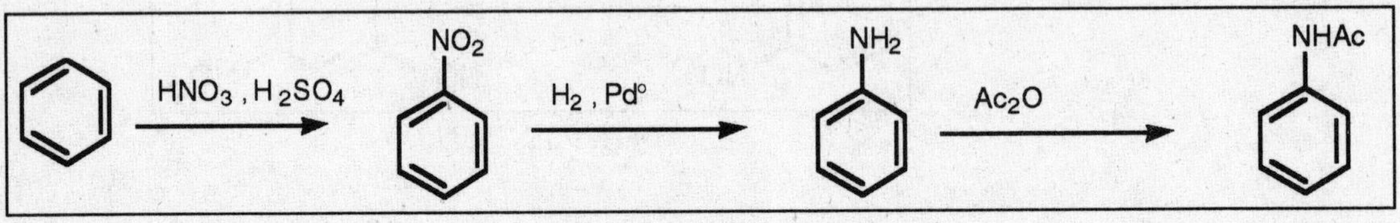

Fig. 9.114

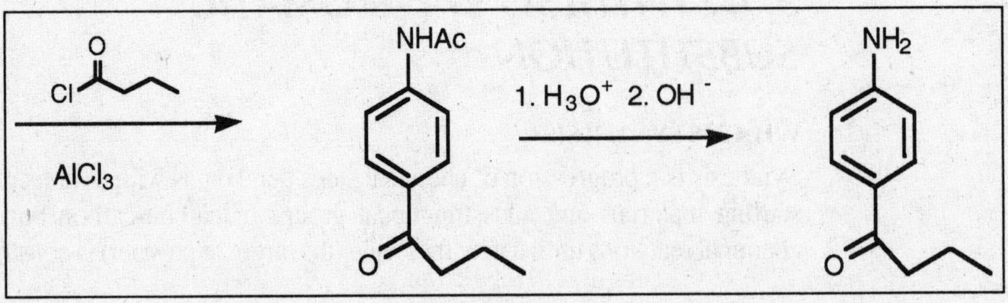

Fig. 9.115, 9.113

Synthesis of Aromatic Derivatives

GIVE A COMPLETE SYNTHESIS FOR 9.117–9.119 FROM THE INDICATED STARTING MATERIAL.

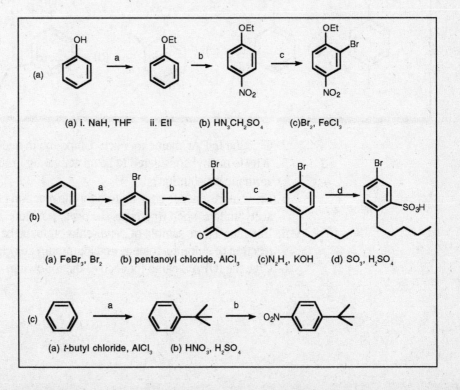

Fig. 9.117–9.119

In this chapter the complexity of chemical transformations increased dramatically. Many different concepts had to be applied to solve various chemical problems. This chapter also offered a contrast between aliphatic chemistry (alkyl halides, alkenes, alkynes, etc.) and aromatic chemistry. Although benzene derivatives contain p-bonds, they clearly do not behave exactly the same way as alkenes or alkynes. Once again, the differences in reactivity are predictable based on the understanding of a few concepts, such as resonance. Just as benzene derivatives behave as nucleophiles in reactions with Lewis bases (in this chapter), so they can behave as electrophilic species under the proper conditions. The following chapter will focus on that aspect of aromatic chemistry.

END OF CHAPTER PROBLEMS

1. Name each of the following molecules using the *ortho*, *meta* or *para* nomenclature.

2. Give the IUPAC name for each compound in question 1.
3. Why is methyl considered to be an activating group in electrophilic aromatic substitution?
4. Draw all resonance contributors for the reaction product of Br⊕ and N-acetylaniline when Br attacks the *ortho* position.
5. How can a pure sample of *ortho*-chlorotoluene be obtained from the reaction of chlorine, toluene and aluminum chloride?
6. Give the IUPAC name for each of the following.

(a) 3,5-di-C₄H₉ benzoic acid (CO₂H); (b) 4-phenylbutanoyl chloride; (c) acyl chloride structure; (d) 3-bromo-4-methylbenzoyl chloride

7. Why does the nitration of anisole give more *ortho* product than does the nitration of toluene under similar reaction conditions?

8. Provide a suitable synthesis for each of the following. Give all intermediate products and show all reagents. Do not give mechanistic intermediates.

9. For each reaction give the major product. If there is no reaction, indicate by N.R.

(a) 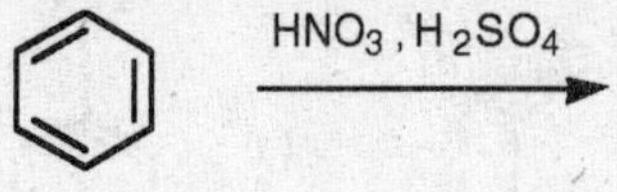 [benzene] →(HNO₃, H₂SO₄)

(b) 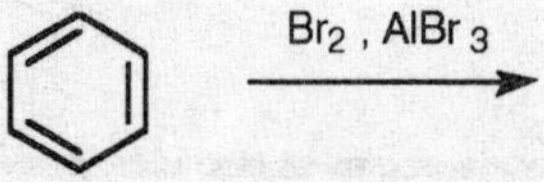 [benzene] →(Br₂, AlBr₃)

(c) 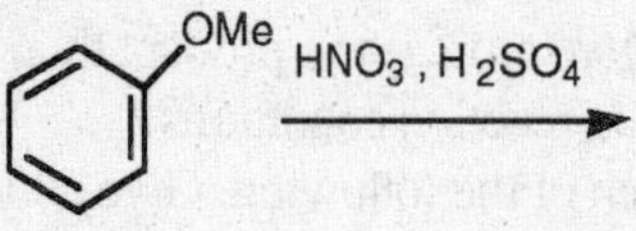 [anisole, OMe] →(HNO₃, H₂SO₄)

(d) 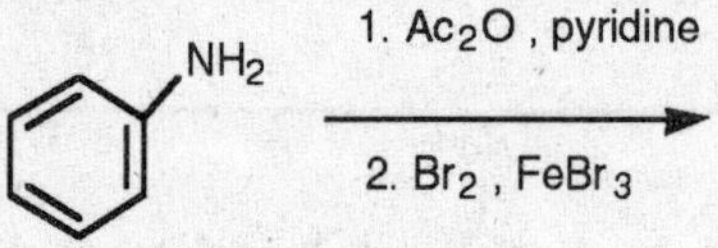 [aniline, NH₂] →(1. Ac₂O, pyridine 2. Br₂, FeBr₃)

(e) 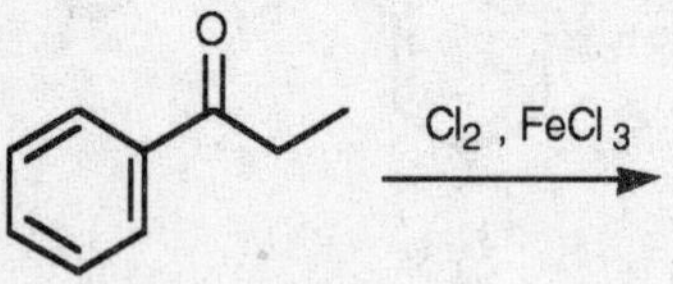 [propiophenone] →(Cl₂, FeCl₃)

(f) 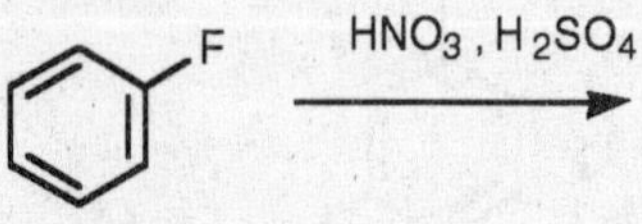 [fluorobenzene, F] →(HNO₃, H₂SO₄)

(g) 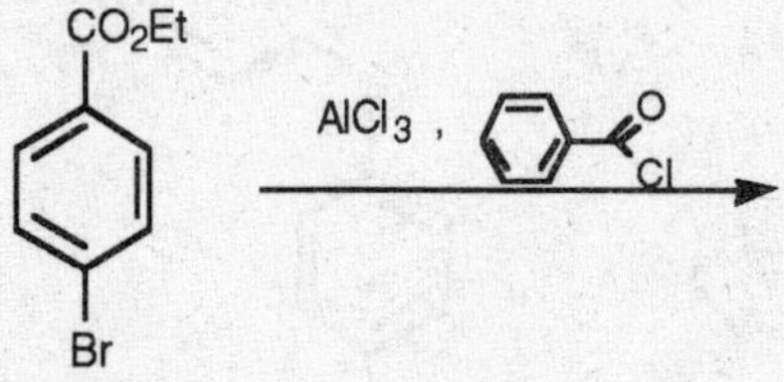 [ethyl 4-bromobenzoate, CO₂Et ... Br] →(AlCl₃, [benzoyl chloride])

(h) 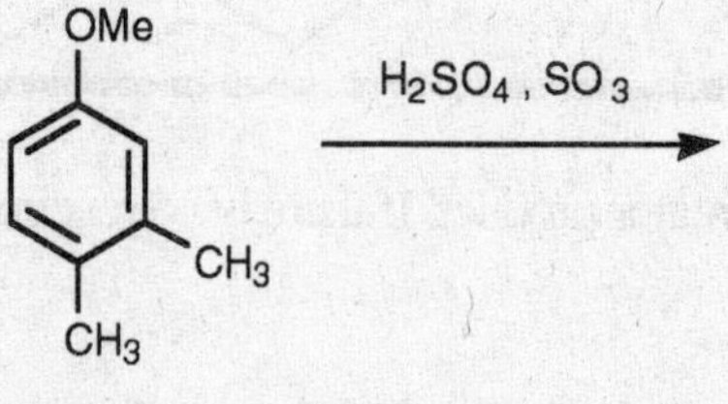 [4-methoxy-o-xylene, OMe, CH₃, CH₃] →(H₂SO₄, SO₃)

(i) 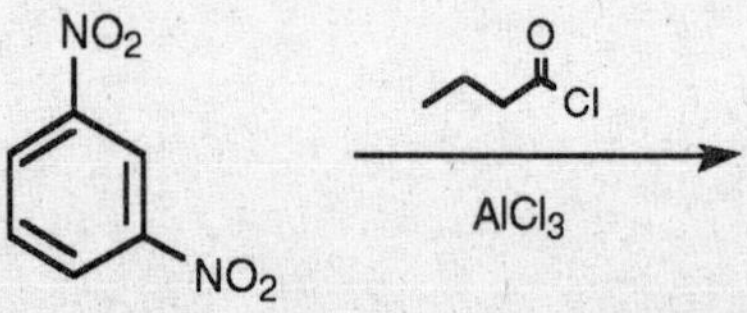 [1,3-dinitrobenzene, NO₂, NO₂] →([butanoyl chloride], AlCl₃)

(j) 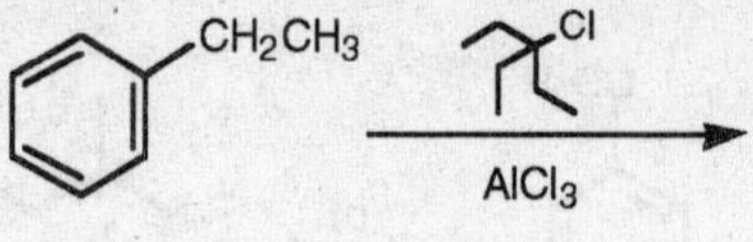 [ethylbenzene, CH₂CH₃] →([3-chloropentane, Cl], AlCl₃)

(k) 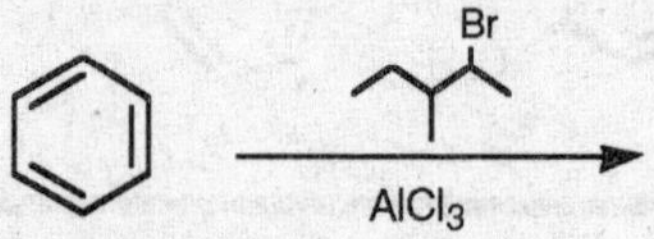 [benzene] →([2-bromo-3-methylbutane, Br], AlCl₃)

(l) 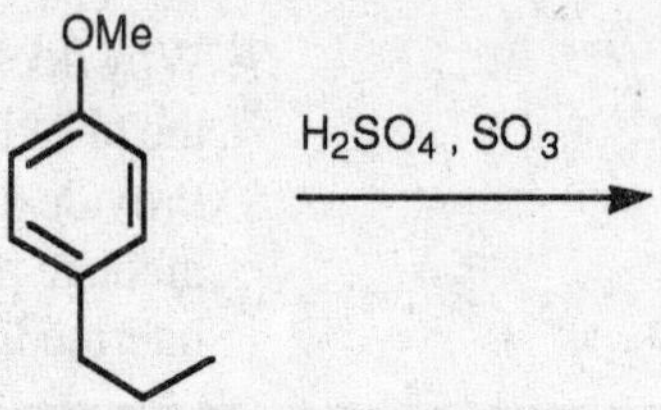 [OMe ... propyl, anisole derivative] →(H₂SO₄, SO₃)

(m) 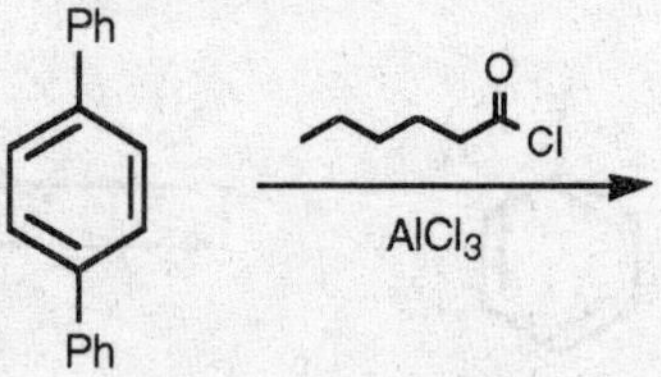 [1,4-diphenylbenzene, Ph, Ph] →([hexanoyl chloride, Cl], AlCl₃)

(n) 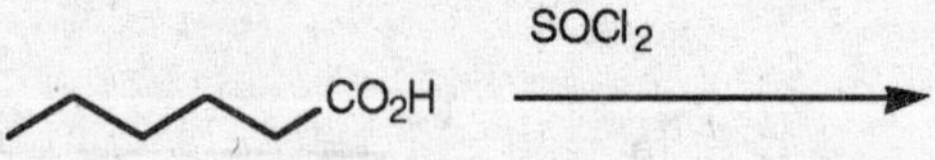 [pentanoic acid, CO₂H] →(SOCl₂)

(o) [benzophenone, Ph, Ph, O] →(aq. KOH, N₂H₄)

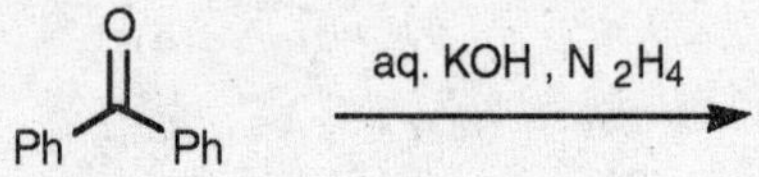

(p) 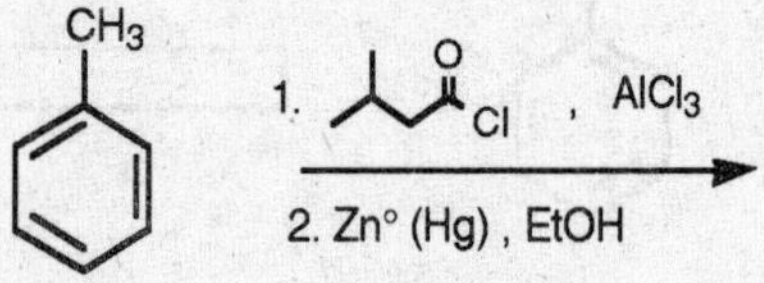 [toluene, CH₃] →(1. [3-methylbutanoyl chloride, Cl], AlCl₃ 2. Zn° (Hg), EtOH)

(q) 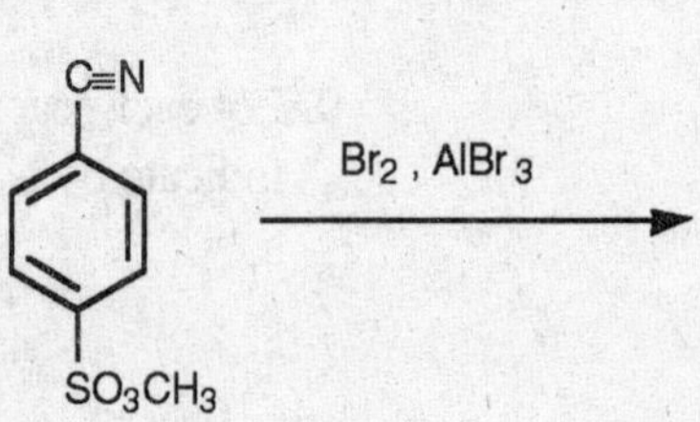 [4-cyanophenyl methanesulfonate, C≡N, SO₃CH₃] →(Br₂, AlBr₃)

10

Nucleophilic Aromatic Substitution

---

*A benzene ring is rich in electrons and is not usually attacked by another nucleophilic species. If substituents are attached to the benzene ring that can withdraw electrons from it, however, nucleophiles can attack the ring and displace halogens in what is known as **nucleophilic aromatic substitution**. It is also possible to attach extraordinarily good leaving groups (such as nitrogen, N_2^+) that are readily displaced under mild conditions. Such leaving groups can also be lost to generate a highly reactive intermediate known as benzyne. These reagents lead to rather novel chemistry that is different from any discussed to this point.*

WHAT IS THE DEFINITION OF NUCLEOPHILIC AROMATIC SUBSTITUTION?

When a leaving group on a benzene ring (such as a halogen) is displaced by a nucleophile, the reaction is known as nucleophilic aromatic substitution. In general such a reaction is less facile than electrophilic aromatic substitution because an electron rich nucleophile must attack an electron rich benzene ring.

10.1. REACTIVITY OF ARYL HALIDES

Aryl halides are the most common partners in nucleophilic reactions of benzene derivatives.

Halobenzenes and Hydroxide

WHAT IS THE PRODUCT WHEN CHLOROBENZENE REACTS WITH KOH OR NaOH IN AQUEOUS MEDIA AT AMBIENT TEMPERATURES?

There is no reaction. Neither KOH nor NaOH are sufficiently nucleophilic to attack a benzene ring and displace the chlorine. For this to occur high temperatures and pressures are required.

Phenol Formation at High Pressures and Temperatures

WHAT IS THE PRODUCT WHEN CHLOROBENZENE REACTS WITH AQUEOUS KOH AT 350°C AND 2000-3000 PSI?

When chlorobenzene reacts with KOH at elevated temperature and pressure the resulting product is phenol, *10.1*.

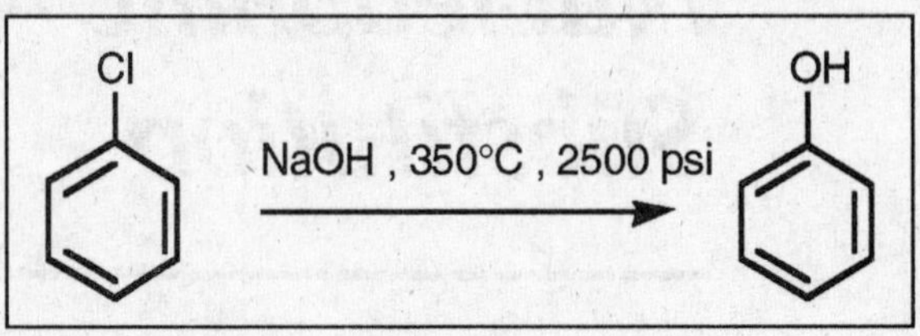

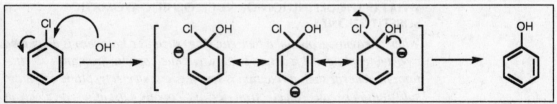

NaOH , 350°C , 2500 psi

Fig. 10.1

WHAT IS THE MECHANISM OF THIS REACTION?

The initial reaction involves collision of hydroxide with the chlorine-bearing carbon of chlorobenzene. The π-bond is broken, dumping the electrons into the ring as in *10.2*. This is a resonance stabilized intermediate and the electrons in the ring can displace the chlorine in the final step to generate phenol. This process has a high activation energy for the initial attack of hydroxide since the negatively charged species must attack a benzene ring that is rich in electron density. This is the reason for the high reaction temperature and pressure. At much lower temperatures and pressures, no reaction occurs.

Fig. 10.2

WHAT IS THE GENERAL NAME FOR THIS REACTION?

Nucleophilic aromatic substitution.

CAN THIS REACTION BE USED FOR A GENERAL SYNTHESIS FOR PHENOLS?

The high reaction temperatures and pressures make it unattractive for the synthesis of all but the most simple phenol derivatives. It is very useful in industrial labs, however, for the production of phenol.

Activating Substituents

ELECTRON WITHDRAWING GROUPS

UNDER WHAT CONDITIONS WILL 2-CHLORONITROBENZENE REACT WITH HYDROXIDE?

The reaction involves treatment with aqueous NaOH at about 150–175°C, and the product is 4-nitrophenol, *10.3*.

UNDER WHAT CONDITIONS WILL 2-CHLORO-1,5-DINITROBENZENE REACT WITH HYDROXIDE?

The reaction involves the use of aqueous sodium carbonate (or hydroxide) at about 125–150°C, and the product is 2,4-dinitrophenol, *10.4*.

UNDER WHAT CONDITIONS WILL 2-CHLORO-1,3,5-TRINITROBENZENE REACT WITH HYDROXIDE?

In this case, heating with warm water converts the chloride to 2,4,6-trinitrophenol, *10.5*.

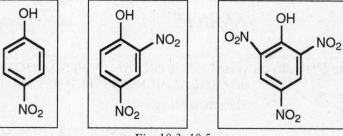

Fig. 10.3–10.5

INFLUENCE ON RESONANCE INTERMEDIATES

EXPLAIN WHY THE REACTION CONDITIONS FOR PHENOL FORMATION BECOME MILDER AS MORE NITRO GROUPS ARE ADDED TO THE BENZENE RING.

Nitro is an electron withdrawing group with a positive charge on the nitrogen. Examination of intermediate *10.6* (from 4-nitro chlorobenzene) reveals that the negative charge is adjacent to the positively charged nitrogen. This allows delocalization of the charge onto the nitro group, formation of another resonance form and increased stability for the intermediate. This allows the overall reaction proceed under milder reaction conditions.

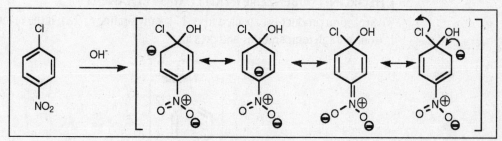

Fig. 10.6

WHAT IS THE PRODUCT WHEN POTASSIUM METHOXIDE REACTS WITH 2-CHLORO-1,5-DINITROBENZENE AT 170°C AT ELEVATED PRESSURES?

The product is 2,4-dinitroanisole.

Deactivating Substituents

WHAT IS THE PRODUCT WHEN 4-CHLOROANISOLE REACTS WITH HYDROXIDE?

There is no reaction. The electron releasing methoxy group makes the nucleophilic attack even more difficult than in chlorobenzene and, in general, no reaction occurs.

10.2. REACTION WITH AMMONIA AND AMINES

Aniline Derivatives

WHAT IS THE PRODUCT WHEN AMMONIA REACTS WITH CHLOROBENZENE AT HIGH TEMPERATURES AND PRESSURES?

The product is aniline.

WHAT IS THE MECHANISM FOR THE REACTION WITH AMMONIA?

The mechanism is nucleophilic aromatic substitution, as noted with reactions of hydroxide and aryl halides. The intermediate for the reaction of chlorobenzene and ammonia is, therefore, that shown in *10.7*.

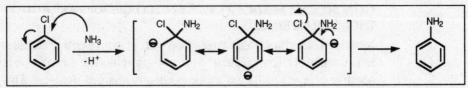

Fig. 10.7

WHAT IS THE PRODUCT WHEN METHYLAMINE REACTS WITH 4-CHLORONITROBENZENE IN REFLUXING ETHANOL?

The reaction product is expected to be N-methylaniline (*10.8*), if the reaction is done at high temperatures and pressures.

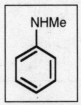

Fig. 10.8

IS THIS A GENERAL SYNTHESIS FOR ANILINE DERIVATIVES?

It is a general synthesis only for simple compounds. The high temperatures and pressures required for unactivated aromatic rings make it unattractive for complex molecules. If there are electron withdrawing groups such as nitro attached to the benzene ring, at the *ortho* and *para* positions relative to the halogen, the reaction conditions are much milder.

Reaction With Amide Bases

WHAT IS THE PRODUCT WHEN SODIUM AMIDE (NaNH$_2$) REACTS WITH CHLOROBENZENE AT HIGH TEMPERATURES AND PRESSURES?

The reaction produces aniline as the product, but the mechanism may not be the same as in nucleophilic aromatic substitution.

WHAT IS THE PRODUCT WHEN SODIUM N,N-DIETHYLAMIDE REACTS WITH 2-CHLORO-1,3,5-TRINITROBENZENE AT ABOUT 100°C?

The reaction is expected to give 2,4,6-trinitro-N,N-diethylaniline, *10.9*.

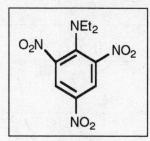

Fig. 10.9

10.3. ELIMINATION REACTIONS

Acidity of Ortho Hydrogens

WHAT IS THE APPROXIMATE pK$_a$ OF THE ORTHO-HYDROGEN OF CHLOROBENZENE?

The pK$_a$ of the *ortho* hydrogen of chlorobenzene is approximately 40. A very powerful base is required for its removal as an acid.

WHAT BASES ARE STRONG ENOUGH TO REMOVE THIS ORTHO HYDROGEN?

Suitable bases for removal of the *ortho* hydrogen are organolithium reagents such as *n*-butyl-lithium and amide bases such as sodium amide (NaNH$_2$).

WHAT IS THE INITIAL PRODUCT IS THE ORTHO HYDROGEN IS REMOVED FROM CHLOROBENZENE?

Deprotonation of chlorobenzene leads to a phenyl carbanion, *10.10*. This is a highly unstable and reactive intermediate.

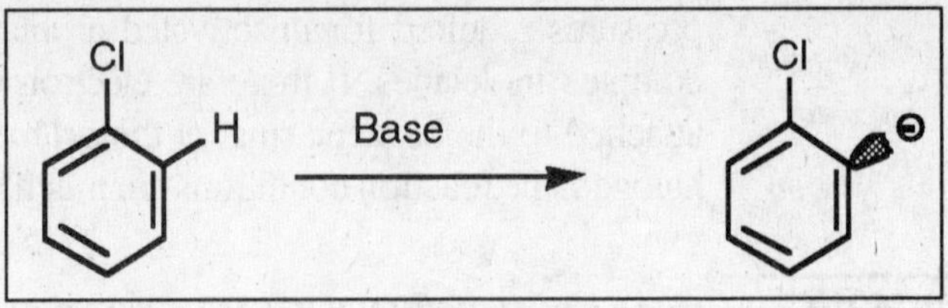

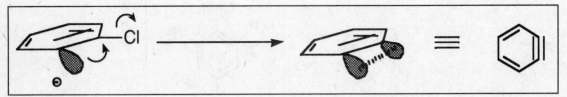

Fig. 10.10

IF THE CHLORINE FUNCTIONS AS A LEAVING GROUP IN *10.10,* WHAT IS THE INTERMEDIATE PRODUCT?

Loss of chlorine from *10.10* (via displacement of Cl by the lone electron pair) leads to a triple bond in the aromatic ring. This new π-bond is perpendicular to the plane of the aromatic π-cloud, as shown in *10.11*. This is usually represented by structure *10.12*.

Fig. 10.11, 10.12

WHAT IS THE NAME OF THIS PRODUCT (*10.12*)?

Structure *10.12* is known as *benzyne*.

FORMATION OF BENZYNE

WHAT AMIDE BASES ARE COMMONLY USED TO GENERATE A BENZYNE?

The sodium, lithium or potassium salts of ammonia or simple primary and secondary amines such as methylamine, ethylamine, diethylamine or diisopropylamine.

WHAT IS THE PRODUCT WHEN POTASSIUM AMIDE REACTS WITH CHLOROBENZENE IN LIQUID AMMONIA?

The product is aniline.

WHAT IS THE MECHANISM OF THIS REACTION?

The reaction proceeds via a benzyne intermediate (*10.12*). Amide adds to the triple bond to form a new carbanion (*10.13*) which removes a proton from the ammonia solvent to give aniline.

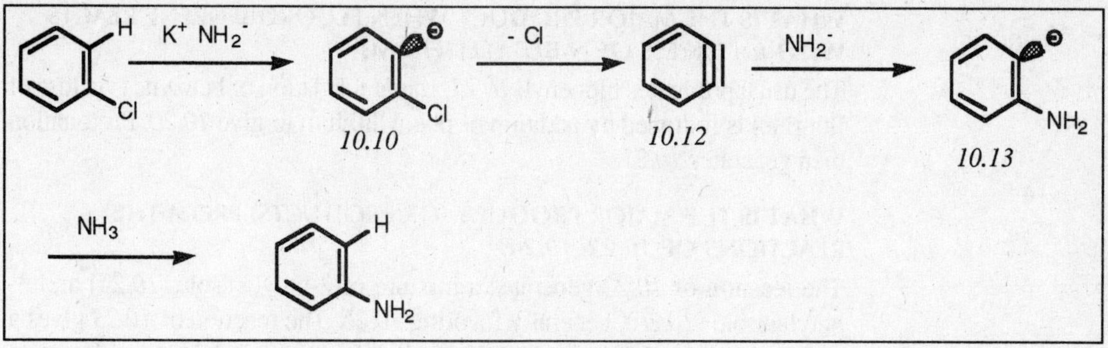

Fig. 10.10, 10.12, 10.13

WHAT IS THE PRODUCT WHEN SODIUM AMIDE REACTS WITH 2-BROMOETHYLBENZENE? DISCUSS THE FORMATION OF TWO MAJOR PRODUCTS?

The two products are 2-ethylaniline (*10.18*) and 3-ethylamine (*10.19*). When the carbanion intermediate (*10.14*) generates the benzyne intermediate (*10.15*), there are two sites capable of being attacked, the C_2 position (leading to *10.16*) and the C_3 position (leading to *10.17*). The electron releasing ethyl group is expected to destabilize the intermediate carbanion at C_2 (*10.16*) relative to the carbanion at C_3 (*10.17*) and *10.19* is expected to be the major product, but only slightly. This usually gives a 40-50:50-60 ratio of products favoring *10.19*.

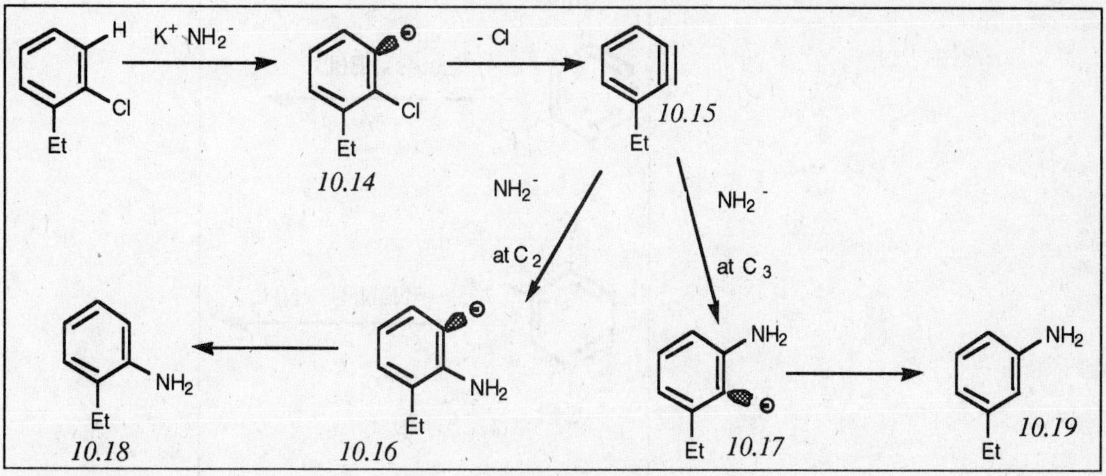

Fig. 10.14–10.19

Alternative Methods of Benzyne Formation

FROM FLUOROBENZENE AND ORGANOLITHIUM BASES

WHY IS PHENYLLITHIUM A SUITABLE BASE FOR THE GENERATION OF BENZYNE?

Phenyllithium is a very powerful base (the pK_a of its conjugate acid, which is benzene, is greater than 40).

WHAT IS THE MAJOR PRODUCT WHEN FLUOROBENZENE REACTS WITH AN EXCESS OF N-BUTYLLITHIUM?

The usual product is biphenyl, *10.21*. Initial formation of benzyne (via loss of fluorine) is followed by addition of phenyllithium to give *10.20*. Protonation then generates *10.21*.

WHAT IS THE MAJOR PRODUCT (OR PRODUCTS) FROM THE REACTIONS OF *10.22–10.24*?

The reaction of *10.22* generates a mixture of 2-butylanisole (*10.25*) and 3-butylanisole (*10.26*), generally favoring *10.26*. The reaction of *10.23* gives a mixture of 4-ethyl-3-aminophenetole (*10.27*) and 4-ethyl-2-aminophenetole (*10.28*), somewhat favoring *10.27*. The final reaction of *10.24* leads to a mixture of *10.29* and *10.30*.

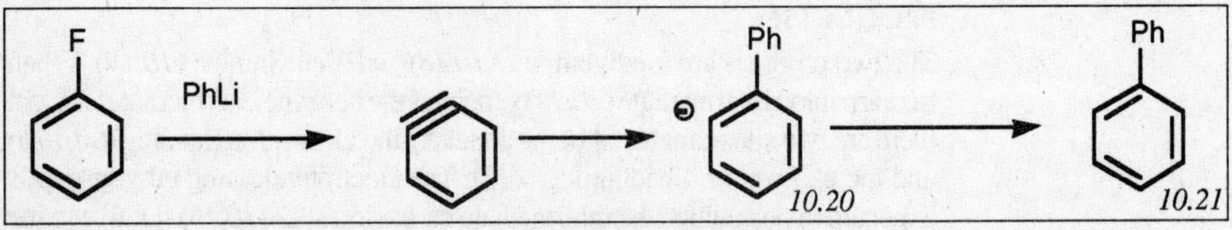

Fig. 10.20, 10.21

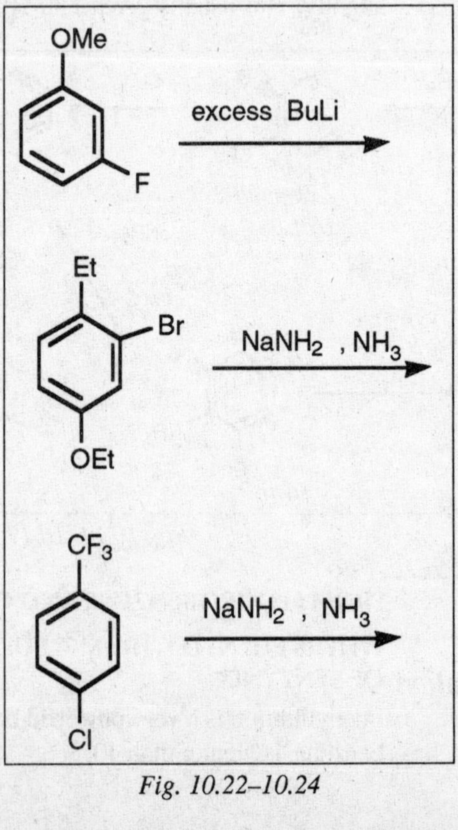

Fig. 10.22–10.24

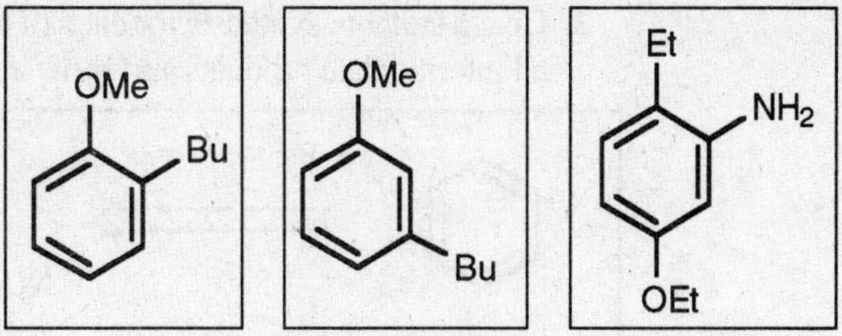

Fig. 10.25–10.27

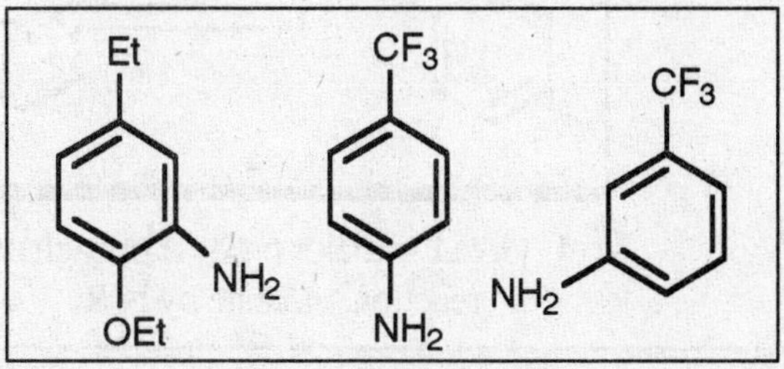

Fig. 10.28–10.30

WHAT IS THE PRODUCT WHEN CHLOROBENZENE IS TREATED WITH *t*-BUTYLLITHIUM? EXPLAIN WHY THIS DIFFERS FROM THE REACTION WITH FLUOROBENZENE.

The *t*-butyl group is rather bulky and a simple exchange reaction usually occurs to give phenyllithium (PhLi) [*t*-BuLi+PhCl → PhLi+*t*-BuCl]. The chlorine is also a much weaker leaving group than fluorine, further diminishing the possibility of forming benzyne. Phenyllithium then behaves as any other organolithium reagent.

*T*his chapter on nucleophilic aromatic substitution closes the section on benzene chemistry for this book. These reactions are used for a wide range of aromatic and heteroaromatic transformations. Some of the principles introduced here will be used again in later chapters. Benzene derivatives will be discussed again in connection with the spectroscopy chapter (chapter 17).

END OF CHAPTER PROBLEMS

1. Draw all resonance contributors to the intermediate of the reaction of KOH and 1-bromo-2,4,6-trinitrobenzene.
2. Describe the new π-bond formed in benzyne when an *ortho* hydrogen is eliminated from chlorobenzene.

3. Give a suitable synthesis for each of the following. In each case give all intermediate products and show all reagents that are used.

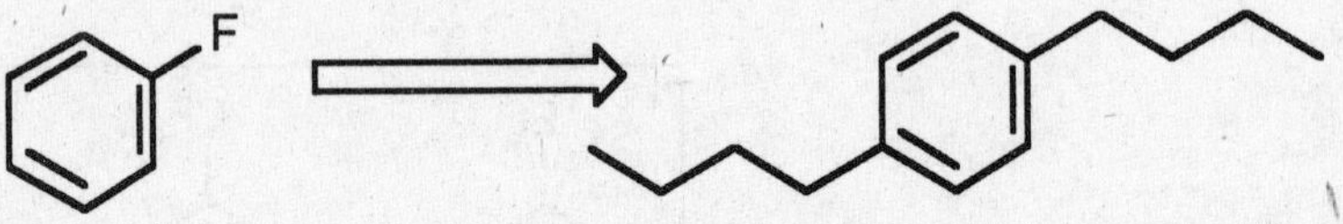

4. Give the major product of each of the following reactions. If there is no reaction, indicate by N.R.

(a) [structure: 4-bromotoluene] → aq. KOH, 350°C, 2500 psi

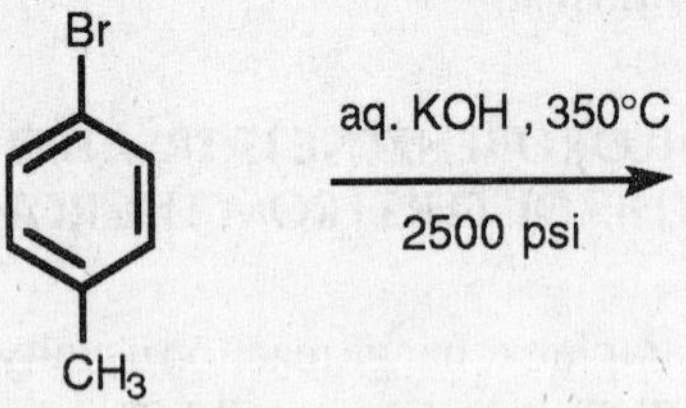

(b) [structure: 2-chloro-1,3,5-trinitrobenzene] → H_2O, reflux

(c) [structure: 2-bromo-1,3,5-trinitrobenzene] → NaOMe, reflux / MeOH

(d) [structure: 2-bromo-1,4-dimethoxybenzene] → aq. KOH, reflux

(e) [structure: bromobenzene] → KNH_2, NH_3, 300°C, 3000 psi

(f) [structure: 4-bromonitrobenzene] → 1. aq. KOH, 200°C 2. H_2, Pd-C

(g) [structure: fluorobenzene] → excess butyllithium

(h) [structure: 1-isopropyl-4-bromobenzene] → $NaNH_2$, NH_3

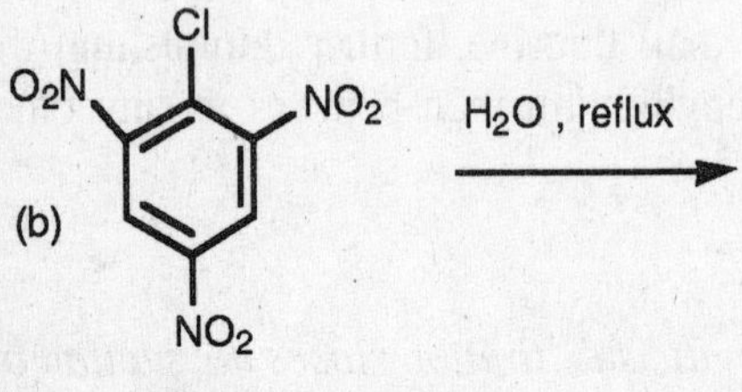

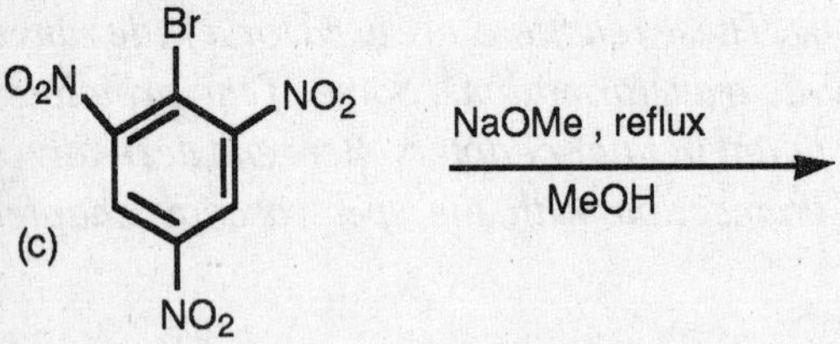

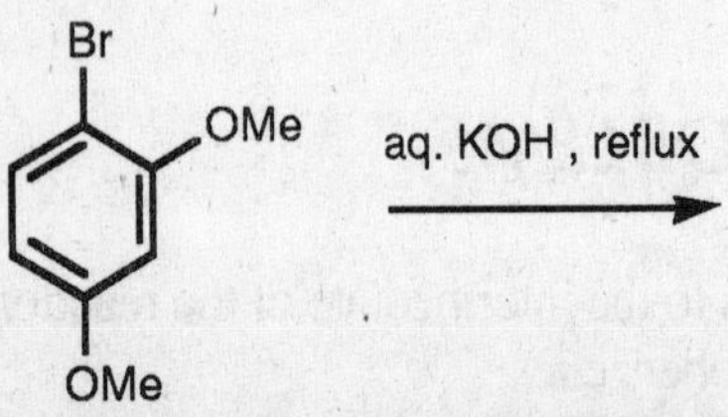

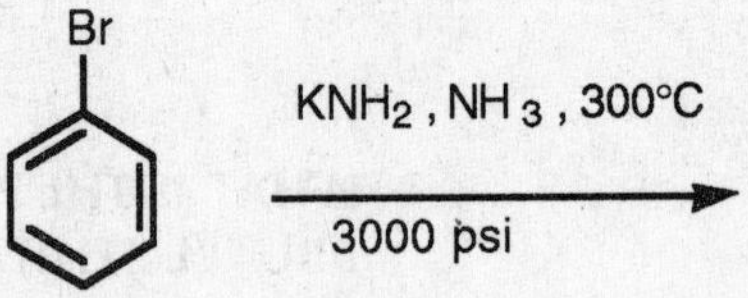

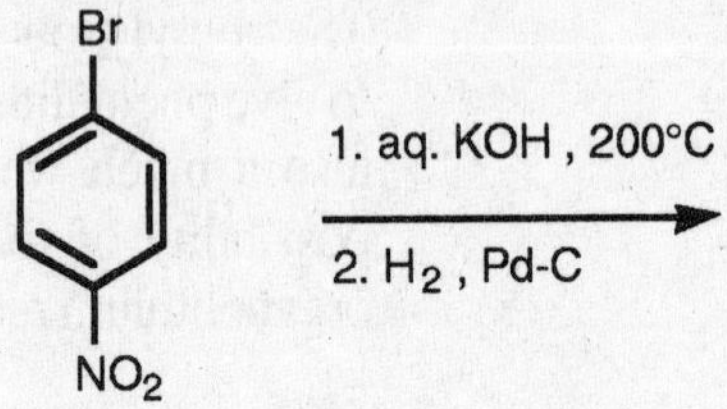

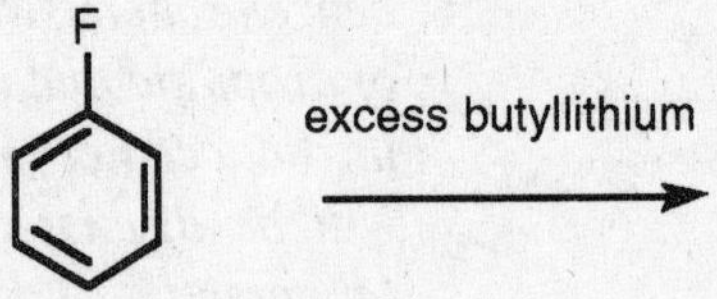

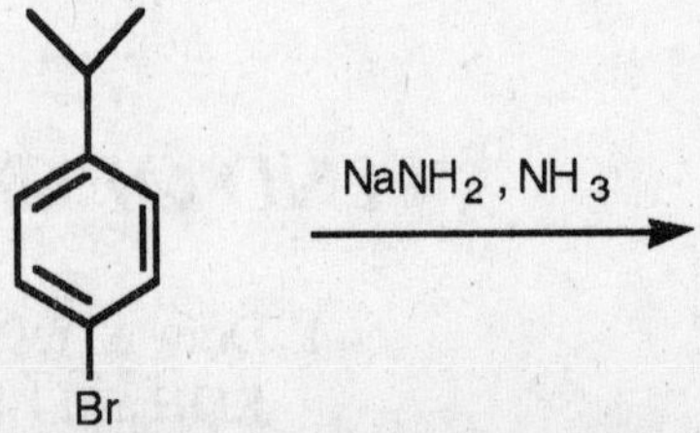

11

Alcohols

*A*lcohols are another of the functional groups that are among the most important in Organic chemistry. Alcohols can be prepared from alkenes, halides, ketones, aldehydes and acid derivatives, as well as other functional groups. Alcohols can be chemically transformed into a wide range of other functional groups, including halides, alkenes, ethers, aldehydes, ketones and acid derivatives. Alcohols are vitally important and this chapter will describe their physical and chemical properties. Reactions that form alcohols and those that transform alcohols will be discussed. Since alcohols are pivotal in the formation of many other functional groups, they will appear in reactions throughout the remainder of this book.

11.1. STRUCTURE

WHAT IS THE DISTINGUISHING FEATURE OF AN ALCOHOL? OF A THIOL?

An alcohol is characterized by a C–O–H bond. A thiol is the sulfur analog of an alcohol and is characterized by a C–S–H bond.

The OH Group and Hydrogen Bonding

WHAT IS THE BOND POLARIZATION FOR AN O–H GROUP?

Since the oxygen is the most electronegative, the oxygen is the negative pole and the hydrogen is the positive pole ($^{\delta}O-H^{\delta\oplus}$). This makes the hydrogen slightly acidic ($pK_a \approx 16-18$).

WHY IS THE INTERMOLECULAR INTERACTION OF TWO O–H GROUPS GREATER THAN THE INTERACTION OF TWO C–O GROUPS?

The O–H bond is more polarized than the C–O bond, leading to a greater attraction of the oxygen of one OH for the hydrogen of another. Since the intermolecular O-----H bond (a hydrogen bond) is quite strong, the OH interactions are stronger than the C–O interaction.

WHAT IS THE ASSOCIATIVE INTERACTION BETWEEN TWO ALCOHOL GROUPS CALLED?

Hydrogen bonding.

Physical Properties **COMPARED TO AN ALKANE, HOW MUCH IS THE BOILING POINT INCREASED BY INTRODUCING AN OH GROUP?**

A comparison of the boiling points of several alkanes with their homologous alcohol derivatives leads to the conclusion that replacing a hydrogen with an OH does not increase the boiling point by a set amount. There is a clear and significant upward trend but the difference in boiling point diminishes as the size of the carbon chain increases.

Ethane, bp = -88.5°C and ethanol, +78.3°C (Δ = 166.8°C);propane, bp = -42°C and propanol, bp = +92.2°C (Δ = 134.2°C);butane, bp = 0°C and butanol, bp = +117.7°C (Δ = 117.7°C);octane, bp = +126°C and octanol, bp = +195°C (Δ = 69°C).

WHY IS THE BOILING POINT OF AN ALCOHOL HIGHER THAN THAT OF AN ETHER WITH APPROXIMATELY THE SAME MOLECULAR WEIGHT?

A comparison of diethyl ether (MW = 74.12, bp = 34.5°C) and 1-butanol (MW 74.12, bp = 117.7°C) clearly shows the trend. The strong hydrogen bonding possible in the alcohol far outweighs the dipole interactions possible in the C–O bond of the ether.

WHAT IS THE GEOMETRY OF AN ALCOHOL IF ATTENTION IS FOCUSED UPON THE OXYGEN?

One cannot "see" the lone electron pairs. If the methyl group and hydrogen of methanol are included with the lone pairs, however, the geometry around the oxygen is 'tetrahedral'. If one only focuses upon the atoms one can see, the geometry is angular or bent around the oxygen (see *11.1*).

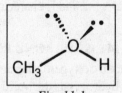

Fig. 11.1

WHAT IS THE APPROXIMATE NUMBER OF CARBONS REQUIRED FOR AN ALCOHOL TO BE SOLUBLE IN WATER?

Low molecular weight alcohols such as methanol and ethanol are very soluble in water. High molecular weight alcohols such as 2-decanol or 1-pentadecanol are generally insoluble. There is a competition between the "water-soluble" (hydrophilic) OH group and the 'water-insoluble' (hydrophobic) hydrocarbon backbone. The 'break point' is about five carbons (pentanol) where 1-butanol has a solubility of 7.4 g/100 mL of water, 1-pentanol has a solubility of 2.7 g/ 100 mL and 1-hexanol has a solubility of 0.8 g/100 mL. Branched chain alcohols are more soluble than linear alcohols [isobutyl alcohol (10g/100 mL) vs. *t*-butanol (infinitely soluble in water)].

11.2. NOMENCLATURE

WHAT IS THE ENDING FOR AN ALCOHOL UNDER THE IUPAC RULES?

The IUPAC ending for an alcohol is -ol, where the -e of the alk*ane* is dropped (or e in alk*ene* or e in alk*yne*)and replaced with -ol, as in ethane → ethanol.

WHY IS THE C$_6$ ALCOHOL WITH THE FORMULA C$_6$H$_{14}$O CALLED HEXANOL RATHER THAN HEXOL?

A six-carbon alcohol could have an alkane backbone:

$$CH_3CH_2CH_2CH_2CH_2CH_2OH \ (Example\ 1),$$

an alkene backbone:

$$CH_3CH=CHCH_2CH_2CH_2OH \ (Example\ 2)$$

or an alkyne backbone:

$$CH_3C \equiv CCH_2CH_2CH_2OH \ (Example\ 3).$$

In order to specify which one is being considered the alkan, alken or alkyn prefix is retained, as in 1-hexanol (*Example 1*), 4-hexen-1-ol (*Example 2*) and 4-hexyn-1-ol (*Example 3*).

GIVE THE IUPAC NAMES FOR *11.2–11.7*.

The names are: 5-ethyl-2-methyl-4-octanol for *11.2*; 3-chloro-2,5,5-triethyl-2-methyl-1-octanol, *11.3*; 2-methyl-6,8-diphenyl-2-decanol, *11.4*; 5-ethyl-oct-6-yn-2-ol, *11.5*; *cis*–3-propylcyclohexanol, *11.6*; tridec-11*E*-en-2-ol, *11.7*.

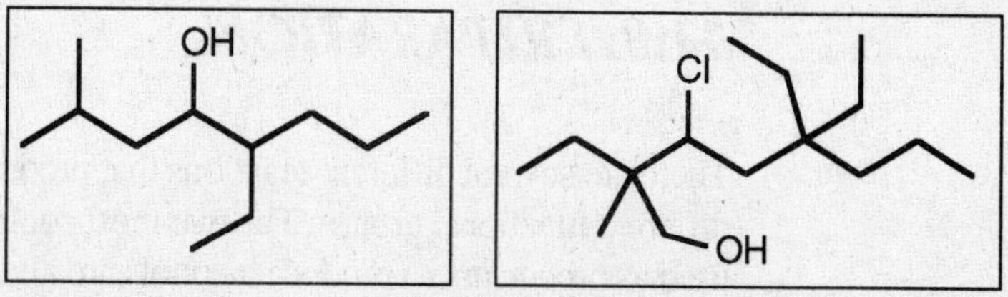

Fig. 11.2, 11.3

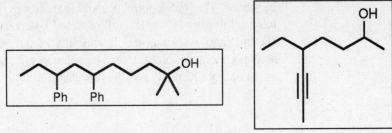

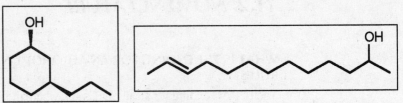

Fig. 11.4, 11.5

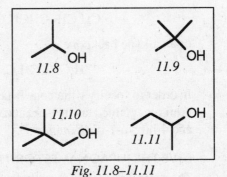

Fig. 11.6, 11.7

GIVE THE COMMON NAMES FOR *11.8–11.11*.

There are several, usually lower molecular weight, alcohols that have common names. The common name of *11.8* is isopropyl alcohol (rubbing alcohol); *11.9* is *tert*-butyl alcohol; *11.10* is neopentyl alcohol and *11.11* is *sec*-butyl alcohol.

Fig. 11.8–11.11

11.3. PREPARATION

There are several different reactions that produce alcohols, involving several different functional groups. The two most common functional groups that are used as precursors to produce alcohols are alkenes and carbonyl compounds (ketones and aldehydes or acid derivatives).

Hydration of Alkenes

When an alkene reacts with an acid such as HCl, a carbocation intermediate is generated. That cation reacts with the nucleophilic counterion of the acid to give the final addition product. In order for this reaction to work, the acid must be strong enough to react with the weakly basic alkene. Weak acids give no reaction unless an acid catalyst is provided.

WHAT IS THE PRODUCT WHEN 2-METHYLCYCLOHEXENE REACTS WITH WATER?

There is no reaction. Water is not a sufficiently strong acid to react with the weak base (the π-bond of the alkene).

IF A CATALYTIC AMOUNT OF H_2SO_4 IS ADDED TO THE REACTION OF 2-METHYLCYCLOHEXENE AND WATER, WHAT IS THE RESULT?

The strong acid catalyst (H_2SO_4) reacts with the alkene moiety to form the more stable cation, *11.12*. Once this cation is formed, water is a sufficiently strong nucleophile to attack the positive center, generating oxonium ion *11.13*. Loss of a proton completes the reaction, giving 1-methyl-1-cyclohexanol (*11.14*) as the final product.

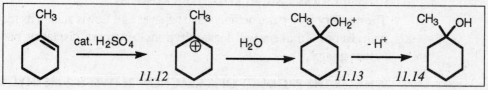

Fig. 11.12–11.14

WHAT IS pTsOH?

This is an abbreviation for *para*-toluenesulfonic acid, RSO_3H, where R = 4-methylphenyl. This organic acid is soluble in most organic solvents and is commonly used as an acid catalyst.

GIVE THE MAJOR PRODUCT FOR THE REACTIONS OF *11.15* AND *11.16*.

The reaction of water with the first alkene (*11.15*) generates 3-methyl-3-hexanol (*11.17*). The second reaction involves a 1,2-methyl shift from the initially formed secondary cation to the more stable tertiary cation. Trapping water leads to the final product, 1,2-dimethyl-1-cycloheptanol (*11.18*).

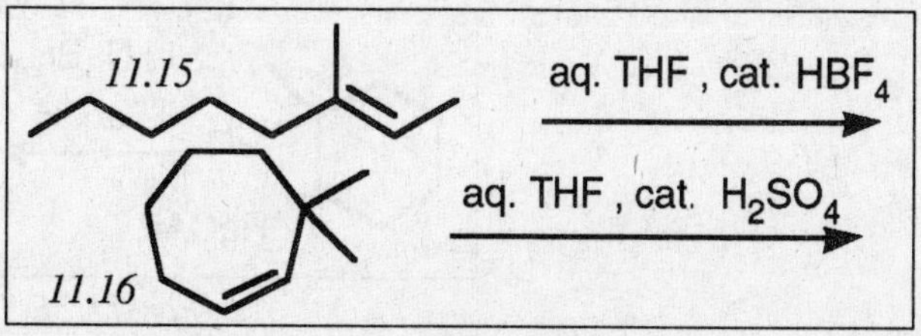

Fig. 11.15, 11.16

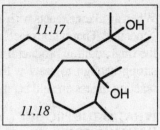

Fig. 11.17, 11.18

Oxymercuration

WHAT IS THE STRUCTURE OF MERCURIC ACETATE?

The structure of mercuric acetate $(Hg(OAc)_2)$ is *11.19*.

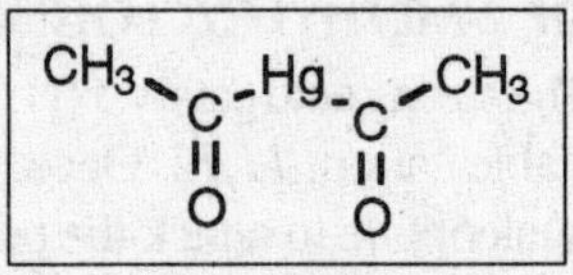

Fig. 11.19

CLASSIFY MERCURIC ACETATE AS A REAGENT.

The mercury is electron deficient and behaves as a Lewis acid in its reactions with alkenes. An alkene will donate electrons to mercury, displacing one of the acetate groups.

WHAT IS THE PRODUCT OF A REACTION BETWEEN 2-METHYL-1-BUTENE AND MERCURIC ACETATE?

The product is the organomercury cation, *11.20*. The mercury atom stabilizes the cation by "back donation" of electrons.

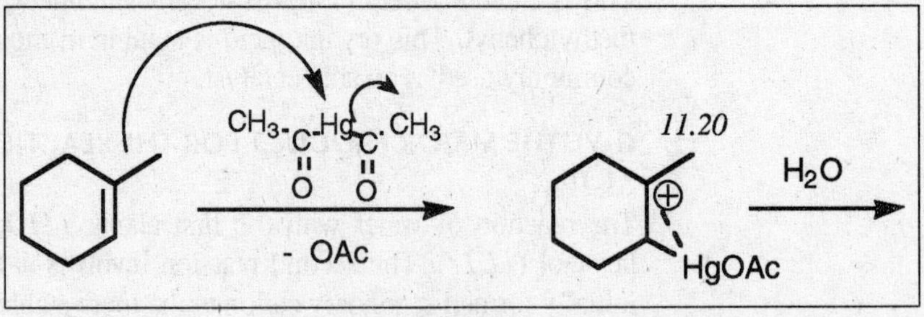

Fig. 11.20

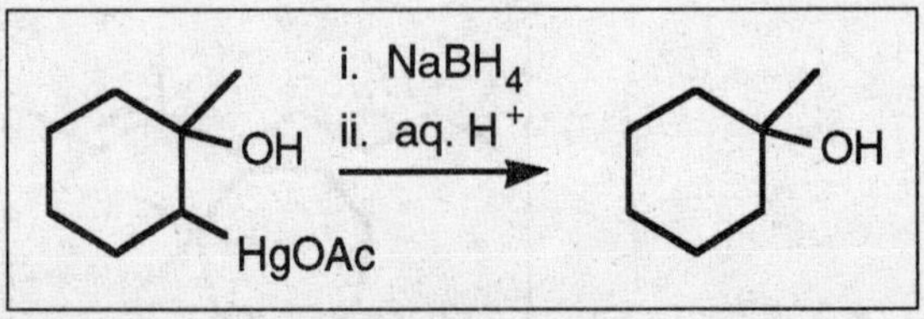

Fig. 11.21. 11.22

IF THE REACTION IS DONE IN AN AQUEOUS MEDIUM, WHAT IS THE PRODUCT?

Organomercury cation *11.20* behaves, more or less, as any other cation and in the presence of a nucleophile such as water will be converted to a hydroxy-mercury compound, *11.21*.

HOW CAN THE MERCURY BE REMOVED FROM THE PRODUCT?

Removal of mercury requires cleavage of the C–Hg bond. This can be done very efficiently by addition of sodium borohydride ($NaBH_4$) to *11.21* followed by aqueous hydrolysis. The final product is the alcohol that is formed by addition of water to the more substituted carbon (*11.22*).

This overall sequence is called *oxymercuration* or, sometimes, *oxymercuration-demercuration*.

WHAT IS THE PRODUCT WHEN MERCURIC ACETATE REACTS WITH 3-METHYL-1-PENTENE? IS THAT PRODUCT THE RESULT OF A REARRANGEMENT? WHY OR WHY NOT?

The product (after treatment with $NaBH_4$) is 3-methyl-2-pentanol. There is no rearrangement of the intermediate mercuric cation. The mercury stabilizes the secondary cationic center by *back donation* of its d-orbitals. This increased stability diminishes the possibility of rearrangement and trapping with water is usually faster than the rearrangement.

GIVE THE PRODUCTS OF THE REACTIONS OF *11.23–11.25*.

The first reaction converts *11.23* into the tertiary alcohol, 2-methyl-2-heptanol (*11.26*). This hydration reaction proceeds as if it were a normal cation intermediate in an addition reaction. The second reaction of *11.25* poses a problem. There is no regiochemical preference for addition of the mercury. The overall sequence will, therefore, produce a roughly 1:1 mixture of two alcohols, *11.27* and *11.28*. In the final reaction, mercury trifluoroacetate is used rather than mercuric acetate. The reaction of *11.25* proceeds normally, however, producing the tertiary alcohol, *11.29*.

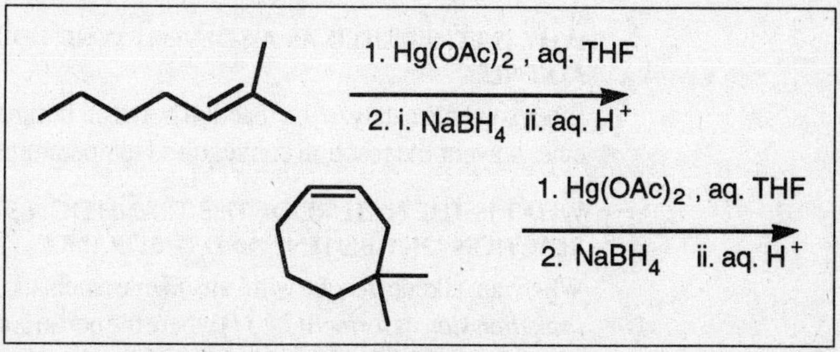

Fig. 11.23, 11.24

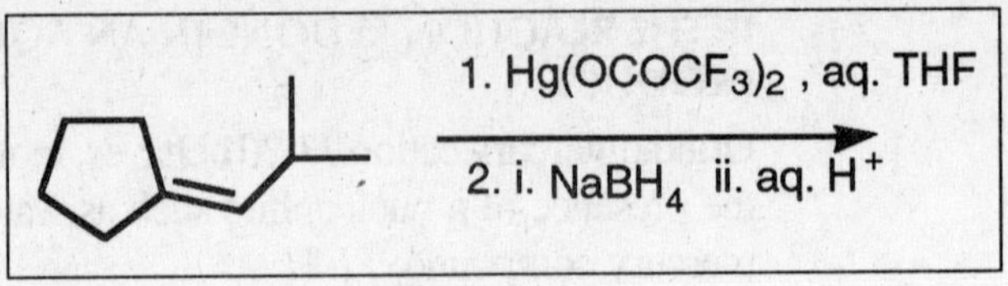

1. Hg(OCOCF$_3$)$_2$, aq. THF

2. i. NaBH$_4$ ii. aq. H$^+$

Fig. 11.25

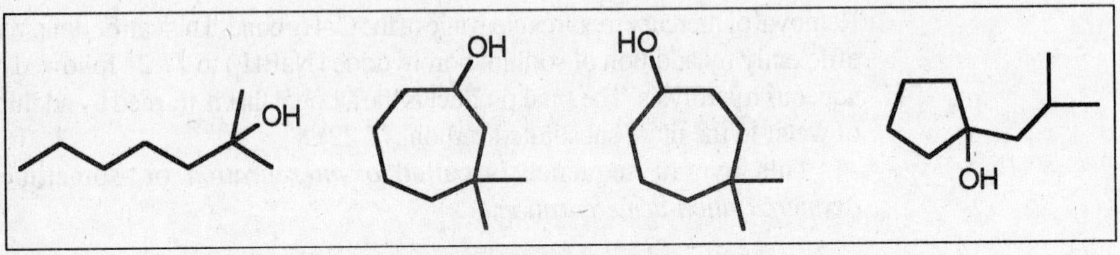

Fig. 11.26–11.29

WHAT IS THE ADVANTAGE OF USING MERCURIC TRIFLUOROACETATE RATHER THAN MERCURIC ACETATE?

Trifluoroacetate is a better leaving group than acetate. In addition, trifluoroacetate withdraws more electron density form mercury, making it more electrophilic. Both of these things combine to make the trifluoroacetate derivative more reactive.

Hydroboration

Hydroboration was introduced and discussed in section 5.5.

WHAT IS THE STRUCTURE OF DIBORANE?

Diborane (B$_2$H$_6$) is a hydrido-bridged dimer, *11.30*.

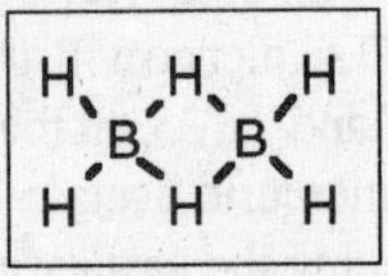

Fig. 11.30

WHY IS ETHER USED AS A SOLVENT WHEN DIBORANE REACTS WITH ALKENES?

Ether solvents catalyze the reaction between borane and alkenes. Without the ether solvent the reaction can required temperatures up to 200-250°C.

WHAT IS THE NATURE OF THE TRANSITION STATE FOR THE REACTION OF 1-BUTENE AND DIBORANE?

When an alkene reacts with an alkene such as 1-butene a *four-centered transition state* is formed (*11.31*) where the boron is delivered to one carbon and a hydrogen of the B–H bond is delivered to the other carbon. The final product is an *organoborane*, in this case *11.32*.

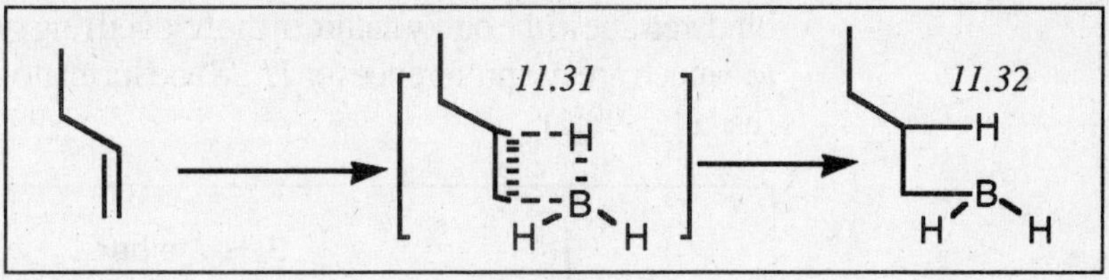

Fig. 11.31, 11.32

WHAT IS THE REGIOCHEMICAL PREFERENCE OF THE REACTION OF 1-BUTENE AND DIBORANE?

The major product is the one where boron is attached to the *less* substituted carbon (see *11.32*), although about 15% of the other isomer (boron attached to the secondary carbon) is also produced.

WHY DOES ONE PRODUCT PREDOMINATE WHEN DIBORANE REACTS WITH 2-METHYL-1-PENTENE?

The two possible transition states are *11.31* and *11.33* (which leads to alkylborane *11.34*). It is clear that the interaction of the ethyl group of the alkene and the BH$_2$ unit in *11.33* causes more steric hindrance than the ethyl-H interaction in *11.31*. Minimization of this steric interaction drives the reaction to give the product where boron is attached to the less substituted carbon.

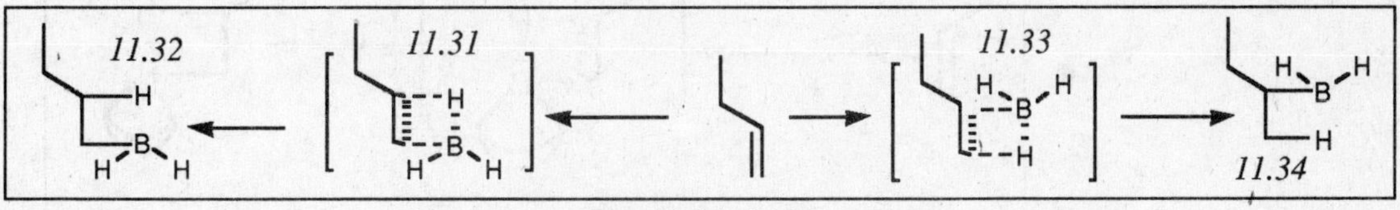

Fig. 11.31–11.34

GIVE THE STRUCTURE AND SHOW A REACTION FOR THE PREPARATION OF DISIAMYLBORANE, THEXYLBORANE AND 9-BBN.

When 2-methyl-2-butene is treated with diborane, a dialkylborane (*11.35*) is formed. This product is given the common name disiamylborane (siamyl = *sec*-isoamyl). When 2,3-dimethyl-2-butene is treated with diborane a monoalkylborane (*11.36*) is formed. The common name of this product is thexylborane (thexyl = *tert*-hexyl). When 1,5-cylcooctadiene is treated with diborane, boron adds to one alkene to form the alkylborane but then adds intramolecularly to the other alkene to give *11.37*, 9-borabicyclo[4.4.1]nonane (9-BBN).

EXPLAIN WHY 9-BBN GIVES A HIGHER PERCENTAGE OF THE 1-SUBSTITUTED PRODUCT WHEN COMPARED TO DIBORANE IN A REACTION WITH 1-BUTENE.

Examination of the two possible transition state (*11.38* and *11.39*) for the reaction of 9-BBN and 1-butene show that *11.39* is much more sterically hindered due to the bulky nature of the bridged ring system of 9-BBN. This leads to a much greater preference for *11.38* and formation of *11.40* rather than *11.41* (usually >99:1).

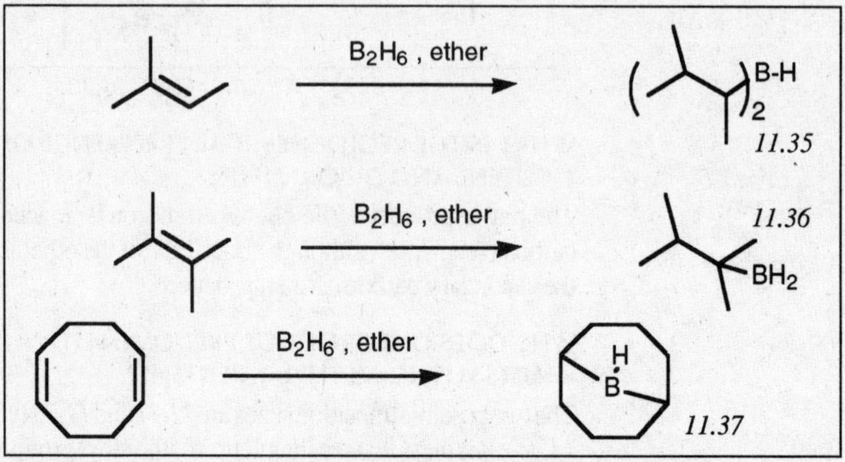

Fig. 11.35–11.37

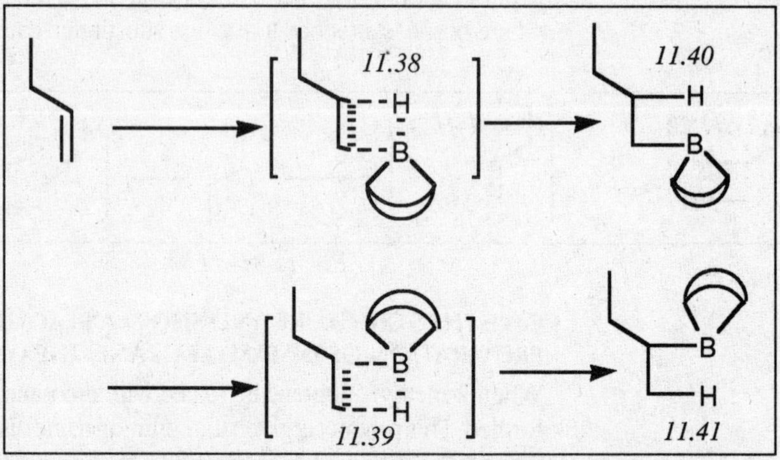

Fig. 11.38–11.41

WHEN THE BORANE PRODUCT RESULTING FROM THE REACTION OF CYCLOPENTENE AND DIBORANE IS TREATED WITH SODIUM HYDROXIDE AND HYDROGEN PEROXIDE, WHAT IS THE PRODUCT?

The product is cyclopentanol.

WHAT IS THE MECHANISM OF THIS REACTION?

The initial reaction is between hydrogen peroxide and hydroxide to produce the hydroperoxide anion (HOO⁻). This attacks the boron of the tricyclopentylborane (*11.42*) to form *11.43*. A B→O carbon shift is accompanied by loss of hydroxide (OH⁻) and leads to the borinate (*11.44*). Two additional reactions of HOO$^\ominus$

followed by the B → O alkyl shift produces boric acid [B(OH)$_3$] and three equivalents of the alcohol (cyclopentanol). In general, a trialkylborane leads to three equivalents of the alcohol and a dialkylborane leads to two equivalents.

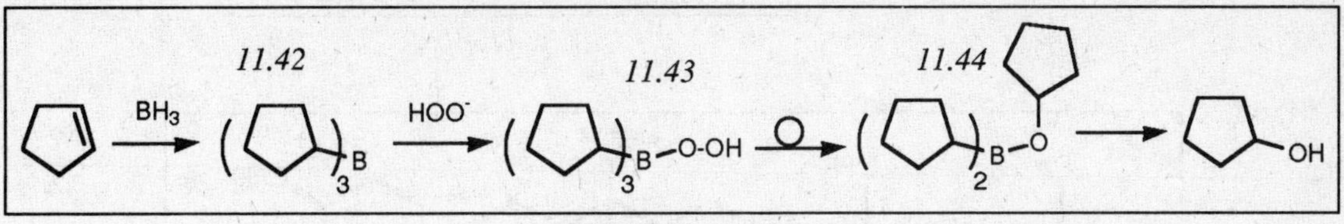

Fig. 11.42–11.44

EXPLAIN WHY THE HYDROBORATION OF 1-METHYLCYCLOPENTENE LEADS TO TRANS-2-METHYLCYCLOHEXANOL WHEN THE HYDROBORATION REACTION INVOLVES A 'CIS-' ADDITION.

The 'cis' addition involves the boron and the hydrogen of the borane. This leads to borane *11.45* where the methyl group is pushed back and is *trans* to the boron. Oxidation with basic hydrogen peroxide attacks the boron, not the carbon, so the relative stereochemistry of the methyl and the boron is retained, leading to *11.46* as the major product. In *11.45*, the groups attached to boron (R) refers to either a hydrogen or the methylcyclopentyl group.

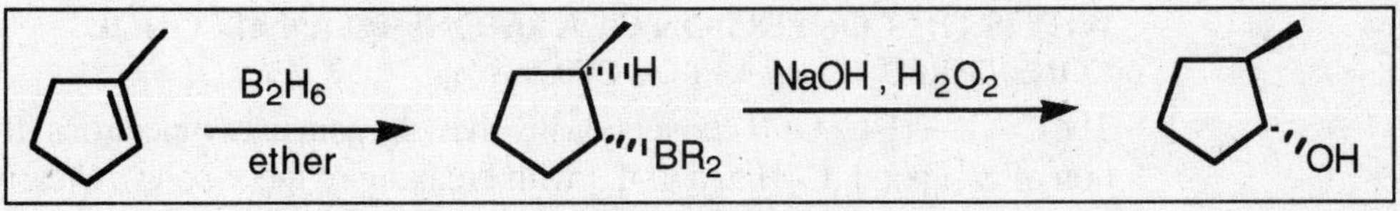

Fig. 11.45, 11.46

GIVE THE MAJOR PRODUCT FOR THE REACTIONS OF *11.47–11.49*.

In the first case, the product is the alcohol formed by 'delivery' of boron (and thereby OH after the oxidation step) to the less substituted carbon of *11.47*. The product is 3-methyl-6-phenyl-2-heptanol (*11.50*). In the second reaction, *11.48* is converted to the secondary alcohol, *11.51*. In the last case, alkene *11.49* (1,2-dimethylcyclohexene) is converted to *11.52* where the 'cis' addition leads to the two methyl groups *cis* to each other but *trans* to the OH.

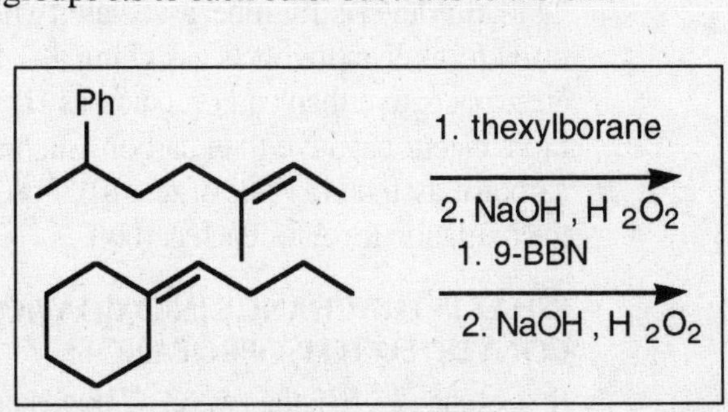

Fig. 11.47, 11.48

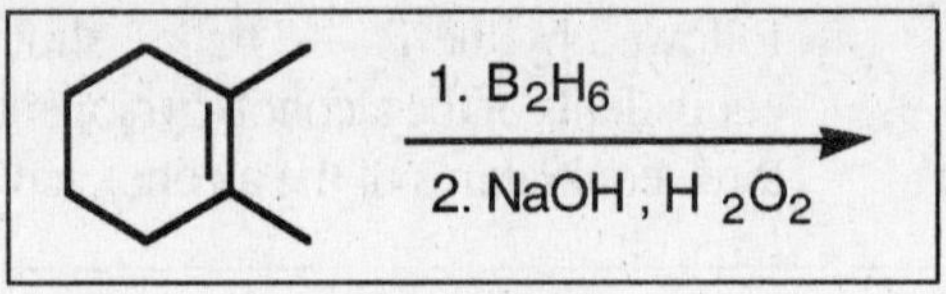

Fig. 11.49

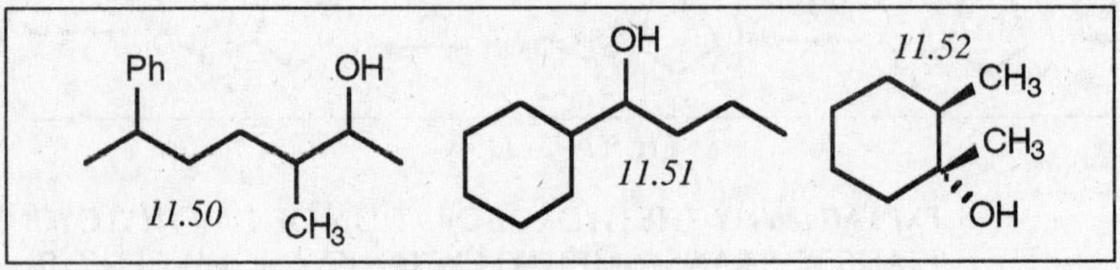

Fig. 11.50–11.52

Reduction of Carbonyl Compounds

WHAT IS THE DEFINITION OF A REDUCTION?

Reduction is defined as a reaction in which two electrons are gained in the final product. A more practical definition is a reaction that adds hydrogen to the molecule or loses an electronegative element (such as oxygen) from the molecule.

WHY IS THE CONVERSION OF A KETONE TO AN ALCOHOL CONSIDERED TO BE A REDUCTION?

The C=O → H–C–O–H conversion involves the gain of two electrons (formation of two bond [C–H and O–H] with breaking of the π-bond). Clearly, the reaction adds two hydrogens to the carbonyl and therefore fits the definition of adding hydrogen to a molecule.

OXIDATION NUMBER AND OXIDATION STATE

WHAT IS OXIDATION NUMBER?

The oxidation number for a molecule is the sum of the oxidation levels for each carbon in the molecule.

WHAT IS AN OXIDATION LEVEL?

Oxidation level is a number associated with gain or loss of electron density. The usual formalism involves assigning a -1 to each attached element that is less electronegative than carbon (such as H); +1 to each attached element that is more electronegative than carbon (such as O, N, Br, etc.). Another attached carbon is assigned a value of zero (0). These numbers are added together to give the oxidation level for each carbon.

WHAT IS THE CHANGE IN OXIDATION NUMBER WHEN ACETONE IS CONVERTED TO ISOPROPANOL?

In acetone (*11.53*), the two C–C bonds are assigned a value of 0 and the two bonds to oxygen (C=O) give a value of +2. The oxidation level for the carbonyl carbon is, therefore, +2. Examination of isopropanol shows the C–O bond is valued at +1, the C–H bond at -1 and each C–C bond is 0. The central carbon of isopropanol has an oxidation level of 0. The conversion from +2 - 0 is a net *gain* of electrons (electrons are negatively charged and increasing electron density leads to a more negative number) and is, therefore, a reduction.

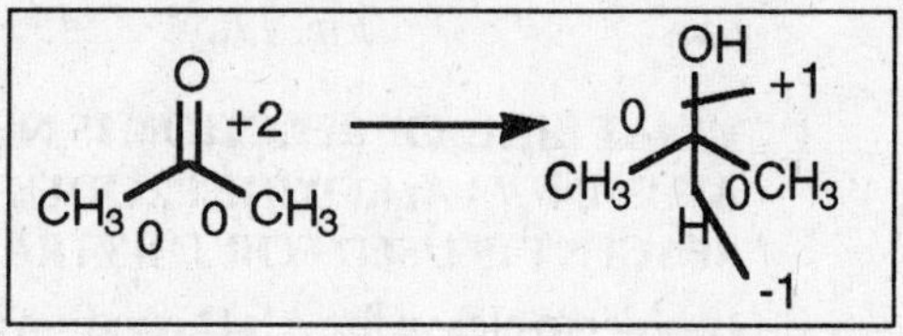

Fig. 11.53

In general, if the change is oxidation number is positive it is an oxidation (see section 11.4) and if it is negative it is a reduction.

IF THE ALCOHOL IS OXIDIZED, WHAT HAPPENS TO THE REAGENT THAT CAUSES THE OXIDATION TO OCCUR?

Oxidation and reduction are linked. If the alcohol is oxidized, the reagent that caused that transformation must be reduced. Conversely, is a ketone is reduced, the reagent that caused that transformation must be oxidized.

WHAT IS THIS REAGENT CALLED?

A reducing agent is a molecule that causes another molecule to be reduced. An oxidation agent is a molecule that causes another molecule to be oxidized.

LITHIUM ALUMINUM HYDRIDE

WHAT IS THE STRUCTURE OF LITHIUM ALUMINUM HYDRIDE?

The structure is $LiAlH_4$, where the active species is tetrahydridoaluminate, AlH_4^-.

WHAT IS THE BOND POLARIZATION FOR THE AL-H BOND OF LITHIUM ALUMINUM HYDRIDE?

Aluminum is less electronegative than hydrogen and the hydrogen takes the negative pole ($H^{\delta-}$). The polarization is $^{\delta+}Al-H^{\delta-}$.

WHAT IS THE MECHANISM OF THE REACTION WHEN LITHIUM ALUMINUM HYDRIDE REACTS WITH 2-BUTANONE?

The reaction proceeds by a four-centered transition state such as *11.54*. The electropositive aluminum is attracted to the electronegative oxygen. The electronegative hydrogen (a hydride) is attracted to the electropositive carbon.

WHAT IS THE PRODUCT OF THE INITIAL REACTION BETWEEN LITHIUM ALUMINUM HYDRIDE AND 2-BUTANONE?

As shown with *11.54*, the initial product of the reaction is an aluminum alkoxide (*11.55*).

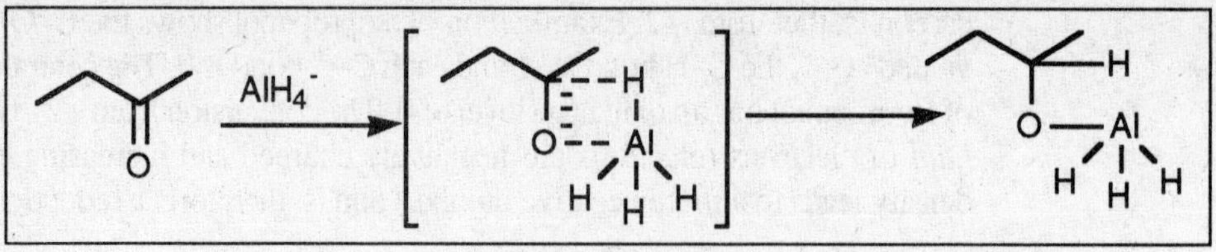

Fig. 11.54, 11.55

WHAT KIND OF REACTION IS NECESSARY TO CONVERT THE ALUMINUM ALKOXIDE PRODUCT INTO AN ALCOHOL? WHAT REAGENT IS USED FOR THIS TRANSFORMATION?

In order to cleave the Al–H bond, an acid-base reaction is necessary. The usual reagent is dilute aqueous acid, although plain water or even aqueous hydroxide can be used. The treatment that leads to the isolation of the alcohol product with the greatest ease is the sequence: i. water ii. 15% aq. NaOH iii. 3n water, where n = number of equivalents of $LiAlH_4$.

WHAT IS THE REACTION PRODUCT WHEN ETHYL BUTANOATE REACTS WITH LITHIUM ALUMINUM HYDRIDE AND THEN IS HYDROLYZED WITH WATER?

The 'acid portion' of an ester (see section 15.2) is reduced by $LiAlH_4$ to an alcohol. The product is an alcohol, 1-butanol. Ethanol (from the alcohol part of the ester) is the other product.

WHAT IS THE PRODUCT WHEN PENTANOIC ACID IS REACTED FIRST WITH LITHIUM ALUMINUM HYDRIDE AND THEN WITH WATER?

Lithium aluminum hydride is a powerful reducing agent and reduces even carboxylic acids to the corresponding alcohol. The product is, therefore, 1-pentanol.

GIVE THE MAJOR PRODUCT OF THE REACTIONS OF *11.56–11.59*.

The product of the reduction of 3-hexanone (*11.55*) is 3-hexanol. Reduction of 3-methylhexanal (*11.57*) is 3-methyl-1-hexanol. When the ester, ethyl cyclohexane-carboxylate (*11.58*) is reduced, cyclohexanemethanol is the product. Reduction of 1-phenyl-1-propanone (*11.59*) leads to 1-phenyl-1-propanol as the product.

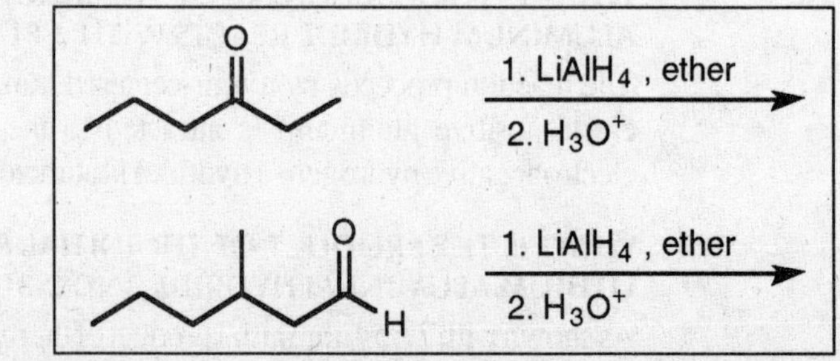

Fig. 11.56, 11.57

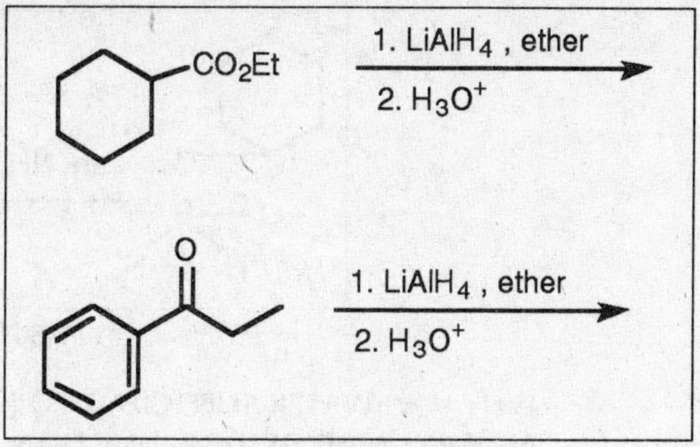

Fig. 11.58, 11.59

SODIUM BOROHYDRIDE

WHAT IS THE STRUCTURE OF SODIUM BOROHYDRIDE?

Sodium borohydride is $NaBH_4$ and the active agent is tetrahydridoborate, BH_4^-.

IS SODIUM BOROHYDRIDE A STRONGER OR A WEAKER REDUCING AGENT WHEN COMPARED TO LITHIUM ALUMINUM HYDRIDE? EXPLAIN.

Sodium borohydride is a much weaker reducing agent than lithium aluminum hydride. It is capable of reducing only a few functional groups (aldehydes, ketones, acid chlorides). Esters can be reduced, but with difficulty, and the yields of alcohol product are often poor. In general the B–H bond is less polarized than the Al–H bond and the hydrogen of the B–H bond is a weaker hydride species.

WHAT IS THE MECHANISM OF THE REACTION BETWEEN SODIUM BOROHYDRIDE AND CYCLOHEXANONE? WHAT IS THE PRODUCT AFTER HYDROLYSIS?

The mechanism of reduction of $NaBH_4$ with ketones and aldehydes is identical to that shown for reduction with $LiAlH_4$. The four-centered transition state (*11.60*) leads to an alkoxyborate product, *11.61*. Hydrolysis of *11.61* leads to cleavage of the B–O bond and formation of cyclohexanol, along with boric acid, $B(OH)_3$.

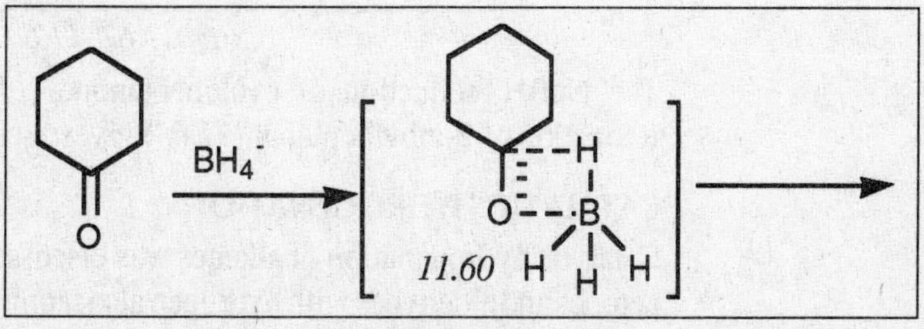

Fig. 11.60

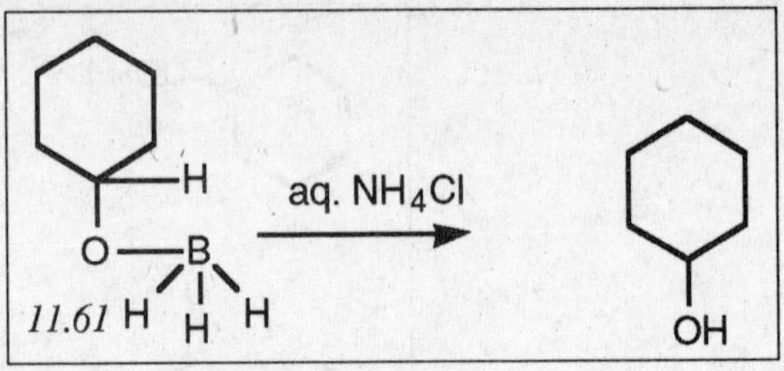

Fig. 11.61

WHY WAS WATER SUFFICIENT TO HYDROLYZE A LITHIUM ALUMINUM HYDRIDE REDUCTION BUT AQUEOUS AMMONIUM CHLORIDE WAS USED WITH THE SODIUM BOROHYDRIDE REDUCTION?

Since $NaBH_4$ is a much weaker reducing agent, it does not react completely with water. Sodium borohydride dissolves in water and reacts to give a mono or dihydroxy borohydride species. An acid stronger than water is required to hydrolyze the B–O bond and the slightly acidic ammonium chloride solution is a mild and excellent choice.

WHAT IS THE REACTION PRODUCT WHEN SODIUM BOROHYDRIDE REACTS WITH ETHYL BUTANOATE?

The generic answer is no reaction since $NaBH_4$ generally does not reduce esters very well. In fact, many esters are reduced to the primary alcohol with $NaBH_4$ although the reaction is often slow. The first *estimate*, however, is to say no reaction.

WHAT IS THE PRODUCT OF EACH OF THE REACTIONS OF 11.62–11.63?

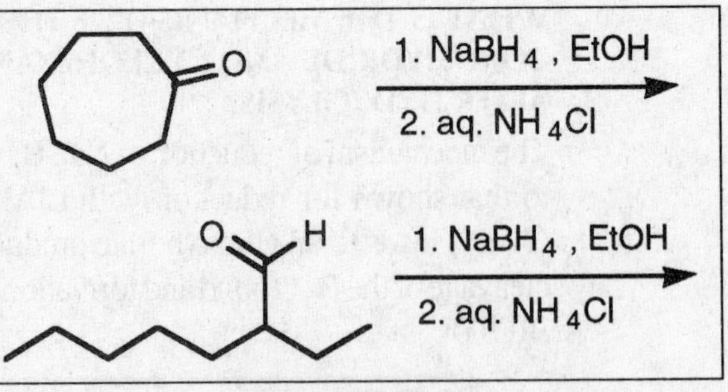

Fig. 11.62–11.63

The $NaBH_4$ reduction of cycloheptanone (*11.62*) leads to cycloheptanol. Reduction of 2-ethylheptanal (*11.63*) gives 2-ethyl-1-heptanol.

CATALYTIC HYDROGENATION

Catalytic hydrogenation of alkenes was discussed in section 5.5. Reduction of ketones and aldehydes with hydrogen also requires a catalyst, usually platinum, and is very similar in mechanism to that shown for alkenes in chapter five.

WHAT IS THE PRODUCT WHEN 2-PENTANONE IS REACTED WITH HYDROGEN GAS?

As with the hydrogenation of alkenes, hydrogen gas does not react with ketones or aldehydes unless a catalyst is present. This attempted hydrogenation gave no reaction.

WHAT IS THE PRODUCT WHEN 2-PENTANONE IS REACTED WITH PLATINUM OXIDE AND HYDROGEN GAS?

In the presence of the platinum derivative catalyst, 2-pentanone is reduced to 2-pentanol.

WHICH FUNCTIONAL GROUP IS EASIER TO REDUCE WITH HYDROGEN, A KETONE OR AN ESTER?

The carbonyl group of an aldehyde or a ketone is much easier to reduce by catalytic hydrogenation than is the carbonyl of an ester. Esters are usually very difficult to reduce with hydrogen.

GIVE THE MAJOR PRODUCT OF THE REACTIONS OF *11.64–11.67*.

Catalytic hydrogenation of 3-octanone (*11.64*) leads to reduction of the carbonyl and formation of 3-octanol. Reduction of 4,4-dimethylhexanal (*11.65*) with hydrogen gives 4,4-dimethyl-1-hexanol. Reduction of 2-propylcyclohexanone (*11.66*) leads to 2-propylcyclo-hexanol. Catalytic hydrogenation of *11.67* (3-methyl-2-phenyl-cyclopentanone) gives 3-methyl-2-phenylcyclopentanol as the major product.

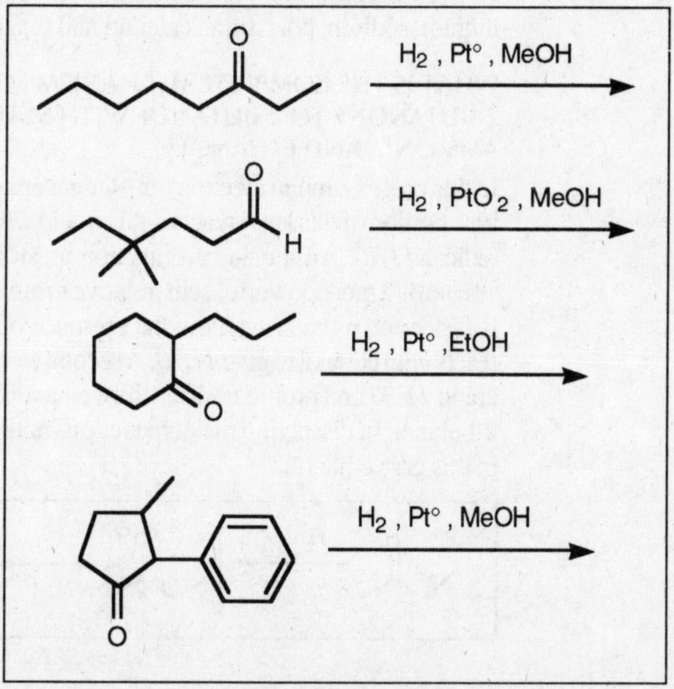

Fig. 11.64–11.67

DISSOLVING METAL REDUCTION

WHEN SODIUM METAL IS MIXED WITH ACETONE, WHAT IS THE INITIAL PRODUCT?

Sodium transfers one electron to the carbonyl, forming a *ketyl* (*11.68*). This resonance stabilized intermediate has characteristics of both a radical and a carbanion (it is an example of a radical anion).

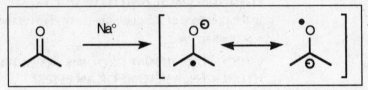

Fig. 11.68

WHY DOES SODIUM METAL TRANSFER AN ELECTRON TO THE π-BOND?

Sodium metal lies in Group I of the Periodic Table. Energetically, it is easier to lose one electron (ionization potential) than to gain seven electrons (electron affinity) to achieve a full octet in the outer shell.

WHAT OTHER METALS ARE CAPABLE OF TRANSFERRING AN ELECTRON IN THIS MANNER?

Most metals in Group I and Group II of the periodic Table are capable of single electron transfer. The most common metals used in this type of reaction are lithium, sodium, potassium, calcium and magnesium.

WHAT IS THE COMPLETE MECHANISM FOR THE REDUCTION OF 2-BUTANONE TO 2-BUTANOL WITH SODIUM METAL IN LIQUID AMMONIA AND ETHANOL?

In this process, initial electron transfer generates a ketyl (*11.69*). The "carbanion" portion of this ketyl reacts with an acid which is in the medium to generate radical *11.70*. Ammonia can function as an acid in this case but the added ethanol is a more powerful acid (relative to ammonia) and the overall reduction is faster and more efficient in the presence of ethanol. Ketyl *11.69* therefore reacts with ethanol to give *11.70*. A second electron transfer from sodium gives anion *11.70* and proton transfer from ethanol completes the reduction to give 2-butanol. In dissolving metal reductions both hydrogens come from the acid, in this case ethanol.

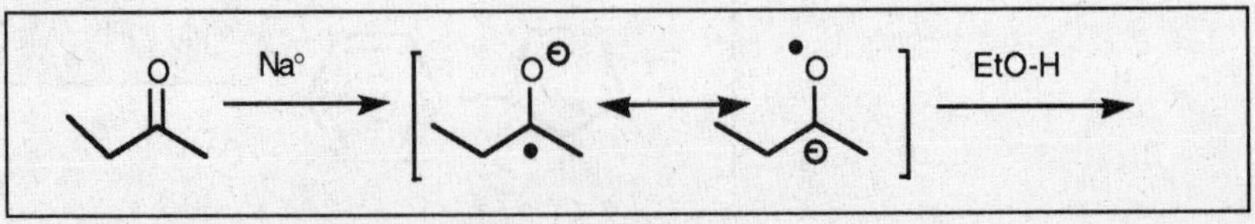

Fig. 11.69

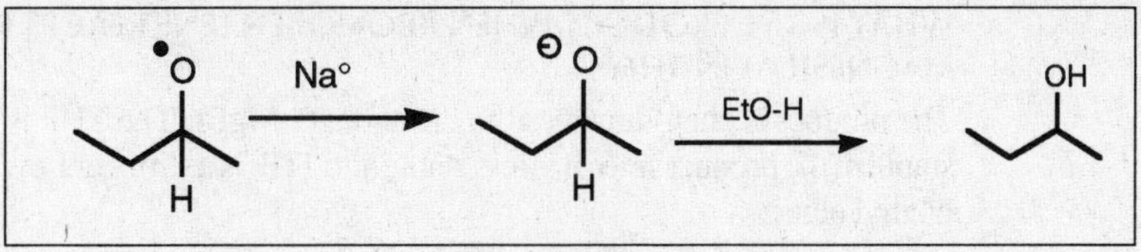

Fig. 11.70, 11.71

WHAT ARE THE MAJOR PRODUCTS OF THE REACTIONS OF *11.72* AND *11.73*?

The dissolving metal reduction of cyclohexanone (*11.72*) with sodium leads to cyclohexanol. Reduction of 4,4-dimethylpentanal (*11.73*) with potassium leads to 4,4-dimethyl-1-pentanol.

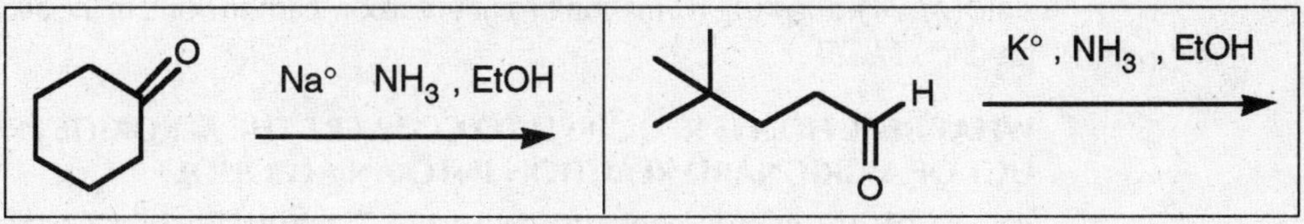

Fig. 11.72, 11.73

From Carbonyl Compounds and Grignard Reagents

The reactions that form Grignard regents from alkyl halides was described in section 4.7.

WHAT IS A GRIGNARD REAGENT?

A Grignard reagent is an organometallic compound possessing a C–Mg–X bond where "C" can be an alkyl or an aryl group and X is a halogen.

WHAT IS THE BOND POLARIZATION OF A C–Mg BOND?

Since Mg is less electronegative than carbon the polarization is: $^{\delta+}Mg-C^{\delta-}$.

WHAT IS THE PRODUCT WHEN 1-BROMOBUTANE REACTS WITH MAGNESIUM IN ETHER? WHAT IS THE NAME OF THIS PRODUCT?

The product is butylmagnesium bromide, $CH_3CH_2CH_2CH_2MgBr$.

WHAT IS THE ROLE OF THE ETHER IN THIS REACTION?

The ether solvent acts as a Lewis base, donating electrons to the electron deficient magnesium, assisting formation of the Grignard reagent and stabilizing it once it is formed.

WHAT IS THE PRODUCT WHEN BUTYLMAGNESIUM BROMIDE REACTS WITH CYCLOHEXANONE?

The product is 1-butylcyclohexanol, resulting from nucleophilic attack of the carbon in the Grignard reagent at the electropositive carbonyl, followed by aqueous hydrolysis of the resulting alkoxide.

WHAT IS THE PRODUCT WHEN BROMOBENZENE REACTS WITH MAGNESIUM IN THF?

The product is phenylmagnesium bromide, PhMgBr. The THF is required to stabilize the product since it is less stable and THF is a stronger Lewis base than diethyl ether.

FOUR-CENTER TRANSITION STATE AND ALKOXIDE FORMATION

WHAT IS THE MECHANISM OF REACTION WHEN METHYLMAGNESIUM BROMIDE REACTS WITH ACETONE?

The nucleophilic carbon of the Grignard is attracted to the electropositive carbonyl of the carbonyl and the electropositive magnesium is attracted to the electronegative oxygen of the carbonyl, leading to a four-centered transition state (*11.74*), allowing formation of a new carbon-carbon bond in the alkoxide product, *11.75*.

WHAT REACTION IS REQUIRED TO CONVERT THE ALKOXIDE PRODUCT OF A GRIGNARD REACTION INTO AN ALCOHOL?

An acid-base reaction is required to convert *11.75* into the final alcohol product, *tert*-butyl alcohol, *11.76*.

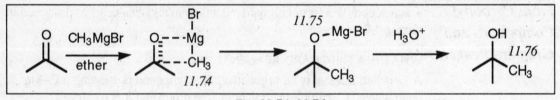

Fig. 11.74–11.76

WHAT IS THE SCHLENK EQUILIBRIUM?

The Schlenk equilibrium describes several organometallic species that comprise the actual structure of a "Grignard reagent" in solution. In its most simple form, the Grignard (RMgX) is described as: $2\,RMgX \leftrightarrows R_2Mg + MgX_2$.

SECONDARY ALCOHOLS FROM ALDEHYDES

WHEN A GRIGNARD REAGENT REACTS WITH AN ALDEHYDE, WHAT IS THE MAJOR PRODUCT AFTER HYDROLYSIS?

The major product is a secondary alcohol.

WHICH ALDEHYDE LEADS TO A PRIMARY ALCOHOL UPON REACTION WITH BUTYLMAGNESIUM BROMIDE?

Formaldehyde.

TERTIARY ALCOHOLS FROM KETONES

WHEN A GRIGNARD REAGENT REACTS WITH A KETONE AND IS FOLLOWED BY HYDROLYSIS, WHAT IS THE MAJOR PRODUCT?

The major product is a tertiary alcohol.

WHAT IS THE PRODUCT OF THE REACTIONS OF *11.77–11.80*?

The reaction of benzaldehyde (*11.77*) and hexylmagnesium chloride is 1-phenyl-1-heptanol (*11.81*). When 4,4,5-trimethyl-2-heptanone (*11.78*) reacts with phenylmagnesium bromide, the product is 4,4,5-trimethyl-2-phenyl-2-heptanol, *11.82*. Reaction of 2-ethylcyclohexanone (*11.79*) and cyclopentylmagnesium iodide leads to formation of 1-cyclopentyl-2-ethylcyclohexanol, *11.83*. Finally, reaction of cyclohexanol (*11.80*) and PBr$_3$ forms the bromide and subsequent reaction with magnesium gives the Grignard reagent. When the Grignard reagent is condensed with benzaldehyde, the product is cyclohexylphenylmethanol, *11.84*.

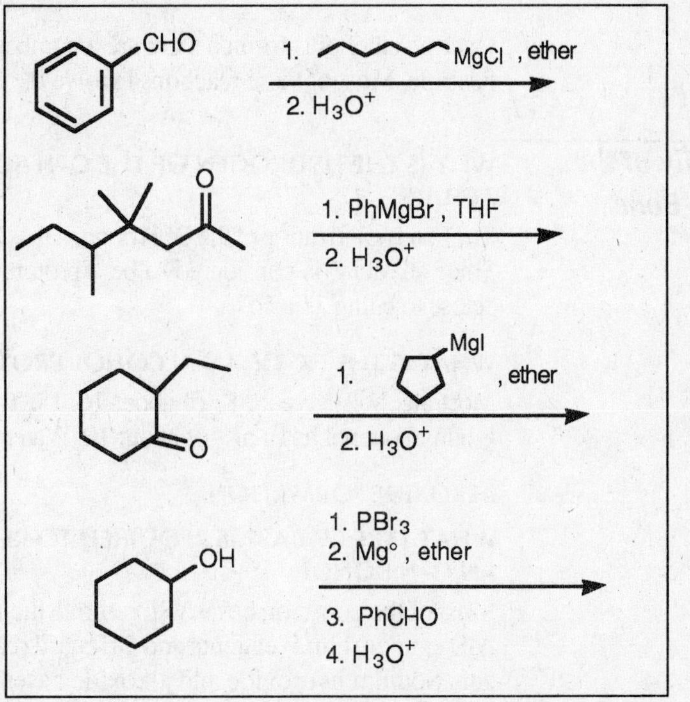

Fig. 11.77–11.80

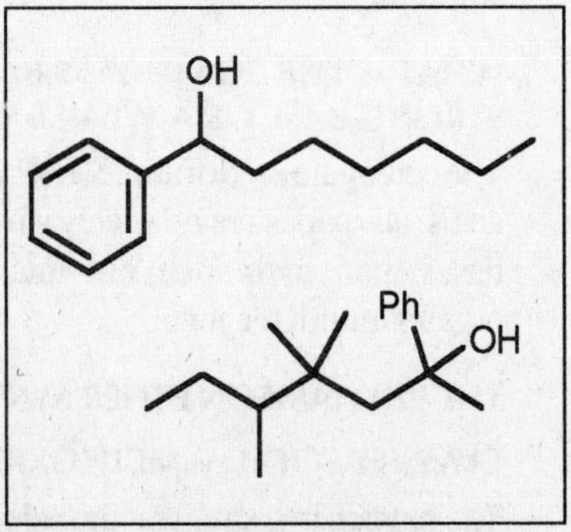

Fig. 11.81, 11.82

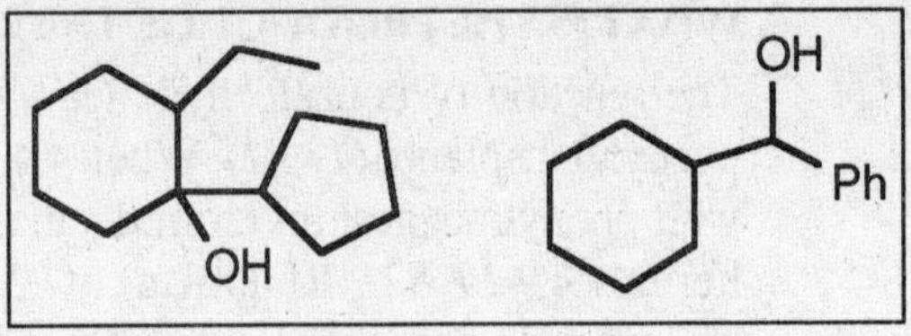

Fig. 11.83, 11.84

11.4. REACTIONS OF ALCOHOLS

Once an alcohol is formed there are a number of important reactions that are possible. Most of these reactions involve the O–H bond.

Acidity of the O–H Bond

WHY IS THE HYDROGEN OF THE O–H BOND CONSIDERED TO BE ACIDIC?

The bond polarization of the O–H bond makes the hydrogen electrophilic ($\delta\oplus$). Since an 'acid' is considered to be a proton, an electropositive hydrogen is "close to being an acid".

WHAT IS THE PK$_a$ OF AN ALCOHOL PROTON?

Most alcohols have a pK$_a$ of about 16–18. The acidic hydrogen of the O–H group in phenol has a pK$_a$ of about 10. Water has a pK$_a$ of 15.8.

ALKOXIDE FORMATION

WHAT TYPE OF BASE IS REQUIRED TO REMOVE THE HYDROGEN OF AN O–H BOND?

Most of the common bases will remove the acidic hydrogen of an alcohol. All organolithium reagents and Grignard reagents will remove that hydrogen. Sodium hydroxide and alkoxide bases such as sodium ethoxide will remove the proton. Sodium hydride (NaH) and amide bases (NR_2^-) are also suitable.

WHAT IS THE CONJUGATE BASE OF AN ALCOHOL CALLED? IS IT A STRONG BASE OR A WEAK BASE?

The conjugate base of an alcohol is an alkoxide. Since alcohols are relative weak acids, alkoxides are relatively strong bases. Alkoxides are somewhat stronger bases than hydroxide but much weaker than carbanion bases such as organolithium reagents.

THE WILLIAMSON ETHER SYNTHESIS

CLASSIFY SODIUM METHOXIDE AS A REAGENT.

The oxygen in sodium methoxide is classified both as a base and a nucleophile.

WHAT IS THE PRODUCT WHEN SODIUM METHOXIDE REACTS WITH 1-IODOETHANE?

In reactions with alkyl halides such as iodoethane, methoxide is a nucleophile (Na is the positive counterion) and will react at the electropositive carbon that bears the iodine. The product of this reaction is an ether, ethyl methyl ether *11.85*.

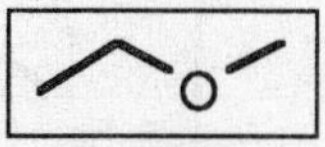

Fig. 11.85

WHAT TYPE OF REACTION IS THIS?

This is a bimolecular substitution reaction, S_N^2.

WHAT IS THE COMMON NAME OF THIS REACTION?

The *Williamson Ether Synthesis*.

WHAT IS THE PRODUCT WHEN POTASSIUM T-BUTOXIDE REACTS WITH 1-IODOETHANE?

The product of the nucleophilic *t*-butoxide and iodoethane is ethyl *t*-butyl ether, *11.86*.

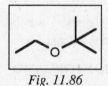

Fig. 11.86

WHAT IS THE PRODUCT WHEN SODIUM ETHOXIDE REACTS WITH 2-BROMO-2-METHYLBUTANE?

The nucleophile is ethoxide but the electrophilic center is a tertiary halide. The S_N^2 reaction will not occur at a tertiary center. Since ethoxide is also a base, removal of a β-hydrogen from 2-bromo-2-methylbutane will lead to an E^2 reaction and the final product will be 2-methyl-2-butene.

GIVE THE MAJOR PRODUCTS OF THE REACTIONS OF *11.87–11.89*.

In the first reaction, phenol reacts with NaH to form the resonance stabilized phenolic anion, a weak nucleophile. This nucleophile can react with iodomethane, however, to produce anisole. In the second reaction, *n*-butyllithium deprotonates 2-pentanol to form the alkoxide. The tertiary halide can also undergo an E^2 reaction, however, and the products are the starting alcohol (2-pentanol) and methylcyclohexene. In the last reaction, deprotonation of 1-methylcyclopentanol generates an alkoxide, which reacts with crotyl bromide to give the ether, *11.90*.

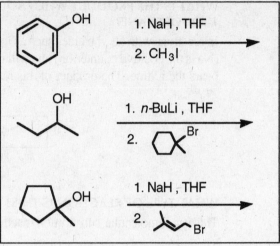

Fig. 11.87–11.89

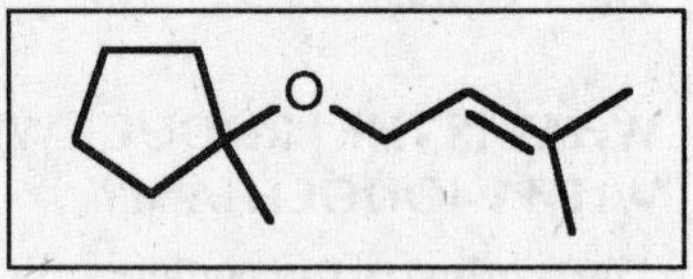

Fig. 11.90

Reaction with Acids

This chemistry was briefly introduced in the formation of alkyl halides in sections 4.2 and 4.6.

CATION FORMATION

WHAT IS THE INITIAL PRODUCT WHEN 2-METHYL-2-PENTANOL REACTS WITH HCl? WHAT IS THE FINAL PRODUCT?

The initial reaction product is an oxonium salt (*11.91*). Loss of water generates a tertiary cation (*11.92*), which traps the nucleophilic chloride (from the HCl) to form 2-chloro-2-methyl-pentane, *11.93*.

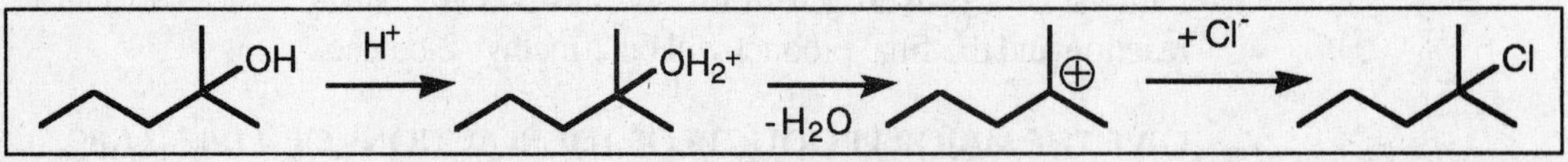

Fig. 11.91–11.93

WHAT IS THE INITIAL PRODUCT WHEN 1-BUTANOL REACTS WITH HCl? WHAT IS THE FINAL PRODUCT?

The initial product is the oxonium ion (*11.94*) but loss of water to form a primary cation is energetically unfavorable. Since water (H_2O) is a good leaving group, the nucleophilic chloride ion displaces water in an S_N^2 reaction to give the chloride, 1-chlorobutane.

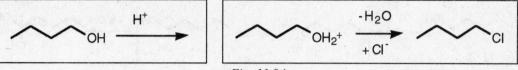

Fig. 11.94

COMPARE THE MECHANISMS OF THE REACTIONS OF 2-METHYL-2-PENTANOL AND 1-BUTANOL WITH HCl.

Formation of *11.93* generates a cation since the tertiary center helps stabilize that intermediate. In addition, the S_N^2 pathway is not possible for the tertiary center. Formation of 1-chlorobutane follows the S_N^2 pathway since displacement from a primary center is very facile and formation of a primary cation is very difficult.

REACTION WITH CARBOXYLIC ACIDS

This chemistry will be fully described with the chemistry of esters in section 15.2.

WHEN PENTANOIC ACID REACTS WITH ETHANOL IN THE PRESENCE OF A CATALYTIC AMOUNT OF SULFURIC ACID, WHAT IS THE PRODUCT?

The product is the ethyl ester of pentanoic acid, ethyl pentanoate, *11.95*.

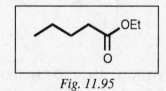

Fig. 11.95

WHAT IS THE FUNCTIONAL GROUP IN THE PRODUCT?

The functional group is the ester group, $R'CO_2R$, where R is the alcohol part of the ester and R' is the carboxylic acid part of the ester.

WHAT IS THE NAME OF THIS PRODUCT?

The name is ethyl pentanoate: ethyl from the alcohol part (ethanol) and pentanoate from the pentanoic acid fragment. The -oate ending is characteristic of esters.

GIVE THE COMPLETE MECHANISM OF THE CONVERSION OF *11.96* INTO *11.95*.

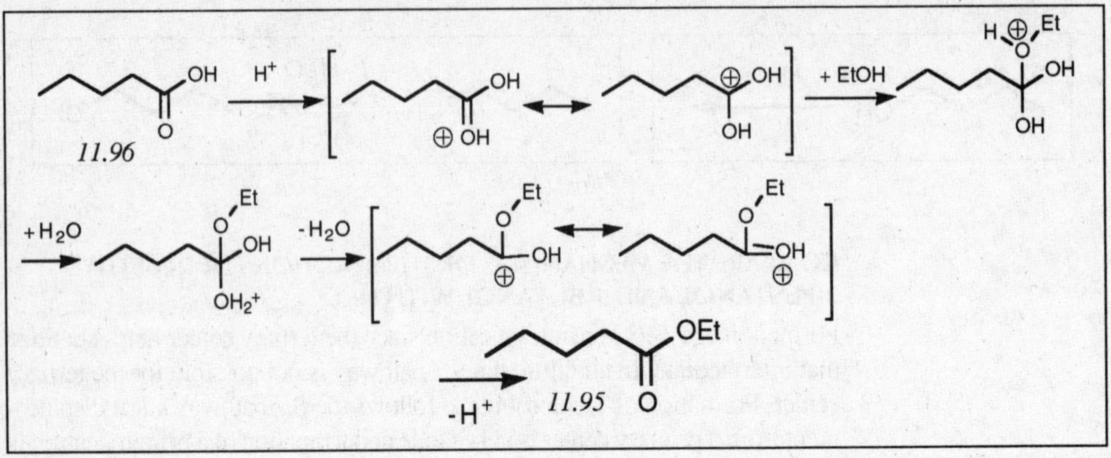

Fig. 11.96–11.95

GIVE THE MAJOR PRODUCT FOR THE REACTIONS OF *11.97* AND *11.98*.

In the first reaction, benzoic acid (*11.97*) reacts with methanol to form the ester, methyl benzoate [$PhCO_2CH_3$]. In the second reaction, 1-heptanol (*11.98*) reacts with butanoic acid to give heptyl butanoate, [$CH_3CH_2CH_2CO_2(CH_2)_6CH_3$].

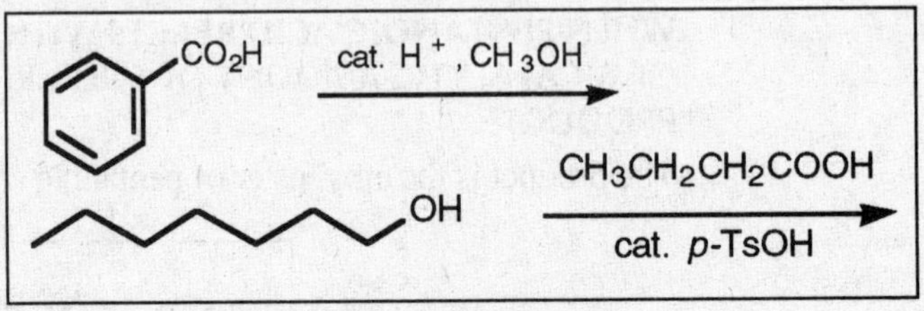

Fig. 11.97, 11.98

WHAT IS AN ACID CHLORIDE?

An acid chloride (discussed in section 9.7) contains a carbonyl and a chlorine on the carbonyl carbon (Cl–C=O). The ending is -oyl chloride. This will be discussed in greater detail in section 15.1.

WHAT IS THE REACTION PRODUCT OF PROPANOYL CHLORIDE AND ETHANOL, IN THE PRESENCE OF PYRIDINE?

The product of this reaction is ethyl propanoate [$CH_3CH_2CO_2Et$]. This chemistry will also be discussed in detail in section 15.3.

REACTION WITH SULFONYL HALIDES

WHAT IS A SULFONYL HALIDE?

A sulfonyl halide is the acid halide of a sulfonic acid. The generic structure is

RSO$_2$Cl (or Br). The name of CH$_3$SO$_2$Cl is methanesulfonyl chloride. The name of PhSO$_2$Cl is benzenesulfonyl chloride. These two sulfonyl chlorides are derived from the corresponding sulfonic acids, methanesulfonic acid (CH$_3$SO$_3$H) and benzenesulfonic acid (PhSO$_3$H).

HOW ARE SULFONYL HALIDES PRODUCED?

Sulfonyl halides are produced by the reaction of halogenating reagents such as thionyl chloride and a sulfonic acid. RSO$_3$H +SOCl$_2$ → RSO$_2$Cl.

WHAT IS THE PRODUCT WHEN BENZENESULFONYL CHLORIDE REACTS WITH 1-BUTANOL IN THE PRESENCE OF PYRIDINE?

Just as an acid chloride from a carboxylic acid reacts with an alcohol to produce an ester, a sulfonyl chloride reacts with an alcohol to produce a sulfonic ester, RSO$_2$R'. In this case the product is butyl benzenesulfonate, PhSO$_2$CH$_2$CH$_2$CH$_2$CH$_3$.

WHAT IS TOSYL CHLORIDE?

Tosyl chloride is the sulfonyl chloride, *para*-toluenesulfonyl chloride (*11.99*), derived from *para*-toluenesulfonic acid. The abbreviation for this group is Ts (TsCl for tosyl chloride).

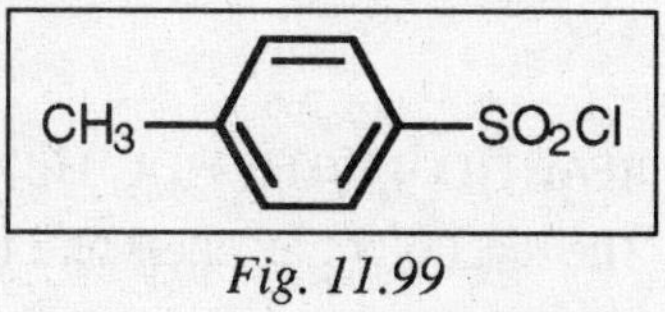

Fig. 11.99

WHAT IS A TOSYLATE?

A tosylate is the sulfonyl ester derived from *para*-toluenesulfonic acid, such as the tosylate derivative of propanol, *11.100*. [CH$_3$CH$_2$CH$_2$OTs].

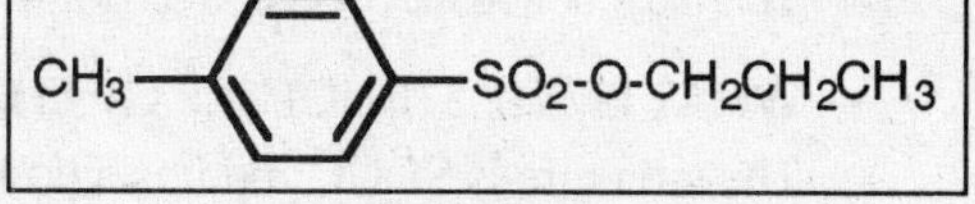

Fig. 11.100

GIVE THE MAJOR PRODUCT FOR THE REACTIONS OF *11.101–11.103*.

In the first reaction, 1-hexanol (*11.101*) reacts with benzenesulfonyl chloride to give the benzenesulfonate ester, *11.104*. Cyclohexanol (*11.102*) reacts with methanesulfonyl chloride (also called *mesyl chloride*) to give the methanesulfonate ester, *11.105* (also called a *mesylate*). In the last case, alcohol *11.103* reacts with tosyl chloride to give the tosyl ester, *11.106*. In each case, pyridine was added as a base to absorbed the HCl by-product.

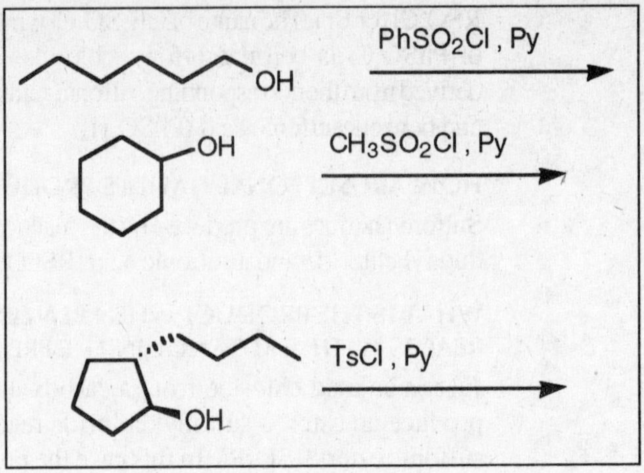

Fig. 11.101–11.103

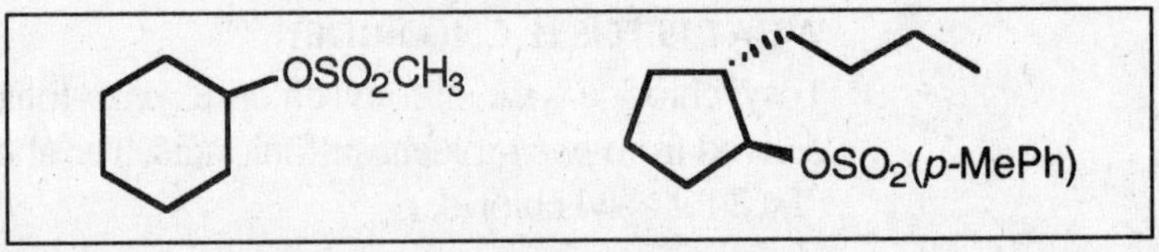

Fig. 11.104–11.106

Halogenation

REACTION WITH HCL, HBR AND HI

The reaction of alcohols and HX reagents was described in section 11.4.

WHAT IS THE PRODUCT WHEN CYCLOHEXANOL IS TREATED WITH HBr?

Cyclohexanol is converted to bromocyclohexane by reaction with anhydrous HBr.

REACTION WITH THIONYL CHLORIDE

This reagent was introduced in section 4.2.

WHAT IS THE STRUCTURE OF THIONYL CHLORIDE?

The structure is $SOCl_2$ and it is a powerful chlorinating reagent.

WHAT IS THE PRODUCT WHEN 1-BUTANOL REACTS WITH THIONYL CHLORIDE?

The product is 1-chlorobutane.

WHAT IS THE MECHANISM OF THIS REACTION?

The mechanism involves an intramolecular transfer of chlorine via a sulfinate ester intermediate (*11.107*) in what is termed an S_N^i *mechanism*. Initial reaction of the alcohol and thionyl chloride generates *11.107* with loss of HCl. Transfer of chlorine to carbon in *11.107* occurs in a *synfacial* manner (the chlorine is delivered on the same side as the oxygen) with loss of sulfur dioxide (SO_2) to give the chloride, here 1-chlorobutane.

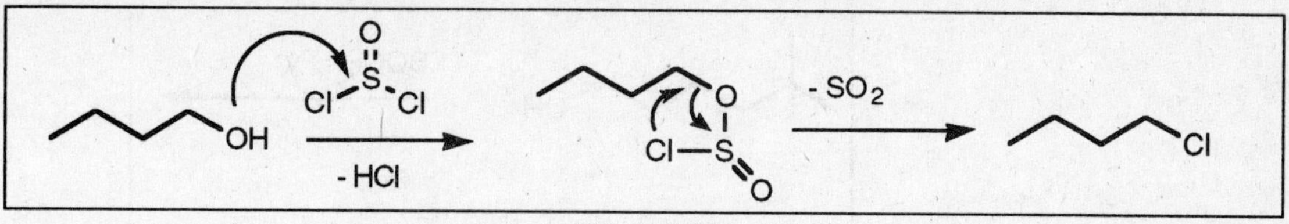

Fig. 11.107

WHY DOES THE REACTION OF R-2-PENTANOL (*11.108*) AND THIONYL CHLORIDE LEAD TO R-2-CHLOROPENTANE (*11.110*) AS THE MAJOR PRODUCT?

As mentioned above, the $S_N{}^i$ mechanism transfers chlorine to carbon on the same face as the oxygen, which is part of the SO_2 leaving group. Since the reaction is intramolecular, chlorine can approach the carbon only from that face. Reaction of R-2-pentanol (*11.108*) generates *11.109* as the intermediate and transfer of chorine from the same face retains the R-stereochemistry in the final product, *11.110*.

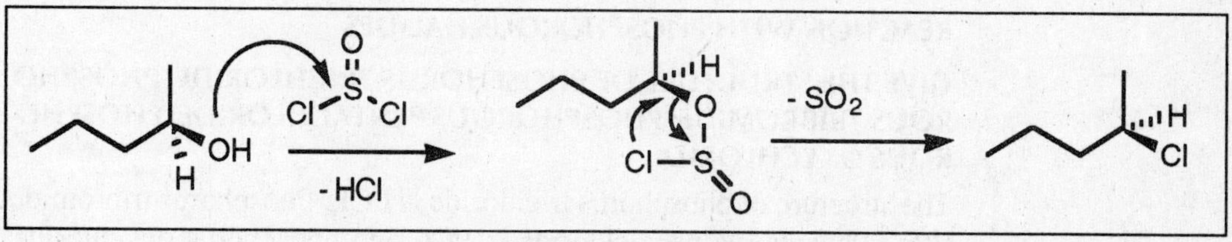

Fig. 11.108–11.110

WHY DOES THE ADDITION OF TRIETHYLAMINE TO THE REACTION OF R-2-PENTANOL AND THIONYL CHLORIDE LEAD TO S-2-CHLOROPENTANE?

Formation of *11.109* is accompanied by release of HCl, which usually escapes from the medium. If triethylamine (or another amine base) is added, HCl is trapped as triethylammonium chloride. With chloride ion present in solution, $S_N{}^2$ displacement of the SO_2Cl group is possible. Since the $S_N{}^2$ mechanism requires inversion of configuration, the R chiral center is transformed into an S chiral center.

WHAT IS THE MAJOR PRODUCT IN THE REACTIONS OF *11.111–11.114*?

Reexamination of these previously used alcohols with thionyl chloride reveals that treatment of 5-methyl 1-hexanol (*11.111*) with thionyl chloride generates 5-methyl 1-chlorohexane. Reaction of 3,3-dimethyl cyclohexan-1-ol (*11.112*) with thionyl chloride generates 3,3-dimethyl-1-chlorocyclohexane. Treatment of *11.113* with thionyl chloride, in the presence of the basic pyridine, gives chloride *11.114* with inversion of configuration at the C–OH carbon.

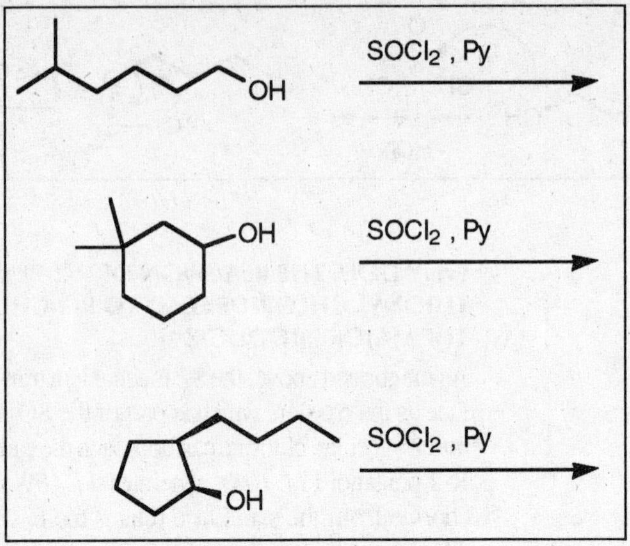

Fig. 11.111–11.114

REACTION WITH PHOSPHOROUS HALIDES

GIVE THE STRUCTURE OF PHOSPHORUS TRICHLORIDE; PHOSPHOROUS TRIBROMIDE; PHOSPHOROUS PENTACHLORIDE; PHOSPHOROUS OXYCHLORIDE.

The structure of phosphorus trichloride is PCl_3. Phosphorus tribromide is PBr_3. Phosphorus pentachloride is PCl_5 and phosphorus oxychloride is $POCl_3$.

IS PHOSGENE A PHOSPHORUS HALIDE?

No. The structure of phosgene is $COCl_2$ [Cl–(C=O)–Cl]. Phosgene is also a chlorinating reagent, however.

WHAT IS THE REACTION PRODUCT WHEN PBr₃ REACTS WITH CYCLOPENTANOL?

The major product is bromocyclopentane.

GIVE THE MAJOR PRODUCT FOR THE REACTIONS OF *11.115–11.118.*

In the first reaction, alcohol *11.115* is converted to the chloride (*11.119*) with phosphorus pentachloride. The allylic alcohol (*11.116*) is converted to the allylic chloride (*11.120*) with phosphorus trichloride. In this case, migration of the double bond leads (to form 3-chlorohept-1-ene as a minor product), presumably via an allylic cation. Reaction of alcohol *11.117* with phosphorus oxychloride leads to chloride *11.121*. Without an amine base, one might expect the stereochemistry of the chlorination to proceed with retention of configuration. With most phosphorus halides, however, the reaction proceeds with low stereoselectivity and *11.121* is a mixture of *cis*-and *trans*-isomers. In the final reaction, alcohol *11.118* is converted to bromide *11.122*.

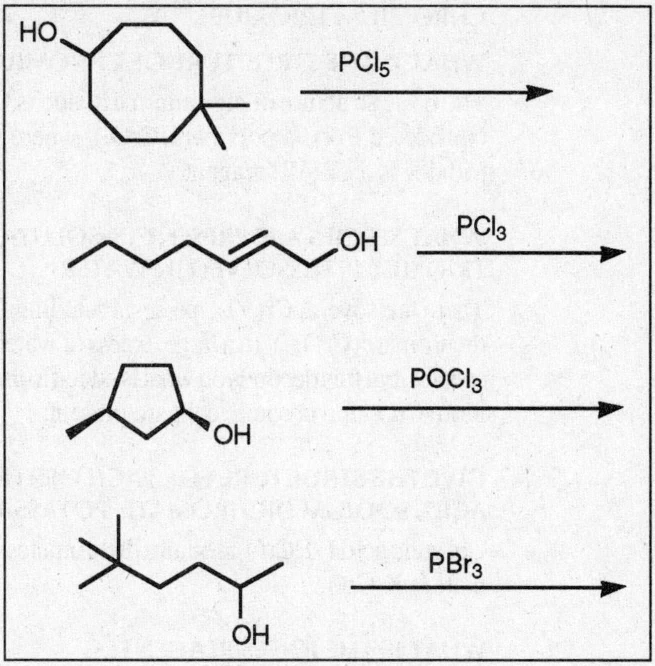

Fig. 11.115–11.118

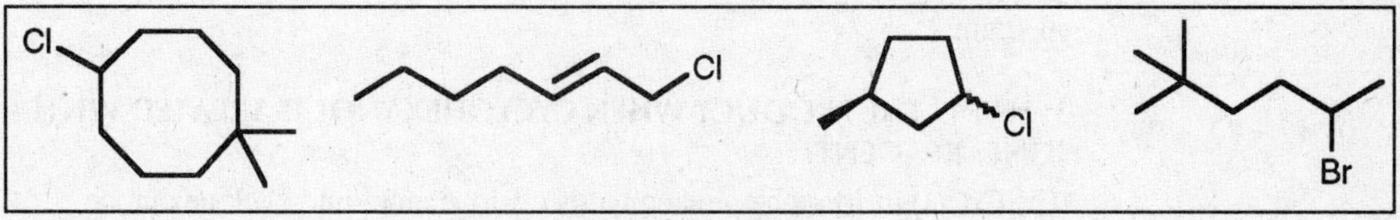

Fig. 11.119–11.122

Oxidation

WHAT IS THE DEFINITION OF AN OXIDATION?

Oxidation is the reverse of reduction and is, therefore a loss of two electrons in the course of a chemical reaction. Oxidation can also be defined as the loss of hydrogen or the gain of heteroatoms such as oxygen.

OXIDATION STATE AND OXIDATION NUMBER

WHAT IS THE CHANGE IN OXIDATION NUMBER WHEN 2-PROPANOL IS CONVERTED TO 2-PROPANONE?

As noted in section 11.3.D, the oxidation level of 2-propanol is 0 and that of 2-propanone is +2. Conversion of the alcohol to the ketone involves a $0 \rightarrow +2$ transition. Going to the more positive number indicates a decrease in electron density (a loss of two electrons).

WHY IS THIS REACTION CONSIDERED TO BE AN OXIDATION?

The reaction involves a loss of two electrons and also involves loss of two hydrogens from the alcohol.

CHROMIUM TRIOXIDE

WHAT IS THE STRUCTURE OF CHROMIUM TRIOXIDE?

The basic structure of chromium trioxide is CrO_3 but this reagent is generally considered to be a polymer, $(CrO_3)_n$ where n is a large number. Chromium trioxide is a Cr (VI) reagent.

WHAT SPECIES ARE PRESENT IN SOLUTION WHEN CHROMIUM TRIOXIDE IS DISSOLVED IN WATER?

There are several Cr(VI) species, including CrO_3, $HCrO_4$ (chromic acid) and dichromate (CrO_7^{-2}). In a large excess of water, dichromate is usually the major species, but this depends on what is added to the solution. In very dilute solutions more CrO_3 and chromic acid are present.

GIVE THE STRUCTURE FOR EACH OF THE FOLLOWING: CHROMIC ACID, SODIUM DICHROMATE, POTASSIUM DICHROMATE.

Chromic acid is $HCrO_4$; sodium dichromate is Na_2CrO_7 and potassium dichromate is K_2CrO_7.

WHAT IS THE JONES REAGENT?

Jones reagent is CrO_3 dissolved in aqueous HCl or aqueous sulfuric acid, generally with an organic solvent such as acetone. It is a powerful oxidizing medium.

WHAT IS THE PRODUCT WHEN CYCLOHEXANOL IS TREATED WITH JONES REAGENT?

The Cr(VI) in Jones reagent converts cyclohexanol into cyclohexanone.

CHROMATE ESTER FORMATION

WHAT IS THE MECHANISM FOR OXIDATION OF AN ALCOHOL TO A KETONE?

This reaction begins with reaction between the alcohol and the chromate species to give a chromate ester (*11.123*). The hydrogen β- to the chromium is now acidic and can be removed by the water that is in the system (water behaves as a base here), expelling the chromium leaving group and forming the ketone.

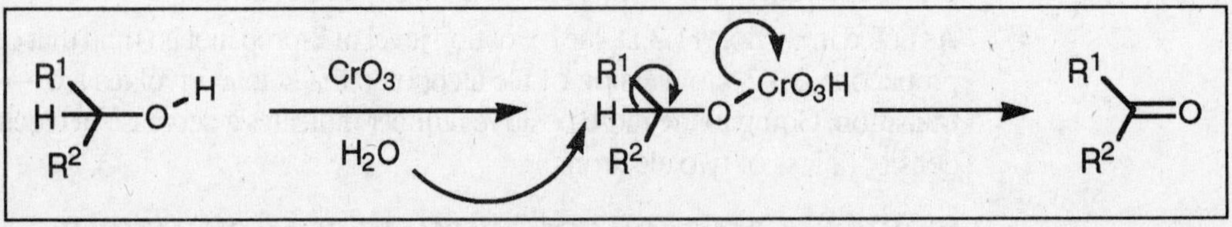

Fig. 11.123

WHAT IS THE NATURE OF A CHROMATE ESTER?

The presence of the chromium species converts CrO_nH into a good leaving group and the H–C–O–Cr moiety makes the a-hydrogen acidic.

HOW IS A CHROMATE ESTER CONVERTED TO THE KETONE?

The β-hydrogen (to the chromium atom) is removed by a base (usually water) to form a carbonyl π-bond and expel the chromium (III) species (which disproportionates) since the chromium is a good leaving group. Since acid (H_3O^+) is formed, the reaction proceeds best in acid media.

WHY IS IT NOT POSSIBLE TO OXIDIZE A TERTIARY ALCOHOL TO A KETONE?

There is no hydrogen β-to the chromate ester of this alcohol and formation of a carbonyl would require breaking a C–C bond.

WHY IS THERE A DIFFERENCE IN REACTION RATE FOR CHROMATE ESTERS *11.124* AND *11.125*?

The chromate ester in *11.124* has a hydrogen that is very difficult to approach due to steric hindrance imposed by the ring system. In *11.125* that hydrogen is relatively accessible. Since the hydrogen in *11.124* in hard to remove, the rate of oxidation is slower since that is the rate determining step.

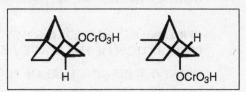

Fig. 11.124, 11.125

SECONDARY ALCOHOLS TO KETONES

GIVE THE MAJOR PRODUCTS FOR THE REACTIONS OF *11.126–11.128*.

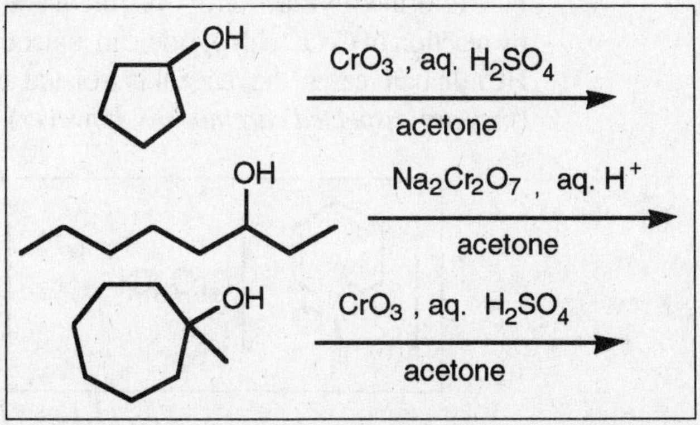

Fig. 11.126–11.128

In the first reaction, cyclopentanol (*11.126*) is converted into cyclopentanone by the Jones reagent. In the second reaction 3-octanol (*11.127*) is converted into 3-octanone and in the final example, methylcycloheptanol (*11.128*) was treated with Jones reagent. Since this is a tertiary alcohol, no oxidation takes place and the correct answer is no reaction.

PRIMARY ALCOHOLS TO ACIDS

WHAT IS THE EXPECTED PRODUCT WHEN A PRIMARY ALCOHOL IS OXIDIZED WITH CR (VI)?

A primary alcohol is expected to be oxidized into an aldehyde ($RCH_2OH \rightarrow RCHO$) but this is not the observed product.

WHAT IS THE ACTUAL PRODUCT WHEN A PRIMARY ALCOHOL IS OXIDIZED WITH CR (VI)? EXPLAIN.

The actual product isolated when a primary alcohol is oxidized with Jones reagent is usually a carboxylic acid ($RCH_2OH \rightarrow RCO_2H$). Chromium (VI) in acidic media is a powerful oxidizing medium and aldehydes are very susceptible to oxidation to acids. Indeed, many low molecular weight aldehydes are oxidized to acids by exposure to oxygen in the air. The initially formed aldehyde from the oxidation will, therefore, be further oxidized to a carboxylic acid.

PYRIDINIUM CHLOROCHROMATE AND PYRIDINIUM DICHROMATE: PREPARATION OF THE REAGENTS

WHAT IS THE STRUCTURE OF PCC? OF PDC?

Pyridinium chlorochromate (PCC, *11.129*) and pyridinium dichromate (PDC, *11.130*) are Cr (VI) reagents that have been structurally modified to diminish their oxidizing power and improve their solubility in organic solvents.

HOW ARE THESE TWO REAGENTS FORMED?

PCC is formed by reaction of CrO_3 in aqueous HCl and pyridine. PDC is formed by reaction of CrO_3 with pyridine in aqueous solution, but without addition of HCl. In both cases, the reagent is isolated and purified as crystalline material (*they are suspected carcinogens, however*).

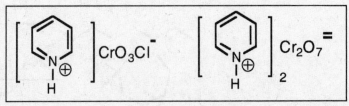

Fig. 11.129, 11.130

PRIMARY ALCOHOLS TO ALDEHYDES

WHY ARE PCC AND PDC USED RATHER THAN JONES REAGENT?

They are significantly milder oxidizing agents and will convert a primary alcohol to an aldehyde without further oxidation to the carboxylic acid. Both PCC and PDC will convert a secondary alcohol to a ketone.

WHAT IS THE PRODUCT OF THE REACTIONS OF *11.131–11.134?*

Cyclohexanol (*11.131* is oxidized to cyclohexanone with PCC. 1-Hexanol (*11.132*) is oxidized to the aldehyde (hexanal) with PCC. PDC will oxide benzyl alcohol (*11.133*) to benzaldehyde. 3-Methyl-3-octanol (*11.134*) is a tertiary alcohol and PCC and PDC will not oxidize this alcohol. The answer here is no reaction. In all cases, the reactions are performed at 25°C using dichloromethane as a solvent. These are typical reaction conditions.

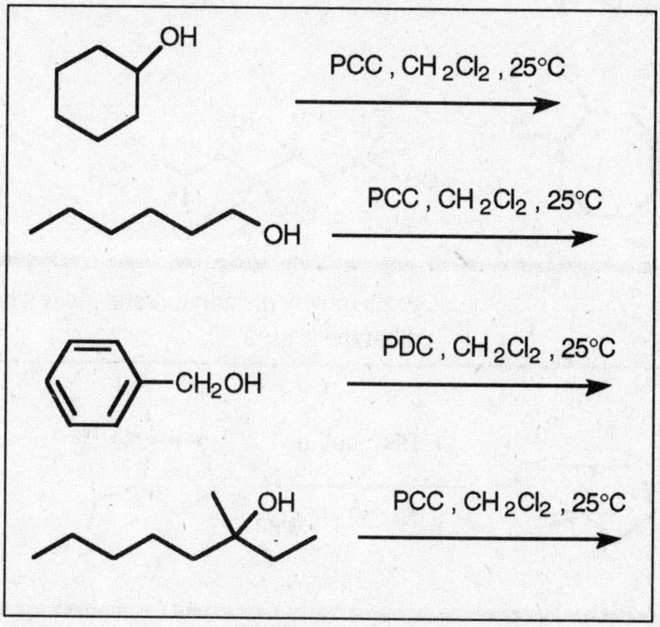

Fig. 11.131–11.134

*I*t is clear from this chapter that alcohols generate the widest range of reactions encountered so far. Many functional groups that were only briefly alluded to in previous chapters have now been discussed in detail. As mentioned, alcohols will appear in most of the remaining chapters and the chemistry and mechanisms presented here will also surface many times.

END OF CHAPTER PROBLEMS

1. Which of the following is likely to have the higher boiling point. Explain: (a) pentene (b) 1-pentanol (c) dodecane (d) dodecanol.
2. The lipophilic character of many drugs is measured against its relative solubility in an octanol/water mixture. Why is the choice of octanol an appropriate one?
3. Give the IUPAC name for each of the following.

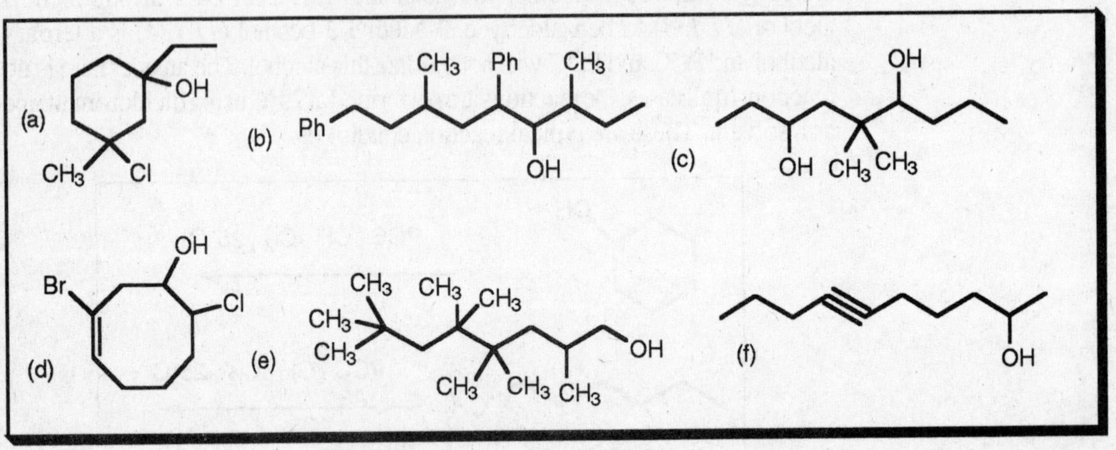

4. Explain why disiamylborane gives a higher percentage of A than when diborane is used.

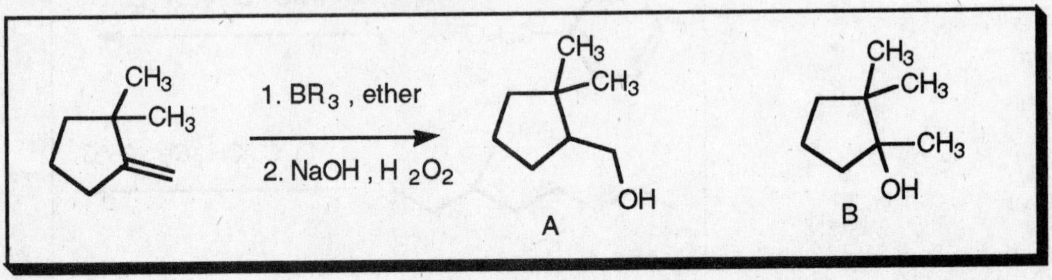

5. Which of the following reactions can be classified as reductions. Calculate the oxidation number of each reactive carbon and determine the net electron change.

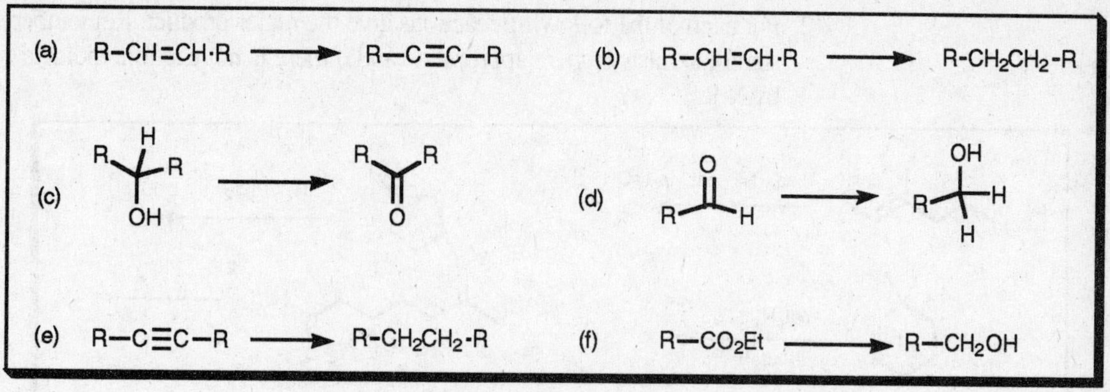

(a) $R-CH=CH \cdot R \longrightarrow R-C \equiv C-R$

(b) $R-CH=CH \cdot R \longrightarrow R-CH_2CH_2-R$

(c) [structure: R-CH(OH)-R → R-C(=O)-R]

(d) [structure: R-CHO → R-CH₂OH]

(e) $R-C \equiv C-R \longrightarrow R-CH_2CH_2 \cdot R$

(f) $R-CO_2Et \longrightarrow R-CH_2OH$

6. Give the mechanism for the following reaction.

[reaction: cyclohexanone + Na°, NH₃ (no ethanol) → cyclohexanol]

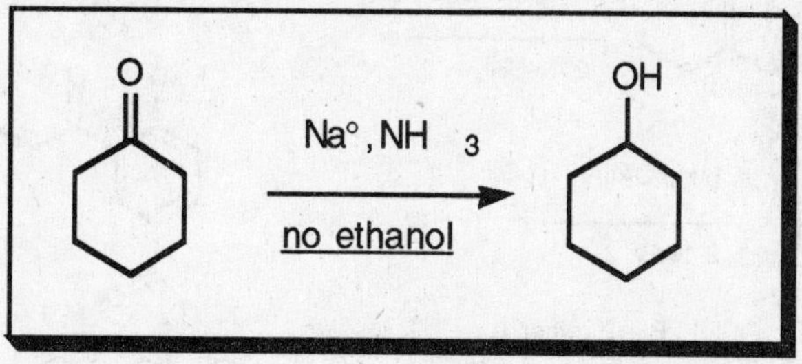

7. Which is the most acidic alcohol: methanol of *t*-butanol? Explain.
8. Is the sodium salt of 2-propen-1-ol resonance stabilized? Explain.
9. Explain why methyl *t*-butyl ether $[CH_3OC(CH_3)_3]$ cannot be formed from 2-methyl-2-iodopropane and ethanol using a Williamson ether synthesis.
10. Give the complete mechanism for the following reaction.

[reaction: methyl hexanoate + H₃O⁺ → hexanoic acid + MeOH]

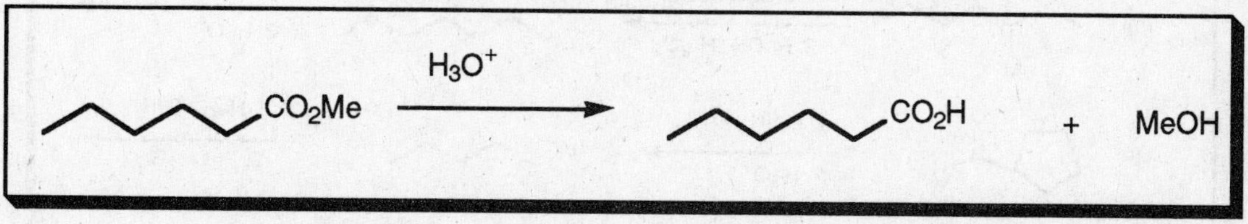

11. Explain why alcohol A is oxidized much slower than alcohol B.

[structures: A is 2,2,4,4-tetramethyl-3-pentanol; B is 2-pentanol]

A   B

12. For each of the following reactions give the major product. Remember stereochemistry where appropriate and if there is no reaction, indicate by N.R.

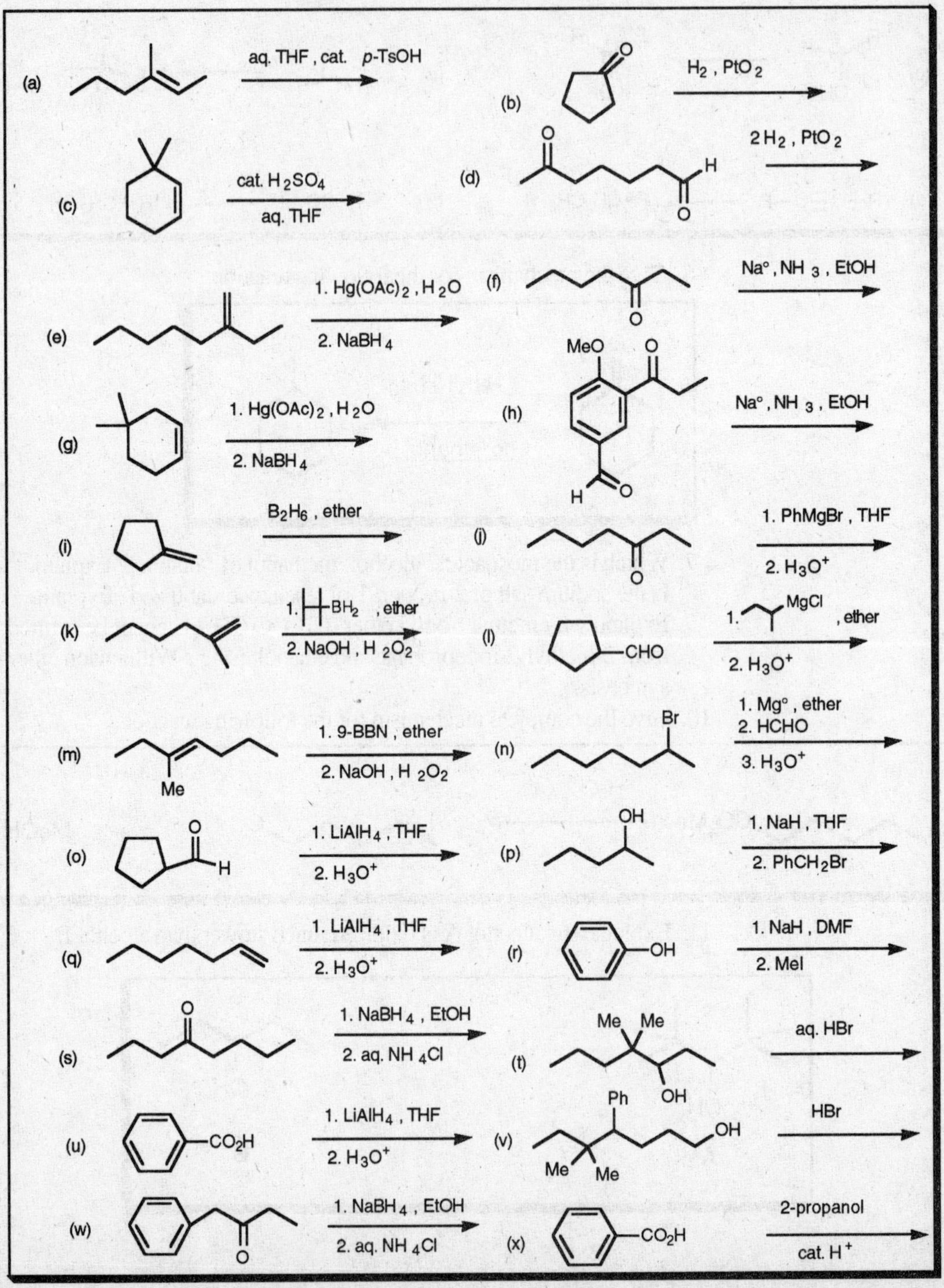

(a) [structure: branched alkene]   aq. THF , cat. *p*-TsOH →

(b) [cyclopentanone]   H₂ , PtO₂ →

(c) [1,1-dimethylcyclohexene]   cat. H₂SO₄ / aq. THF →

(d) [diketoaldehyde]   2 H₂ , PtO₂ →

(e) [branched alkene with exocyclic double bond]   1. Hg(OAc)₂ , H₂O   2. NaBH₄ →

(f) [ketone]   Na° , NH₃ , EtOH →

(g) [dimethylcyclohexene]   1. Hg(OAc)₂ , H₂O   2. NaBH₄ →

(h) [aromatic with MeO, ketone, CHO]   Na° , NH₃ , EtOH →

(i) [methylenecyclopentane]   B₂H₆ , ether →

(j) [ketone]   1. PhMgBr , THF   2. H₃O⁺ →

(k) [branched alkene]   1. H–BH₂ , ether   2. NaOH , H₂O₂ →

(l) [cyclopentane-CHO]   1. [MgCl reagent] , ether   2. H₃O⁺ →

(m) [alkene with Me]   1. 9-BBN , ether   2. NaOH , H₂O₂ →

(n) [alkyl bromide]   1. Mg° , ether   2. HCHO   3. H₃O⁺ →

(o) [cyclopentanecarbaldehyde]   1. LiAlH₄ , THF   2. H₃O⁺ →

(p) [2-butanol]   1. NaH , THF   2. PhCH₂Br →

(q) [terminal alkene]   1. LiAlH₄ , THF   2. H₃O⁺ →

(r) [phenol]   1. NaH , DMF   2. MeI →

(s) [ketone]   1. NaBH₄ , EtOH   2. aq. NH₄Cl →

(t) [Me Me branched alcohol]   aq. HBr →

(u) [PhCO₂H]   1. LiAlH₄ , THF   2. H₃O⁺ →

(v) [Ph, Me Me branched diol]   HBr →

(w) [Ph-CH₂-C(O)-Et]   1. NaBH₄ , EtOH   2. aq. NH₄Cl →

(x) [Ph-CO₂H]   2-propanol / cat. H⁺ →

(y)

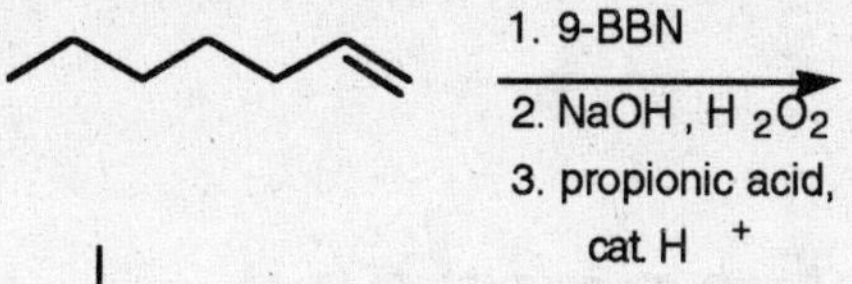

1. 9-BBN
2. NaOH , H$_2$O$_2$
3. propionic acid, cat. H$^+$

(z)

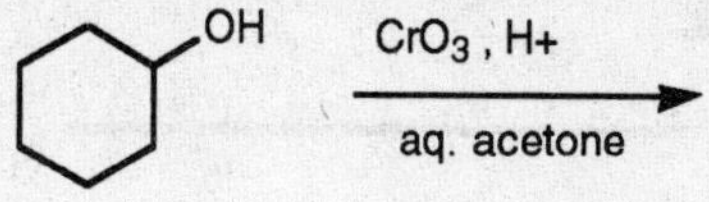

CrO$_3$, H+

aq. acetone

(aa)

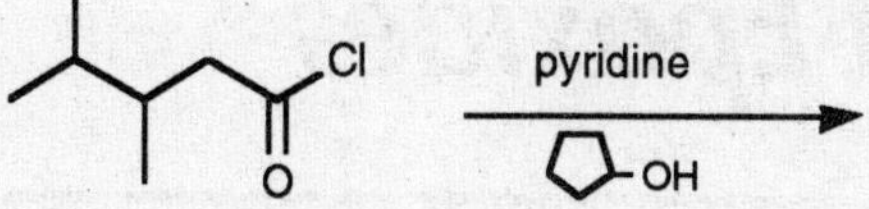

pyridine

⬠-OH

(ab)

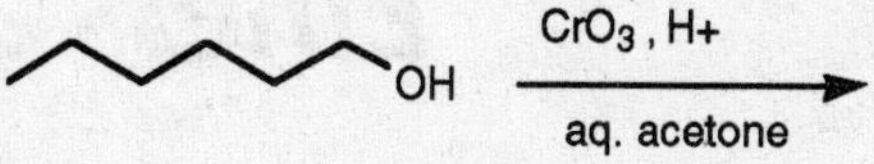

CrO$_3$, H+

aq. acetone

(ac)

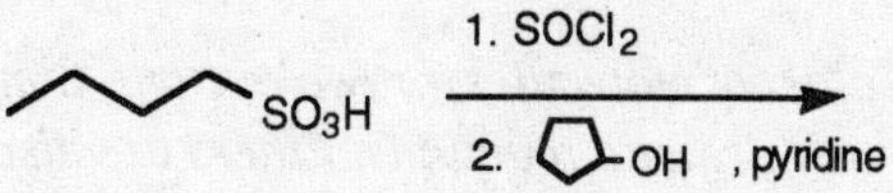

1. SOCl$_2$
2. ⬠-OH , pyridine

(ad)

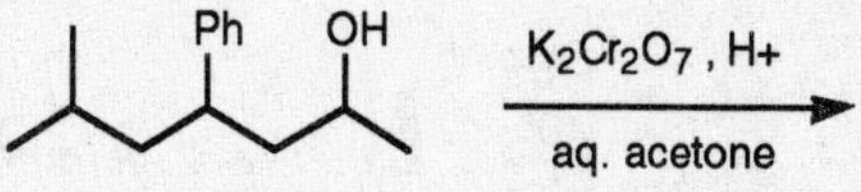

K$_2$Cr$_2$O$_7$, H+

aq. acetone

(ae)

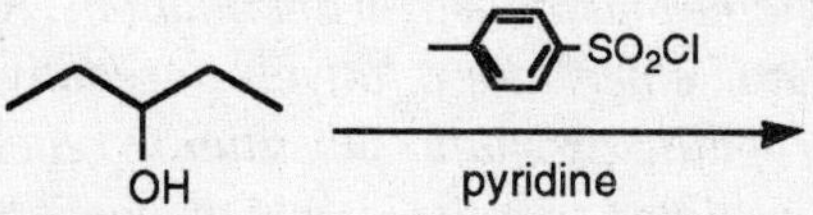

⬡-SO$_2$Cl

pyridine

(af)

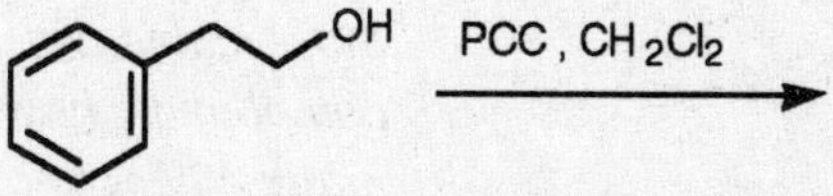

PCC , CH$_2$Cl$_2$

(ag)

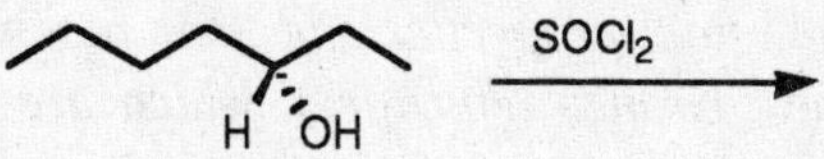

SOCl$_2$

(ah)

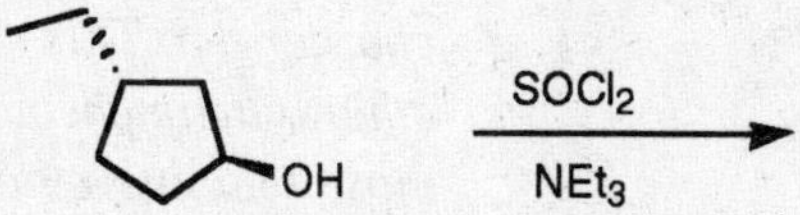

SOCl$_2$

NEt$_3$

(ai)

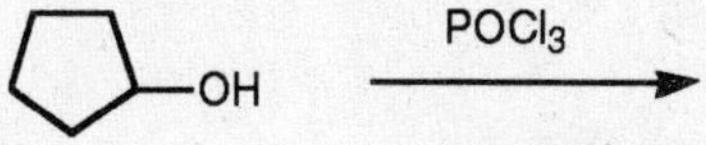

POCl$_3$

(aj)

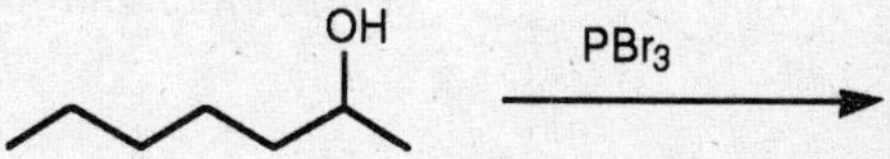

PBr$_3$

(ak)

PCl$_5$

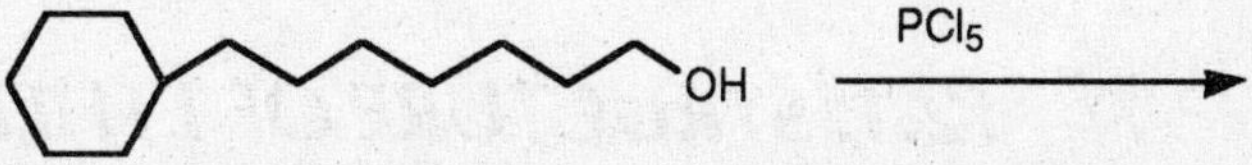

12

Ethers and Epoxides

Ethers are an important class of molecules for two reasons. Simple ethers are used as solvents in many organic reactions. Ethers are also found as structural components of many naturally occurring molecules as well as those molecules used in medicine and industrial applications. As a class of compounds, however, aliphatic ethers are relatively unreactive, but aromatic ethers undergo electrophilic aromatic substitution reactions. Aromatic ethers are chemically related to anisole, which was introduced in chapter ten. This chapter will discuss the various methods of preparing ethers, their chemical and physical properties and their reactions. The most reactive ethers are the oxiranes (epoxides), which are common compounds and highly useful in chemical transformations.

12.1. STRUCTURE OF ETHERS

WHAT IS AN ETHER?

An ether is a molecule containing an oxygen but it does not have the OH for C=O functional groups.

WHAT FUNCTIONAL GROUP IS ASSOCIATED WITH AN ETHER?

The functional group associated with an ether is the C–O–C moiety.

Alkyl Ethers

WHAT IS AN ALKYL ETHER?

An alkyl ether is an ether with two alkyl groups on either side of the oxygen (R–O–R^1).

GIVE TWO DIFFERENT EXAMPLES OF ALKYL ETHERS.

Two examples are ethylmethyl ether ($CH_3CH_2OCH_3$) and diethyl ether ($CH_3CH_2OCH_2CH_3$).

WHAT IS THE STRUCTURE OF TETRAHYDROFURAN?

Tetrahydrofuran is a cyclic ether where the oxygen is part of a five-membered ring (*12.1*). This is also called oxolane.

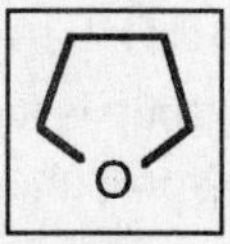

Fig. 12.1

GIVE EXAMPLES OF CYCLIC ETHERS IN A FOUR-MEMBERED RING, SIX-MEMBERED RING AND SEVEN-MEMBERED RING.

The four-membered ring ether is oxetane (*12.2*), the six membered ring ether is oxane (also called tetrahydropyran, *12.3*) The seven membered ring ether is *12.4*.

Fig. 12.2–12.4

Aryl Ethers

WHAT IS AN ARYL ETHER?

An aryl ether has an aryl group as at least one of the carbon groups attached to oxygen.

GIVE TWO DIFFERENT EXAMPLES OF ARYL ETHERS.

Two examples are anisole ($PhOCH_3$) and diphenyl ether (PhOPh).

GIVE TWO DIFFERENT EXAMPLES OF ARYLALKYL (ARALKYL) ETHERS.

The term "Aralkyl" ether is used to describe an ether with one aryl group and one alkyl group, as in anisole. Another example is phenylpropyl ether ($PhOCH_2CH_2CH_3$).

12.2. NOMENCLATURE

WHAT IS THE BASIC ENDING ASSOCIATED WITH AN ETHER?

Ethers are usually named as "ethers" or as alkoxy derivatives.

NAME THE FOLLOWING COMPOUNDS USING THE 'ETHER' NOMENCLATURE SYSTEM.

a) $CH_3CH_2CH_2CH_2OCH_2CH(CH_3)_2$ b) $PhOC(CH_3)_3$ c) $(CH_3)_2CHCHOCH_2CH_3$

Ether (a) is named butyl isobutyl ether as a common name or 1-butyl-3-methylpropylether. Ether (b) is phenyl *t*-butyl ether or phenyl 1,1,-dimethylethyl ether. Ether (c) is ethyl isopropyl ether or ethyl 1-methylethyl ether.

DESCRIBE THE 'ALKOXY' NOMENCLATURE SYSTEM FOR ETHERS.

The RO group is an alkoxy group. $ROCH_2CH_2CH_3$ could, therefore, be called a 1-alkoxypropane.

NAME THE FOLLOWING COMPOUNDS USING THE 'ALKOXY' NOMENCLATURE SYSTEM.

a)$CH_3CH_2CH_2CH_2OCH_2CH(CH_3)_2$ b)$PhOC(CH_3)_3$ c)$(CH_3)_2CHCHOCH_2CH_3$

Ether (a) is 1-butoxy-3-methylpropane. Ether (b) is 1-phenoxy-1,1,-dimethylethane and (c) is 1-ethoxy-1-methylethane.

Note that the IUPAC names for the cyclic ethers (oxetane, oxolane and oxane, were given above.

12.3. PREPARATION OF ETHERS

There are two main preparation of ethers, the Williamson ether synthesis (see section 11.4) and alkoxymercuration (see sections 5.5 and 11.3).

Williamson Ether Synthesis

WHAT IS THE MAJOR PRODUCT WHEN 1-BUTANOL IS TREATED FIRST WITH NaH AND THEN WITH IODOMETHANE?

The product is butoxide ($CH_3CH_2CH_2CH_2O^- Na^+$).

DESCRIBE A SYNTHETIC ROUTE TO ETHYL T-BUTYL ETHER FROM MOLECULES CONTAINING FOUR CARBONS OR LESS.

The synthesis requires the use of *t*-butanol and its conversion to an alkoxide (with NaH), followed by reaction with bromoethane (iodoethane is more reactive) to give the product, *12.5*. It is not possible to begin with ethanol and make sodium ethoxide since the subsequent reaction with the tertiary halide will give elimination rather than substitution.

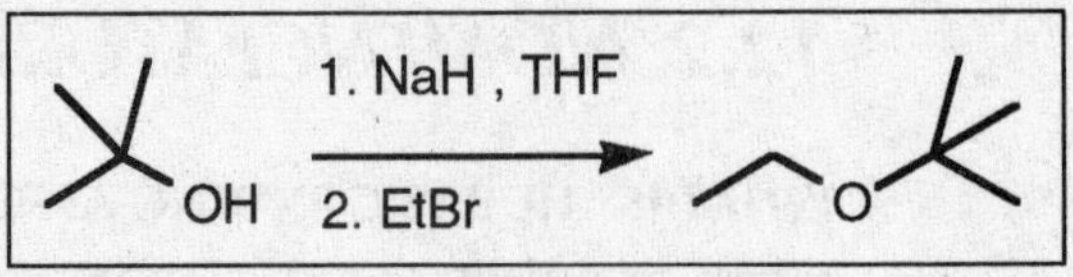

Fig. 12.5

IS IT POSSIBLE TO PREPARE ETHERS VIA AN S_N^1 MECHANISM? IF SO GIVE AN EXAMPLE.

Yes, it is possible. If *t*-butanol is treated with a catalytic amount of acid in ethanol solvent, the initially formed tertiary cation (*12.6*) can react with ethanol to give *12.7*. Subsequent loss of a proton from this oxonium intermediate gives ethyl *t*-butyl ether, *12.5*.

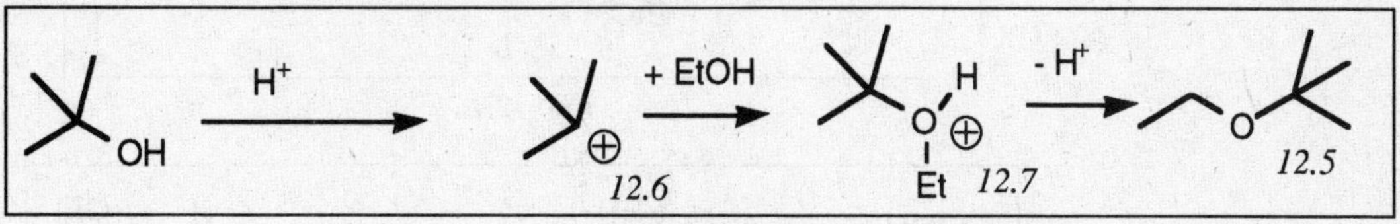

Fig. 12.6, 12.7

WHAT IS THE PRODUCT WHEN 4-BROMOBUTANOL IS TREATED WITH NaH IN ETHER?

Reaction of chlorohydrin *12.8* with NaH will form the alkoxide, *12.9*. This initially formed alkoxide will react with the bromide at the end of the molecule in an intramolecular Williamson ether synthesis to give tetrahydrofuran.

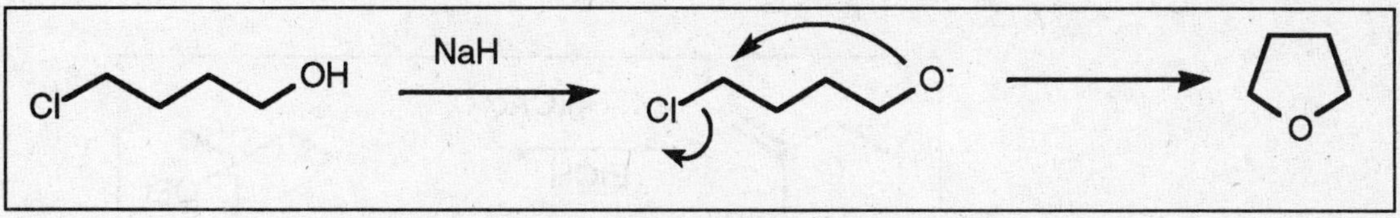

Fig. 12.8–12.9

REDUCTION OF 5-CHLOROPENTANAL (*12.10*) WITH SODIUM BOROHYDRIDE MAY PRODUCE A SMALL AMOUNT OF A BY-PRODUCT OTHER THAN THE EXPECTED 5-CHLOROPENTANOL. WHAT IS THIS MINOR PRODUCT AND HOW IS IT FORMED?

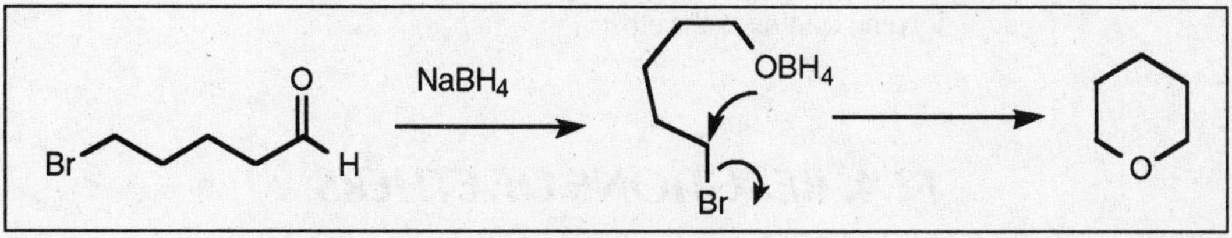

Fig. 12.10, 12.11

Initial reduction of the aldehyde will generate an alkoxide (*12.11*), which can react with the terminal chloride to give tetrahydropyran as a by-product by the Williamson ether reaction. Since the product *12.11* is not a completely ionic alkoxide but is bound to the boron, the oxygen is not as nucleophilic, accounting for only a small amount of this ether by-product.

Alkoxymercuration **DRAW THE PRODUCT WHEN 1-PENTENE IS TREATED WITH MERCURIC ACETATE IN ETHANOL.**

The initial product is the mercuric cation (*12.12*) which reacts with the only available nucleophile (ethanol) to produce the ethoxy product, *12.13*. Treatment with $NaBH_4$ leads to the final product, 2-ethoxypentane (*12.14*).

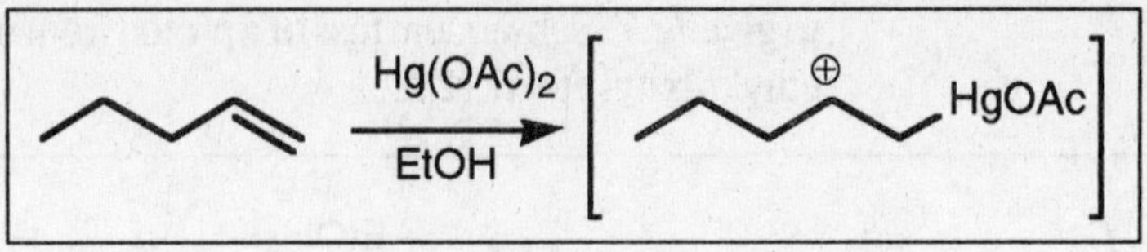

Fig. 12.12

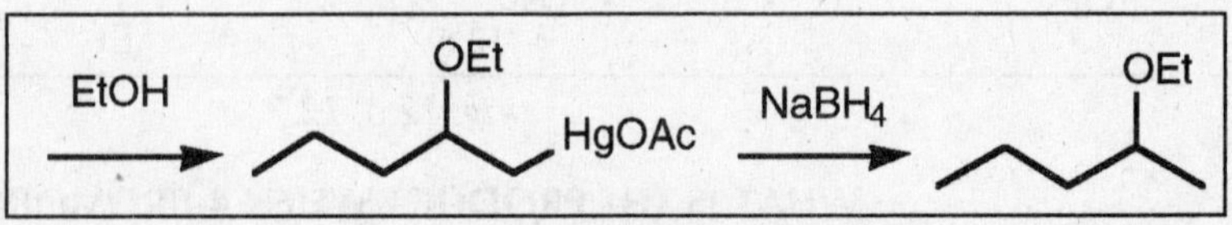

Fig. 12.13, 12.14

DRAW THE PRODUCT WHEN 2-METHYL-1-BUTENE IS TREATED FIRST WITH MERCURIC ACETATE IN ETHANOL AND THEN WITH NABH₄.

The product is the result of attack by ethanol at the tertiary carbon, giving ether *12.15*.

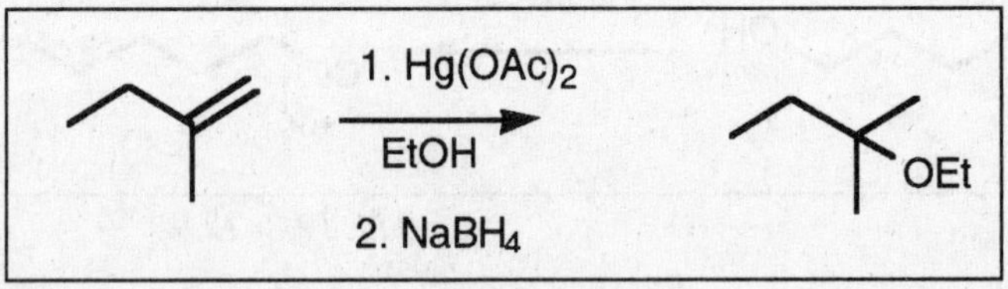

Fig. 12.15

WHY DOES THIS PROCESS LEAD TO AN ETHER RATHER THAN AN ALCOHOL (AS WITH OXYMERCURATION)?

The only nucleophilic species provided to the cation intermediate is the alcohol solvent, leading to the ether.

12.4. REACTIONS OF ETHERS

Ethers give only a limited number of reactions, as described below.

Alkyl Ethers

CLEAVAGE WITH ACID

WHAT IS THE REACTION PRODUCT WHEN DIETHYL ETHER IS TREATED WITH HYDROIODIC ACID (HI)?

The powerful acid HI cleaves diethyl ether into ethanol and iodoethane.

GIVE A MECHANISTIC RATIONALE FOR HOW AN ALKYL ETHER IS CLEAVED BY ACID.

The reaction occurs by protonation of the ether oxygen to give an oxonium ion such as *12.16* (the ether oxygen is basic in the presence of the powerful acid).

The nucleophilic iodide counterion attacks the less sterically hindered carbon, displacing ethanol and forming iodoethane.

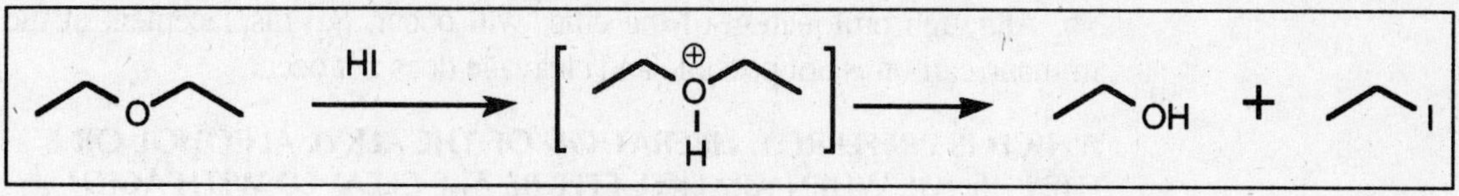

Fig. 12.16

WHAT IS THE PRODUCT WHEN METHYL ISOPROPYL ETHER (*12.17*) IS TREATED WITH HI?

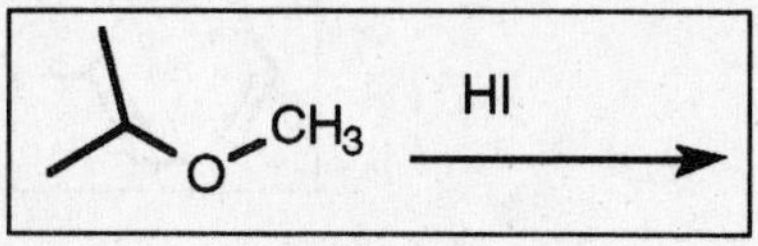

Fig. 12.17

The products are isopropanol and iodomethane. The oxygen of *12.17* is protonated to give *12.18*. Iodide attacks the less sterically hindered carbon in an S_N^2 displacement, as shown, to give the product. Very little attack at the secondary carbon is observed.

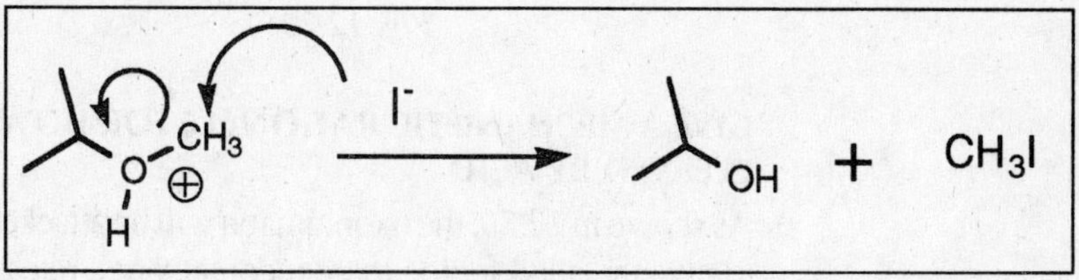

Fig. 12.18

WHAT ACID OR ACIDS ARE CAPABLE OF CLEAVING ALKYL ETHERS?

Very few protonic acids are strong enough to cleave ethers. Hi is the most common. Relatively strong Lewis acids will also cleave ethers. The most commonly used reagent is boron tribromide, BBr_3.

LEWIS BASICITY

IF AN ALKYL ETHER IS A BASE, IS IT A STRONG BASE OR A WEAK BASE?

Ethers are relatively weak Lewis bases, requiring strong Lewis acids for a reasonable reaction.

WHAT ACIDS WOULD BE STRONG ENOUGH TO PROTONATE AN ETHER?

HI is the most common and any acid stronger than HI would also protonate an ether.

Aryl and Aralkyl Ethers

CLEAVAGE WITH ACID

IS DIPHENYL ETHER CLEAVED WITH HI?

No. Although protonation of the ether will occur, S_N^2 displacement at the aromatic carbon is not possible and cleavage does not occur.

WHICH IS PREFERRED, LIBERATION OF THE ALKYL ALCOHOL OR THE PHENOL WHEN ARALKYL ETHERS ARE CLEAVED WITH ACID?

An alkyl aryl ether will be protonated (as anisole, *12.19*, gives *12.20*) but attack by iodide is possible only at the alkyl fragment. This cleavage will always liberate the phenol and an alkyl iodide.

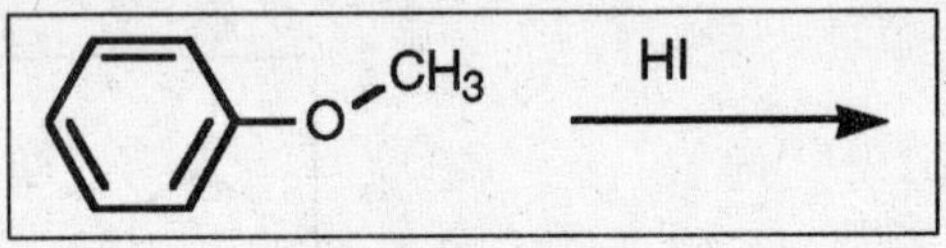

Fig. 12.19

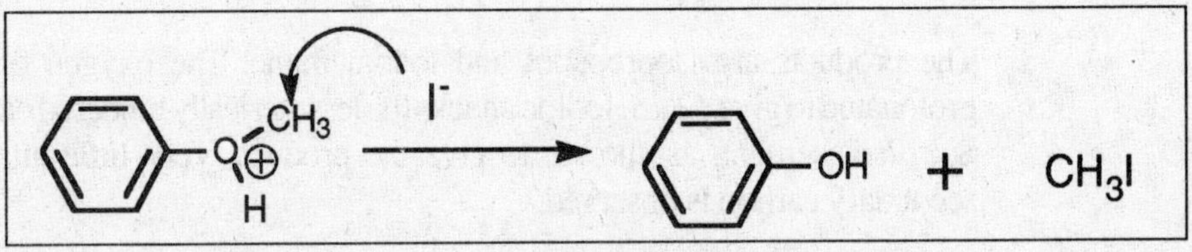

Fig. 12.20

GIVE A MECHANISTIC RATIONALE FOR HOW AN ARALKYL ETHER IS CLEAVED BY ACID.

As shown in *12.20*, the oxonium ion will be attacked only at the alkyl fragment to give the alkyl iodide (here iodomethane), releasing the aromatic hydroxyl derivative (here, phenol).

GIVE THE MAJOR PRODUCT OR PRODUCTS OF THE REACTIONS OF 12.21–12.23.

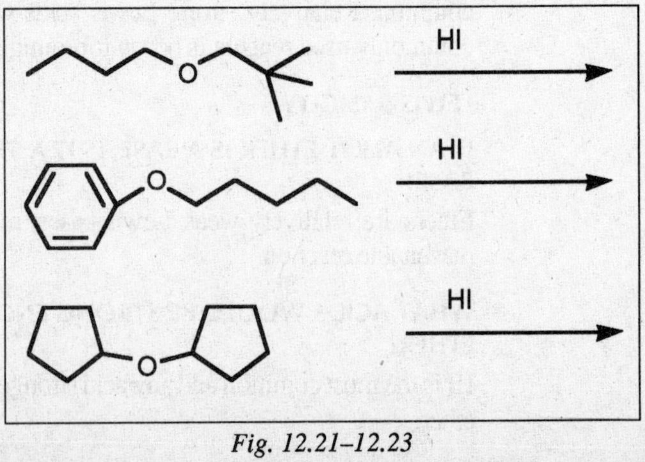

Fig. 12.21–12.23

Cleavage of ether *12.21* will give neopentyl alcohol (2,2-dimethyl-1-propanol) and iodobutane. Nucleophilic attack at the neopentyl carbon (adjacent to the tertiary center) is too sterically hindered for the S_N^2 process. In the second reaction, ether *12.22* is cleaved to give phenol and iodopentane. In the last reaction, dicyclopentyl ether (*12.23*) is cleaved to one molecule of cyclopentanol and one molecule of iodocyclopentane.

ELECTROPHILIC AROMATIC SUBSTITUTION

This chemistry was described in chapter nine (section 9.5).

GIVE THREE DIFFERENT EXAMPLES OF AROMATIC ETHERS CAPABLE OF UNDERGOING ELECTROPHILIC AROMATIC SUBSTITUTION.

Anisole ($PhOCH_3$), phenetole ($PhOCH_2CH_3$) and phenyl *t*-butyl ether $[PhOC(CH_3)_3]$ will all undergo electrophilic aromatic substitution with a variety of reagents.

WHAT IS THE PRODUCT (OR PRODUCTS) WHEN PHENYL ETHYL ETHER REACTS WITH BROMINE AND FERRIC BROMIDE?

As discussed in section 9.5, bromination of phenyl ethyl ether (phenetole) leads to a mixture of 2-bromophenetole and 4-bromophenetole.

Reduction

WHAT IS THE PRODUCT WHEN DIETHYL ETHER IS TREATED WITH LiAlH₄?

There is no reaction. Ethers are not reactive with $LiAlH_4$ (an exception will be the epoxides discussed in section 12.5). Ethers are generally used as solvents in $LiAlH_4$ reductions.

WHAT IS THE PRODUCT WHEN DIETHYL ETHER IS TREATED WITH HYDROGEN AND A PALLADIUM CATALYST?

Diaryl and most alkyl ethers are unreactive with catalytic hydrogenation and this gives no reaction.

WHAT IS THE PRODUCT WHEN ETHYL BENZYL ETHER IS TREATED WITH HYDROGEN AND A PALLADIUM CATALYST?

Benzyl ethers are particularly reactive and cleavage of the C–O bond (adjacent to the benzyl group) is facile with palladium catalyzed hydrogenation. This reaction is generically referred to as *hydrogenolysis*. In this case the products are toluene and ethanol:

$$CH_3CH_2OCH_2Ph + H_2 \text{ (Pd catalyst)} \rightarrow CH_3CH_2OH + CH_3Ph$$

12.5. EPOXIDES

Three membered ring ethers are special cases. The three-membered ring is highly strained, making these compounds significantly more reactive than other cyclic ethers.

Structure and Bonding

DESCRIBE THE HYBRIDIZATION IN A THREE-MEMBERED RING ETHER.

The hybridization of an epoxide is similar to that of cyclopropane. The sigma bonds are weaker than sp^3 hybrids and stronger than sp^2 hybrids. These bonds are usually said to have $sp^{2.33}$ hybridization.

WHY IS A THREE-MEMBERED RING ETHER EXPECTED TO BE MORE REACTIVE THAN OTHER CYCLIC ETHERS?

The strain inherent to a three-membered ring makes the electron density between the nuclei (the σ-bond) distort to a position away from the line between the nuclei. There is less electron density between the nuclei and the bond is weaker.

'BENT' BONDS

WHY ARE THE SIGMA BONDS OF A THREE-MEMBERED RING CONSIDERED TO BE 'BENT'?

As described above, the strain of the three-membered ring makes the σ-bonds "bend" away from the line between the nuclei. This leads to "bent" bonds (sometimes called "banana bonds"), as shown in *12.24*. This leads to the idea of $sp^{2.33}$ hybridization.

Fig. 12.24

WHAT EFFECT DOES THIS HAVE ON THE RELATIVE STRENGTH OF THE SIGMA BOND?

Since there is less electron density between the nuclei, the bonds are significantly weaker.

Nomenclature

The generic name of three-membered ring ethers is 'epoxides'. An epoxide can be named by three nomenclature systems.

THE 'EPOXY' NOMENCLATURE

Epoxides can be named as an 'epoxy' alkane. The epoxide formed from 1-pentene, for example, is known as 1,2-epoxypentane.

GIVE THE NAME OF EACH OF *12.25–12.27*.

The name of *12.25* is 4-chloro-1-cyclopentyl-1,2-epoxyhexane. Epoxide *12.26* is 1,2-epoxycyclohexane. Epoxide *12.27* is called 1,4-diphenyl-1,2-epoxyhexane.

THE 'OXIDE' NOMENCLATURE

Epoxides can also be named as oxides when the alkene is named with one of the common names: ethylene, styrene, propylene, etc. The epoxide derived from ethylene is then called ethylene oxide. This nomenclature system is considered to be a 'common name'. The simplest alkene (ethylene) is a precursor for the simplest epoxide (oxirane), called ethylene oxide.

GIVE THE NAMES FOR *12.25–12.27* BY THIS SYSTEM.

Epoxide *12.25* is 4-chloro-1-cyclopentyl-1-hexene oxide; *12.26* is cyclohexene oxide; *12.27* is 1,4-diphenyl-1-hexene oxide.

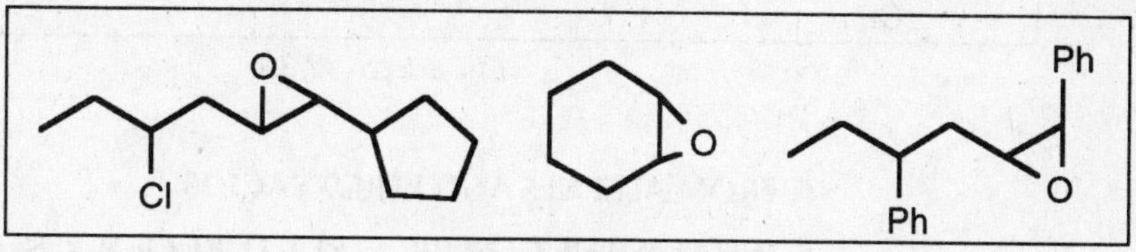

Fig. 12.25–12.27

THE 'OXIRANE' NOMENCLATURE

The epoxide derived from ethene (ethylene oxide) is given the IUPAC name oxirane. It is, therefore, reasonable to name epoxides as oxirane derivatives. The epoxide derived from 1-propene is called 1-methyloxirane.

GIVE THE NAME OF *12.25–12.27* USING THE IUPAC NOMENCLATURE.

Epoxide *12.25* is 1-cyclopentyl-2-(2-chlorobutyl)oxirane; *12.26* is 1,2-tetramethyleneoxirane; *12.27* is 1-phenyl-2-(2-phenylbutyl)oxirane.

Preparation

Epoxides are generally prepared by two synthetic routes, from halo alcohols and from alkenes.

S_N^2 FROM CHLOROHYDRINS

WHAT IS A CHLOROHYDRIN?

A chlorohydrin is a molecule containing both a chlorine and an alcohol in the same molecule.

HOW IS 2-CHLORO-1-BUTANOL FORMED FORM 1-BUTENE?

Reaction of 1-butene with hypochlorous acid (HOCl—see section 5.5) leads to this chlorohydrin, *12.28*.

GIVE A MECHANISTIC EXPLANATION OF HOW TREATMENT OF 2-CHLORO-1-BUTANOL (*12.28*) WITH NaH LEADS TO 1-ETHYLOXIRANE (*12.30*).

When *12.28* is treated with the base (NaH), alkoxide *12.29* is formed. An intramolecular S_N^2 displacement of the chloride leads to the epoxide, *12.30*. This is another example of an intramolecular Williamson ether synthesis.

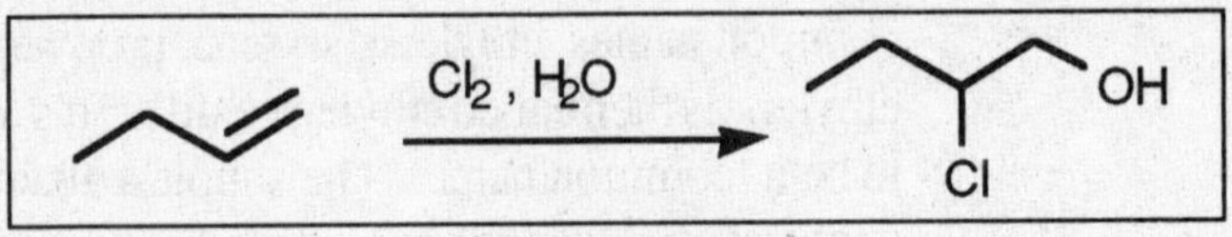

Fig. 12.28

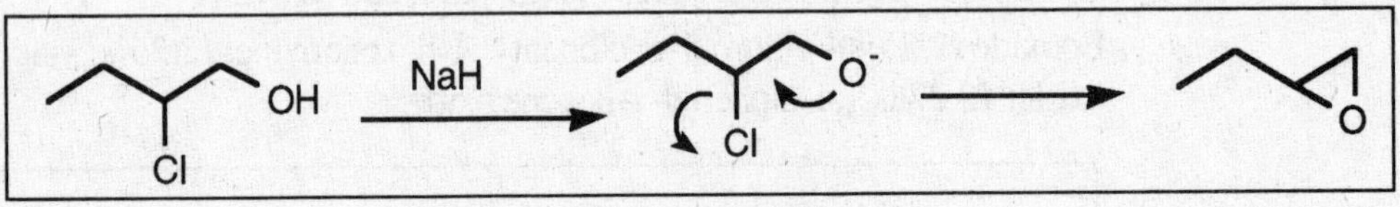

Fig. 12.28–12.30

FROM ALKENES AND PEROXYACIDS

WHAT IS THE GENERIC STRUCTURE OF A PEROXY ACID?

A peroxy acid has the generic formula RCO_3H and is characterized by a R–(C=O)–OOH unit.

HOW ARE PEROXYACIDS NAMES?

The word peroxy is added to the front of the carboxylic acid name (either the IUPAC name or the common name). Formic acid becomes peroxyformic acid, benzoic acid becomes peroxybenzoic acid, butanoic acid becomes peroxybutanoic acid and acetic acid becomes peroxyacetic acid.

WHAT IS THE PRODUCT WHEN CYCLOPENTENE REACTS WITH PEROXYBENZOIC ACID?

The products are the epoxide (cyclopentene oxide) and the carboxylic acid, benzoic acid.

GIVE A MECHANISTIC RATIONALE FOR CONVERSION OF CYCLOPENTENE TO THE EPOXIDE WITH PEROXYBENZOIC ACID.

The bond polarization of the peroxyacid is such that the 'second' oxygen from the carbonyl is electrophilic ($\delta^\oplus$) and is attacked by the electrons in the π-bond of cyclopentene. There is no intermediate and this reaction is thought to proceed by a concerted mechanism involving transition state *12.31*. In this transition state, the alkene attacks the electropositive oxygen, transfers the hydrogen to the oxygen of the peroxyacid. Synchronous bond breaking leads to formation of the second bond of the epoxide (*12.32*) and expulsion of benzoic acid, the by-product. In this reaction, part of the driving force for the reaction is loss of the leaving group, benzoic acid. This is a generic mechanism in that alkenes attack the electropositive oxygen of a peroxyacid, form the epoxide and expel the corresponding carboxylic acid.

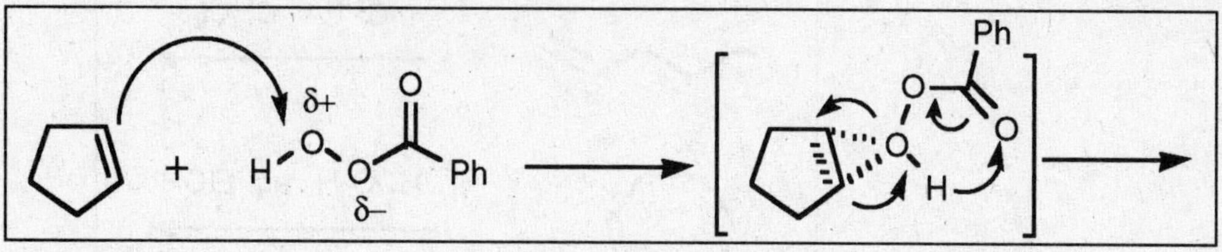

Fig. 12.31

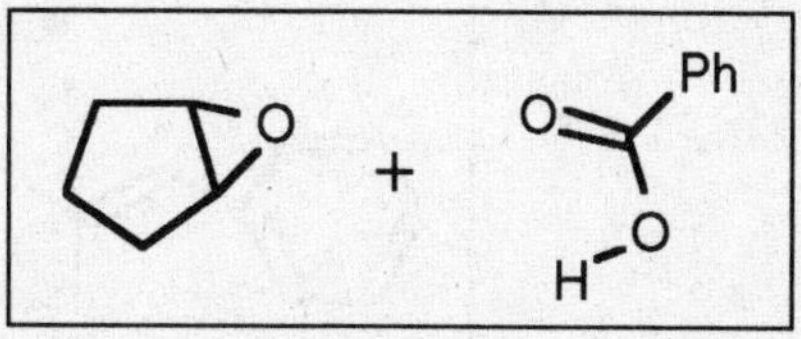

Fig. 12.32

EXPLAIN WHY PEROXY ACIDS REACT FASTER WITH MORE HIGHLY SUBSTITUTED ALKENES THAN WITH LESS SUBSTITUTED ALKENES.

The initial reaction involves attack of the alkene π-bond on the electropositive oxygen of the peroxyacid. The more electron density in that π-bond, the faster the reaction. Since carbon substituents are electron releasing, more highly substituted alkenes are richer in electron density and react faster.

WHAT IS THE STRUCTURE OF META-CHLOROBENZOIC ACID AND WHY IS IT A POPULAR CHOICE FOR EPOXIDATIONS?

The structure is *12.33*. It is popular because it is commercially available, a crystalline solid that is readily purified, stable to storage and gives *meta*-chlorobenzoic acid which is usually easily removed from the product.

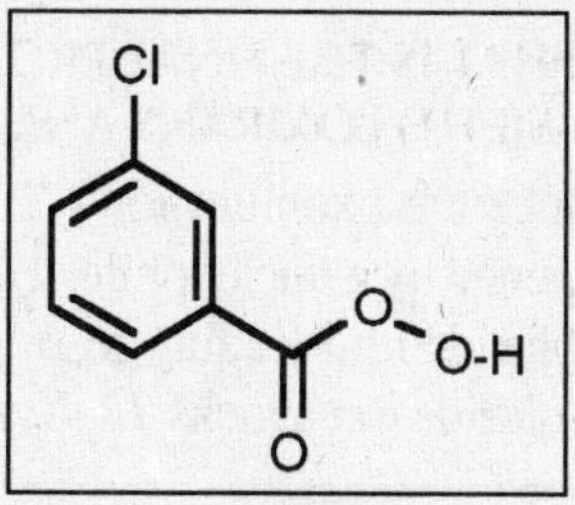

Fig. 12.33

GIVE THE MAJOR PRODUCT FOR THE REACTIONS OF *12.34–12.36*.

Epoxidation of 1-hexene with *m*-chloroperoxybenzoic acid give 1-hexene oxide (*12.37*). Epoxidation of cycloheptene gives cycloheptene oxide (*12.38*) and epoxidation of *12.36* leads to the epoxide *12.39*.

Reactions

Epoxides are highly strained molecules and react with a variety of reagents. The most common reactions involve opening the three-membered ring with acid or with a nucleophile and reduction with various reducing agents.

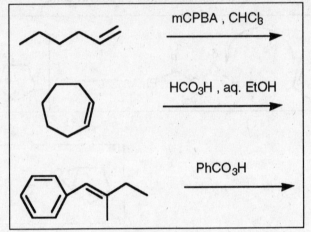

mCPBA , CHCl3
HCO3H , aq. EtOH
PhCO3H

Fig. 12.34–12.36

O
O
O

Fig. 12.37–12.39

ACID CATALYZED RING OPENING

WHAT IS THE INITIAL PRODUCT WHEN 1-METHYLOXIRANE REACTS WITH HCl?

As with any other ether, an oxirane reacts with HCl to form an oxonium ion, in this case, *12.40*.

WHAT IS THE FINAL PRODUCT OF THE REACTION OF 1-METHYLOXIRANE AND HCl?

Once the oxonium ion (*12.40*) is formed, the three-membered ring will be opened by a nucleophile. The only available nucleophile in this reaction is the chloride ion, leading to ring opening and formation of chlorohydrin *12.41*. Chloride ion attacks *12.40* at the least sterically hindered carbon.

CH3
O
HCl
H
⊕
O
CH3
Cl-
OH
CH3
Cl

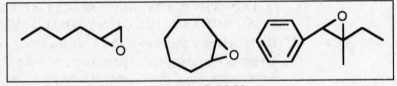

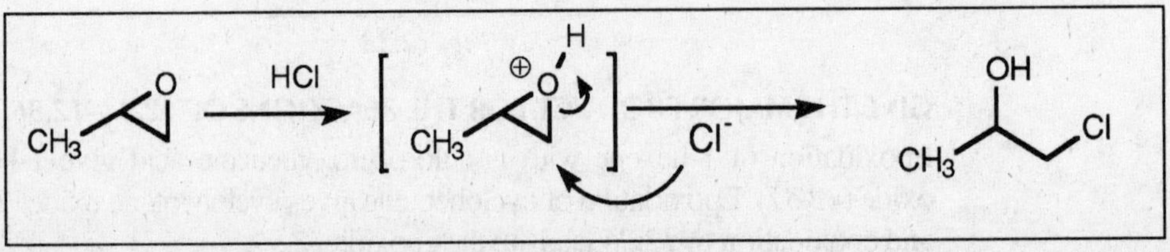

Fig. 12.40, 12.41

WHY DOES THIS REACTION FAVOR OPENING THE THREE-MEMBERED RING?

The highly strained three-membered ring is converted to an oxonium ion, making the "OH" unit an excellent leaving group. The combination of these two facts makes opening the epoxide by even weak nucleophiles very favorable.

NUCLEOPHILIC RING OPENING

Since the carbon atoms of an epoxide are electrophilic, reaction with various nucleophilic reagents is facile.

COMMON NUCLEOPHILES

WHAT IS THE PRODUCT WHEN 1-METHYLOXIRANE REACTS WITH SODIUM HYDROXIDE?

It is not necessary to first protonate the ether oxygen to induce ring opening. Epoxides are sufficiently strained that reaction with good nucleophiles give the ring opened product. In this case, 1-methyloxirane is opened by hydroxide to give the diol, 1,2-propanediol, *12.42*, after hydrolysis. The nucleophile attacks the least sterically hindered carbon in what is essentially an S_N^2 process.

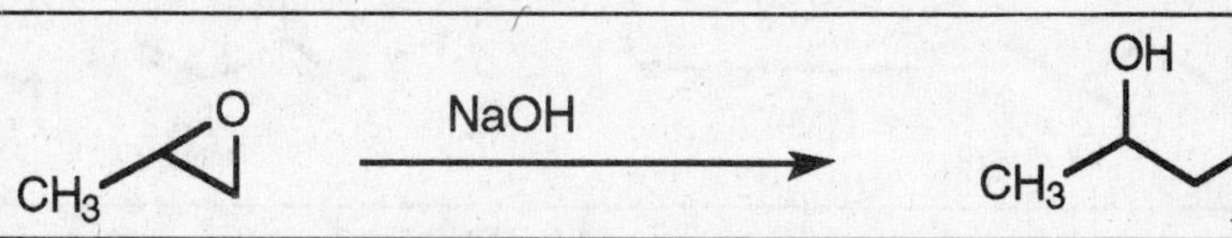

Fig. 12.42

EXPLAIN WHY THE REACTION IS HIGHLY REGIOSELECTIVE FOR THE LESS SUBSTITUTED CARBON OF THE EPOXIDE.

If this reaction is an S_N^2 process, the transition state for the less sterically hindered carbon is lower in energy than that for the more highly substituted carbon.

WHAT IS THE PRODUCT WHEN CYCLOHEXENE EPOXIDE REACTS WITH: A) NaN₃ B) NaCN C) NaI D) SODIUM ACETYLIDE E) Na C≡C–ET?

The first reaction generates the azido alcohol (*12.43*). Reaction with cyanide give the cyanohydrin, *12.44*. Iodide opens the epoxide ring to give the iodohydrin, *12.45*. Acetylide is a powerful nucleophile and the anion derived from acetylide gives *12.46* whereas that derived from 1-butyne gives *12.47*.

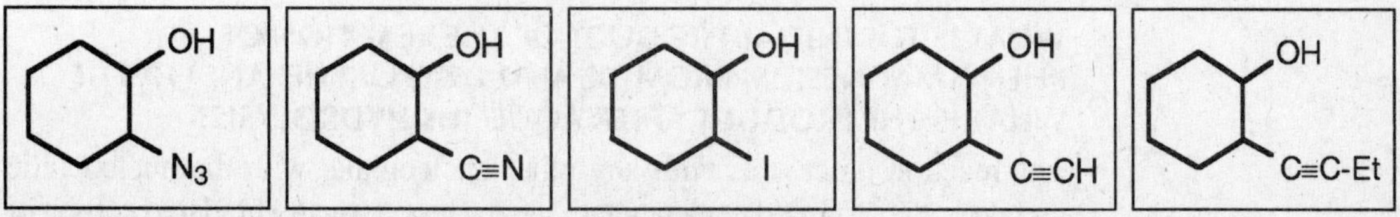

Fig. 12.43–12.47

WHY ARE THE REACTIONS OF EPOXIDES AND CYANIDE OR ACETYLIDE DERIVATIVES PARTICULARLY IMPORTANT?

In both cases a new carbon-carbon bond is formed in one of the few reactions capable of forming a C–C bond. This is important since the synthesis of a molecular target relies on constructing the carbon skeleton by a series of carbon-carbon bond forming reactions.

WHAT IS THE PRODUCT OR PRODUCTS WHEN SODIUM CYANIDE REACTS WITH 2,3-EPOXYHEXANE (*12.48*)? EXPLAIN.

The cyanide will attack the less sterically hindered carbon of the epoxide if given a 'choice'. In this case, *12.48* has a similar substitution pattern at each carbon and there is little difference between methyl and propyl. In such cases, a mixture of two products is expected from attack at both carbons of the epoxide. In this reaction the two products are cyanohydrins *12.49* and *12.50*. There may be a slight preference for *12.49* since the methyl group is slightly smaller than the propyl.

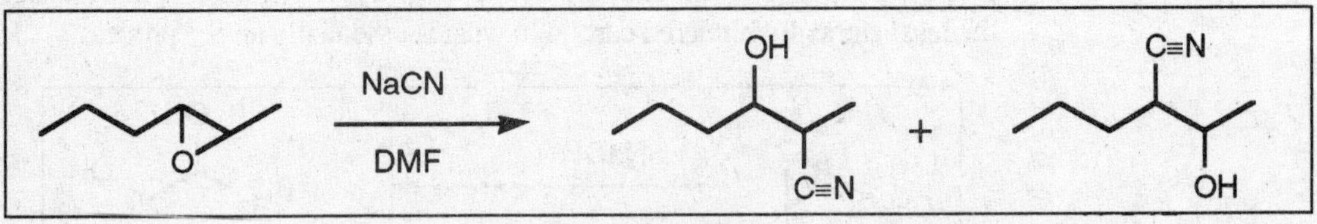

Fig. 12.48–12.50

WHAT SOLVENTS ARE MOST FAVORED FOR NUCLEOPHILIC RING OPENING REACTIONS WITH EPOXIDES?

Since this is considered to be an S_N^2 process, polar aprotic solvents such as ether, THF, DMSO or DMF are the most commonly used.

REACTION WITH GRIGNARD REAGENTS

The formation and general reactivity of Grignard reagents is discussed in sections 4.7 and 11.3.

EXPLAIN WHY A GRIGNARD REAGENT SHOULD REACT WITH AN EPOXIDE.

A Grignard reagent is a source of nucleophilic carbon. This nucleophilic carbon will attack and open the electropositive carbon of an epoxide, generally at the less sterically hindered site.

WHAT IS THE INITIAL PRODUCT OF THE REACTION OF PHENYLMAGNESIUM BROMIDE AND 1,2-EPOXYHEXANE (*12.51*)? WHAT IS THE PRODUCT AFTER AQUEOUS HYDROLYSIS?

The reaction process as with any other nucleophile, with the nucleophilic carbon of the Grignard reagent attacking the less sterically hindered carbon of the epoxide (*12.51*) to give an alkoxide. Hydrolysis gives 1-phenyl-3-hexanol, *12.52*.

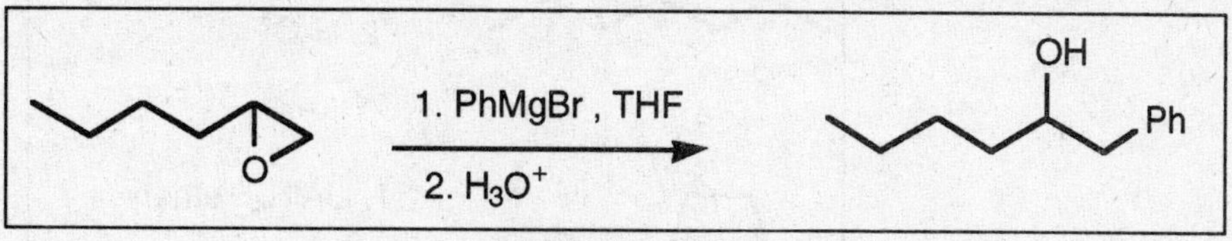

Fig. 12.51, 12.52

WHAT IS THE PRODUCT (OR PRODUCTS) WHEN 3,4-EPOXYHEPTANE (*12.53*) REACTS WITH ETHYLMAGNESIUM IODIDE?

As with other nucleophiles, ethyl magnesium iodide will react at both electropositive carbons of *12.53*. Both carbons are equally substituted and the result will be a roughly equal mixture of two alcohols, 3-ethyl-4-heptanol (*12.54*) and 4-ethyl-3-heptanol (*12.55*).

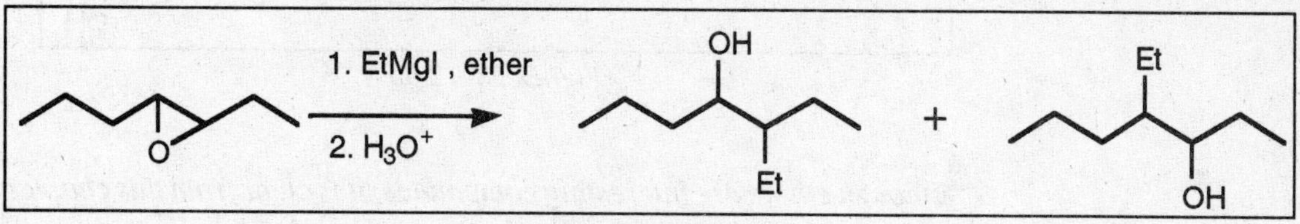

Fig. 12.53–12.55

HYDRIDE REDUCTION

It is also possible to reduce an epoxide and generate an alcohol. See section 11.3.

WHAT IS THE MAJOR PRODUCT WHEN 1,2-EPOXYCYCLOHEXANE IS TREATED FIRST WITH LiAlH₄ AND THEN WITH DILUTE AQUEOUS ACID?

In this reaction, the hydride reagent behaves as a 'nucleophile' delivering the "H⁻" to the less substituted carbon of the epoxide. When this symmetrical epoxide is reduced, the product is cyclohexanol.

EXPLAIN WHY 'HYDRIDE' IS GENERALLY DELIVERED TO THE LESS SUBSTITUTED CARBON OF THE EPOXIDE.

In the four-centered transition state required for reaction of LiAlH₄ with the electropositive carbon of the epoxide, the hydride will be delivered to the less sterically hindered carbon so that all steric interactions are minimized.

GIVE THE MAJOR PRODUCT FOR THE REACTIONS OF *12.56* AND *12.57*.

In the first reaction, epoxide *12.56* is reduced to a mixture of 2-heptanol (*12.58*) and 3-heptanol (*12.59*) due to the lack of a less substituted carbon on the epoxide. Reduction of *12.57* shows the expected delivery of hydride to the less substituted carbon, forming 1-cyclopentyl-1-ethanol, *12.60*.

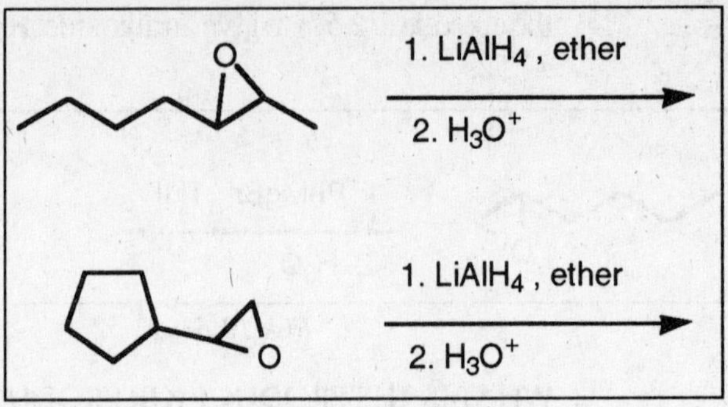

Fig. 12.56, 12.57

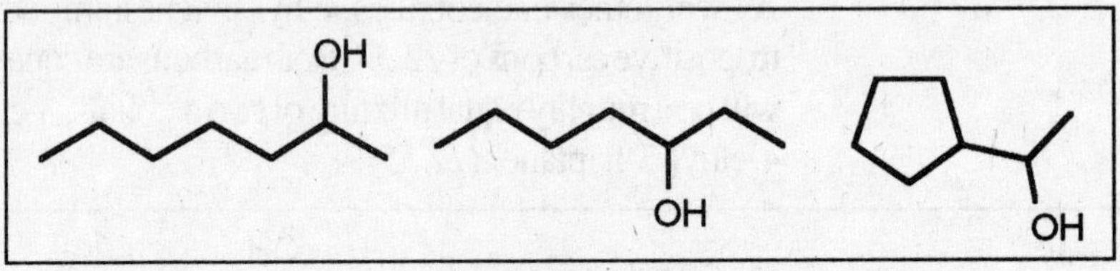

Fig. 12.58–12.60

Although ethers are interesting compounds, it is clear from this chapter that the most chemically useful ethers are the epoxides. Epoxides will appear in other chapters as one functional group is transformed into another. The most common occurrence of ethers, however, will be the use of diethyl ether or tetrahydrofuran as solvents.

END OF CHAPTER PROBLEMS

1. Give the correct IUPAC names for each of the following.

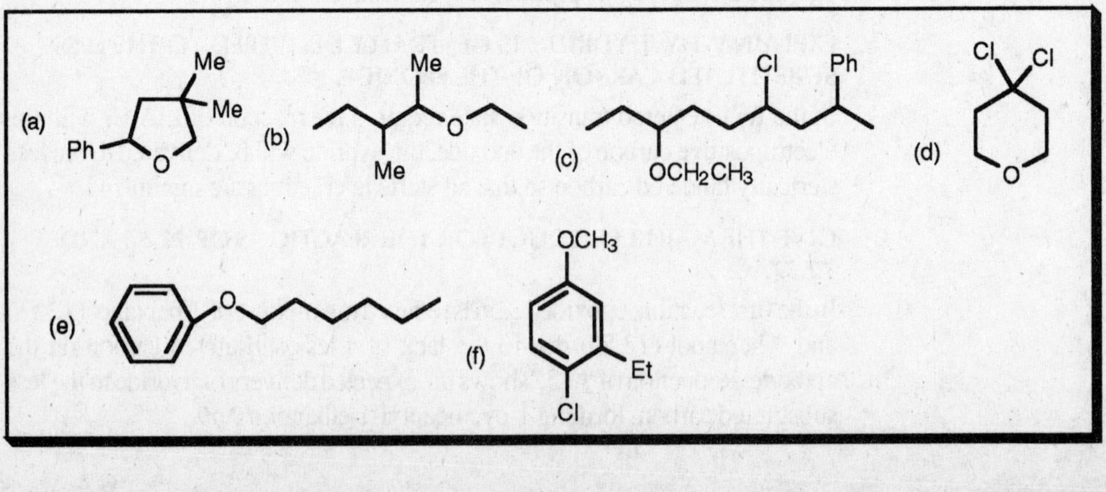

2. Give the complete mechanism for the following reaction.

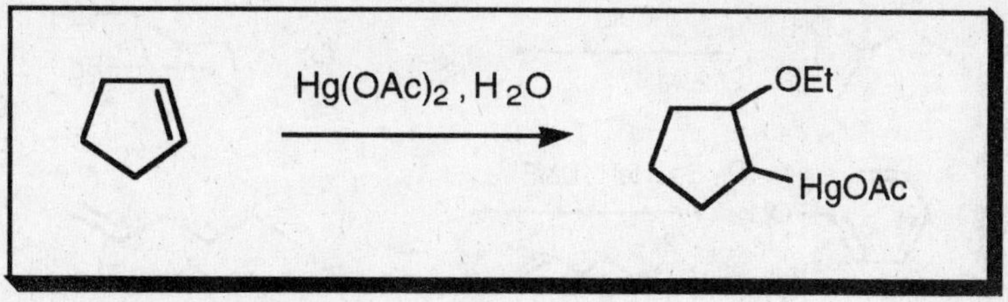

3. What is the product of this reaction? Explain.

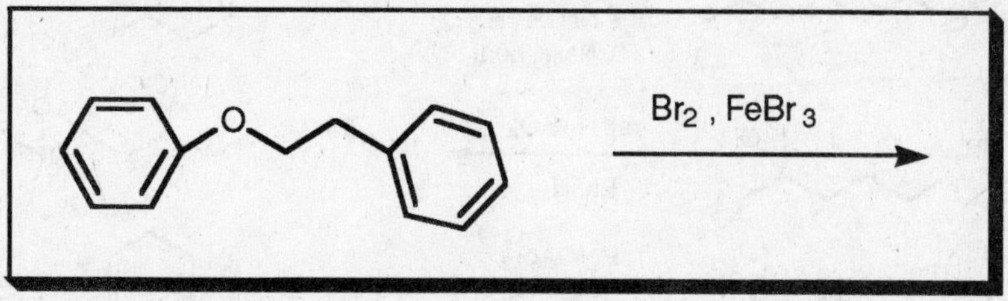

4. Give the IUPAC name for each of the following.

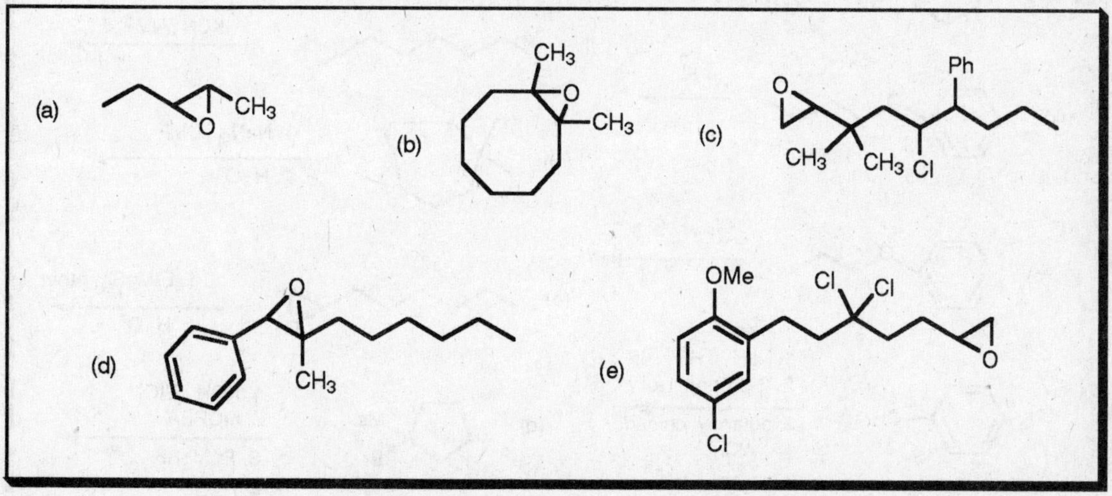

5. In each case give the structure of the major product. Remember stereochemistry where appropriate and if there is no reaction, indicate by N.R.

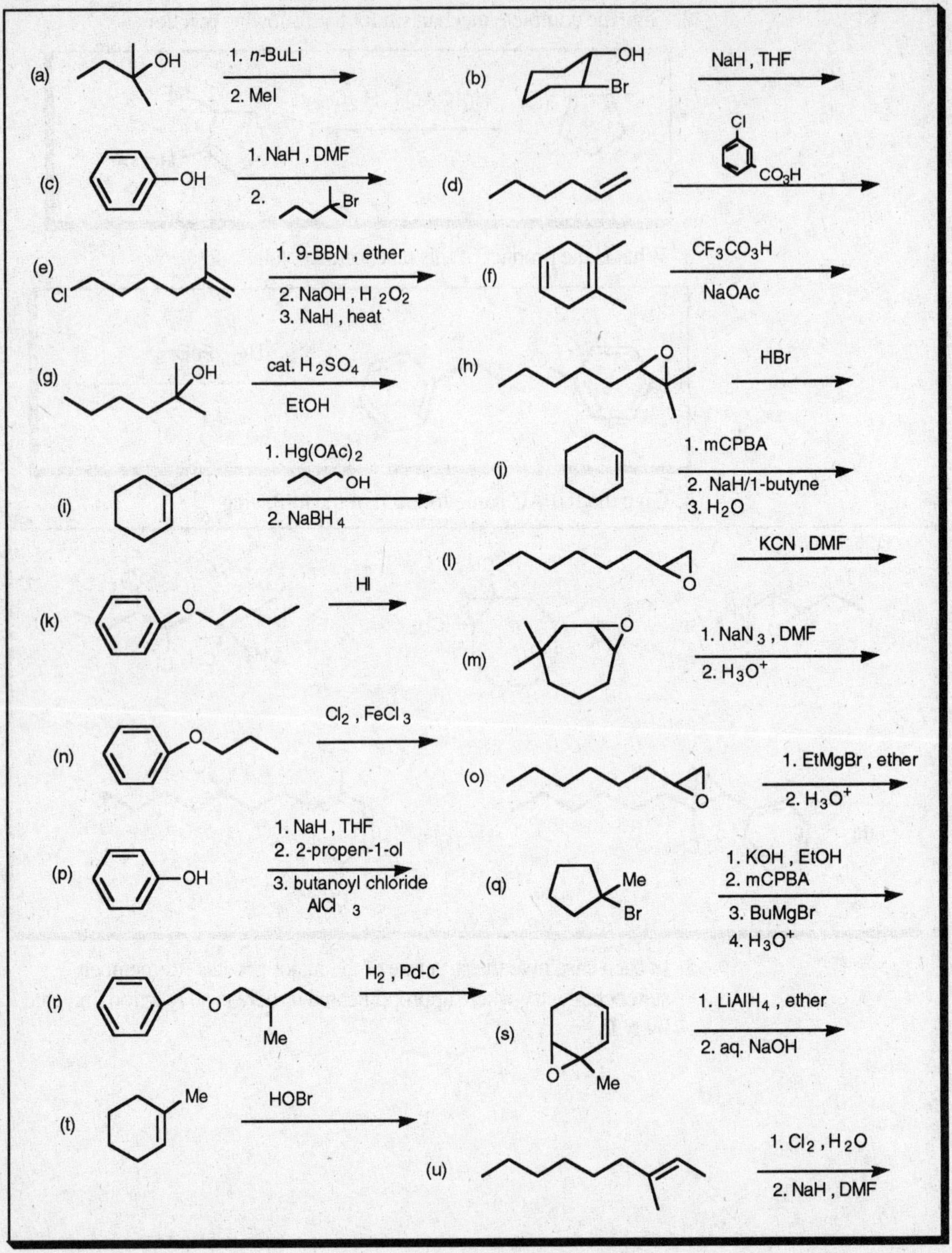

(a) 1. *n*-BuLi 2. MeI

(b) NaH , THF

(c) 1. NaH , DMF 2. (Br structure)

(d) (Cl) CO₃H — CO_3H with Cl on ring

(e) 1. 9-BBN , ether 2. NaOH , H$_2$O$_2$ 3. NaH , heat

(f) CF$_3$CO$_3$H NaOAc

(g) cat. H$_2$SO$_4$ EtOH

(h) HBr

(i) 1. Hg(OAc)$_2$ (OH) 2. NaBH$_4$

(j) 1. mCPBA 2. NaH/1-butyne 3. H$_2$O

(k) HI

(l) KCN , DMF

(m) 1. NaN$_3$, DMF 2. H$_3$O$^+$

(n) Cl$_2$, FeCl$_3$

(o) 1. EtMgBr , ether 2. H$_3$O$^+$

(p) 1. NaH , THF 2. 2-propen-1-ol 3. butanoyl chloride AlCl$_3$

(q) Me Br — 1. KOH , EtOH 2. mCPBA 3. BuMgBr 4. H$_3$O$^+$

(r) H$_2$, Pd-C   Me

(s) Me / O — 1. LiAlH$_4$, ether 2. aq. NaOH

(t) Me HOBr

(u) 1. Cl$_2$, H$_2$O 2. NaH , DMF

13

Aldehydes and Ketones

Ketones and aldehydes, along with alkenes and alcohols, are among the most common and most used class of organic molecules. The carbonyl group (C=O) can be formed from alcohols by a variety of oxidative methods. Indeed, oxidation will be discussed in greater detail in this chapter than in any previous chapter. The importance of ketones and aldehydes, however, lies in the ability to add nucleophilic reagents to the carbon of the carbonyl, generating new carbon-carbon bonds. Many of the most important carbon-carbon bond forming reactions known in Organic chemistry (addition of Grignard reagents, the Aldol Condensation, the Wittig reaction are examples) will be discussed in this chapter. Many functional group transformations are also possible using ketones and aldehydes. The chemical and physical properties of carbonyl compounds will be discussed, along with methods for their preparation and their transformation into other molecules. By necessity, several derivatives of carboxylic acids will be introduced in this chapter, despite the fact that they will be discussed in greater detail in chapters fourteen and fifteen. Several of the important methods of preparing aldehydes and ketones, particularly when aromatic derivatives are involved, use acid derivatives.

13.1. THE CARBONYL GROUP

The carbonyl group is the main characteristic of aldehydes and ketones. A ketone has two carbon groups on either side of the carbonyl [R(C=O)R] whereas an aldehyde has at least one hydrogen attached to the carbonyl [R(C=O)H].

A Polarized π-Bond DRAW A PICTURE OF A CARBONYL.

As shown by *13.1*, a carbonyl consists of a C–O unit with one strong σ-bond and a weak π-bond. The geometry of the carbonyl is trigonal planar, with the two attached groups (R^1 and R^2) coplanar with the C and O. The lone electron pairs on oxygen are also in the same plane as the atoms but the electrons of the π-bond are perpendicular to the plane of the atoms.

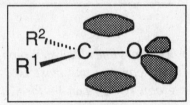

Fig. 13.1

CONTRAST AND COMPARE A CARBON-CARBON DOUBLE BOND WITH A CARBON-OXYGEN DOUBLE BOND.

The double bond of an alkene is very similar to that of a carbonyl in that there is a weak π-bond and a strong σ-bond. The carbonyl is polarized, however, due to the presence of the oxygen ($C^{\delta+}$ and $O^{\delta-}$). This leads to significant differences in reactivity since nucleophiles will attack the electropositive carbon of the carbonyl. Such chemistry is not possible with an alkene.

Structures of Ketones and Aldehydes   WHAT IS THE GENERIC STRUCTURE OF AN ALDEHYDE?

An aldehyde has at least one hydrogen attached to the carbonyl, as in *13.2*. This is usually abbreviated as RCHO.

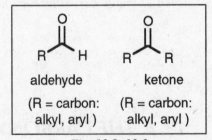

Fig. 13.2, 13.3

WHAT IS THE GENERIC STRUCTURE OF A KETONE?

A ketone has two carbon groups attached to the carbonyl, as in *13.3*.

WHAT IS THE ONLY ALDEHYDE WITH TWO HYDROGENS ATTACHED TO THE CARBONYL GROUP?

Formaldehyde (HCHO). Monomeric HCHO is a gas but there are solid forms as well. These include a trimer $(HCHO)_3$ and a polymer called para formaldehyde (HCHO).

WHICH IS MORE REACTIVE, AN ALDEHYDE OR A KETONE? EXPLAIN.

An aldehyde is usually more reactive. There is less steric hindrance to approach of a reagent to the electropositive carbonyl since there is at least one hydrogen (it is less sterically hindered than any alkyl or aryl group).

Ultraviolet Characteristics

WHAT IS THE GENERIC λ_{MAX} OF A CARBONYL GROUP?

For unconjugated carbonyls, absorption occurs at 150 nm or lower, which is typically invisible to most ultraviolet spectrophotometers. A weak absorption appears at 260-290 nm which is typical of ketones and aldehydes. For conjugated carbonyls, a peak appears around 230 nm and around 300-310 nm.

WHAT TRANSITIONS ARE POSSIBLE FOR A CARBONYL?

The signal at 150 nm signal is due to a $\pi \rightarrow \pi^*$ transition. The 260-290 nm signal is weak and due to a $n \rightarrow \pi^*$ absorption. For conjugated carbonyls, the 230 nm absorption is the $\pi \rightarrow \pi^*$ absorption and the 300-310 signal is the weaker $n \rightarrow \pi^*$ transition.

HOW CAN UV SPECTROSCOPY DISTINGUISH BETWEEN A KETONE OR ALDEHYDE AND AN ALKENE?

Ultraviolet spectroscopy cannot distinguish between an aldehyde and a ketone but alkenes show a $\pi \rightarrow \pi^*$ transition at around 170-200 nm and no $n \rightarrow \pi^*$ transition.

13.2. NOMENCLATURE

WHAT IS THE BASE NAME FOR AN ALDEHYDE?

The IUPAC name for an aldehyde uses the alkane, alkene or alkyne prefix with the ending -al. Drop the -ane (or -ene, or -yne) ending and add -al, as in hexanal.

WHAT IS THE BASE NAME FOR A KETONE?

The IUPAC name for a ketone uses the alkane, alkene or alkyne prefix with the ending -one. Drop the -ane (or -ene, or -yne) ending and add -one, as in 2-hexanone, hex-3-en-2-one and hex-4-yn-2-one.

WHY IS THE POSITION NUMBER OF THE CARBONYL USUALLY OMITTED WITH AN ALDEHYDE BUT NOT WITH A KETONE?

Since the carbonyl (C=O) is the functional group, the carbon of the carbonyl receives the lowest possible number when it is part of the longest continuous chain. Aldehydes always contain at least one hydrogen attached to the carbonyl carbon, which *must* be C_1. For this reason the number is usually omitted.

GIVE THE CORRECT IUPAC NAMES FOR *13.4–13.7*.

The name of *13.4* is cyclohexanone. For *13.5*, this aldehyde is named 4-chloro-4-phenylheptanal. Ketone *13.6* is named 6,6-diphenyl-3-heptanone. When an aldehyde is attached to a ring, the naming system is changed somewhat. The parent aldehyde of *13.7* is cycloheptane carboxaldehyde. The name of *13.7* is, therefore, 2-hexylcylcoheptane carboxaldehyde.

Fig. 13.4, 13.5

Fig. 13.6, 13.7

HOW ARE PHENYL ALKYL KETONES NAMED WITH THE IUPAC SYSTEM?

When the phenyl group is attached to C_1 the ketone is named normally with the exception that the carbonyl carbon is C_1. An example is *13.8* which is 1-phenyl-1-propanone. If the phenyl group is not attached to C_1, the C_6H_5 unit is treated as a substituent and named as phenyl.

WHAT IS THE IUPAC NAME OF 'DIPHENYL KETONE'?

Benzophenone, *13.9*.

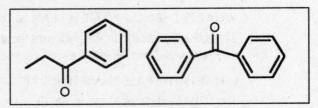

Fig. 13.8, 13.9

13.3. PREPARATION OF KETONES AND ALDEHYDES

There are several different methods for the preparation of ketones and aldehydes.

Oxidation of Alcohols

The most common method for the preparation of a ketone or aldehyde is the oxidation of an alcohol. In general, oxidation of a secondary alcohol is expected to give a ketone and oxidation of a primary alcohol gives either an aldehyde or a carboxylic acid, depending on the oxidizing agent.

CHROMIUM TRIOXIDE

The chemistry of this reagent was discussed in section 11.4.

WHAT IS THE MAJOR PRODUCT WHEN CYCLOHEXANOL IS TREATED WITH CHROMIUM TRIOXIDE IN AQUEOUS ACID?

The major product is cyclohexanone.

WHAT IS THE PRODUCT WHEN 1-HEPTANOL IS TREATED WITH CHROMIUM TRIOXIDE IN AQUEOUS ACID? EXPLAIN.

Since CrO_3 in aqueous acid is a powerful oxidizing agent, a primary alcohol is oxidized to a carboxylic acid. In this case, 1-heptanol is oxidized to heptanoic acid.

PDC AND PCC

This chemistry was discussed in section 11.4.

WHAT IS THE PRODUCT WHEN 1-OCTANOL IS TREATED WITH PCC IN DICHLOROMETHANE?

Since PCC is a much milder and more selective oxidizing agent, 1-octanol is oxidized to the aldehyde, octanal.

WHAT IS THE PRODUCT WHEN 2-METHYLCYCLOPENTANOL IS TREATED WITH PDC IN DICHLOROMETHANE?

Both PCC and PDC are capable of oxidizing secondary alcohols to ketones. Reaction of 2-methylcyclopentanol with PDC, therefore, gives 2-methylcyclopentanone as the product.

Friedel-Crafts Acylation

Friedel Crafts acylation was discussed in section 9.7. The product of an acid chloride and an aromatic derivative, in the presence of a Lewis acid, is an aryl ketone.

WHAT IS THE REACTIVE SPECIES WHEN PROPANOYL CHLORIDE IS MIXED WITH ALUMINUM CHLORIDE?

An acylium ion $(RC \equiv O)^{\oplus}$ is the intermediate. In this case, $R = CH_3CH_2$.

WHAT IS THE PRODUCT WHEN ANISOLE IS TREATED WITH PROPANOYL CHLORIDE AND FERRIC CHLORIDE?

An acylium in reacts with aromatic rings to form an aralkyl ketone. Since the OMe group of anisole is activating and an *ortho/para* director, the products are

1-(2-methoxyphenyl)-1-propanone (*13.10*) and 1-(4-methoxyphenyl)-1-propanone (*13.11*).

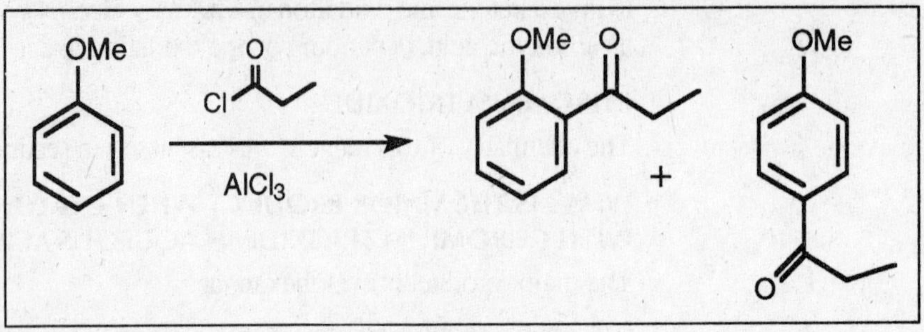

Fig. 13.10, 13.11

WHAT IS THE PRODUCT WHEN NITROBENZENE REACTS WITH PROPANOYL CHLORIDE AND AlCl$_3$?

A strongly deactivating group such as nitro makes the benzene ring too unreactive for a Friedel-Crafts acylation reaction. In this case, the correct answer is no reaction.

CAN ALDEHYDES BE PREPARED BY FRIEDEL-CRAFTS ACYLATION WITH ACID CHLORIDES?

The required acid chloride would be the acid chloride of formic acid (methanoyl chloride), which is a rather unstable species. Formation of benzaldehyde derivatives by this method is, therefore, very difficult. The problem is not the Friedel-Crafts acylation but rather the availability of the requisite acid chloride.

From Acid Derivatives

Ketones and aldehydes can be prepared, in some cases, from carboxylic acid derivatives. Friedel-Crafts acylation is one example. There are often problems in other reactions, and specialized reagents are often necessary.

ACID CHLORIDES AND ORGANOCUPRATES

WHAT IS THE USUAL PRODUCT WHEN AN ACID CHLORIDE IS TREATED WITH A GRIGNARD REAGENT? EXPLAIN.

When a Grignard reagent reacts with an acid chloride, the initial product is a ketone (*13.12*) but this can also react with the Grignard and the final product, after hydrolysis, is the tertiary alcohol, *13.13*.

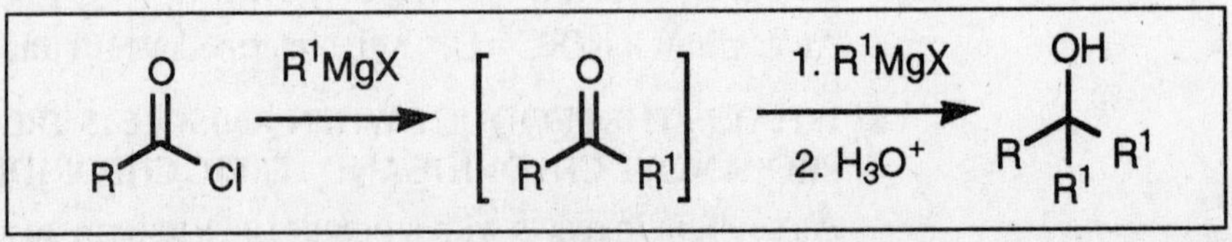

Fig. 13.12, 13.13

WHAT IS THE EXPECTED PRODUCT WHEN BENZOYL CHLORIDE IS REACTED WITH ETHYLMAGNESIUM BROMIDE?

The product is 3-phenyl-3-pentanol, as described above.

WHAT IS AN ORGANOCUPRATE?

An organocuprate is a product formed by the reaction of excess organolithium reagents (RLi) and a cuprous [Cu (I)] derivative such as cuprous iodide (CuI). When these reagents are mixed at temperatures lower than -10°C, in ether solvents, the result is a lithium dialkyl cuprate, R_2CuLi, which is a source of nucleophilic carbon.

WHAT IS THE PRODUCT WHEN BUTANOYL CHLORIDE IS TREATED WITH LITHIUM DI-*N*-BUTYL CUPRATE?

Lithium di-*n*-butyl cuprate $(n\text{-Bu})_2CuLi$ is prepared by reaction of *n*-butyllithium and cuprous iodide. When this reagent reacts with butanoyl chloride, the product is 4-octanone. Under these conditions, the organocuprate does *not* react with the ketone product.

WHY DOES THE ORGANOCUPRATE PRODUCE A KETONE RATHER THAN A TERTIARY ALCOHOL?

An organocuprate is much less reactive than a Grignard reagent. It is strong enough to react with a highly reactive species such as an acid chloride but not strong enough to react with the less reactive ketone.

ACID CHLORIDES AND DIALKYLCADMIUM REAGENTS

WHAT IS THE STRUCTURE OF A DIALKYLCADMIUM REAGENT? SHOW THE STRUCTURE OF DIETHYL CADMIUM.

A dialkylcadmium reagent has the structure R_2Cd. An example is diethylcadmium, Et_2Cd.

HOW IS DIETHYL CADMIUM PREPARED?

Diethylcadmium is prepared by the reaction of ethyllithium with cadmium chloride $(CdCl_2)$. All organocadmium reagents are prepared in this way (from the appropriate organolithium) but the reaction demands anhydrous $CdCl_2$.

WHAT IS THE PRODUCT WHEN PENTANOYL CHLORIDE REACTS WITH DIBUTYLCADMIUM?

As with organocuprates, when a dialkyl cadmium reacts with an acid chloride, the product is a ketone. In this case, pentanoyl chloride reacts with dibutylcadmium to give 5-nonanone.

WHY IS THE TERTIARY ALCOHOL NOT FORMED IN DIALKYL CADMIUM REACTIONS?

Dialkylcadmium reagents are relatively weak nucleophiles. They are strong enough to react with the highly reactive acid chloride but not strong enough to react with the less reactive ketone product of the reaction.

FROM NITRILES AND GRIGNARD REAGENTS

Nitriles are also discussed in sections 15.1, 15.2 and 15.3.

WHAT IS THE STRUCTURE OF BUTANENITRILE?

The structure is $CH_3CH_2CH_2C \equiv N$.

WHY DOES ETHYL MAGNESIUM BROMIDE REACT WITH BUTANENITRILE? AT WHAT ATOM DOES THE GRIGNARD REAGENT REACT?

The carbon of the nitrile group polarized with a $\delta+$ charge ($^{\delta+}C \equiv N^{\delta-}$) and the nucleophilic carbon of the Grignard reagent will be attracted to that electropositive atom. In this regard, the nitrile carbon shows many analogies to a carbonyl carbon.

WHAT IS THE INITIAL PRODUCT OF THE REACTION OF ETHYLMAGNESIUM BROMIDE AND BUTANENITRILE?

The initial product is an iminium salt, *13.14*. When the Grignard attacks the nitrile carbon, a new carbon-carbon bond is formed and one of the π-bonds is broken, 'dumping' those electrons on the nitrogen (the most electronegative atom).

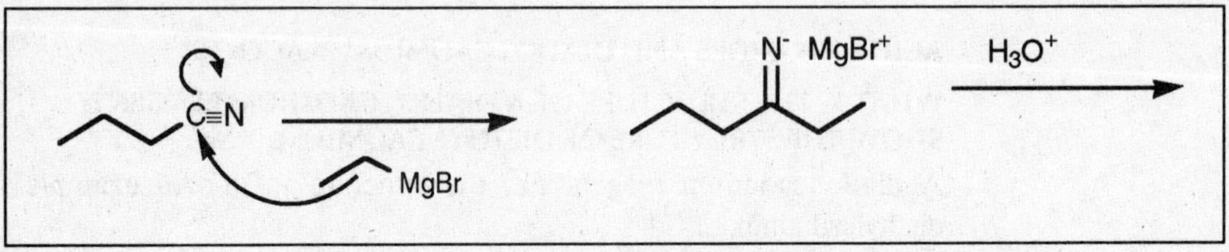

Fig. 13.14

WHAT IS THE PRODUCT WHEN THE INITIAL PRODUCT IS REACTED WITH AQUEOUS ACID?

Aqueous hydrolysis of an iminium salt (with acid) leads to a ketone, in this case 3-hexanone, *13.15*.

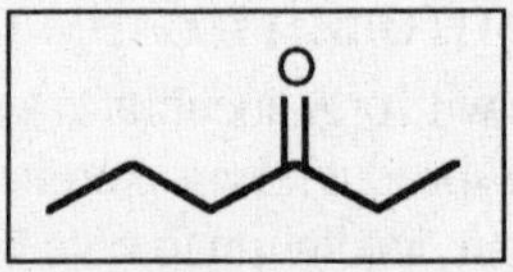

Fig. 13.15

GIVE THE MECHANISM FOR THIS LATTER REACTION.

The initially formed iminium salt (*13.14*) is protonated to give an imine and then protonated a second time to give an iminium salt, *13.16*. The carbon of this iminium salt is electropositive and is attacked by water (the only nucleophile in the system) to give *13.17*, which loses a proton. The proton is transferred to the more basic atom (nitrogen) in *13.18* and loss of ammonia (a good leaving group) generates the protonated carbonyl, *13.19*. Loss of a proton from *13.19* completes the hydrolysis to generate the ketone, *13.15*.

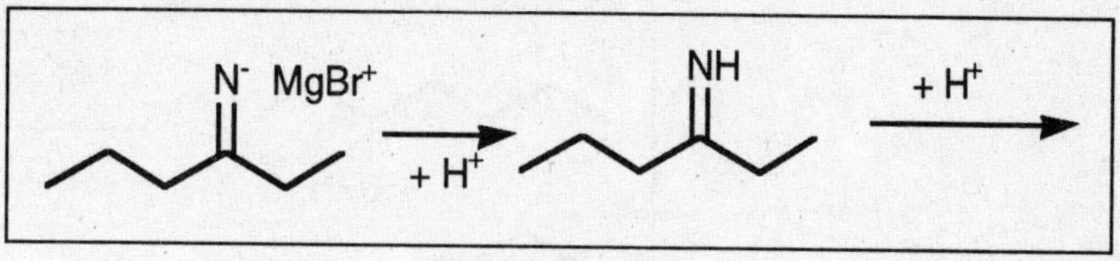

Fig. 13.14, 13.15

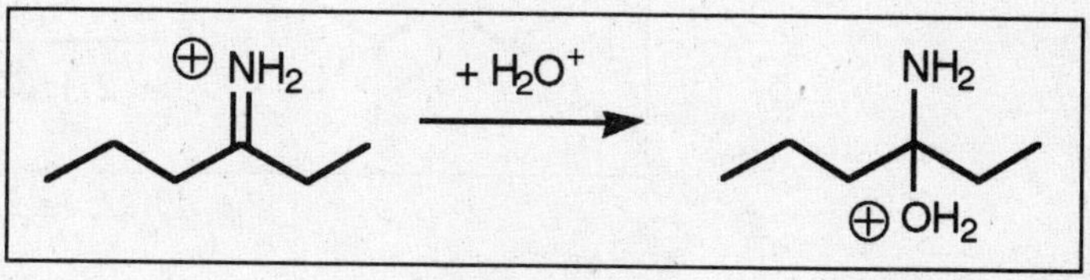

Fig. 13.16, 13.17

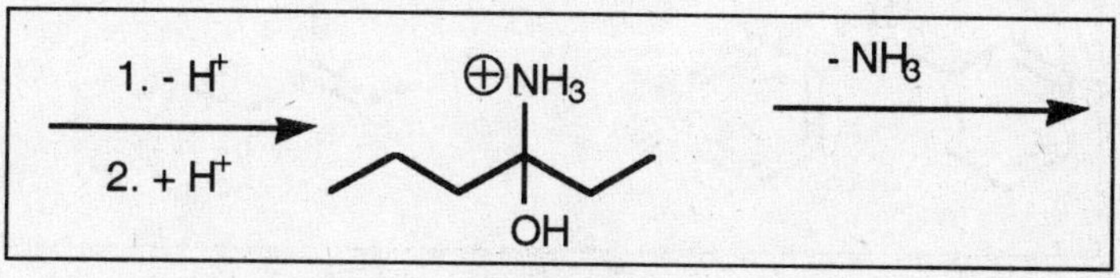

Fig. 13.18

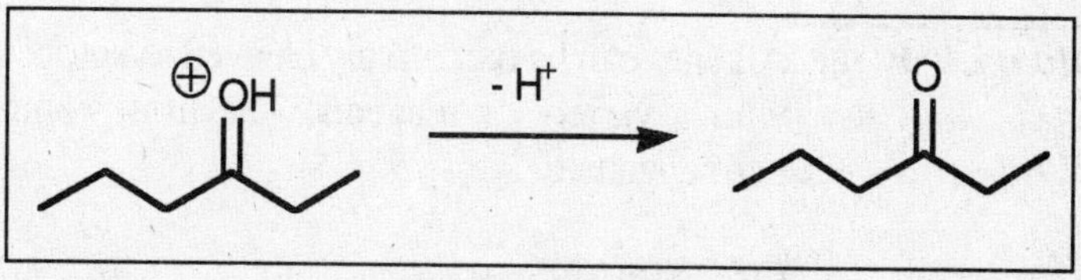

Fig. 13.19, 13.20

GIVE THE MAJOR PRODUCT FOR THE REACTIONS OF *13.20–13.22*.

In the first reaction, benzonitrile (*13.20*) reacts with phenylmagnesium bromide to give benzophenone (*13.23*), after acid hydrolysis. In the second reaction, 2-ethylhexanenitrile (*13.21*) is treated with cyclopentylmagnesium chloride to give the corresponding ketone, *13.24*. In the last example, *13.22* is treated with methylmagnesium iodide. In such sterically hindered nitriles, the reaction with a Grignard is sluggish and requires more vigorous conditions. The imine product is also sterically hindered and the hydrolysis can be slow, requiring vigorous conditions. The ketone product would be *13.25*.

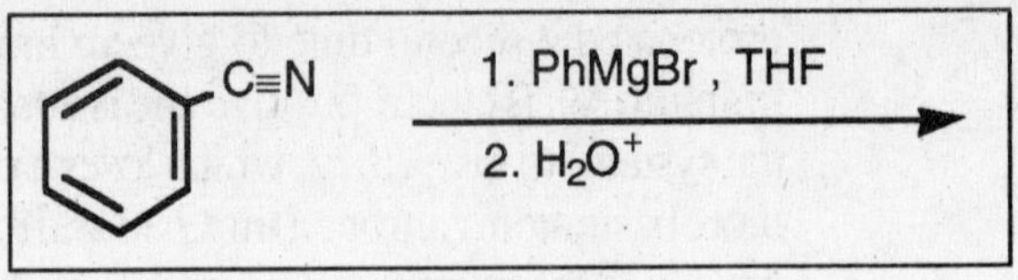

Fig. 13.20

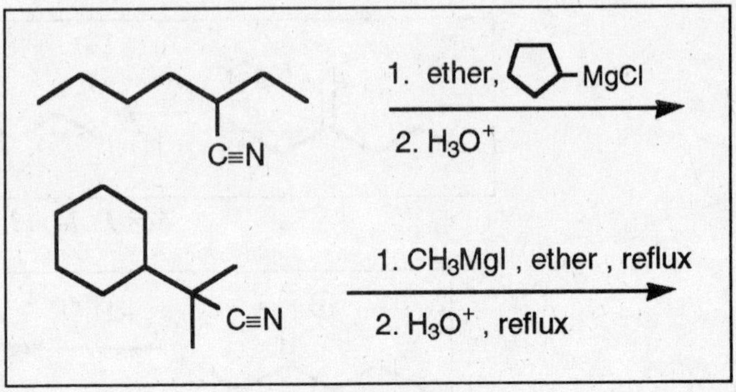

Fig, 13.21, 13.22

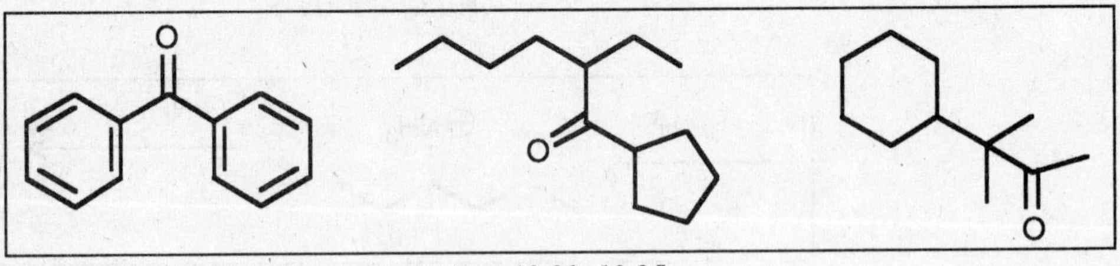

Fig. 13.23–13.25

Oxidative Cleavage   Alkenes can be oxidatively cleaved to ketones, aldehydes or carboxylic acids with a variety of reagents. The most common are ozone and potassium permanganate.

OZONOLYSIS

Ozonolysis was discussed in section 5.5.

GIVE THE PRODUCTS OF OZONOLYSIS AND HYDROGEN PEROXIDE WORKUP OF 1-PENTENE.

1-Pentene is oxidatively cleaved to the ozonide and the oxidative workup with hydrogen peroxide will give formic acid and butanoic acid as the products.

GIVE THE PRODUCTS OF OZONOLYSIS AND HYDROGEN PEROXIDE WORKUP OF 2,3-DIMETHYL-2-HEXENE.

Under these conditions, this alkene is cleaved to a mixture of acetone and 2-pentanone.

GIVE THE PRODUCTS OF OZONOLYSIS AND DIMETHYL SULFIDE WORKUP OF 2-METHYL-2-PENTENE.

The ozonolysis with reductive workup gives acetone and propanal as the products.

PERIODIC ACID CLEAVAGE OF 1,2-DIOLS

WHAT IS THE STRUCTURE OF PERIODIC ACID?

Periodic acid is usually written as HIO_4 but exists as the dihydrate, written as H_5IO_6, (see *13.26*). The two structures are used interchangeably.

WHAT IS THE PRODUCT OF THE REACTION OF 1,2-CYCLOHEXANEDIOL AND PERIODIC ACID?

Periodic acid cleaves 1,2-diols into aldehydes. In this case, the product is a dialdehyde, 1,6-hexanedial [$OHC–(CH_2)_4–CHO$].

WHAT IS THE PRODUCT WHEN 2,3-BUTANEDIOL IS TREATED WITH PERIODIC ACID?

The product is two equivalents of acetaldehyde (ethanal).

WHAT IS THE GENERAL MECHANISM OF THIS REACTION?

Periodic acid (*13.26*) reacts with the 1,2-diol to form a cyclic periodate ester (*13.27*). A concerted electronic rearrangement allows cleavage of the carbon-carbon bond, liberating two equivalents of the carbonyl compound (here ethanal) and iodic acid.

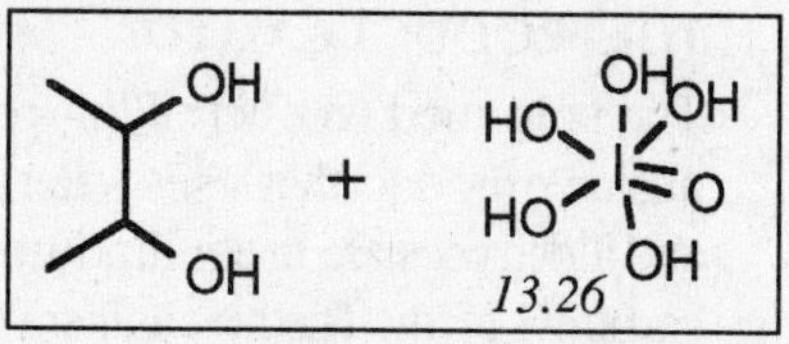

Fig. 13.26

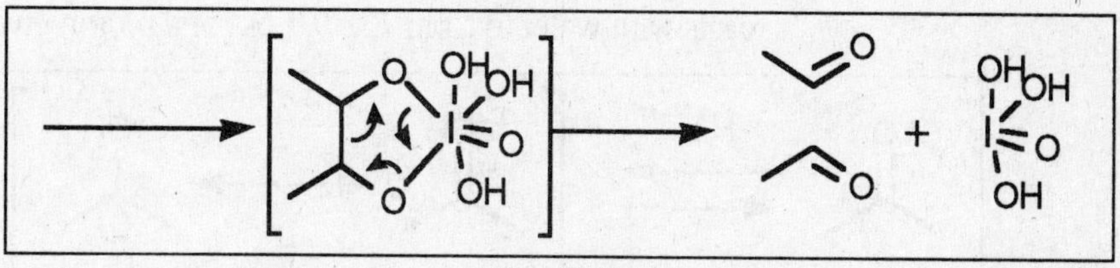

Fig. 13.27

HOW ARE 1,2-DIOLS USUALLY FORMED?

As discussed in section 5.5, 1,2-diols are usually formed by treatment of an alkene with dilute $KMnO_4$ and hydroxide or with OsO_4 and sodium thiosulfite.

WHAT IS THE PRODUCT WHEN 2-HEPTENE IS TREATED WITH A MIXTURE OF OSMIUM TETROXIDE AND HIO_4?

In this case the OsO_4 converts 2-heptene to the 1,2-diol, in the presence of HIO_4.

The HIO_4 then cleaves the diol into carbonyl compounds, in this case ethanal and pentanal.

13.4. REACTIONS

Aldehydes and ketones react primarily by the polarized carbonyl group. The most common reactions are nucleophilic acyl addition and acid-base reactions involving protonation of the carbonyl oxygen.

Nucleophilic Acyl Addition

This reaction involves addition of a nucleophile to the carbon of a carbonyl, accompanied by cleavage of the π-bond to form an alkoxide.

WATER AND HYDRATES

WHAT IS THE MECHANISM FOR REACTION OF ACETONE AND WATER?

Water is not a sufficiently strong nucleophile to add to the carbonyl of a ketone. In this case, acetone is soluble in water but does not react with it.

WHAT IS THE MECHANISM OF REACTION BETWEEN ACETONE AND WATER WITH A CATALYTIC AMOUNT OF ACID PRESENT? WHAT IS THE PRODUCT CALLED?

The presumed product of this reaction is a hydrate (*13.28*) but this is a very unstable product that loses water and reverts back to acetone. In general ketones and aldehydes are in equilibrium with a hydrate and the equilibrium favors the carbonyl form. The mechanism of reaction involves initial protonation of the carbonyl oxygen to give *13.29*, which is resonance stabilized. This intermediate reacts with water to form *13.30*. Loss of a proton gives the hydrate (*13.28*).

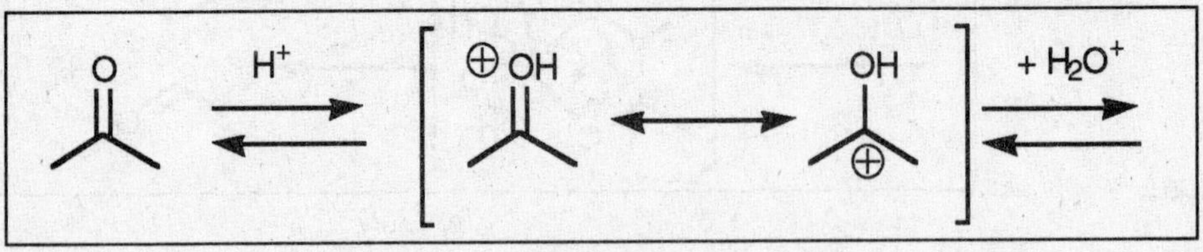

Fig. 13.29

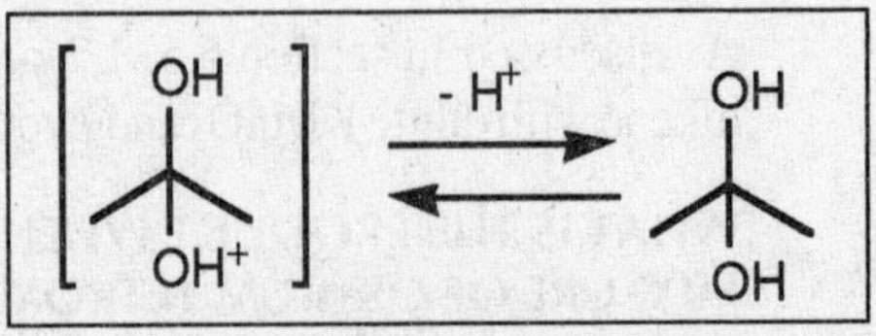

Fig. 13.30, 13.28

WHY ARE HYDRATES SO DIFFICULT TO ISOLATE?

Hydrates are in equilibrium with the carbonyl precursor. The hydrate is more sterically hindered than the carbonyl, driving the equilibrium to the left (to the carbonyl compound). In addition, two OH groups withdraw a significant amount of electron density from the central carbon, further destabilizing it.

WHY IS CHLORAL HYDRATE A STABLE PRODUCT?

Choral hydrate (*13.32*) is the hydrate of choral (2,2,2-trichloroethanal, *13.31*). The chlorines withdraw electrons from the α-carbon which, in turn, pulls electrons from the carbonyl carbon. The carbonyl carbon withdraws electrons from both oxygens of the C–O bonds, strengthening those bonds and stabilizing the hydrate (the equilibrium is shifted in favor of the hydrate). This only occurs when strongly electron withdrawing groups are attached to the α-carbon of the ketone or aldehyde.

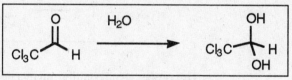

Fig. 13.31, 13.32

ALCOHOLS

Alcohols can add to a carbonyl but the reaction usually requires an acid catalyst.

ACETALS

WHAT IS THE PRODUCT WHEN BUTANAL IS REACTED WITH AN EXCESS OF ETHANOL IN THE PRESENCE OF A CATALYTIC AMOUNT OF *p*-TOLUENESULFONIC ACID?

This is analogous to the hydrate forming reaction. Rather than water, the alcohol (ethanol) is the nucleophilic species, leading to a geminal diethoxy compound called an acetal (from an aldehyde) or a ketal (from a ketone). In this case, butanal generates 1,1-diethoxybutane (*13.33*).

GIVE THE COMPLETE MECHANISM FOR THIS REACTION?

Initial protonation of butanal gives *13.34* which adds ethanol to give *13.35*. Loss of a proton generates *13.36*, which is called a *hemiacetal*, and addition of another proton gives intermediate *13.37*. If the OEt group is reprotonated, rather than the OH, the equilibrium is driven back towards the carbonyl. If the OH group is protonated, however, (as in *13.37*) loss of water gives a new resonance stabilized cation, *13.38*. Addition of a second molecule of ethanol gives *13.39* and loss of a proton from this intermediate completes the sequence to give the acetal, *13.33*.

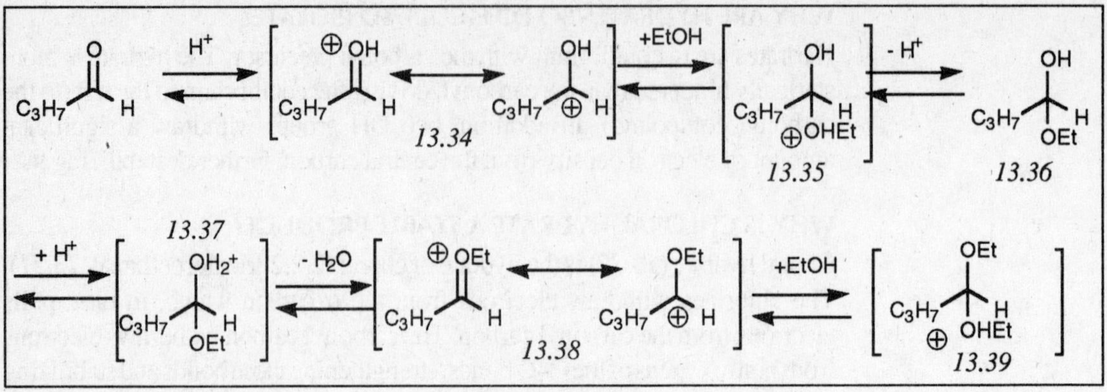

Fig. 13.34–13.39

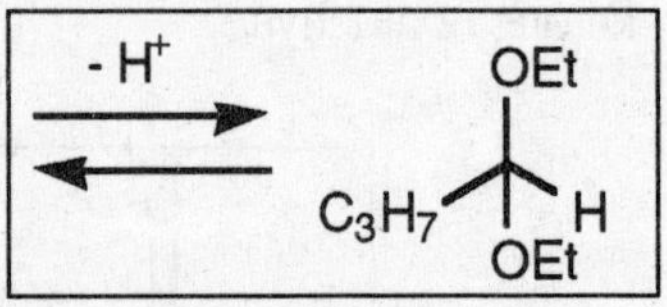

Fig. 13.33

This process is an equilibrium reaction. Removing water from the reaction drives the product towards the acetal. Adding a large excess of water drives it back to the carbonyl. Alternatively, the acetal product could be removed by distillation, again driving the equilibrium to the right.

IF WATER IS REMOVED FROM THIS REACTION AS IT IS FORMED, WHAT IS THE EFFECT ON THE REACTION?

As mentioned, removal of one of the reaction products (water) will drive the equilibrium towards the right, to the acetal product.

WHAT ARE SOME METHODS THAT CAN BE USED TO REMOVE WATER FROM A REACTION?

Drying agents such as calcium chloride ($CaCl_2$) or magnesium sulfate ($MgSO_4$) can be added, although these are not very efficient. A zeolite (molecular sieve) can be added that has a pore size sufficiently large to accommodate water but not the larger organic molecules present in the mixture. The molecular sieves most commonly used are molecular sieves 3Å and 4Å. Another method for removing water is the use of a Dean-Stark trap (see end of chapter problem #7). This glass apparatus relies on azeotropic distillation (ethanol-water mixtures form an azeotrope, which is a constant boiling mixture of the two liquids boiling lower than each individual liquid). The azeotropic distillate is a fixed ratio of the two liquids. The Dean-Stark trap relies on a mixture of a solvent (such as benzene) in which water is mostly insoluble, but with which it forms an azeotrope. The azeotropic mixture distills off and is collected, the water sinks to the bottom (it is more dense than benzene) and the benzene eventually overflows back into the reaction vessel. The water collected in this manner is removed from the reaction.

WHAT IS THE PRODUCT WHEN AN ACETAL IS REACTED WITH AQUEOUS ACID?

As mentioned, if this equilibrium mixture of acetal (or ketal) and aldehyde (or ketone) is treated with aqueous acid, the excess of water will drive the reaction back to the carbonyl. In effect, this will remove the acetal group and replace it with the carbonyl group. In the mechanism shown above, replace ethanol with water and the equilibrium shifts to the left.

WHAT IS THE PRODUCT WHEN ACETAL *13.40* IS REACTED WITH AQUEOUS ACID?

The product is hexanal.

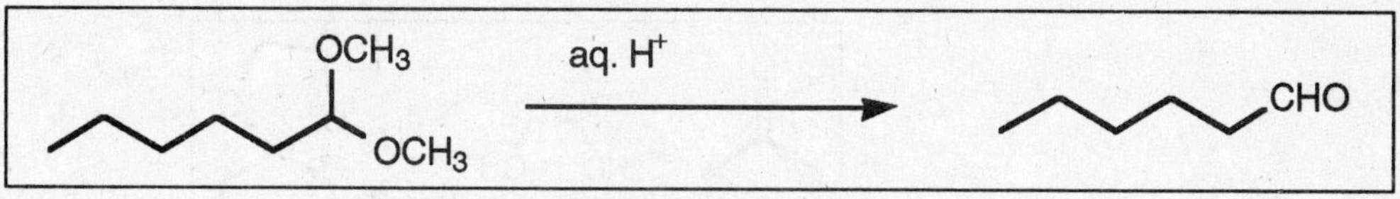

Fig. 13.40

WHAT IS THE PRODUCT WHEN BUTANAL IS TREATED WITH 1,2-ETHANEDIOL AND A CATALYTIC AMOUNT OF ACID?

In this case, the two alcohol units are tied together. The acetal formed will be a cyclic species (*13.41*) called a 1,3-dioxolane.

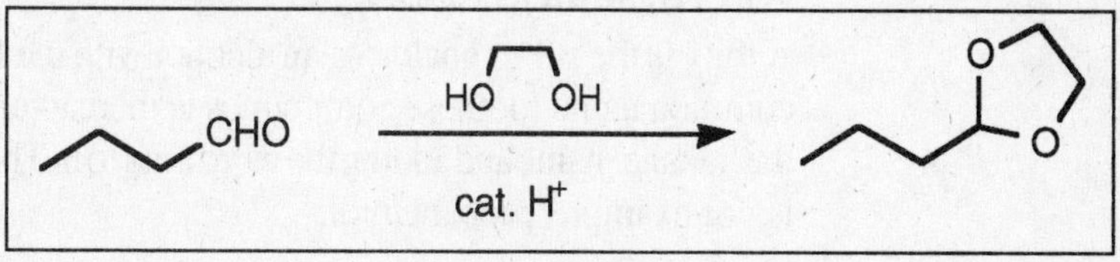

Fig. 13.41

KETALS

WHAT IS THE PRODUCT WHEN 2-PENTANONE IS REACTED WITH AN EXCESS OF PROPANOL IN THE PRESENCE OF A CATALYTIC AMOUNT OF *p*-TOLUENESULFONIC ACID?

The product is 2,2-dipropoxypentane, *13.42*.

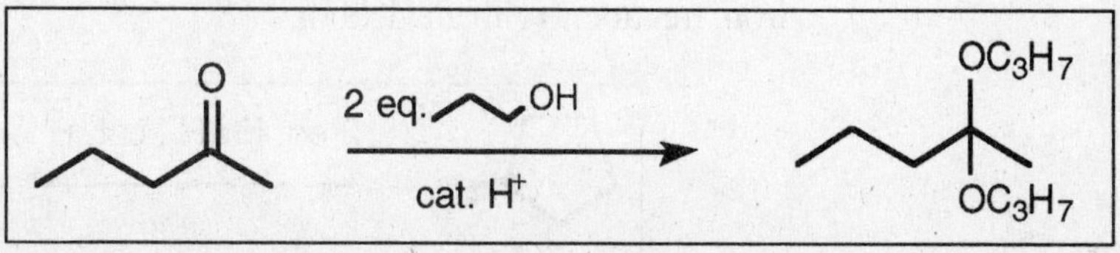

Fig. 13.42

WHAT IS THE MECHANISM FOR THIS REACTION?

The mechanism is identical to that presented above. Substitute 2-pentanone for butanal and substitute 1-propanol for ethanol.

WHAT IS THE PRODUCT WHEN A KETAL IS REACTED WITH AQUEOUS ACID?

As with acetals, treatment of a ketone with aqueous acid shifts the equilibrium back to the carbonyl derivative. Treatment of *13.42* with aqueous acid will, for example, regenerate 2-pentanone and propanol.

WHAT IS THE PRODUCT WHEN CYCLOHEXANONE IS TREATED WITH 1,2-ETHANEDIOL AND A CATALYTIC AMOUNT OF ACID?

As with dioxolane formation from aldehydes, ketones also form dioxolanes upon treatment with ethylene glycol. The product is *13.43*.

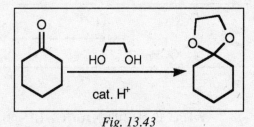

Fig. 13.43

DITHIOKETALS AND DITHIOACETALS

WHAT IS THE STRUCTURE OF A THIOL? WHAT IS A COMMON NAME FOR THESE MOLECULES?

A thiol is the sulfur analog of an alcohol with the functional group R–SH. The common name for these compounds is mercaptan. They are named by taking the 'alkane' name and adding the word thiol to it. The mercaptan $CH_3CH_2CH_2SH$ is, for example, propanethiol.

HOW WOULD YOU PREDICT A THIOL TO REACT?

A thiol should react, more or less, in a manner similar to an alcohol, at least in reactions with carbonyl derivatives.

WHAT IS THE PRODUCT WHEN CYCLOPENTANONE IS TREATED WITH AN EXCESS OF ETHANETHIOL AND A CATALYTIC AMOUNT OF ACID?

The product is a dithioketal (*13.44*), exactly analogous to formation of a ketal from treatment with an alcohol.

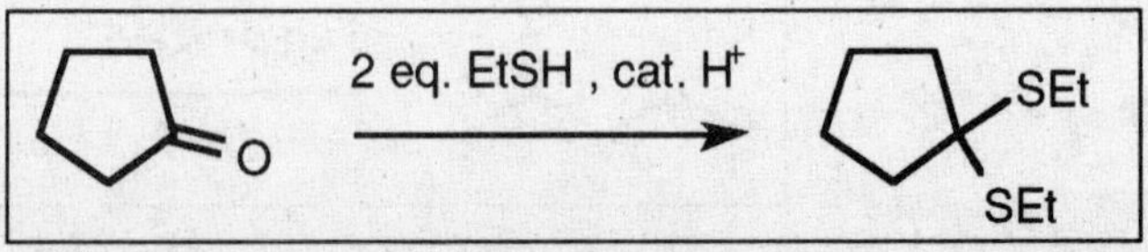

$$\text{2 eq. EtSH , cat. H}^+$$

Fig. 13.44

WHAT IS THE PRODUCT WHEN PENTANAL IS TREATED WITH 1,3-PROPANEDITHIOL IN THE PRESENCE OF A CATALYTIC AMOUNT OF ACID?

The product is a cyclic dithioacetal (*13.45*), exactly analogous to formation of an acetal from treatment with a cyclic diol. Similar six-membered ring compounds with two sulfur atoms are called 1,3-dithianes.

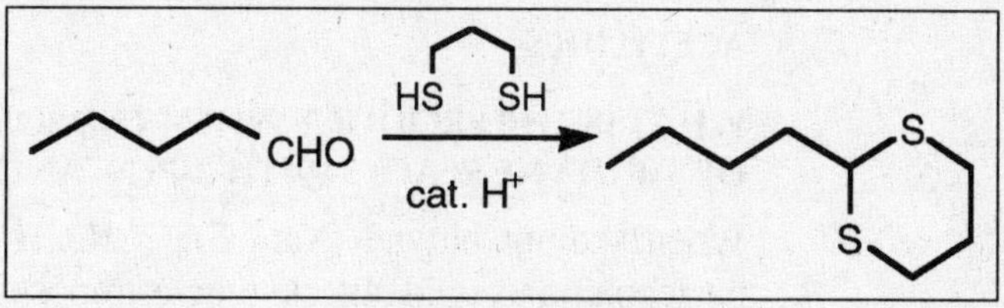

Fig. 13.45

WHAT IS THE PRODUCT WHEN 2,2-(DIMETHYLTHIO)HEXANE IS REACTED WITH RANEY NICKEL IN HOT ACETONE? EXPLAIN.

Nickel has a strong affinity for sulfur. Raney nickel is specially prepared and has a considerable amount of hydrogen adsorbed on the surface of the finely divided nickel. When a dithioketal is treated with this reagent, complete removal of the sulfur occurs, with reduction to a -CH_2- group. In this case, the final product is the alkane, hexane.

CYANIDE

WHAT IS THE PRODUCT WHEN SODIUM CYANIDE REACTS WITH ACETONE?

The product is *13.46*. The nucleophilic cyanide attacks the electropositive carbonyl group. A proton source (usually the acidic workup) is required to generate the alcohol group from the initially formed alkoxide. This reaction works best with an acid catalyst to provide the proton.

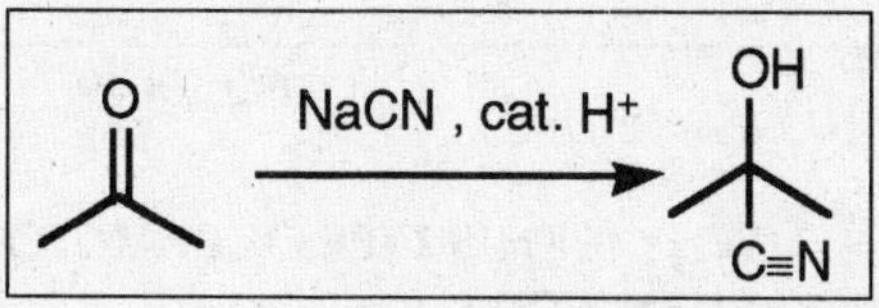

Fig. 13.46

WHAT IS THE COMMON NAME FOR THIS TYPE OF PRODUCT?

A cyanohydrin.

WHAT IS THE PRODUCT WHEN CYCLOHEXANONE REACTS WITH HCN?

This reaction also generates a cyanohydrin, *13.47*.

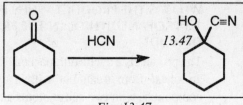

Fig. 13.47

ACETYLIDES

WHAT IS THE PRODUCT WHEN THE SODIUM SALT OF 1-BUTYNE REACTS WITH 2-PENTANONE?

When sodium butyne (Na^+ $^-C{\equiv}CCH_2CH_3$) reacts with 2-pentanone, the nucleophilic acetylide attacks the electropositive carbonyl carbon to produce an alkoxide. Hydrolysis liberates the alcohol product, 4-methyl-oct-3-yn-4-ol (*13.48*).

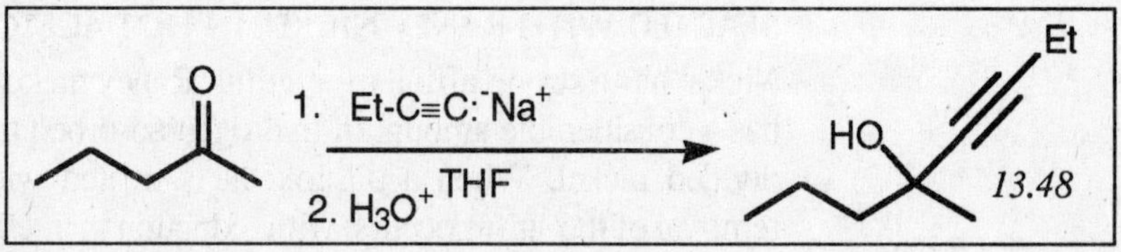

Fig. 13.48

WHAT IS THE PRODUCT WHEN THE SODIUM SALT OF ACETYLENE REACTS WITH BENZALDEHYDE?

The product is 1-phenylprop-2-yn-1-ol, *13.49*.

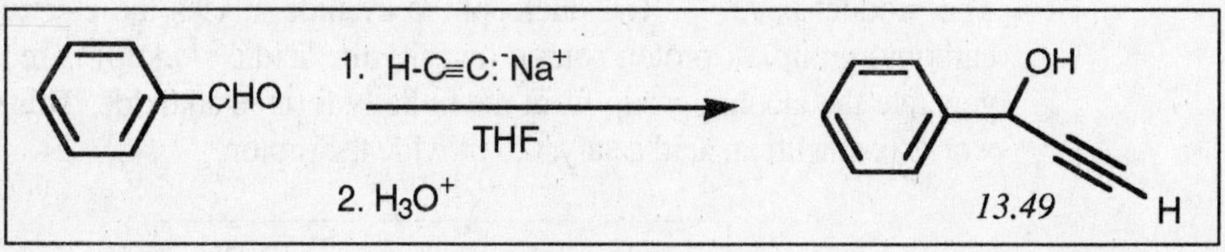

Fig. 13.49

WHY IS THIS TYPE OF REACTION IMPORTANT IN ORGANIC CHEMISTRY?

It is important because it is one of the few chemical reactions that form a new carbon-carbon bond, and the product contains other functionality that will allow further chemical transformations. In this case, two functional groups, an alcohol and an alkyne, are introduced into the same molecule.

GRIGNARD REAGENTS

This reaction was discussed previously in section 11.3.

WHAT IS THE PRODUCT OF THE REACTION BETWEEN PHENYLMAGNESIUM BROMIDE AND CYCLOHEXANONE?

The product is 1-phenylcyclohexanol where the nucleophilic carbon of the Grignard reagent attacks the electropositive carbonyl carbon, forming a new carbon-carbon bond and producing an alkoxide. Hydrolysis gives the alcohol product.

WHAT IS THE PRODUCT OF THE REACTION BETWEEN BUTYLMAGNESIUM CHLORIDE AND HEXANAL?

The product, after hydrolysis, is 5-decanol.

WHAT ALDEHYDE REACTS WITH ETHYLMAGNESIUM BROMIDE TO PRODUCE A PRIMARY ALCOHOL?

Formaldehyde. When ethylmagnesium bromide reacts with formaldehyde (HCHO), hydrolysis gives the alcohol, 1-propanol.

WHY IS THE REACTION OF A KETONE OR ALDEHYDE AND A GRIGNARD REAGENT NOT REVERSIBLE?

A strong carbon-carbon bond is formed when the π-bond of the carbonyl is broken by $C^{\delta\ominus}$ of the Grignard reagent. The strength of the carbon-carbon bond makes the reverse reaction highly endothermic. The reverse reaction also has a high activation energy relative to the forward reaction.

Reduction to Alcohols

As discussed in section 11.3, ketones and aldehydes are reduced to alcohols with various reducing agents including hydrides, catalytic hydrogenation and dissolving metal reductions.

HYDRIDES
See section 11.3.

WHAT IS THE MAJOR PRODUCT WHEN CYCLOHEPTANONE IS REACTED WITH LiAlH₄ AND THEN WATER?

The product is an alcohol resulting from 'nucleophilic' attack of the hydride (via a four-centered transition state) on the electropositive carbonyl carbon. In this case, cyclopentanone is converted into cycloheptanol.

WHAT IS THE MAJOR PRODUCT WHEN BENZALDEHYDE IS REACTED WITH NABH₄ AND THEN AQUEOUS AMMONIUM CHLORIDE?

The product is benzyl alcohol (1-phenylmethanol).

GIVE THE MAJOR PRODUCT FOR THE REACTIONS OF *13.50* AND *13.51*.

5-Methylhept-4-enal (*13.50*) is reduced with LiAlH₄ to give corresponding alcohol, 5-methyl-hept-4-en-1-ol (*13.52*). In the second example, conjugated ketone *13.51* is reduced to the alcohol, *13.53*.

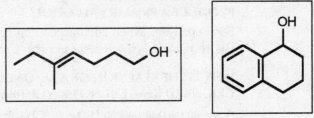

Fig. 13.50, 13.51

Fig. 13.52, 13.53

CATALYTIC HYDROGENATION

See section 5.5. As with alkenes, hydrogen in the presence of a suitable transition metal catalyst (usually platinum) reduces carbonyls of aldehydes and ketones to the corresponding alcohol.

GIVE THE MAJOR PRODUCT FOR THE REACTIONS OF *13.54* AND *13.55*.

Keto-aldehyde *13.54* contains two carbonyl groups, an aldehyde and a ketone. When reduced with excess hydrogen (Platinum oxide—sometimes called Adam's catalyst—is the catalyst) a diol (2-ethyl-1,5-hexanediol, *13.56*) is formed. Reduction of 2-methylcyclopentanone (*13.55*) leads to a mixture of the *cis*-alcohol (*13.57*) and the *trans*-alcohol (*13.58*).

Fig. 13.54, 13.55

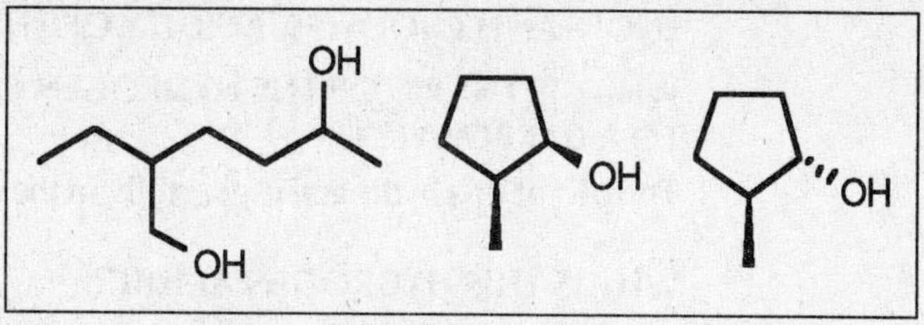

Fig. 13.56–13.58

DISSOLVING METAL REDUCTION

See section 11.3. As previously discussed, metals such as sodium and potassium reduce carbonyls via a single electron transfer mechanism, where the hydrogen is introduced into the molecule from an acidic solvent (NH_3 or EtOH). The intermediate in carbonyl reduction is a resonance stabilized ketyl and the end-product is an alcohol.

GIVE THE MAJOR PRODUCT FOR THE REACTIONS OF *13.59* AND *13.60.*

The reduction of cyclohexane carboxaldehyde (*13.59*) gives cyclohexanemethanol (*13.61*). Both of the ketone functions in *13.60* are reduced under these conditions to 4,5-dimethyl-2,6-octanediol, *13.62*.

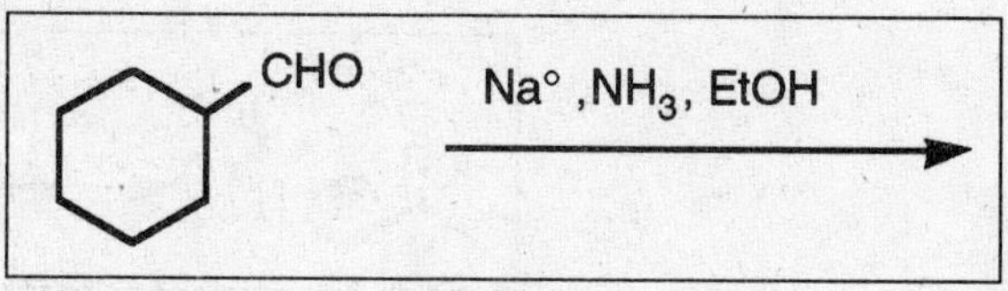

Fig. 13.59

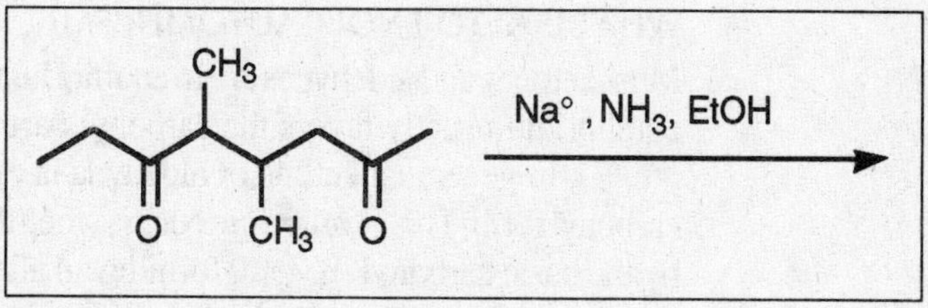

Fig. 13.60

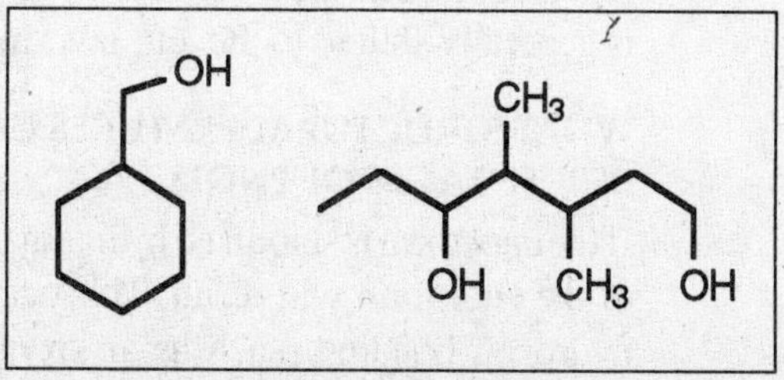

Fig. 13.61, 13.62

ENOLS AND ENOLATES: ACIDITY OF THE α-HYDROGEN

WHAT IS THE PK$_a$ OF THE HYDROGEN ON THE CARBON ATTACHED TO A CARBONYL?

The pK$_a$ of this hydrogen is generally in the range 20–22.

WHY IS THIS HYDROGEN ACIDIC?

The electron withdrawing carbon group of the carbonyl induces a δ^+ charge on that hydrogen, making it susceptible to attack by a base. In addition, most ketones and aldehydes are in equilibrium with an enol (see below) which has an acidic O–H moiety.

WHEN THE α-CARBON IS SUBSTITUTED, WHAT IS THE EFFECT ON THE ACIDITY OF THAT α-PROTON?

Since a carbon group is electron releasing, its presence makes the α-hydrogen less acidic (larger pK$_a$) by about one pK$_a$ unit for each alkyl substituent.

KETO-ENOL TAUTOMERISM

WHAT IS AN ENOL?

An enol is a molecule that has an OH group directly attached to a carbon-carbon double bond, as in *13.63*.

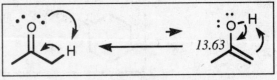

Fig. 13.63

WHAT IS KETO-ENOL TAUTOMERISM?

Most ketones and aldehydes are in equilibrium with an enol form (*13.63*). This equilibrium usually favors the carbonyl partner to a very great extent (often >99%). In general, a ketone or aldehyde is expected to exist primarily in the carbonyl form. This equilibrium occurs when the acidic α-hydrogen is removed by the basic carbonyl oxygen, forming an alkene group. The reverse reaction has the less basic alkene π-bond removing the acidic hydrogen form the O–H, regenerating the carbonyl. Since O–H is more acidic than C–H, the equilibrium is generally shifted to the left, favoring the carbonyl.

WHAT STRUCTURAL FEATURES CAN LEAD TO GREATER PERCENTAGES OF ENOL?

If the enol form is stabilized by internal hydrogen bonding, a higher percentage of the enol form will result. This occurs primarily when an atom capable of hydrogen bonding (such as an oxygen) is located at the position β-to the carbonyl carbon, as in 1,3-dicarbonyl compounds (see *13.64*).

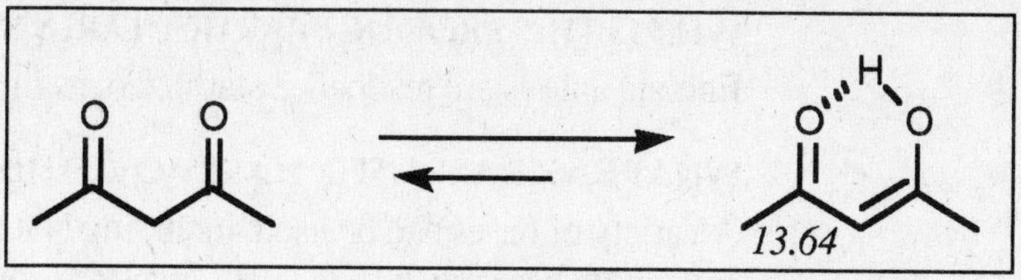

Fig. 13.64

WHAT IS THE RELATIVE PK$_a$ OF 2,4-PENTANEDIONE? EXPLAIN.

The pK$_a$ of the hydrogens on the -CH$_2$- group between the carbonyls (the presence of two C=O groups make these hydrogens the most acidic) is about 9. This is explained primarily by the enol content of this compound (*13.64*) which is present in >90% in hydrocarbon solvents. Removal of this acidic hydrogen is much more facile than from the enol form of a simple ketone (*13.63*) which has a pK$_a$ of about 20. It is noted that the common name of 2,4-pentanedione is acetylacetone.

COMPARE THE ACIDITY OF H$_a$ IN *13.65* AND *13.66*.

H$_a$ in 1,3-cyclopentanedione (*13.65*) is very acidic (pK$_a$ ≈9–10 due to its proximity to two carbonyls the high percentage of enol. Both H$_a$ and H$_b$ in *13.66* have the same pK$_a$ (≈ 21). The enol content is about the same as in a simple ketone, as is the pK$_a$, due to the fact that the carbonyl groups are not close enough to provide internal hydrogen bonding which would stabilize the enol form.

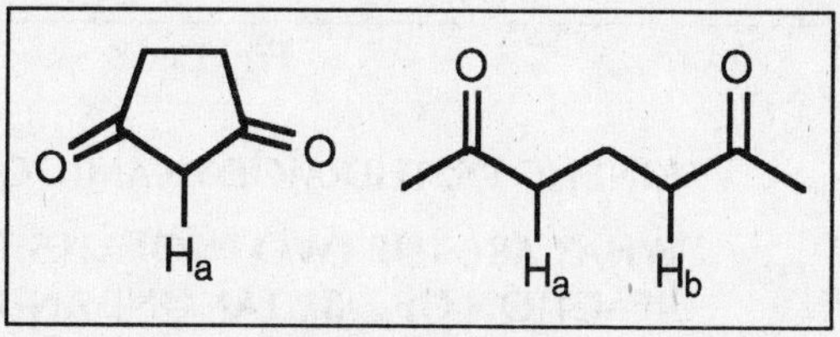

Fig. 13.65, 13.66

FORMATION OF ENOLATE ANIONS

WHEN THE ACIDIC α-PROTON OF A KETONE IS REMOVED, WHAT IS THE PRODUCT?

If one assumes the hydrogen is removed from the enol form of *13.66*, the product is an enolate anion (*13.67*), which is a resonance stabilized anion.

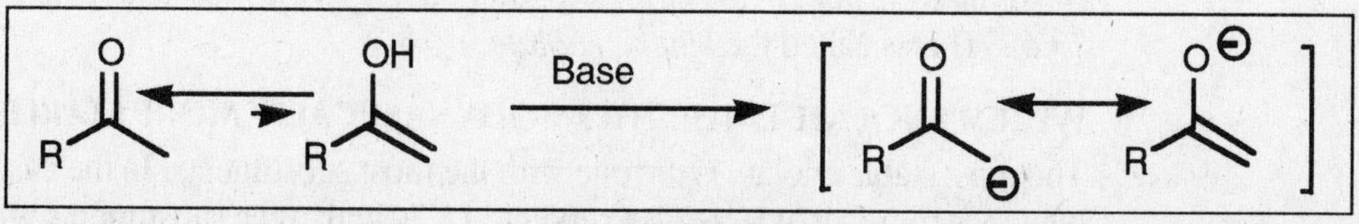

Fig. 13.66, 13.67

WHY IS THIS PRODUCT PARTICULARLY STABLE?

Enolate anions are resonance stabilized, as in *13.67*.

WHAT BASES ARE USED TO REMOVE THIS ACIDIC PROTON?

A variety of bases can be used, including NaOEt, NaOH, NaOMe, KOt-OBu and amide bases such as $NaNH_2$, $NaNR_2$, $LiNH_2$ and $LiNR_2$.

WHAT ARE 'NON-NUCLEOPHILIC' BASES?

Non-nucleophilic bases are usually amide bases (NR_2^-) where the R groups are bulky. This causes steric hindrance as the nitrogen approaches a carbon (behaving as a nucleophile) but does not hinder approach to a hydrogen (behaving as a base). The most commonly used non-nucleophilic base is lithium diisopropyl amide [$LiN(iPr)_2$], often abbreviated LDA.

WHAT IS THE PRODUCT WHEN 2,4-PENTANEDIONE IS REACTED WITH LDA? WITH SODIUM ETHOXIDE?

In both cases, the product is the same, enolate *13.68* (as the Li or Na salt, respectively) The presence of the second carbonyl group makes this enolate anion even more stable than *13.67*.

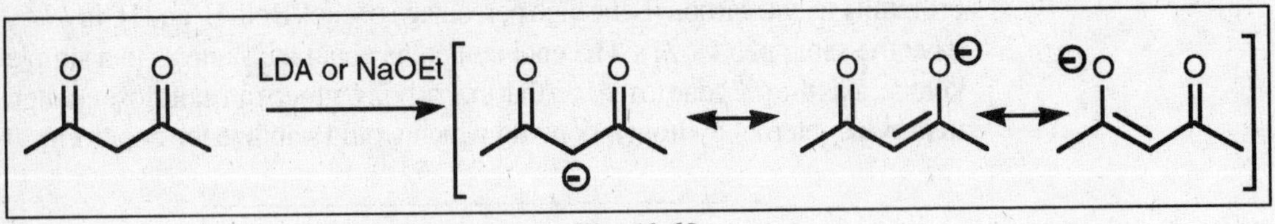

Fig. 13.68

KINETIC VS. THERMODYNAMIC CONTROL

WHAT ARE THE TWO ENOLATES THAT ARE POSSIBLE FROM THE REACTION OF 2-BUTANONE AND A SUITABLE BASE?

There are two acidic α-protons, H_a and H_b. Removal of H_a generates *13.69* and removal of H_b generates *13.70*. When these isomeric enolate anions react, isomeric products can result from reaction with *13.69* and/or *13.70*.

WHICH ENOLATE IS FORMED BY REMOVING THE MOST ACIDIC HYDROGEN?

Since an alkyl group is electron releasing, its presence will make the α-proton *less* acidic. The most acidic hydrogen will, therefore, be attached to the *less substituted carbon*. In the case of 2-butanone, H_a is the most acidic, leading to *13.69*. This is called the *kinetic enolate*.

WHICH ENOLATE IS THE THERMODYNAMICALLY MORE STABLE?

The most stable enolate is the one with the most substituents. In the case of 2-butanone removal of H_b leads to enolate *13.70* with three substituents whereas

13.69 has only two substituents. In this case *13.70* is the most stable enolate. This is called the *thermodynamic enolate*.

IF THE MOST ACIDIC HYDROGEN IS ALWAYS REMOVED FIRST, HOW CAN THE THERMODYNAMIC ENOLATE EVER FORM?

The only way to generate the thermodynamic enolate from the kinetic enolate is to establish an equilibrium between *13.69*, 2-butanone and *13.70*. Since removal of H_a or H_b is an acid-base reaction, which is inherently an equilibrium process, reaction conditions that promote this equilibrium will lead to the thermodynamic enolate, *13.70*.

Fig. *13.69, 13.70*

WHAT CONDITIONS FAVOR THE KINETIC ENOLATE?

Since the kinetic enolate is formed faster (and first) and an equilibrium is required to convert the kinetic enolate into a thermodynamic enolate, conditions that disfavor an equilibrium will favor the kinetic enolate. In general these conditions are: a polar, aprotic solvent (no acidic proton is available to reprotonate the enolate once it is formed); low temperatures (0 to -78°C are typical, which makes the proton transfer required for an equilibrium much slower); a strong base (such as LDA which removes the proton in a fast reaction and, most importantly, *does not produce a conjugate acid with an acidic proton*). If NaOEt is used, EtOH is the conjugate acid ($pK_a \approx 17$) which is strong enough to reprotonate the enolate. If LDA is used, the conjugate acid is diisopropylamine ($PK_a \approx 25$) which is not strong enough to quickly reprotonate the enolate anion. Short reaction times also favor the kinetic enolate.

WHAT CONDITIONS FAVOR THE THERMODYNAMIC ENOLATE?

Any reaction conditions that promote an equilibrium will favor the thermody-namic enolate and, of course, those conditions will be the exact opposite of the kinetic conditions. In general, a protic (acidic) solvent such as water or an alcohol is used (also an amine such as ethylamine or ammonia) since the acidic proton can be transferred to the enolate anion, regenerating the ketone and promoting the equilibrium. Higher reaction temperatures (mild heating to reflux) will promote the equilibrium, as will long reaction times. A base that generates a stronger conjugate acid (NaOEt, NaOH, etc.) will also favor thermodynamic control.

GIVE THE MAJOR PRODUCT FOR REACTIONS OF *13.71–13.73*. IDENTIFY EACH AS KINETIC OR THERMODYNAMIC CONTROL CONDITIONS.

In the first reaction, cyclohexanone (*13.71*) is deprotonated under thermodynamic control conditions. Since this is a symmetrical molecules both kinetic and thermodynamic control gives the same enolate (*13.74*). Aldehyde *13.72* has only one acidic a-proton and both kinetic and thermodynamic conditions will remove it. For reasons involving reactivity, kinetic control conditions (shown) are superior and will generate enolate *13.75*. In the last case, ketone *13.73* will give enolate *13.76* under the kinetic control conditions shown.

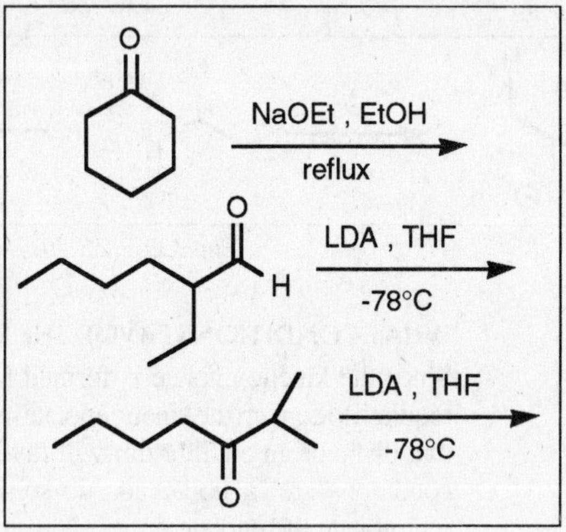

Fig. 13.71–13.73

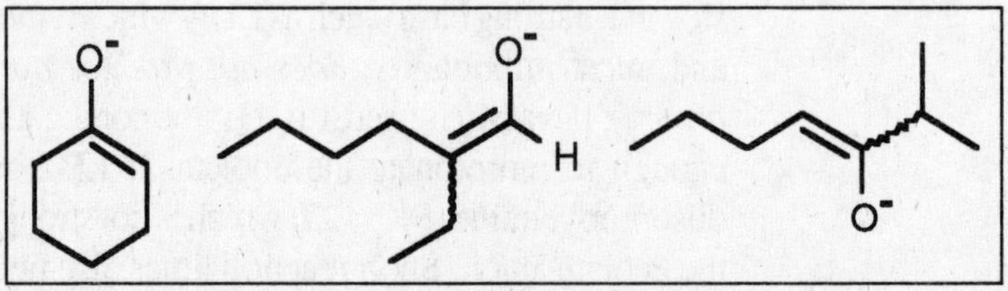

Fig. 13.74–13.76

WHAT TYPE OF REAGENTS ARE ENOLATES EXPECTED TO REACT WITH?

The carbon of the enolate anion is very nucleophilic and is expected to react with suitable electrophilic carbons. Typical reaction partners and alkyl halides and other carbonyl derivatives (ketones, aldehydes and acid derivatives).

ENAMINES

WHAT IS AN ENAMINE?

An enamine is a molecule that has an amino group (NR_2) attached directly to a carbon-carbon double bond, as in *13.77*. This particular example is the diethylamino enamine of 2-pentanone [named 2-(N,N-diethylamino)-1-pentene].

HOW ARE ENAMINES FORMED?

Enamines such as *13.77* are formed by reaction of a ketone with a *secondary* amine (HNR_2), usually in the presence of an acid catalyst.

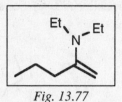

Fig. 13.77

GIVE THE MECHANISM FOR THE REACTION OF CYCLOPENTANONE AND DIETHYLAMINE IN THE PRESENCE OF A CATALYTIC AMOUNT OF ACID.

The reaction begins by formation of the protonated carbonyl species (*13.78*) with the acid catalyst. Addition of diethylamine to the anionic intermediate leads to *13.79* and loss of the proton give the amino alcohol *13.80*. Reprotonation of the amine leads back to the carbonyl but protonation of the OH group (see *13.81*) allows expulsion of water by the amine to give iminium salt *13.82*. Excess amine or even water can remove the hydrogen as H^+ to give the final enamine product, *13.83*. This is a general mechanism for the reaction of secondary amines and ketones. It is noted that the proton in *13.79* can be shifted to oxygen, giving *13.81* directly.

Fig. 13.78

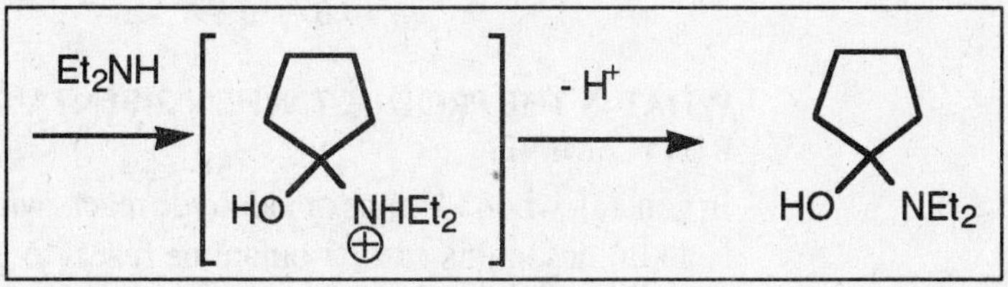

Fig. 13.79, 13.80

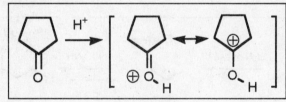

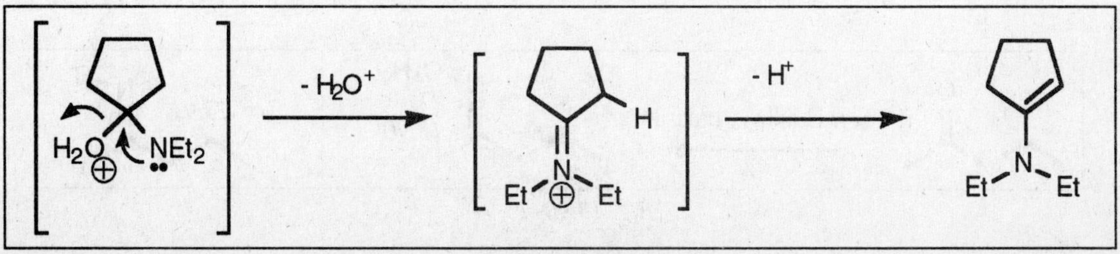

Fig. 13.81–13.83

WHAT AMINES ARE COMMONLY USED TO FORM ENAMINES?

The most common secondary amines used to form enamines are diethylamine (Et$_2$NH, dimethylamine (Me$_2$NH), pyrrolidine (*13.84*), piperidine (*13.85*) and morpholine (*13.86*). See sections 16.1 and 16.2.

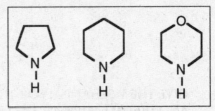

Fig. 13.84–13.86

WHAT IS THE PRODUCT WHEN BUTANAL REACTS WITH DIETHYLAMINE AND A CATALYTIC AMOUNT OF ACID?

The initial product is 1,1-(*bis*-diethylamino)butane (*13.87*). The term *bis*-refers to the presence of two diethylamine species in the molecule. This product arises from intermediate *13.88*, which reacts with additional diethylamine to form the disubstituted amino compound. *In most cases*, this geminal diamine will eliminate diethylamine to form iminium salt *13.88* as the major product. In many cases, however, *13.87* is the isolated product and must be reacted with base to give *13.89*.

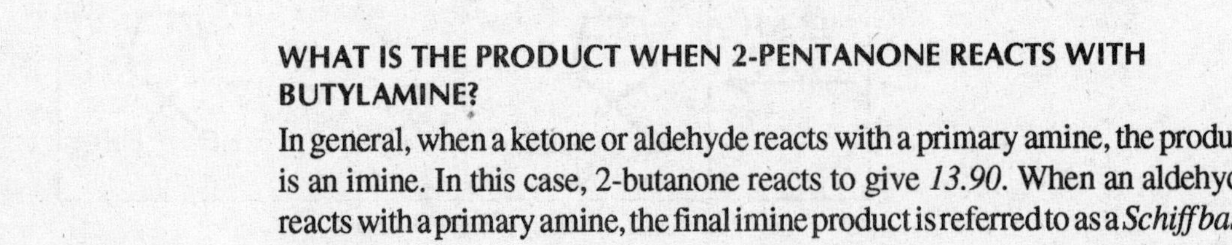

Fig. 13.87–13.89

WHAT IS THE PRODUCT WHEN 2-PENTANONE REACTS WITH BUTYLAMINE?

In general, when a ketone or aldehyde reacts with a primary amine, the product is an imine. In this case, 2-butanone reacts to give *13.90*. When an aldehyde reacts with a primary amine, the final imine product is referred to as a *Schiff base* (*13.91*).

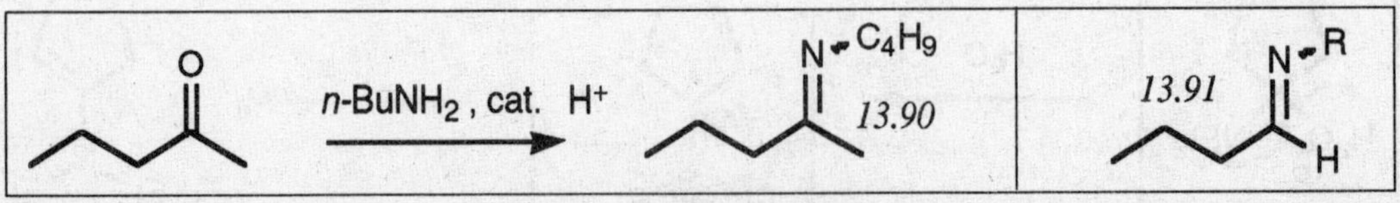

Fig. 13.90, 13.91

HOW ARE ENAMINES RELATED TO ENOLATE ANIONS?

An enolate anion can donate electrons from oxygen to an electrophile (E^+), making the α-carbon nucleophilic (as in *13.92*) Similarly, electrons can be donated from the nitrogen of an enamine, again making the α-carbon nucleophilic (as in *13.93*). In a very practical sense, an enamine can be considered as a nitrogen enolate.

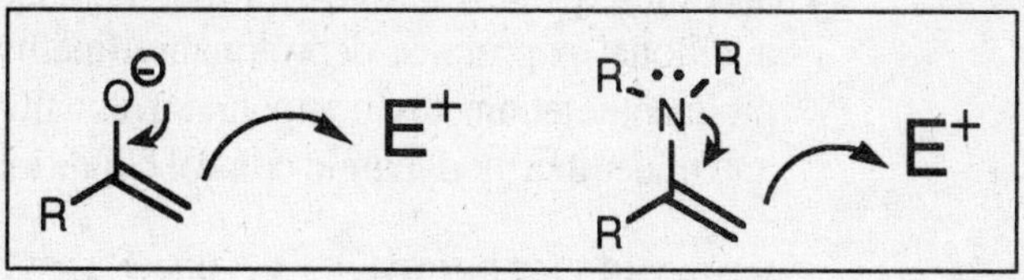

Fig. 13.92, 13.93

Enolate Alkylation   Enolates are carbon nucleophiles and react with alkyl halides to produce substituted aldehydes or ketones. In addition, enolate anions react with epoxides to produce hydroxy ketones or aldehydes. Enamines behave as 'nitrogen enolates' to produce alkylated derivatives upon reaction with alkyl halides. These reactions are generally S_N^2-like in their reactivity and stereochemistry.

REACTION WITH ALKYL HALIDES

WHEN THE KINETIC ENOLATE DERIVED FROM 2-PENTANONE IS REACTED WITH BENZYL BROMIDE, WHAT IS THE MAJOR PRODUCT?

The product is 1-phenyl-3-hexanone, *13.94*.

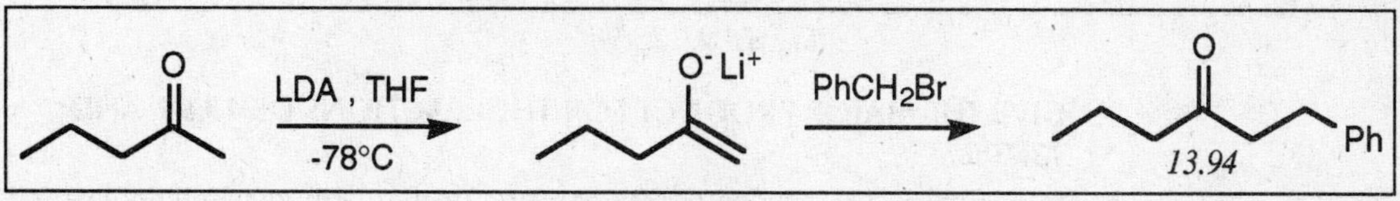

Fig. 13.94

WHEN 2-METHYLCYCLOHEXANONE IS REACTED WITH SODIUM ETHOXIDE IN ETHANOL AND THEN WITH IODOMETHANE, WHAT IS THE EXPECTED MAJOR PRODUCT?

Since these are thermodynamic control conditions, the most highly substituted enolate will form (*13.95*) and then react with iodomethane to give 2,2-dimethylcyclohexanone (*13.96*) as the major product.

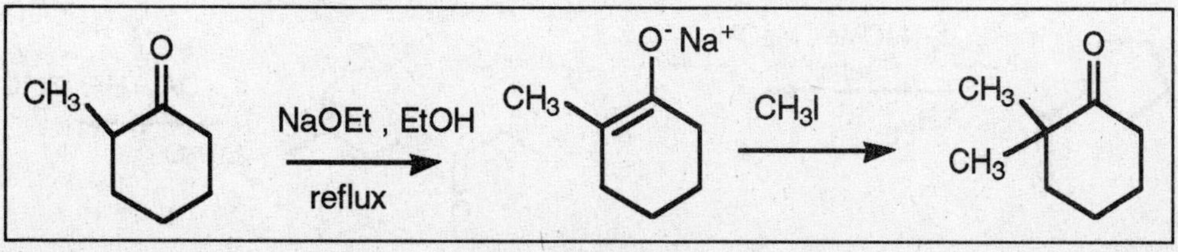

Fig. 13.95, 13.96

EXPLAIN HOW THE REACTION OF CYCLOHEXANONE WITH SODIUM AMIDE IN AMMONIA AND TREATMENT WITH A LARGE EXCESS OF IODOMETHANE CAN LEAD TO SMALL AMOUNTS OF 2,2,6,6-TETRAMETHYLCYCLOHEXANONE.

The initially formed enolate of cyclohexanone will react with iodomethane to form 2-methylcyclohexanone. This can react with more $NaNH_2$ to form *13.95* and subsequent reaction with iodomethane will give *13.96*. Since there are additional α-protons, deprotonation-methylation can occur sequentially to produce the tetramethyl compound. This will occur only with excess iodomethane and under thermodynamic control conditions with a relatively strong base.

WHAT IS THE PRODUCT WHEN 2,4-CYCLOPENTANEDIONE IS REACTED WITH SODIUM HYDRIDE AND THEN WITH ALLYL CHLORIDE? WHY CAN NaH BE USED RATHER THAN A MORE POWERFUL BASE?

The initially formed enolate (*13.97*) reacts with allyl chloride to form *13.98*. The presence of two carbonyls makes the proton on the 'middle' -CH_2- moiety very acidic (pK_a ≈ 9). Therefore, a much weaker base such as NaH can be used for the deprotonation.

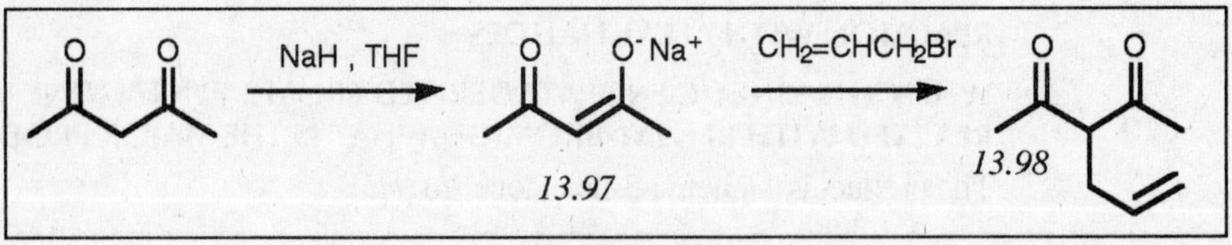

Fig. 13.97, 13.98

GIVE THE MAJOR PRODUCT FOR THE REACTIONS OF *13.99* AND *13.100*.

In the first reaction, ketone *13.99* is converted to the thermodynamic enolate and reaction with bromoethane leads to the highly substituted product, *13.101*. In the second reaction, diketone *13.100* has four acidic positions. Since the two carbonyls have a 1,4-relationship rather than a 1,3-relationship, there is no special acidity of the 'inside' protons nor special stability for those enolates. These are kinetic control conditions and quenching with deuterium oxide will transfer a D (^2H) to the less substituted carbon (*13.102*).

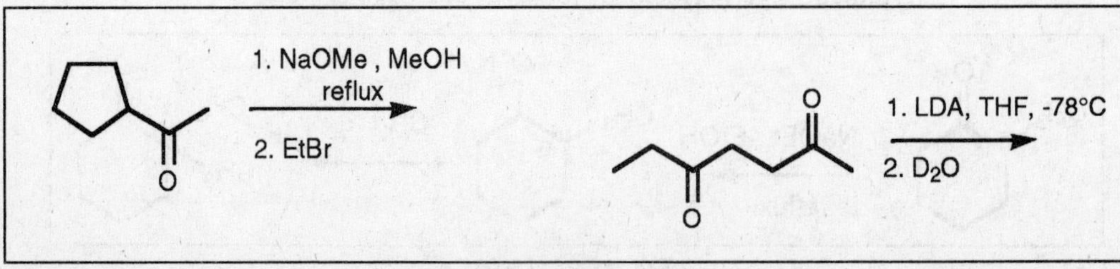

Fig. 13.99, 13.100

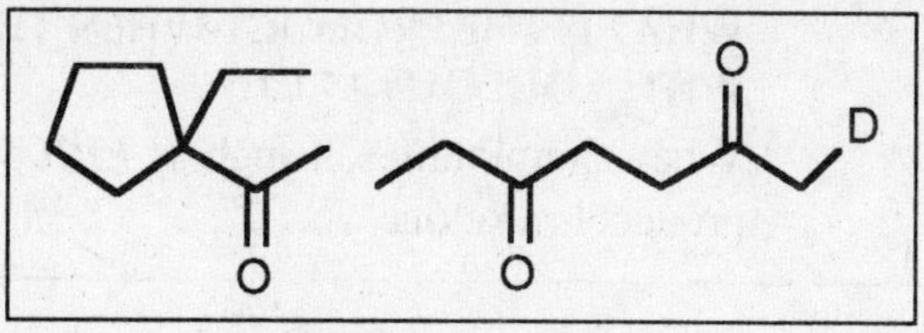

Fig. 13.101, 13.102

REACTION WITH EPOXIDES

WHAT IS THE PRODUCT WHEN THE KINETIC ENOLATE OF 2-HEXANONE REACTS WITH 1-ETHYLOXIRANE FOLLOWED BY HYDROLYSIS?

The electropositive carbon of an epoxide is subject to attack by a nucleophile such as an enolate. The nucleophile generally attacks the less sterically hindered (less substituted) carbon of the epoxide. In this case, the product is *13.103*.

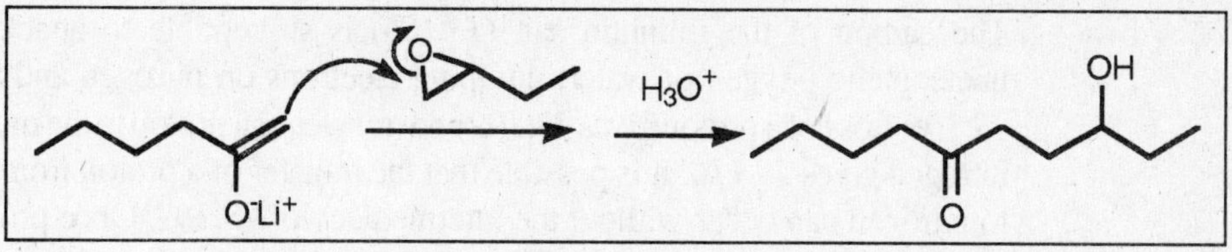

Fig. 13.103

EXPLAIN WHY EPOXIDE *13.104* DOES NOT REACT WITH THE ENOLATE OF ACETOPHENONE, EVEN UNDER THESE CONDITIONS.

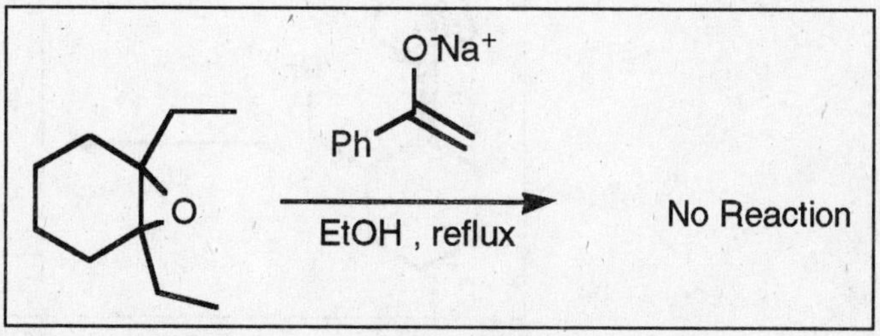

Fig. 13.104

The reaction of an enolate anion and an epoxide can be viewed essentially as a S_N^2 reaction. The two tertiary centers of the epoxide are, therefore, too unreactive with the nucleophilic enolate to permit the reaction.

ALKYLATION OF ENAMINES

WHAT IS THE INITIAL PRODUCT WHEN THE PYRROLIDINE ENAMINE OF CYCLOHEXANONE (*13.105*) REACTS WITH BENZYL BROMIDE?

When the α-carbon of the enamine attacks the electropositive carbon of benzyl bromide, the product is an iminium salt, *13.106*.

WHAT IS THE PRODUCT WHEN THE ABOVE PRODUCT IS TREATED WITH AQUEOUS ACID?

When an iminium salt such as *13.106* is treated with aqueous acid, the final product is a ketone, *13.107*.

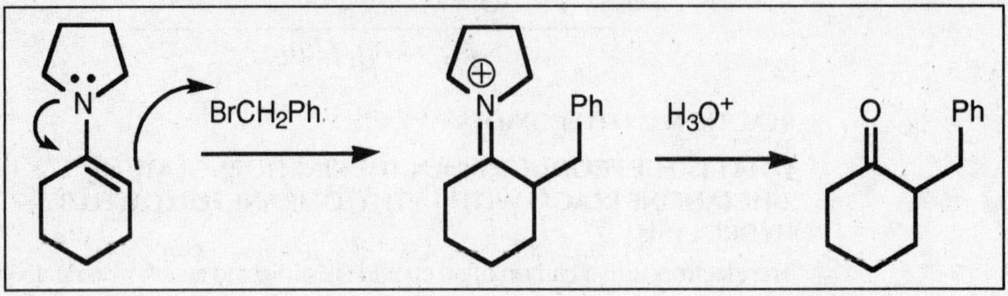

Fig. 13.105–13.107

GIVE THE MECHANISM FOR THIS LATTER REACTION.

The carbon of the iminium salt (*13.106*) is susceptible to attack by the nucleophilic oxygen of water, dumping electrons on nitrogen and forming *13.108*. Loss of a proton gives *13.109* and transfer of a proton to the more basic nitrogen gives *13.110*. It is possible that the transfer of a proton from oxygen to nitrogen can occur without the intermediacy of *13.109*. Once protonated, pyrrolidine becomes a good leaving group and its loss gives the protonated carbonyl (*13.111*) and simple loss of a proton gives the final product, *13.107* (2-benzylcyclohexanone).

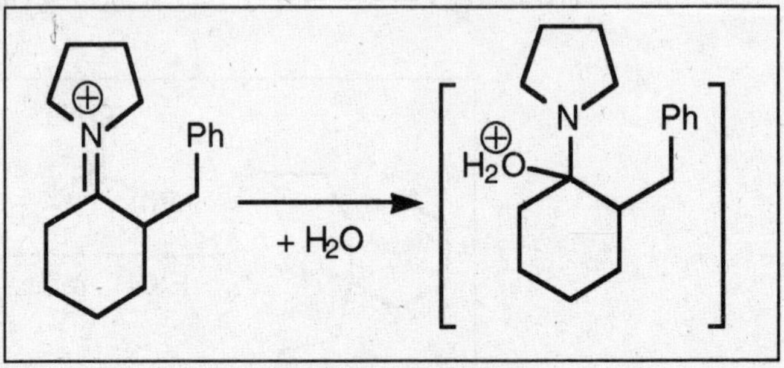

Fig. 13.106, 13.108

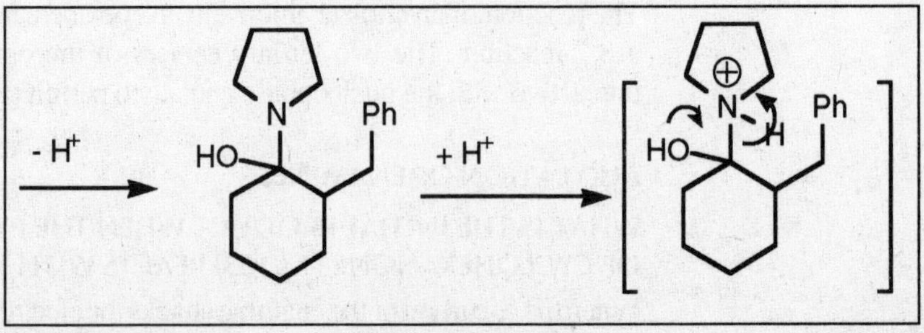

Fig. 13.109, 13.110

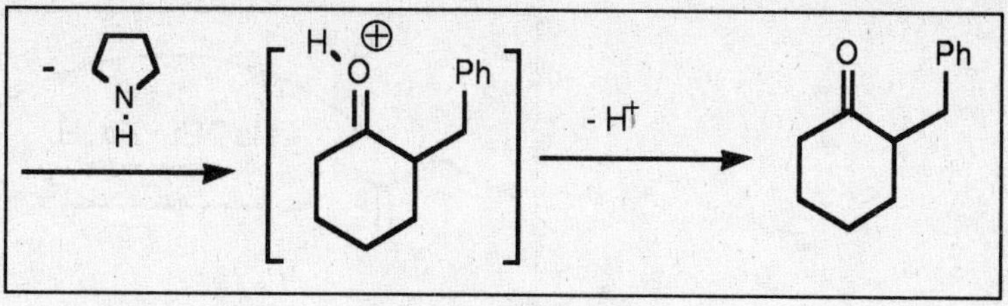

Fig. 13.111, 13.107

Enolate Condensation

An enolate condensation is the reaction of an enolate of a ketone or aldehyde with another carbonyl compound. There are many variations: enolates of aldehydes, ketones or acid derivatives can be condensed with aldehydes, ketones or acid derivatives. In this section only the condensation of aldehyde or ketone enolates with aldehydes or ketones will be considered. See section 15.4 for the condensation reactions of acid derivatives.

THE ALDOL CONDENSATION

WHAT IS THE PRODUCT OF THE REACTION BETWEEN THE KINETIC ENOLATE OF 2-BUTANONE AND CYCLOPENTANONE?

The nucleophilic carbon of the enolate will attack the electropositive carbon of the cyclopentanone carbonyl to form a new carbon-carbon bond, dump the electrons on oxygen and form alkoxide *13.112* as the initial product. Hydrolysis liberates the final alcohol product, *13.113*. Such β-hydroxyketones (or β-ketoalcohol) are known generically as aldols.

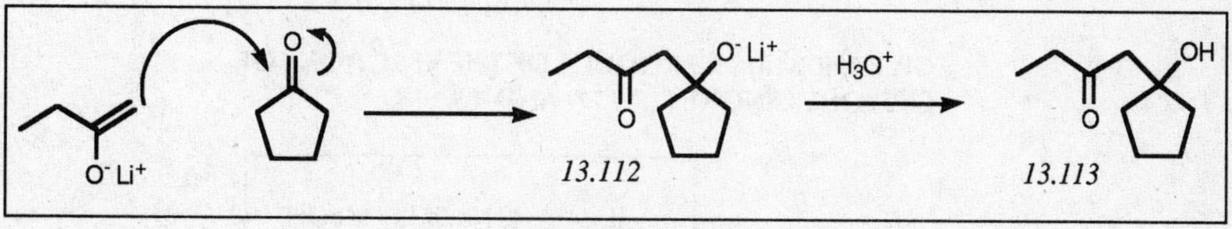

Fig. 13.112, 13.113

WHAT IS THE REACTION PRODUCT WHEN 2-BUTANONE IS TREATED WITH SODIUM ETHOXIDE IN ETHANOL?

When 2-butanone is converted to the thermodynamic enolate, significant amounts of base *and unreacted 2-butanone* are present in the equilibrium mixture. It is therefore reasonable to conclude that the enolate of 2-butanone (*13.114*) will react with unchanged 2-butanone in a condensation reaction that produces the alkoxide as the product. Hydrolysis gives the aldol, *13.115*.

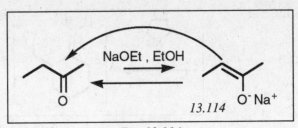

Fig. 13.114

WHAT IS THE NAME OF THIS REACTION?

It is the *Aldol Condensation*, named after the β-hydroxy carbonyl product (an aldol).

EXPLAIN WHY CONJUGATED KETONES OR ALDEHYDES ARE OFTEN ISOLATED FROM THIS REACTION WHEN THE PRODUCT IS TREATED WITH AQUEOUS ACID OR IS HEATED.

Loss of water (dehydration) is very facile since the final product (a conjugated carbonyl derivative such as *13.116*) is more stable than an unconjugated carbonyl derivative, *13.115*. Dehydration can be induced thermally (by heating the aldol product) or during the aqueous acid workup (H⁺ will catalyze dehydration). It is important to note, however, that dehydration does *not* occur in all cases with the acid workup and isolation of the aldol product is often straightforward.

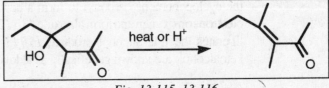

Fig. 13.115, 13.116

GIVE THE MAJOR PRODUCT OF THE REACTIONS OF CYCLOHEXANONE (*13.117*) AND *13.118*.

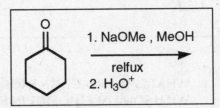

Fig. 13.117

Cyclohexanone is expected to react with itself, under thermodynamic conditions, to give the aldol product (after hydrolysis), *13.119*. In the second example, *13.118* is converted to the kinetic enolate under kinetic control conditions. No 'self-condensation' can occur since all of the ketone was converted to the enolate. In order to get this condensation, a second equivalent of *13.118* must the added to the enolate, allowing condensation and formation of the aldol product, *13.120* (after hydrolysis).

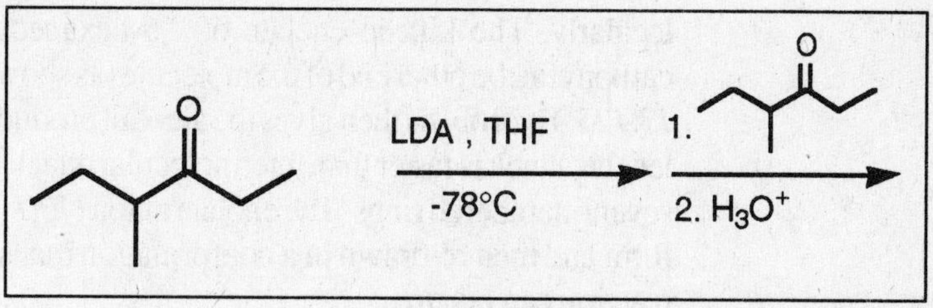

Fig. 13.118

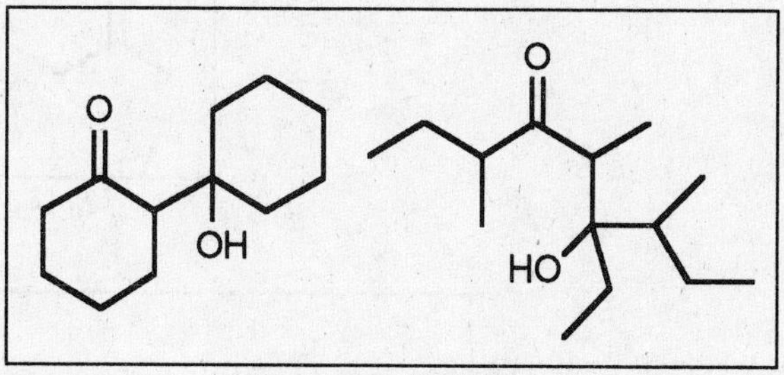

Fig. 13.119, 13.120

THE 'MIXED' ALDOL

WHAT IS A 'MIXED' ALDOL CONDENSATION?

Formation of *13.113* by condensing 2-butanone and cyclopentanone is an example of a mixed aldol. It simply means that the enolate of one ketone or aldehyde is reacted with a different ketone or aldehyde.

WHY ARE THERMODYNAMIC CONDITIONS NOT USED VERY OFTEN TO PRODUCE MIXED ALDOLS?

If two different ketones are present in a reaction under thermodynamic control, two different enolates can be formed, and each enolate can react with both ketones (which remain in solution), leading to four different aldol condensation products. As an example, the enolate of 2-butanone could react with both 2-butanone and cyclopentanone. Alternatively, the enolate of cyclopentanone could react with both 2-butanone and cyclopentanone.

WHAT IS THE ADVANTAGE OF USING KINETIC CONTROL IN FORMING MIXED ALDOL PRODUCTS?

Under kinetic control conditions, the enolate is formed essentially irreversibly. A second carbonyl partner is then added, giving a single 'mixed Aldol' product. Under thermodynamic control conditions, both carbonyls must be present at the same time. This is not true for kinetic control conditions.

THE INTRAMOLECULAR ALDOL

WHAT IS THE PRODUCT WHEN 2,5-HEXANEDIONE (*13.121*) IS REACTED WITH LDA AND THEN HYDROLYZED?

Aldol condensation reactions can occur intramolecularly as well as intermolecularly. The kinetic enolate of 2,5-hexanedione (*13.122*) will attack the carbonyl at the other end of the molecule (as shown) to form the cyclic alkoxide, *13.123*. Hydrolysis then gives the alcohol product, *13.124*. In general, intramolecular attack is faster than intermolecular attack for formation of five-, six- and seven-membered rings. The enolate anion (*13.122*) is drawn as the 'carbanion' form and then re-drawn in a conformation that shows how the intramolecular reaction can occur.

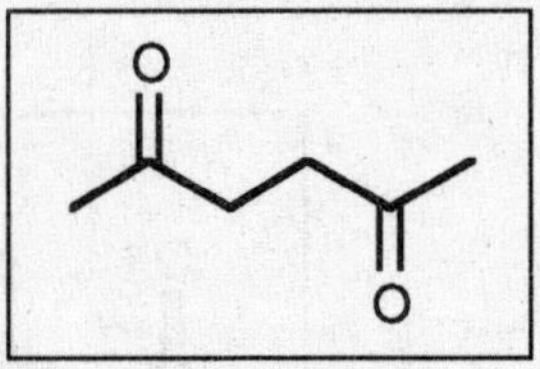

Fig. 13.121

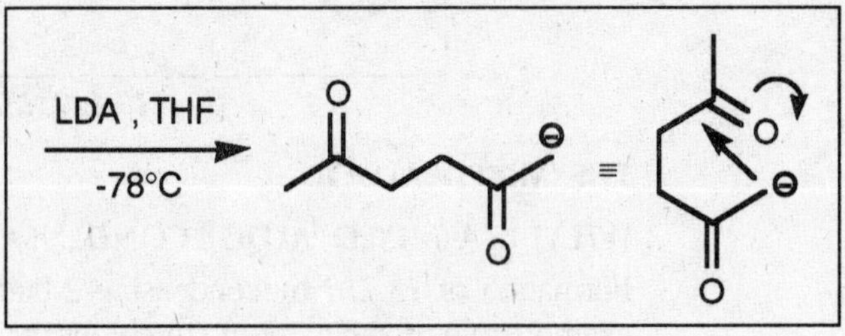

Fig. 13.122

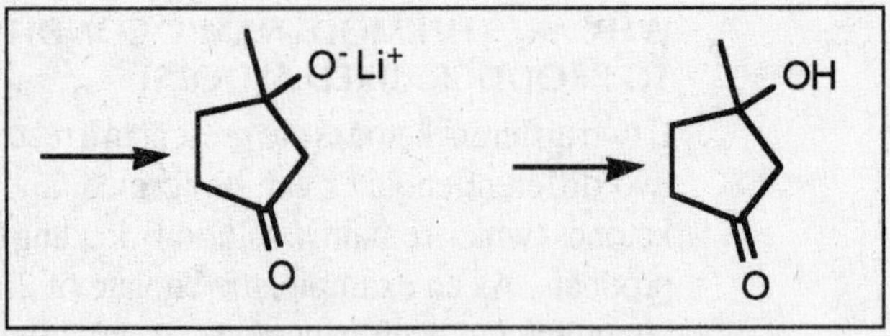

Fig. 13.123, 13.124

WHAT IS THE PRODUCT WHEN 2,5-HEXANEDIONE IS TREATED WITH SODIUM METHOXIDE IN METHANOL AND THEN HYDROLYZED?

The major product is the cyclopentanone derivative, *13.127*. Under thermodynamic conditions, enolates *13.125* and *13.122* are in equilibrium with the dione (*13.121*). The intramolecular Aldol condensation of *13.125* would generate a three-membered ring (*13.126*) which is energetically unfavorable when compared to formation of the five-membered ring derivative (*13.127*) from enolate *13.122*. Due to the relative ease of forming the five-membered ring product, the "kinetic" enolate leads to the product, even under thermodynamic control conditions. Remember, thermodynamic control implies that the *most stable product* is formed.

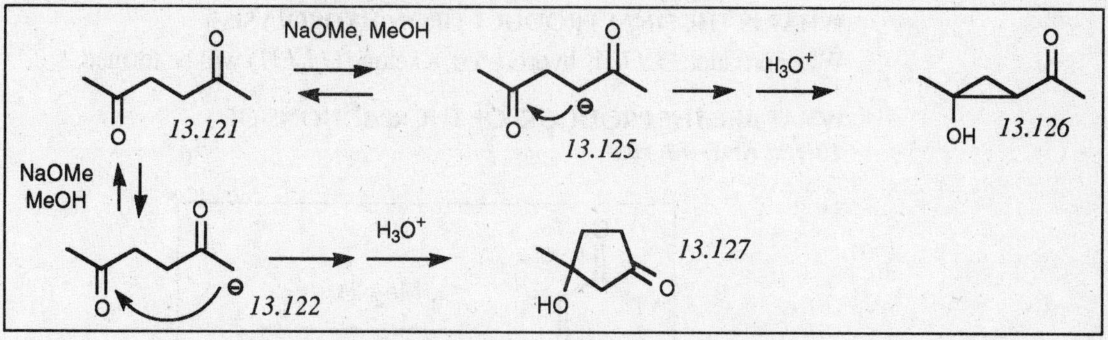

Fig. 13.121, 13.122, 13.125, 13.126, 13.127

MICHAEL ADDITION

WHAT IS A MICHAEL ADDITION?

Michael addition is the reaction of a nucleophile with a conjugated (α,β-unsaturated) ketone or aldehyde (usually a ketone) where the nucleophile adds to the π-bond of the alkene rather than to the carbonyl carbon.

WHY IS THE TERMINAL CARBON OF A CONJUGATED KETONE SUBJECT TO ATTACK BY A NUCLEOPHILE?

Analysis of *13.128* shows that bond polarization extends from the electronegative oxygen through the bonds to the β-carbon, making it electropositive.

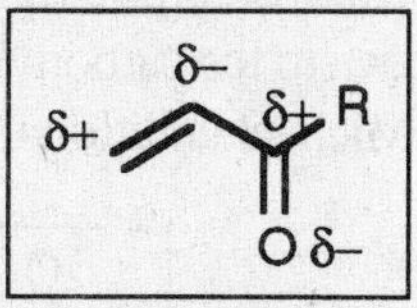

Fig. 13.128

WHAT IS THE INITIAL PRODUCT WHEN A NUCLEOPHILE REACTS WITH METHYL VINYL KETONE?

Reaction of methyl vinyl ketone (*13.129*) and a nucleophile will produce an enolate (*13.130*) via Michael addition.

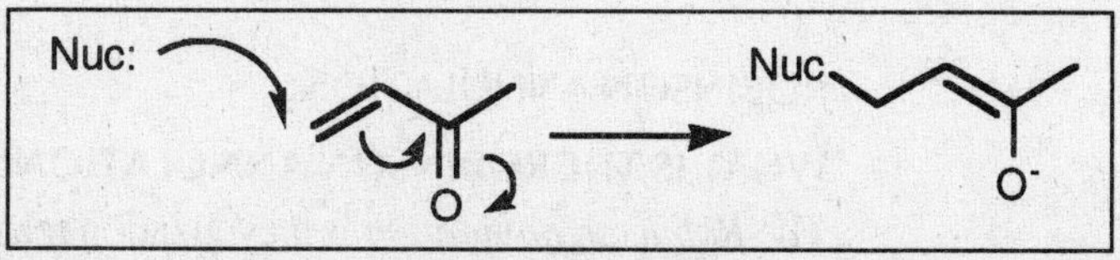

Fig. 13.129, 13.130

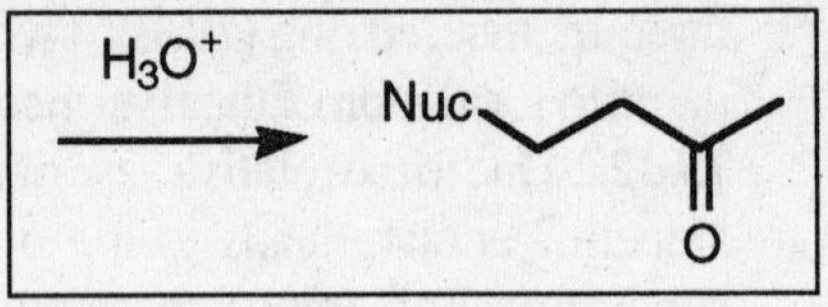

Fig. 13.131

WHAT IS THE FINAL PRODUCT UPON HYDROLYSIS?

When product *13.130* is hydrolyzed, a ketone (*13.131*) will be formed.

WHAT ARE THE PRODUCTS OF THE REACTIONS OF *13.132* AND *13.133*?

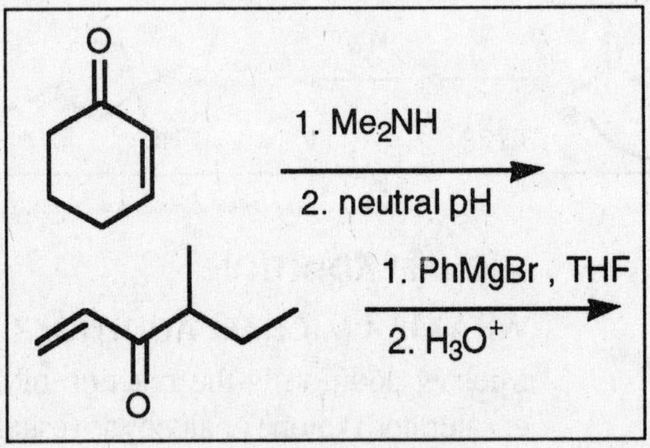

Fig. 13.132, 13.133

If a Michael addition occurs with cyclohexenone (*13.132*), the 3-dimethylamino product (*13.134*) will be the result, after careful neutralization of the amino ketone product. These *Michael adducts* are often unstable and are usually sensitive to heat and acid, losing the amine to reform the conjugated ketone. In the second case, the Grignard reagent adds to the double bond primarily because approach to the carbonyl is somewhat hindered by the adjacent alkyl substituents. Michael addition to *13.133* leads to the phenyl derivative, *13.135*.

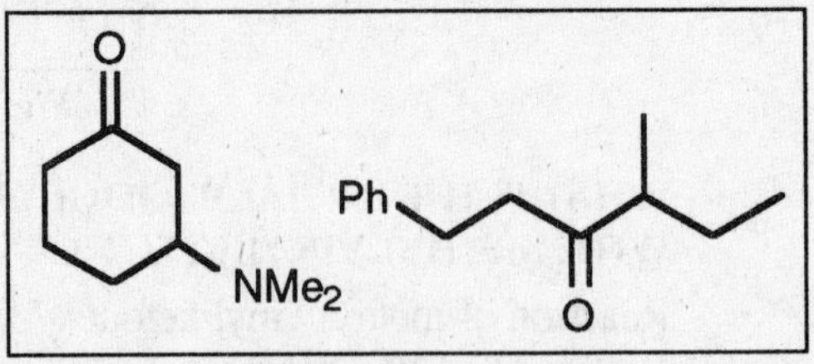

Fig. 13.134, 13.135

ROBINSON ANNULATION

WHAT IS THE ROBINSON ANNULATION?

The *Robinson annulation* is a cyclization reaction that combines an intramolecular Aldol condensation with an initial Michael addition. When cyclopentenone is treated with 2,4-pentane-dione under thermodynamic conditions, the product after hydrolysis is *13.136*. This is a classical example of the Robinson annulation.

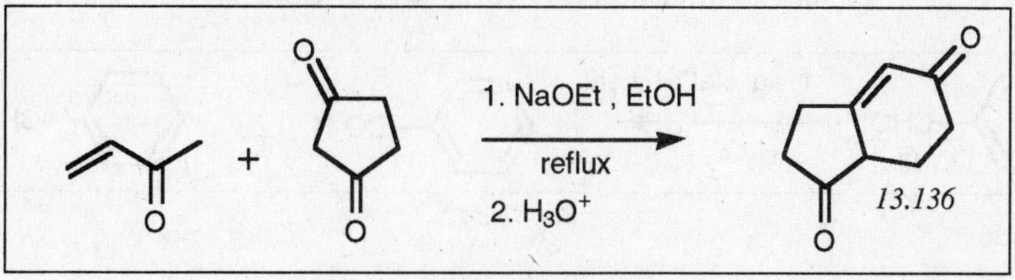

Fig. 13.136

GIVE A MECHANISTIC RATIONALE FOR WHY THE ROBINSON ANNULATION LEADS TO A SIX-MEMBERED RING.

The initial enolate (*13.137*) adds to methyl vinyl ketone to produce enolates *13.138* and *13.139* via a Michael addition. An intramolecular Aldol condensation from *13.138* would form a higher energy four-membered ring and is disfavored. Since under equilibrium conditions enolate *13.139* is also present, a six-membered ring can be formed via an intramolecular Aldol condensation. This alkoxide (*13.140*) is protonated by hydrolysis to give *13.141*. In many cases this is the isolated product. Heating or hydrolysis with strong aqueous acid will induce dehydration to give the conjugated ketone, *13.136*.

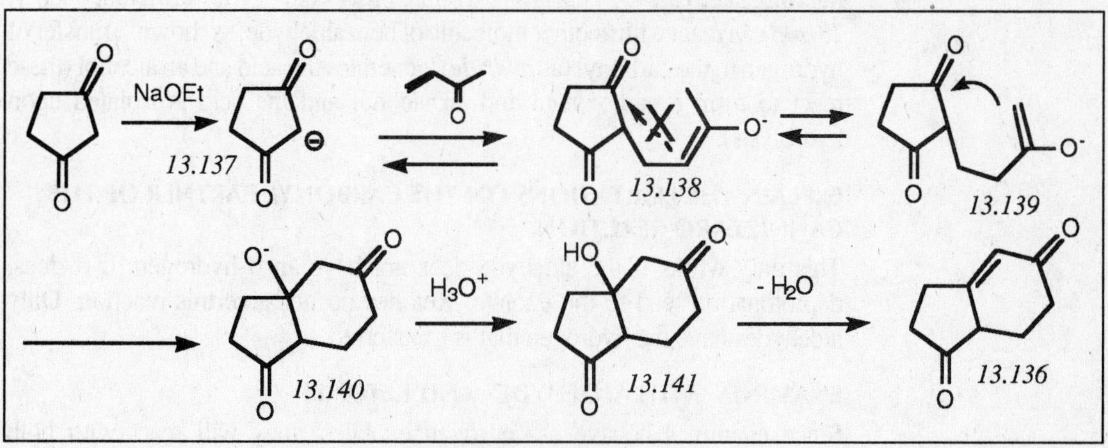

Fig. 13.137–13.141, 13.136

THE CANNIZZARO REACTION

WHAT IS THE CANNIZZARO REACTION?

The *Cannizzaro Reaction* is a condensation reaction of aromatic aldehydes (or other aldehydes that do not have an α-hydrogen) that is induced by treatment with hydroxide. Two products are formed, an oxidation product (an acid) and a reduction product (an alcohol). This 'self oxidation-reduction' type of reaction is known as *disproportionation*. An example is the conversion of benzaldehyde (*13.142*) to benzoic acid and benzyl alcohol upon treatment with aqueous hydroxide, followed by neutralization.

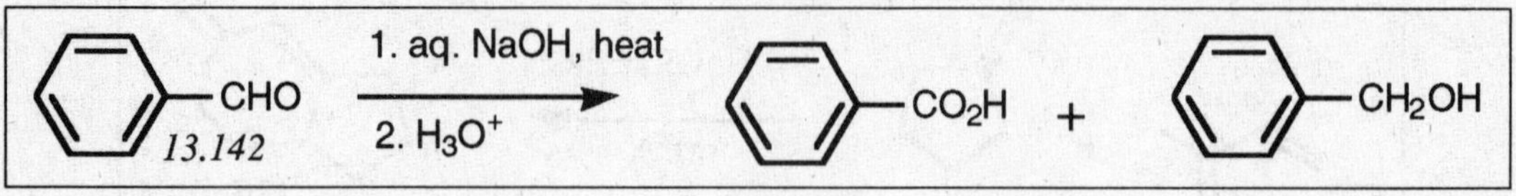

Fig. 13.142

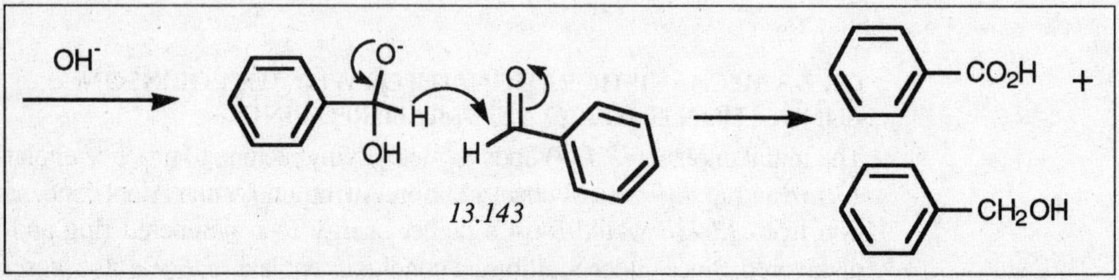

Fig. 13.143

GIVE A MECHANISTIC RATIONALE FOR THIS REACTION.

Hydroxide attacks the carbonyl of benzaldehyde to produce an alkoxide intermediate, *13.143*. This is a reversible process but given sufficient energy, *13.143* can react with another molecule of benzaldehyde, as shown. Transfer of hydrogen to the carbonyl (as *hydride*), generates the acid and an alcohol (these react to form a carboxylate and an alcohol and the acid is isolated upon hydrolysis).

EXPLAIN THE LIMITATIONS ON THE CARBONYL PARTNER OF THE CANNIZZARO REACTION.

This only works if the aldehyde does not have an α-hydrogen. If it does, deprotonation lead to the enolate. Ketones do not give this reaction. Only aldehydes have the hydrogen that is transferred.

ENAMINES WITH ALDEHYDES AND KETONES

Since enamines behave as 'nitrogen enolates' they will react with both aldehydes and ketones to produce iminium salts. Hydrolysis will then produce Aldol-like products.

GIVE THE MAJOR PRODUCT FOR THE REACTIONS OF *13.144* AND *13.145*.

In the first reaction the diethylamino enamine of cyclohexanone (*13.144*) is condensed with cyclopentanone to give, after hydrolysis, *13.146*. The second enamine (*13.145*) is condensed with butanal and gives, after hydrolysis, *13.147*.

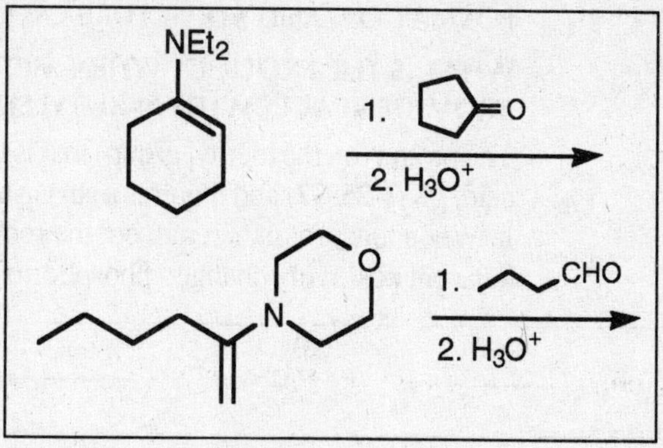

Fig. 13.144, 13.145

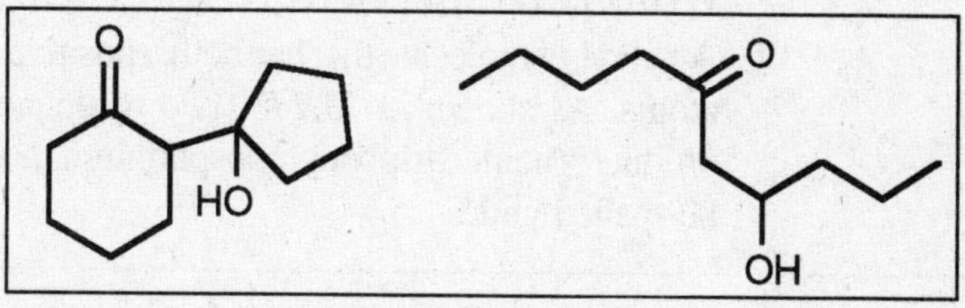

Fig. 13.146, 13.147

13.5. THE WITTIG REACTION

An ylid reacts with ketones or aldehydes to produce an alkene in what is known at the Wittig reaction or Wittig olefination.

Formation of Phosphoranes

WHAT IS THE STRUCTURE OF TRIPHENYLPHOSPHINE?

Phosphines are the phosphorus analogs to amines. Triphenylphosphine is Ph_3P.

WHAT IS THE CLOSEST ANALOGY TO THE REACTION OF A PHOSPHINE?

Since phosphorus is beneath nitrogen in the Periodic Table, phosphines are expected to react similarly to amines, R_3N.

WHAT IS THE PRODUCT WHEN TRIPHENYLPHOSPHINE REACTS WITH IODOMETHANE?

The phosphorus of triphenylphosphine behaves as a nucleophile, displacing iodide from iodomethane to form methyltriphenylphosphonium iodide [$Ph_3PMe^+ I^-$].

FORMATION AND STRUCTURE OF YLIDS

WHAT IS THE PRODUCT WHEN METHYLTRIPHENYLPHOSPHONIUM BROMIDE REACTS WITH N-BUTYLLITHIUM?

The proton (on the methyl group) that is α- to the phosphorus is acidic (a weak acid, $pK_a \approx 25\text{-}32$) and requires a strong base such as n-butyllithium to remove it. When this proton is removed, the remaining carbanion is stabilized by the adjacent positively changed phosphorus, as shown in *13.148*.

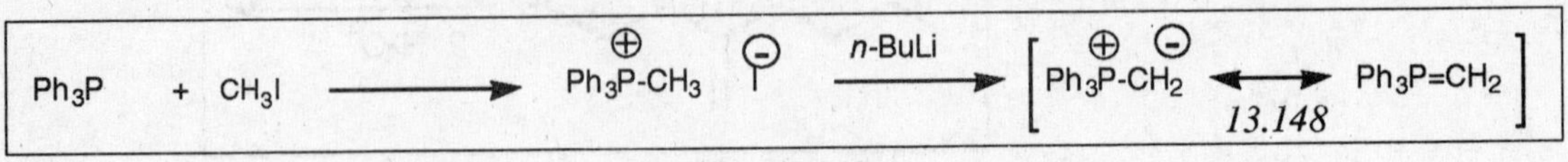

Fig. 13.148

WHAT IS THE DEFINITION OF AN YLID?

An ylid is a molecule that has both a positive and a negative charge on adjacent atoms. As shown in *13.148*, two resonance structures can be drawn. This product is named triphenylphosphonium methylid. It is noted that ylid can also be spelled ylide.

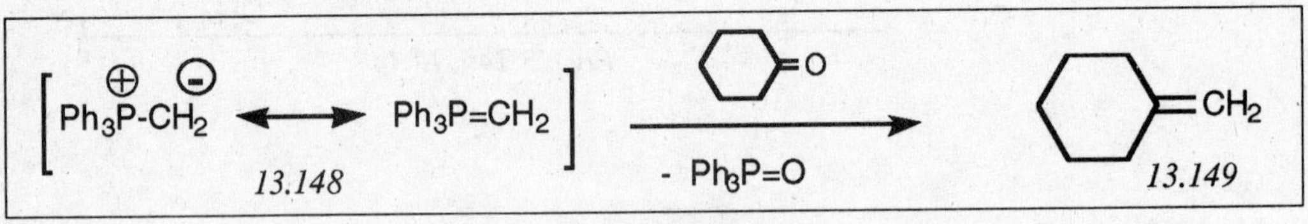

Fig. 13.149

OXAPHOSPHETANE AND BETAINE INTERMEDIATES

WHEN TRIPHENYLPHOSPHONIUM METHYLID REACTS WITH CYCLOHEXANONE WHAT IS THE MAJOR PRODUCT?

When a phosphonium ylid reacts with a ketone or aldehyde, an alkene is formed, along with triphenylphosphine oxide [$Ph_3P=O$]. In this case, *13.148* reacts with cyclohexanone to form methylene cyclohexane, *13.149*.

HOW DOES THIS REACTION WORK?

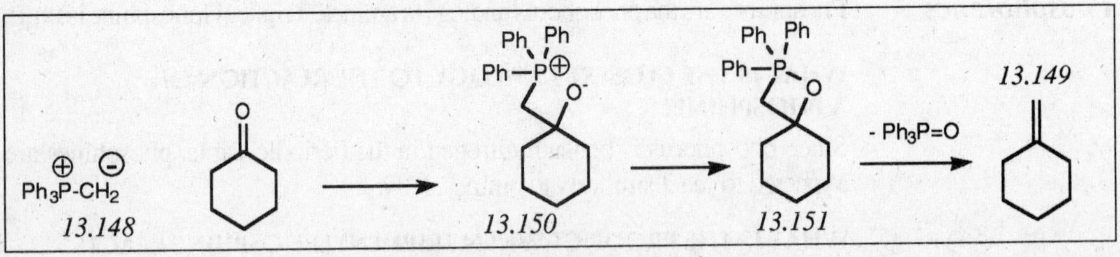

Fig. 13.150, 13.151, 13.149

The ylid initially reacts with the carbonyl to form a dipolar ion, *13.150*. The four-membered ring closes to generate *13.151*. The P–O is very strong and its formation (exothermically) drives the cleavage of the four membered ring differently than its formation. The C–P and C–O bonds are cleaved, forming the alkene (*13.149*) and triphenylphosphine oxide.

WHAT IS THE DISTINCTION BETWEEN AN OXAPHOSPHETANE AND A BETAINE?

The betaine is the dipolar ion, *13.150*. An oxaphosphetane is a four-membered ring containing both a phosphorus and an oxygen, such as *13.151*.

WHAT IS THE 'DRIVING FORCE' FOR THE WITTIG OLEFINATION REACTION?

Formation of the very strong P–O bond.

ALKENE FORMATION VIA THE WITTIG REACTION

GIVE THE MAJOR PRODUCT FOR THE REACTIONS OF *13.152–13.154*.

Aldehyde *13.152* reacts with the ylid to produce the linear alkene, *13.155*. The sensitive molecule cyclobutanone (*13.153*) reacts to form the exocyclic methylene compound, methylenecyclobutane, *13.156*. In the last example, a methyl group is incorporated in the conversion of ketone *13.154* into the tetrasubstituted alkene, *13.157*.

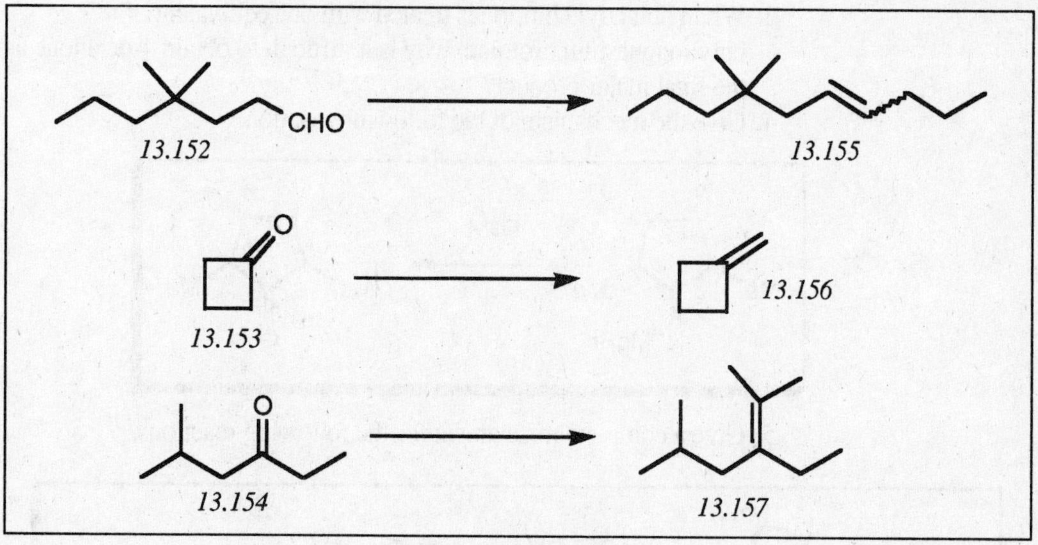

Fig. 13.152–13.157

*T*his is the first chapter where a major focus has been on the formation of carbon-carbon bonds. If chemists want to make a molecule, they usually start with a 'small' molecule and add carbons by chemical reactions, eventually forming 'large' molecules. Ketones and aldehydes are very important partners in reactions that form carbon-carbon bonds. They also play a role in many other transformations, particularly reductions to form alcohols. It is clear they are vitally important and the chemistry discussed in this chapter will be used in many other applications.

END OF CHAPTER PROBLEMS

1. How can one distinguish between cyclohexanone and 2-cyclohexenone using spectroscopy?
2. Give the IUPAC name for each of the following.

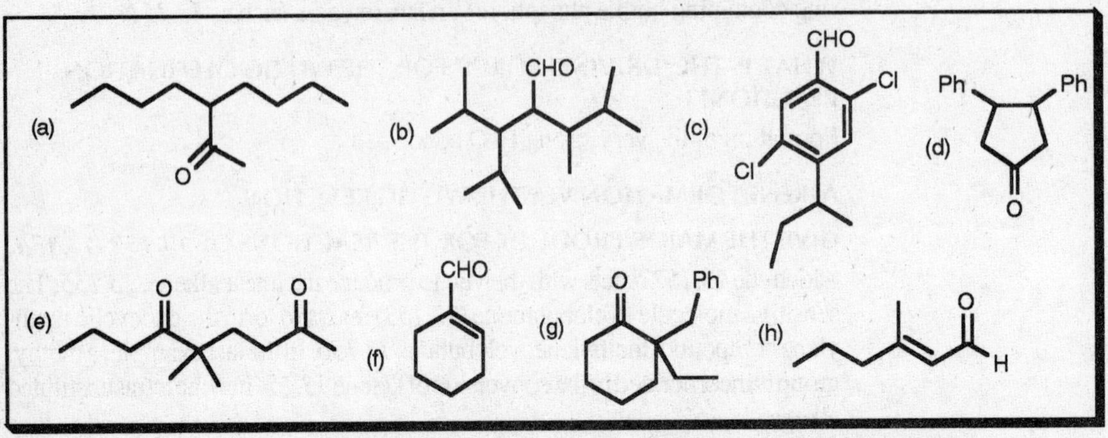

3. When butanoyl chloride is treated with one equivalent of butylmagnesium bromide, why is it difficult to obtain 4-octanone as the final major product?
4. Give the mechanism of the following reaction.

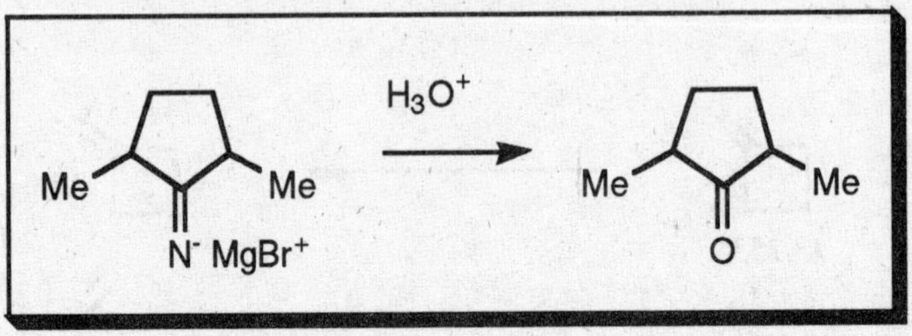

5. Give a complete mechanism for the following reactions.

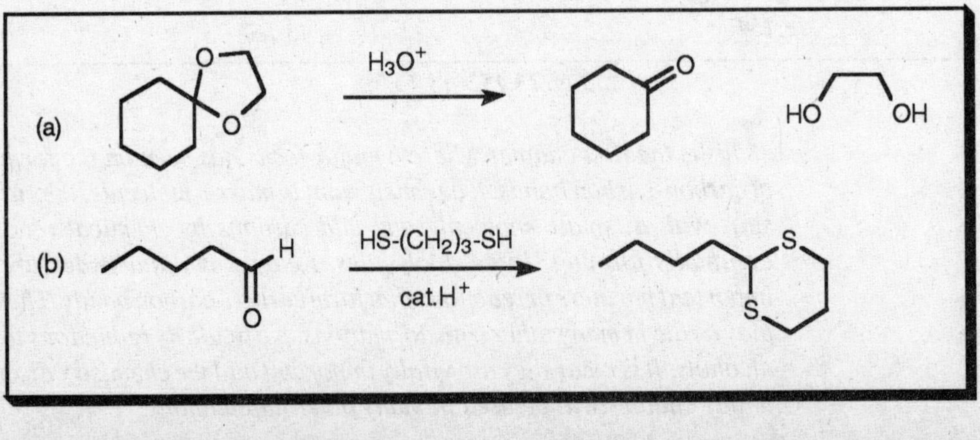

6. What is the initial product when the hydrate of 2-butanone loses water? How is this converted back to 2-butanone?
7. Draw a picture of a Dean-Stark apparatus.
8. Give the structures of 1,3-dioxane, of 1,3-dioxolane, of 1,3-dithiane and of 1,3-dithiolane.
9. Give the IUPAC name of each of the following.

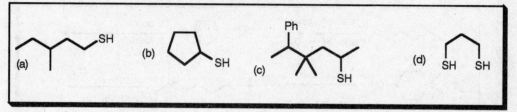

10. What is the most acidic hydrogen in each of the following molecules?

11. Which of the following has the highest enol content? Explain.

12. What reaction conditions favor kinetic control in forming an enolate anion from 2-butanone?
13. Give the mechanism of the following reaction.

14. Give all Aldol products that are possible from the following reaction.

15. Predict the product from the reaction of but-3-en-2-one and lithium dibutylcuprate.

16. Why does the Cannizzaro reaction *not* occur with pentanal and aqueous sodium hydroxide?

17. In each case give the major product. Remember stereochemistry where appropriate and if there is no reaction, indicate by N.R.

(a)
1. 9-BBN , ether
2. NaOH , H$_2$O$_2$
3. PCC

(b)
1. OsO$_4$
2. NaHSO$_3$
3. H$_5$IO$_6$

(c)
CrO$_3$, aq. H$^+$

(d)
1. O$_3$
2. H$_2$O$_2$

(e)
PDC , CH$_2$Cl$_2$

(f)
1. KOH , EtOH
2. O$_3$
3, Me$_2$S

(g)
Ph–C(=O)–Cl
NEt$_3$

(h)
OsO$_4$, H$_5$IO$_6$

(i)
1. SOCl$_2$
2. AlCl$_3$

(j)
cat. p-TsOH , EtOH

(k) Cl$_3$C–CHO
H$_2$O

(l) O$_2$N––NO$_2$
AlCl$_3$

(m)
1. HSCH$_2$CH$_2$SH, cat. H$^+$
2. Ni(R) , acetone

(n)
CO$_2$H
1. SOCl$_2$
2.3 MeMgBr
3. H$_3$O$^+$

(p) CHO
1. cat. H$^+$, HO   OH
2. H$_3$O$^+$

(o)
Br
1. Li° , ether
2. 1/2 CdCl$_2$
3.   Cl
        O

(q)
HCN

(r)
O
Cl
Bu$_2$CuLi , ether
–10°C

(s)
O
1. EtC≡C:$^-$, DMF
2. H$_3$O$^+$

(t)
O
Cl
Et$_2$Cd

(u)
1. NaNH$_2$, THF
2. 2-butanone
3. H$_3$O$^+$

(v)
C≡N
1. C$_3$H$_7$MgBr
2. H$_3$O$^+$, heat

(w)
OH
1. CrO$_3$, aq. H$^+$
2. EtMgBr , ether
3. H$_3$O$^+$

(x)
Br
1. KCN , DMF
2. PhMgBr
3. H$_3$O$^+$, heat

(y)
Br
1. Mg° , ether
2. HCHO
3. H$_3$O$^+$

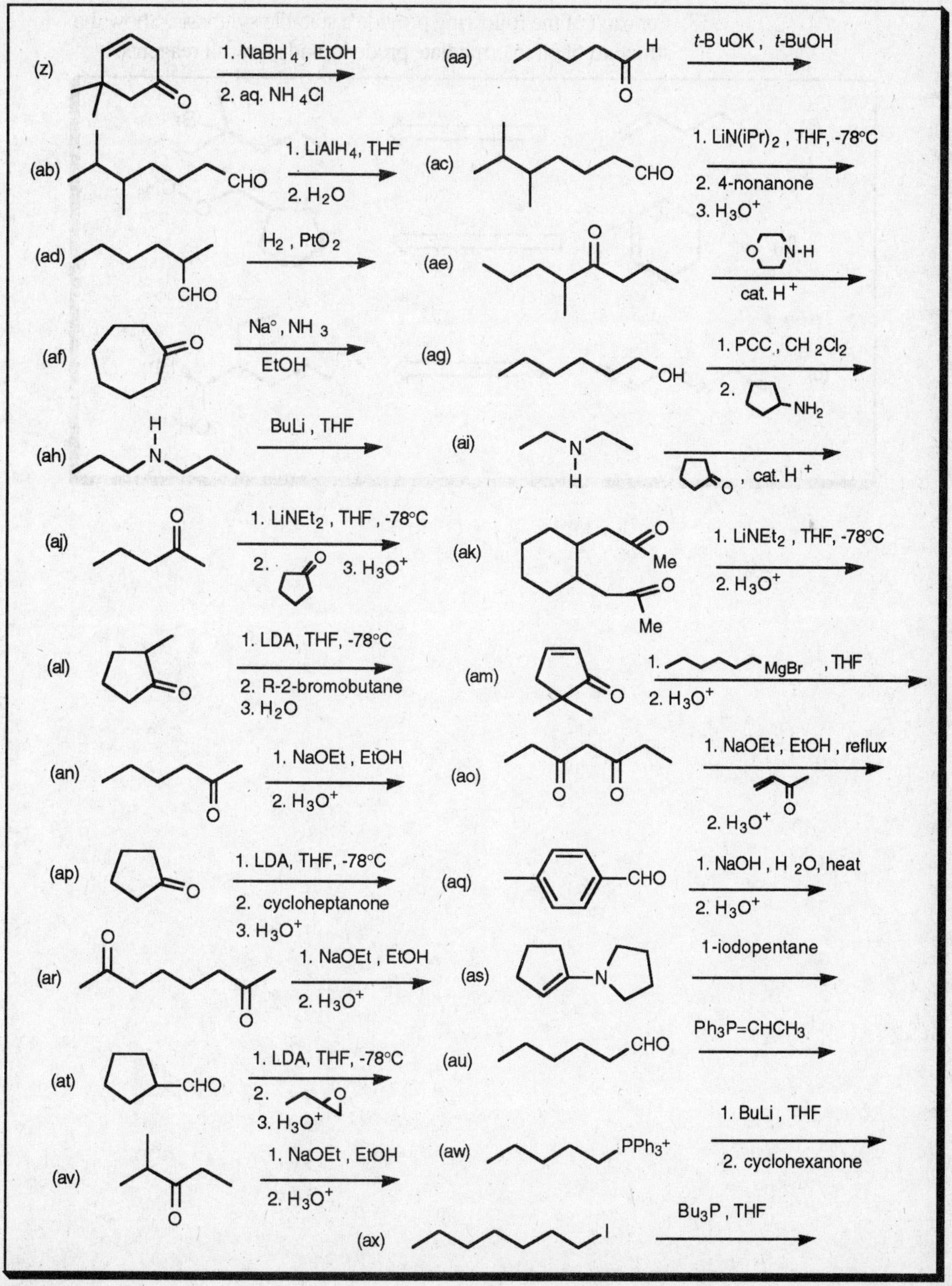

(z)
1. NaBH 4 , EtOH
2. aq. NH 4Cl
O
(aa)
H
O
t-B uOK , t-BuOH
(ab)
CHO
1. LiAlH4, THF
2. H2O
(ac)
CHO
1. LiN(iPr)2 , THF, -78°C
2. 4-nonanone
3. H3O+
(ad)
CHO
H2 , PtO 2
(ae)
O
N-H
cat. H +
(af)
O
Na° , NH 3
EtOH
(ag)
OH
1. PCC , CH 2Cl2
2.
NH2
(ah)
H
N
BuLi , THF
(ai)
N
H
O
, cat. H +
(aj)
O
1. LiNEt2 , THF , -78°C
2.
O
3. H3O+
(ak)
O
Me
O
Me
1. LiNEt2 , THF, -78°C
2. H3O+
(al)
O
1. LDA, THF, -78°C
2. R-2-bromobutane
3. H2O
(am)
O
1.
MgBr
, THF
2. H3O+
(an)
O
1. NaOEt , EtOH
2. H3O+
(ao)
O
O
1. NaOEt , EtOH , reflux
O
2. H3O+
(ap)
O
1. LDA, THF, -78°C
2. cycloheptanone
3. H3O+
(aq)
CHO
1. NaOH , H 2O, heat
2. H3O+
(ar)
O
O
1. NaOEt , EtOH
2. H3O+
(as)
N
1-iodopentane
(at)
CHO
1. LDA, THF, -78°C
2.
O
3. H3O+
(au)
CHO
Ph3P=CHCH3
(av)
O
1. NaOEt , EtOH
2. H3O+
(aw)
PPh3+
1. BuLi , THF
2. cyclohexanone
(ax)
I
Bu3P , THF

18. For each of the following provide a suitable synthesis. Show the structure of all intermediate products and show all reagents.

(a)

(b)

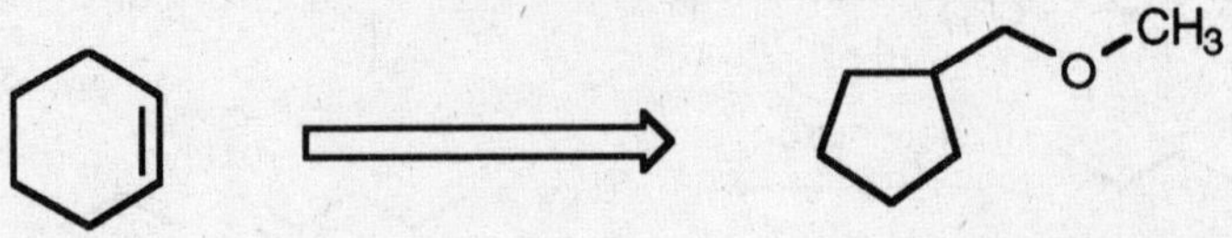

(c)

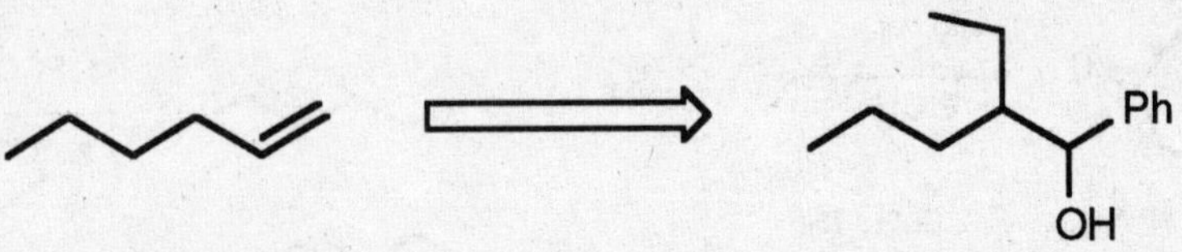

14

Carboxylic Acids

*C*arboxylic acids are the prototype organic acid. They comprise an entire family of molecules called acid derivatives. The name 'acid' describes much of their chemistry. These organic acids are important building blocks for the formation of other functional groups. Their acid properties are important in such diverse applications as giving important physical and chemical properties to amino acids (see chapter eighteen) to their use as acid catalysts in cationic reactions of alcohols and alkenes. This chapter will focus on the acid properties of carboxylic acids and the factors which influence acidity. This chapter will also show how carboxylic acids can be transformed into other 'acid derivatives' such as acid chlorides, esters, anhydrides and amides.

14.1. STRUCTURE OF CARBOXYLIC ACIDS

The Carboxyl Group

WHAT IS THE BASIC UNIT REFERRED TO A CARBOXYL GROUP?
A carbonyl with an OH attached to it, HO–C=O.

WHAT IS THE DISTINGUISHING FEATURE OF A CARBOXYL GROUP?
A carboxyl group is characterized by the presence of a very acidic hydrogen (O–H) along with an electropositive carbonyl carbon of the C=O.

Hydrogen Bonding

DESCRIBE THE BOND POLARITY IN A CARBOXYL GROUP.
The O–H group in *14.1* is polarized such that the H is acidic and the carbonyl carbon is electrophilic.

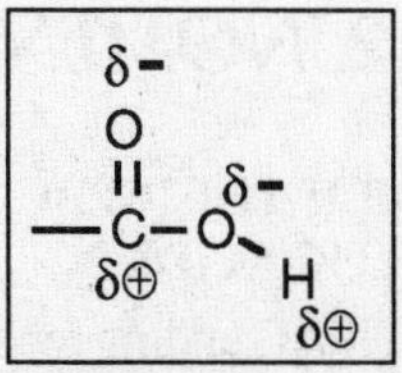

Fig. 14.1

HOW EXTENSIVE IS THE HYDROGEN BONDING CAPABILITY OF A CARBOXYL GROUP?

The acidic hydrogen of the OH group is strongly hydrogen bonded to the carbonyl oxygen of a second carboxyl, as illustrated in *14.2*.

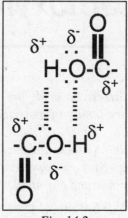

Fig. 14.2

Physical Properties

WHEN COMPARED TO AN ALCOHOL OF SIMILAR MOLECULAR WEIGHT A CARBOXYLIC ACID GENERALLY HAS A MUCH HIGHER BOILING POINT. WHY?

As seen in chapter one, a carbonyl group is capable of extensive hydrogen bonding, much more extensive and stronger than observed with alcohols. This strong hydrogen bonding must be disrupted to bring the carboxylic acid into equilibrium with both gas and liquid (boiling point), requiring higher temperatures than with an alcohol.

DOES A CARBOXYLIC ACID EXHIBIT IMPORTANT UV ABSORPTION?

There are no important UV bands that can be used for unique identification of a carboxylic acid relative to another functional group.

WHAT IS THE RELATIVE POLARITY OF A CARBOXYLIC ACID?

A carboxyl group is very polar, with the dipole moment generally directed at an angle between the O–C=O bond.

14.2. NOMENCLATURE

WHAT IS THE IUPAC ENDING THAT IS CORRELATED WITH A CARBOXYLIC ACID?

The IUPAC ending for a carboxylic acid is -oic acid. The C_6 straight-chain acid is hexanoic acid (drop -ane from hexane and add -oic acid).

WHY IS THE NUMERICAL POSITION OF THE CARBOXYL GROUP USUALLY OMITTED FROM THE NAME OF A CARBOXYLIC ACID?

Since the carbonyl carbon of the carbonyl *must* have the lowest number (it is the functional group) and that carbon contains the OH, it *must* be C_1. For this reason (as with aldehydes) the number is usually omitted.

WHY IS A C_6 ACID CALLED HEXANOIC ACID RATHER THAN HEXOIC ACID?

A C_6 acid could have an alkane, alkene or alkyne backbone. The -an, en or yn must be included to show which is present. This will lead to hexanoic acid, hexenoic acid and hexynoic acid for the three cases mentioned. In the last two cases, a number must be assigned to the C=C or C≡C group (as in hex-4-enoic acid or hex-5-ynoic acid, $CH_3CH=CHCH_2CH_2COOH$ and $HC≡CCH_2CH_2CH_2COOH$, respectively).

GIVE THE CORRECT STRUCTURE FOR THE FOLLOWING ACIDS.

(a) 3,5-diphenylheptanoic acid (b) 3,5-dichlorobenzoic acid (c) 3-ethyl-4-(3-methylbutyl)nonanoic acid (d) 3-cyclopentylbutanoic acid

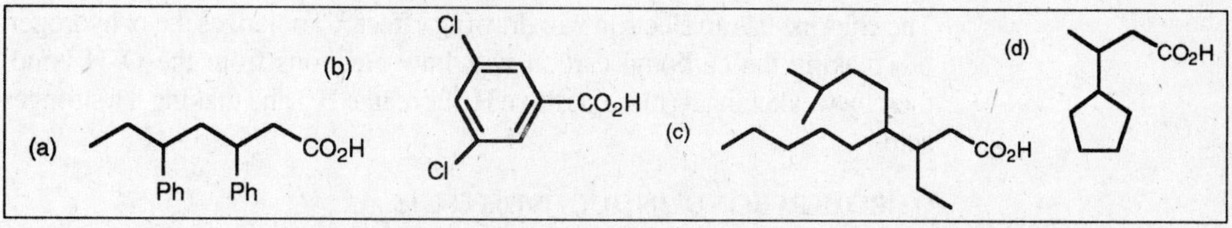

GIVE THE COMMON NAME OF THE FOLLOWING ACIDS.

(a) CH_3CO_2H
(b) HCO_2H
(c) $PhCH_2CO_2H$
(d) $CH_3CH_2CH_2CH_2CH_2CH_2CH_2CO_2H$

The common name of (a) is acetic acid and (b) is called formic acid. Using the acetic acid nomenclature, the common name of (c) is phenylacetic acid. Case (d) is an 8-carbon acid with the common name of caprylic acid. Many of the common lower molecular weight acid have common names, especially those with an even number of carbons:

C_5 = valeric acid; C_6 = caproic acid; C_{10} = capric; C_{12} = lauric; C_{14} = myristic; C_{16} = palmitic; C_{18} = stearic.

14.3. ACIDITY

Perhaps the most distinguishing feature of carboxylic acids is that they are protonic acids and react with a variety of suitable bases.

pK_a of Alkyl Acids

WHAT IS THE PK_a OF ACETIC ACID (ETHANOIC ACID)?

The pK_a of acetic acid (ethanoic acid) is 4.76.

GIVE THE PK_a VALUES OF THE FOLLOWING CARBOXYLIC ACIDS: A) PROPANOIC ACID B) BUTANOIC ACID C) FORMIC ACID.

(a) propanoic = 4.89; (b) butanoic acid = 4.82; (c) formic acid = 3.75.

Structure and Acidity

WHY IS ACETIC ACID A WEAKER ACID THAN FORMIC ACID?

Acetic acid has a methyl group attached to the electropositive carbonyl. Relative to hydrogen (in formic acid) methyl is an electron releasing group. This "pushes" electrons towards the O–H bond, strengthening it, and making that hydrogen less acidic (less positive = less like H⁺).

WHAT IS THE PK_a OF 2-CHLOROETHANOIC ACID (CHLOROACETIC ACID)?

The pK_a of chloroacetic acid is 2.85.

WHY IS THIS A STRONGER ACID THAN ACETIC ACID?

The chlorine has an electron withdrawing effect (Cl polarizes the α-hydrogen δ+, making the carbonyl carbon withdraw electrons from the O–H bond, thereby weakening it (more positive H, more like H⁺) and making it a stronger acid.

'THROUGH BOND' INDUCTIVE EFFECTS

Certain electronic effects are transmitted from nucleus to nucleus thorough the adjacent covalent bonds and these are collectively called *'through-bond' effects*, a type of *inductive effect*.

WHEN AN ELECTRON WITHDRAWING GROUP IS ATTACHED TO THE CARBONYL OF A CARBOXYL, WHAT IS THE EFFECT ON THE O–H BOND?

The electron withdrawing group induces a δ+ charge on the α-carbon, which is adjacent to the δ+ charge on the carbonyl carbon. This is destabilizing and to compensate the carbonyl carbon withdraws electrons from neighboring atoms to diminish the electron withdrawing effects of the α-carbon. This makes the O–H bond more polarized, the H more positive and more acidic.

WILL AN ELECTRON WITHDRAWING SUBSTITUENT INCREASE OR DECREASE ACIDITY?

In general, electron withdrawing groups increase acidity (larger K_a, smaller pK_a).

EXPLAIN WHY 3-CHLOROBUTANOIC ACID IS A WEAKER ACID THAN 2-CHLOROBUTANOIC ACID.

The electron withdrawing chlorine atom is further away from the carbonyl carbon in 3-chloroacetic acid than in 2-chloroacetic acid. The electron withdrawing ability of an atom or group diminishes as the distance from the O–H group and the carbonyl increases.

EXPLAIN WHY 2,2,2-TRICHLOROETHANOIC ACID IS A STRONGER ACID THAN 2-CHLOROETHANOIC ACID.

If one chlorine atom withdraws electrons from the α-carbon and this makes the O–H bond weaker, the presence of three electron withdrawing chlorines will withdraw even more electron density. This will make the α-carbon more positive and the O–H bond weaker, and therefore more acidic. If the pK_a of 2-chloroethanoic acid (listed above) is 2.89, the pK_a of 2,2,2-trichloroethanoic acid is 0.64, making the latter a significantly stronger acid.

WILL AN ELECTRON RELEASING SUBSTITUENT INCREASE OR DECREASE ACIDITY?

An electron releasing substituent 'feeds' electrons towards the electropositive carbonyl and that carbonyl carbon will withdraw *less* electron density from the O–H bond. The O–H bond is stronger and the acid is a weaker acid (more difficult to remove the H from O–H).

EXPLAIN WHY 4-NITROBENZOIC ACID IS A STRONGER ACID THAN 4-METHOXYBENZOIC ACID.

The nitro group is strongly electron withdrawing. This effect is transmitted through the aromatic ring to the carbonyl carbon, making the acid stronger. When attached to benzene, the OMe group is electron releasing (relative the benzene ring) and when this effect is transmitted through the aromatic ring, the acid is weaker.

IN EACH OF THE FOLLOWING SERIES, INDICATE THE STRONGEST ACID.

(a) benzoic acid or 4-methoxybenzoic acid (b) 3-chloropropanoic acid or 3-chloropentanoic acid (c) 2-methoxyethanoic acid or propanoic acid (d) 4-nitrobenzoic acid or p-toluic acid (4-methyl-benzoic acid).

In (a) the electron releasing methoxy group makes 4-methoxybenzoic acid the weaker acid relative to benzoic acid [pK_a of benzoic acid = 4.19 and the pK_a of 4-methoxybenzoic acid = 4.46]. In (b) both acids have an electron withdrawing chlorine at C_3 but 3-chloropentanoic acid also has an ethyl group attached to C_3. The presence of the electron releasing alkyl group, which is missing in 3-chloropropanoic acid, will make 3-chloropentanoic acid a weaker acid. Therefore, 3-chloropropanoic acid is the stronger acid. In (c) methoxy is electron withdrawing, primarily by through-space effects (see below), whereas the methyl (attached to the α-carbon of acetic acid, respectively) is electron releasing. Since methoxy is electron withdrawing, 2-methoxyethanoic acid is expected to be the stronger acid [pK_a of methoxyacetic acid = 3.6; pK_a of propionic acid = 4.9]. In (d) the nitro group is electron withdrawing and will make it a stronger acid than toluic acid, which has an electron releasing methyl group at the *para-* position [the pK$_a$ of 4-nitrobenzoic acid is 3.41 and the pK$_a$ of toluic acid = 4.34].

'THROUGH SPACE' FIELD EFFECTS

When a heteroatom group is sufficiently close in space to the acidic hydrogen of the carboxyl, 'through-space' electronic effects (often called field effects) will influence the acidity of the acid. These through-space effects are usually a stronger influence on the acidity than the through-bond effects.

EXPLAIN WHY 2-NITROBENZOIC ACID IS A STRONGER ACID THAN 4-NITROBENZOIC ACID.

In 2-nitrobenzoic acid, the electron withdrawing group is closer to the carboxyl group. As shown in *14.3*, the H of the O–H bond is physically close to the electronegative oxygens of the nitro group. A "through-space" hydrogen bonding effect will weaken the O–H bond and strength the acid. Since the nitro group in the *para-* position *cannot* assume such an intramolecular hydrogen bonding array, it will be a weaker acid.

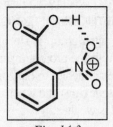

Fig. 14.3

DESCRIBE THE RELATIVE ACIDITY OF ETHANOIC ACID AND 2-CHLOROETHANOIC ACID IN TERMS OF A THROUGH-SPACE EFFECT.

Examination of *14.4* shows that the chlorine and the H of the OH can hydrogen bond (through space) in what is effectively a five-membered ring. This is energetically accessible and the electron withdrawing effect of this through space hydrogen bonding is very strong, making chloroacetic acid a stronger acid.

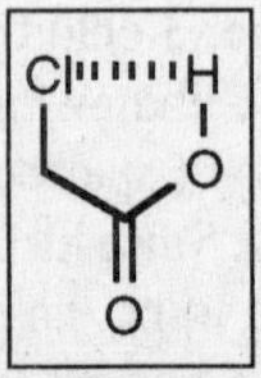

Fig. 14.4

WHY IS 2-METHOXYBENZOIC ACID A STRONGER ACID THAN 4-METHOXYBENZOIC ACID ALTHOUGH BOTH ARE ELECTRON RELEASING AND, IN PRINCIPLE WEAKEN ACIDITY?

In *14.5* the oxygen of the methoxy is sufficiently close to the carbonyl that hydrogen bonding can occur between the lone electrons of oxygen and the acidic hydrogen of the acid. This makes the *ortho*-methoxy derivative more acidic than the *para*-methoxy derivative (*14.6*) where intramolecular hydrogen bonding is not possible. This enhancement in acidity due to the presence of a heteroatom in the *ortho*- position is often called the ortho effect.

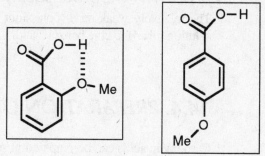

Fig. 14.5, 14.6

EXPLAIN WHY 2-METHOXYBENZOIC ACID IS A STRONGER ACID THAN 2-METHYLBENZOIC ACID.

This is another example of the ortho effect. The oxygen of the methoxy group can hydrogen bond with the acidic hydrogen of the carbonyl group when OMe is in the *ortho*- position. The methyl, of course, has no heteroatom for hydrogen bonding.

Nature of Carboxylate Anions

WHAT IS THE STRUCTURE OF THE CARBOXYLATE ANION, FORMED BY REMOVAL OF THE ACIDIC HYDROGEN FROM THE ACID?

Treatment of a carboxylic acid with a base ($NaHCO_3$ is a sufficiently strong base for this reaction) generates the carboxylate anion, *14.7*. This ion is resonance stabilized, with the charge dispersed to both oxygens. The carboxylate anion is a weak nucleophile and a relatively weak base.

$$R \overset{O}{\underset{O-H}{||}} \xrightarrow{NaHCO_3} \left[R \overset{O}{\underset{O^-}{||}} \longleftrightarrow R \overset{O^-}{\underset{O}{||}} \right]$$

Fig. 14.7

WHY IS THE CARBOXYLATE ANION CONSIDERED TO BE VERY STABLE?

As shown in *14.7*, the carboxylate anion is resonance stabilized. The negative charge is delocalized over three atoms (O–C–O).

HOW DOES THE SPECIAL STABILITY OF THE CARBOXYLATE ANION INFLUENCE ACIDITY?

The product (the carboxylate anion) is resonance stabilized and an equilibrium reaction will be influenced by the relative stability of the species that make up that equilibrium A more stable product tends to shift the equilibrium towards that product. In this case, if the equilibrium is shifted towards the carboxylate, K_a is larger. A large K_a is indicative of a stronger acid.

WHAT IS THE PRODUCT WHEN POTASSIUM BENZOATE IS DISSOLVED IN AQUEOUS SOLUTION AT pH 4?

The relatively weak base (potassium benzoate) is protonated in the acidic solution (pH 4) to give benzoic acid.

14.4. PREPARATION OF ACIDS

Carboxylic acids can be prepared in several different ways but oxidation of alcohols or alkenes is probably the most common method. Hydrolysis of cyanides, derived from alkyl halides is another very common preparative method.

Oxidation of Aldehydes

This chemistry was discussed in section 13.3.

WHAT IS THE PRODUCT WHEN 1-PENTANOL IS REACTED WITH CHROMIUM TRIOXIDE IN AQUEOUS ACID?

Chromium trioxide (in aqueous acid it is usually called Jones reagent) is a powerful oxidizing agent. The initially formed aldehyde (from the primary alcohol) is further oxidized to a carboxylic acid. The product of oxidizing 1-pentanol is, therefore, pentanoic acid.

IS THIS A USEFUL METHOD FOR THE PREPARATION OF CARBOXYLIC ACIDS OR DOES IT USUALLY GIVE MIXTURES OF PRODUCTS?

When Jones reagent is used for the oxidation of primary alcohols, the carboxylic acid is almost always the major product, often the exclusive product. Since the acidic carboxylic acid and the neutral aldehyde and alcohol starting material are both neutral, the acid is easily separated, making this a useful preparative method for the synthesis of carboxylic acids.

Oxidative Cleavage of Alkenes

This chemistry was described in section 5.5. Alkenes are oxidatively cleaved to produce carboxylic acids if the carbon of the C=C group has at least one hydrogen attached to it.

OZONOLYSIS
The chemistry was described in section 5.5.

WHAT IS THE MAJOR PRODUCT OR PRODUCTS WHEN 2-OCTENE IS REACTED WITH OZONE AND THEN WITH HYDROGEN PEROXIDE?
Cleavage of 2-octene with ozone with an oxidative workup leads to a mixture of ethanoic acid and hexanoic acid.

GIVE THE MAJOR PRODUCTS FOR THE REACTIONS OF *14.8* AND *14.9*.
In the first reaction, oxidative cleavage of methylcyclo-hexene (*14.8*) leads to a ketoacid (*14.10*). In the second reaction, oxidative cleavage of 3-ethyl-3-nonene (*14.9*) leads to a mixture of two products, 3-pentanone and hexanoic acid.

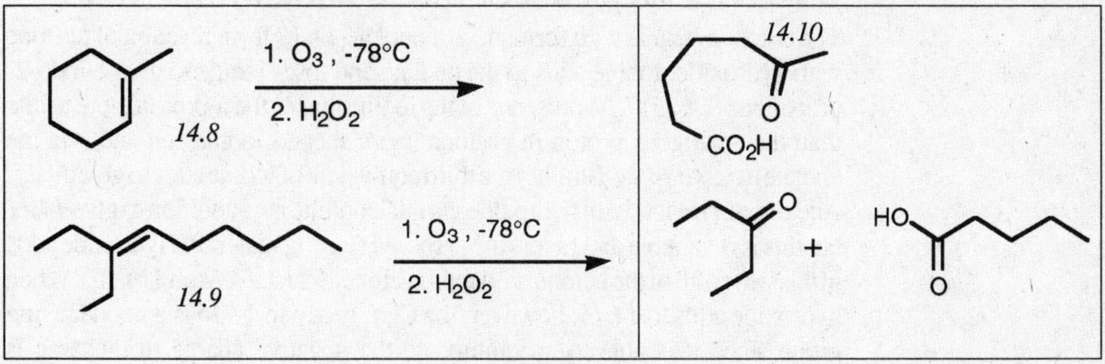

Fig. 14.8–14.10

POTASSIUM PERMANGANATE
This reagent was introduced in section 5.5.

WHAT IS THE MAJOR PRODUCT WHEN 3-HEXENE IS TREATED WITH HOT CONCENTRATED POTASSIUM PERMANGANATE?
Since 3-hexene is symmetrical, oxidative cleavage leads to propanoic acid as the major product.

WHAT IS THE PRODUCT WHEN 3-HEXENE IS TREATED WITH COLD AND DILUTE POTASSIUM PERMANGANATE?
As described in section 5.5, these conditions lead to a 1,2-diol rather than oxidative cleavage. The product of this reaction is 3,4-hexanediol.

WHAT IS THE PRODUCT WHEN 2,3-BUTANEDIOL IS TREATED WITH HOT AND CONCENTRATED POTASSIUM PERMANGANATE?
Hot and concentrated permanganate is capable of cleaving 1,2-diols to the corresponding carboxylic acids via oxidative cleavage. In this case, cleavage of the symmetrical diol leads to ethanoic acid (acetic acid).

THE HALOFORM REACTION

WHAT IS A HALOFORM?

A haloform has the structure HCX_3 where X = F, Cl, Br, I.

WHAT IS THE PRODUCT WHEN 2-BUTANONE IS TREATED WITH BROMINE AND AQUEOUS SODIUM HYDROXIDE.

This reaction leads to oxidative cleavage of the C–C bond in methyl ketones. In this case there are two products, bromoform ($HCBr_3$) and propanoic acid.

WHAT IS THE PRODUCT WHEN ACETONE IS TREATED WITH IODINE AND AQUEOUS SODIUM HYDROXIDE?

Iodine and base also gives oxidative cleavage to iodoform (HCI_3) and ethanoic acid.

WHAT IS THE MECHANISM OF THIS REACTION WITH ACETONE?

The reaction begins with formation of enolate *14.12* from reaction of acetone with hydroxide. Iodine adds to the enolate and loses iodide to give 1-iodo-2-propanone (*14.13*). The presence of the iodine makes the a-proton more acidic than the analogous proton in acetone and a second iodine can add (via the enolate) to give *14.14*. Similarly, a third equivalent of iodine adds to give *14.15*. Acetone also reacts with hydroxide via nucleophilic acyl addition to give *14.11* but this is reversible and favors the carbonyl starting material. Hydroxide adds in this way to all of the ketone products (acetone, *14.13*, *14.14* and *14.15*). When hydroxide adds to *14.15*, however, the CCI_3 group in *14.16* is a good leaving group since it is able to accommodate the negative charge (the charge is stabilized in *14.17*). This allows cleavage to acetic acid and *14.17*. Since *14.17* is a strong base, it deprotonates the acid to give the carboxylate salt and iodoform, *14.18*.

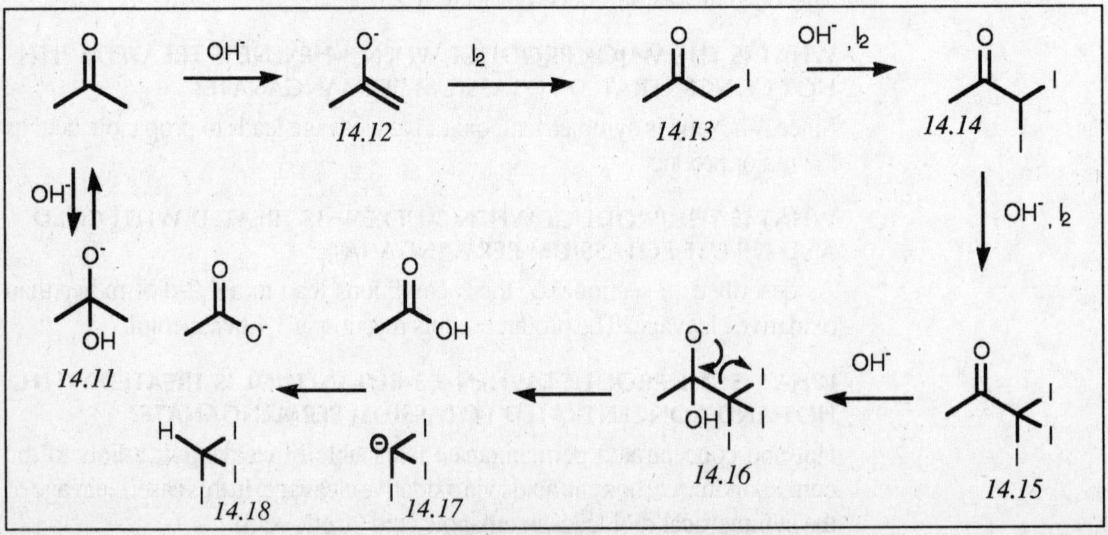

Fig. 14.11–14.18

WHAT IS THE IODOFORM TEST? WHAT FUNCTIONAL GROUP DOES IT DETECT?

The iodoform test mixes a suspected methyl ketone (the functional group is a methyl group attached to a carbonyl [CH_3–C=O]) with iodine and aqueous hydroxide. If the methyl ketone functional group is present, a yellow precipitate of iodoform is observed. The reaction also works with methyl carbinols (HO–C–CH_3).

FROM CYANIDES

When a nitrile is reacted with aqueous acid, under rather vigorous conditions (heat and relatively concentrated acid), a carboxylic acid is formed. Often, the nitrile can be converted to an amide and then further hydrolyzed to the acid.

S_N^2 REACTIONS WITH HALIDES AND HYDROLYSIS

WHAT IS THE PRODUCT WHEN 1-BROMOBUTANE IS REACTED WITH SODIUM CYANIDE IN DMF?

Cyanide behaves as a carbon nucleophile, giving pentanenitrile ($CH_3CH_2CH_2CH_2C\equiv N$) via a S_N^2 reaction (see section 4.4).

WHAT IS THE PRODUCT WHEN HEXANENITRILE IS TREATED WITH COLD AND DILUTE AQUEOUS HCl?

Nitriles can be hydrolyzed to carboxylic acids or amides but this usually requires strong acid and vigorous reaction conditions. If any reaction occurs at all under these milder conditions, the product will be the amide, pentanamide. It is more likely that the nitrile will be recovered unchanged from this reaction medium.

WHAT IS THE PRODUCT WHEN A 6 N SOLUTION OF HCL IS ADDED TO PENTANENITRILE AND HEATED TO 80°C FOR SEVERAL HOURS?

Under these vigorous reaction conditions, pentanenitrile is converted to the carboxylic acid, pentanoic acid. Since the reaction proceeds by initial hydrolysis to pentanamide, some pentanamide may also be isolated from this reaction. Given sufficient time, the acid will become the major product, however.

FROM CYANOHYDRINS

WHAT IS A CYANOHYDRIN?

A cyanohydrin is a molecule that has both a hydroxyl (OH) and a nitrile ($C\equiv N$) group in it.

HOW ARE CYANOHYDRINS FORMED?

Cyanohydrins are usually formed by reaction of a ketone or aldehyde with sodium (or potassium) cyanide (to give *14.20*), followed by quenching with aqueous acid to give the cyanohydrin, *14.19*. Alternatively, treatment of an aldehyde or ketone with HCN will lead to a cyanohydrin, *14.19*.

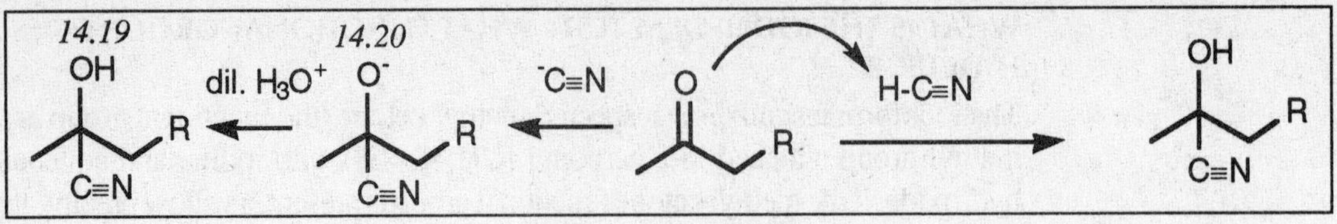

Fig. 14.19, 14.20

WHAT IS THE PRODUCT WHEN A CYANOHYDRIN IS HYDROLYZED?

Hydrolysis will convert the nitrile group to a carboxylic acid. Since the hydroxyl group will remain, the product will be an α-hydroxy acid. In many cases, however, treatment with acid induces loss of water (via protonation of the OH) and the product is an α,β-unsaturated acid.

FROM GRIGNARD REAGENTS AND CARBON DIOXIDE

IN WHAT WAY IS CARBON DIOXIDE RELATED TO FORMALDEHYDE?

Carbon dioxide is a carbonyl compound [O=C=O] just as formaldehyde [$H_2C=O$] contains a carbonyl. Both compounds can react with nucleophiles.

WHEN ETHYLMAGNESIUM BROMIDE REACTS WITH CARBON DIOXIDE, WHAT IS THE INITIAL PRODUCT? WHAT IS THE PRODUCT AFTER HYDROLYSIS?

The nucleophilic Grignard reagent will attack the carbonyl of CO_2 to produce a carboxylate salt (*14.21*). Hydrolysis will convert the salt to the acid, propanoic acid in this case.

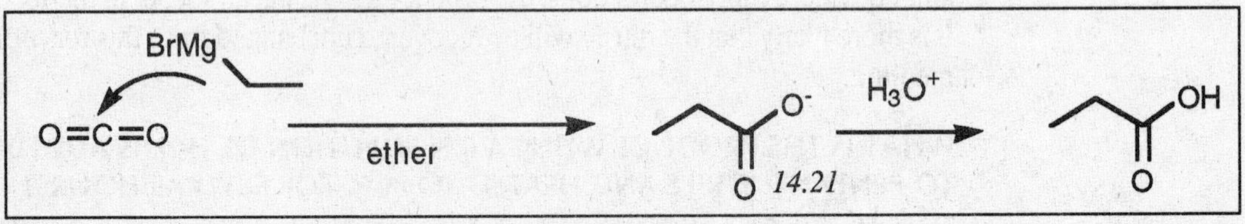

Fig. 14.21

GIVE THE MAJOR PRODUCTS FROM THE REACTIONS OF *14.22* AND *14.23*.

When bromobenzene (*14.22*) reacts with magnesium, phenylmagnesium bromide is formed. This Grignard reagent reacts with CO_2 to give benzoic acid, after hydrolysis. When 2-heptanol reacts with PBr_3, 2-bromoheptane is produced. Subsequent reaction with Mg leads to the Grignard reagent and condensation with CO_2 leads to 2-ethylhexanoic acid.

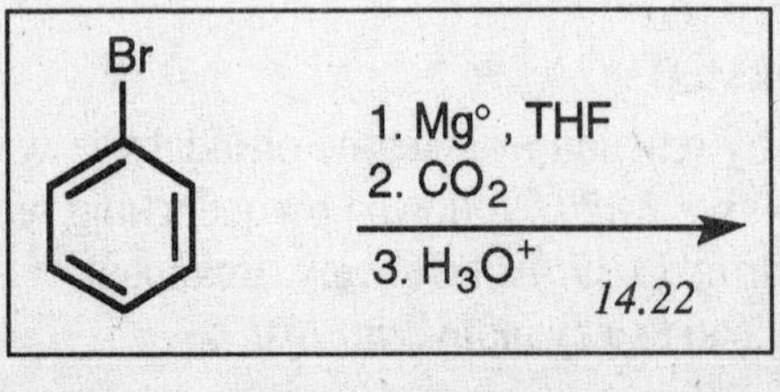

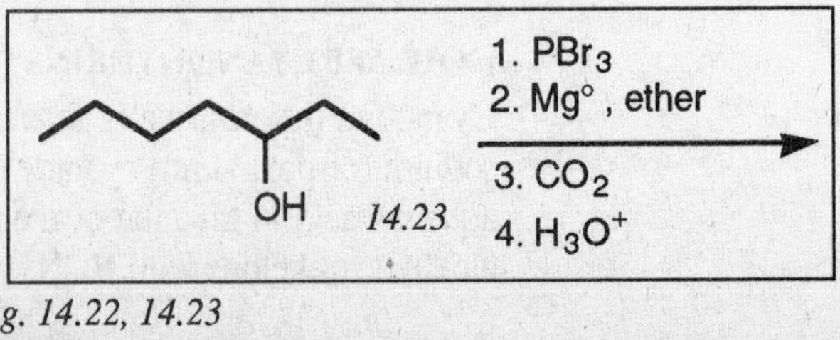

Fig. 14.22, 14.23

14.5. REACTIONS OF CARBOXYLIC ACIDS

Carboxylic acids can be converted into a variety of acid derivatives (see chapter 15) but there are also many other reactions that can be useful.

Reduction

In general, when a carboxylic acid is reduced, a primary alcohol is the product.

LITHIUM ALUMINUM HYDRIDE

WHAT IS THE PRODUCT OF THE REACTION OF PENTANOIC ACID AND LiAlH$_4$?

LiAlH$_4$ reduces acids to the corresponding primary alcohol, in this case 1-pentanol.

WHAT IS THE PRODUCT OF THE REACTION BETWEEN BUTANOIC ACID AND NaBH$_4$?

NaBH$_4$ is not powerful enough to reduce the acid to the alcohol. NaBH$_4$ reacts with butanoic acid in an acid-base reaction to form the carboxylate salt of butanoic acid.

BORANE

WHAT IS THE PRODUCT WHEN PROPANOIC ACID IS TREATED WITH BORANE AND THEN HYDROLYZED WITH DILUTE ACID?

Borane has a great affinity for reaction with carboxylic acid, giving the corresponding alcohol. Borane will reduce propanoic acid to 1-propanol.

EXPLAIN WHY BORANE IS OFTEN CALLED 'THE REAGENT OF CHOICE' FOR THE REDUCTION OF CARBOXYLIC ACIDS.

Borane will reduce an acid faster than an ester, a nitro compound, a nitrile or many other functional groups. If both an ester an a carboxylic acid are present in the same molecule (as in *14.24*) reaction with borane will give selective reduction of the acid, to give *14.25*.

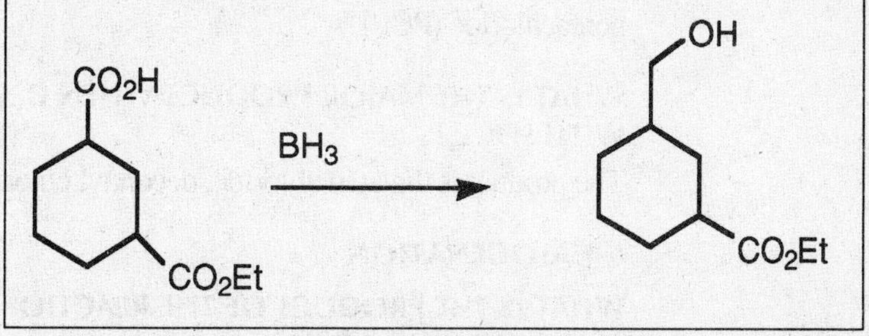

Fig. 14.24, 14.25

Halogenation

Halogenation of carboxylic acids can occur both at the carboxyl group and at the α-carbon.

PREPARATION OF ACID CHLORIDES

WHAT IS THE STRUCTURE OF AN ACID CHLORIDE?

An acid chloride has a chlorine attached directly to a carbonyl, as in *14.25*.

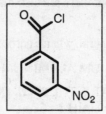

Fig. 14.25

WHAT IS THE IUPAC NOMENCLATURE SYSTEM FOR ACID CHLORIDES?

Drop the -oic acid ending of the parent carboxylic acid and add -oyl chloride. Pentanoic acid give pentanoyl chloride, for example (see section 15.1).

GIVE THE IUPAC NAME *14.26* AND *14.27*.

Acid chloride *14.26* is named 3-chlorobutanoyl chloride. Derivative *14.25* is 3-nitrobenzoyl chloride and *14.27* is 5-methyl-4-phenylhexanoyl chloride.

Fig. 14.26, 14.27

WHAT REAGENTS ARE CAPABLE OF CONVERTING BENZOIC ACID INTO BENZOYL CHLORIDE?

Common halogenating reagents are thionyl chloride ($SOCl_2$), phosphorus oxychloride ($POCl_3$), phosphorus trichloride (PCl_3) and phosphorus pentachloride (PCl_5).

WHAT IS THE MAJOR PRODUCT WHEN DECANOIC ACID IS TREATED WITH $SOCL_2$?

The product is the acid chloride, decanoyl chloride [$CH_3(CH_2)_7CH_2COCl$].

α-HALOGENATION

WHAT IS THE PRODUCT OF THE REACTION BETWEEN BROMINE AND BUTANOIC ACID?

The reaction of a carboxylic acid and bromine or chlorine is very slow. For all practical purposes, there is no reaction since a halogen must react with the enol form of the acid, which is present in very small concentration. If the % of enol can be increased, halogenation is more viable.

WHAT IS THE HELL-VOLHARD-ZELINKSY REACTION?

The conversion of a carboxylic acid to an α-halo acid by treatment with a halogen (usually bromine) and a halogenating agent such as PCl_3 is the *Hell-Volhard-Zelinsky* reaction. An example is the conversion of butanoic acid to 2-bromobutanoic acid. Initial reaction with PCl_3 gives the acid chloride, which has a relatively high enol content (*14.28*). The enol will then attack the bromine, as shown, displacing bromide and forming the α-bromo acid chloride (*14.29*). This acid chloride usually reacts with the starting acid to produce the final product, α-bromobutanoic acid (*14.30*) and the acid chloride, which can be recycled. For this reason, only a catalytic amount of PCl_3 is required.

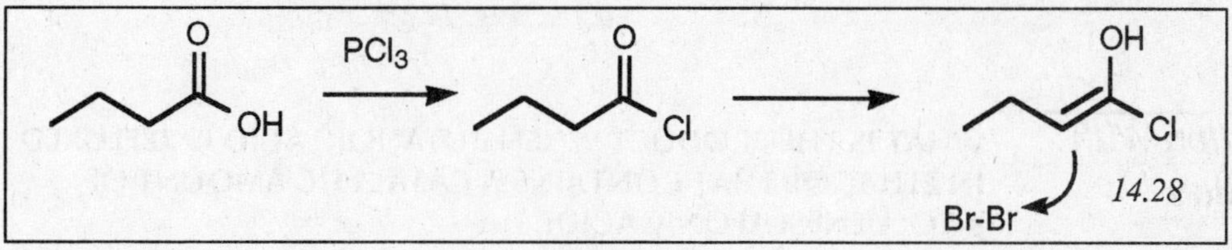

Fig. 14.28

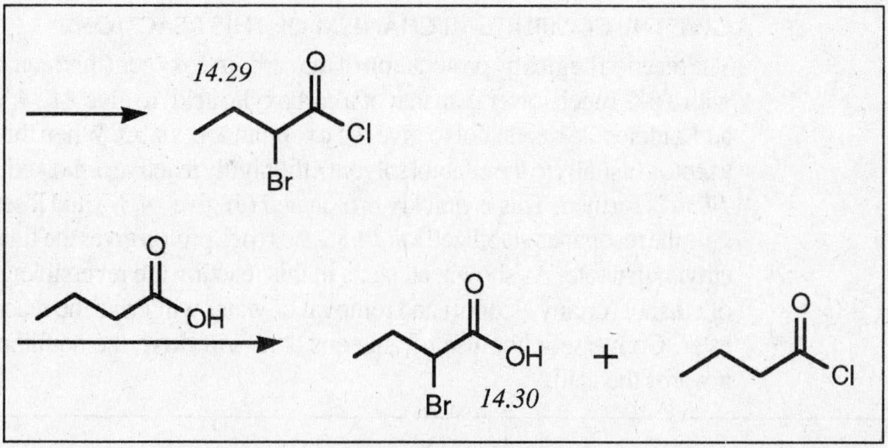

Fig. 14.29, 14.30

DESCRIBE THE REACTION OF 2-CHLOROETHANOIC ACID AND SODIUM PHENOXIDE. EXPLAIN THE PRODUCT

The chlorine at the 2-position is very susceptible to nucleophilic attack, usually reacting faster than nucleophilic attack at the acyl carbon. In this case, the basic phenoxide will form the carboxylate (*14.31*) and a second equivalent of phenoxide will give the final substitution product, the phenyl ether, *14.32*.

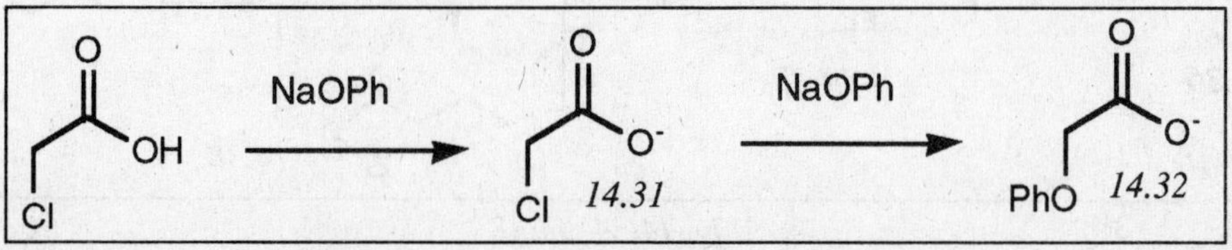

Fig. 14.31, 14.32

WHAT IS THE PRODUCT OF THE REACTION OF 2-BROMOPROPANOIC ACID AND AQUEOUS SODIUM CARBONATE, WHEN FOLLOWED BY TREATMENT WITH DILUTE AQUEOUS ACID?

Under these conditions, the bromine is displaced by OH to give 2-hydroxy-propanoic acid, *14.33*.

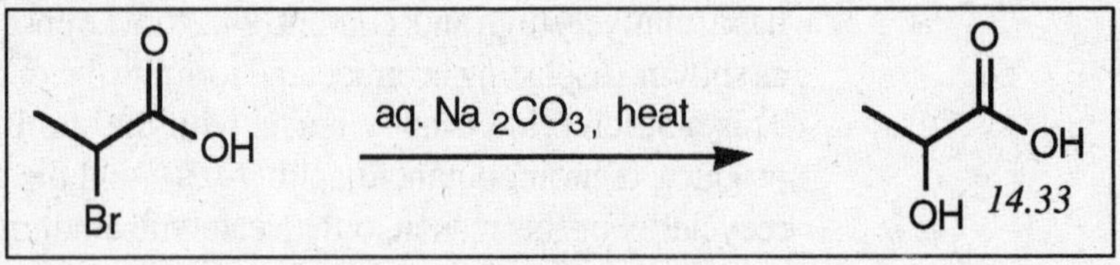

Fig. 14.33

Reaction With Alcohols

WHAT IS THE PRODUCT WHEN BUTANOIC ACID IS REFLUXED IN ETHANOL THAT CONTAINS A CATALYTIC AMOUNT OF p-TOLUENESULFONIC ACID?

The product is an ester, ethyl butanoate [$CH_3CH_2CH_2CO_2Et$].

GIVE THE COMPLETE MECHANISM OF THIS REACTION.

The reaction begins by protonation of the carbonyl oxygen (this requires an acid with a pK_a much lower than that of a carboxylic acid) to give *14.34*, which can add a molecule of ethanol to give the oxonium ion, *14.35*. When this ion loses a proton (usually to the ethanol solvent), the highly reactive orthoacid derivative *14.36* is formed. This is quickly protonated (to give *14.37*) and loses water to give the resonance stabilized ion *14.38*. Loss of a proton gives the final product, ethyl butanoate. As shown, all steps in this reaction are reversible. An excess of ethanol (or any alcohol) and removal of water will drive the reaction to the ester. Conversely, the use of aqueous acid will drive the equilibrium back towards the acid.

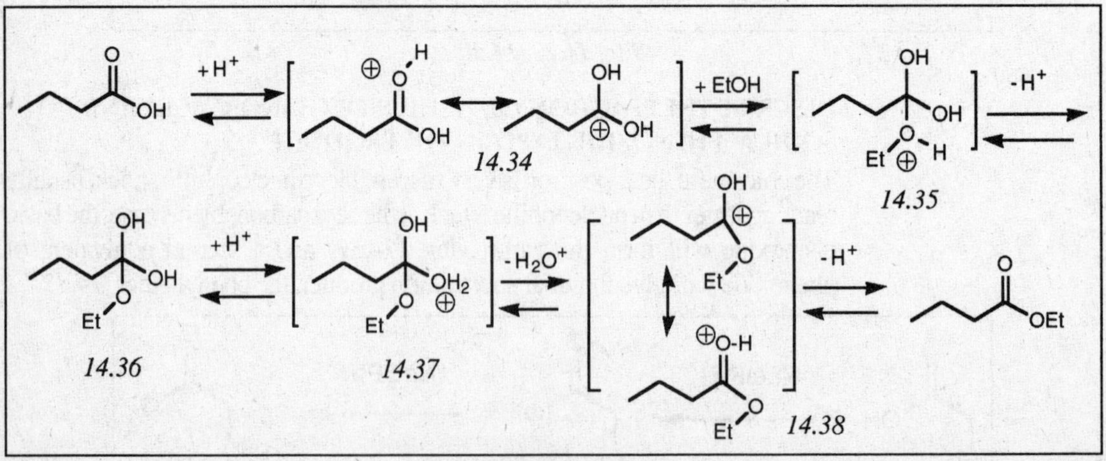

Fig. 14.34–14.38

WHAT IS THE GENERIC NAME OF THE PRODUCT OF THIS REACTION?

This type of product is called an ester.

WHAT IS THE IUPAC NOMENCLATURE SYSTEM FOR ESTERS?

The -oic acid ending of the parent acid is dropped and -oate is added. The alcohol used to form the ester is also part of the name. If ethanol is used the name is ethyl, methanol leads to methyl, propanol leads to propyl, etc. The name of $CH_3CH_2CH_2CH_2CH_2CO_2CH_2CH_3$, for example, is ethyl hexanoate [ethyl from the ethanol precursor and hexanoate from the hexanoic acid precursor], as described in section 15.1.

WHAT IS THE MAJOR PRODUCT OF THE REACTIONS OF 14.39–14.41?

Benzoic acid (*14.39*) is converted to ethyl benzoate (*14.42*) upon treatment with ethanol and an acid catalyst. The second acid (*14.40*, 5-cyclohexyl-3-methylpentanoic acid) is converted to methyl 5-cyclo-hexyl-3-methylpentanote (*14.43*) under these conditions. In the last example, ethyl hexanoate is hydrolyzed with aqueous acid to ethanol and hexanoic acid.

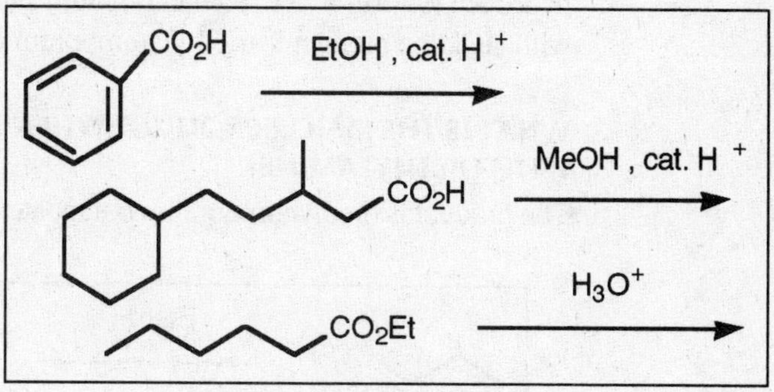

Fig. 14.39–14.41

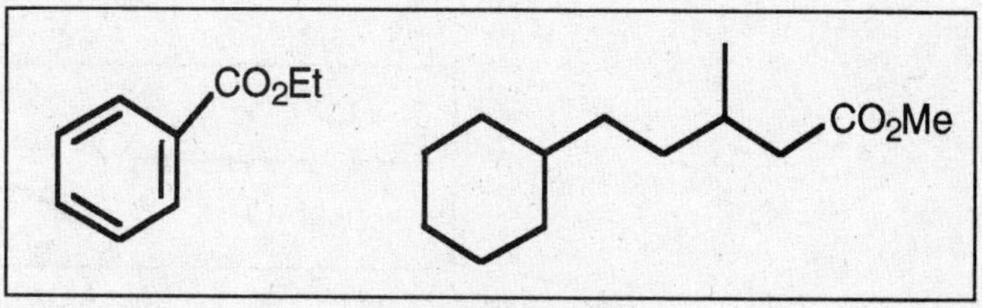

Fig. 14.42, 14.43

Reaction With Amines

WHAT IS THE STRUCTURE OF AN AMIDE?

An amide has a NR_2 group attached to a carbonyl. A primary amide has structure *14.44*, an example of a secondary amide is *14.45* and an example of a tertiary amide is *14.46*.

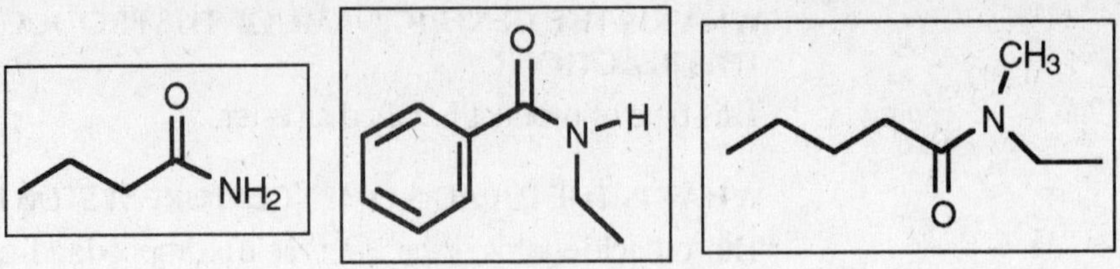

Fig. 14.44–14.46

HOW ARE AMIDES NAMED BY THE IUPAC SYSTEM?

The -oic acid is dropped from the pertinent acid and the word amide is added. Pentanoic acid produces pentanamide and benzoic acid produces benzamide. Amide *14.44* is butanamide. If a substituent is attached to the nitrogen, it is identified by using N- in the name. The name of *14.45* is N-ethylbenzamide and *14.46* is N-ethyl, N-methylpentanamide (see section 15.1).

CONVERSION OF AMMONIUM SALTS TO AMIDES

WHAT IS AN AMMONIUM SALT?

When an amine (NR_3) reacts with an acid, the basic nitrogen accepts the hydrogen to form R_3NH^+, an ammonium salt. If triethylamine [NEt_3] reacts with HCl, the product is triethylammonium chloride [$Et_3NH^+ Cl^-$].

WHAT IS THE MAJOR PRODUCT WHEN BUTANOIC ACID IS MIXED WITH DIETHYLAMINE?

The product is diethylammonium butanoate, *14.47*.

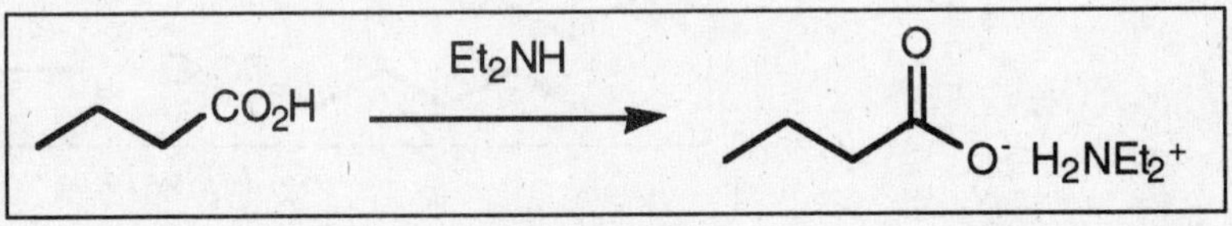

Fig. 14.47

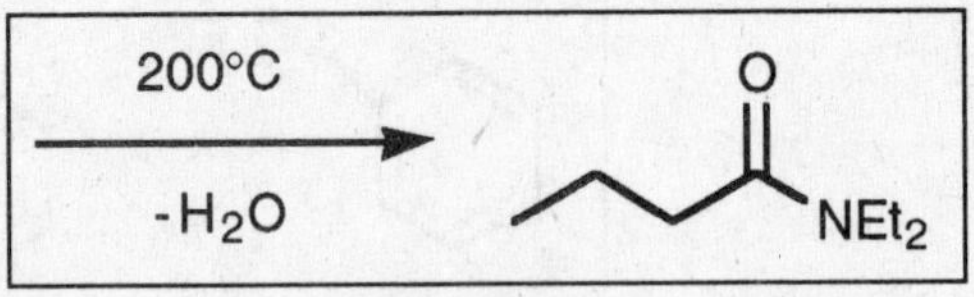

Fig. 14.48

WHAT IS THE MAJOR PRODUCT WHEN THE DIETHYLAMMONIUM SALT OF BUTANOIC ACID IS HEATED TO 200°C?

If the ammonium carboxylate is heated to a sufficiently high temperature, water is expelled to generate an amide. In this case, the product is N,N-diethylbutanamide, *14.48*.

OTHER PREPARATIONS OF AMIDES

WHAT IS THE MAJOR PRODUCT WHEN PENTANOYL CHLORIDE IS MIXED WITH BUTYLAMINE IN THE PRESENCE OF PYRIDINE?

The product is an amide, N-butylpentanamide, *14.49*. The pyridine acts as a base to react with the HCl by-product (producing pyridinium chloride).

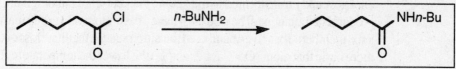

Fig. 14.49

WHAT IS THE PRODUCT WHEN ETHYL PENTANOATE IS HEATED WITH AMMONIA?

An amide is generally more stable than an ester. In other words, the ester is much more reactive than the amide. When ammonia is heated with an ester, ammonia behaves as a nucleophile, attacking the carbonyl and leading to loss of ethanol to form the amide, pentanamide.

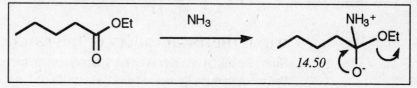

Fig. 14.50

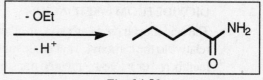

Fig. 14.51

WHAT IS THE PRODUCT WHEN METHYL BENZOATE IS HEATED WITH DIETHYLAMINE?

The product is N,N-diethyl-benzamide *14.52*.

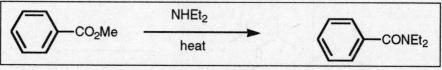

Fig. 14.52

___

Decarboxylation When a carboxyl group is conjugated to a π-bond, heating often induces the loss of carbon dioxide in a reaction called decarboxylation.

THERMAL LOSS OF CARBON DIOXIDE FROM β-KETO-ACIDS

DESCRIBE HOW CO_2 CAN BE LOST FROM 3-KETOPENTANOIC ACID.

The carbonyl oxygen can attack the acidic hydrogen of the acid via a six-centered transition state (illustrated by the arrows in *14.53*). The electron flow will break the C–C bond, generate CO_2 (O=C=O) and the *enol*, *14.54*. Since the enol is quickly transformed to the ketone via keto-enol tautomerism, the final product is 2-butanone. The acid *must* have a basic atom on a group that can form a six-membered or a five-membered transition state to facilitate loss of CO_2. The more basic that atom (O > C for example) the lower the temperature for loss of CO_2. Loss of CO_2 in this manner is called *decarboxylation*.

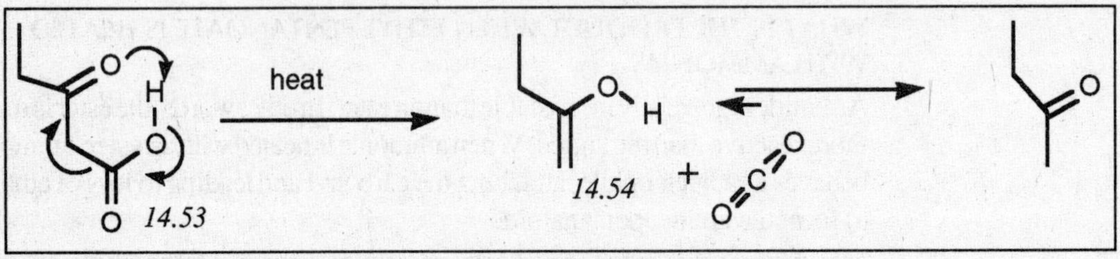

Fig. 14.53, 14.54

WHY IS THE FINAL PRODUCT OF THIS REACTION A KETONE?

Since the initial product is an enol, tautomerism favors the carbonyl form (it is thermodynamically more stable), as introduced in section 13.4.

WHAT ARE THE REQUIREMENTS FOR THERMAL LOSS OF CARBON DIOXIDE FROM β-KETOACIDS?

The acid must have a carbonyl, an alkene or an aromatic ring in the β-position relative to the carbonyl. That group must have a basic atom that can form a six-membered or a five-membered transition state with the acidic hydrogen.

GIVE THE MAJOR PRODUCTS FROM THE REACTIONS OF *14.55–14.57*.

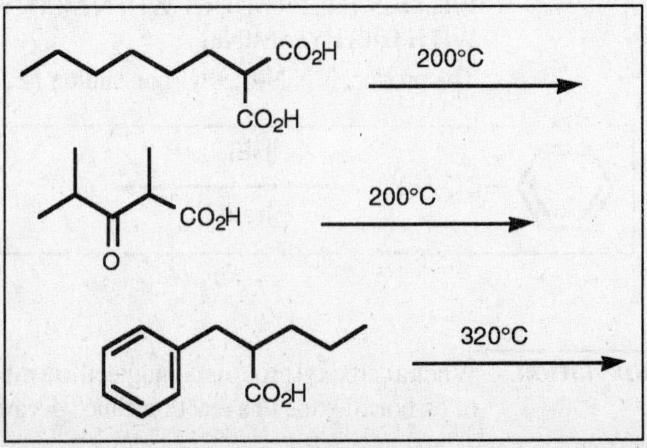

Fig. 14.55–14.57

In the first case the carboxyl carbonyl at the β-position can remove the hydrogen from OH. Such 1,3-diacids decarboxylate thermally to give the mono-acid. Heating *14.55* leads to octanoic acid. The carbonyl that is β- to the acid group in *14.56* is a ketone and decarboxylation by heating leads to 2-methyl-3-pentanone. In the final case, there is no carbonyl β- to the acid but there is an aromatic ring. Since the C=C group is much less basic than the C=O group of a carbonyl, higher temperatures are required for decarboxylation. Loss of CO_2 does occur, however and *14.57* is converted into 1-phenylpentane.

FROM MALONIC ACID DERIVATIVES

WHAT IS THE STRUCTURE OF MALONIC ACID?

Malonic acid is 1,3-propanedioic acid, $HO_2C–CH_2–CO_2H$.

WHY DOES HEATING 2-HEXYLMALONIC ACID (*14.55*) LEAD TO OCTANOIC ACID?

The decarboxylation reaction of *14.55* is facile since 1,3-diacids are capable of losing CO_2 thermally. The C=O of one carboxyl can remove the acidic hydrogen of the other carbonyl.

IS DECARBOXYLATION OF MALONIC ACID DERIVATIVES MORE OR LESS FACILE THAN β-KETOACIDS? EXPLAIN.

In general the carbonyl of an acid is somewhat less basic than the carbonyl of a ketone. For this reason, removal of the hydrogen via decarboxylation is slower with the carbonyl. It therefore requires somewhat higher reaction temperatures and is slightly less facile.

14.6. DIBASIC CARBOXYLIC ACIDS

When a molecule contains two carboxyl groups it is referred to as a dibasic acid. The IUPAC nomenclature system uses the ending dioic acid with each carboxyl identified by a number.

WHAT IS THE IUPAC NOMENCLATURE SYSTEM FOR DIBASIC ACIDS?

The carbon chain is indicted by the usual alkane, alkene or alkyne name, followed by dioic acid, where di- shows the presence of two carboxyl groups. The position of the carbonyl groups is given by numbers. An example is $HO_2C–(CH_2)_8–CO_2H$, which is named 1,10-decanedioic acid.

WHAT IS THE IUPAC NAME FOR COMPOUNDS *14.58–14.60*?

The name of the first diacid is 2-ethyl-1,6-hexanedioic acid (*14.58*). The second example (*14.59*) is named 2,4-diethyl-1,4-butanedioic acid. The aromatic diacid (*14.60*) is named 1,3-benzenedicarboxylic acid. Note the name change for aromatic acids.

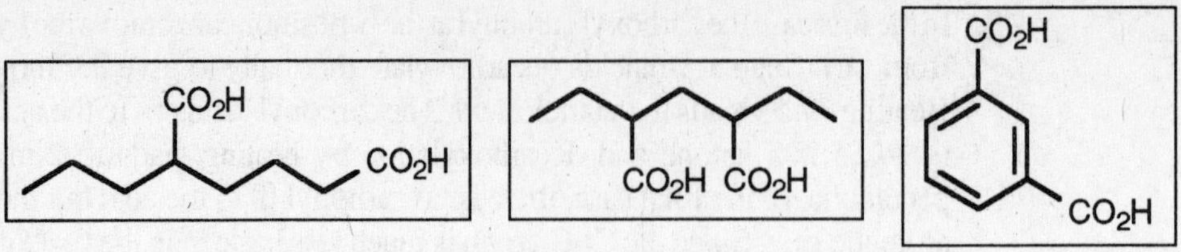

Fig. 14.58–14.60

Oxalic Acid

STRUCTURE

WHAT IS THE STRUCTURE OF OXALIC ACID?

Oxalic acid is the common name of ethanedioic acid, $HO_2C–CO_2H$.

WHAT IS THE IUPAC NAME OF OXALIC ACID?

Ethanedioic acid.

ACIDITY

THERE ARE TWO DIFFERENT PK_a VALUES FOR OXALIC ACID. EXPLAIN.

There are two carboxyl groups and two acidic hydrogens. One of the hydrogens has a pK_a of 1.27 but the second pK_a is 4.27. Examination of *14.61* shows that internal hydrogen bonding via a five-centered interaction is expected to greatly enhance the acidity of one of the carboxyl hydrogens in the diacid. In addition, the carboxyl group is electron withdrawing, strengthening the first pK_a by an inductive effect. The carboxylate (*14.62*, after removal of the first hydrogen) is less electron withdrawing and the internal hydrogen bonding is less extensive, weakening the acid. Removal of both acidic hydrogens generates the dicarboxylate salt, *14.63*.

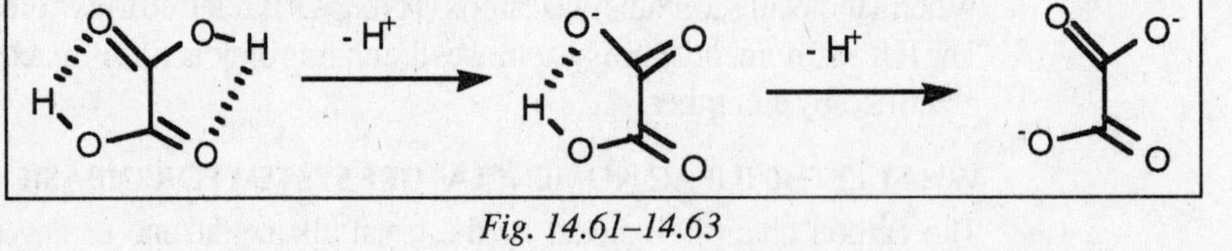

Fig. 14.61–14.63

COMPARE THE FIRST PK_a OF OXALIC ACID WITH THAT OF ACETIC ACID.

The pK_a of acetic acid is 4.76 The first pK_a of oxalic acid is 1.27 and the second is 4.27. These values show the strong electron withdrawing effect of a second carboxyl. Even the second pK_a of oxalic acid indicates that the second carboxyl is more acidic than acetic acid, again the result of the electron withdrawing carboxyl group.

Malonic Acid

STRUCTURE

WHAT IS THE STRUCTURE OF MALONIC ACID?

Malonic acid is the common name of 1,3-propanedioic acid, $HO_2C–CH_2–CO_2H$.

WHAT IS THE IUPAC NAME OF MALONIC ACID?

The IUPAC name is 1,3-propanedioic acid.

ACIDITY

GIVE THE FIRST AND SECOND pK_a'S OF MALONIC ACID.

The first pK_a is 2.86 and the second pK_a is 5.70.

COMPARE THE FIRST AND SECOND pK_a VALUE OF MALONIC ACID WITH THOSE OF OXALIC ACID.

The first pK_a of malonic acid shows it to be a significantly weaker acid than oxalic. Likewise, the second pK_a is much higher, again reflecting a much weaker acid, weaker even than acetic acid. The reason for these changes is the presence of the -CH_2- group between the carboxyls. The increased distance between the acidic hydrogens and the carboxyls diminishes the inductive effects and hydrogen bonding is weaker due to the increased distance between the carbonyl group and the acidic hydrogen.

Higher Order Diacids

GIVE THE IUPAC NAME AND STRUCTURE OF THE C_3–C_6 DIBASIC ACIDS WHERE THE CARBOXYL GROUPS ARE AT THE TWO EXTREME ENDS OF EACH MOLECULE.

The C_3 acid is $HO_2CCH_2CO_2H$ (1,3-propanedioic acid), the C_4 acid is $HO_2C(CH_2)_2CO_2H$ (1,4-butanedioic acid), the C_5 acid is $HO_2C(CH_2)_3CO_2H$ (1,5-pentanedioic acid) and the C_6 acid is $HO_2C(CH_2)_4CO_2H$ (1,6-hexanedioic acid).

WHAT IS THE STRUCTURE AND IUPAC NAME OF SUCCINIC ACID? OF GLUTARIC ACID?

Succinic acid is the common name of 1,4-butanedioic acid [$HO_2C(CH_2)_2CO_2H$] and glutaric acid is the common name of 1,5-pentanedioic acid [$HO_2C(CH_2)_3CO_2H$].

EXPLAIN WHY GLUTARIC ACID IS A SIGNIFICANTLY WEAKER ACID THAN MALONIC ACID.

The first pK_a of glutaric acid is 4.34 and the second pK_a is 5.27. This decrease in acidity reflects the increased distance between the carboxyl groups and the diminished inductive effects.

WHAT IS THE STRUCTURE OF MALEIC ACID? GIVE THE IUPAC NAME.

Maleic acid is the common name of *cis*-2-buten-1,4-dioic acid (*14.64*).

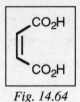

Fig. 14.64

WHAT IS THE STRUCTURE OF FUMARIC ACID? GIVE THE IUPAC NAME.

Fumaric acid is the common name of *trans*-2-buten-1,4-dioic acid (*14.65*).

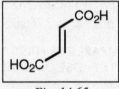

Fig. 14.65

EXPLAIN WHY MALEIC ACID IS A STRONGER ACID THAN FUMARIC ACID.

In maleic acid (*14.64*) the carboxyl groups are on the same side of the molecule and intramolecular hydrogen bonding (a through-space inductive effect) will make the acid much stronger (see *14.66*). When the carboxyl groups are on opposite sides of the molecule as in fumaric acid (*14.65*), this interaction is not possible and the result is a weaker acid. The first pK_a of maleic acid is 2.0 and the second pK_a is 6.3. The first pK_a of fumaric acid is 3.0 and the second pK_a is 4.4.

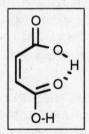

Fig. 14.66

This discussion of carboxylic acids is necessary for an understanding of the chemistry of acid derivatives to be discussed in the following chapter. Several interesting chemical transformations that are novel to acids were presented. Perhaps the most novel new reaction is the removal of a functional group from a molecule, as in decarboxylation. This is also one of the first chapters to focus attention on multi-functional molecules, that is, molecules that contain two or more functional groups. Clearly, diacids have physical and chemical properties that result from the presence and interaction of two functional groups. In later chapters, two different functional groups will be introduced into molecules with even more interesting chemical consequences.

END OF CHAPTER PROBLEMS

1. Give the IUPAC name for each of the following.

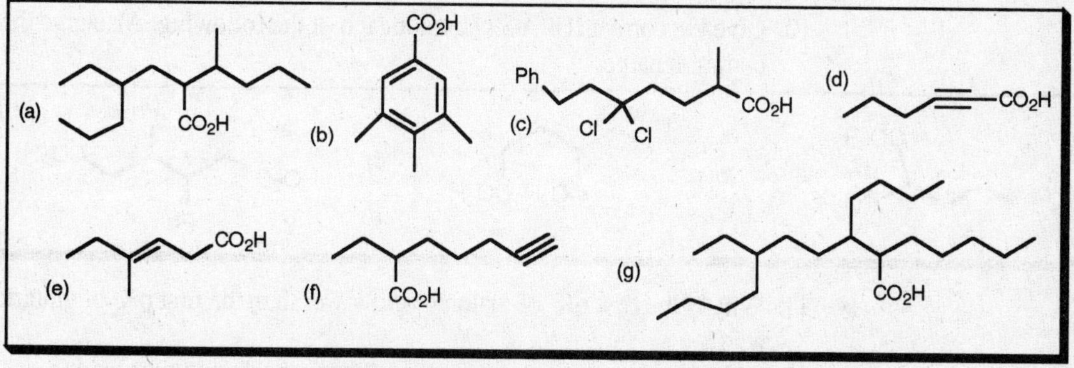

2. Which of the following is the strongest acid? Explain.

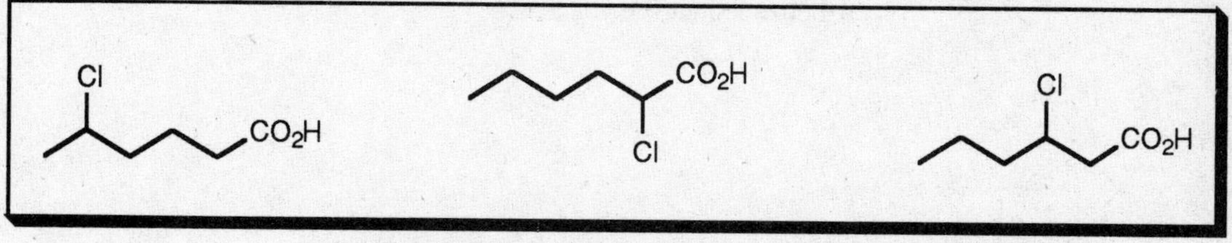

3. Why is *ortho*-chlorobenzoic acid a stronger acid than *para*-chlorobenzoic acid?

4. Draw a diagram to illustrate through-space inductive effects in 4-chloropropanoic acid.

5. Why is acetic acid a stronger acid in water than in ethanol?

6. How can the 'iodoform test' be used to give information about the structure of ketones?

7. When 4-hydroxybutanoic acid was prepared and heated, the final product was not acidic as expected. Explain this observation.

8. Give the complete mechanism for the following reaction.

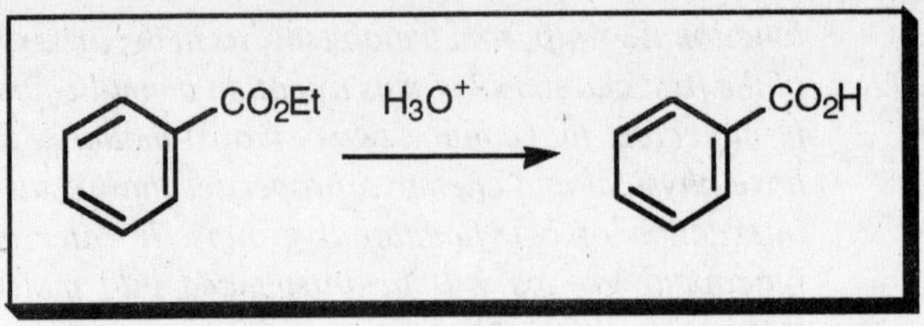

9. Give the complete mechanism for the following reaction.

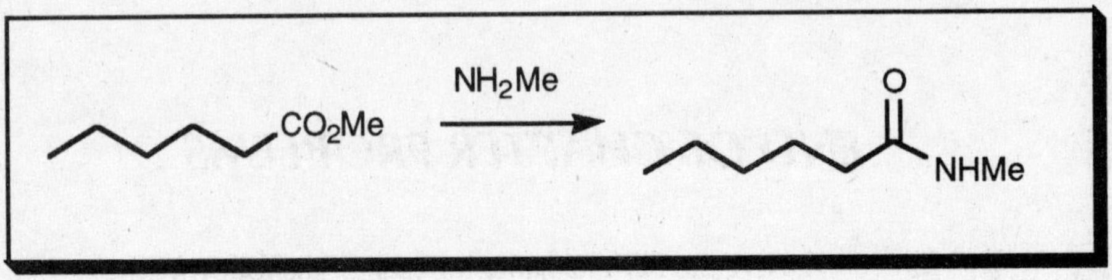

10. Give the correct IUPAC name for each of the following. Also give the common name.

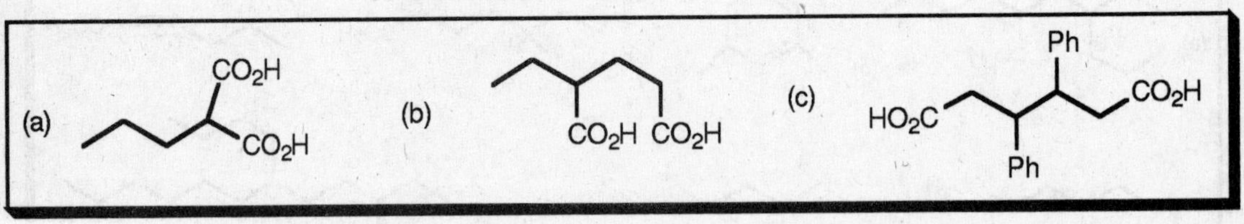

11. Why is the first pK_a of malonic acid lower than the first pK_a of glutaric acid?

12. What is the common name of (a) 1,2-benzenedicarboxylic acid (b) 1,4-benzenedicarboxylic acid?

13. In each case give the major product. If there is no reaction, indicate by N.R.

(a) (structure: 3-methylbutan-1-ol with OH) → CrO$_3$, aq. acetone / HCl

(b) (cyclohexyl-CH$_2$-CO$_2$H) → SOCl$_2$

(c) (structure) → 1. O$_3$ 2. H$_2$O$_2$

(d) (structure) → 1. O$_3$ 2. H$_2$O$_2$ 3. SOCl$_2$ 4. Pyridine, (cyclopentanol, OH)

(e) (styrene) → 1. O$_3$ 2. Me$_2$S

(f) (structure with CO$_2$H) → PCl$_3$, Br$_2$

(g) (1-methylcyclohexene) → conc. KMnO$_4$ / aq. OH$^-$, 100°C

(h) (structure with Ph, CO$_2$H, Cl) → NaCN, THF

(i) (ketone structure) → I$_2$, aq. NaOH

(j) (structure with CO$_2$H, I) → NaH, THF

(k) (structure with Ph and ketone) → Br$_2$, aq. NaOH

(l) (structure with Cl) → aq. EtOH, KCN

(m) (cyclopentane structure with Br) → 1. KCN, DMF 2. H$_3$O$^+$

(n) (cyclopentane-CH$_2$-CO$_2$H) → iPrOH, cat. H$^+$

(o) (structure with CHO) → 1. HCN 2. H$_3$O$^+$

(p) Ph-CH$_2$-CO$_2$H → MeNH$_2$, 200°C

(q) (aryl structure with isopropyl, methyl, Br) → 1. Mg°, THF 2. CO$_2$ 3. H$_3$O$^+$

(r) (structure with OH) → 1. CrO$_3$, H$^+$, heat 2. SOCl$_2$ 3. butylamine, pyridine

(s) (structure with Br) → 1. Mg°, THF 2. CO$_2$ 3. H$_3$O$^+$

(t) (structure with C≡N and CO$_2$Et) → NH$_3$, heat

(u) (structure with CHO) → 1. CrO$_3$, H$^+$ 2. LiAlH$_4$ 3. H$_3$O$^+$

(v) (keto acid structure with CO$_2$H) → 200°C

(w) EtO$_2$C—(structure)—CO$_2$H → BH$_3$

(x) (cyclopentane with OH and CH$_2$OH) → 1. CrO$_3$, H$^+$ 2. 200°C

(y) (structure with CO$_2$Et, CO$_2$Et) → 1. H$_3$O$^+$ 2. 200°C

14. Provide a suitable synthesis for each of the following. Provide all reagents and show all intermediate products.

15

Carboxylic Acid Derivatives

*C*arboxylic acids can be easily converted into several important derivatives: acid chlorides, anhydrides, esters, amides and nitriles. Each of these derivatives can be converted back to its parent carboxylic acid or transformed in a variety of other ways. Of particular interest are the chemical transformations of acid derivatives, not only into other acid derivatives, and back into carboxylic acids, but also into functional groups such as alcohols, alkenes, ketones and aldehydes and amines. Several new carbon-carbon bond forming reactions will be presented that are clearly related to those first seen with aldehydes and ketones in chapter thirteen. The Claisen Condensation, the Dieckmann condensation, the Knoevenagel Condensation and the Reformatsky reaction are notable carbon-carbon bond forming reactions that involve acid derivatives. In particular, this chapter will tie together carboxylic acid derivatives with most of the other functional groups presented in previous chapters.

15.1. STRUCTURE AND NOMENCLATURE

Acid Chlorides

Acid chlorides were introduced in section 14.5.

WHAT IS THE BASIC STRUCTURE OF AN ACID CHLORIDE?
An acid chloride has a chlorine attached directly to a carbonyl [Cl–C=O].

WHAT IS THE IUPAC NOMENCLATURE SYSTEM FOR AN ACID CHLORIDE?
The -oic acid ending of the parent carboxylic acid is dropped and replaced with -oyl chloride. The acid chloride of hexanoic acid is hexanoyl chloride. Using the common name acetic acid, the acid chloride is acetyl chloride.

GIVE THE STRUCTURE OF EACH OF THE FOLLOWING COMPOUNDS.

(a) 5-phenyl-3,3-dimethyloctanoyl chloride (b) malonyl chloride (c) oxalyl chloride (d) 4-methoxy-benzoyl chloride (e) phenylacetyl chloride.

The structure of (a) is *15.1*, (b) is *15.2*, (c) is *15.3*, (d) is *15.4* and (e) is *15.5*.

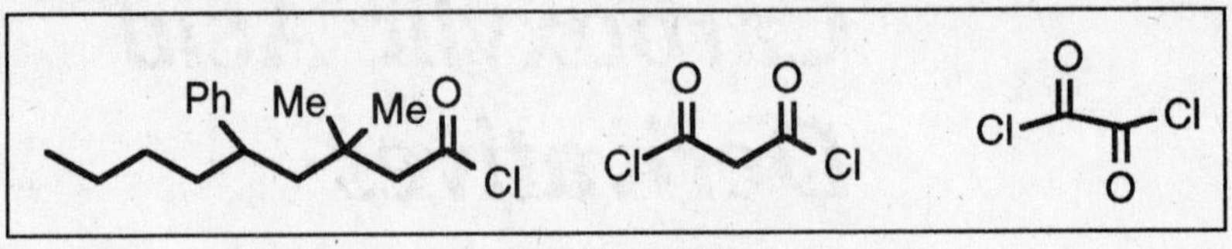

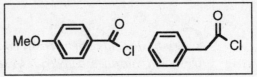

Fig. 15.1–15.3

Fig. 15.4, 15.5

Acid Anhydrides

WHAT IS THE BASIC STRUCTURE OF AN ACID ANHYDRIDE?

An acid anhydride is characterized by a O=C–O–C=O structure. A generic example is *15.6*, where R is alkyl or aryl.

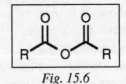

Fig. 15.6

WHAT IS THE IUPAC NOMENCLATURE SYSTEM FOR A SYMMETRICAL ACID ANHYDRIDE?

Acid anhydrides are essentially composed of two acid functionalities that are joined together. There are, therefore, two acyl groups (RCO). If both of the acyl groups are the same, the acid ending of the acid is dropped and replaced with the word anhydride. Anhydride *15.7* is ethanoic anhydride (the common name is acetic anhydride) and *15.8* is butanoic anhydride.

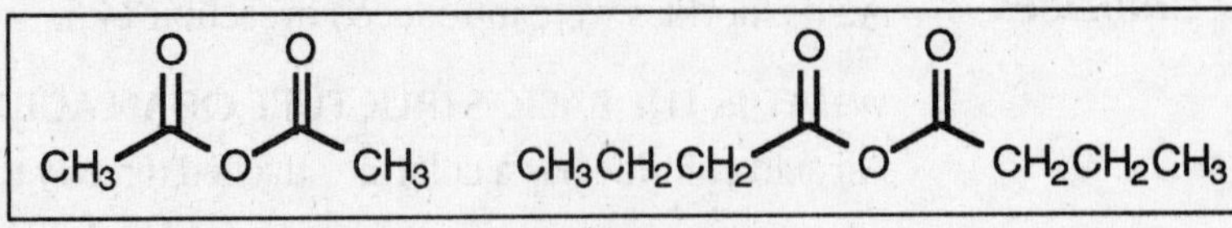

Fig. 15.7, 15.8

WHAT IS A 'MIXED' ANHYDRIDE?

A mixed anhydride has two different acyl groups as part of the anhydride, as in *15.9*.

HOW ARE MIXED ANHYDRIDES NAMED?

The two acyl groups are arranged in alphabetical order followed by the word anhydride. Anhydride *15.9* is named butanoic hexanoic anhydride.

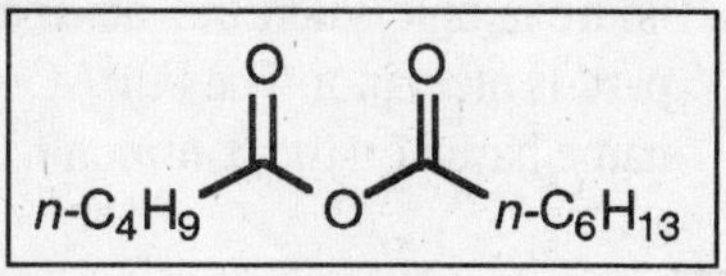

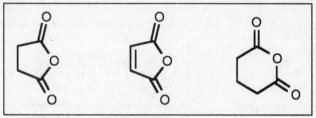

Fig. 15.9

WHAT ARE THE COMMON CYCLIC ANHYDRIDES DERIVED FROM SUCCINIC ACID, MALEIC ACID AND GLUTARIC ACID? GIVE THEIR NAME.

Succinic acid gives succinic anhydride (*15.10*), maleic acid gives maleic anhydride (*15.11*) and glutaric acid gives glutaric anhydride (*15.12*). In general, dicarboxylic acids of four carbons up to six-carbons give cyclic anhydrides. Diacids of less than four carbons would lead to highly strained three- or four-membered rings which are difficult to form. Larger chain diacids must form eight and larger membered rings and this is very difficult for C_8–C_{13} compounds.

Fig. 15.10–15.12

WHAT IS PHTHALIC ACID? WHAT IS PHTHALIC ANHYDRIDE?

Phthalic acid is benzene 1,2-dicarboxylic acid (see *15.13*) and the corresponding anhydride is *15.14*.

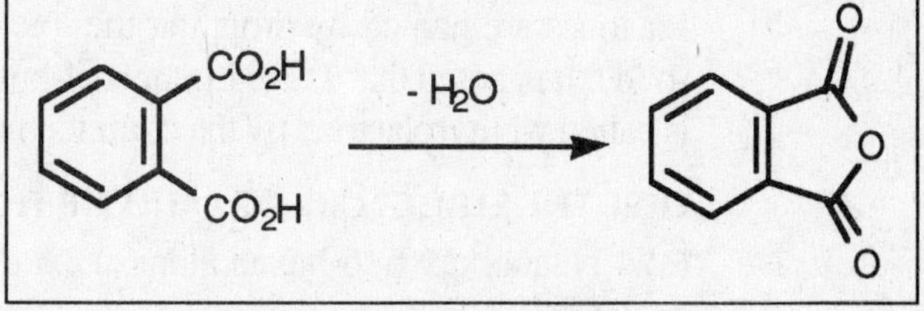

Fig. 15.13, 15.14

Esters

Esters were briefly introduced in section 14.5.

WHAT IS THE BASIC STRUCTURE OF AN ESTER?

An ester has an OR group attached to a carbonyl [RO–C=O].

WHAT IS THE IUPAC NOMENCLATURE SYSTEM FOR AN ESTER?

The -oic acid ending of the parent acid is dropped and replaced with -oate. The 'alcohol' portion of the ester is put in front of the 'acid portion'. $CH_3CO_2CH_3$ is an example where the 'acid part' is ethanoic acid (acetic acid) and the 'alcohol part' is methanol. The IUPAC name is methyl ethanoate (methyl acetate is the name based on the common name for the acid).

Acyclic Esters

HOW ARE ACYCLIC ESTERS NAMED?

The IUPAC system just described is used for acyclic esters. Acyclic esters do not contain a ring that includes the CO_2 group.

GIVE THE IUPAC NAME OF *15.15–15.17.*

The name of *15.15* is propyl heptanoate. The name of *15.16* is 1-methylethyl 1-cycloheptenoate (also called isopropyl cycloheptenoate). The name of *15.17* is methyl 2,4-dichlorobenzoate.

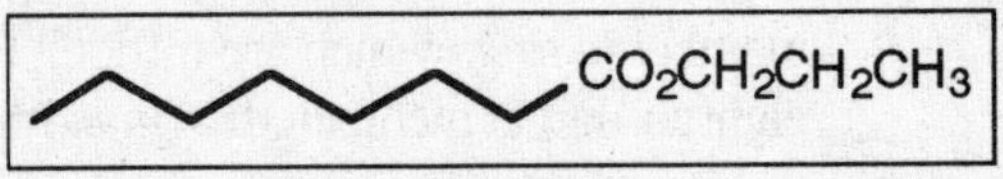

Fig. 15.15

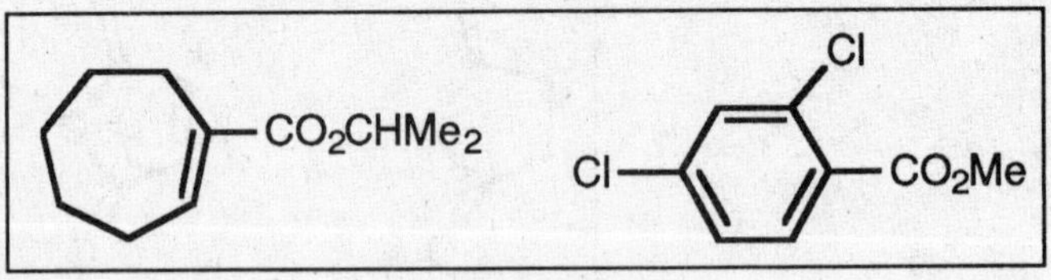

Fig. 15.16, 15.17

Lactones

WHAT IS THE DEFINITION OF A LACTONE?

A lactone is a cyclic ester, as in structure *15.18*.

HOW ARE LACTONES NAMED?

Lactones are named by dropping the -oic acid ending and replacing it with -olide. It is noted that *15.18* is named 4-butanolide by the IUPAC system but is called γ-butyrolactone by the common nomenclature.

GIVE THE STRUCTURE OF EACH OF THE FOLLOWING.

(a) 4-butanolide (b) 6-hexanolide (c) 2,3-diphenyl-6-hexanolide (d) 4-but-2-enolide

Lactone (a) is *51.18*, (b) is *15.19*, (c) is *15.20* and (d) is *15.21*.

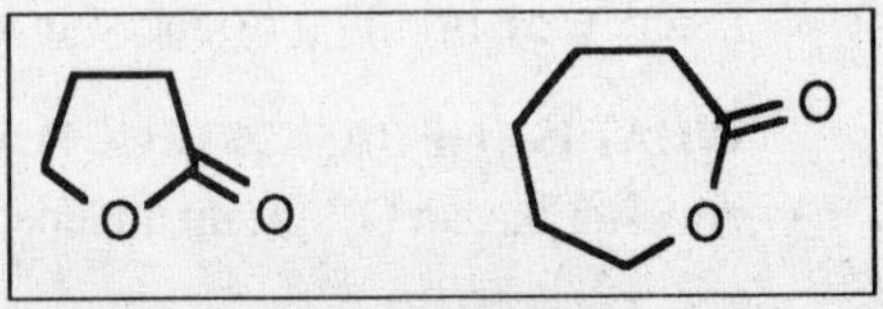

Fig. 15.18, 15.19

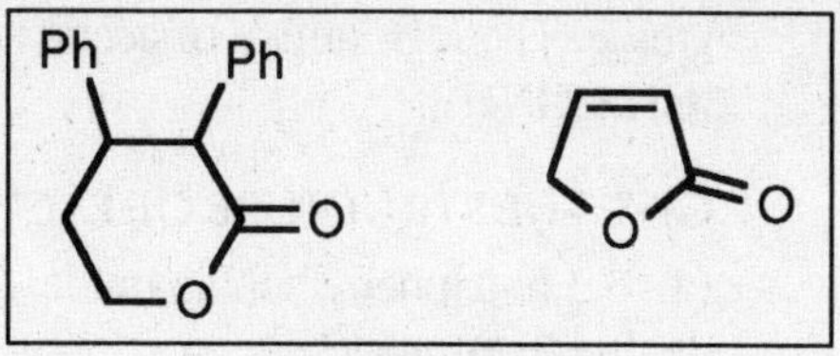

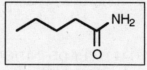

Fig. 15.20, 15.21

Amides

WHAT IS THE BASIC STRUCTURE OF AN AMIDE?

The fundamental structure of an amide has an amino group attached directly to a carbonyl, as in *15.22* [O=C–NR$_2$]. There are primary amides (-NH$_2$), secondary amides (-NHR) and tertiary amides (NR$_2$).

Fig. 15.22

WHAT IS THE IUPAC NOMENCLATURE SYSTEM FOR AN AMIDE?

The -oic acid of the parent carboxylic acid is dropped and replaced with amide. The amide of propanoic acid is, therefore, propanamide [CH$_3$CH$_2$CONH$_2$]. Amide *15.22* is named pentanamide.

WHAT IS THE NOMENCLATURE PROTOCOL WHEN SUBSTITUENTS APPEAR ON THE NITROGEN OF AN AMIDE?

When substituents appear on the nitrogen (as in *15.23*), the position of the substituent is given by using N- in front of the substituent. Amide *15.23* is N-ethyl-N-methylhexanamide and *15.24* is N,N,4-trimethylbenzamide. Note that the term N is used to position substituents on the nitrogen just as the traditional number (4) is used to position the methyl group on the benzene ring.

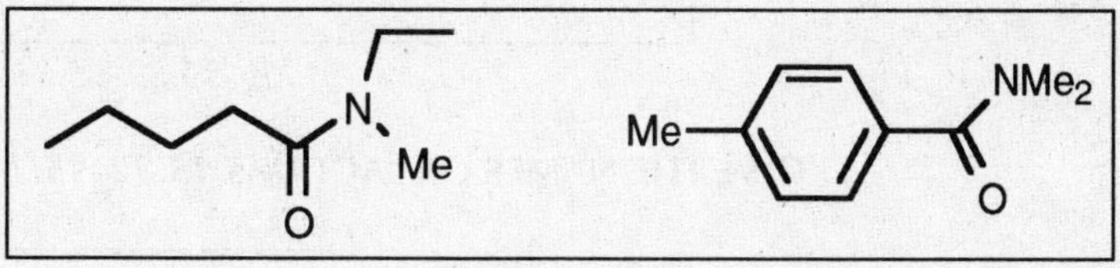

Fig. 15.23, 15.24

ACYCLIC AMIDES

HOW ARE ACYCLIC AMIDES NAMED?

The nomenclature system described above is for acyclic amides (the -CON unit is not part of a ring). If pentanoic acid is the parent, replacing the -OH with NR$_2$ leads to dropping the -oic acid and replacing it with amide. If the common name of the acid is used (such as acetic acid), the -ic acid is dropped and replaced with amide. The NH_2 amide of acetic acid is, therefore, ethanamide or acetamide [CH_3CONH_2].

GIVE THE STRUCTURE OF EACH OF THE FOLLOWING.

(a) 3,3,N-triphenylheptanamide (b) N-ethyl-3-chlorobenzamide (c) N,N-diethylacetamide

The structure of (a) is *15.26*, (b) is *15.27* and (c) is *15.28*.

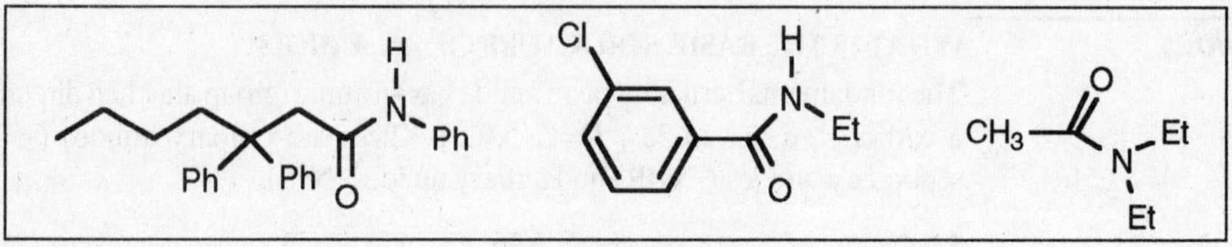

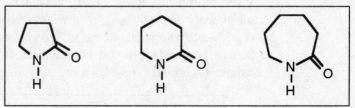

Fig. 15.26–15.28

Lactams

WHAT IS THE DEFINITION OF A LACTAM?

A lactam is a cyclic amide where the carbonyl and the nitrogen are part of a ring.

HOW ARE LACTAMS NAMED?

The names are based on a few specialized cyclic structures (derived from the reduced form of a heterocyclic base). The base names focus on 2-pyrrolidinone (*15.29*), 2-piperidone (*15.30*, also called tetrahydropyridin-2-one) and hexahydroazepin-2-one (*15.31*). There is also a common nomenclature system, based on the common name of the acid, which includes the word lactam. Lactam *15.29* is γ-butyrolactam, *15.30* is δ-valerolactam and *15.31* is caprolactam.

Fig. 15.29–15.31

GIVE THE NAMES OF LACTAMS *15.32–15.34*.

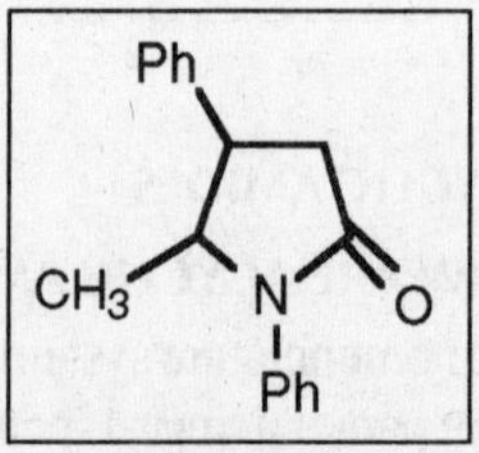

Fig. 15.32

Lactam *15.32* is 5-methyl-4,N-diphenyl-2-pyrrolidinone. Lactam *15.33* is N-butyl-3,5-dimethylhexahydroazepin-2-one. Lactam *15.34* is 3-(2-methyl-butyl)-5-cyclopentyl-2-pyrrolidinone.

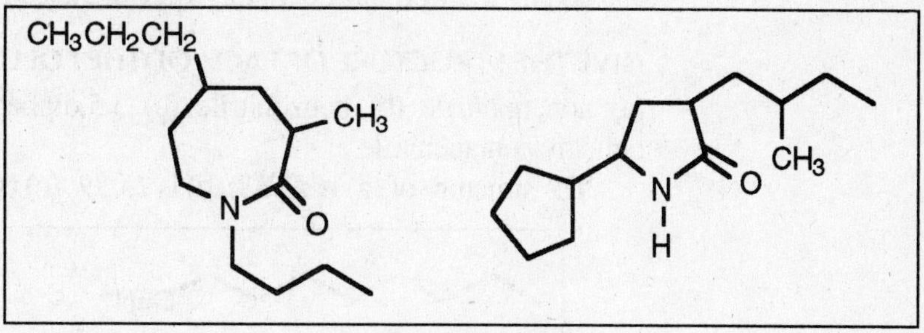

Fig. 15.33, 15.34

Imides

WHAT IS THE DEFINITION OF A IMIDE?

An imide is the nitrogen equivalent of an anhydride (see below) and is characterized by the O=C–N–C=O group.

HOW ARE IMIDES NAMED?

The fundamental name of an imide uses the word imide. EtCONHCOEt is known as diethylimide.

GIVE THE STRUCTURES AND NAMES OF THE CYCLIC IMIDES DERIVED FROM THE DIACIDS SUCCINIC ACID, GLUTARIC ACID AND PHTHALIC ACID.

The imide derived from succinic acid is succinimide (*15.35*), glutaric acid gives glutarimide (*15.36*) and phthalic acid leads to phthalimide (*15.37*).

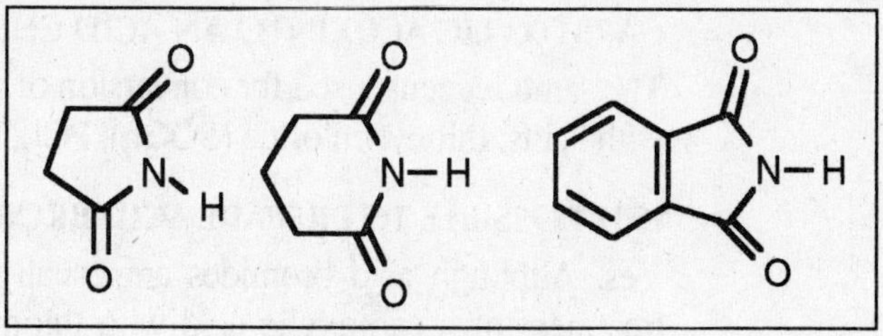

Fig. 15.35–15.37

Nitriles

WHAT IS THE BASIC STRUCTURE OF A NITRILE?

A nitrile is characterized by the presence of a cyanide group $-C\equiv N$. An example of a nitrile is $CH_3CH_2CH_2CH_2C\equiv N$.

HOW ARE NITRILES NAMED BY THE IUPAC SYSTEM?

Nitriles are considered to be carboxylic acid derivatives. They are named by dropping the -oic acid ending of the parent acid and replacing it with the word nitrile. The C_5 nitrile shown above is derived from pentanoic acid and is named pentanonitrile. It can also be named by using the alkane, alkene or alkyne base and adding the word nitrile. In this system, the C_5 nitrile is pentanenitrile.

GIVE THE STRUCTURE OF EACH OF THE FOLLOWING NITRILES.

(a) nonanonitrile (b) benzonitrile (c) 3,5,diphenylhexanonitrile (d) 3,3-dimethylpentanenitrile

The structure of (a) is *15.38*; (b) is *15.39;* (c) is *15.40* and (d) is *15.41.*

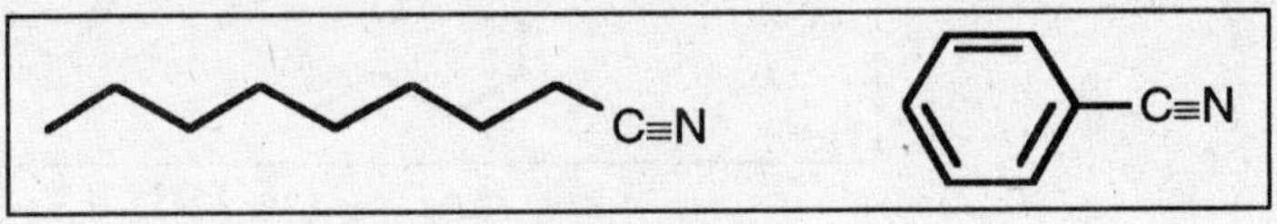

Fig. 15.38, 15.39

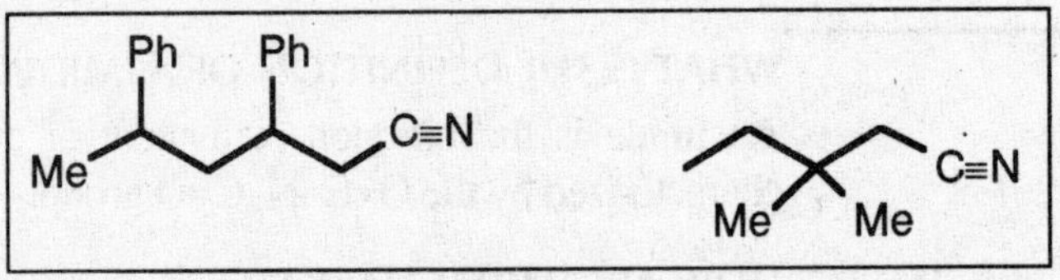

Fig. 15.40, 15.41

15.2. PREPARATION OF ACID DERIVATIVES

Acid Chlorides

GIVE AT LEAST THREE DIFFERENT REAGENTS THAT TRANSFORM A CARBOXYLIC ACID INTO AN ACID CHLORIDE.

The same reagents used for conversion of alcohols to chlorides are effective with acids: thionyl chloride ($SOCl_2$), PCl_3, PCl_5 and $POCl_3$ are all effective.

IS IT POSSIBLE TO PREPARE ACID BROMIDES?

Yes. Although acid bromides are usually less stable than acid chlorides, treatment of a carboxylic acid with thionyl bromide ($SOBr_2$) or PBr_3 will produce the acid bromide.

WHY ARE ACID FLUORIDES AND ACID IODIDES ALMOST NEVER OBSERVED?

Both are very unstable and difficult to isolate. It is also true that thionyl fluoride or iodide are not usable reagents and phosphorus iodides are relatively unstable. The latter reagents are usually formed *in situ* by reaction of phosphorous with iodide. POF_3 is known but the acid fluoride derived from reaction with an acid is too unstable to isolate.

WHAT ARE THE UV PROPERTIES OF ACID CHLORIDES?

There are no diagnostic absorption peaks in the UV spectrum that are used to identify this class of compounds.

Acid anhydrides WHAT IS THE BASIC STRUCTURE OF AN ACID ANHYDRIDE?

The basic functional group is O=C–O=C=O, where alkyl or aryl groups are attached to each carbonyl, RCO_2OR' (see *15.42*). If R and R' are the same this is called a symmetrical anhydride. If R and R' are different it is called an unsymmetrical anhydride.

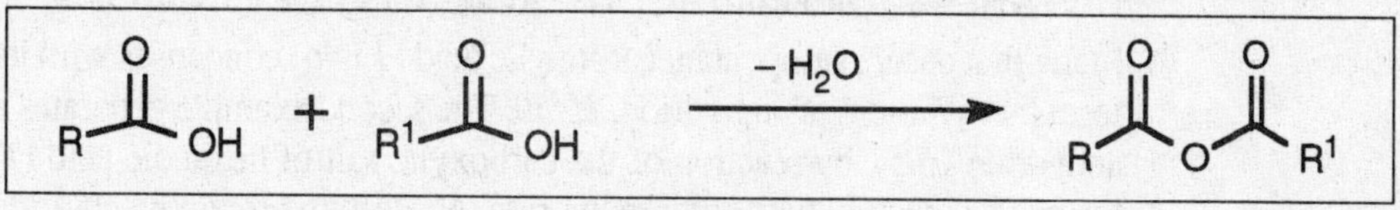

Fig. 15.42

GIVE A GENERIC REACTION FOR THE PREPARATION OF AN ANHYDRIDE.

In the simplest reaction type, two carboxylic acids combine, with loss of a molecule of water, to form the anhydride. The anhydride therefore consists of two acid fragments.

SYMMETRICAL ANHYDRIDES

HOW ARE SYMMETRICAL ANHYDRIDES PREPARED?

A carboxylic acid can be heated with a dehydrating agent such as phosphorus pentoxide (P_2O_5) to produce the anhydride. The carboxylate salt of an acid can be reacted with the acid chloride of that acid.

WHY IS AN ACID CHLORIDE MORE USEFUL FOR PREPARATION OF AN ANHYDRIDE THAN A CARBOXYLIC ACID?

An acid chloride is more reactive than the acid to acyl addition reactions. It is also true that mixed anhydrides are easier to prepare via the acid chloride/carboxylate salt route.

MIXED ANHYDRIDES

WHY IS THE PREPARATION OF MIXED ANHYDRIDES OFTEN ACCOMPANIED BY LOW YIELDS AND SIGNIFICANT AMOUNTS OF SYMMETRICAL ANHYDRIDES?

If two different acids such as ethanoic acid and butanoic acid are heated with a dehydrating agent, ethanoic acid can condense with itself or with butanoic acid. Likewise, butanoic acid can condense with itself or with ethanoic acid. This reaction, therefore, produces three anhydrides in a 1:2:1 ratio: *15.43, 15.44* and *15.45*.

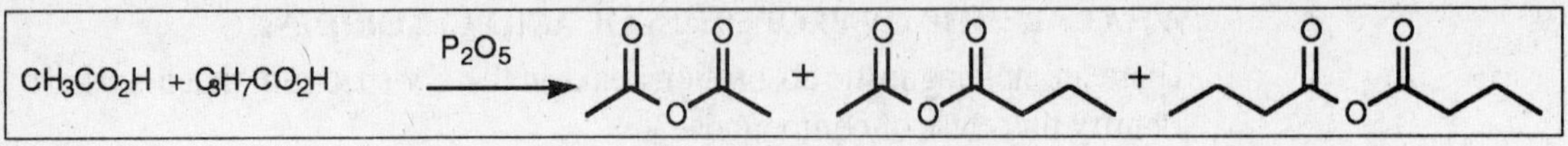

$$CH_3CO_2H + C_3H_7CO_2H \xrightarrow{P_2O_5}$$

Fig. 15.43–15.45

HOW CAN THESE PROBLEMS BE OVERCOME?

The best method for producing mixed anhydrides is to condense the acid chloride of one acid (such as butanoyl chloride) with the carboxylate salt of the other (such as sodium ethanoate). In this example, reaction of these two species will produce *15.44*, exclusively.

GIVE THE MAJOR PRODUCT THE REACTIONS OF *15.46–15.49*.

In the first case, cyclopentanecarboxylic acid (*15.46*) condenses with itself to form the symmetrical anhydride, *15.50*. The second example generates mixed anhydride *15.51* by reaction of the carboxylic salt of hexanoic acid (*15.47*), formed by reaction with sodium hydride [NaH] with propanoyl chloride. The third example also produces a mixed anhydride (*15.52*) by reaction of benzoyl chloride (*15.48*) with the sodium salt of hexanoic acid. The last example condenses *15.49* with itself to produce the symmetrical anhydride, *15.53*.

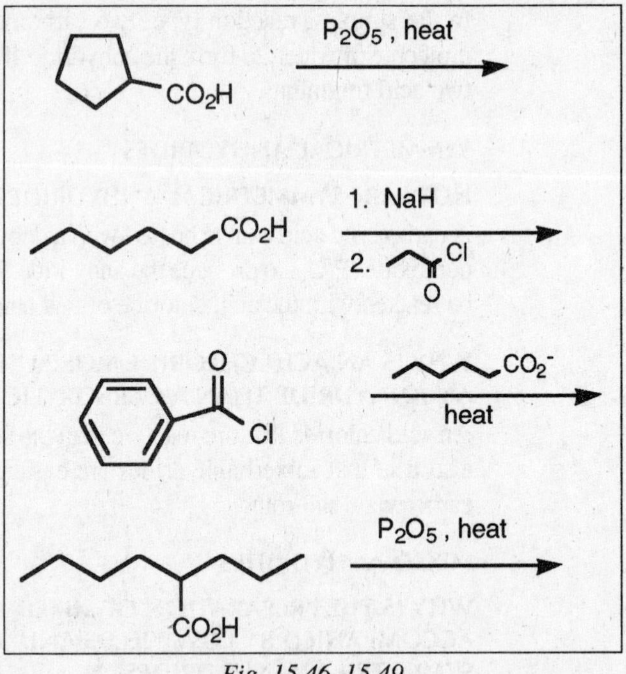

Fig. 15.46–15.49

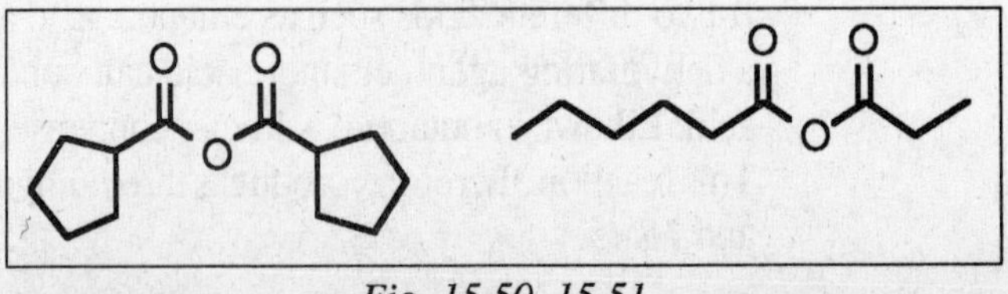

Fig. 15.50, 15.51

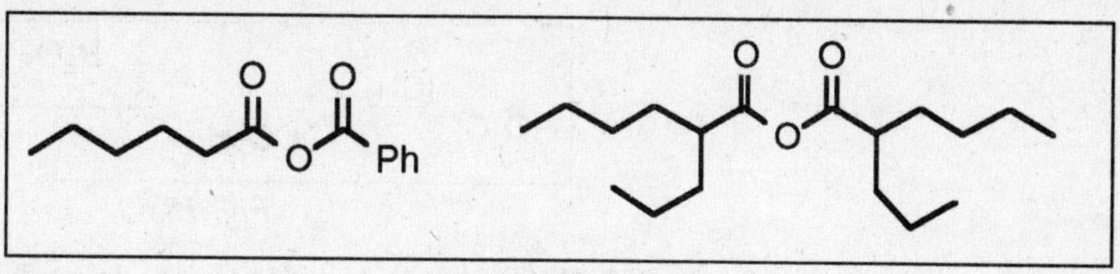

Fig. 15.52, 15.53

CYCLIC ANHYDRIDES

WHAT TYPE OF ACID DERIVATIVE LEADS TO A CYCLIC ANHYDRIDE?

A dibasic acid such succinic acid or glutaric acid will form a cyclic anhydride upon dehydration. In general, cyclization of dicarboxylic acids to produce five-, six- and seven-membered ring anhydrides is favorable. Cyclization to form most, but not all, larger ring anhydrides in this manner is usually very difficult.

GIVE THE NAME OF *15.54–15.58.*

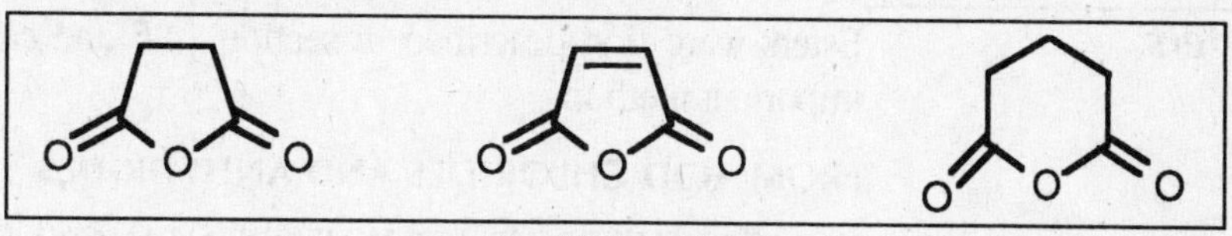

Fig. 15.54–15.56

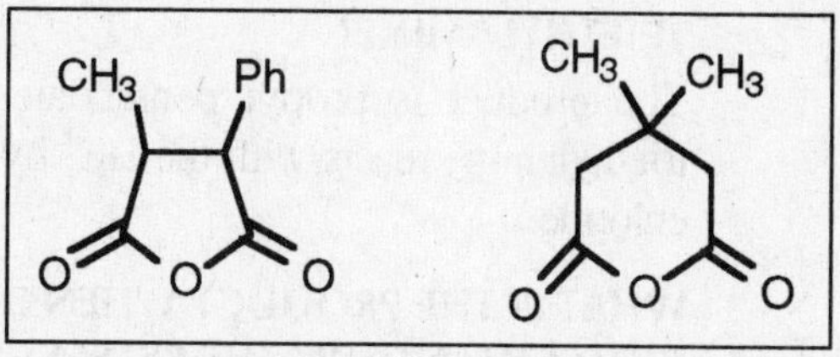

Fig. 15.57, 15.58

The first anhydride (*15.54*) is succinic anhydride (the IUPAC name is 1,4-butanedioic anhydride). The second anhydride (*15.55*) is maleic anhydride (2-butene-1,4-dioic anhydride). The third (*15.56*) is glutaric anhydride (1,5-pentanedioic anhydride). Anhydride *15.57* is 2-methyl-3-phenyl-1,4-butanedioic anhydride (2-methyl-3-phenylsuccinic anhydride) and *15.58* is 3,3-dimethyl-1,5-pentanedioic anhydride (3,3-dimethylglutaric anhydride).

GIVE THE MAJOR PRODUCT FROM THE REACTIONS OF *15.59* AND *15.60.*

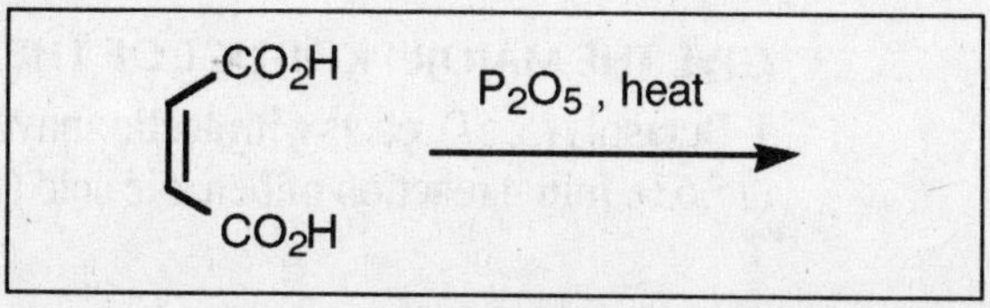

Fig. 15.59

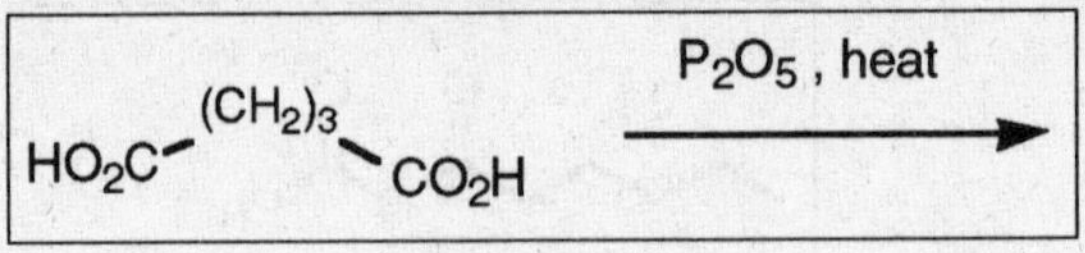

Fig. 15.60

Maleic acid (*15.59*) is dehydrated to give maleic anhydride (*15.55*) and glutaric acid (*15.60*) is dehydrated to give glutaric anhydride, *15.56*.

EXPLAIN WHY FUMARIC ACID (TRANS-2-BUTENEDIOIC ACID) DOES NOT GIVE A CYCLIC ANHYDRIDE UPON TREATMENT WITH P_2O_5.

Unlike maleic acid (*15.59*) which has the carboxyl groups on the same side and close enough for those group to interact to lose water, fumaric acid has the carbonyl groups on opposite sides of the double bond. They cannot get close enough to interact and if water is lost to form an anhydride it will be an acyclic anhydride.

Esters

Esters were first described in section 14.5 and can be prepared by several important methods.

FROM ACID CHLORIDES AND ANHYDRIDES

WHAT IS THE PRODUCT WHEN PENTANOYL CHLORIDE REACTS WITH PROPANOL IN BENZENE SOLUTION IN THE PRESENCE OF TRIETHYLAMINE?

The product is propyl pentanoate [$CH_3CH_2CH_2O_2C(CH_2)_4CH_3$]. The triethylamine reacts with the HCl by-product to produce triethylammonium chloride.

WHAT IS THE PRODUCT WHEN BUTANOYL ANHYDRIDE REACTS WITH ETHANOL IN THE PRESENCE OF TRIETHYLAMINE?

The anhydride reacts with ethanol, in the presence of an amine, to produce ethyl butanoate [$CH_3CH_2O_2CCH_2CH_2CH_3$] and butanoic acid. The triethylamine will react with butanoic acid to produce triethylammonium butanoate (the acid salt), driving the reaction towards the ester.

WHICH IS MORE REACTIVE, AN ACID CHLORIDE OR AN ESTER? EXPLAIN.

An acid chloride is somewhat more reactive than an acid anhydride but they are close in reactivity. The reason for the enhanced reactivity of the acid chloride is because chlorine is a better leaving group than an acyl group in acyl addition reactions.

GIVE THE MAJOR PRODUCT OF THE REACTIONS OF *15.61–15.62*.

1-Butanol (*15.61*) reacts with acetic anhydride to form the ester, ethyl butanoate (*15.63*). Initial reaction of benzoic acid (*15.62*) with SOCl₂ generates the acid chloride, which reacts with cycloheptanol to form cycloheptyl benzoate, (*15.64*).

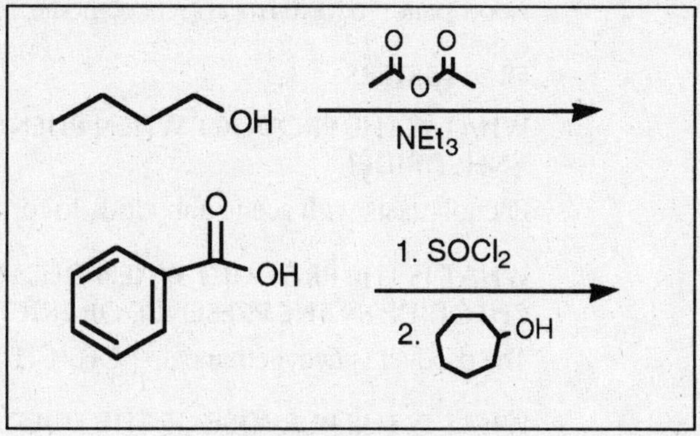

Fig. 15.61, 15.62

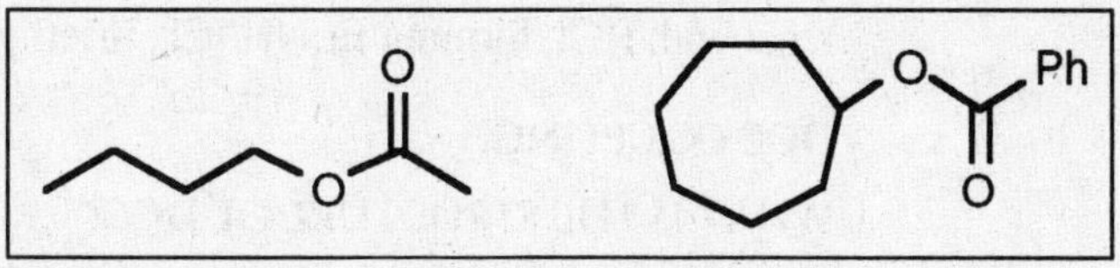

Fig. 15.63, 15.64

ACID CATALYZED REACTION OF ACIDS AND ALCOHOLS

See section 14.5 and 11.4 (alcohols).

WHEN BUTANOIC ACID IS DISSOLVED IN ETHANOL AND HEATED, IN THE PRESENCE OF AN ACID CATALYST, WHAT IS THE MAJOR PRODUCT?

The product is ethyl butanoate.

WHAT IS THE MECHANISM OF THIS REACTION?

This complete mechanism was given in section 14.5.

WHAT IS THE MAJOR PRODUCT OF THE REACTIONS OF *15.65* AND *15.66*?

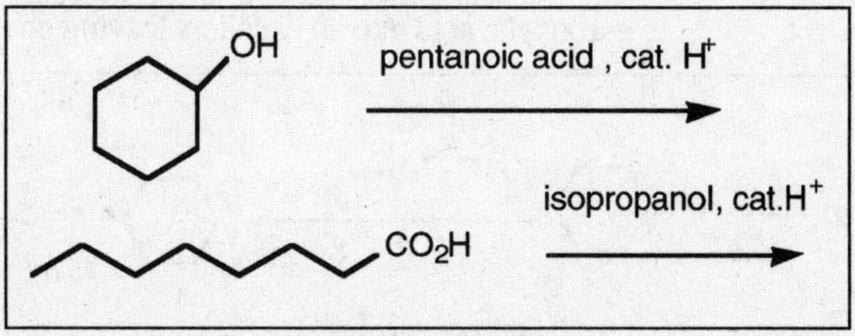

Fig. 15.65, 15.66

In the first reaction, cyclohexanol (*15.65*) reacts with pentanoic acid to form cyclohexyl pentanoate. In the second reaction, octanoic acid (*15.66*) reacts with isopropanol to form isopropyl octanoate.

FROM ESTERS

WHAT IS THE PRODUCT WHEN PHENOL REACTS WITH ACETIC ANHYDRIDE?

Phenol reacts with acetic anhydride to form phenyl acetate (CH_3CO_2Ph).

WHAT IS THE PRODUCT WHEN DECANOL REACTS WITH ETHANOYL CHLORIDE IN THE PRESENCE OF TRIETHYLAMINE?

The product is decyl ethanoate [$CH_3(CH_2)_8CH_2O_2CCH_3$].

WHAT IS THE PURPOSE OF THE TRIETHYLAMINE?

The by-product of this reaction is HCl. The triethylamine functions as a base to react with HCl, forming $Et_3NH^+ Cl^-$, (triethylammonium chloride).

DCC COUPLING

WHAT IS THE STRUCTURE OF DCC?

The structure of DCC (dicyclohexyl carbodiimide) is *15.67*.

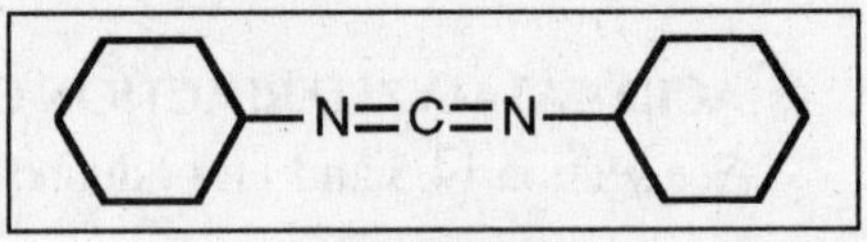

Fig. 15.67

WHAT IS THE PRODUCT OF THE REACTION BETWEEN PROPANOIC ACID AND ETHANOL IN THE PRESENCE OF DCC?

The products are the ester, ethyl propanoate (*15.69*), and dicyclohexyl urea (*15.70*).

WHAT IS THE MECHANISM OF THIS REACTION?

The initial reaction between DCC and the acid generates *15.68*. The acyl carbon is attacked by the alcohol oxygen, displacing dicyclohexyl urea (*15.70*) and generating the ester. For all practical purposes, the DCC converts the OH of the carboxylic acid into an excellent leaving group (the urea).

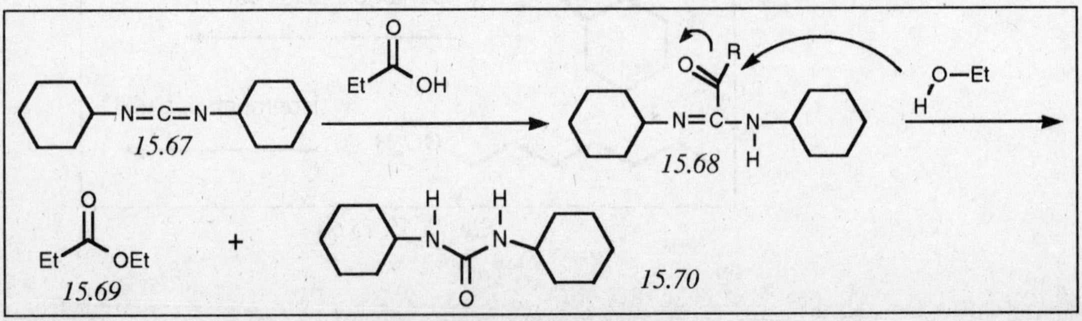

Fig. 15.67–15.70

WHAT IS THE PRODUCT OF THE REACTIONS OF *15.62, 15.65* AND *15.71*?

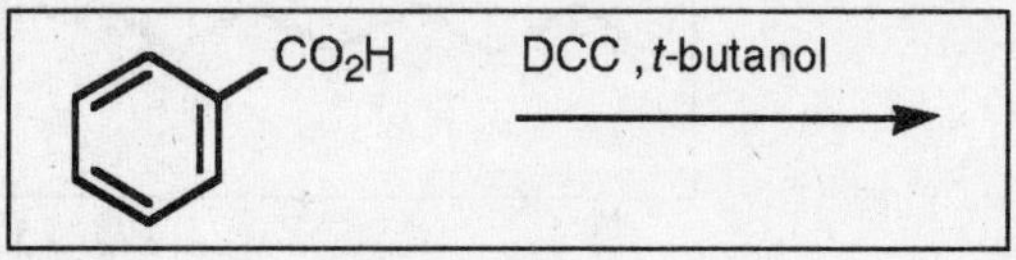

Fig. 15.62

Benzoic acid (*15.62*) reacts with *t*-butanol to form *t*-butyl benzoate (*15.72*). Cyclohexanol (*15.65*) reacts with benzoic acid to form cyclohexyl benzoate (*15.73*) and 2,4-dimethyl-hexanoic acid (*15.71*) reacts with 1-butanol to give butyl 2,4-dimethylhexanoate, *15.74*.

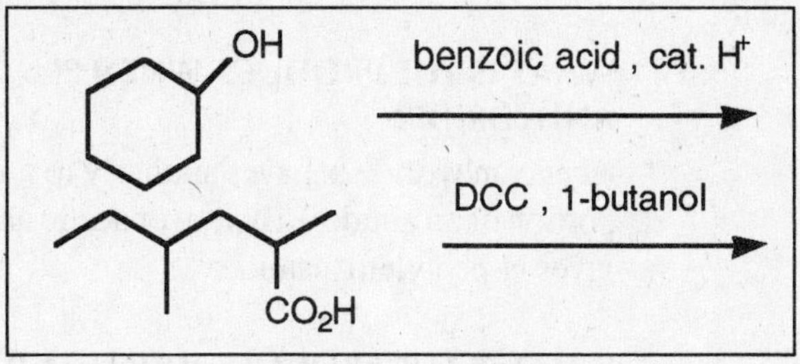

Fig. 15.65, 15.71

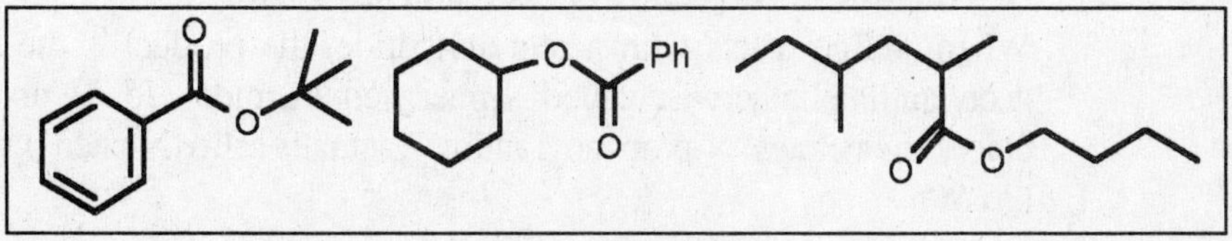

Fig. 15.72–15.74

Amides

See section 14.5.

THERMOLYSIS OF AMMONIUM SALTS

WHAT IS THE PRODUCT OF THE REACTIONS OF *15.75* AND *15.76*?

Reaction of acid *15.75* and dimethylamine generates the dimethylammonium carboxylate salt. Thermolysis dehydrates the salt to produce amide *15.77*. Similarly, reaction of N-methyl-cyclooctylamine (*15.76*) with butanoic acid gives a salt and thermolysis liberates the amide, *15.78*.

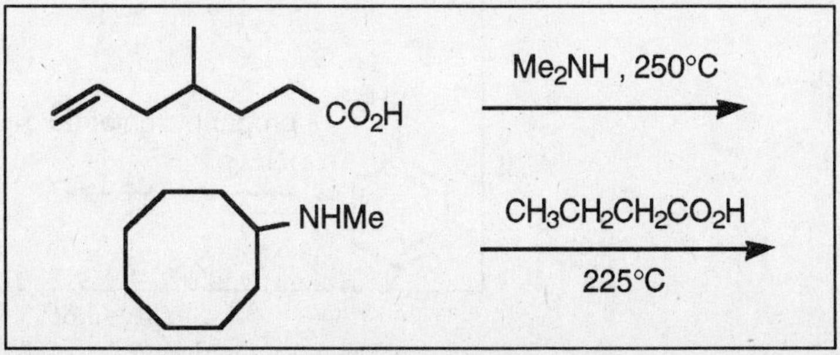

Fig. 15.75, 15.76

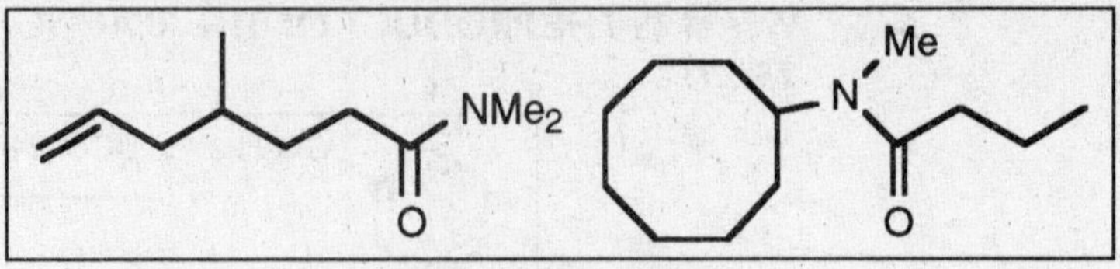

Fig. 15.77, 15.78

FROM ACID CHLORIDES AND ANHYDRIDES

WHAT IS THE MAJOR PRODUCT WHEN BUTANOYL CHLORIDE REACTS WITH BUTYLAMINE IN THE PRESENCE OF TRIETHYLAMINE?

The product is the amide, N-butylbutanamide [BuNH(C=O)Bu].

WHAT IS THE PRODUCT WHEN PENTYLAMINE REACTS WITH ACETIC ANHYDRIDE?

Acetic anhydride behaves similarly to an acid chloride and provides the acyl portion of an amide. Reaction of acetic anhydride and pentylamine, therefore, gives N-pentylethanamide.

WHAT IS THE PRODUCT WHEN ANILINE REACTS WITH ACETIC ANHYDRIDE? WITH PROPANOYL CHLORIDE?

When aniline reacts with acetic anhydride, the product is the amide, "N-acetylaniline" otherwise called N-phenylethanamide, (*15.79*) and propanoyl chloride generates "N-propanoyl aniline", actually called N-phenylpropanamide (*15.80*).

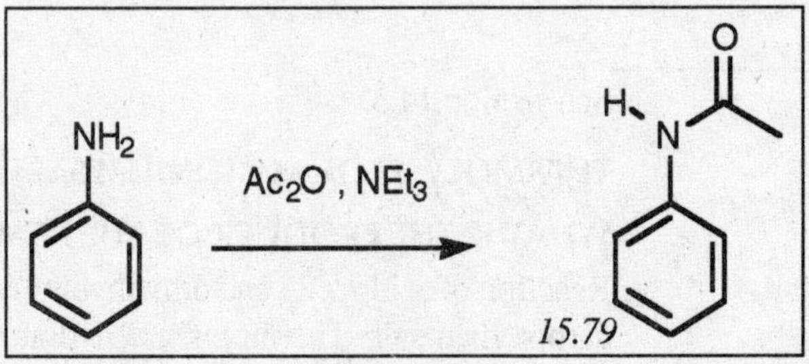

Fig. 15.79

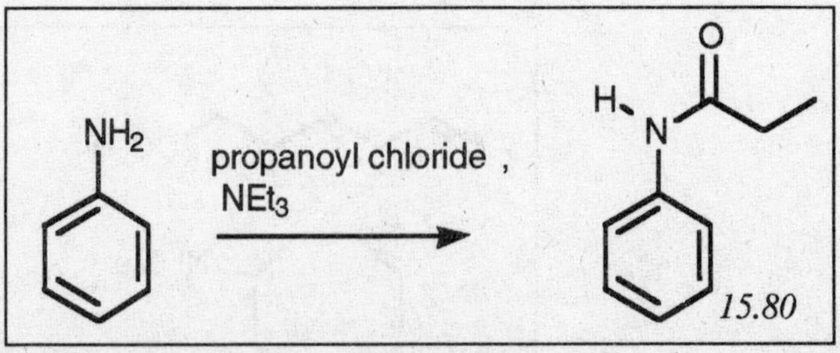

Fig. 15.80

FROM ESTERS

WHAT IS THE PRODUCT WHEN ETHYL PENTANOATE REACTS WITH AMMONIA UNDER CONDITIONS OF HIGH HEAT AND PRESSURE?

Under these conditions an amide is formed (pentanamide) where the ammonia displaces ethanol via acyl addition and substitution.

WHAT IS THE PRODUCT WHEN CH_3NH_2 REACTS WITH γ-BUTYRO-LACTONE?

Once again, the nitrogen displaces the 'alcohol' via acyl addition. The OH is converted to OH_2^+ and displacement by the nitrogen (under high heat and pressure) to form the lactam, *15.81*.

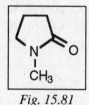

Fig. 15.81

GIVE THE MAJOR PRODUCT OF THE REACTIONS OF *15.82* AND *15.83*.

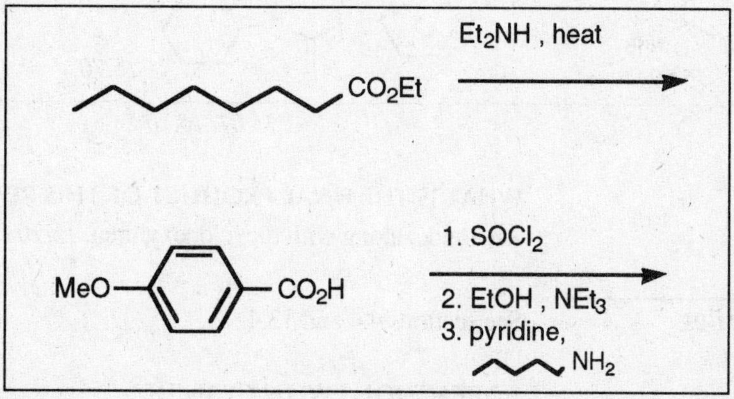

Fig. 15.82, 15.83

In the first reaction, *15.82* reacts with diethylamine to form the N,N-diethyl amide, *15.84*. In the second reaction, conversion of *15.83* to the acid chloride allows esterification. Subsequent reaction with pentylamine leads to the amide, *15.85*.

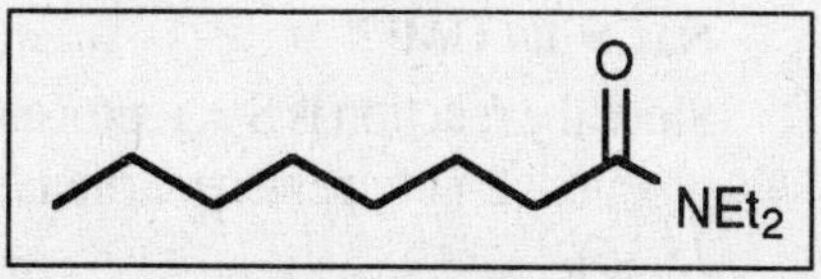

Fig. 15.84

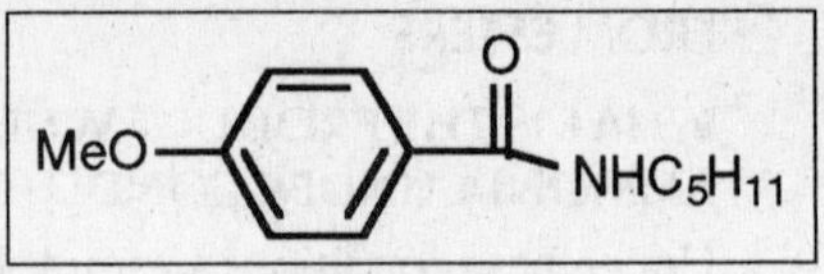

Fig. 15.85

DCC COUPLING WITH ACIDS AND AMINES

BY ANALOGY WITH THE DCC REACTION OF ALCOHOLS AND ACIDS, WHAT IS THE KEY INTERMEDIATE IN THE DCC REACTION OF AN AMINE WITH A CARBOXYLIC ACID?

As with the coupling of acids and alcohols, when DCC (*15.67*) reacts with the carboxylic acid, the key intermediate is *15.68*. The DCC portion of the molecule functions as a 'leaving group' and attack by the amine generates the amide and dicyclohexylurea (*15.70*).

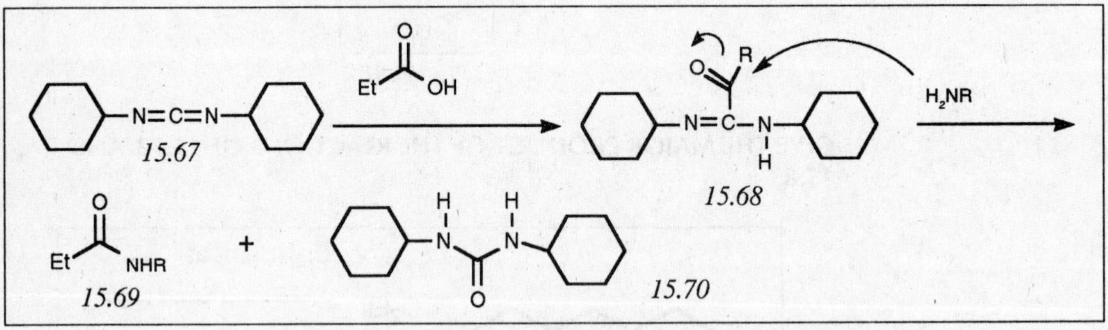

Fig. 15.67–15.70

WHAT IS THE FINAL PRODUCT OF THIS REACTION?

An amide, along with dicyclohexylurea, *15.70*.

Nitriles

See sections 4.4 and 13.4.

S$_N$² REACTIONS WITH CYANIDE

WHAT IS THE MAJOR PRODUCT WHEN 1-IODOPENTANE REACTS WITH KCN IN HOT DMF?

The product is pentanenitrile, $CH_3CH_2CH_2CH_2C \equiv N$.

WHAT IS THE PRODUCT WHEN S-3-BROMOHEPTANE REACTS WITH NaCN IN DMF?

Since the reaction is S$_N$², it proceed with 100% inversion of configuration. The product is 2-ethylpentanenitrile and the chiral center is R (R-2-ethylpentanenitrile, *15.86*).

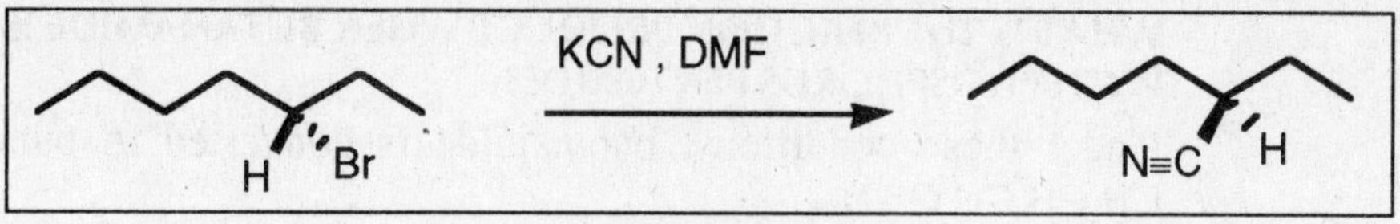

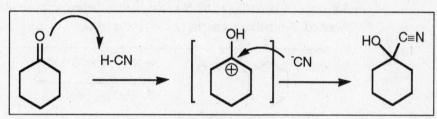

Fig. 15.86

CYANOHYDRINS VIA NUCLEOPHILIC ACYL SUBSTITUTION

WHAT IS THE PRODUCT WHEN CYCLOHEXANONE REACTS WITH HCN?

The product is a cyanohydrin, 1-cyanocyclohexanol, *15.88.* Initial reaction of the carbonyl oxygen and HCN generates the cation (*15.87*), which is then attacked by the nucleophilic cyanide ion.

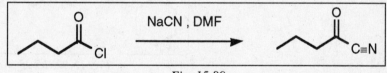

Fig. 15.87, 15.88

WHAT IS THE PRODUCT OF THE REACTION BETWEEN BUTANOYL CHLORIDE AND NaCN IN DMF?

The cyanide behaves as a nucleophile and displaces the chloride (nucleophilic acyl substitution) to product 1-cyano-1-butanone, *15.89.*

Fig. 15.89

DEHYDRATION OF AMIDES

WHAT IS A DEHYDRATION AGENT?

A dehydrating agent is a reagent that reacts with water and removes it from the reaction medium or reacts with a molecule to remove the elements of water.

WHAT ARE COMMON DEHYDRATING AGENTS?

The most common dehydrating agent is probably phosphorus pentoxide (P_2O_5 — NOTE: the actual formula of this reagent is P_4O_{10} — the other formula was thought to be correct and accounts for the name). Sulfuric acid is sometimes used as a dehydrating agent in relatively simple molecules.

WHAT IS THE REACTION PRODUCT WHEN BUTANAMIDE IS HEATED WITH PHOSPHORUS PENTOXIDE?

Under these conditions, butanamide is converted to butanenitrile, $CH_3CH_2CH_2C\equiv N$.

WHAT IS THE PRODUCT WHEN BENZOIC ACID IS TREATED WITH: i. SOCl$_2$ ii. NH$_3$, HEAT iii. P$_2$O$_5$, HEAT?

The product is benzonitrile, $Ph-C\equiv N$.

WHAT IS THE MAJOR PRODUCT OF THE REACTIONS *15.90* AND *15.91*?

The reaction of cyclohexane carboxylic acid (*15.90*) and ammonia leads to the amide (with heating). Subsequent dehydration gives the corresponding nitrile, cyclohexane carbonitrile, *15.92*. Similarly, when 2-ethylhexanamide (*15.91*) is dehydrated, 2-ethylhexanenitrile (*15.93*) is the product.

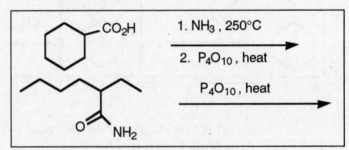

Fig. 15.90, 15.91

Fig. 15.92, 15.93

15.3. REACTIONS OF ACID DERIVATIVES

Aqueous Hydrolysis

Virtually all acid derivatives can be converted to their parent carboxylic acid by either acid or base hydrolysis.

ACIDS FROM ACID HALIDES

WHAT IS THE MECHANISM FOR THE BASE HYDROLYSIS OF BUTANOYL CHLORIDE?

Hydroxide attacks the carbonyl carbon (acyl addition) to form *15.94*. The electrons on the alkoxide oxygen expels chlorine (which is a good leaving group), forming the carboxylic acid (*15.95*). Under the basic conditions of the reaction, this acid reacts with NaOH to form the carboxylate, *15.96*.

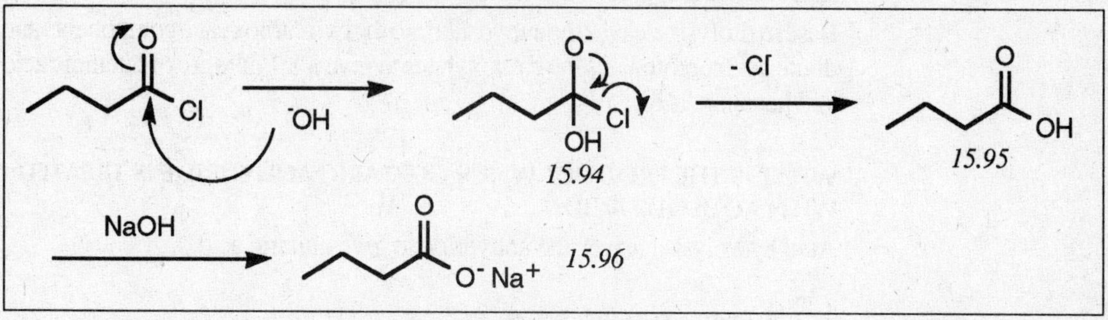

Fig. 15.94–15.96

WHAT IS THE MECHANISM OF ACID HYDROLYSIS OF BUTANOYL CHLORIDE TO THE ACID?

The initial reaction is protonation of the carbonyl oxygen to give the resonance stabilized ion, *15.97*, followed by reaction with water to give *15.98*. Loss of a proton gives *15.99*, which allows expulsion of chloride ion to give *15.100*. Final loss of a proton gives the acid, *15.95*. The loss of H^+ and Cl^- is formally equivalent to losing HCl.

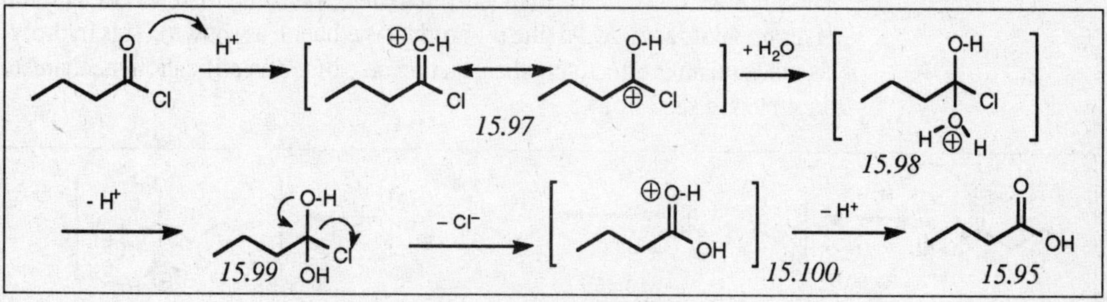

Fig. 15.97–15.100, 15.95

ACIDS FROM ACID ANHYDRIDES

WHAT IS THE PRODUCT WHEN ETHANOIC ANHYDRIDE IS TREATED WITH AQUEOUS ACID?

Acid hydrolysis converts an anhydride to a mixture of the two component acids. In this case, ethanoic anhydride (acetic anhydride) gives two equivalents of ethanoic acid (acetic acid) upon aqueous acid hydrolysis.

WHY IS IT NOT IMPORTANT TO THE FINAL PRODUCT DISTRIBUTION WHICH CARBONYL OF ETHANOIC PROPIONIC ANHYDRIDE IS ATTACKED BY HYDROXIDE IN BASE HYDROLYSIS?

Ethanoic anhydride is symmetrical and hydroxide can attack either carbonyl to give the same product.

WHAT ARE THE PRODUCTS WHEN BUTANOIC HEXANOIC ANHYDRIDE IS TREATED WITH i. AQ. NaOH ii. DIL. ACID?

Base hydrolysis cleaves the anhydride into the two carboxylate components and dilute acid reprotonates the carboxylates to give a 1:1 mixture of butanoic acid and hexanoic acid.

WHAT IS THE PRODUCT WHEN GLUTARIC ANHYDRIDE IS TREATED WITH AQUEOUS ACID?

Acid hydrolysis cleaves the anhydride to give glutaric acid.

ACIDS FROM ESTERS

WHAT IS THE MECHANISM FOR THE CONVERSION OF ETHYL BUTANOATE TO BUTANOIC ACID AND ETHANOL UNDER ACIDIC CONDITIONS?

The mechanism for ester hydrolysis is essentially identical to that given for acid hydrolysis of an acid chloride (butanoyl chloride—see above). In this case, the leaving group is OEt rather than Cl. Initial reaction with acid gives the resonance stabilized cation (*15.101*), which is attacked by water to give *15.102*. Loss of a proton is followed by transfer of the proton to the OEt moiety, to give *15.103*. This allows expulsion of ethanol, the leaving group, and final loss of a proton gives butanoic acid, *15.95* (the by-product is ethanol, as shown). This hydrolysis mechanism is effectively the exact reverse of the esterification mechanism presented in section 14.5.

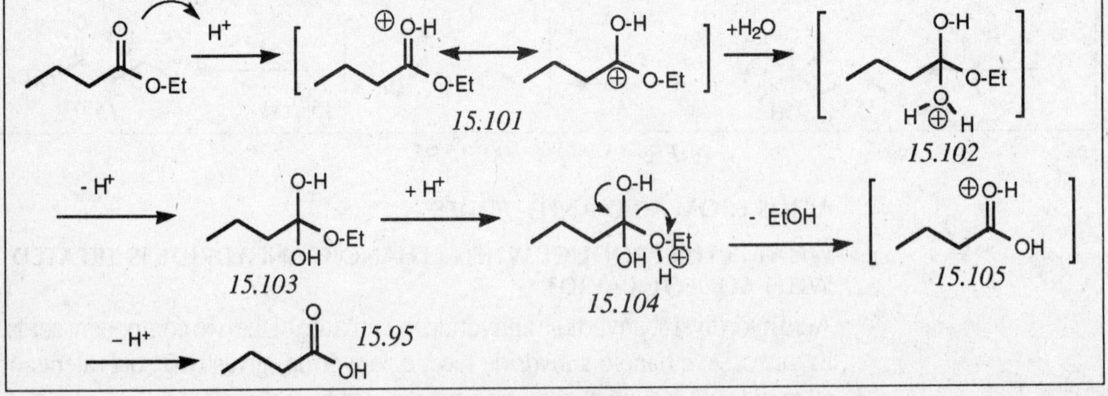

Fig. 15.101–15.104, 15.95

WHAT IS SAPONIFICATION?

Saponification is a term used for the manufacture of soap. It involves treatment of fats (triglyceryl esters) with lye (hydroxide) to form the sodium salt of fatty acids (soap). Triglycerides are formed from glycerol (the alcohol) and long chain fatty acids. The term saponification has come to be used for the reaction: base hydrolysis of esters. The mechanism is identical to that shown for acid chlorides where Cl is replaced with OR.

ACIDS FROM AMIDES

WHAT IS THE MECHANISM FOR THE ACID CATALYZED HYDROLYSIS OF N,N-DIMETHYLPENTAMIDE?

The mechanism is identical to that for acid chlorides and esters, where the 'leaving group' is now the amine (HNEt$_2$).

WHY IS THE HYDROLYSIS OF AN AMIDE MORE DIFFICULT THAN THE HYDROLYSIS OF AN ESTER?

The amine group is a poorer leaving group than OEt and the amide group is bulkier, making attack of water at the carbonyl more difficult. The reaction begins the same way with protonation of the carbonyl oxygen to give *15.105* and addition of water to give *15.106*. Loss of a proton will give *15.107* but the proton must be transferred to the nitrogen to convert it into a good leaving group, *15.108*. It is noted that this hydrogen transfer may occur intramolecularly, avoiding the need to form *15.107*. Loss of diethylamine gives *15.109* and loss of a proton gives butanoic acid, *15.95*.

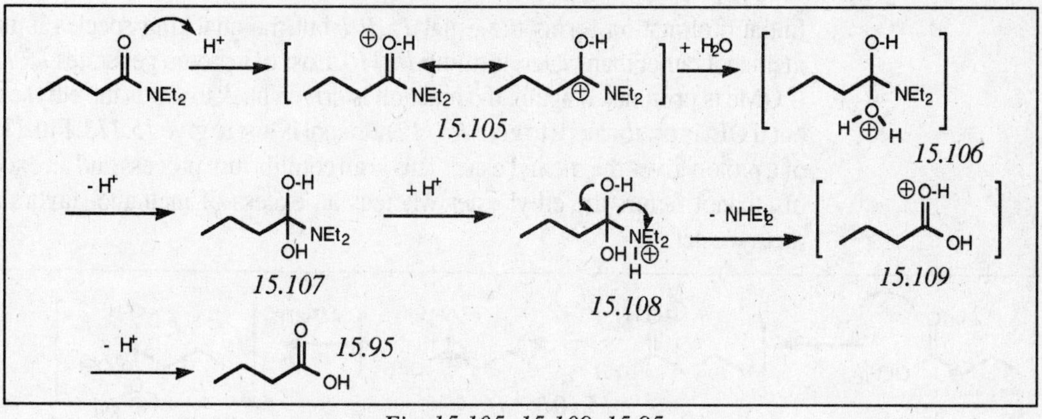

Fig. 15.105–15.109, 15.95

ACIDS FROM NITRILES

WHAT IS THE PRODUCT OF THE 'PARTIAL HYDROLYSIS' OF HEXANENITRILE?

The complete hydrolysis of a nitrile gives the carboxylic acid. "Partial hydrolysis" refers to limiting the hydrolysis conditions to isolate the amide, which is an intermediate product on the path to the carboxylic acid. In this case, partial hydrolysis leads to hexanamide. In general relatively dilute acid and relatively mild conditions give the amide.

WHAT CONDITIONS ARE REQUIRED FOR THE CONVERSION OF A NITRILE TO A CARBOXYLIC ACID?

If concentrated aqueous acid and vigorous reaction conditions (refluxing conditions for a long period of time) are used, the nitrile is converted directly to the carboxylic acid.

Reaction With Alcohols

ESTERS FROM ACID CHLORIDES AND ANHYDRIDES

As noted in sections 11.4 and 14.5, the reaction of an acid chloride or an anhydride leads to an ester.

TRANSESTERIFICATION

WHAT DOES THE TERM TRANSESTERIFICATION MEAN?

Transesterification refers to exchanging the OR group of an ester with a new alcohol group (OR^1). Conversion of a methyl ester to an ethyl ester is an example of transesterification.

WHAT IS THE PRODUCT WHEN ETHYL BUTANOATE IS DISSOLVED IN METHANOL WITH A CATALYTIC AMOUNT OF ACID?

The product is methyl butanoate.

WHAT IS THE MECHANISM OF THIS REACTION?

Initial protonation forms the usual 15.101 but the attacking species is now methanol rather than water, forming 15.110. Loss of a proton generates 15.111. If OMe is protonated again, the reaction is driven back towards the ethyl ester but if OEt is protonated (to give 15.112) ethanol is lost to give 15.113. Final loss of a proton gives the methyl ester. This is an equilibrium process and an excess of ethanol favors the ethyl ester whereas an excess of methanol favors the methyl ester.

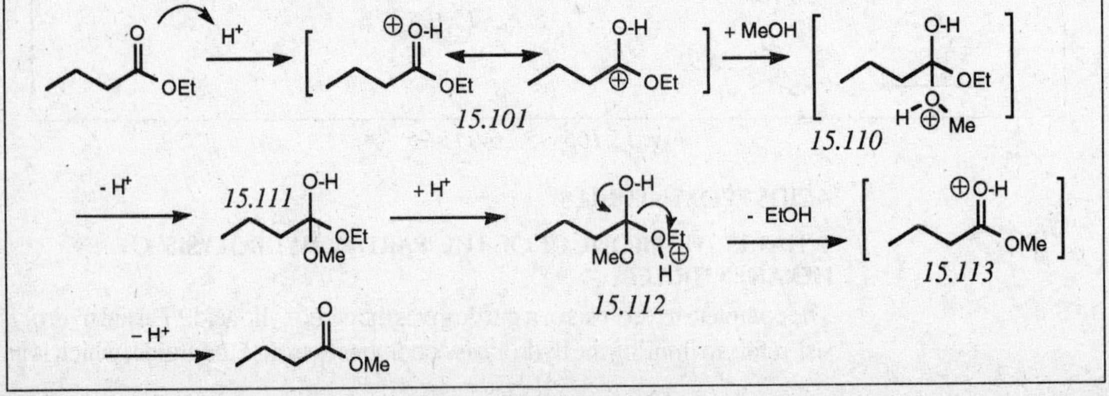

Fig. 15.101, 15.110–15.114

ESTERS OF DIACIDS

WHAT IS THE PRODUCT WHEN SUCCINIC ACID IS DISSOLVED IN ETHANOL WITH A CATALYTIC AMOUNT OF ACID?

The product is the diester, diethyl succinate, *15.115*.

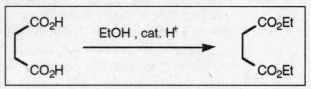

Fig. 15.115

IS IT POSSIBLE TO FORM THE 'HALF-ESTER' OF A DIBASIC ACID?

Yes. It is usually difficult to stop an equilibrium reaction (catalytic H⁺ and an alcohol, for example) but if the half-acid chloride can be made, the half ester can be prepared by standard techniques.

Reaction With Amines

AMIDES FROM ACID CHLORIDES AND ANHYDRIDES

As described in sections 14.5 and 15.2, reaction of amines with acid chlorides and anhydrides leads to amides.

AMIDES FROM ESTERS

As described in section 15.2, heating an ester with ammonia or an amine leads to an amide.

LACTAMS FROM LACTONES

WHAT IS THE PRODUCT WHEN δ-VALEROLACTONE IS HEATED WITH AMMONIA? WITH METHYLAMINE?

A lactone is a cyclic ester. Reaction of an ester with an amine leads to formation of an amide. It is therefore reasonable to conclude that reaction of a cyclic ester (a lactone) with an amine or ammonia will lead to a cyclic amide (a lactam). When δ-valerolactone (*15.116*) is heated with ammonia, the product is δ-valerolactam (2-piperidone, *15.117*). Similarly, when *15.116* is heated with methylamine, N-methyl-2-piperidone, *15.118*. Depending on the size of the ring, lactones of greater than eight members are opened by this reaction to give the open chain amino acid.

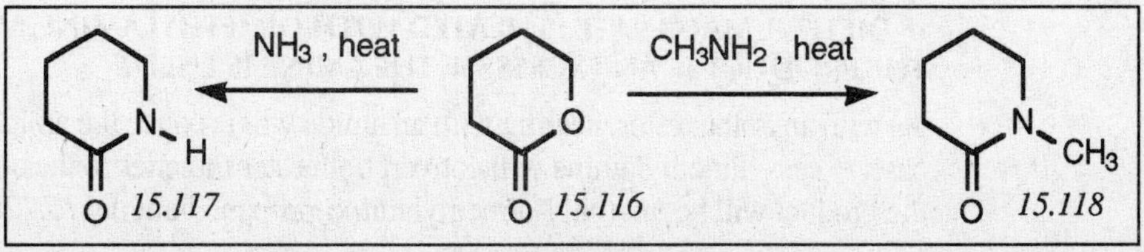

Fig. 15.116–15.118

WHY DOES HEATING A NINE-MEMBERED RING LACTONE WITH AMMONIA LEAD TO AN OPEN CHAIN HYDROXY AMIDE RATHER THAN A LACTAM?

Nine-membered rings are high in energy due to *transannular* steric effects (the result of crowding hydrogen atoms inside the cavity of the ring). If a nine-membered ring is being formed, the molecule assumes a conformation analogous to a nine-membered ring in the transition state. The high transannular strain destabilizes that transition state and inhibits formation of the ring. Since cyclization to the nine-membered ring lactam is very difficult, the molecule simply opens to an amino acid (9-aminononanoic acid in this case).

AMIDES OF DIACIDS

WHEN SUCCINIC ANHYDRIDE IS HEATED WITH AMMONIA, WHAT IS THE PRODUCT?

Just as lactones are converted to lactams, anhydrides are converted to imides upon heating with ammonia or an amine. In this case, succinic anhydride is converted to succinimide, *15.119*.

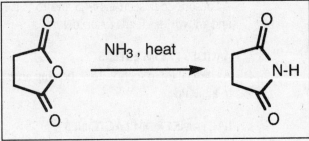

Fig. 15.119

WHY IS IT DIFFICULT TO CONVERT DIETHYL MALONATE INTO A LACTAM?

If diethyl malonate were to form a lactam, it would be a four-membered ring lactam (a so-called β-lactam). In general, the strain inherent to four-membered rings makes their formation by this route difficult, but not impossible. There are many alternative synthetic routes to β-lactams that will not be discussed in this book.

IF DIETHYL MALONATE IS HEATED WITH DIMETHYLAMINE, WHAT IS THE PRODUCT IF AN EXCESS OF THE AMINE IS USED?

As with any other ester, heating with an amide will produce the amide. In this case, excess dimethylamine will convert both ester moieties to the amide and the product will be *bis*-(N,N-dimethylamino)propanediamide, *15.120*.

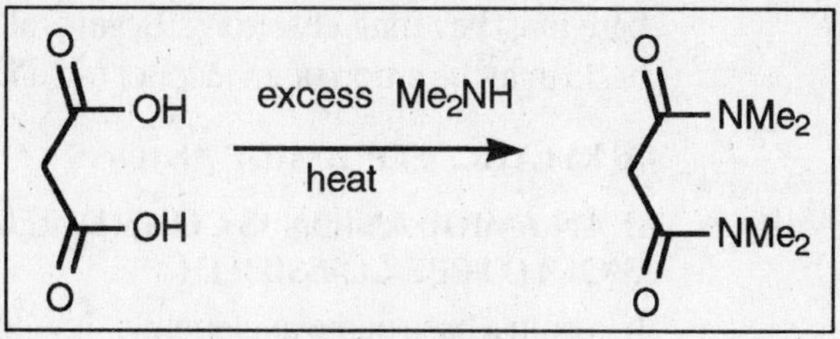

Fig. 15.120

ACIDITY OF AMIDES: PK$_a$ OF AMIDE N–H BONDS

WHAT IS THE PKA OF A TYPICAL AMIDE N–H?

The pK$_a$ of the hydrogen attached to an amide nitrogen is in the range of 15–17, very similar to the acidity of the O–H group of an alcohol.

IS THE AMIDE N–H MORE OR LESS ACIDIC THAN AN AMINE?

An amide is significantly more acidic than the NH of an amine (a typical amine N–H shows a pK$_a$ of about 25–30). The carbonyl group on the nitrogen of the amide serves as an electron withdrawing group to stabilize the amide base (after removal of a the hydrogen) and to make the N–H more polarized (more acidic).

WHAT TYPE OF BASE IS REQUIRED TO MAKE THE N–H BOND OF AN AMIDE AN ACID?

A relatively strong base is required such as NaNH$_2$, NaNR$_2$, an organolithium reagent such as *n*-butyllithium, or a base such as sodium hydride.

STRUCTURE AND STABILITY OF AMIDE ANIONS

WHAT IS THE STRUCTURE OF AN AMIDE ANION?

Removal of the acidic proton of an amide generates an resonance stabilized amide anion, *15.121*.

HOW STABLE IS AN AMIDE ANION?

It is quite stable due to the resonance contributors that are possible, dispersing the change on both nitrogen and the carbonyl oxygen.

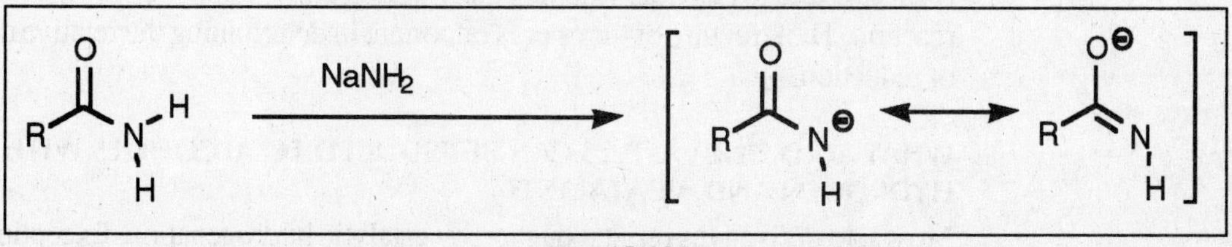

Fig. 15.121

IS AN AMIDE ANION A STRONG BASE?

Yes. Since an acid with a pK$_a$ of 15-17 is a relatively weak acid, the conjugate base must be relatively strong. In general, the anion of an amide is slightly less basic than the anion of an alcohol (an alkoxide).

ALKYLATION OF AMIDE ANIONS

IF AN AMIDE ANION IS CONSIDERED TO BE A REAGENT, HOW WOULD IT BE CLASSIFIED?

It is both a base and a nucleophile. It will, therefore, react with a suitable acid (to regenerate the amide) or with an electrophilic carbon (such as an alkyl halide) to form an N-substituted amide.

WHAT IS THE REACTION PRODUCT WHEN THE AMIDE ANION DERIVED FROM BUTANAMIDE IS TREATED WITH 1-BROMOBUTANE?

The product is N-butylbutanamide, *15.122*.

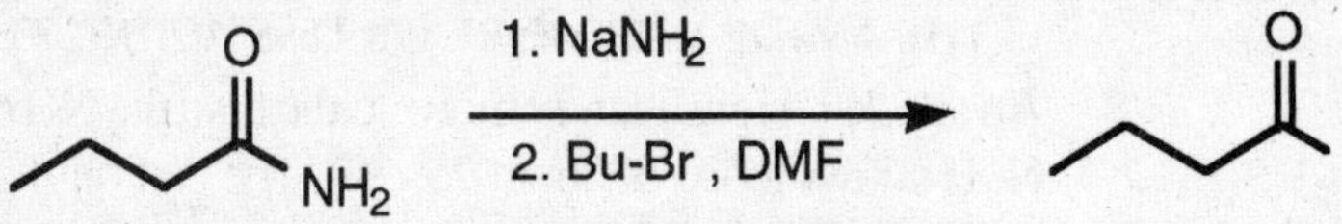

Fig. 15.122

Reduction

In general, acid derivatives are reduced to an alcohol. Amides and nitriles are exceptions, where reduction usually leads to an amine if the reducing agent is powerful enough.

REDUCTION TO ALCOHOLS

WHAT IS THE MAJOR PRODUCT WHEN ETHYL BENZOATE IS REDUCED WITH LiAlH$_4$ AND THEN TREATED WITH WATER?

The 'acid portion' is reduced to benzyl alcohol (PhCH$_2$OH) and the 'alcohol portion' is "released" giving, in this case, ethanol.

HOW EFFICIENT IS THE REDUCTION OF AN ESTER TO AN ALCOHOL WITH NaBH$_4$?

Sodium borohydride is much weaker reducing agent than LiAlH$_4$ and NaBH$_4$ reduces esters to alcohols with difficulty. It is usually (but not always) a slow reaction. The structure of the ester is important in determining the relative rate of reduction.

WHAT ACID DERIVATIVES CAN BE REDUCED TO ALCOHOLS WITH HYDROGEN AND A CATALYST?

Most acid derivatives resist reduction by catalytic hydrogenation. Exceptions are acid chlorides and acid anhydrides, which are readily reduced to alcohols. Acids, esters and amides are very difficult to reduce by this method and usually give no reaction.

WHAT IS THE PRODUCT WHEN δ-VALEROLACTONE IS REDUCED WITH LiAlH₄?

The product is 1,5-pentanediol [$HOCH_2CH_2CH_2CH_2CH_2OH$].

WHAT IS THE PRODUCT WHEN DIETHYL SUCCINATE IS REDUCED WITH LiAlH₄?

Reduction of diethyl succinate gives 1,4-butanediol [$HOCH_2CH_2CH_2CH_2OH$].

REDUCTION TO AMINES

WHAT IS THE PRODUCT WHEN N-ACETYL ANILINE IS REDUCED WITH LiAlH₄?

In most cases, the carbonyl portion of the amide is reduced to a hydrocarbon [C=O → -CH₂-]. In this case, the product is N-ethylaniline.

WHAT IS THE PRODUCT WHEN N,N-DIETHYLPENTANAMIDE IS REDUCED WITH HYDROGEN AND PALLADIUM CATALYST?

Amides are very resistant to reduction with hydrogen. The correct answer here is, therefore, no reaction.

WHAT IS THE PRODUCT WHEN BENZONITRILE IS REDUCED WITH LiAlH₄?

Benzonitrile is reduced to benzylamine ($PhCH_2NH_2$). In general, nitriles are reduced to primary amines upon reaction with LiAlH₄.

GIVE THE MAJOR PRODUCT WHEN *15.123–15.125* ARE REDUCED WITH LiAlH₄?

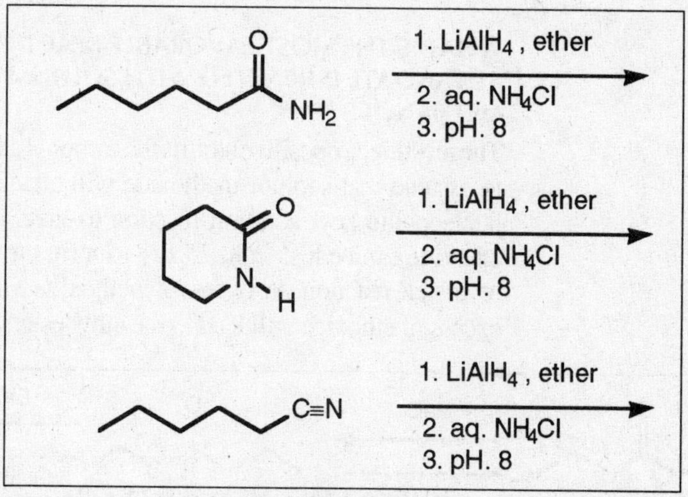

Fig. 15.123–15.125

Reduction of hexanamide (*15.123*) leads to hexanamine (1-aminohexane, *15.126*). Lactams are also reduced to amines with LiAlH₄. In this case, 2-piperidone (*15.124*) is reduced to piperidine (*15.127*). In the last case, hexanenitrile (*15.125*) is reduced to 1-aminohexane (*15.126*). In all cases, after the acid workup of the hydride, the pH is adjusted to about 8 to facilitate isolation of the basic amine product.

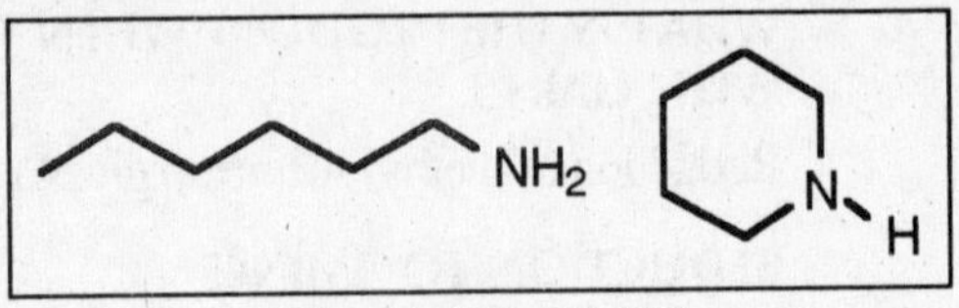

Fig. 15.126, 15.127

15.4. ENOLATES OF ACID DERIVATIVES

The carbonyl of an acid derivative makes the α-hydrogen acidic just as in ketones and aldehydes. This hydrogen can be removed by a suitable base to form an enolate anion, which can react with alkyl halides in an alkylation reaction or with carbonyl derivatives in a condensation reaction.

Enolate Formation and Stability

WHAT IS THE PRODUCT WHEN BUTANOIC ACID IS REACTED WITH SODIUM ETHOXIDE?

Since sodium ethoxide is a strong base, the acidic hydrogen (O–H) of butanoic acid is removed to form the sodium salt of the acid, sodium benzoate.

WHAT IS THE MOST FAVORABLE REACTION WHEN ETHYL BUTANOATE IS REACTED WITH SODIUM METHOXIDE IN METHANOL?

The most electropositive atom is the carbonyl carbon. It is, therefore, reasonable to assume that sodium methoxide will attack the carbonyl via a reversible nucleophilic acyl addition reaction to give *15.128*. It is also possible that ethoxide can be lost from *15.128* to form the methyl ester, and this is also a reversible reaction. An excess of methoxide will lead to the methyl ester and an excess of ethoxide will lead to the ethyl ester.

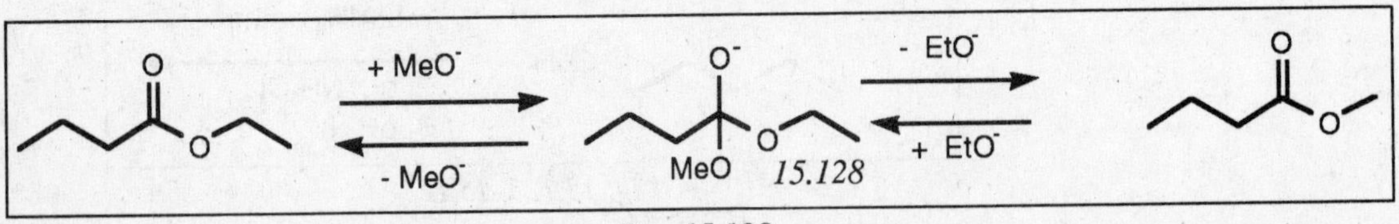

Fig. 15.128

WHAT IS THE PRODUCT WHEN ETHYL BUTANOATE IS REACTED WITH LITHIUM DIETHYLAMIDE IN THF, AT -78°C?

Lithium diethylamide is a powerful but non-nucleophilic base. The usual nucleophilic attack at the carbonyl is, therefore, slow. The hydrogen on the carbon adjacent to the carbonyl (the α-carbon) is acidic and can be removed by this strong base. The product is the enolate anion, *15.129*.

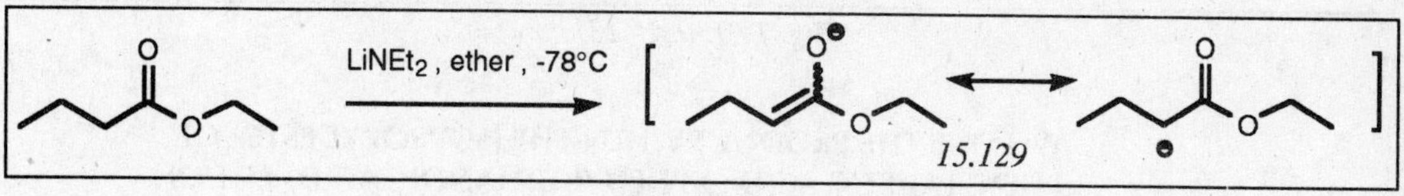

Fig. 15.129

WHAT IS THE RELATIVE PK$_a$ OF THE α-HYDROGEN OF ETHYL BUTANOATE WHEN COMPARED TO THE TWO ACIDIC PROTONS OF 2-BUTANONE?

The α-hydrogens of 2-butanone have a pK$_a$ of 20 and 21 (for C$_1$ and C$_3$, respectively). The α-hydrogen of ethyl butanoate (the carbon next to the carbonyl, *not* next to the oxygen of the ester) has a pK$_a$ of about 24-25.

DISCUSS THE ENOLATES DERIVED FROM ETHYL BUTANOATE UNDER BOTH KINETIC AND THERMODYNAMIC CONTROL CONDITIONS.

In both cases the enolate anion that is formed is *15.129*. Under kinetic control (aprotic solvents, low temperature, strong non-nucleophilic base) *15.129* is formed in an effectively irreversible manner. Under thermodynamic control (protic solvent, alkoxide bases, higher reaction temperatures) the reaction is reversible and *15.129* is in equilibrium with the starting ester. If methoxide is used as the base, the addition product (*15.128*) can be present. Similarly, if ethoxide is used, the OEt derivative can be present.

IF THERMODYNAMIC CONDITIONS ARE USED TO DEPROTONATE AN ESTER, WHAT ARE THE LIMITATIONS ON THE BASE THAT CAN BE USED?

Examination of *15.128* clearly shows that a transesterification reaction can occur if the alkoxide base is different from the alcohol portion of the ester. For this reason, NaOEt is used with ethyl ester, NaOMe with methyl esters, etc.

Enolate Alkylation

Just as with the enolates derived from aldehydes and ketones, ester enolates are nucleophilic and react with alkyl halides to give the substitution product.

MONOBASIC ESTER ENOLATES AND ALKYL HALIDES

WHAT IS THE PRODUCT WHEN METHYL PROPIONATE IS REACTED FIRST WITH SODIUM METHOXIDE IN METHANOL AND THEN WITH IODOMETHANE?

The initial reaction gives the enolate (*15.130*) which reacts with iodomethane to give methyl 2-methylpropionate, *15.131*.

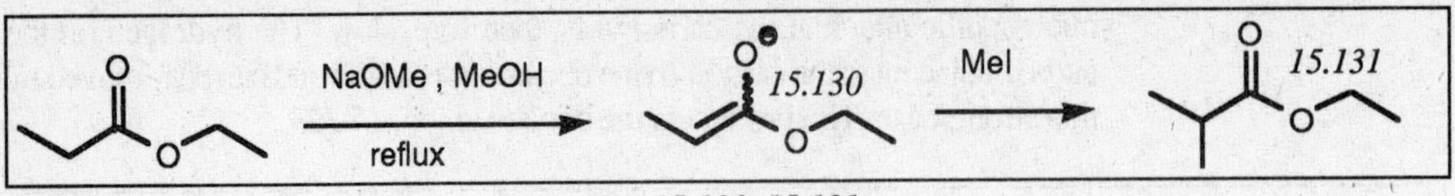

Fig. 15.130, 15.131

WHAT IS THE PRODUCT WHEN THE ISOPROPYL ESTER OF PHENYLACETIC ACID (2-PHENYL ETHANOIC ACID, *15.132*) IS REACTED FIRST WITH LDA (-78°C, THF) AND THEN WITH BENZYL BROMIDE?

The enolate is formed and alkylation with benzyl bromide gives *15.133*.

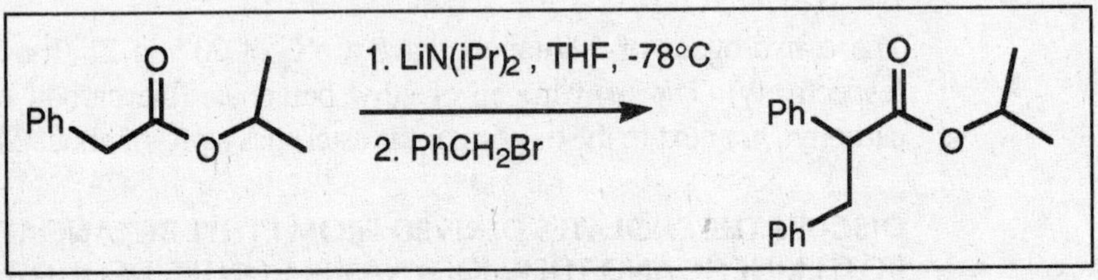

Fig. 15.132, 15.133

DIBASIC ESTER ENOLATES

DISCUSS THE ACIDITY OF THE α-HYDROGEN OF A DIBASIC ACID SUCH AS DIETHYL MALONATE.

The hydrogens on the carbon between the two carbonyl groups have a pK_a of 12.9. The inductive effects of two carbonyl groups greatly enhance the acidity of those hydrogens.

DISCUSS THE RELATIVE STABILITY OF THE ENOLATE DERIVED FROM DIETHYL MALONATE.

The presence of the second carbonyl in the enolate anion of diethyl malonate (*15.134*) leads to an additional resonance structure and greater stability when compared to the enolate anion derived from a monocarboxylic acid.

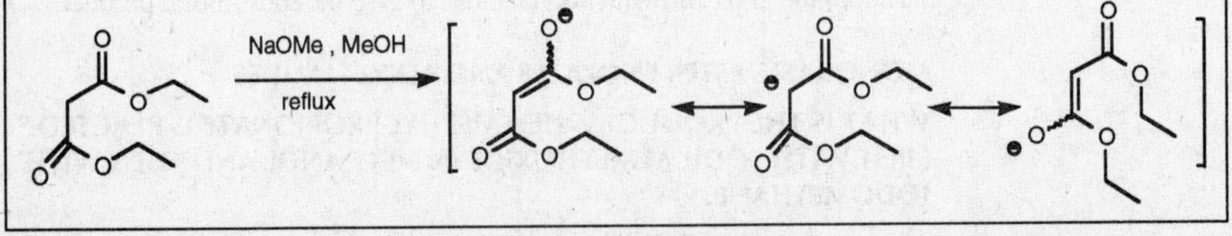

Fig. 15.134

ARE ESTER ENOLATES DERIVED FROM DIBASIC ACIDS MORE OR LESS REACTIVE THAN ESTER ENOLATES DERIVED FROM MONOBASIC ACIDS? EXPLAIN.

They are more stable, due to the resonance stability of the anion (see *15.134*, the enolate of diethyl malonate) which makes them *less reactive*.

WHAT IS THE PRODUCT WHEN DIETHYL MALONATE IS REACTED WITH: I. NaOEt, ETOH II. PhCH$_2$Br? IF THIS PRODUCT IS THEN REACTED WITH I. NaOEt II. CH$_3$I, WHAT IS THE FINAL PRODUCT?

The first product is the 2-alkylated product, diethyl 2-benzylmalonate (*15.135*). If *15.135* is treated with additional base, a new enolate is formed (*15.136*) which then reacts with iodomethane to form diethyl 2-benzyl-2-methyl malonate, *15.137*.

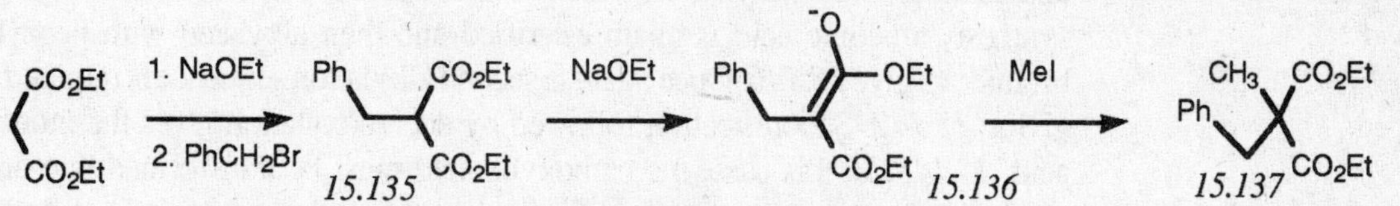

15.135 *15.136* *15.137*

Fig. 15.135–15.137

MALONIC ESTER SYNTHESIS

SHOW HOW MALONIC ACID CAN BE CONVERTED INTO 2-ETHYL-2-PROPYL MALONIC ACID (WHAT IS THE IUPAC NAME OF THIS COMPOUND?).

The first step is to convert diethyl malonate (or another ester) into the 2-ethyl derivative (*15.138*) by treatment with NaOEt followed by EtI. Repetition of this base-halide sequence with iodopropane leads to *15.139*. When this ester is saponified (1. aq. NaOH 2. pH 5), the corresponding malonic acid derivative (*15.140*) is produced. The IUPAC name of *15.140* is 2-ethyl-2-propyl-1,3-propanedioic acid.

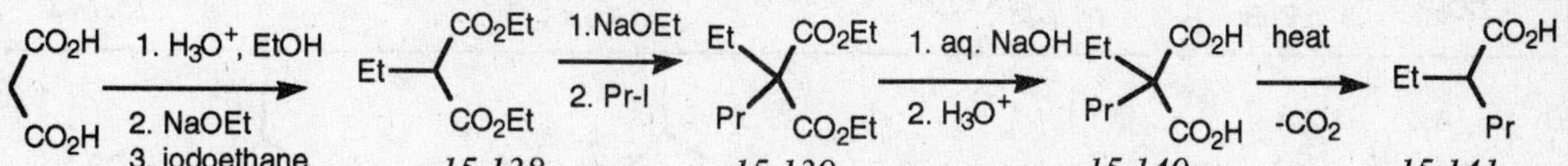

15.138 *15.139* *15.140* *15.141*

Fig. 15.138–15.141

IF THIS PRODUCT IS HEATED, WHAT IS THE RESULTING PRODUCT?

Since malonic acid is a 1,3-dicarbonyl acid, heating will lead to decarboxylation (loss of CO_2) and the product will be butanoic acid, *15.141*. See section 14.5.

WHAT IS THE NAME OF THIS OVERALL TRANSFORMATION?

The reaction sequence that converts malonic acid into a mono carboxylic acid via alkylation-decarboxylation is called the malonic ester synthesis. This sequence is very powerful for the synthesis of highly substituted carboxylic acids.

PROVIDE A SUITABLE SYNTHESIS FOR *15.142* AND *15.143*.

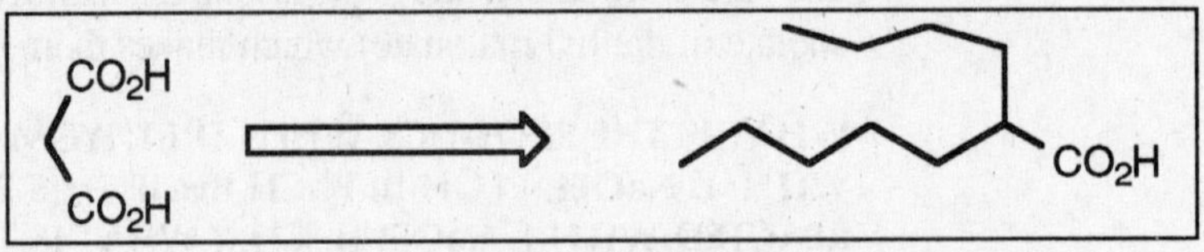

Fig. 15.142

In the first step, malonic acid is converted to the diester and then alkylated with bromobutane to give *15.144*. A second alkylation inserts the pentyl group via enolate alkylation Saponification leads to the malonic acid derivative (*15.145*) and thermal decarboxylation gives the final target, *15.142*. In the second synthesis, malonic acid is again esterified and then alkylated with benzyl bromide to give *15.146*. Once again, a second alkylation sequence is required, giving *15.147*. Saponification followed by decarboxylation gives the mono acid, *15.148*. In this case, the carboxylic acid must be transformed into an aldehyde. One way to do this is to first reduce the acid to an alcohol (*15.149*) with LiAlH$_4$. Subsequent treatment with PCC (pyridinium chlorochromate— see section 11.4) gives the final aldehyde target, *15.143*.

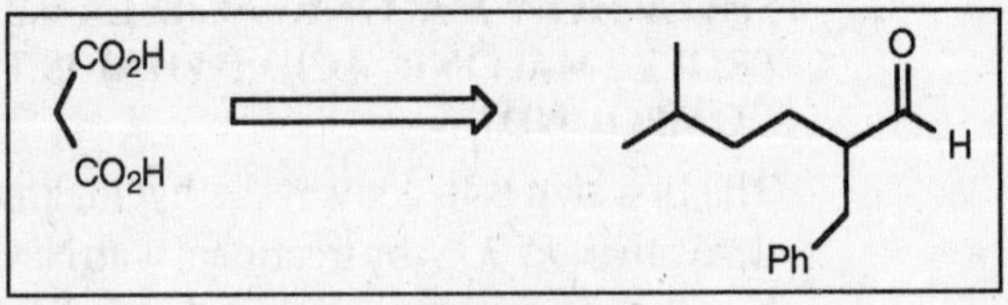

Fig. 15.143

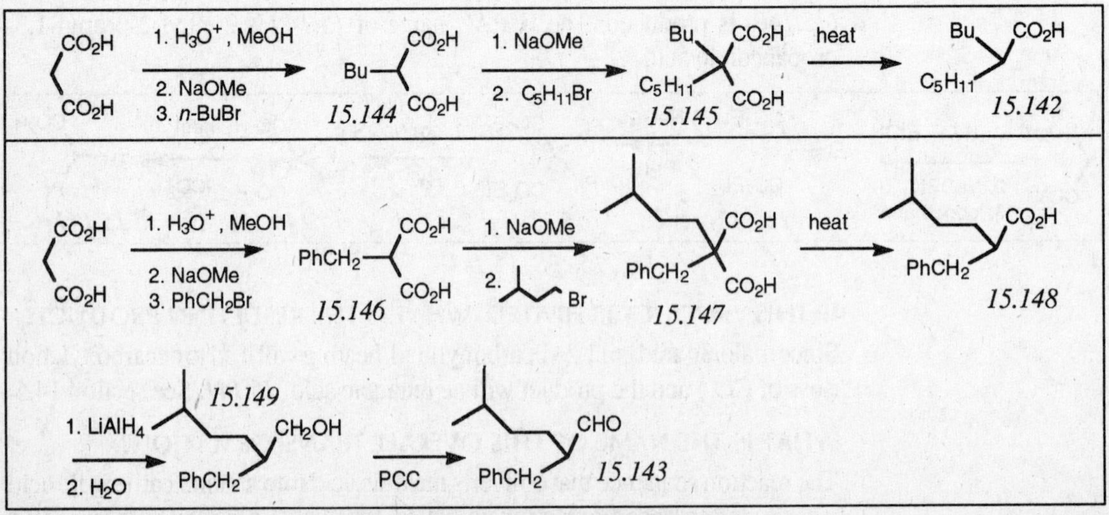

Fig. 15.144–15.149, 15.142, 15.143

SUCCINIC ESTER DERIVATIVES

IF THE DIETHYL ESTER OF SUCCINIC ACID IS TREATED WITH i. NaOEt ii. ALLYL BROMIDE, WHAT IS THE MAJOR PRODUCT?

Succinic esters behave as any other ester since the carbonyls are not conjugated. This sequence will therefore produce the 2-allyl derivative, *15.150*.

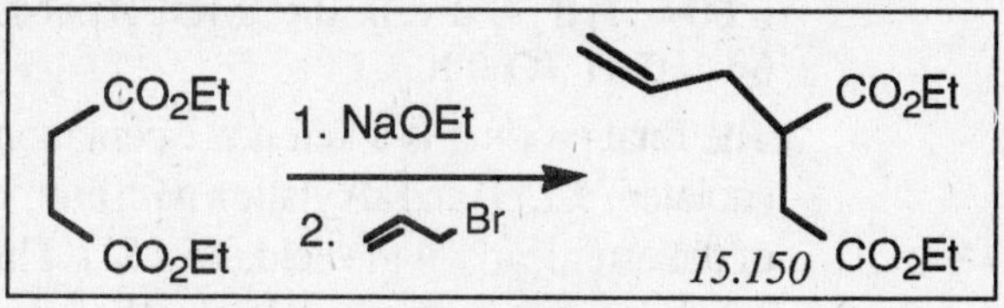

Fig. 15.150

WHAT IS THE PK$_a$ OF THE α-HYDROGEN OF DIETHYL SUCCINATE?

It is very close to that of propionic acid esters. Ethyl propionate has a pK$_a$ of 22-23 and diethyl succinate also has a pK$_a$ of about 22.

IF 2-BUTYL-1,4-BUTANEDIOIC ACID IS FIRST ESTERIFIED (ETHYL ESTER) AND THEN REACTED WITH i. LDA, THF, -78°C ii. CH$_3$I, WHAT IS THE MAJOR PRODUCT? EXPLAIN.

The product is the ethyl ester of 2,3-diethyl-1,4-butanedioic acid (*15.151*). These are kinetic control conditions and the most acidic hydrogen will be removed (attached to the less substituted carbon). Alkylation will then lead to the 2,3-dimethyl derivative rather than the 2,2-dimethyl derivative.

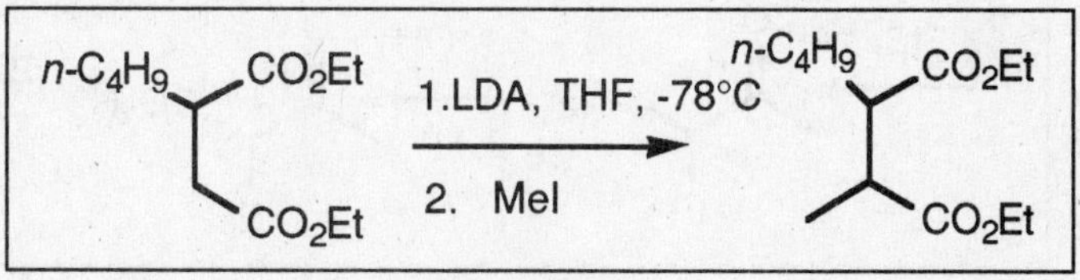

Fig. 15.151

ACETOACETIC ESTER SYNTHESIS

WHAT IS ACETOACETIC ACID? WHAT IS THE IUPAC NAME?

Acetoacetic acid has the structure *15.152*. The IUPAC name is 3-keto-butanoic acid.

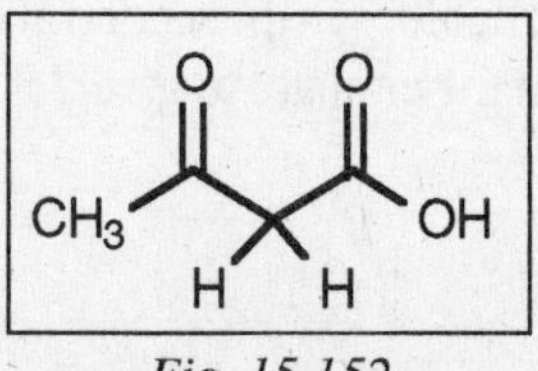

Fig. 15.152

WHAT IS THE PK$_a$ OF THE MOST ACIDIC HYDROGEN IN THE ETHYL ESTER OF THIS MOLECULE? IDENTIFY THAT HYDROGEN.

The most acidic hydrogens are those between the two carbonyl groups, as in malonic acid esters. The pK$_a$ of those hydrogens in *15.152* is about 11.

WHAT IS THE PRODUCT IF ETHYL ACETOACETATE IS TREATED WITH: i. LDA, THF, -78°C ii. BROMOETHANE iii. AQ. KOH iv. ADJUST TO PH 6 v. HEAT TO 200°C?

The final product is a ketone, 2-pentanone. The initial reaction generates the enolate (*15.153*) and alkylation with bromoethane gives *15.154*. Saponification of the ester leads to the acid (*15.155*). This acid can be decarboxylated (it is a 1,3-dicarbonyl compound) to give the ketone as the final product, (2-pentanone).

WHAT IS THE NAME OF THIS OVERALL PROCESS?

This synthetic sequence is known as the *acetoacetic ester synthesis*.

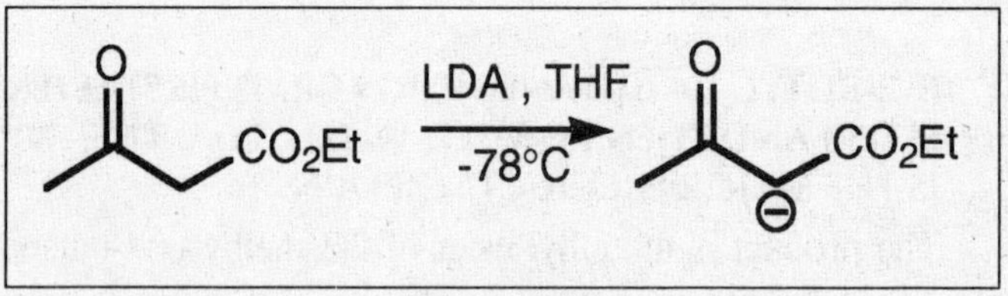

Fig. 15.153

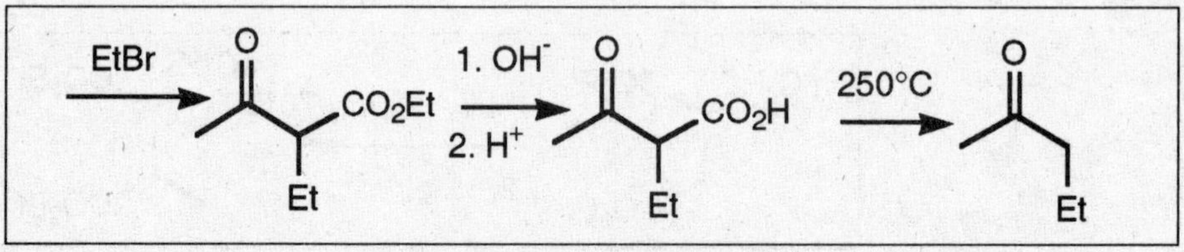

Fig. 15.154, 15.155

PROVIDE A SUITABLE SYNTHESIS FOR THE PREPARATION OF *15.156* AND *15.157*.

In the first case, acetoacetic ester is alkylated (via the enolate) to give *15.158*. Note that the more bulky group is put in first and the smaller group second. This usually maximizes the yield since the reverse alkylation order might lead to difficulties in the second alkylation. The second step is to insert the ethyl group, via the enolate, to give *15.159*. Saponification of the ester gives acid *15.160*, which is thermally decarboxylated to the ketone, *15.156*. In the second case, a ring is formed. Initial alkylation of the enolate, under thermodynamic conditions, with 1,5-dibromo-pentane gives *15.161*. Under thermodynamic control conditions, *15.161* is converted to its enolate (*15.162*) and reacts with the bromine intramolecularly to give the keto ester product (*15.163*). Saponification and decarboxylation gives the final ketone product, *15.157*.

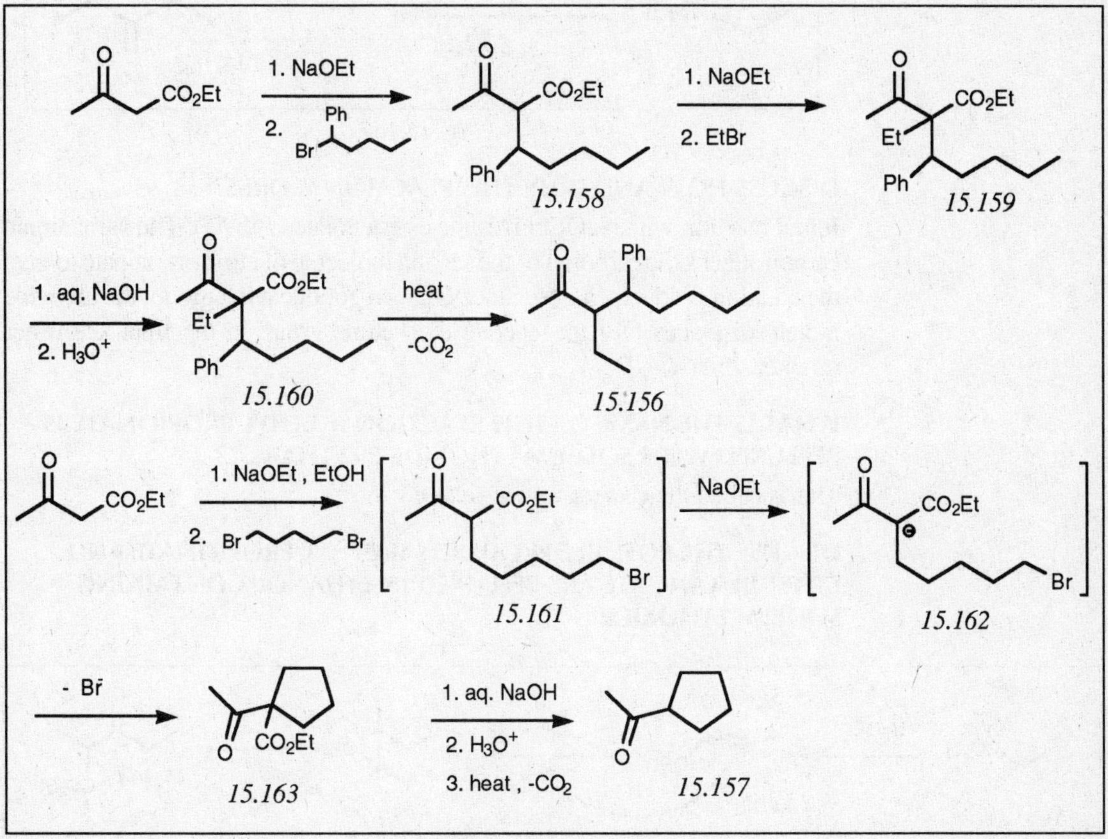

Fig. 15.156–15.163

Enolate Condensations

Just as the enolates of aldehydes and ketones react with other aldehydes and ketones in the Aldol condensation, ester enolates react with a variety of carbonyl derivatives.

THE CLAISEN CONDENSATION

WHAT IS THE PRODUCT WHEN ETHYL PROPANOATE IS REACTED WITH: i. LDA, THF, -78°C ii. ETHYL PROPANOATE?

The product is a β-keto ester, *15.164*.

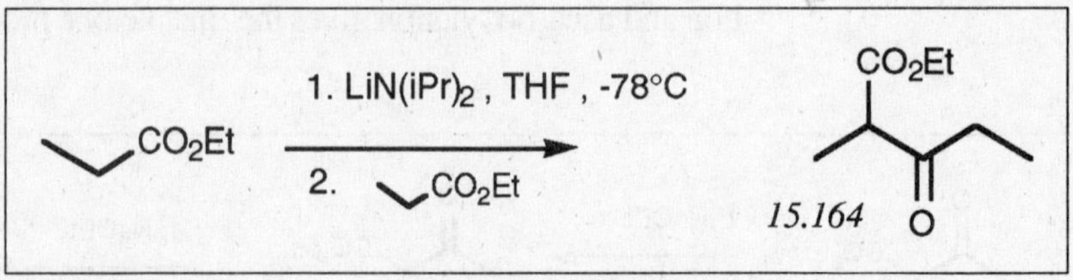

Fig. 15.164

DISCUSS HOW AND WHY THIS REACTION WORKS?

Initial reaction with NaOEt gives the ester enolate (*15.165*). The carbanionic carbon attacks the carbonyl of the second molecule of ethyl propionate to give the addition product, *15.166*. Since OEt is a good leaving group, the alkoxide moiety displaces OEt to generate the ketone group in the final keto-ester product, *15.164*.

WHAT IS THE NAME OF THIS REACTION IF ETHYL PROPIONATE IS REFLUXED WITH SODIUM ETHOXIDE IN ETHANOL?

This is called the *Claisen condensation*.

DISCUSS THE POSSIBLE PRODUCTS IF ETHYL PROPIONATE AND ETHYL BUTANOATE ARE REFLUXED IN ETHANOL CONTAINING SODIUM ETHOXIDE.

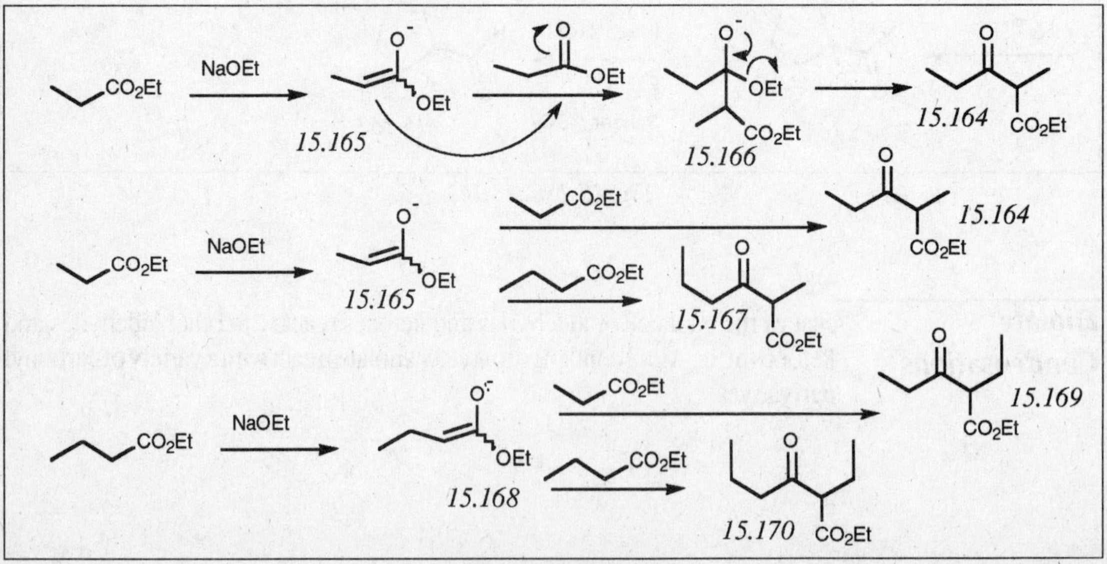

Fig. 15.165–15.170

Under these conditions, *both* esters give an enolate in the equilibrium conditions. Ethyl propionate gives *15.165* and ethyl butanoate will give *15.168*. Since these enolates are in equilibrium with the free ester, *15.165* can react with ethyl propionate to give *15.167* but it can also react with ethyl butanoate to give *15.164*. Similarly, *15.168* can react with ethyl propionate to give *15.169* or with ethyl butanoate to give *15.170*. The equilibrium conditions with two different esters therefore leads to four possible ester products.

WHAT IS A 'MIXED' CLAISEN CONDENSATION?

The reaction of two different esters to produce the Claisen product is a mixed Claisen. The enolate of one ester condenses with the carbonyl of the other ester.

WHICH ARE BETTER CONDITIONS FOR A MIXED CLAISEN, KINETIC CONTROL OR THERMODYNAMIC CONTROL CONDITIONS? EXPLAIN.

Although both conditions will generate the same enolate, kinetic control conditions are better for mixed Claisen condensations. Reaction of ethyl propionate with LDA, for example, will give *15.165* as the only enolate and either ethyl propionate or ethyl butanoate can be added to give the appropriate mixed Claisen product (*15.164* or *15.170*, respectively). Under these conditions both esters are not present at the time the enolate is formed and the chemist has control of which ester is added as the carbonyl partner, and in what order.

WHAT IS THE PRODUCT OR PRODUCTS WHEN ETHYL BUTANOATE IS TREATED WITH SODIUM METHOXIDE IN METHANOL?

Under these equilibrium conditions, enolate *15.168* is formed but since ethyl butanoate is the only ester present, *15.168* is the only enolate and it can only react with itself, to give *15.170*.

GIVE THE MAJOR PRODUCT OF THE FOLLOWING SEQUENCE WITH ETHYL BUTANOATE: i. LDA, THF, -78°C ii. METHYL PROPIONATE iii. SAPONIFICATION iv. HEATING TO 200°C.

Under these kinetic control conditions, the initial Claisen product is *15.170*. Saponification liberates the free carboxylic acid and heating leads to decarboxylation (this is a 1,3-dicarbonyl compound) to give the ketone, 3-hexanone.

GIVE THE MAJOR PRODUCT OF THE REACTIONS OF *15.171* AND *15.172*.

In the first reaction, ethyl hexanoate (*15.171*) is condensed with itself under thermodynamic conditions to give the 'symmetrical' Claisen product, *15.173*. The second example generates the enolate from ethyl cycloheptane carboxylate (*15.172*) and then reacts it with ethyl benzoate [PhCO₂Et] to give the 'mixed' Claisen product, *15.174*.

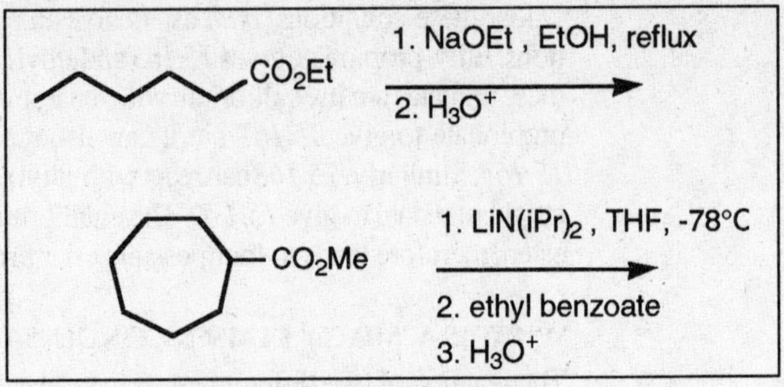

Fig. 15.171, 15.172

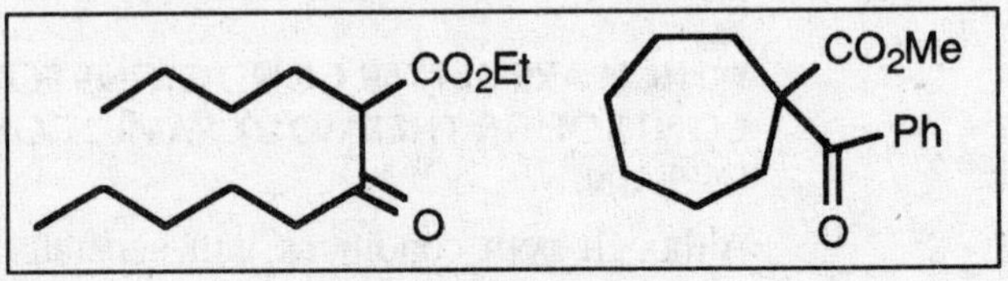

Fig. 15.173, 15.174

THE DIECKMANN CONDENSATION

WHAT IS THE MAJOR PRODUCT WHEN THE DIETHYL ESTER OF 1,6-HEXANEDIOIC ACID (*15.175*) IS REACTED WITH SODIUM ETHOXIDE IN ETHANOL?

This is an intramolecular Claisen condensation and the product is the cyclic keto-ester, *15.176*.

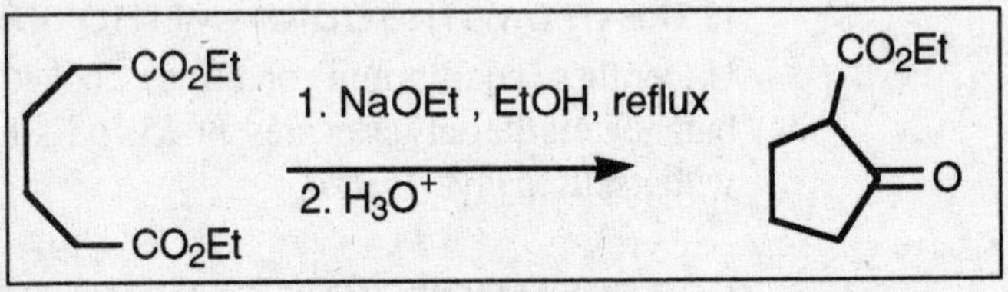

Fig. 15.175, 15.176

WHAT IS THE NAME OF THIS REACTION?

It is called the *Dieckmann Condensation*.

WHAT RING SIZES ARE FORMED BY THIS CYCLIZATION REACTION?

Rings of three-seven members can be formed by this technique. Formation of cyclic ketones of 8-13 members is very difficult by this method although larger rings can be prepared by high dilution techniques.

GIVE THE MAJOR PRODUCT OF THE FOLLOWING SEQUENCE WITH THE DIETHYL ESTER OF 1,7-HEPTANEDIOIC ACID: i. LDA, THF, -78°C ii. SAPONIFICATION iii. HEATING TO 200°C.

The Claisen product is the keto ester but saponification and decarboxylation leads to the final product, cyclohexanone.

GIVE THE MAJOR PRODUCT OF THE REACTIONS OF *15.177–15.179.*

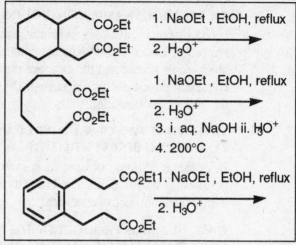

Fig. 15.177–15.179

Dieckmann condensation with diester *15.177* leads to the bicyclic keto-ester, *15.180*. In the second case, diethyl 1,8-octanedioate (*15.178*) is cyclized under Dieckmann conditions but saponification and decarboxylation gives cycloheptanoate (*15.181*) as the final product. In the last example, diester *15.179* is cyclized to keto-ester *15.182*.

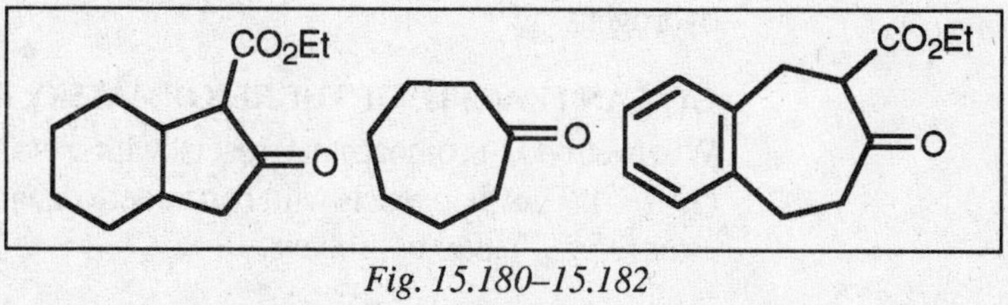

Fig. 15.180–15.182

CONDENSATION WITH ALDEHYDES AND KETONES

IF THE ENOLATE OF METHYL 2-PHENYLETHANOATE (*15.183*) IS TREATED WITH CYCLOHEXANONE, WHAT IS THE MAJOR PRODUCT AFTER HYDROLYSIS?

The ester enolate (*15.183*) reacts with cyclohexanone to give the β-hydroxy-ester, *15.184* after hydrolysis.

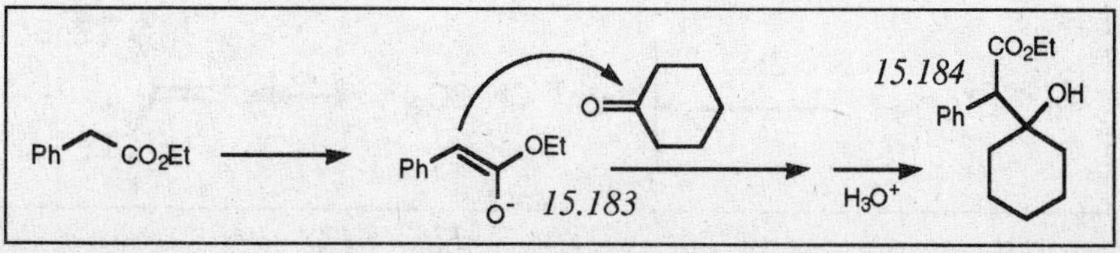

Fig. 15.183, 15.184

WHICH IS BETTER FOR THE CONDENSATION OF AN ESTER ENOLATE AND AN ALDEHYDE, KINETIC CONTROL CONDITIONS OR THERMODYNAMIC CONTROL CONDITIONS?

In order to prevent a Claisen condensation of the ester, kinetic control conditions are better. Under thermodynamic control conditions, especially when both aldehyde or ketone and the ester are present in the same reaction, an Aldol condensation could also compete with the Claisen condensation, in addition to the 'mixed' condensation.

WITH WHAT TYPE OF ALDEHYDE CAN THERMODYNAMIC CONTROL CONDITIONS BEST BE UTILIZED?

If an aldehyde does not have an α-carbon with acidic hydrogens (such as benzaldehyde), it can be added directly into the flask with the ester, under thermodynamic control conditions.

GIVE THE MAJOR PRODUCT OF THE FOLLOWING SEQUENCE WITH ETHYL BUTANOATE: i. LDA, THF, -78°C ii. 5-METHYL-2-HEXANONE iii. SAPONIFICATION iv. HEATING TO 200°C.

The product is 4,7-dimethyl-4-octanol.

THE REFORMATSKY REACTION

WHAT IS THE REFORMATSKY REACTION?

The *Reformatsky* reaction is the condensation of a *zinc enolate* of an ester (formed from an α-halo ester) and an aldehyde, usually an aldehyde with no α-hydrogens.

GIVE AN EXAMPLE OF THE REFORMATSKY REACTION.

When ethyl 2-bromoacetate reacts with zinc, the zinc enolate is formed (*15.185*). This then reacts with benzaldehyde via *15.186* to give the hydroxy-ester (*15.187*) after hydrolysis.

IN WHAT WAYS IS THE REFORMATSKY REACTION SIMILAR TO THE ENOLATE REACTIONS DESCRIBED ABOVE?

The Reformatsky is an enolate condensation reaction of an ester with an aldehyde. It is a metal enolate but zinc is used rather than lithium or sodium, as in the usual Claisen type condensations. Since the zinc enolate is usually generated in the presence of the aldehyde partner, aldehydes with no enolizable hydrogens are usually required and reaction with ketones is difficult.

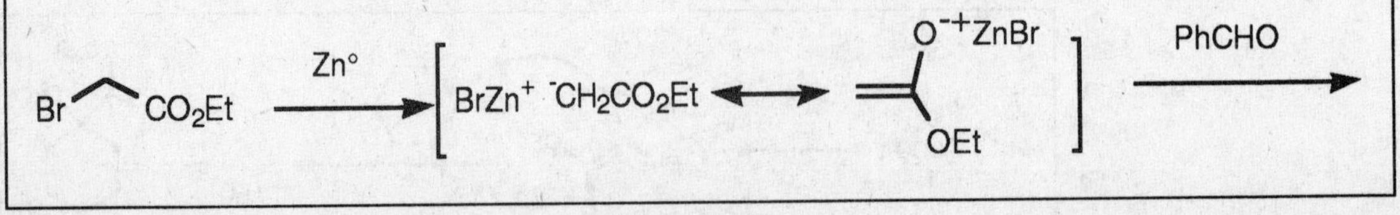

Fig. 15.185

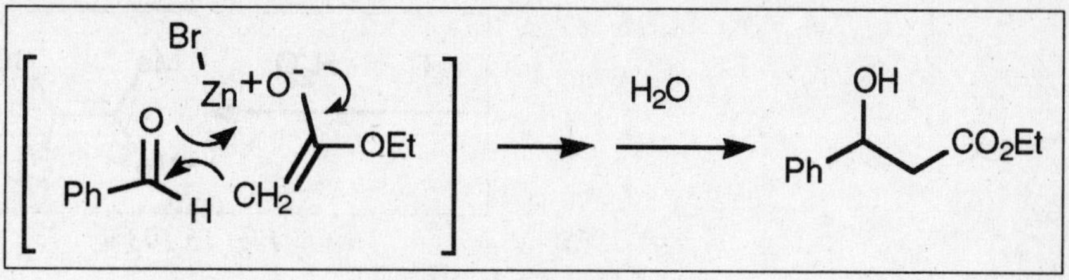

Fig. 15.186, 15.187

HOW ARE α-HALO ESTERS PREPARED?

A common method for the preparation of α-halo acids is the reaction of an acid such as acetic acid with phosphorus and chlorine or bromine (P, Cl_2 or P, Br_2).Under these conditions, PCl_3 or PBr_3 is formed and reacts to give 2-chloroacetyl chloride (*15.188*) or 2-bromoacetyl chloride (*15.189*) which is then hydrolyzed to the corresponding acid. Such α-halo-acids are converted to the corresponding ester by the usual methods. The conversion of an acid to an α-halo acid chloride is called the *Hell-Volhard-Zelinsky* reaction.

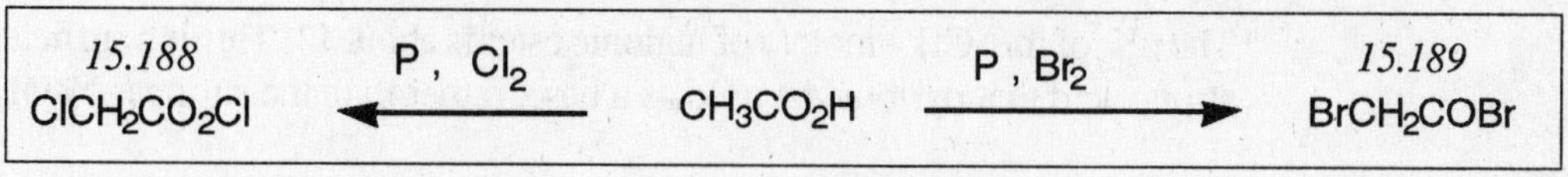

Fig. 15.188, 15.189

THE KNOEVENAGEL CONDENSATION

WHAT IS THE MAJOR PRODUCT WHEN ETHYL MALONATE IS TREATED WITH i. NaOEt ii. ACETONE iii. H_3O^+?

The initially formed malonate anion (*15.190*) reacts with acetone to give the alkoxide (*15.191*). Aqueous hydrolysis gives the alcohol (*15.192*) but the alcohol usually dehydrates under these conditions to the alkylidene derivative, *15.193*. Note that the great acidity of the malonic ester allowed the use of a weaker base such as pyridine.

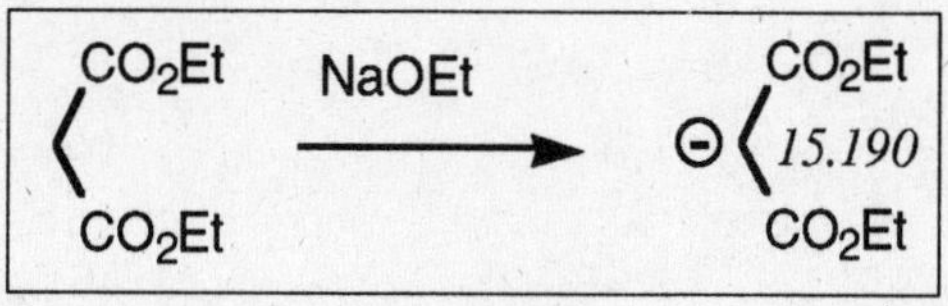

Fig. 15.190

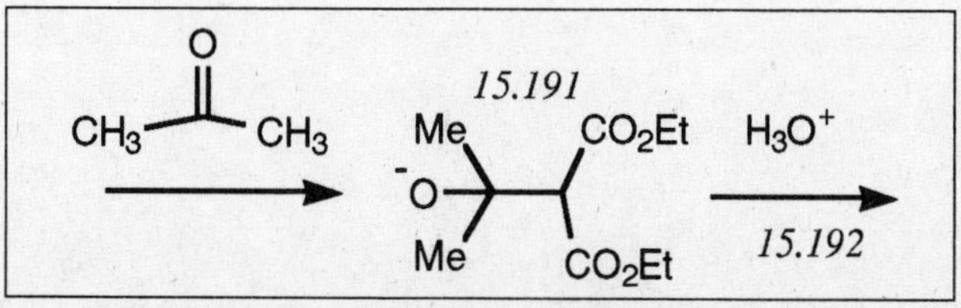

Fig. 15.191, 15.192

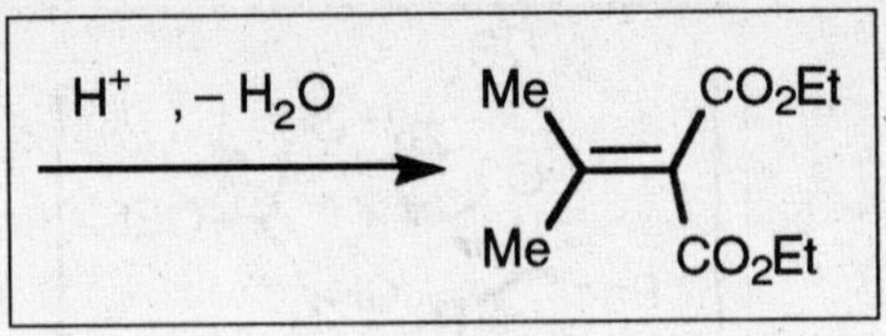

Fig. 15.193

WHY IS THE MAJOR PRODUCT USUALLY AN ALKENE?

The proximity of the alcohol moiety to two carbonyl lead to extensive hydrogen bonding and facile loss of water under the acidic conditions of the workup (conversion of the alkoxide product to the alcohol).

WHAT IS THE NAME OF THIS TYPE OF CONDENSATION?

This is known as the *Knoevenagel condensation*.

WHY CAN AN AMINE BE USED FOR THE BASE RATHER THAN NaOEt?

The pK_a of the $-CH_2-$ moiety of malonic ester is about 11. This is a sufficiently strong acid that pyridine be used as a base, rather than the stronger NaOEt.

It is clear from this chapter why acid derivatives are so important. The scope of their reactivity extends to most of the functional groups discussed in this book and to several carbon-carbon bond forming reactions. Along with chapter thirteen, discussing aldehydes and ketones, an understanding of this chapter provides an excellent review of most of the key concepts and reactions in organic chemistry.

END OF CHAPTER PROBLEMS

1. Give the IUPAC name for the following molecules.

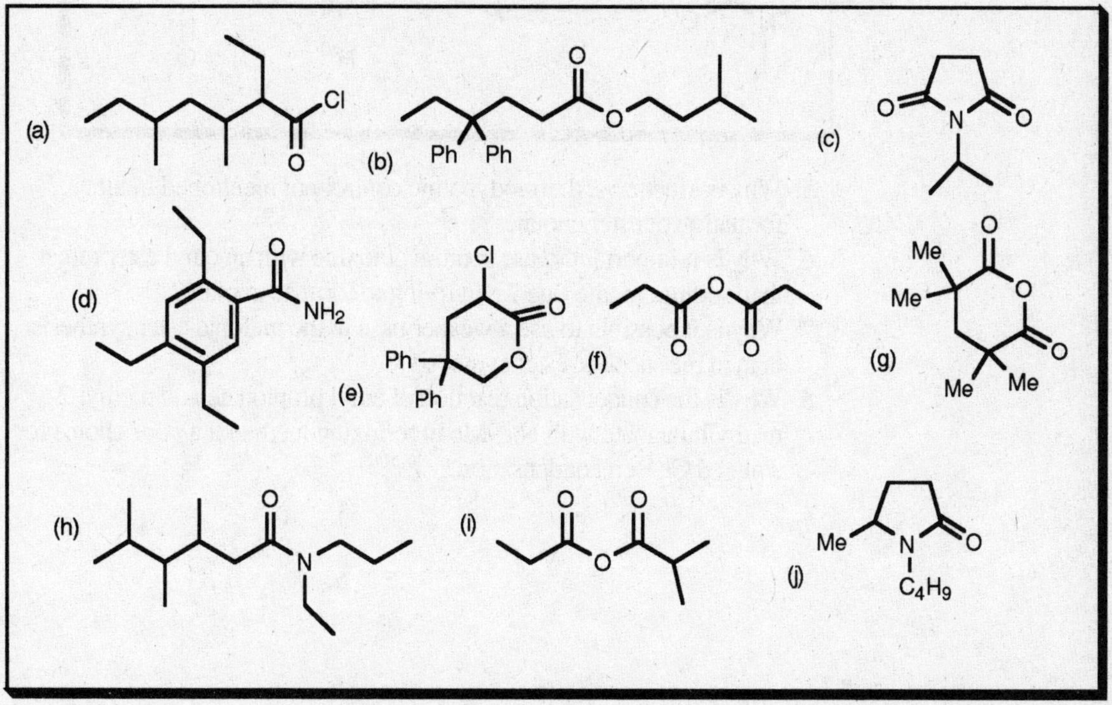

(a)

(b) Ph Ph

(c)

(d) NH$_2$

(e) Cl Ph Ph

(f)

(g) Me Me Me Me

(h) N

(i)

(j) Me N C$_4$H$_9$

2. Why is it possible to prepare amides from esters but not esters from amides?

3. Give the complete mechanism for the following reaction.

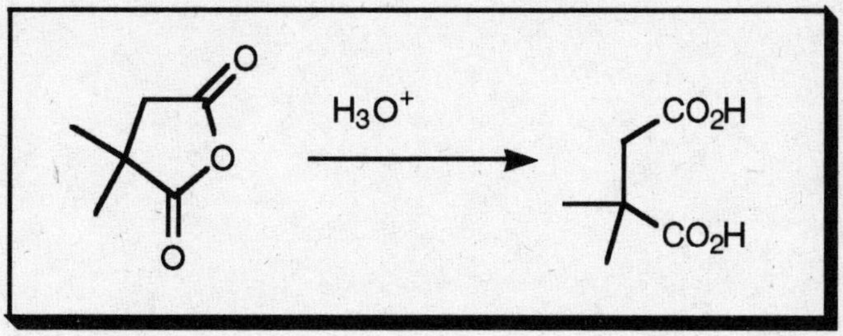

H$_3$O$^+$ → CO$_2$H CO$_2$H

4. Give the complete mechanism for the following reaction.

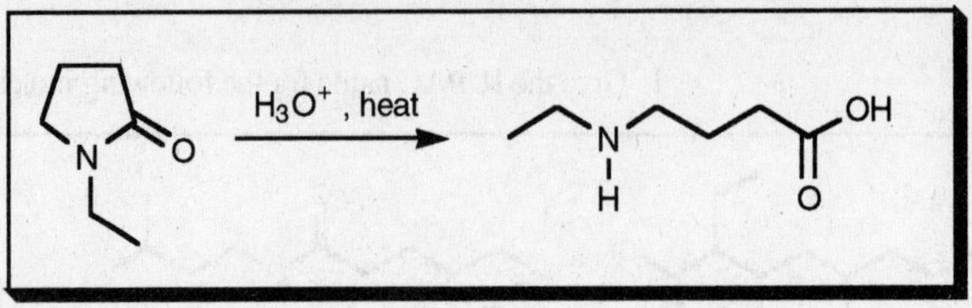

5. Why is kinetic vs. thermodynamic control not mentioned in the formation of ester enolates?

6. Why is it important to use sodium ethoxide with an ethyl ester rather than sodium methoxide when trying to form an enolate?

7. Why is it possible to use a weaker base in the malonic ester synthesis than in the succinic ester synthesis?

8. Why is the condensation reaction of ethyl propionate and methyl 2-methylbutanoate with NaOMe in refluxing methanol a *poor* choice for a mixed Claisen condensation?

9. In each case give the major product. If there is no reaction, indicate by N.R.

(a) [structure: cyclohexylmethanol, CH2OH] → 1. CrO_3, aq. H^+ 2. $SOCl_2$

(b) [structure: heptene] → 1. $Hg(OAc)_2$, H_2O 2. $NaBH_4$ 3. CrO_3, aq. H^+ 4. NH_3, heat

(c) [structure: CO_2H chain] → $POCl_3$

(d) [structure: acyl chloride, C(=O)Cl] → 1. NH_3 2. P_4O_{10}

(e) [structure: branched CO_2H] → 1. NaH, DMF 2. heat, [acyl chloride structure]

(f) [structure: cyclopentane with C(=O)NEt2] → P_4O_{10}

(g) [cyclopentene] → 1. O_3 2. H_2O_2 3. P_2O_5

(h) [glutaric anhydride structure] → 1. aq. NaOH 2. pH 7

(i) [cyclohexylmethanol, CH2OH] → pyridine, [acyl chloride]

(j) [branched alkyl bromide, Br] → 1. KCN, DMF 2. H_3O^+, 30°C

(k) [cyclopentanol, OH] → Ac_2O, pyridine

(l) [γ-butyrolactone] → EtOH, cat. H^+

(m) [ketone chain] → 1. $LiAlH_4$, THF 2. H_2O 3. Ac_2O, pyridine

(n) [structure: CO_2Et chain] → MeOH, cat. H^+

(o) [structure: secondary alcohol OH] → PhCOOH, [cyclohexyl-N=C=N-cyclohexyl]

(p) [succinic anhydride structure] → MeOH, cat. H^+

(q) [structure: CO_2H, neopentyl] → DCC, 2-butanol

(r) [structure: $(CH_2)_{13}$ lactone, C=O] → H_3O^+, heat

(s) [cyclopentane-NHEt] → [acyl chloride], pyridine

(t) [structure: EtHN, Me, imide with N-H] → *n*-BuLi, THF

(u) [anhydride structure] → $PhNH_2$, pyridine

(v) [lactone structure] → 1. $LiAlH_4$, THF 2. H_3O^+

(w) [bicyclic lactone] → $EtNH_2$, heat

(x) [structure: amide, NH_2] → 1. $LiAlH_4$, THF 2. H_3O^+

(y) [structure: CO_2Et chain] → NH_3, heat

(z) Ph—N(H)—Ac → 1. $LiAlH_4$, THF 2. H_3O^+

(aa) [structure] 1. KCN ,THF → 2. LiAlH₄ , ether 3. H₂O

(ab) [structure] CO₂Et 1. LDA, THF, -78°C → 2. MeI

(ac) [structure] CO₂Me 1. LDA, -78°C, THF → 2. S-2-iodopentane

(ad) [structure] CO₂Me 1. LDA, -78°C, THF → 2. ethyl benozate

(ae) [structure] CO₂Et 1. NaOEt , EtOH, reflux → 3. H₃O⁺

(af) [structure] 1. O₃ 2. H₂O₂ → 3. SOCl₂; EtOH/pyridine 4. NaOEt, EtOH; H₃O⁺

(ag) [structure] CO₂Et 1. LDA, -78°C, THF → 2. 4-phenyl-3-methyl-2-hexanone

(ah) [structure] 1. O₃ 2. H₂O₂ → 3. EtOH, H⁺ 4. LDA, -78°C, THF 5. 4-phenyl-2-hexanone

(ai) EtO₂C [structure] CO₂Et 1. NaOEt , EtOH, reflux → 3. H₃O⁺

(aj) [structure] CO₂Et PhCHO → NaOEt

(ak) [structure] CO₂Et / CO₂Et 1. NaH , THF 2. benzyl bromide → 3. NaH , THF 4. iodoethane

(al) [structure] CO₂Me PhCO₂Me, NaOMe →

(am) [structure] CO₂Et / CO₂Et 1. NaH, THF 2. iodohexane → 3. aq. NaOH; H₃O⁺ 4. 200°C

(an) [structure] Br / CO₂Me Zn°, EtOH → [naphthalene]CHO

(ao) HO₂C [structure] CO₂H 1. H⁺ , EtOH → 2. LDA, THF, -78°C 3. [structure] Br

(ap) [structure] CO₂H P°, Br₂ →

(aq) [structure] CO₂Et (O) 1. NaH, THF 2. [structure] CHO → 3. H₃O⁺

(ar) [structure] CO₂Et / CO₂Et 1. NaOEt , PhCHO → 2. H₃O⁺

(as) [structure] (O) CO₂Et 1. NaH , THF 2. [structure] I → 3. aq. NaOH; H₃O⁺ 4. 200°C

(at) [structure] CO₂Et / CH₃ (O) 1. NaOEt , PhCHO → 2. H₃O⁺ 3. saponification 4. 200°C

(au) [structure] CO₂Et 1. SOCl₂ → 2. MeOH, pyridine 3. NaOEt, EtOH, reflux

10. In each case provide a suitable synthesis. Show all reagents and
intermediate products.

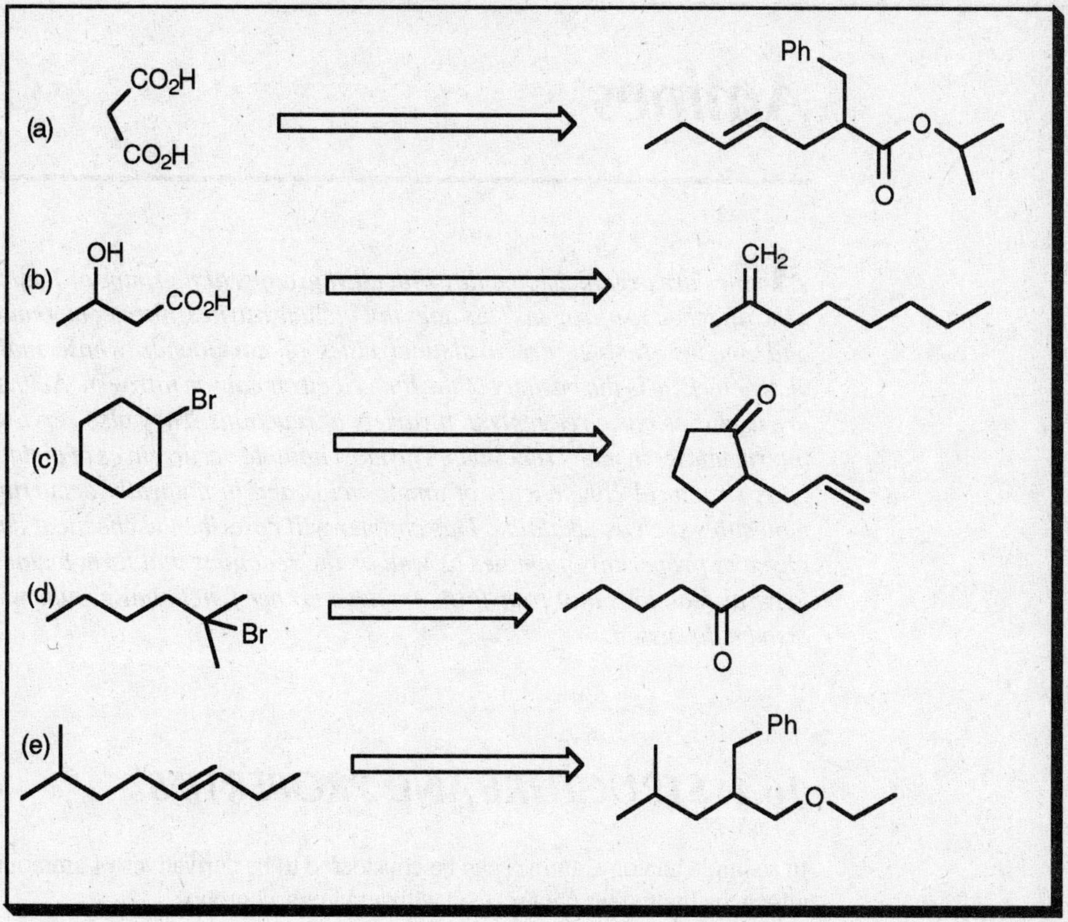

(a)

(b)

(c)

(d)

(e)

16

Amines

Amines are organic molecules with alkyl groups, aryl groups or hydrogens attached to nitrogen. This does not include nitriles, nitro compounds and amides. Amines are a distinct class of compounds whose main characteristic is the basicity of the lone electron pair on nitrogen. Amines are useful as basic reagents in a variety of reactions. They also serve as intermediates in many reactions. The most notable occurrences of amines is as structural components of amino acids and in naturally occurring molecules such as alkaloids. This chapter will describe the chemical and physical properties of amines as well as the reactions that form amines. Several reactions that transform amines in other functional groups will also be discussed.

16.1. STRUCTURE AND PROPERTIES

In a simple analogy, amines can be considered to be derivatives of ammonia where the hydrogens are replaced with alkyl or aryl groups.

Primary, Secondary and Tertiary Amines

GIVE GENERIC EXAMPLES OF A PRIMARY AMINE, A SECONDARY AMINE AND A TERTIARY AMINE.

A primary amine is characterized by two hydrogens on the nitrogen (RNH_2). A secondary amine is characterized by one hydrogen on the nitrogen (R_2NH) and a tertiary amine is characterized by no hydrogens on the nitrogen (R_3N).

WHAT IS THE DISTINGUISHING FEATURE OF A TERTIARY AMINE?

It has three alkyl or aryl groups on the nitrogen and no hydrogens.

Basicity

CLASSIFY AN AMINE AS A REAGENT.

An amine is both a nucleophile (if it reacts with carbon) and a base (if it reacts with a proton or a Lewis acid).

WHAT IS THE PRODUCT WHEN AN AMINE REACTS WITH HCL?

The product is an ammonium chloride. For a secondary amine, the reaction is $R_2NH+HCl \rightarrow R_2N^+H_2\ Cl^-$.

WHICH IS MORE BASIC, A PRIMARY AMINE, A SECONDARY AMINE OR A TERTIARY AMINE? EXPLAIN.

A secondary amine is the most basic. The electron releasing alkyl groups suggest that the more groups on nitrogen the more basic it will be ($3° > 2° > 1°$) but there is a steric effect of the alkyl groups around the nitrogen. With a tertiary amine, the alkyl groups inhibit approach of the nitrogen to the acid, decreasing the basicity. Another important factor is the presence of N–H groups in the ammonium salt product (the product after the amine reacts with the acid). These N–H groups are capable of hydrogen bonding with the solvent [N----H-----OH_2], further stabilizing the product. This suggests $1° > 2° > 3°$. With secondary amines the electronic effects, solvent effects and steric effects are balanced to make it the most basic. The *usual order of basicity* is $2° > 1° ≈ 3°$).

WHAT IS THE PRODUCT WHEN AN AMINE REACTS WITH $AlCl_3$?

The product is the usual Lewis acid-Lewis base complex:$R_2HN^+: ^-AlCl_3$.

WHICH IS MORE BASIC, R_2NH OR R_2N^-? EXPLAIN.

In R_2N^- the charge is concentrated on the nitrogen with a formal charge of -1. This is clearly a stronger base than the neutral amine, which has only a δ- charge on nitrogen due to the unshared electron pair.

Nucleophilic Strength

WHICH IS THE STRONGEST NUCLEOPHILE, A PRIMARY AMINE, SECONDARY AMINE OR A TERTIARY AMINE? EXPLAIN?

For essentially the same reasons described for basicity, secondary amines are usually the most nucleophilic.

WHAT IS THE PRODUCT OF THE REACTION BETWEEN TRIMETHYLAMINE (TERTIARY AMINE) AND IODOMETHANE?

The product is tetramethylammonium iodide: $Me_4N^+\ I^-$.

Physical Properties

WHAT IS A DISTINGUISHING FEATURE OF AMINES THAT CAN BE CORRELATED WITH THEIR SOLUBILITY CHARACTERISTICS?

Amines have a polarized C–N bond and also a polarized N–H bond for primary and secondary amines. The strong dipole of the C–N bond in small molecular weight amines promotes solubility in polar solvents. For primary and secondary amines, the ability to hydrogen bond to the N–H moiety makes solubility in water and other protic solvents very high, *if* the molecular weight of the amine is not too great.

IF AN AMINE CONTAINS THREE DIFFERENT GROUPS (RR'R²N), IS THE NITROGEN CHIRAL? WHY OR WHY NOT?

Such amines are considered to be chiral, racemic molecules. Although there are three different alkyl groups and the lone electron pair can be considered a fourth 'group', there is rapid inversion of configuration around nitrogen (see *16.1*) that generates a racemic mixture of the possible enantiomers. For this reason, the nitrogen of such cyclic amines is not considered when determining the absolute configuration of chiral centers (they are chiral but exist as a racemic mixture).

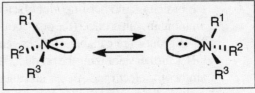

Fig. 16.1

HOW CAN THE RAPID INVERSION CHARACTERISTIC OF AN AMINE BE PREVENTED BY STRUCTURAL MODIFICATION OF THE AMINE?

If the alkyl groups are 'tied back', as in 1-azabicyclo[2.2.2]octane (*16.2*) inversion around nitrogen is not possible, the nitrogen is an asymmetric center and *16.2* is a chiral, non-racemic molecule.

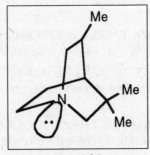

Fig. 16.2

WHICH IS EXPECTED TO HAVE THE HIGHER BOILING POINT, A PRIMARY AMINE OR A TERTIARY AMINE?

Since primary amines have two N–H units that can hydrogen bond, it is expected to have a higher boiling point than the tertiary amine, which cannot hydrogen bond if the molecular weights are approximately equal.

DO AMINES HAVE A DISTINGUISHING UV ABSORPTION?

Amines do not have a distinguishing absorption in the UV.

16.2. NOMENCLATURE

WHAT IS THE IUPAC NOMENCLATURE SYSTEM FOR ALKYL AMINES?

Amines can be named as with an alkylamine or as an alkanamine. The primary amine $CH_3CH_2CH_2CH_2NH_2$ is, therefore, butylamine or butanamine (note the -e of -ane is dropped).

WHAT IS THE IUPAC NOMENCLATURE SYSTEM FOR ARYL AMINES?

They are generally named as the parent aromatic amine. Aniline, 2-bromoaniline and 3-nitro-aniline are typical examples. If a methyl group is also attached to the benzene ring, the common name is *ortho*-toluidine, *meta*-toluidine and *para*-toluidine.

HOW ARE SUBSTITUENTS ON NITROGEN TREATED IN THE IUPAC SYSTEM?

When a group is attached to the nitrogen, it is placed in the name with a N- preceding it. An example is $CH_3CH_2NHCH_2CH_3$, which is named N- ethylpropanamine. If there are two groups on nitrogen, each uses the N- designation. The amine $CH_3CH_2CH_2N(CH_3)_2$ is named N,N-dimethyl- propanamine and $PhN(CH_3)Et$ is N-ethyl-N-methylaniline.

16.3. PREPARATION OF ALKYL AMINES

Alkyl amines are prepared by several different routes involving several different functional groups. In general, substitution and reduction reactions are the most important.

S_N^2 Reactions with Alkyl Halides

Since amines are nucleophiles, they can react with alkyl halides via a S_N^2 process to produce new amines. Since amines are also basic, however, E^2 reactions may be competitive with substitution for 2° amines and will dominate for 3° amines.

POLYALKYLATION

WHAT IS THE EXPECTED PRODUCT WHEN BUTANAMINE REACTS WITH IODOMETHANE?

Since the nitrogen of butanamine is a nucleophile, it will displace iodide (in an S_N^2 reaction) to give the ammonium salt, $BuNH_3^+ I^-$.

WHICH IS THE MOST NUCLEOPHILIC, BUTANAMINE OR N-METHYLBUTANAMINE?

The secondary amine, N-methylbutanamine, is more nucleophilic since there are two alkyl groups releasing electrons to nitrogen.

DISCUSS WHY MONOALKYLATION OF A PRIMARY AMINE IS VERY DIFFICULT.

If ethanamine reacts with iodomethane, the initial product is the ammonium iodide of N-methylethanamine ($EtNH_2Me^+$). Since ethanamine is also a base, it will deprotonate the ammonium salt to give the secondary amine, EtNHMe. Secondary amines are more nucleophilic than primary amines and EtNHMe will likely react with MeI faster than will $EtNH_2$, leading to a tertiary amine. Since the products of the initial reaction with $EtNH_2$ are more reactive than the starting material, it is difficult to stop the reaction at the secondary amine stage.

HOW CAN POLYALKYLATION BE MINIMIZED IN REACTIONS OF AMINES?

If a large excess of the primary amine is used, polyalkylation is minimized.

COMPETITIVE ELIMINATION

WHY IS ELIMINATION A PROBLEM WHEN AMINES REACT WITH ALKYL HALIDES?

With secondary and especially tertiary halides, elimination of the halide leaving group will lead to an alkene via an E^2 reaction. Since all amines are relatively good bases, the can initiate the E^2 reaction if the rate of the S_N^2 reaction is competitively low.

WHAT IS THE PRODUCT WHEN 2-BROMO-2-METHYLPENTANE REACTS WITH TRIETHYLAMINE?

This is an E^2 reaction and the product is 2-methyl-2-pentene.

IS ELIMINATION A MAJOR PROBLEM WHEN PRIMARY AMINES REACT WITH ALKYL HALIDES? WHY OR WHY NOT?

In general, elimination is slower than substitution for primary halides. The ammonium intermediate ($RCH_2NR_3^+$) is susceptible to both S_N^2 and E^2 reactions since $-NR_3^+$ is a good leaving group. For primary amines, substitution is faster than elimination so elimination is usually not a significant problem in alkylation reactions of primary amines.

EXPLAIN WHY REACTION OF A TERTIARY ALCOHOL WITH THIONYL CHLORIDE AND TRIETHYLAMINE LEADS DIRECTLY TO AN ALKENE.

Thionyl chloride first converts the alcohol to the tertiary chloride and triethylamine induces an E^2 elimination, *in situ*, to give the alkene directly.

The Gabriel Synthesis

WHAT IS THE STRUCTURE OF PHTHALIMIDE?

Phthalimide has the structure *16.3*, and is the imide of phthalic acid.

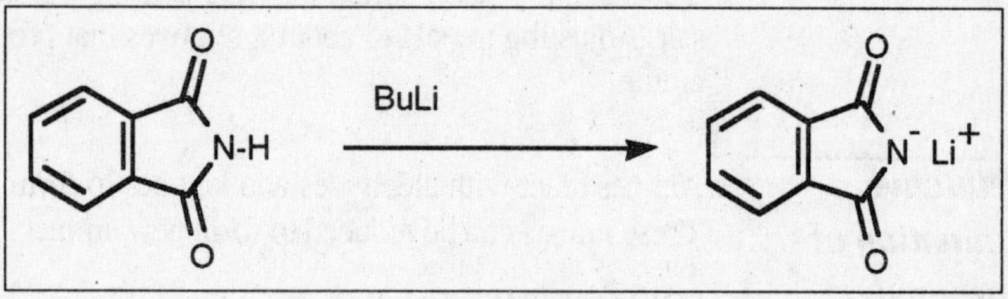

Fig. 16.3, 16.4

WHAT IS THE PRODUCT WHEN PHTHALIMIDE REACTS WITH N-BUTYLLITHIUM?

The imide N–H is quite acidic (pK_a of about 17) and treatment with a strong base such as butyllithium will give the imide anion, *16.4*.

WHAT IS THE PRODUCT WHEN THE SODIUM SALT OF PHTHALIMIDE REACTS WITH 1-BROMOPENTANE?

The phthalimide anion *16.4* is a potent nucleophile and reacts with 1-bromopentane to give N-pentylphthalimide, *16.5*.

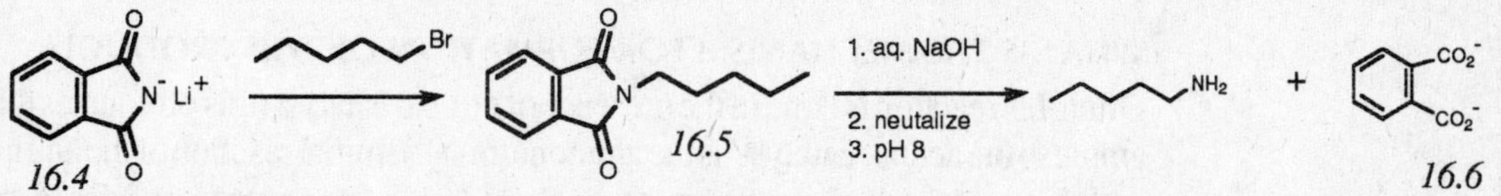

Fig. 16.4–16.6

EXPLAIN WHY POLYALKYLATION IS NOT A PROBLEM WITH PHTHALIMIDE.

The product of the alkylation is an imide, which is significantly less basic than the imide anion. There is, therefore, virtually no chance of the product reacting competitively with *16.4*.

IF N-PENTYL PHTHALIMIDE IS REACTED WITH: i. AQ. KOH ii. NEUTRALIZE, WHAT IS THE PRODUCT?

There are two products. The primary amine (pentanamine) is 'released' along with phthalic acid. The initial product is phthalic acid and the ammonium salt. Mild basification (to pH 8, for example) deprotonates the ammonium salt to give the amine and converts phthalic acid into the dianion *16.6*.

IF N-BUTYL PHTHALIMIDE IS HYDROLYZED WITH ACID, WHY MUST THE pH OF THAT SOLUTION BE ADJUSTED TO ABOUT 8 PRIOR TO ATTEMPTS TO ISOLATE THE AMINE?

Under slightly acidic conditions, amines are protonated to give the ammonium salt. Adjusting the pH to about 8 removes that proton and 'liberates' the free amine.

Reductive Amination of Carbonyls

Amines react with aldehydes and ketones to form imines (see section 16.5). These imines can be reduced to form new amines.

FORMALDEHYDE

WHAT IS THE PRODUCT OF THE REACTION BETWEEN PENTANAMINE AND FORMALDEHYDE?

In general, aldehydes react with primary amines to form an imine, which is generically known as a *Schiff Base*. In this example, the initial product is an iminium salt (*16.7*) which can be deprotonated to give the imine, *16.8*. In this particular case, imine *16.8* is very reactive and difficult to isolate.

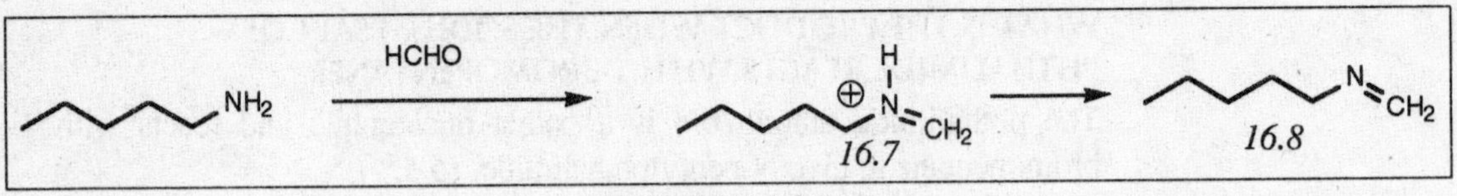

Fig. 16.7, 16.8

WHAT IS THE MECHANISM FOR FORMATION OF THIS PRODUCT?

Often this reaction is done in the presence of an acid catalyst (this protonates the amine so the actual 'catalyst' is the ammonium salt). Initial reaction of the amine with formaldehyde gives the amino alcohol (*16.9*) after a proton transfer form nitrogen to oxygen. If the oxygen is then protonated, to give *16.10*, water is lost to give the iminium salt, *16.7* (with a proton transfer to nitrogen). Loss of the proton from nitrogen (to the amine or during a slightly basic workup) will 'liberate' the imine product, *16.8*.

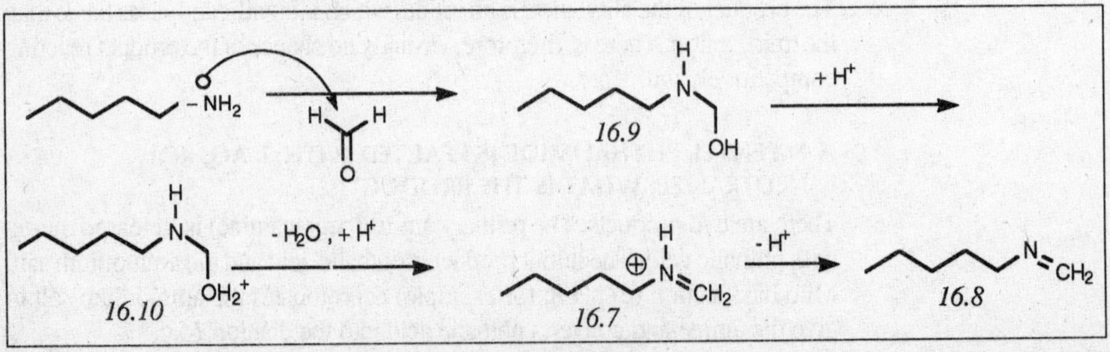

Fig. 16.9, 16.10

IF FORMALDEHYDE WERE REACTED WITH PENTANAMINE IN THE PRESENCE OF HYDROGEN AND A PALLADIUM CATALYST, WHAT IS THE PRODUCT?

With a palladium catalyst, the iminium salt (*16.7*) and the imine (*16.8*) will both be reduced to the corresponding amine. In this case the product is N-methylpentanamine.

WHAT IS THE GENERIC NAME FOR THIS PROCESS?

Reductive amination.

IMINES AND SCHIFF BASES

WHAT IS A SCHIFF BASE?

A Schiff base is the imine (usually N-alkyl) derived from reaction of a primary amine and an aldehyde (generally not formaldehyde). Reaction of ethanamine and ethanal, for example, leads to $CH_3CH_2N=CHCH_3$.

WHAT IS THE PRODUCT OF THE REACTION BETWEEN A SCHIFF BASE AND LiAlH$_4$?

The powerful reducing agent $LiAlH_4$ is capable of reducing the C=N bond to the amine via delivery of hydride to the $C^{\delta+}$ of the C=N bond. If $R-N=CR'_2$ is reacted with $LiAlH_4$ and hydrolyzed under slightly basic conditions, the amine product will be $RNHCHR'_2$.

WHAT IS THE PRODUCT BETWEEN A SCHIFF BASE AND HYDROGEN, IN THE PRESENCE OF A CATALYST?

The product will be the amine, via reductive amination (see reaction with formaldehyde).

WHAT IS THE PRODUCT WHEN THE IMINE DERIVED FROM ANILINE AND BUTANAL IS TREATED WITH NaBH$_4$?

Aniline and butanal will form the Schiff base, $PhN=CHCH_2CH_2CH_3$. Sodium borohydride reduces imines, although with some difficulty, to the amine, $PhNHCH_2CH_2CH_2CH_3$, although the reaction can be slow in the absence of an acid catalyst.

Reduction of Nitriles

WHAT IS THE PRODUCT WHEN HEXANENITRILE IS REDUCED WITH LiAlH$_4$?

When hexanenitrile is reduced, the product is hexanamine.

WHAT IS THE PRODUCT WHEN BENZONITRILE (PhC≡N) IS REDUCED WITH HYDROGEN AND A PALLADIUM CATALYST?

The product is benzylamine ($PhCH_2NH_2$).

WHAT IS THE PRODUCT OF THE LiAlH$_4$ REDUCTION OF 1,6-HEXANEDINITRILE?

The product is the diamine, 1,6-hexanediamine [$H_2N-(CH_2)_6-NH_2$].

Reduction of Amides

WHAT IS THE PRODUCT WHEN N-ETHYLPENTANAMIDE IS TREATED WITH LiAlH$_4$?

As first mentioned in section 15.3, amides are reduced to amines. In this case, the product is N-ethylpentanamine.

WHAT IS THE PRODUCT WHEN 2-PYRROLIDINONE IS REACTED WITH LiAlH$_4$?

Reduction of lactams gives cyclic amines. Reduction of 2-pyrrolidinone gives pyrrolidine.

S$_N$² Reactions of Alkyl halides and Azide

STRUCTURE AND REACTIVITY OF SODIUM AZIDE

WHAT IS THE STRUCTURE OF SODIUM AZIDE?

Sodium azide has the structure NaN$_3$. The azide anion is N$_3^-$.

DISCUSS THE RELATIVE STABILITY OF THE AZIDE ANION.

Azide anion is a resonance stabilized structure, *16.11*.

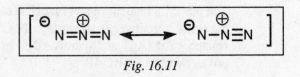

Fig. 16.11

CLASSIFY AZIDE AS A REAGENT.

Azide anion is a strong nucleophile but a rather weak base. It will react with primary and secondary halides via a S$_N$² reaction to form alkyl azides (RN$_3$).

WHAT IS THE MAJOR PRODUCT OF THE REACTION BETWEEN SODIUM AZIDE AND 1-IODOHEXANE?

The product is 1-azidohexane, CH$_3$CH$_2$CH$_2$CH$_2$CH$_2$CH$_2$N$_3$.

HYDRIDE REDUCTION OF AZIDES

WHAT IS THE MAJOR PRODUCT WHEN 1-AZIDOPENTANE REACTS WITH LiAlH$_4$? WITH H$_2$ AND A CATALYST?

In both cases, the azide is reduced to the primary amine. In this case, the product is pentanamine.

CAN THE REACTION OF AZIDE AND ALKYL HALIDES BE USED TO PRODUCE SECONDARY OR TERTIARY AMINES?

Not directly. Reduction of -N$_3$ always leads to -NH$_2$, the primary amine.

16.4. PREPARATION OF ARYL AMINES

AROMATIC AMINES ARE GENERALLY CONSIDERED TO BE DERIVATIVES OF WHAT SIMPLE COMPOUND?

Aniline, $PhNH_2$.

Reduction of Nitrobenzene Derivatives

HOW IS NITROBENZENE SYNTHESIZED FROM BENZENE?

Reaction of benzene with nitric and sulfuric acid gives nitrobenzene. This chemistry was discussed, in detail, in section 9.3.

CATALYTIC HYDROGENATION

WHAT IS THE MAJOR PRODUCT WHEN NITROBENZENE IS REACTED WITH HYDROGEN AND A PALLADIUM CATALYST?

Reduction with hydrogen leads to aniline as the product.

WHY DO THESE CONDITIONS NOT REDUCE THE BENZENE RING?

The benzene ring is aromatic (resonance stabilized) and an excess of hydrogen and very vigorous conditions (heat and pressure) are required to reduce it. The nitro group is relatively easy to reduce and the mild conditions used will not affect the benzene ring.

FORMATION OF DIAZO COMPOUNDS WITH $LiAlH_4$

WHAT IS THE MAJOR PRODUCT OF THE REACTION BETWEEN $LiAlH_4$ AND NITROBENZENE?

The product is *not* the amine (aniline) but rather a diazo compound, *16.12*.

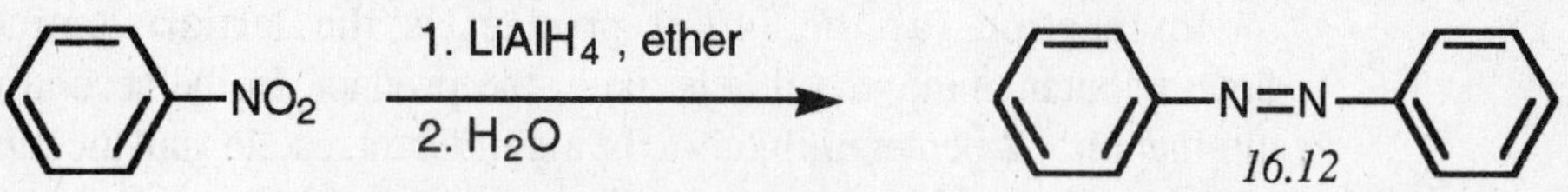

Fig. 16.12

WHAT IS THE MAJOR PRODUCT OF THE REACTION BETWEEN 1-NITROBUTANE AND $LiAlH_4$?

Unlike aromatic nitro compounds, alkyl nitro derivatives are cleanly reduced to the amine. In this case, the product is 1-butanamine ($CH_3CH_2CH_2CH_2NH_2$).

IS REDUCTION OF AROMATIC NITRO COMPOUNDS WITH $LiAlH_4$ A VIABLE SYNTHETIC ROUTE TO AROMATIC AMINES?

No. In general, diazo compounds are produced rather than amines.

Nucleophilic Aromatic Substitution

This chemistry was discussed in sections 10.2 and 10.3.

WHAT REACTION CONDITIONS ARE REQUIRED FOR AMMONIA TO REACT WITH BROMOBENZENE?

High temperatures and pressures (200-300°C, 2000-3000 psi) and high concentrations of ammonia. Under these nucleophilic aromatic substitution conditions, bromobenzene is converted into aniline.

WHY DOES THE PRESENCE OF A NITRO GROUP AT THE ORTHO AND PARA POSITION OF A BENZENE RING INCREASE THE REACTIVITY OF AMMONIA WITH THE ARYL HALIDE?

As discussed in section 10.2, the intermediate for this reaction is a carbanion and the nitro groups will delocalize that negative charge onto the nitro groups. This leads to additional resonance structures and increased stability. The increased stability of the intermediate makes the overall reaction faster.

16.5. REACTIONS OF ALKYL AMINES

With Alkyl Halides

These reactions were described in section 16.3.

SUBSTITUTION

Amines react with aliphatic alkyl halides to form new amines via a S_N^2 reaction. As noted in section 16.3, polyalkylation is a serious problem.

WHAT IS THE MAJOR PRODUCT OF EACH OF THE FOLLOWING REACTIONS?

(a) 1-bromobutane and dimethylamine (b) 2-iodopentane and butylamine.

In reaction (a) the initial product is the tertiary amine, N,N-dimethylbutanamine and this is likely the product. In the second reaction, elimination to 2-pentene is likely to be a significant reaction but the substitution process will give N-butyl-2-methylbutanamine and the major product. The steric hindrance of this second amine will make the subsequent reaction rather slow, especially if an excess of butylamine is used.

E² ELIMINATION

When a tertiary amine such as triethylamine or pyridine is used in the reaction of a tertiary (and occasionally a secondary) alcohol with thionyl chloride, the alkene is the product via an E² pathway. See section 16.1.B.

WHAT IS THE MAJOR PRODUCT FROM THE REACTIONS OF *16.13* AND *16.14*?

In the first reaction, 1-bromo-1-methylcyclohexane (*16.13*) is treated with pyridine (the base) to produce 1-methylcyclohexene (*16.15*) via an E² reaction.

In the second case, diene *16.16* is formed from alcohol *16.14* by the thionyl chloride/pyridine combination.

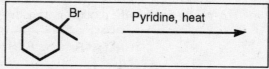

Fig. 16.13

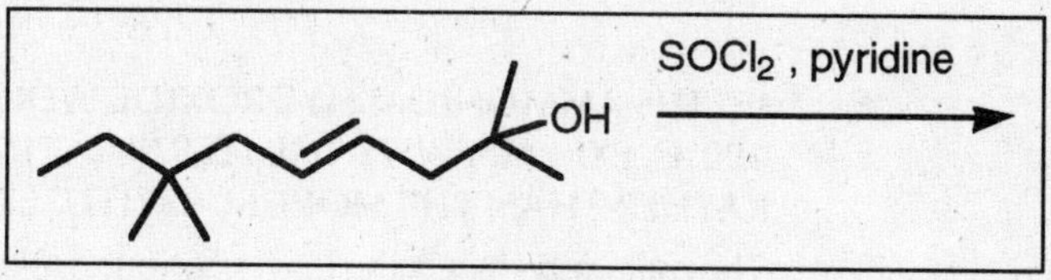

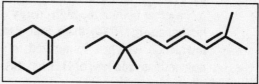

Fig. 16.14

Fig. 16.15, 16.16

HOFMANN ELIMINATION

The bimolecular elimination reaction (E^2) was discussed in section 5.4.

IF THE BASE REQUIRED FOR AN E^2 REACTION WERE SOMEHOW 'TETHERED' TO THE MOLECULE SO AN INTERMOLECULAR REACTION WAS IMPOSSIBLE, WHAT RELATIONSHIP MUST THE β-HYDROGEN AND THE BASE HAVE IN ORDER TO REACT?

They must have a 'syn' relationship (eclipsed).

WHAT IS THE RELATIONSHIP OF THE β-HYDROGEN AND THE LEAVING GROUP IN THIS ROTAMER?

The leaving group and the β-hydrogen are syn (eclipsed).

GIVE THE MAJOR PRODUCT WHEN TRIMETHYLAMINE IS TREATED WITH 2-BROMOPENTANE?

Although there could be a significant amount of elimination, the major substitution product will be trimethylpentylammonium bromide, *16.17*.

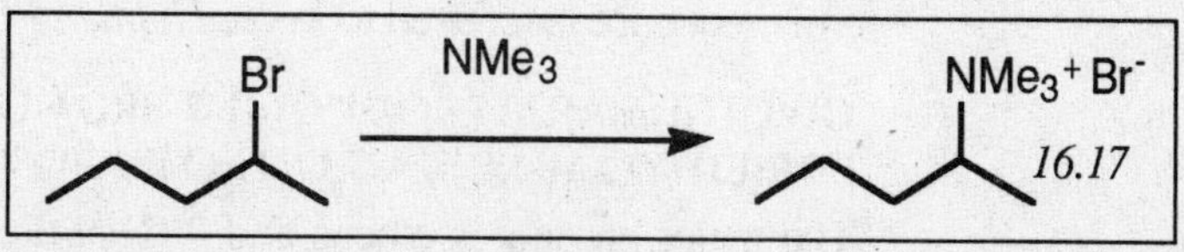

Fig. 16.17

IF THIS PRODUCT WERE REACTED WITH SILVER OXIDE AND ONLY ONE EQUIVALENT OF WATER, WHAT IS THE PRODUCT?

Under these conditions, the bromide counterion is replaced with a hydroxide counterion and the product is trimethylpentylammonium hydroxide, *16.18*.

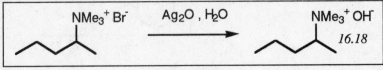

Fig. 16.18

IF THIS AMMONIUM HYDROXIDE WERE HEATED TO ABOUT 150–200°C, EXPLAIN WHY THE LESS SUBSTITUTED ALKENE IS FORMED RATHER THAN THE MORE SUBSTITUTED ALKENE.

The major product is the less substituted alkene, 1-pentene. The tethered base can only reach the β-hydrogen via an eclipsed conformation. Examination of the Newman projections for removal of the two β-hydrogens (H_a and H_b) reveals that both of the high energy eclipsed rotamers have significant steric hindrance. In *16.19*, there is a steric interaction due to the methyl-alkyl interaction which is minimized in *16.20*. The lower energy rotamer will predominate and loss of H_a from this rotamer will lead to the less substituted alkene, 1-pentene.

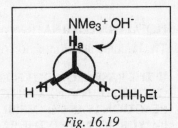

Fig. 16.19

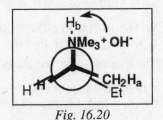

Fig. 16.20

WHAT IS THE NAME OF THIS REACTION SEQUENCE?

This sequence is referred to as the *Hofmann Elimination*.

GIVE THE MAJOR PRODUCT IF 2-BROMOPENTANE IS TREATED WITH i. TRIETHYLAMINE ii. AG₂O, H₂O iii. 200°C. EXPLAIN YOUR ANSWER.

The major product is ethene and 2-(N,N-diethylamino)pentane, *16.22*. The requisite ammonium hydroxide (*16.21*) will give syn elimination at the less sterically hindered and less substituted site, *which is on one of the ethyl groups.*

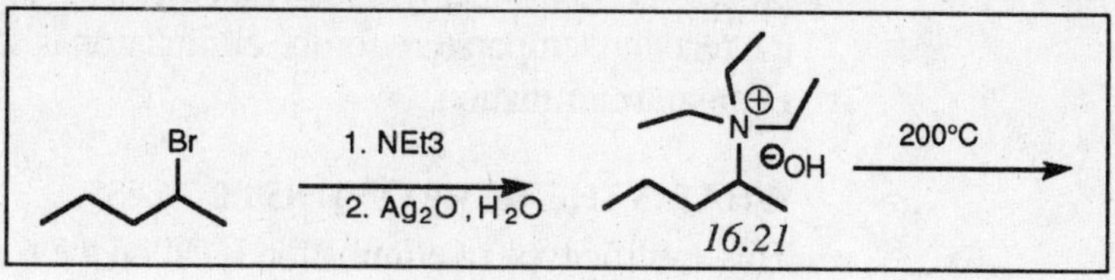

Fig. 16.21

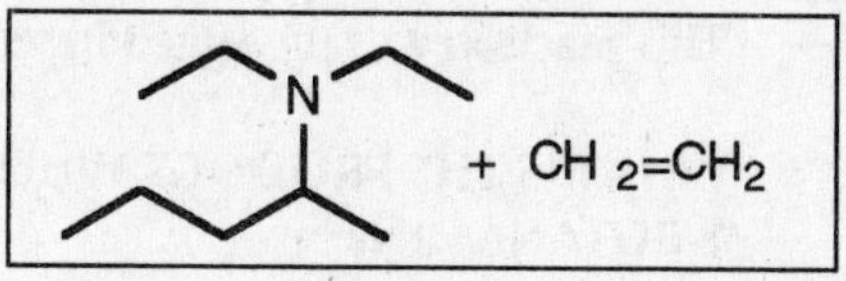

Fig. 16.22

HOW DOES 'SYN ELIMINATION' DIFFER FROM 'ANTI ELIMINATION'?

The leaving group and the β-hydrogen are *syn* (eclipsed) in syn elimination but they are *anti* in the E² reaction. The *syn* elimination process is more difficult and slower, requiring significantly higher reaction temperatures. The *syn* elimination process will always give the less substituted alkene as the major product whereas *anti* elimination (E²) will always give the more substituted alkene as the major product.

COPE ELIMINATION

WHAT IS THE PRODUCT WHEN A TERTIARY AMINE IS OXIDIZED WITH A REAGENT SUCH AS HYDROGEN PEROXIDE, A PEROXYACID OR NaIO₄?

These oxidizing agents convert a tertiary amine into an N-oxide such as *16.23*.

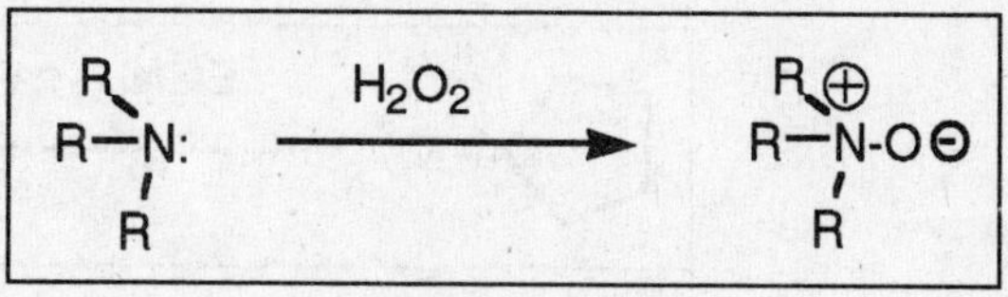

Fig. 16.23

IF THE N-OXIDE OF 2-(N,N-DIMETHYLAMINO)HEXANE (*16.24*) IS HEATED WHAT IS THE EXPECTED PRODUCT?

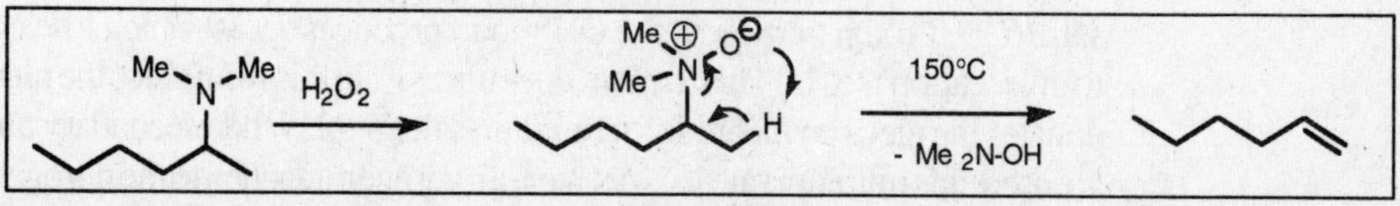

Fig. 16.24

Oxidation of *16.24* generates N-oxide *16.25*. Heating leads to syn elimination and formation of the less substituted alkene, 1-hexene. The leaving group in this process is N,N-dimethylhydoxylamine, Me_2N-OH. As noted in the reaction, the reaction temperature for the elimination is somewhat lower than with the Hofmann elimination.

WHAT IS THE NAME OF THIS PROCESS?

This specific type of elimination is called the *Cope elimination*.

With Aldehydes — Formation of Schiff Bases

This reaction was presented in sections 13.4 and 16.5.

WHAT IS THE PRODUCT WHEN CYCLOPENTANONE REACTS WITH 1-BUTANAMINE?

The product is N-butylcyclopentylimine, *16.26*.

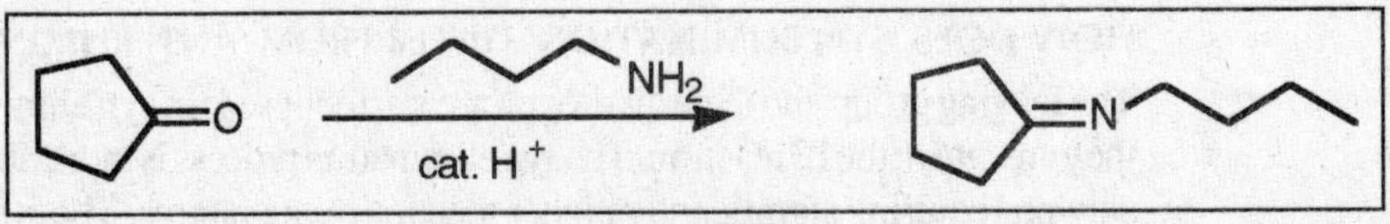

Fig. 16.26

Enamine Formation

WHAT IS AN ENAMINE?

An enamine is a molecule that has an amino group (NR_2) attached directly to a carbon-carbon double bond [$C=C–NR_2$], as discussed in section 13.4.

WHEN CYCLOPENTANONE REACTS WITH DIETHYLAMINE, WHAT IS THE PRODUCT?

This reaction produces the enamine, *16.27*.

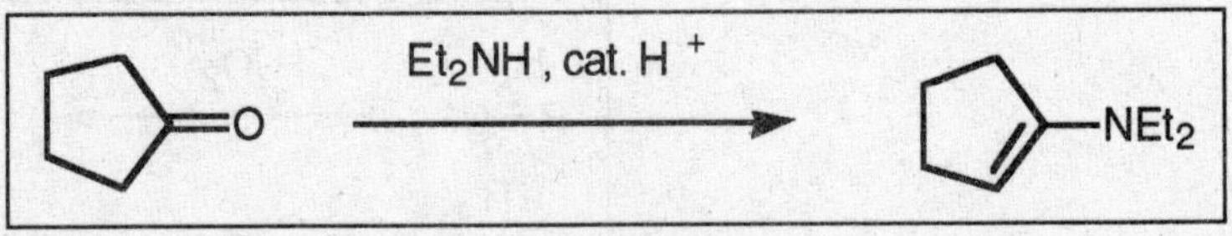

Fig. 16.27

GIVE A MECHANISTIC RATIONALE FOR ENAMINE FORMATION.

Initial protonation of cyclopentanone by the acid catalyst promotes the reaction by forming *16.28*. This cation is attacked by diethylamine to form ammonium salt *16.29*. Proton transfer to the OH group produces *16.30* which loses water to give 'cation' *16.31*. This 'cation' does not exist in this form since the nitrogen donates the electron pair to form iminium salt *16.32*. When secondary amines are used, this iminium salt does not have a hydrogen attached to the nitrogen that can be removed to form an imine. Only primary amines will produce an iminium salt that can be converted to an imine. In the case of iminium salt *16.32*, the α-hydrogen is acidic (much as in a ketone that produces an enolate anion) and removal of that hydrogen with a base (usually the amine) generates the enamine, *16.27*. In fact, depending on the solvent, enamine *16.5.15* and iminium salt *16.32* are in equilibrium, with the equilibrium generally favoring the enamine.

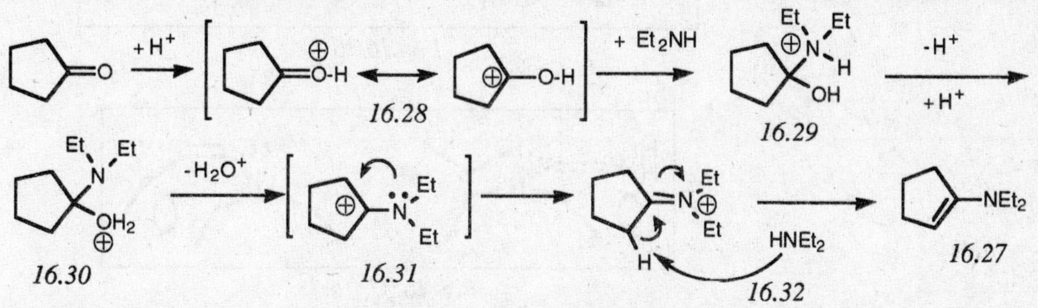

Fig. 16.28–16.32, 16.27

WHAT IS THE PRODUCT WHEN AN ALDEHYDE REACTS WITH A SECONDARY AMINE?

When an aldehyde such as butanal reacts with a secondary amine such as diethylamine, the initially formed iminium salt (*16.33*) reacts with diethylamine to form the geminal diamine, *16.34*. In the presence of a base (usually the amine) *16.34* eliminates a molecule of diethylamine to form the enamine, *16.35*.

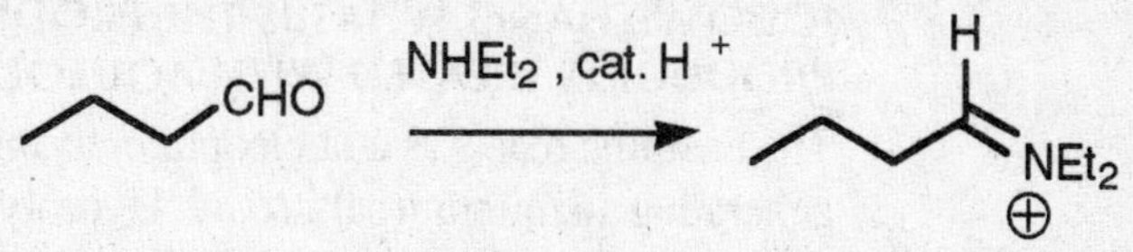

Fig. 16.33

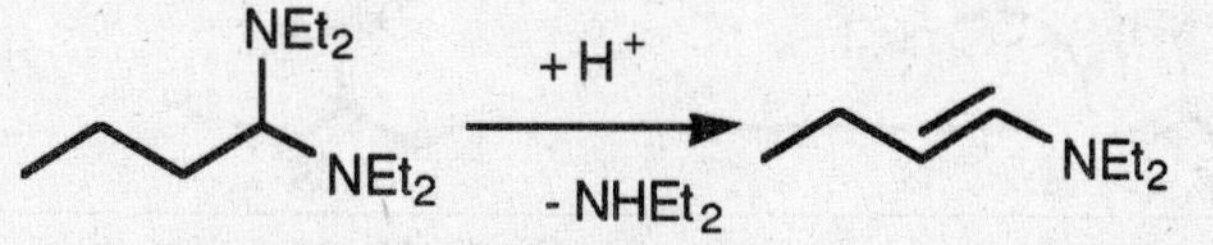

Fig. 16.34, 16.35

WHEN DIETHYLAMINE REACTS WITH 2-PENTANONE, WILL THE ENAMINE HAVE A MORE HIGHLY SUBSTITUTED OR THE LESS SUBSTITUTED DOUBLE BOND? EXPLAIN.

The major product of this reaction is enamine *16.36*, where the double bond has the fewest substituents. This is explained by a comparison of enamine *16.36* (redrawn as *16.37*) with the other possible isomer, *16.38*. The planar nature of this molecule around nitrogen makes the steric interaction of the ethyl groups on nitrogen with the groups on the alkenyl carbons severe. This interaction is minimized in *16.37*, making *16.36* the major product.

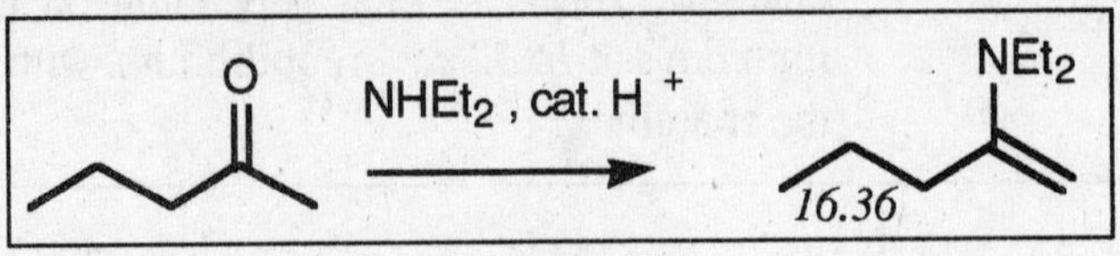

Fig. 16.36

Fig. 16.37, 16.38

PREDICT HOW ENAMINES SHOULD REACT WITH ALKYL HALIDES OR WITH KETONES AND ALDEHYDES.

The electron pair on nitrogen can be donated to the C=C group, making the terminal carbon of the $R_2N-C=C$ system nucleophilic. The best way to think about an enamine is: it behaves as a nitrogen 'enolate', forming a new carbon-carbon bond with the terminal carbon of C=C.

WHAT IS THE MAJOR PRODUCT WHEN *16.36* REACTS WITH IODOMETHANE? WHAT IS THE PRODUCT WHEN THIS INITIAL PRODUCT IS TREATED WITH AQUEOUS ACID?

The enamine reacts as a nucleophile, forming a new carbon-carbon bond and generating an iminium salt, *16.39*. Hydrolysis of the iminium salt (as observed in previous sections) generates a ketone with loss of diethylamine to give 3-hexanone, *16.40*.

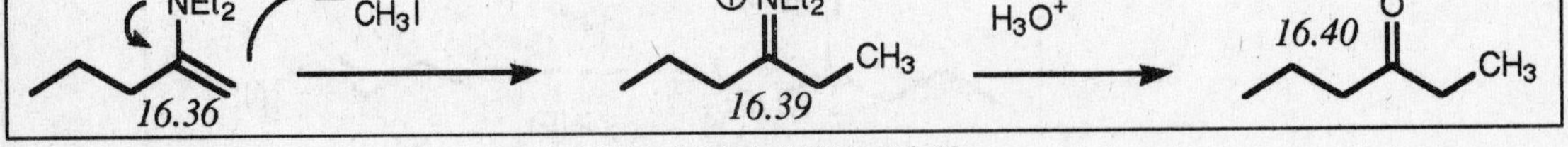

Fig. 16.36, 16.39, 16.40

With Acid Derivatives

FORMATION OF AMIDES

The chemistry was discussed in sections 14.5 and 15.3.

WHAT IS THE PRODUCT WHEN AN AMINE REACTS WITH A CARBOXYLIC ACID?

An amine is a base and reacts with the acidic hydrogen of the carboxyl group to give an ammonium carboxylate [R_3NH^+ ^-O_2CR].

WHY DOES HEATING THE REACTION PRODUCT OF AN AMINE AND A CARBOXYLIC ACID PRODUCE AN AMIDE?

Thermally, the ammonium salt protonates another molecule of the ammonium salt, allowing thermal dehydration (loss of water) to form the amide.

WHAT IS THE PRODUCT WHEN N-METHYLPENTANAMINE REACTS WITH BENZOYL CHLORIDE?

In this case, the product is an amide, *16.41*.

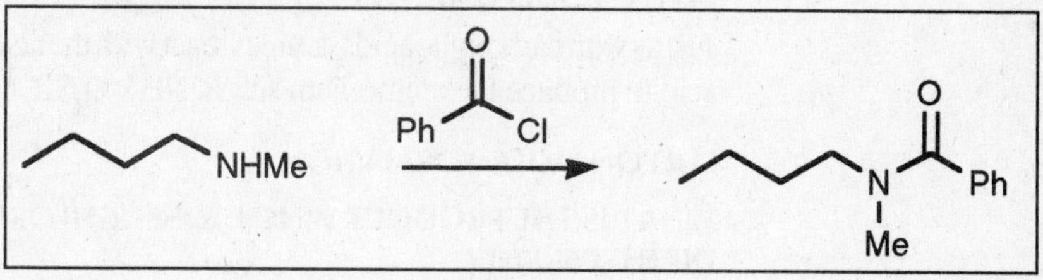

Fig. 16.41

REACTION WITH SULFONIC ACID DERIVATIVES

WHAT IS THE STRUCTURE OF A SULFONIC ACID?

A sulfonic acid has the structure RSO_2OH. The R group can be alkyl or aryl.

HOW ARE SULFONIC ACIDS PREPARED?

Aromatic sulfonic acids are prepared by sulfonation of an aromatic ring with SO_3 and an acid (usually sulfuric). Alkyl sulfonic acids are generally prepared from the thiol (RSH) by oxidation with $KMnO_4$ (HNO_3 can also be used).

WHAT IS THE STRUCTURE OF BENZENESULFONIC ACID? OF TOSIC ACID? OF METHANESULFONIC ACID?

Benzenesulfonic acid has the structure $PhSO_3H$ and methanesulfonic acid has the structure CH_3SO_3H.

HOW IS A SULFONYL CHLORIDE MADE?

Just as treatment of a carboxylic acid with $SOCl_2$ or PCl_3 gives the acid chloride, so reaction of a sulfonic acid with $SOCl_2$ (usually in the presence of a base such as pyridine to react with the HCl by-product) gives the sulfonic acid: $RSO_3H + SOCl_2 \rightarrow RSO_2Cl$, where RSO_2Cl is the generic structure of the sulfonyl chloride.

WHAT IS TOSYL CHLORIDE? MESYL CHLORIDE?

Tosyl chloride is the common name for *para*-toluenesulfonyl chloride (*16.42*) and mesyl chloride is the common name for methanesulfonyl chloride (*16.43*).

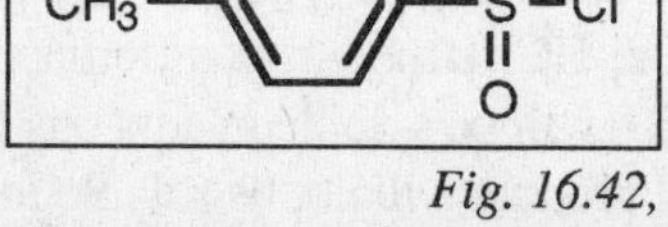

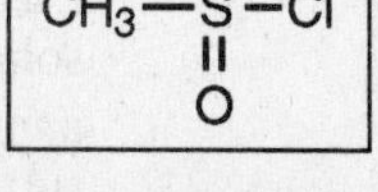

Fig. 16.42, 16.43

WHAT IS THE STRUCTURE OF A SULFONAMIDE?

A sulfonamide is the amide form of the sulfonic acid and has the generic structure $R'SO_2NR_2$. The R group on the nitrogen can be H,H (primary amide), alkyl or aryl,H = secondary amide or alkyl,aryl/alkyl,aryl = tertiary amide.

SALT FORMATION

WHAT IS THE PRODUCT WHEN DIETHYLAMINE REACTS WITH BENZENESULFONIC ACID?

Just as with carboxylic acids, amines react with the acidic hydrogen of a sulfonic acid to produce the ammonium salt: R_3NH^+ $^-O_3SR'$.

SULFONAMIDE FORMATION

WHAT IS THE PRODUCT WHEN TOSYL CHLORIDE REACTS WITH DIETHYLAMINE?

If tosyl chloride is represented as TsCl, the product is the sulfonamide, $TsNEt_2$ [$p\text{-}MeC_6H_4SO_2NEt_2$].

WHAT IS THE PRODUCT WHEN BENZENESULFONYL CHLORIDE REACTS WITH AMMONIA?

The product is benzene sulfonamide, $PhSO_2NH_2$.

HINSBERG TEST

WHAT IS THE PRODUCT WHEN A PRIMARY AMINE REACTS WITH BENZENESULFONYL CHLORIDE IN THE PRESENCE OF HYDROXIDE?

The product is the sulfonamide: RCH_2NHSO_2Ph.

WHAT IS THE PRODUCT WHEN A SECONDARY AMINE REACTS WITH BENZENESULFONYL CHLORIDE IN THE PRESENCE OF HYDROXIDE?

The product is the sulfonamide: R_2NSO_2Ph.

WHAT IS THE PRODUCT WHEN A TERTIARY AMINE REACTS WITH BENZENESULFONYL CHLORIDE IN THE PRESENCE OF HYDROXIDE?

The product is the ammonium salt: R_3NH^+ ^-O_3SPh.

DESCRIBE THE HINSBERG TEST.

The Hinsberg test is used to determine if an amine is primary, secondary or tertiary. The amine is, presumably, insoluble in water. The amine is converted to the benzenesulfonamide and placed in aqueous sodium hydroxide. A sulfonamide derived from a primary amine will have an acidic N–H that is deprotonated by NaOH to give a soluble product. A secondary amine will give a sulfonamide with no acidic hydrogen and will not be soluble in aqueous NaOH. If the sulfonamide is insoluble in aqueous NaOH, it is then treated for solubility in aq. HCl. If the amine is a tertiary amine, no sulfonamide was formed and $R_3NH^+Cl^-$ will be soluble in aqueous HCl. If the amine is secondary, the sulfonamide product will not be soluble in aqueous HCl.

The test is, therefore: If the product of the amine and PhSO$_2$Cl is soluble in aqueous NaOH it is a primary amine. If it is insoluble in NaOH but soluble in aqueous HCl, it is a tertiary amine. If it is insoluble in both aqueous NaOH and aqueous HCl, it is a secondary amine.

IF AN AMINE IS TREATED WITH PhSO$_2$Cl AND THE PRODUCT IS SOLUBLE IN AQ. NaOH AND INSOLUBLE IN AQ. HCl IS IT PRIMARY, SECONDARY OR TERTIARY?

It is a primary amine.

IF AN AMINE IS REACTED WITH PhSO$_2$Cl AND THE PRODUCT IS INSOLUBLE IN AQ. NaOH BUT SOLUBLE IN AQ. HCl IS THE PRIMARY, SECONDARY OR TERTIARY?

It is a tertiary amine.

16.6 REACTIONS OF ARYL AMINES

Electrophilic Aromatic Substitution

This chemistry was described in chapter 9.

ANILINE DERIVATIVES

WHAT IS THE REACTION PRODUCT WHEN ANILINE IS REACTED WITH AlCl$_3$?

Since AlCl$_3$ is a powerful Lewis acid, aniline will function as a Lewis base, generating the usual complex: PhNH$_2$: AlCl$_3$.

IF ANILINE IS REACTED WITH BROMINE AND NO LEWIS ACID CATALYST, EXPLAIN WHY A TRIBROMOANILINE IS FORMED.

The NH$_2$ group on the benzene ring strongly activates that ring to electrophilic aromatic substitution. So strong is the activation that bromine reacts, without a catalyst, to give not only the monosubstitution product but the tribromo derivatives (the specific product is 2,4,6-tribromoaniline).

ACETANILIDE DERIVATIVES

WHAT IS THE PRODUCT WHEN N-ACETYLANILINE IS TREATED WITH A MIXTURE OF NITRIC ACID AND SULFURIC ACID?

The amide group is a strong activating group and is an *ortho/para* director. The products of this nitration are, therefore, a mixture of the 2-nitro- and 4-nitroacetanilide derivatives.

Nucleophilic Aromatic Substitution

This reaction was described in chapter 10.

Nitrosation

REACTION WITH NITROUS ACID — DIAZONIUM SALTS

WHAT IS THE STRUCTURE OF SODIUM NITRITE?

$NaNO_2$.

WHAT IS THE REACTIVE SPECIES IN AN AQUEOUS SOLUTION OF SODIUM NITRITE AND HCl?

Nitrous acid, HONO.

WHAT IS THE PRODUCT WHEN ANILINE IS TREATED WITH NANO$_2$ IN AQ. HCl?

The product is benzenediazonium chloride: $PhN_2^+ Cl^-$.

HOW STABLE ARE BENZENEDIAZONIUM SALTS?

Aromatic diazonium salts are usually stable when kept in aqueous solution. If one attempts to isolate them in pure, anhydrous form, they are very dangerous and often (if not usually) decompose violently (explode). Diazonium salts should *always* be handled only in aqueous solution.

HOW REACTIVE ARE BENZENEDIAZONIUM SALTS?

They are very reactive to nucleophilic aromatic substitution reactions where water, CuX (X = CN, Br, Cl, I) or activated aromatic rings are the nucleophiles.

FORMATION OF PHENOLS

GIVE AN EXAMPLE OF A REACTION THAT PRODUCES PHENOLS FROM BENZENEDIAZONIUM CHLORIDE.

If benzenediazonium chloride is heated with water, phenol is the product.

FORMATION OF ARYL HALIDES

SHOW A REACTION THAT PRODUCES CHLOROBENZENE FROM BENZENEDIAZONIUM CHLORIDE?

If benzenediazonium chloride is heated with cuprous chloride, chlorobenzene is the product: $PhN_2^+ Cl^- + CuCl \rightarrow Ph–Cl$.

WHAT IS THE PRODUCT OF THE REACTION BETWEEN NITROBENZENE AND i. HNO$_3$, H$_2$SO$_4$ ii. NaNO$_2$, HCl iii. CuBr?

The product is bromobenzene, Ph–Br.

WHAT IS THE PRODUCT OF THE REACTION BETWEEN ANILINE AND i. HONO ii. CuCN?

The product is benzonitrile, $Ph–C \equiv N$.

REDUCTION OF DIAZONIUM SALTS

WHAT IS THE PRODUCT WHEN BENZENEDIAZONIUM CHLORIDE IS REACTED WITH H$_3$PO$_2$? WITH NaBH$_4$?

In both cases, these reducing agents convert PhN_2^+ to Ph–H.

COUPLING OF DIAZONIUM SALTS

WHAT IS THE PRODUCT WHEN BENZENEDIAZONIUM CHLORIDE IS TREATED WITH ANISOLE?

The product is a diazo compound, *16.45*.

EXPLAIN HOW THIS PRODUCT IS FORMED.

It is formed by the anisole attacking the electrophilic nitrogen of the diazonium salt. This reaction forms the coupling product (cation *16.44*) which loses a proton (usually to the water solvent) to reform the aromatic ring in the final product, *16.45*. Since the OMe activates the *ortho* and *para* positions by an electron releasing inductive effect, these are the carbons that attack the nitrogen. Attack via the *ortho* position is usually sterically hindered and the major product is attack via the *para* carbon to give *16.45*.

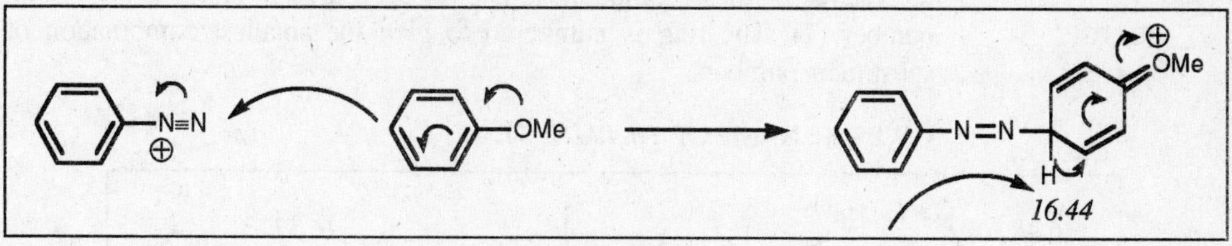

Fig. 16.44

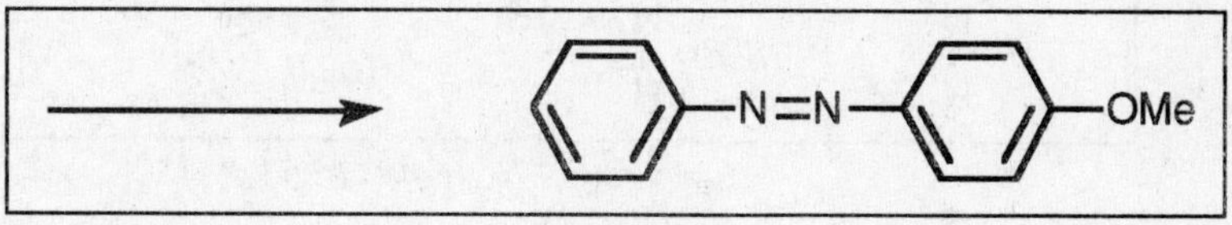

Fig. 16.45

WHAT IS THE FAMILY NAME FOR THIS TYPE OF PRODUCT?

This type of reaction is called azo coupling. Since many of these compounds have strong absorption in the visible region of the electromagnetic spectrum, they can be used as dyes. A common name for this type of compound is aza dye.

16.7. HETEROCYCLIC AMINES

A heterocyclic amine is defined as an aromatic compound that contains nitrogen in a ring. The most common monocyclic members are pyrrole and pyridine.

Structures of Representative Amines

WHAT IS THE STRUCTURE OF PYRROLE?

Pyrrole is a five-membered aromatic ring compound that contains one nitrogen. Its structure is *16.46*.

WHAT IS THE STRUCTURE OF PYRIDINE?

Pyridine is a six-membered aromatic ring that contains one nitrogen. Its structure is *16.47*.

Fig. 16.46, 16.47

DISCUSS THE NOMENCLATURE SYSTEM FOR SUBSTITUTED PYRROLES AND PYRIDINES.

The name pyrrole and pyridine constitute the IUPAC base name of all derivatives of these compounds. The nitrogen always receives the lowest number (1). The ring is numbered to give the smallest combination of substituent numbers.

GIVE THE NAME OF *16.48–16.51*.

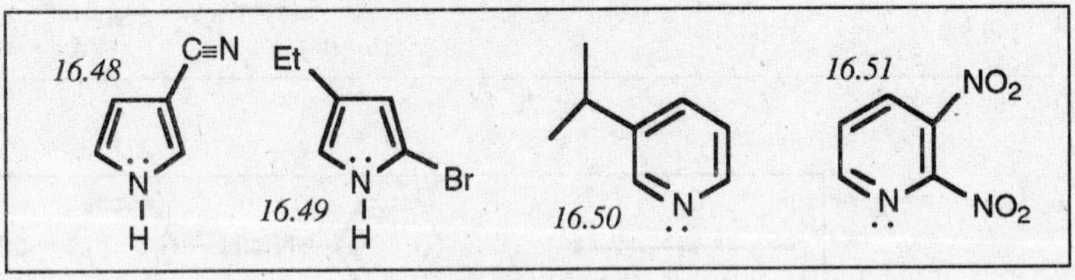

Fig. 16.48–16.51

Amine (*16.48*) is named 3-cyanopyrrole. Amine (*16.49*) is 2-bromo-4-ethylpyrrole. Amine (*16.50*) is 3-isopropylpyridine [3-(1-methylethyl)pyridine is the proper IUPAC name] and amine (*16.51*) is 2,3-dinitropyridine.

Aromatic Character

WHY IS PYRIDINE AROMATIC?

There are two formal sigma bonds to nitrogen, leaving two lone pairs of electrons. One of those electron pairs is parallel with the π-bonds and provides the last two electrons for the requisite six electrons in the aromatic cloud (see *16.52*). Note that the second lone electron pair on nitrogen is perpendicular to the aromatic π-cloud. See section 8.2.

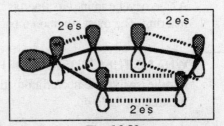

Fig. 16.52

IS THE HYDROGEN ATTACHED TO NITROGEN IN PYRROLE PERPENDICULAR OR PARALLEL TO THE π-BONDS IN THE RING? EXPLAIN.

The hydrogen of the N–H unit is perpendicular to the π-bonds. The lone electron pair of the nitrogen is part of the six-electron aromatic cloud, forcing the hydrogen to be perpendicular.

WHICH IS MORE BASIC, PYRIDINE OR PYRROLE?

Pyridine is more basic. The electron pair on nitrogen in pyrrole is 'tied up' as part of the aromatic cloud but the electron pair on nitrogen in pyridine is not part of the aromatic system. In pyridine, the electron pair on nitrogen is perpendicular to the aromatic system and is relatively unhindered (easily accessible).

WHICH IS MORE BASIC, PYRIDINE OR PIPERIDINE?

Pyridine is about as basic an aniline, which is generally less basic than secondary alkyl amines. On this basis, piperidine would be expected to be the more basic of the two.

Reactions

ELECTROPHILIC AROMATIC SUBSTITUTION

WHAT IS THE MAJOR PRODUCT WHEN PYRROLE REACTS WITH BROMINE AND ACETIC ACID?

The product is that of electrophilic aromatic substitution (see section 9.5) and the major product is 2-bromopyrrole, *16.53*.

GIVE A MECHANISTIC RATIONALE FOR THIS PRODUCT.

When bromonium ion is attacked by pyrrole, both the C_2 and the C_3 positions are susceptible to formation of the new C–Br bond. Attack at C_2 generates resonance intermediate *16.54* where there are three canonical forms, including one that includes delocalization of the charge onto nitrogen. Attack at C_3, however, can only give two canonical forms (*16.55*) and is less stable. This usually leads to electrophilic aromatic substitution at the C_2 position in five-membered heterocyclic rings, including furan and thiophene.

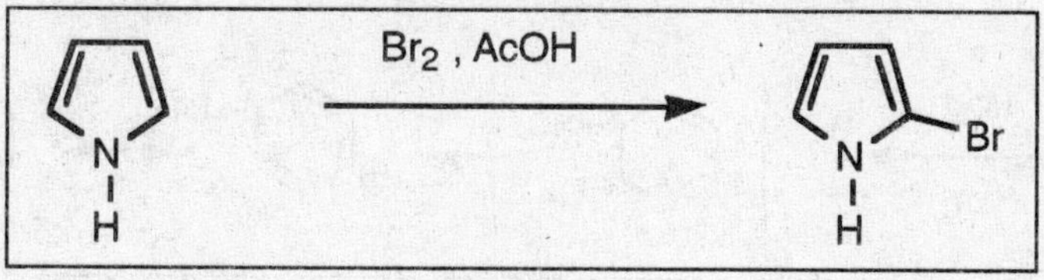

Fig. 16.53

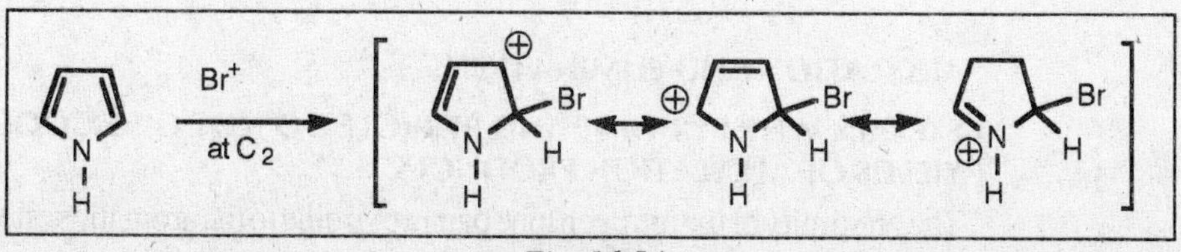

Fig. 16.54

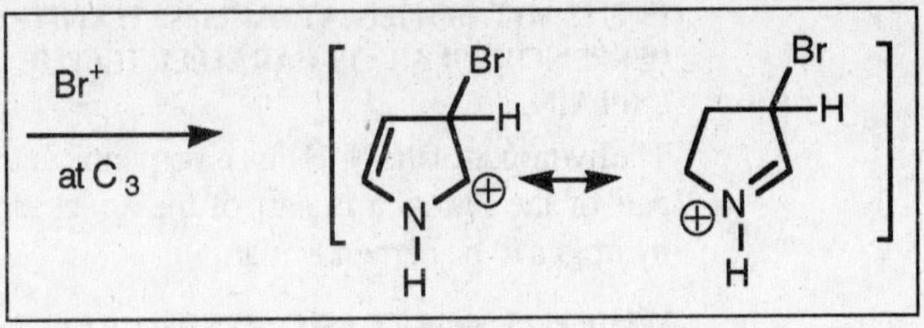

Fig. 16.55

WHAT IS THE MAJOR PRODUCT WHEN PYRIDINE REACTS WITH NITRIC ACID AND SULFURIC ACID?

Electrophilic aromatic substitution of pyridine usually gives the 3-substituted product. In this case, the major product is 3-nitropyridine, *16.56*. It is important to note that the reaction requires high temperatures. In general, pyridine reacts poorly in electrophilic aromatic substitution reactions and often requires very vigorous conditions.

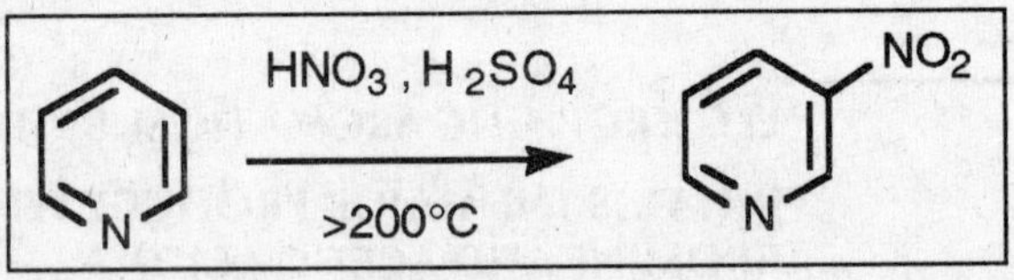

Fig. 16.56

WHAT IS THE MECHANISTIC RATIONALE FOR THIS REACTION.

When NO_2^+ reacts with pyridine at C_2 (or at C_4), one of the resonance forms places a positive charge on an electron deficient nitrogen (see *16.57*), and is particularly unstable. Attack at C_3, however, does not place the positive charge directly on nitrogen. Attack at C_3 (to give *16.58*) is preferred since it gives the most stable cationic intermediate.

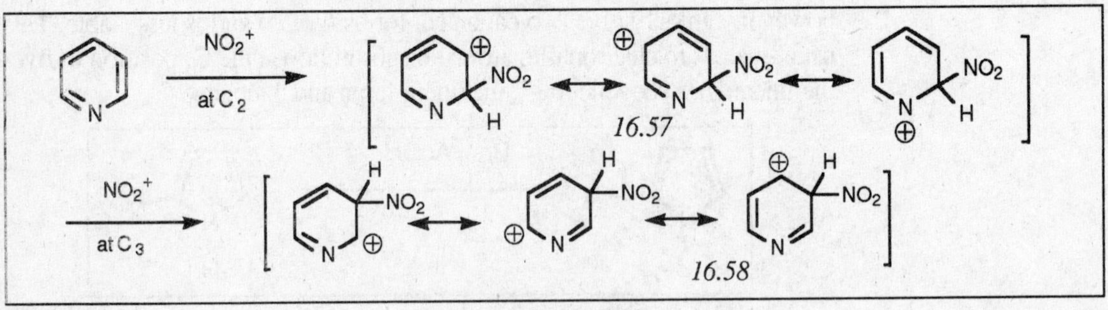

Fig. 16.57, 16.58

ALKYLATION AND ELIMINATION

EXPLAIN WHY PYRIDINE AND PYRROLE DO NOT GIVE GOOD YIELDS OF ALKYLATION PRODUCTS.

The proximity of the nitrogen lone pair in pyridine to the aromatic system makes pyridine a poor nucleophile. Pyrrole is even weaker since the electron pair on nitrogen is tied up in the aromatic system.

WHY IS PYRIDINE OFTEN USED IN E² ELIMINATION REACTIONS?

Pyridine is sufficiently basic to remove a β-hydrogen of an alkyl halide and induce an E² reaction. It is generally unreactive to other reactions and is not very nucleophilic. Its poor nucleophilic strength makes it particularly attractive for an E² reaction, where S_N^2 is usually competitive if a nucleophilic base is used with a secondary halide.

WHY IS PYRIDINE ADDED TO THE REACTION OF A CARBOXYLIC ACID AND THIONYL CHLORIDE?

Pyridine is a base and reacts with the HCl by-product, producing pyridinium hydrochloride.

*I*t is clear from this chapter that there are many useful reactions involving amines. Some of the reactions that form amines are important in the synthesis of amino acids, to be discussed in chapter eighteen. This chapter also introduced heterocyclic amines. Although the discussion was brief, heterocyclic chemistry is one of the most important areas in organic chemistry, particularly for industrial preparations and pharmaceutical products. Some of the chemistry is unique to hetereocyclics but most of it is characteristic of aromatic compounds. The chemistry of amines will also be important in biological systems such as amino acids, peptides, DNA and RNA.

END OF CHAPTER PROBLEMS

1. Which of the following is the more basic?

2. Choose the more basic atom in each pair. Explain your choice.

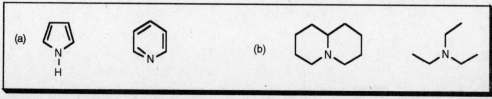

3. Give the IUPAC name for each of the following.

(a)

(b)

(c)

(d)

(e)

(f)

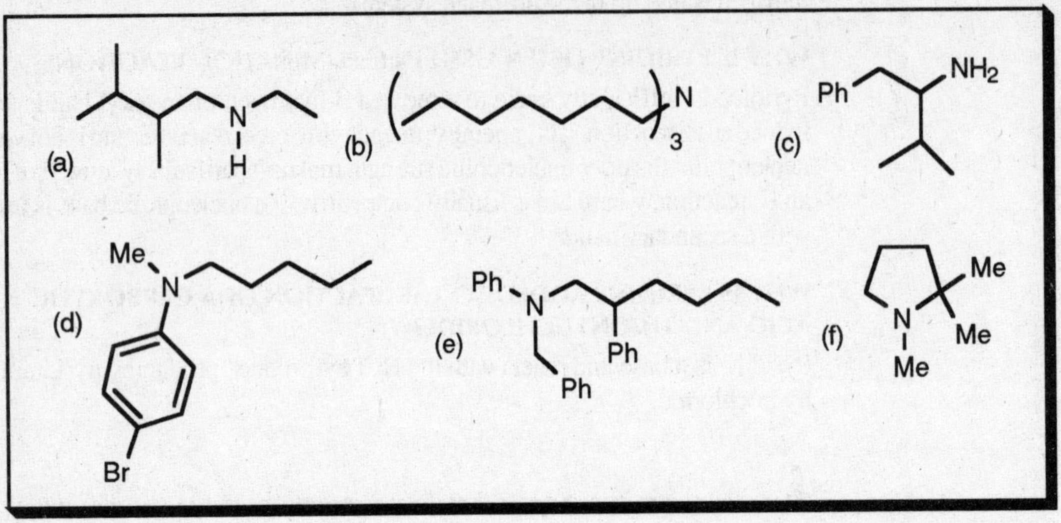

4. 1-Bromopentane is reacted with a large excess of methylamine. How can one prove the major product is a secondary amine, without using spectroscopy?

5. Give the correct name for each of the following.

(a)

(b)

(c)

(d)

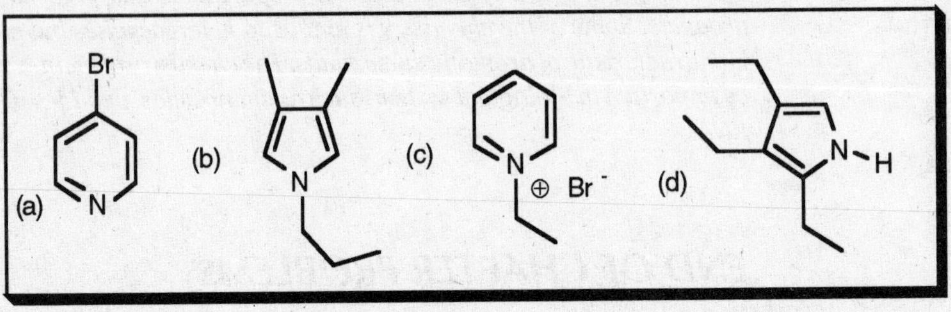

6. Give the major product for each of the following reactions. If there is no reaction, indicate by N.R.

(a) [benzenamine structure with -NH₂] →(AlCl₃)→

(b) [1-bromoethylcyclohexane structure] →(1. NMe₃ 2. Ag₂O, H₂O 3. 150°C)→

(c) [(CH₂)₃N tri-substituted amine] →(allyl bromide, Br)→

(d) [amine structure with NMe₂] →(1. MeI 2. Ag₂O, H₂O 3. 150°C)→

(e) PPh₃ →(iodopentane)→

(f) [1-methylcyclohexanol structure, OH] →(POCl₃, pyridine)→

(g) [N,N-dimethylaniline, NMe₂] →(H₂O₂, 25°C)→

(h) [tertiary bromide structure, Br] →(pyridine, heat)→

(i) [structure with NMe₂] →(H₂O₂, 180°C)→

(j) [diethyl phthalate, CO₂Et, CO₂Et] →(1. NH₃, heat 2. BuLi 3. benzyl bromide 4. saponification)→

(k) [3-pentanone, O] →(morpholine O–N-H, cat. H⁺)→

(l) [phenylacetaldehyde, CHO] →(C₃H₇NH₂, H₂, Pd-C)→

(m) [1-(1-buten-2-yl)pyrrolidine structure] →(1. iodopropane 2. H₃O⁺)→

(n) [2-aminohexane, NH₂] →(PhCHO, cat. H⁺)→

(o) [pyrrolidine, N-H] →(pentanoic acid CO₂H, 250°C)→

(p) [N-butylcyclohexanimine, =N–C₄H₉] →(1. HCl 2. NaBH₄)→

(q) [N-ethyl secondary amine, NHEt] →(CH₃SO₂Cl)→

(r) [1-bromopentane, Br] →(KCN, DMF)→

(s) [aniline, NH₂] →(TsCl, aq. NaOH)→

(t) [N-methylpiperidinone, O, N–Me] →(1. LiAlH₄, THF 2. aq. NaOH)→

(u) [aniline, NH₂] →(1. NaNO₂, HCl 2. H₂O, reflux)→

(v) [1-bromohexane, Br] →(1. NaN₃, THF 2. LiAlH₄, THF 3. aq. NaOH)→

(w) [aniline, NH₂] →(1. Ac₂O 2. AlCl₃, butanoyl chloride 3. saponification)→

(x) [benzene ring]—NO₂ $\xrightarrow{\text{1. LiAlH}_4\text{ , ether}}$ (y) [benzene ring]—N₂⁺Cl⁻ $\xrightarrow{\text{CuBr}}$
      2. aq. NaOH

(z) [benzene ring with C₄H₉ and NO₂] $\xrightarrow{\text{1. H}_2\text{ , Pd-C}}$ (aa) [benzene ring with Me, OMe, Me] $\xrightarrow{\text{PhN}_2^+\ \text{Cl}^-}$
      2. Ac₂O , pyridine

(ab) [pyridine ring] $\xrightarrow{\text{Br}_2\text{ , AcOH}}$ (ac) [pyrrole ring with Me groups and N-Me] $\xrightarrow{\text{Cl}_2\text{ , AcOH}}$

(ad) [N-Me pyrrole ring] $\xrightarrow{\text{HNO}_3\text{ , AcOH}}$ (ae) [pyridine ring] $\xrightarrow{\text{AlCl}_3\text{ , Cl}_2}$

7. In each case provide a suitable synthesis. Show all reagents and intermediate products.

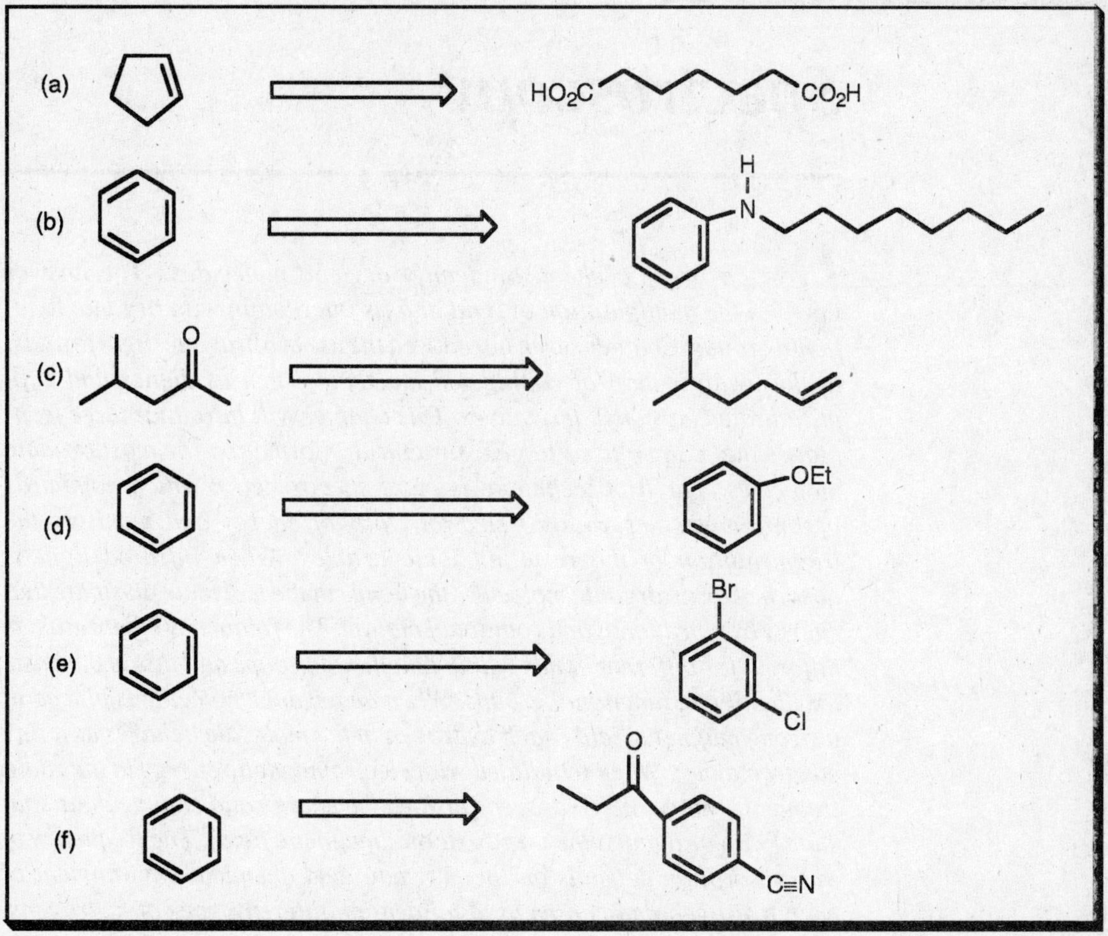

(a)

(b)

(c)

(d)

(e)

(f)

17

Spectroscopy

---

*H*ow do organic chemists identify organic molecules? The answer involves the manipulation of light and its interaction with organic functional groups. Chapter seven introduced the use of ultraviolet light to assist in the identification of conjugated molecules such as dienes and α,β-unsaturated carbonyl derivatives. This chapter will introduce three techniques that can be used to give structural information for most organic molecules. The first technique is mass spectrometry, which bombards organic molecules with 70 electron volts of energy and monitors the fragmentation of the resulting ionic articles. When infrared light is absorbed by an organic molecule, the bonds in the molecule dissipate that energy by vibrational and rotational motion. The frequency of vibration is different for different bonds within functional groups and this is the basis for identifying functional groups. When an organic molecule is placed in a strong magnetic field , each hydrogen in the molecule behaves as a tiny electromagnet. When irradiated with electromagnetic energy in the radio frequency range, the hydrogens absorb the energy and change their spin state (with or against the large external magnetic field). The frequency of this absorption depends on the magnetic and chemical environment of each hydrogen and can be used to identify different types of hydrogens. These three techniques can be used to identify the structure of an organic molecule.

17.1. THE ELECTROMAGNETIC SPECTRUM

WHAT IS THE ELECTROMAGNETIC SPECTRUM?

The electromagnetic spectrum is simply the range of energies associated with various forms of 'light'. This includes not only ultraviolet, visible and infrared light but also low energy microwaves and high energy x-rays and cosmic rays.

A simplified version of the electromagnetic spectrum is shown in both wavelength (in meters, m) and frequency (in hertz, ν).

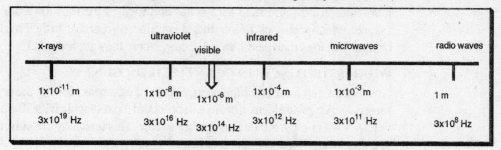

WHAT IS THE RELATIONSHIP BETWEEN WAVELENGTH (λ) AND FREQUENCY (ν)?

They are inversely proportional, by the equation $c = \nu\lambda$, where c is the speed of light (3 x 10^8 m/sec). In general, a high frequency is related to a small wavelength.

WHICH IS HIGHER IN ENERGY, INFRARED OR ULTRAVIOLET LIGHT?

High energy is associated with a high frequency (low wavelength) and low energy is associated with low frequency (high wavelength). Since ultraviolet light has a lower frequency than infrared light, UV light is higher in energy. Similarly, x-rays are very high energy radiation and radiowaves are very low energy radiation.

AT WHAT WAVELENGTHS DO MOLECULES ABSORB INFRARED LIGHT?

The general absorption frequency range for organic molecules is 2.5×10^{-6} m to 16×10^{-6} m. Since an angstrom (Å) is 1×10^{-8} meters, infrared light absorbs in the range 2500-1600 Å.

ARE RADIO WAVES MORE OR LESS ENERGETIC THAN INFRARED LIGHT?

Radio waves are much lower in energy than infrared light.

17.2. MASS SPECTROMETRY

Theory

THE MASS SPECTROMETER

WHAT IS A MASS SPECTROMETER?

A mass spectrometer is an instrument that bombards an organic molecule (or any other molecule) with high energy electrons to ionize the molecule (usually to a radical cation although other ions can also be produced under the proper conditions). Usually, the initially formed ion fragments into other (smaller) mass ions. An electric field accelerates and focuses the ions toward a large magnet, which separates the ions that are produced according to their mass and charge. The ions then pass into a detector, where they are recorded.

WHAT IS THE FUNCTION OF AN ELECTRON GUN?

An electron gun focuses a high energy beam of electrons towards the organic molecule. A typical electron beam will bombard the molecule with 70 electron volts (eV) of energy, although this is adjustable. This is usually enough energy to cause ionization and fragmentation.

HOW MANY KILOCALORIES CORRELATE WITH ONE ELECTRON VOLT (EV)?

One electron volt is equivalent to 22.85 (about 23) kcal/mole of energy.

WHAT IS THE PURPOSE OF THE MAGNETIC FIELD PORTION OF THE MASS SPECTROMETER?

The ion produced by electron bombardment is accelerated by the applied voltage and passes into a strong magnetic field. The magnetic field deflects the flight path of the ion. 'Heavy' ions are deflected most for a given magnetic field strength and a given velocity, whereas 'light' ions are deflected least. Ions that are too heavy or too light will not traverse the instrument but will "crash" into its sides and be lost (not detected). By adjusting both the magnetic field and accelerating voltage, this separation of 'heavy' and 'light' can be refined to separate ions differing by fractions of a mass unit.

ELECTRON IMPACT MASS SPECTROMETRY

HOW ARE MOLECULAR IONS ACCELERATED IN THE MASS SPEC-TROMETER?

If a positively charged ion is forced into a chamber that is positively charged, the electronic repulsion will accelerate the ion out of the chamber.

WHAT IS THE GENERAL RESULT OF A MOLECULE BEING BOMBARDED WITH HIGH ENERGY ELECTRONS?

The high energy electron will expel an electron from the molecule, forming a radical cation (*17.1*). In this example, 2-pentanone is bombarded with an electron beam, expelling one electron (probably from oxygen) and leaving a positively charged oxygen atom that also has an unshared electron. This ion is a radical cation.

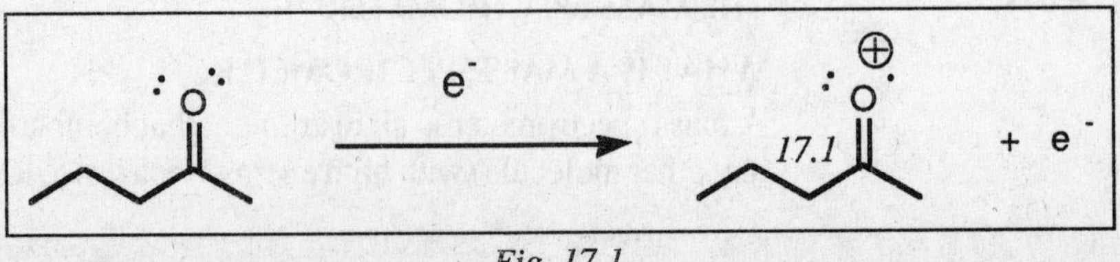

Fig. 17.1

The Parent Ion

When a molecule is bombarded with electrons, an electron is ejected form the molecule to form a radial cation. This initial product has the same mass as the parent molecule that was introduced into the mass spectrometer and is called the *parent ion*.

FORMATION OF THE PARENT

HOW IS A PARENT ION FORMED?

Ion *17.1* is an example of a parent ion. It is formed by ejection of a single electron from the molecule to form the radical cation.

WHAT IS THE SIGNIFICANCE OF THE PARENT ION?

The parent ion has the same mass as the neutral molecule, *if* the charge of the ion is +1. The unit of measure used for the mass is actually m/z (m = mass, z = charge). Mass spectrometry and identification of the parent ion therefore allows determination of the molecular weight of the molecule.

WHAT UNIT IS USED TO IDENTIFY THE PARENT ION IN MASS SPECTROMETRY?

The mass to charge ratio, m/z.

ISOTOPES

WHAT ARE THE NATURAL ABUNDANCE ISOTOPIC RATIOS OF ^2H, ^{13}C, ^{34}S, ^{18}O, ^{37}Cl, ^{15}N AND ^{81}Br?

For deuterium (^2H) the natural abundance is 0.015%; ^{13}C is 1.11%; ^{34}S is 4.22%; ^{18}O is 0.204%; ^{37}Cl is 24.47% and ^{81}Br is 49.46%.

FOR A GIVEN ORGANIC MOLECULE, WHAT IS THE NATURAL % OF DEUTERIUM AND ^{13}C IN THE MOLECULE?

In organic molecules composed of carbon and hydrogen, the 'hydrogen' atoms in that molecule are actually a mixture of 99.985% ^1H and 0.015% of ^2H. Similarly, the carbon atoms are a mixture of 98.89% ^{12}C and 1.11% of ^{13}C.

IF THE PARENT ION INCLUDES A DEUTERIUM, WHAT IS THE M/Z VALUE FOR THAT FRAGMENT?

The m/z value will be the parent m/z + 1. If the parent m/z is 90 without ^2H it is 91 with ^2H.

THE P+1 AND P+2 FRAGMENTS

IF THE PARENT ION REPRESENTS THE MOLECULAR WEIGHT, WHY ARE THERE FRAGMENTS WITH M/Z OF P+1 AND P+2 (P=PARENT)?

The parent ion is due to a molecule containing only atoms of the highest natural abundance. These are the isotope peaks that arise from small amounts of ^{13}C, ^{15}N and ^2H. All three of these isotopes contribute to the parent ion + 1. The isotope of oxygen (^{18}O) will contribute to the parent ion + 2.

WHAT IS THE SIGNIFICANCE OF THE P+1 FRAGMENT?

Since the isotopic ratios of $^{12}C/^{13}C$, $^{2}H/^{1}H$ and $^{15}N/^{14}N$ are fixed, The ratio of the P+1 to the P (parent) ion allows calculation of the number of carbons and nitrogens in the parent ion. The isotopic ratio of deuterium is so small that calculation of the number of hydrogens is not useful by this method.

WHAT IS THE SIGNIFICANCE OF THE P+2 FRAGMENT?

Since the isotopic ratios of $^{18}O/^{16}O$, $^{34}S/^{32}S$, $^{37}Cl/^{35}Cl$ and $^{81}Br/^{79}Br$ are fixed, the P+2 ion can be used to calculate the number of oxygens, sulfur, chorine and bromine atoms in the molecular ion.

DETERMINATION OF MOLECULAR FORMULA

BASED ON THE ISOTOPIC RATIOS OF ATOMS, HOW CAN THE P+1 FRAGMENT BE USED TO CALCULATE THE NUMBER OF CARBONS AND NITROGEN ATOMS IN THE MOLECULE?

The ratio %P+1 to %P can be used to determine the formula:

$$P+1 = \left[\frac{\#C}{1.11}\right] + 0.37\,(\#N).$$

If the ratio of P/P+1 is 6.66% this implies a total of 6 carbons. Important in this calculation is an estimation of the number of nitrogens. If the molecular weight is *odd*, the molecule must contain an *odd* number of nitrogens (1,3,5,7,.....) and the first assumption is the presence of 1 nitrogen rather than 3 or more. If the molecular weight is *even*, the molecule must contain an *even* number of nitrogens (0,2,4,6,8,......). The first assumption is that there are zero nitrogens rather than 2. If the molecular weight is 100, one assumes #N = 0, and if the P+1 is 6.66% of P, the are 6 carbons in the molecule.

In these calculations, the parent is assumed to be 100% and the P+1 is some % of P.

HOW CAN THE P+2 FRAGMENT BE USED TO CALCULATE THE NUMBER OF OXYGENS IN THE MOLECULE?

The isotopic ratios lead to the formula

$$P+2 = \left[\frac{\{[\#C][1.11]\}^2}{200}\right] + 0.20\,(\#O).$$

The first term is the contribution of naturally occurring tritium (^{3}H) and the second term is due to isotopic oxygen. This formula could be extended to include ....+ 4.22 (#S) + 24.47 (#Cl) + 100 (#Br) but these terms are usually omitted since the calculation is relatively obvious and all of these terms are sufficiently large that they will 'swamp out' the smaller number for oxygen. For a molecule with a molecular weight of 100, the P+1 term indicates 6 carbons and the P+2 term is measured to be 0.42. For 6 carbons, the first term is 0.22 and solving for #O leads to one (1) oxygen. The formula will therefore be C_6O. *The hydrogens must be calculated by difference with the molecular ion.* The mass of the C_6O fragment is 88 and $100 - 88 = 12$. These are assumed to be H atoms. The formula will therefore be $C_6H_{12}O$.

IF AN ORGANIC MOLECULE CONTAINS AN ODD NUMBER OF NITROGEN ATOMS, WILL THE MOLECULAR WEIGHT BE EVEN OR ODD? WHAT IS THE SIGNIFICANCE OF THIS OBSERVATION?

With an odd number of nitrogens, the molecular weight will also be odd. The allows one to estimate the number of nitrogens in the P+1 term. Molecules with 3 or more nitrogens are somewhat rare in this case and one assumes that a molecule with an odd mass will have one (1) nitrogen. Likewise, a molecule with an even number of nitrogens will have an even mass. Since molecules with or more nitrogens are somewhat unusual in this case (the presence of 2 nitrogens are common however) one assumes either zero (0) or two (2) nitrogens. For simple molecular weights, always assume zero nitrogens in that first calculation (it should *always* be checked, however).

IF THE P+1 PEAK IS 13.69% OF THE PARENT AND THE P+2 PEAK IS 1.09% OF THE PARENT, WHAT IS THE EMPIRICAL FORMULA OF A MOLECULE WITH A MOLECULAR ION M/Z OF 191?

The odd mass suggests one (1) nitrogen. Using the P+1 formula, one nitrogen leads to P+1 = (13.69 - 0.37)/1.11 = 12 C. Using the P+2 formula for C_{12}, P+2 = (1.09-0.89)/0.2 = 1 O. The partial formula is, therefore, $C_{12}NO$ (mass = 174). The number of hydrogens are calculated by 191-174 = 7H and the final formula is $C_{12}H_{17}NO$.

GIVEN THE APPROPRIATE P+1 AND P+2 RATIOS, CALCULATE THE EMPIRICAL FORMULA FOR EACH OF THE FOLLOWING.

(a) P+1 = 9.99, P+2 = 0.50; (b) P+1 = 7.77, P+2 = 0.50; (c) P+1 = 9.25, P+2 = 0.39; (d) P+1 = 10.36, P+2 = 0.70.

The formula for (a) is C_9H_{20}; (b) is $C_7H_{14}O$; (c) is $C_8H_{19}N$; (d) is $C_9H_{11}NO$.

WHAT IS THE SIGNIFICANCE OF A P+2 PEAK THAT IS 25-33% OF THE PARENT?

This is a clear indication that there is one chlorine in the molecule. The [37]Cl isotope is about 25-33% of the [35]Cl peak.

WHAT IS THE SIGNIFICANCE OF A P+2 PEAK THAT IS 100% OF THE PARENT?

This is a clear indication that there is one bromine in the molecule (the [79]Br and [81]Br isotopes have about the same abundance.

WHAT IS THE SIGNIFICANCE OF A P+2 PEAK THAT IS ABOUT 4-5% OF THE PARENT?

This is consistent with one sulfur in the molecule where the [34]S is about 4% of the [32]S.

Fragmentation of the Parent

DOES THE PARENT ION REMAIN INTACT OR DOES IT FRAGMENT INTO SMALLER FRAGMENTS? EXPLAIN.

In general, the 70 eV ion beam contains enough energy to cause the molecular ion (parent ion) to fragment into smaller radical cations. Each of these fragmentation ions can be accelerated and separated by the mass spectrometer and detected.

WHAT ARE THE SMALLER FRAGMENT IONS CALLED?

Daughter ions.

THE MASS SPECTRUM

WHAT IS A MASS SPECTRUM?

A mass spectrum is the plot of m/z ions as a function of the abundance of those ions. The abundance is usually taken as the ratio of each ion to the most abundant ion but it does not have to be done this way. A typical mass spectrum is shown in *17.2*.

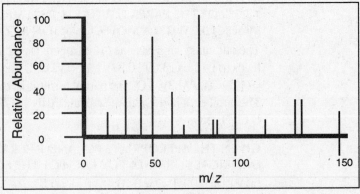

Fig. 17.2

WHAT PEAKS IN THE MASS SPECTRUM ARE TAKEN TO BE THE MOST IMPORTANT?

The parent ion (along with the P+1 and P+2 peaks if they are strong enough) and the most abundant ion, which is called the base peak. In spectrum 17.2, the base peak (B) appears at about 75-80 (obviously this will be determined exactly) and the parent ion will be the highest mass ion (in this case m/z = 150). Other important peaks will be those ion fragments that give structural information, but this will vary with the molecule.

WHAT IS THE MOST CONVENIENT WAY TO SHOW THE RELATIONSHIP OF A FRAGMENT ION TO THE PARENT ION?

The easiest method is to report both the m/z value and also the *difference in m/z* between the daughter ion of interest and the parent. This is reported as P-? (P-15, P-28, P-56, etc.).

WHAT IS THE BASE PEAK?

The base peak is that daughter ion (sometimes it is also the parent) that has the highest abundance (more ions of this m/z migrate through the machine and are recorded by the detector). Often this represents the most stable ion or the lowest energy fragmentation mode.

WHAT IS THE EXPECTED MASS SPECTRUM FOR A LONG CHAIN ALKANE?

The mass spectrum of a long chain alkane such as decane will look something like the spectrum *17.3*. In general, it will show a weak parent ion since there is extensive fragmentation. There is a consistent pattern of P–CH_2 (P-14) for cleavage of each C–C bond. This leads to a characteristic pattern where the higher mass fragments show very low abundance and the lower mass fragments are prominent (m/z 85, 71, 57, 43 and 29 usually show up in the mass spectrum of a linear alkane).

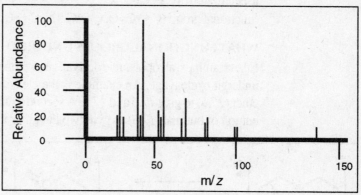

Fig. 17.3

IMPORTANT FRAGMENTATIONS

WHAT FRAGMENT IS ASSOCIATED WITH A P-15 PEAK? P-29? P-43?

A P-15 fragment is usually associated with loss of methyl (-CH_3), P-29 with loss of ethyl (-CH_2CH_3) and P-43 is loss of C_3H_7 which could be isopropyl or *n*-propyl.

WHAT DAUGHTER ION IS ASSOCIATED WITH M/Z = 91 IN MOLECULES CONTAINING A BENZYL GROUP?

This ion is usually the tropylium ion (*17.4*), which is very stable and very prominent. The presence of this daughter ion is usually taken as evidence for the presence of a benzyl group in the molecule.

WHAT IS A P-1 FRAGMENT ASSOCIATED WITH?

A P-1 peak is usually loss of a single hydrogen (loss of H from N–H in an amine, for example).

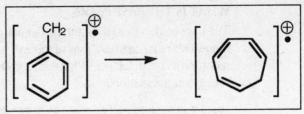

Fig. 17.4

SUGGEST POSSIBLE STRUCTURES FOR M/Z = 57.

A daughter ion with m/z of 57 is probably C_4H_9. This could be *n*-butyl, isobutyl, *sec*-butyl or *t*-butyl, pointing up the ambiguity of assigning specific structures via mass spectrometry based only on fragmentation of the molecular ion.

WHAT IS α-CLEAVAGE?

The fragmentation of an ion at the bond between a carbon and a carbon bearing a heteroatom (C↔C–O, C↔C–S, C↔C–N) or between a carbon and a functional group (C↔C=O, C↔C≡N, C↔CO₂R, etc) is called α-cleavage.

WHAT FUNCTIONAL GROUPS UNDERGO α-CLEAVAGE?

Ethers, amines, alcohols, acid derivatives, ketones and aldehydes and nitriles all undergo α-cleavage. An example is the cleavage of the parent ion of diethyl ether (*17.5*) to give *17.6* and *17.7*. A second example is the cleavage of the parent ion of butanal (*17.8*) to give two daughter ions, *17.9* and *17.10*.

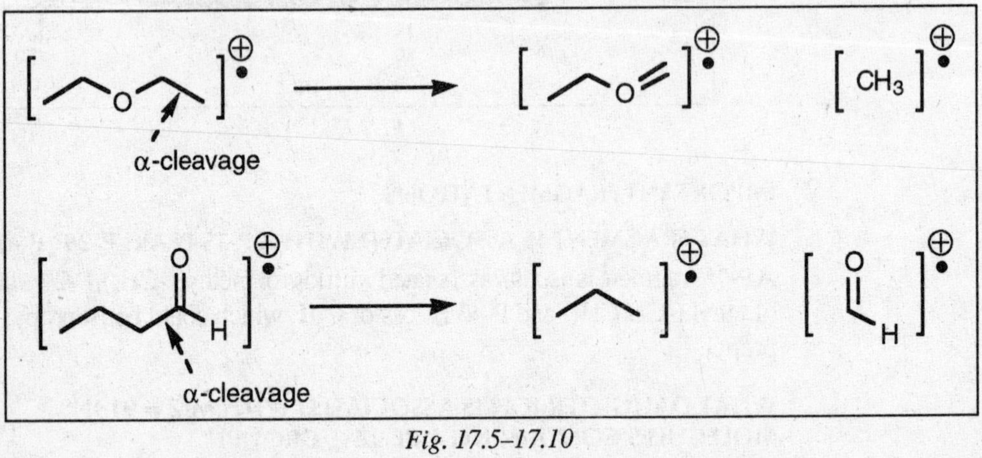

Fig. 17.5–17.10

WHY DOES AN ALCOHOL USUALLY EXHIBIT A P-18 FRAGMENT?

A mass of 18 corresponds to water and P-18 is characteristic of a molecule that loses a molecule of water (dehydration). Under ion bombardment, most alcohols readily lose water from the parent ion. Usually, the parent ion is not observed at all and the first ion actually observed in significant concentration is the P-18 daughter ion.

WHAT IS A MCLAFFERTY REARRANGEMENT?

A McLafferty rearrangement occurs in aldehydes and ketones that have a hydrogen attached to a γ-carbon (the γ-carbon is the third carbon away from a carbonyl, C–C–C–C=O). In a typical example, the hydrogen is transferred to oxygen via a 6-centered transition state (see *17.11*) to form a neutral alkene and an enol daughter ion (*17.12*).

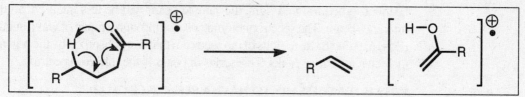

Fig. 17.11, 17.12

SHOW A MCLAFFERTY REARRANGEMENT FOR 2-HEXANONE.

The McLafferty rearrangement for this ion is shown in the conversion of *17.13* to *17.14*.

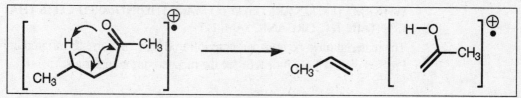

Fig. 17.13, 17.14

17.3. INFRARED SPECTROSCOPY

Theory

INFRARED RADIATION

WHAT IS THE WAVELENGTH RANGE FOR INFRARED LIGHT IN THE ELECTROMAGNETIC SPECTRUM?

Infrared radiation appears at 7.8×10^{-7} m to 1×10^{-4} m (78Å to $10,000$Å). This also can be converted to 7.8×10^{-5} cm to 1×10^{-2} cm (in wavelength) or 0.78 μm to 100 μm (where a μm is 10^{-4} cm or 10^{-6} meters -*usually abbreviated as* μ, or microns). The wavelength (λ) unit is, therefore, mm. This energy range can also be expressed in frequency ($\tilde{v}$) where the unit is cm⁻¹ (reciprocal centimeters or *wavenumbers*). The frequency range for infrared radiation is 12821 cm⁻¹ to 100 cm⁻¹ (1.282-0.01 μ).

WHAT WAVELENGTH RANGE IS USED IN INFRARED SPECTROSCOPY?

In most infrared spectrophotometers, the infrared radiation is measured between *4000-625 cm⁻¹* or 2.5-16 μ. Most organic molecules absorb infrared radiation in this energy range.

THE INFRARED SPECTROMETER

DESCRIBE HOW AN INFRARED SPECTROPHOTOMETER WORKS.

Infrared light is directed towards a prism and split into two equal parts. These two beams are focused by a mirror system, one passing through the sample and the other through a reference cell. The beams are refocused with mirrors and another prism and the two are compared. If an organic molecule in the sample beam absorbed infrared light, the sample beam will be less intense than the reference beam. The spectrophotometer scans through a range of wavelengths (2.5-16 μ) and those regions of the spectrum that were absorbed by the organic molecule appear as peaks. This series of peaks is the infrared spectrum.

WHY IS IT NECESSARY TO HAVE A REFERENCE CELL?

It is essential to compare the amount of light directed at the sample (incident radiation) with the amount of infrared radiation after absorption by the sample. Comparison of the two signals allows the instrument to determine how much infrared light was absorbed.

WHAT MATERIALS ARE USED TO MAKE THE INFRARED CELLS THAT CONTAIN THE ORGANIC SAMPLE?

The material must be transparent to infrared light (not absorb infrared light). Pressed plates of NaCl or KBr are the most common materials.

Absorption of Infrared light

VIBRATIONAL TRANSITIONS

WHEN AN ORGANIC MOLECULE ABSORBS INFRARED LIGHT, WHAT HAPPENS TO THE MOLECULE?

If a molecule absorbs infrared light, this excess energy is dissipated by molecular vibrations. Bending and stretching vibrations are the most common. There are symmetric and asymmetric stretching vibrations as well as symmetric and asymmetric bending vibrations (both 'in plane' and 'out of plane'). These vibrations occur at different infrared frequencies (wavelengths) and lead to the various 'peaks' in the infrared spectrum.

HOW DOES A CHANGE IN DIPOLE MOMENT FOR A BOND INFLUENCE INFRARED ABSORPTION?

If the dipole moment of a bond changes during a bending or stretching vibration, that absorption is particularly strong. The larger the change in dipole moment, the stronger the absorption. If the vibration is not accompanied by a change in dipole moment, it is usually a very weak absorption. When a symmetrical bond (such as C–C) vibrates, the infrared absorption is very weak. The C–C signal in the infrared is very weak (essentially non-existent).

WHAT TYPES OF BONDS ARE EXPECTED TO GIVE STRONG INFRARED SIGNALS? WEAK INFRARED SIGNALS?

Bonds with significant dipole moments will give strong signals in the infrared. Examples are O–H, C–O, C=O, N–H, Cl–C=O and N–C=O which will usually give strong signals. Bonds that give weak signals are C–C, O–O and N–N. Interestingly, the C–H signal is relatively strong.

HOOK'S LAW

WHAT IS HOOK'S LAW?

Hook's Law is an equation that describes the vibrational frequency of two masses connected by a spring. The frequency of the vibration is a function of both the mass of the two objects connected to the spring as well as the strength of the spring. This is an excellent model for predicting vibrational frequencies of two atoms connected by a bond capable of vibrational motion. Hook's Law is:

$$\tilde{v} = \left(\frac{1}{2\pi c} \right) \sqrt{\frac{k}{m}}$$

where c = speed of light = 3×10^{10} cm sec^{-1}; k = force constant (a parameter to describe the tightness of the spring) and m = mass. For organic molecules, the *reduced mass* is used

$$\mu = \left(\frac{mM}{m + M} \right)$$

since the small mass of both atoms are close in magnitude.

IF HOOK'S LAW IS USED TO DESCRIBE TWO MASSES CONNECTED BY A SPRING, DESCRIBE THE RELEVANCE OF THIS LAW TO A COVALENT BOND.

Two atoms function as masses and the covalent bond functions as a spring. As the bond strength (force constant) increases, the vibrational frequency is lower whereas a weaker bond leads to a higher vibrational frequency. As the two atoms change, of course, there will also be differences in the frequency.

AS A BOND GETS STRONGER, IS THE WAVELENGTH OF INFRARED ABSORPTION EXPECTED TO INCREASE OR DECREASE?

A stronger bond absorbs infrared light at a lower frequency (higher wavelength). A comparison of the C $\equiv$ C bond with the C=C bond reveals that C $\equiv$ C absorbs at 2100-2260 cm^{-1} (4.76-4.42 μ), at higher frequency (higher energy) than the absorption for C=C at 1650-1670 cm^{-1} (6.06-5.99 μ).

WHICH IS ASSOCIATED WITH HIGHER ENERGY, HIGH INFRARED WAVELENGTH OR LOWER INFRARED WAVELENGTH?

Since short wavelengths are generally of higher energy, a low infrared wavelength (2.0-4.0 μ for example as compared to 11-14 μ) will be of higher energy. Analysis of the triple bond vs. the double bond shows this to be true. It takes more energy to make the stronger C $\equiv$ C bond vibrate than it does for the weaker C=C bond.

WHAT IS THE REDUCED MASS FOR A C–O BOND?

$$\text{Reduced mass} = \frac{mM}{m+M}$$

where m is the mass of the smaller atom (C) and M is the mass of the larger atom (O). It is important to remember that this is the mass of the individual atom, *not* the atomic mass for a mole of the atom. This mass is the atomic weight divided by Avagadro's number. For C,

$$m = \frac{12.00}{6.023 \times 10^{23}} = 1.992 \times 10^{-23}$$

and for O,

$$M = \frac{15.9994}{6.023 \times 10^{23}} = 2.656 \times 10^{-23}.$$

With these masses, the reduced mass is

$$\frac{\left[1.992 \times 10^{-23}\right]\left[2.656 \times 10^{-23}\right]}{1.992 \times 10^{-23} + 2.656 \times 10^{-23}} = \frac{5.29 \times 10^{-46}}{4.648 \times 10^{-23}} = 1.14 \times 10^{-23}.$$

THE INFRARED SPECTRUM

WHAT IS AN INFRARED SPECTRUM?

An infrared spectrum is the plot of either absorbance or % transmittance as a function of wavelength and/or frequency. When an organic molecule absorbs infrared energy of a particular wavelength, it will appear as a 'peak'. If the signal absorbs a large amount of infrared radiation it will show as a strong absorption (weak % transmittance) and if little energy is absorbed the peak will show a small absorption (large % transmittance).

WHAT LABELS ARE APPLIED TO THE AXES OF AN INFRARED SPECTRUM?

Most infrared spectrophotometers are calibrated in % transmittance with the scale linear in frequency (cm^{-1}). The wavelength scale (μ) is also shown on the spectrum, *17.15*.

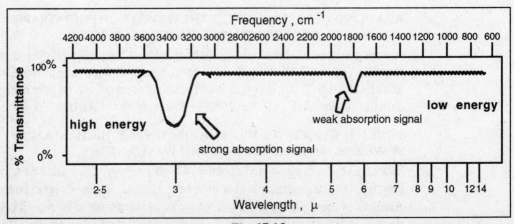

Fig. 17.15

WHAT IS BEERS LAW?

The most common form of Beer's Law (actually the *Beer-Lambert Law*) is:

$$T = \frac{I}{I_o}$$

where T = % transmittance. Absorbance (A) is related to T by: $A = -\log_{10}(T)$ and $T = 10^{-A}$. In this equation, I = intensity of the sample beam and I_o is the intensity of the incident (reference) beam.

IS 90%T ASSOCIATED WITH A STRONG SIGNAL OR A WEAK SIGNAL?

If 90% of the light is transmitted, only 10% was absorbed so this is a weak signal.

IS 70% A ASSOCIATED WITH A STRONG SIGNAL OR A WEAK SIGNAL?

If 70% of the light was absorbed this is a strong signal.

WHAT IS THE RELATIONSHIP BETWEEN WAVELENGTH AND FREQUENCY?

They are inversely proportional:

$$v = \left(cm^{-1}\right) = \frac{10000}{\lambda(\mu)}$$

WHAT UNITS ARE USED FOR WAVELENGTH IN INFRARED SPECTROSCOPY?

Wavelength (λ) uses microns (μ) as the basic unit ($1\,\mu = 1\times10^{-4}$ cm).

WHAT UNITS ARE USED FOR FREQUENCY IN INFRARED SPECTROSCOPY?

Frequency (v) uses reciprocal centimeters as the unit (cm^{-1}).

IS 700 CM⁻¹ ASSOCIATED WITH HIGH ENERGY OR LOWER ENERGY?

An infrared absorption at 700 cm^{-1} is at the low energy end of the spectrum and would be associated with a weaker bond.

IS 3.45 μ ASSOCIATED WITH HIGH ENERGY OR LOW ENERGY?

This is a short wavelength absorption and is, therefore, higher in energy.

WHICH IS THE LOWER ENERGY ABSORPTION, 10.57 μ OR 2335 CM⁻¹?

An absorption at 10.57 μ is equivalent to 946 cm^{-1}. This signal is much lower in energy than the signal at 2335 cm^{-1}.

The Functional Group Region

WHY IS AN O-H GROUP EXPECTED TO ABSORB IN GENERALLY THE SAME REGION OF THE INFRARED, REGARDLESS OF WHAT ELSE IN THE MOLECULE?

Infrared spectroscopy focuses on the vibrations of individual bonds. The O–H bond will give stretching and bending vibrations characteristic of the strength of that bond and the masses of O and H. Electronic effects will clearly play a role but the fundamental absorption frequency will be generally the same for all molecules containing an OH group. This absorption appears at 3400-3640 cm^{-1} (or at 2.94-2.75 μ as a strong, broad signal).

WHICH IS EXPECTED TO ABSORB AT HIGHER ENERGY, AN O–H GROUP OR A C–H GROUP? EXPLAIN.

The bond dissociation energy for O–H (from methanol) is 102 kcal/mol and the bond dissociation energy for C–H (from methane) is 104 kcal/mole. They are obviously rather close and bond dissociation energy does not provide an answer. Using Hook's Law, the greater mass of oxygen, relative to carbon, might be expected to push the OH absorption to higher energy. The OH absorbs at 3400-3640 cm^{-1} and C–H generally absorbs at 2850-2960 cm^{-1} (3.51-3.38 m) making the OH signal the higher energy. The O–H bond is significantly more polarized than the C–H bond and should, therefore, give a much stronger absorption. In fact, the OH absorption is very strong (usually 0-10%T) and quite broad. Hydrogen bonding will increase the relative bond polarity of the O–H and the more extensive the hydrogen bonding the broader the signal (broad = larger range of infrared absorption frequencies).

WHICH GROUP IS EXPECTED TO GIVE THE LOWEST ENERGY INFRARED ABSORPTION, C–C, C=C OR C≡C? EXPLAIN.

The weakest bond is the C–C bond and it is expected to have the lowest energy absorption. For the C–C bond, this is so weak it is usually not reported, perhaps appearing at 1000-1100 cm^{-1} [10-9 μ]. The C=C bond absorbs at 1650-1670 cm^{-1} [6.06-5.99 μ] and the C≡C bond absorbs at 2100-2260 cm^{-1} [4.76-4.42 μ].

WHAT IS THE 'FUNCTIONAL GROUP REGION' OF THE INFRARED IN BOTH WAVELENGTH AND FREQUENCY?

Most common functional groups (OH, NH, CH, C=O, COOH, C≡C, C≡N) appear at the high energy region of the infrared spectrum, usually between 4000-1400 cm^{-1} (2.5-7.0 μ). This region is called the *functional group region*.

The Fingerprint Region

WHAT IS THE FINGERPRINT REGION OF THE INFRARED?

The low energy portion of the infrared spectrum between 1400-625 cm^{-1} (7.0-16 μ) contains a few functional group absorptions (C=C, C–O, C-halogen, C-aromatic and aromatic carbons) but is usually the region where low energy bending and stretching vibrations absorb. Each individual molecule will have its own peculiar set of bending, stretching, rocking, twisting, and wagging vibrations due to the 'backbone' of the molecule. The combination of these vibrations leads to a 'fingerprint' of the molecule that can often be used to identify a specific molecule by 'matching fingerprints' *if* a library of known compounds is available. This region of the infrared spectrum is generally called the *fingerprint region*.

WHAT IS THE USE OF THE FINGERPRINT REGION?

If there is an unknown organic molecule and you have a 'library' of prerecorded infrared spectra, the fingerprint region can be used to find the proper 'match'. Fingerprinting the molecule in the library allows its identification. Obviously, if your molecule is not in the library, you cannot use this technique to identify it.

WHAT FUNCTIONAL GROUPS APPEAR IN THE FINGERPRINT REGION?

As mentioned above, C=C, C–O, C-halogen and aromatic carbons usually absorb in the fingerprint region of the infrared.

Functional Group Correlation Chart

GIVE GENERIC INFRARED ABSORPTIONS FOR THE FOLLOWING MAJOR FUNCTIONAL GROUPS: A) ALCOHOLS B) KETONES C) ALDEHYDES D) CARBOXYLIC ACIDS E) AMINES F) ESTERS G) AMIDES H) NITRILES I) ALKENES J) ALKYNES K) BENZENE DERIVATIVES L) ETHERS M) ACID CHLORIDES N) ACID ANHYDRIDES O) ALKYL HALIDES.

(a) *alcohols:* $O–H$ [3400-3610 cm^{-1}, 2.94-2.77 μ] and $C–O$ [1050-1150 cm^{-1}, 9.52-8.70 μ]

(b) *ketones:* $C=O$ [1725-1680 cm^{-1}, 5.80-5.95 μ]

(c) *aldehydes:* $C=O$ [1740-1695 cm^{-1}, 5.75-5.90 μ] and O=$C–H$ [2816 cm^{-1}, 3.55 μ]

(d) *carboxylic acids:* O=C–O–H [3300-2500 cm^{-1}, 3.03-4.0 μ], $O=C$–OH [1725-1680 cm^{-1}, 5.80-5.95 μ]

(e) *amines:* 1° amines $N–H$ [3550-3300 cm^{-1} - a doublet of peaks for each N–H, 2.82-3.03 μ] 2° amines $N–H$ [3550-3400 cm^{-1} a single peak for the only N–H, 2.82-2.94 μ]

(f) *esters:* $O=C$–O–C [1780-1715 cm^{-1}, 5.61-5.83 μ], O=C–O–C [1050-1100 cm^{-1}, 9.52-9.09 μ]

(g) *amides:* $O=C$–N– Amide I – 1° [1690 cm^{-1}, 5.92 μ] 2° [1700-1670 cm^{-1}, 5.88-6.00 μ]. The Amide II band is - 1° [1600 cm^{-1}, 6.25 μ] 2° [1550-1510 cm^{-1}, 6.45-6.62 μ]. amide $N–H$ – 1° [3500 cm^{-1}, 2.86 μ], 2° [3460-3400 cm^{-1}, 2.89-2.94 μ]

(h) *nitriles:* $C\equiv N$ [2260-2200 cm^{-1}, 4.42-4.56 μ]

(i) *alkenes:* C=C–H [3040-3010 cm^{-1}, 3.29-3.32 μ]; $C=C$ [this is a relatively weak to moderate signal at 1680-1620 cm^{-1} [5.95-6.17 μ];

(j) *alkynes:* $C\equiv C$–H [3300 cm^{-1}, 3.03 μ], $C\equiv C$ [terminal, 2140-2100 cm^{-1}, 4.67-4.76 μ; nonterminal, 2260-2150 cm^{-1}, 4.42-4.65 μ];

(k) *benzene derivatives:* Ar–H [3040-3010 cm^{-1}, 3.29-3.32 μ], Ar $C=C$ [about 1600 and 1510 cm^{-1}, 6.25 and 6.63 μ]

(l) *ethers:* C–O [1150-1060 and 1140-900 cm^{-1}, 8.70-9.43 and 8.77-11.11 μ];

(m) *acid chlorides:* $O=C$–Cl [1815-1750 cm^{-1}, 5.51-5.71 μ], C–Cl [730-580 cm^{-1}, 13.70-17.24 μ];

(n) *acid anhydrides:* $(O=C)_2O$ [1850-1780 and 1790-1710 cm^{-1}, 5.41-5.62 and 5.59-5.85 μ];

(o) *alkyl halides:* C–Cl [730-605 cm^{-1}, 13.70-16.53], C–Br [645-605 cm^{-1}, 15.50-16.53 μ], C–I [600-560 cm^{-1}, 16.67-17.86 μ].

WHAT IS THE EFFECT OF CONJUGATION ON THE ABSORPTION OF A CARBONYL (COMPARE CYCLOHEXANONE WITH CYCLOHEXENONE)?

In general, conjugation shifts the absorption to longer wavelengths (shorter frequencies)—lower energy. The C=O group of cyclohexanone, for example absorbs at 1725-1705 cm^{-1} [5.80-5.87 μ] but the conjugated C=O group of cyclohexenone will absorb at 1685-1665 cm^{-1} [5.93-6.01 μ]. The absorption was shifted to lower energy (longer wavelength) by conjugation.

IDENTIFY EACH OF THE FOLLOWING FUNCTIONAL GROUPS BASED ENTIRELY ON THE PROVIDED MOLECULAR FORMULA AND THE INFRARED SPECTRUM.

(a) C_4H_8O.

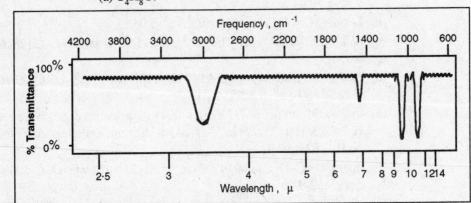

(b) $C_6H_{12}O_2$.

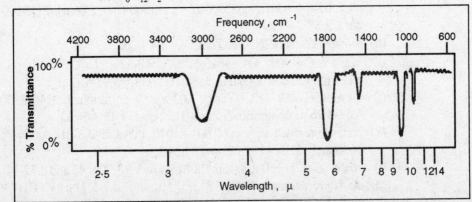

(c) $C_4H_{10}O$.

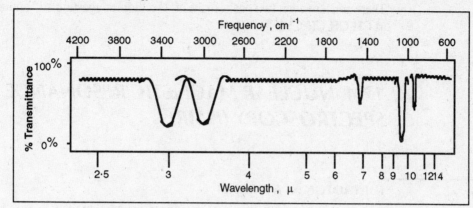

(d) $C_5H_{13}N$.

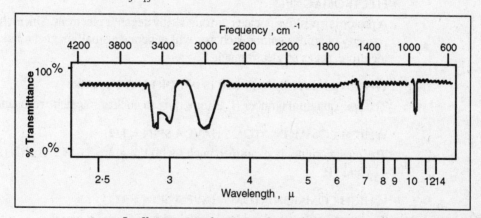

In all cases note the strong absorption at 2850 cm⁻¹ (3.50 μ). This absorption almost always appears but is not due to a functional group. It is the C–H absorption and does not give useful information about structure, unless it is absent. In infrared (a), the molecule has only one oxygen, limiting the functional group choices to a ketone or aldehyde, an ether or an alcohol. There is no O–H absorption nor is there a C=O absorption. This molecule is, therefore, likely to be an ether such as $CH_2CH_2OCH_2CH_3$. Infrared (b) has two oxygens, expanding the possible choices to include carboxylic acids and esters. The molecule has a strong C=O absorption that could be an aldehyde, ketone acid or ester. With two oxygens there would have to be two aldehyde units, two ketone units or one aldehyde and one ketone. There is also a strong band in the 8-10 micron region suggesting a C–O bond and there is no O–H. This molecule is probably an ester such as ethly butanoate. In (c) there is a strong O–H absorption and no C=O. There is also the C–O band and with only one oxygen, this molecule is likely to be an alcohol such as 1-butanol. In (d), the molecule contains one nitrogen and could be an amine or a nitrile. There is no CN absorption and the molecule cannot be a nitrile. If it is an amine, there are three choices, 1°, 2° or 3°. If it were a 3° amine, there would be *no* N–H absorption. There are, however, two peaks in the N–H region, suggesting a 1° amine such as $CH_3CH_2CH_2CH_2CH_2NH_2$.

17.4. NUCLEAR MAGNETIC RESONANCE SPECTROSCOPY (NMR)

Theory

THE PROTON AS A MAGNET

WHY CAN A PROTON BE CONSIDERED TO BE A SMALL ELECTROMAGNET?

A proton is a positive nucleus surrounded by negative electrons. Since it has the property of spin, a spinning charge will generate a small magnetic field and, therefore, act as an electromagnet.

WHAT QUANTUM NUMBER IS IMPORTANT IN NMR?

The spin quantum number (I) is important to nuclear magnetic resonance.

WHICH COMMON ATOMS HAVE A SPIN = 1/2?

The most commonly examined nuclei with $I = \frac{1}{2}$ are ^1H, ^{13}C, ^{19}F, ^{15}N (spin = $-\frac{1}{2}$) and ^{31}P.

WHICH COMMON ATOMS HAVE A SPIN = 1?

The most commonly examined nuclei with $I = 1$ are ^2H and ^6Li.

WHICH COMMON ATOMS HAVE NO SPIN?

Many nuclei commonly found in organic molecules have no spin ($I = 0$) and can *not* be used in an NMR experiment. The most common are ^{12}C, ^{16}O and ^{32}S.

INFLUENCE OF AN EXTERNAL MAGNET

WHAT EFFECT DOES A LARGE EXTERNAL MAGNET HAVE ON THE SMALL MAGNETIC PROTON?

The spin of the small magnet (the proton) can be aligned in parallel (with) the external magnetic field or can be opposed to it (see *17.16*). When the proton field is aligned opposite the external field, it requires more energy than when it is aligned with the field. This creates an energy gap (ΔE). This energy difference is usually of about the same frequency as radio waves ($\nu = 3 \times 10^6$-3×10^8 Hz).

COMPARE THE INFLUENCE OF A 14,100 GAUSS MAGNET VS A 63450 GAUSS MAGNET ON A PROTON.

When the magnetic field is 14,100 gauss, the ΔE for the proton will be about 60

MHz (5.7×10^{-6} kcal/mole). When the magnet field strength is increased to 63,450 gauss, ΔE for the proton will increase to 270 MHz (25.7×10^{-6} kcal/mol)

IRRADIATION AND ABSORPTION OF A RADIO SIGNAL

WHAT IS THE ENERGY RANGE OF THE ΔE IMPOSED BY INTRODUCTION OF A PROTON INTO A MAGNETIC FIELD?

This ΔE is in the range of radio waves (1000×10^{-4} - 100000×10^{-4} cm [1000-100000 λ])= 10.0-0.1 cm^{-1}.

WHAT ENERGY SOURCE CAN CAUSE THE PROTON TO ABSORB ENERGY = ΔE?

A radio signal of controlled frequency is directed towards the sample inside the strong magnetic field.

WHAT HAPPENS WHEN A PROTON IN A MAGNETIC FIELD IS BOMBARDED WITH ENERGY EQUAL TO ΔE?

A proton with spin will *absorb* ΔE, and the nuclei will change its spin state (flips its spin state) as outlined in *17.16*.

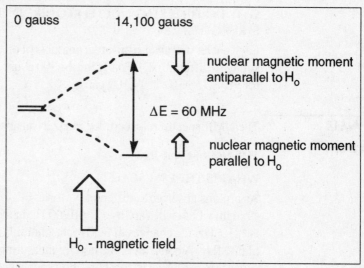

Fig. 17.16

IS THIS AN ABSORPTION OR EMISSION PROCESS?

This is an absorption process.

IS ΔE LARGER OR SMALLER AS THE MAGNETIC FIELD STRENGTH INCREASES?

As the magnetic field strength increases, ΔE will become larger for a given nuclei. IMPORTANT: If the ΔE is kept constant, say at 60 MHz, then the magnetic field strength due to different nuclei (protons in different magnetic environments) will change slightly and these differences can be measured.

THE NMR SPECTROMETER

DESCRIBE HOW AN NMR SPECTROMETER WORKS.

A sample is dissolved in an appropriate solvent and placed in a thin glass tube. This tube is lowered into a magnetic field and spun (to average out inhomogeneous areas in the magnetic field). A radio signal (linked to the magnetic field strength —a 14,100 gauss magnet requires a 60 MHz radio signal for protons to absorb the energy) is applied to the sample. The holder into which the sample tube is lowered is surrounded by a radio generating coil. The radio signal is kept constant and the magnetic field is varied slightly. Those protons that absorb the radio signal at the various magnetic field strengths will be recorded as absorption 'peaks'. The collection of these absorption peaks is the NMR spectrum.

WHAT PROCESS IS EXAMINED IN THE NMR?

The absorption of energy by a nucleus with spin, in a magnetic field. The most commonly examined nuclei are the proton (^{1}H) and ^{13}C. Other nuclei can also be examined, however, including ^{2}H, ^{6}Li, ^{15}N and ^{19}F.

WHY DO DIFFERENT NUCLEI REQUIRE DIFFERENT MAGNETIC FIELD STRENGTHS?

Each nuclei will absorb different amounts of energy for a given magnetic field strength (different ΔE). For ^{1}H in a 14,100 gauss magnet, ΔE is 60 MHz but ΔE for ^{13}C is 15 MHz at 14,100 gauss.

The NMR Spectrum

The NMR spectrum is recorded in Hz as an absorption spectrum.

THE NMR SCALE IN PPM

WHAT IS THE PPM SCALE?

As protons absorb ΔE, different protons will show changes in magnetic field strength which will vary by <1 to 1200 Hz in the 60 MHz field. Since 1 MHz is 1×10^6 Hz, the changes in field represent millionths of the total field strength of 60 MHz. A convenient method for measuring the position of an absorption signal is in Hz. There is a problem, however, since a signal at 60 Hz in a 60 MHz instrument will appear at 300 Hz in a 300 MHz instrument. To consolidate these data, the ppm scale was created. In this scale the absorption signal (in Hz) is divided by the field strength (in MHz). A signal at 60 Hz in a 60 MHz field will then be calculated to be

$$\left(\frac{60 \text{ Hz}}{60 \times 10^6 \text{ Hz}} \right) = 1 \times 10^{-6}$$

or one part-per-million (1 ppm). The same signal at 300 MHz will be

$$\frac{300 \text{ Hz}}{300 \times 10^6 \text{ Hz}} = 1 \times 10^{-6} = 1 \text{ ppm}.$$

In this way absorption signals at different field strengths can be identified as the same signal. This is called the *ppm scale*.

WHY IS A SPECTRUM RECORDED IN PARTS PER MILLION?

When the magnetic field strength changes for a fixed 60 MHz signal, each proton comes into resonance at a slightly different field strength. If the field is changed to a large magnet, the absorption signals will change proportionally. The ppm scale allows the absorption process to be normalized and compared from one machine to another.

IF AN NMR IS RECORDED AT 60 MHZ AND A SIGNAL APPEARS AT 345 HZ, WHAT IS THE ABSORPTION IN PPM?

This signal will appear at

$$\frac{345\,\text{Hz}}{60 \times 10^6\,\text{Hz}} = 5.45\,\text{ppm}.$$

IF A SIGNAL APPEARS AT 4.50 PPM AT 60 MHZ WHERE IS THE SIGNAL, IN PPM, AT 500 MHZ?

The position of the signal in ppm will not change with field strength. This signal will, therefore, also appear at 4.50 ppm at both 500 MHz and at 60 MHz.

IF A SIGNAL APPEARS AT 3.25 PPM AT 60 HZ, WHERE IS THE SIGNAL, IN HZ, AT 400 MHZ?

A signal at 3.25 ppm (3.25×10^{-6}) appears at $3.25 \times 10^{-6} (60 \times 10^6) = 195$ Hz. At 400 MHz, the 3.25 ppm signal appears at $3.25 \times 10^{-6} (400 \times 10^6) = 1300$ Hz.

WHERE IS THE 'ZERO POINT' IN NMR?

The 'zero point' in NMR is the absorption signal for tetramethylsilane (TMS) which is added to the sample. The instrument is adjusted so that the TMS signal is set on zero.

WHAT SOLVENTS ARE USED TO PREPARE SAMPLES IN THE NMR?

Typical solvents are $CDCl_3$, d_6-acetone, D_2O, and d_6-DMSO. Deuterated solvents are used so they will not contribute strong signals in the proton NMR that can obscure sample peaks.

TETRAMETHYLSILANE AS AN INTERNAL STANDARD

WHY IS AN INTERNAL STANDARD USED IN NMR?

There has to be a 'zero point'. Since the absorption peaks are measured in ppm, the scale makes no sense unless there is a point zero of ppm to be used as a reference standard. This must be taken as 0 ppm in all samples under all conditions. All absorption peaks are therefore reported in ppm with reference to the standard. The most common standard in NMR is the chemical tetramethylsilane (TMS).

WHAT IS THE STRUCTURE OF TETRAMETHYLSILANE?

Tetramethylsilane has the structure $(Me_3)_4Si$.

WHY IS TETRAMETHYLSILANE AN IDEAL INTERNAL STANDARD?

Tetramethylsilane absorbs at a position in most magnetic fields at higher energy (higher local field strength) than most protons in most organic molecules. In a typical NMR spectrum (shown in *17.17*) absorptions at higher energy appear on the right hand side of the spectrum and signals of lower field strength appear to the left. The TMS reference signal (assigned 0 ppm) will appear to the far right (high field) and all signals due to the organic sample will appear at lower energy, to its left (downfield). As the absorption position in ppm increase the field strength decreases. This means that a signal at 9 ppm is of lower field strength than a signal at 2 ppm.

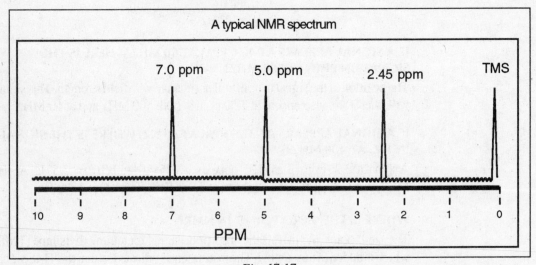

Fig. 17.17

THE SIGNAL FOR TMS APPEARS AT ____ PPM IN THE NMR AT 100 MHZ.

At all field strengths and all radio frequencies, TMS appears at zero (0) ppm since the instrument is adjusted to *make* the signal for TMS = zero.

Chemical Shift

The position of an absorption relative to TMS is referred to as the chemical shift for that signal.

ABSORPTION RELATIVE TO TMS

WHAT IS AN UPFIELD SIGNAL? A DOWNFIELD SIGNAL?

An upfield signal appears at low ppm relative to TMS (close to TMS). A signal at 0.5 ppm is considered to be 'upfield'. A downfield signal appears at larger ppm relative to TMS (the signal at 7.0 ppm in the above spectrum is 'downfield'. These terms can be used in a relative sense. The signal at 5.0 ppm is 'upfield' of the signal at 7.0 ppm. The signal at 5.0 ppm is 'downfield' of the signal at 2.45 ppm.

IS HIGH FIELD ASSOCIATED WITH ABSORPTIONS CLOSER TO 8 PPM OR CLOSER TO 1 PPM?

High field (up field) is associated with signals closer to 1 ppm.

IS THE CHEMICAL SHIFT FOR A GIVEN FUNCTIONAL GROUP AS CONSTANT AS IN INFRARED SPECTROSCOPY?

No. The variations in local structure of a molecule can greatly influence the absorption in ppm. This is because the change in signal relative to the applied field is very small (parts-per-million). Small local variations can lead to changes of 0.5-2.0 ppm (these are arbitrary numbers), which is a significant change in a 10 or 20 ppm scale.

WHY ARE PPM FOR A GIVEN GROUP REPORTED AS A RANGE OF NUMBERS?

For a given group, local variation can led to a range of absorption frequencies. If the hydrogen attached to the carbon of a bromide (Br–C–*H*) appears at about 3.5 ppm, the signal could vary between about 3.2-3.9 ppm, depending on what other groups or atoms are in proximity to this proton. Usually, the variation is less than 0.5 ppm for a given functional group.

SHIELDING EFFECTS

IF A PROTON IS ADJACENT TO AN ELECTRON RELEASING GROUP, HOW DOES THAT INFLUENCE THE INTERACTION WITH THE EXTERNAL FIELD?

An electron releasing substituent will increase the electron density around the proton, increasing the net magnetic moment of the proton. This requires more of an external field to bring the proton into resonance, making the absorption more upfield. Protons adjacent to an electron releasing group generally appear between 2-3 ppm.

IF A PROTON IS ADJACENT TO AN ELECTRON WITHDRAWING GROUP, HOW DOES THAT INFLUENCE THE INTERACTION WITH THE EXTERNAL FIELD?

The electron withdrawing substituent will decrease the electron density around the proton, decreasing the net moment of the proton. This requires less of an external field to bring the proton into resonance, making the absorption more downfield. Protons adjacent to an electron withdrawing group generally appear between 2-6 ppm, although the signal can be as far downfield at 15-18 ppm.

WHAT IS A SHIELDING EFFECT?

A shielding effect is the label for an electron releasing group that causes the absorption to occur upfield. A shielded proton will absorb upfield.

IS SHIELDING ASSOCIATED WITH AN UPFIELD OR DOWNFIELD CHEMICAL SHIFT?

Shielding is associated with an upfield shift.

WHAT ARE COMMON FUNCTIONAL GROUPS THAT CAUSE SHIELDING EFFECTS?

Silane groups (such as Me_4Si) induce large shielding effects. This is why TMS appears far upfield relative to most other organic molecules. Alkyl groups are shielding relative to C–O, C–N, C-halogen, C–C=O, etc.

DESHIELDING EFFECTS

WHAT IS A DESHIELDING EFFECT?

A deshielding effect is associated with an electron withdrawing group, pushing the absorption downfield. A deshielded proton absorbs downfield.

IS DESHIELDING ASSOCIATED WITH AN UPFIELD OR DOWNFIELD CHEMICAL SHIFT?

Deshielding is associated with a downfield shift.

WHAT ARE COMMON FUNCTIONAL GROUPS THAT CAUSE DESHIELDING EFFECTS?

Most electron withdrawing groups induce downfield shifts via deshielding. These include C=O, C≡N, OR, NR_2, Ph, C=C, etc.

WHICH FUNCTIONAL GROUP WILL CAUSE A GREATER DOWNFIELD SHIFT, C=O OR Br?

The Br induces greater bond polarization and, thereby, greater deshielding. A proton adjacent to a bromine (*H*–C–Br) absorbs at about 2.70-4.10 ppm whereas the carbonyl leads to chemical shifts of 2.10-2.50 ppm for *H*–C–C=O.

MAGNETIC ANISOTROPY

WHY IS THE SIGNAL FOR A PROTON ATTACHED TO A C=C GROUP FURTHER DOWNFIELD THAN THAT ATTACHED TO A Cl?

The π-electrons in the C=C double bond induce a secondary magnetic field that is opposed to the external field (see *17.18*). If a proton is held in the center part of this secondary field, it will be shielded and moved upfield. If it is held in the outer portion of the secondary field, however, it will be deshielded and moved downfield. Since the proton attached to the C=C is held in the deshielding portion of the secondary field, it absorbs further downfield than is usual. This effect is in addition to the usual electron withdrawing effects and *H*–C=C absorbs between 4.5-6.5 ppm whereas *H*–C–Cl absorbs between 3.1-4.1 ppm.

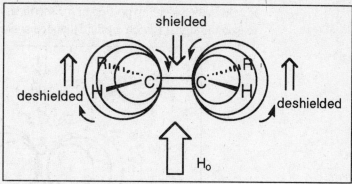

Fig. 17.18

WHAT IS THE NAME OF THIS EFFECT?

Magnetic anisotropy.

WHY DOES THE HYDROGEN ON A BENZENE RING APPEAR AT 6.8-7.2 PPM?

There are significantly more π-electrons in benzene and the magnetic anisotropy effect is much greater. As shown in *17.19*, the protons on the benzene ring are in the deshielding portion of the secondary field, pushing the signal far downfield (to 6.5-8.5 ppm).

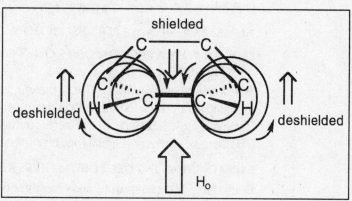

Fig. 17.19

EXPLAIN WHY THE PROTON OF AN ALDEHYDE APPEARS AT 9-10 PPM BUT THE PROTON ON AN ALKENE APPEARS AT 5-6 PPM.

In both cases the H–C= proton is deshielded by magnetic anisotropy. The aldehyde proton, however, is also highly polarized, further pushing that signal downfield of the polarized C=C bond.

EXPLAIN WHY THE PROTON ATTACHED TO AN ALKYNE IS UPFIELD OF THE PROTON ABSORPTION FOR AN ALKENE.

The presence of two π-bonds changes the orientation of the molecule with respect to the external field (H_o). A shown in *17.20*, the proton attached to C ≡ C is held in the shielding portion of the secondary field and is shielded. For this reason the signal is more upfield than the analogous *H*–C=C signal.

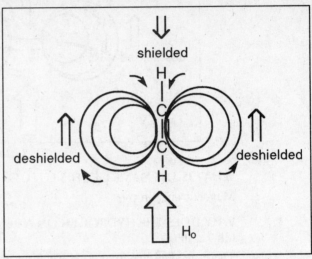

Fig. 17.20

Multiplicity

Multiplicity is defined as the number of signal that appears for each absorption. A single peak is called a singlet, two peaks a doublet, three peaks a triplet, four peaks a quartet, five peaks a pentet, etc.

NUMBER OF SIGNALS PER ABSORPTION

EXPLAIN WHY A PROTON GIVES ONLY ONE SIGNAL PER ABSORPTION.

With a spin quantum number (I) of $\frac{1}{2}$, there are only two orientations for the spin moment of the proton [Number of orientations = (2*I)+1]. For two orientations (for and against the external field) there is only one possible signal. Each proton (^1H) therefore gives one signal (one absorption).

EXPLAIN WHY ONE DEUTERIUM GIVES RISE TO THREE SIGNALS.

Deuterium (^2H) has a spin of 1 and gives three orientations [(2*1)+1]. For three orientations (A,B,C) there are three signals [A→B, A→C, B→C]. Each atom of ^2H therefore gives three signals per absorption.

HOW MANY SIGNALS PER ABSORPTION ARE ASSOCIATED WITH ^{13}C? WITH ^{15}N? WITH ^{16}O?

Both ^{13}C and ^{15}N has a spin of $\frac{1}{2}$ and give one absorption per nuclei. Since ^{16}O has a spin of zero (0) it does not exhibit a signal in the NMR.

ADJACENT HYDROGENS AND SECONDARY FIELDS

IF A PROTON HAS ONE HYDROGEN NEIGHBOR, WHAT IS THE INFLUENCE OF THAT NEIGHBOR?

The neighboring proton will exhibit a small external field, and will split the signal for the proton of interest into two peaks (a doublet).

HOW MANY SIGNALS APPEAR FOR EACH NEIGHBORING HYDROGEN?

Each neighboring hydrogen will split the proton signal of interest into two peaks (a doublet).

WHY DOES AN ISOLATED GROUP GIVE ONLY ONE SIGNAL?

All three of the protons of the methyl group are magnetically equivalent. For this reason, the protons are not considered to be neighbors but are identical and absorb as a single unit (see *17.22*).

COUPLING CONSTANTS

WHAT IS THE COUPLING CONSTANT?

When a signal is split into two peaks, the two peaks will be separated by some number of Hz. This distance (in Hz) is referred to as the *coupling constant* (J), as in *17.21*.

WHAT UNITS ARE USED TO DESCRIBE THE COUPLING CONSTANT?

The units of the coupling constant are hertz (Hz).

OF WHAT MAGNITUDE ARE COUPLING CONSTANTS?

Typical values of J are 0-15 Hz although much larger values are possible and are occasionally observed.

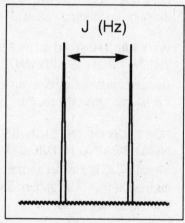

Fig. 17.21

THE N+1 RULE

IF A PROTON HAS ONE NEIGHBOR, HOW MANY SIGNALS WILL BE GENERATED?

For *n* neighbors, a proton will be split into *n+1* signals. For three neighbors (*17.22*), the proton will appear as four signals (a quartet, *17.25*); two neighbors lead to three signals (a triplet, *17.24*); one neighbors gives two signals (a doublet, *17.23*). A proton that appears as a single peak will have no neighbors.

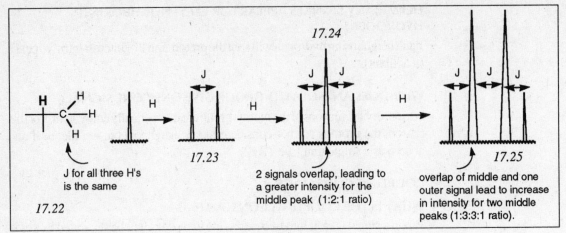

Fig. 17.22–17.25

EXPLAIN WHY THREE NEIGHBORING HYDROGEN LEAD TO FOUR SIGNALS FOR A GIVEN PROTON.

When each identical neighboring proton splits the signal of interest, the coupling constant will be identical, leading to overlap of the signals. The overlap leads to a total four signals in an intensity ratio of 1:3:3:1.

WHAT IS THE N+1 RULE?

For n neighbors there will be n+1 peaks, if the neighboring hydrogens all have the same coupling constant (J).

WHY ARE THESE MULTIPLE SIGNALS ALWAYS SYMMETRICAL WHEN THE N+1 RULE IS APPLIED?

Because the coupling constant (J) is the same for all neighboring hydrogens. If J is not the same, the resulting signal will be asymmetric.

FOR EACH OF THE SIGNALS *17.26–17.28*, GIVE THE NUMBER OF NEIGHBORING HYDROGENS.

Signal *17.26* is a triplet and results from 2 neighbors. Signal *17.27* is a quartet and results from 3 neighbors. Signal *17.28* is a heptet (7 peaks) and results from 6 identical neighbors.

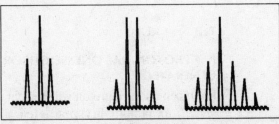

Fig. 17.26–17.28

WHAT IS A MULTIPLET?

A multiplet is a cluster of several peaks but it is not possible to count them. This may be due to very low intensity for the outermost (satellite) signals or due to unsymmetrical overlap of peaks.

NEIGHBORS WITH DIFFERENT COUPLING CONSTANTS

IF A PROTON HAS TWO DIFFERENT KINDS OF HYDROGEN NEIGHBORS, WHAT IS THE RESULT?

The multiplet pattern will be asymmetric, reflecting one hydrogen splitting a proton into a doublet with one coupling constant. Each of those peaks will then be split into new doublets, but with a different coupling, leading to little or no overlap of peaks.

IF THE COUPLING CONSTANT FOR NEIGHBOR A IS 2 HZ AND THE COUPLING CONSTANT FOR NEIGHBOR B IS 5 HZ, WHAT IS THE SIGNAL FOR A GIVEN PROTON IS THERE ARE TWO H_a AND TWO H_b?

The result of these asymmetric splitting patterns is the final 9 peak multiplet shown in *17.29*. Both the 2 Hz and 5 Hz coupling constants can be discerned in this multiplet. Working 'backwards' from the multiplet, the number of neighbors and each coupling constant can be determined.

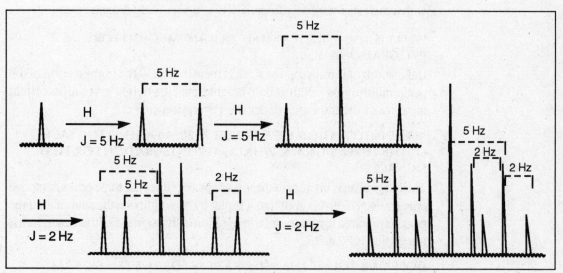

Fig. 17.29

WHAT IS AN AB QUARTET?

An AB quartet arises when two hydrogens have almost the same coupling constant but those hydrogens have slightly different magnetic environments. The asymmetric coupling leads to 4 peaks with the distinctive pattern shown in *17.30*.

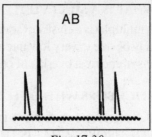

Fig. 17.30

Integration

Each absorption signal appears as a 'peak' or a cluster of 'peaks'. If the area under these peaks is measured (integrated) comparing the peak area of one signal with another allows one to determine the relative ratio of hydrogens (1:1, 1:2, 2:5, etc.). This does not give the actual number of hydrogens unless the empirical formula is known.

THE AREA UNDER AN ABSORPTION SIGNAL

IF ONE SIGNAL (PEAK A) HAS A PEAK AREA OF 120 AND ANOTHER (PEAK B) HAS A PEAK AREA OF 40, WHAT IS THE INTEGRATION FOR THE NMR?

The integration (ratio) of A:B = $\frac{120}{40}$ and $\frac{40}{40}$ = 3:1. This ratio would be consistent with a molecule with 4 hydrogens, 8 hydrogens, 12 hydrogens, etc.

WHAT IS THE 'WIDTH AT HALF HEIGHT' METHOD FOR INTEGRATION?

If the width of the absorption peak is measured at $\frac{1}{2}$ the highest point of the peak, multiplying width at half-height times the height gives an excellent measure of the total area under the absorption curve.

IF THE INTEGRATION OF A TRIPLET IS 20, 40 AND 20 FOR EACH OF THE THREE SIGNALS, WHAT IS THE INTEGRATION FOR THAT SIGNAL?

The integration is the sum of these three peaks. Since the three peaks comprise only one signal that is split into a triplet by its neighbors, the sum of all three peaks is required to give the total integration of that signal. For this example, the integration is 80 units.

DOES ONE COUNT THE INTEGRATION FOR THE TMS SIGNAL?

No.

THE RELATIVE RATIO OF ABSORPTION PEAKS

IF THERE ARE THREE PEAKS WITH AN INTEGRATION OF 1:2:6, WHAT EMPIRICAL FORMULAS ARE POSSIBLE?

This integration means there are a total of 9 hydrogens (3 different kinds of hydrogens in a ratio of (1:2:6). This would fit any formula that had 9 or a multiple of 9 hydrogens in it (9, 18, 27, 36, 45, etc.). This integration refers only to protons and says nothing about the number of carbons or other atoms in the formula.

WHAT INFORMATION IS REQUIRED TO DETERMINE EXACTLY HOW MANY PROTONS ARE ASSOCIATED WITH A GIVEN NMR?

The molecular weight and the empirical formula (usually determined from the mass spectrum) are required. In the example above. If given a choice between $C_9H_{18}O$ or $C_9H_{20}O$, the only possibility is $C_9H_{18}O$, for the example given above.

WHY IS THE INTEGRATION ALWAYS GIVEN AS A RATIO OF SIGNALS?

The exact number of hydrogens is unknown without the specific empirical formula and molecular weight. The integration is based on the ratio of the peak with the smallest area being divided into all other peaks.

IF THE EMPIRICAL FORMULA FOR A NMR IS $C_6H_{12}O$, IDENTIFY THE NUMBER OF PROTONS ASSOCIATED WITH EACH SIGNAL IN THE NMR *17.31*.

The integration in *17.31* is 1:3 (4 protons). Since the empirical formula indicates there are twelve hydrogens, each integration signal must be multiplied by 3 to give the 12 protons. The signal at 0.9 ppm is, therefore, worth 9 hydrogens and the signal at 2.3 ppm is worth 3 hydrogens.

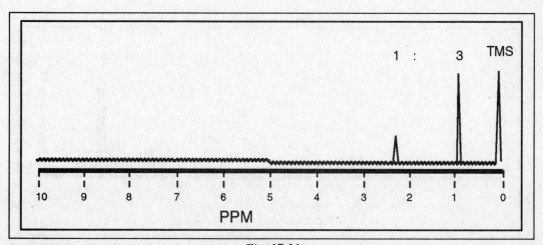

Fig. 17.31

Correlating
NMR Data
With Structure

DUPLICATED SIGNALS

THERE ARE SIX PROTONS IN ACETONE BUT ACETONE GIVES ONLY ONE SIGNAL (A SINGLET) IN THE NMR. EXPLAIN.

All six hydrogens in acetone are identical, magnetically and chemically (they have the same magnetic and chemical environments). They will therefore absorb the radio signal at exactly the same strength, leading to a single peak.

WHAT IS THE NMR FOR BENZOPHENONE?

Benzophenone [$Ph_2C=O$] has a total of 10 identical protons. They will absorb as one signal (a singlet) at about 7.2 ppm (the typical chemical shift for benzene derivatives).

WHAT IS THE NMR FOR 2,6-DIMETHYL-4-HEPTANONE?

This molecule has a formula of $C_9H_{18}O$. Since it is symmetrical, it will exhibit only three different signal: one for the two isopropyl groups and one for the two -CH_2- groups attached to the carbonyl. The integration is 1:0.5:3 or 2:1:6. Since there are a total of 18 hydrogens, this represents four hydrogens for the doublet at 2.3 ppm, 2 hydrogens for the heptet centered at about 1.7 ppm and 12 hydrogens for the doublet at about 1.3 ppm (see *17.32*).

STRUCTURE AND CHEMICAL SHIFT

IS NMR *17.33* ASSOCIATED WITH PROPANOL OR PROPANOIC ACID?

The triplet at 1.2 ppm and the quartet at 3.0 ppm are characteristic of an ethyl group (see *17.33*). The chemical shift of 3.0 ppm for the -CH_2- group is somewhat downfield for attachment to a carbonyl [CH_3CH_2–$C=O$], which normally appears at 2.2-2.6 ppm. The signal for one proton at 13.6 ppm is characteristic of a very deshielded proton on a carboxylic acid. This NMR spectrum is therefore due to propanoic acid rather than 1-propanol.

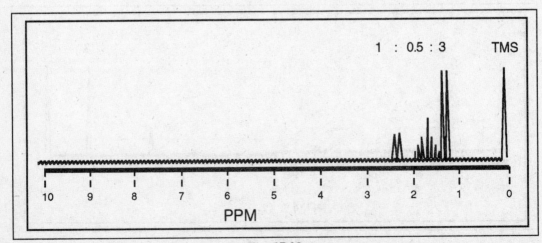

Fig. 17.32

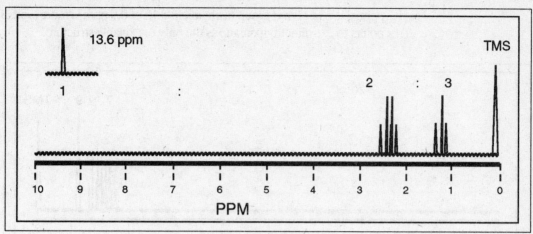

Fig. 17.33

IS NMR *17.34* ASSOCIATED WITH BUTANAL OR 2-BUTANONE?

The triplet worth three hydrogens in *17.34* is a methyl group split by two neighbors (-CH$_2$-). The triplet at 2.4 ppm (attached to a carbonyl) is a CH$_2$ group split by two neighbors (-CH$_2$-). The multiplet at about 1.8 ppm cannot be easily analyzed. The singlet (worth one hydrogen) at 9.2 is very characteristic of an aldehyde (O=C–H) and coupled with the other information clearly identifies this spectrum as coming from butanal rather than butanone.

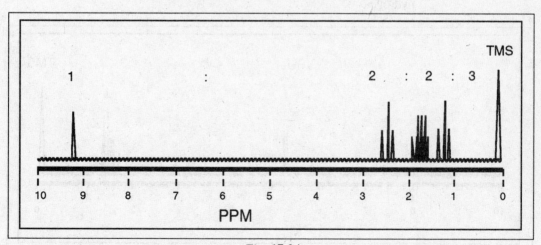

Fig. 17.34

IS NMR *17.4.20* ASSOCIATED WITH 2,2,-DIMETHYLPENTANE OR 2-METHYLPENTANE?

The distinctly upfield nature of the chemical shifts for the signals in *17.35* suggests an alkane. A clearly discernible signal is the 9 hydrogen singlet at

~1.2 ppm, due to a *t*-butyl group (a chemical shift of 0.9 ppm is more typical). This points to 2,2-dimethylpentane as the only reasonable structure.

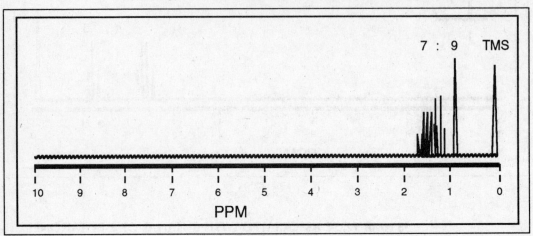

Fig. 17.35

IS NMR *17.36* ASSOCIATED WITH CYCLOHEXENE OR BENZENE?

If this were benzene, it would show a singlet at about 7.1 ppm. NMR *17.36* shows a multiplet (more characteristic of an alkene) between 1.8-2.2 ppm and the signal (worth two hydrogens for cyclohexene) that is characteristic of alkene hydrogens.

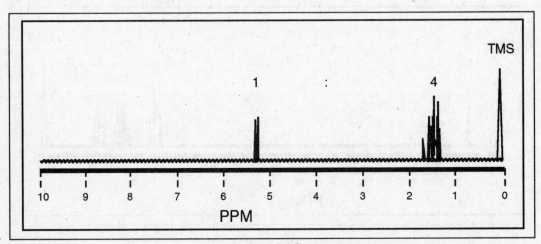

Fig. 17.36

IS NMR *17.37* ASSOCIATED WITH DIETHYL ETHER OR METHYL PROPYL ETHER?

The singlet at about 3.0 ppm in *17.37* is a methyl group attached to an oxygen (3.3-3.5 ppm is more typical) and the -CH$_2$- group (triplet at 3.8 ppm) also indicates the group -CH_2–O. The methyl (triplet at 1.1 ppm) is attached to a -CH_2- and this evidence points to methyl propyl ether. Diethyl ether is symmetrical and would show only an ethyl group with the -CH_2- signal at about 3.3 ppm and the methyl signal at about 1.5 ppm.

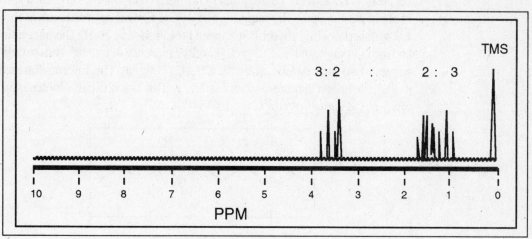

Fig. 17.37

WHAT IS THE NMR OF HEXACHLOROBENZENE?

The proton NMR will show *no* signals at all since this molecule does not contain a hydrogen.

USING COUPLING CONSTANTS

IF THE SIGNAL AT 3.6 PPM SHOWS J = 12.0 HZ AND THE SIGNAL AT 2.3 PPM SHOWS J = 7.0 HZ, DETERMINE THE STRUCTURE OF THE MOLECULE BASED ON NMR *17.38* AND A MOLECULAR FORMULA OF $C_8H_{15}NO_4$.

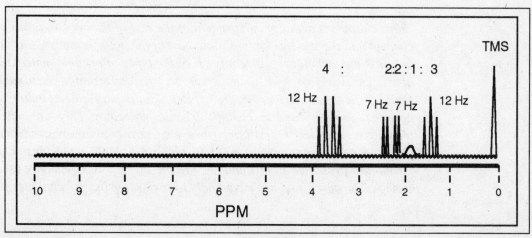

Fig. 17.38

The triplet at 1.4 ppm and the quartet at 3.6 ppm are coupled together (same J) and constitute an ethyl group. The chemical shift of the -CH_2- of the ethyl suggests O–CH_2CH_3. The two doublets at 2.2 and 2.4 ppm are coupled together and each is a -CH_2- next to a -CH_2- (X–CH_2–CH_2–Y). The position of the -CH_2- suggests -CH_2–C=O but there is also a nitrogen (which shows chemical shifts of about 2.3-2.5 ppm. This suggests N–CH_2CH_2C=O. The broad peak at about 1.9 ppm is probably a hydrogen bonded proton such as N–H. The integration and formula suggests two EtO groups and the presence of four oxygens strongly suggests two ester groups, given the CH_2–C=O signal. This information leads to the conclusion that the structure is *17.39*. This is a difficult problem since many of the signals overlap.

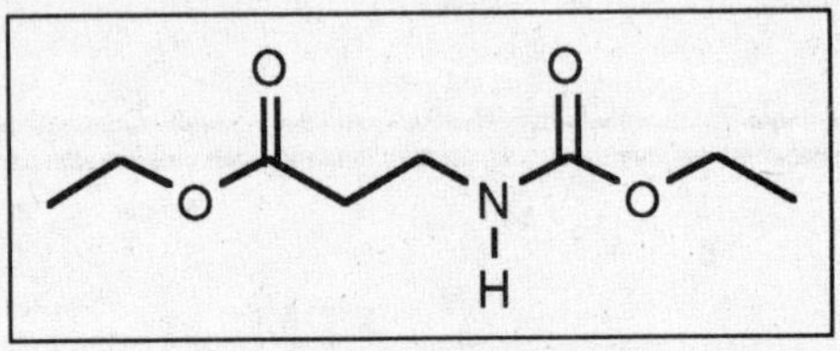

Fig. 17.39

EXPLAIN HOW ONE CAN CORRELATE WHICH CH$_2$ IS ATTACHED TO THE PHENYL IN 5-PHENYL-1-PENTANONE.

In this molecule one must distinguish between a -CH_2Ph, HO–CH_2- and two -CH_2- groups attached to a -CH_2- group. The CH_2 connected to OH will absorb at about 3.3-3.5 ppm and the -CH_2- groups connected to other -CH_2 units will absorb below 2 ppm. The CH_2 group connected to Ph will have a chemical shift of 2.2-2.5 ppm and should set apart from the other signals and be easily identified.

*T*his chapter is actually independent of the rest of the book in terms of concept and theory. It is an important part of the book, however, since it presents the techniques to identify all of the types of organic molecules discussed. This is a brief introduction to spectroscopy techniques and each topic can be discussed in much greater detail for a good understanding of how that topic is used to identify organic molecules. Ther are other techniques, such as ^{13}C NMR, microwave spectroscopy, x-ray spectrometry and others that can be used to identify organic molecules. The techniques presented in this chapter are the three most commonly used methods, however, and are meant only to review the basic techniques.

END OF CHAPTER PROBLEMS

1. Interchange each of the following:
   (a) 4.87×10^{-8} m = _____ Hz   (b) 2350 Å = _____ cm
   (c) 6.91×10^{14} Hz = _____ nm   (d) 3800 nm = _____ μ
   (e) 6.43 m = _____ Hz   (f) 1641 cm^{-1} = _____ m
   (g) 875 cm^{-1} = _____ nm.

2. Interchange each of the following.
   (a) 70 eV = _____ kcal = _____ kJ (b) 30 eV = _____ kcal = _____ kJ
   (c) 1200 kcal = _____ eV   (d) 2145 kcal = _____ eV

3. Draw the parent ion for each of the following:
   (a) 2-butanone (b) N,N-dimethylbutanamine
   (c) 1-propene (d) ethanenitrile

4. Calculate the P, P+1 and P+2 ratios for each of the following.
   (a) $C_5H_{10}O$ (b) $C_8H_{17}N$ (c) $C_5H_{12}O_2$ (d) $C_{10}H_{21}NO$

5. Calculate the empirical formula for each of the following (molecular weight in brackets).
   (a) P (136) 100%, P+1 (137) 8.88%, P+2 (138) 0.794%.
   (b) P (113) 14.5 mm, P+1 (114) 1.18 mm, P+2 (115) 0.044 mm.
   (c) P (98) 79.8 mm, P+1 (99) 5.02 mm, P+2 (100) 0.123 mm.
   (d) P (100) 100%, P+1 (101) 6.66%, P+2 (102) 0.22%.

6. What can be gleaned form the following data?
   (a) P 100%, P+1 7.78%, P+2 100%.
   (b) P 100%, P+1 11.1%, P+2 4.7%.
   (c) P 100%, P+1 8.88%, P+2 31%.

7. Suggest possible fragments for each of the following:
   (a) P-15 (b) P-18 (c) P-28 (d) P-29 (e) P-43 (f) P-45

8. Which of the following can undergo a McLafferty rearrangement. Show the actual fragmentation in those cases.

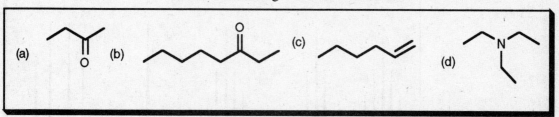

9. Why is it important not to take an infrared spectrum in an aqueous solution when using pressed KBr cells?

10. What is a 'bending' vibration? A stretching vibration?

11. Does the $C \equiv C$ or the C–O bond give the most intense infrared absorption? Which gives the lowest energy absorption?

12. Calculate the reduced mass for (a) C–Cl (b) C–N (c) C–C

13. Describe the important infrared absorption bands for
    (a) 2-butanone (b) 4-cyclohexyl-2-pentanol (c) 6-bromohexanoic acid.

14. Identify how many signals each of the following nuclei will generate in the NMR.
    (a) ^2H (b) ^1H (c) ^{13}C (d) ^{15}N (e) ^6Li (f) ^{12}C

15. If a 14000 gauss magnet required a ΔE of 60 MHz for resonance and this is assumed to be the standard, calculate ΔE for each of the following magnetic fields.
    (a) 28,574 (b) 125,672 (c) 297,113

16. Calculate each of the following in ppm.
    (a) 625 Hz at 120 MHz   (b) 1475 Hz at 90 MHz
    (c) 432 Hz at 60 MHz   (d) 2122 Hz at 500 MHz

17. Draw the magnetic anisotropy field for the N-methyl imine of acetone.

18. For the following pairs of signals identify which one will absorb further upfield.
    (a) HC–Br HC–NR$_2$ (b) H–C=O H–C–C=O
    (c) O=C–O–H C=C–C–H (d) C≡C–H C=C–H

19. Identify all magnetically equivalent hydrogens in each molecule.

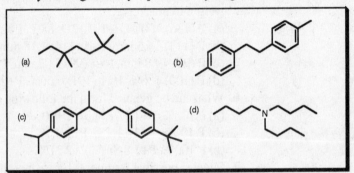

20. For each NMR signal indicate how many neighboring hydrogens it will have.

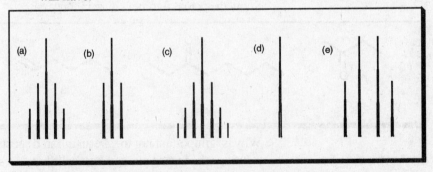

21. What is the actual signal for a hydrogen with 3 neighbors J = 12.0 Hz) and also 2 neighbors (coupling constant 8.0 Hz)?

22. Give the chemical structure for each of the following based on the spectra provided.

(a)

Infrared Stretching Frequencies
3350-2400 (bd, strong), 1675 (s), 1338-1220 (bd, strong), 996, 921, 683 cm^{-1}

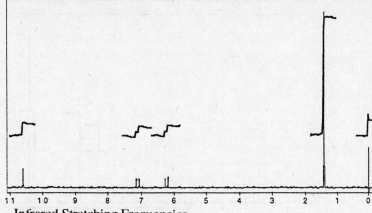

(b)

Infrared Stretching Frequencies
2933, 2770, 1613, 1209, 813 cm^{-1}

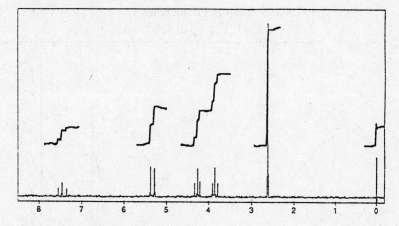

(c)

Infrared Stretching Frequencies
2950, 1721 (s), 1105, 735, 695 cm^{-1}

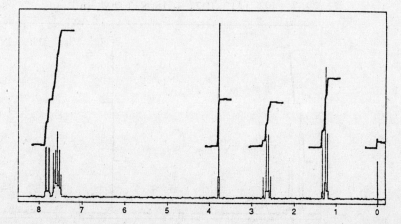

(d)

Infrared Stretching Frequencies
2941, 2833 (w), 1718 (s), 1366, 1220, 1079 cm⁻¹

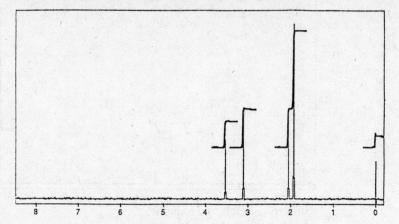

(e)

Infrared Stretching Frequencies
3448 (s), 2941, 1160, 1078, 833 cm⁻¹

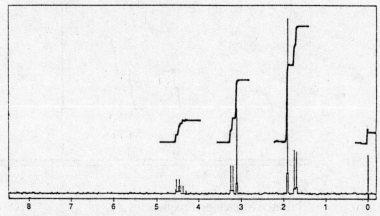

(f)

Infrared Stretching Frequencies
2262, 1493, 1412, 1071, 1015, 833, 794 cm⁻¹

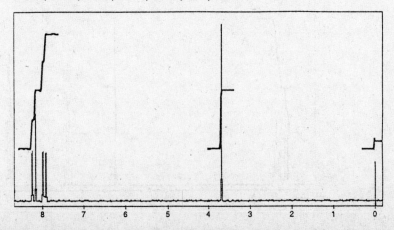

18

Amino Acids, Peptides and Proteins

*O*rganic molecules that contained two or more functional groups have been seen only sparingly in this book. This chapter discusses one of the most important classes of organic molecules, amino acids. Amino acids are important biologically as constituents of mammalian peptides and proteins. They are important chemically since their properties and chemical reactions graphically illustrate the problems that arise when two different functional groups are in a single molecule and what happens when those groups interact with each other. This chapter will present the chemical and physical properties of amino acids, both their reactions and methods of their preparation. Since amino acids are the important building blocks of proteins and peptides, a brief overview of that chemistry will be given as well.

18.1 AMINO ACIDS

An amino acid is a difunctional molecule that contains an amino group (NH_2) and a carboxylic acid group (CO_2H).

Structure

GIVE THE GENERIC STRUCTURE OF AN α-AMINO ACID.
The general structure will be $HO_2CCH(R)NH_2$.

WHAT IS THE ABSOLUTE CONFIGURATION OF MOST ESSENTIAL AMINO ACIDS?
These amino acids will have the S-configuration, as in *18.1*. This amino acid is also shown in its Fisher projection (*18.2*).

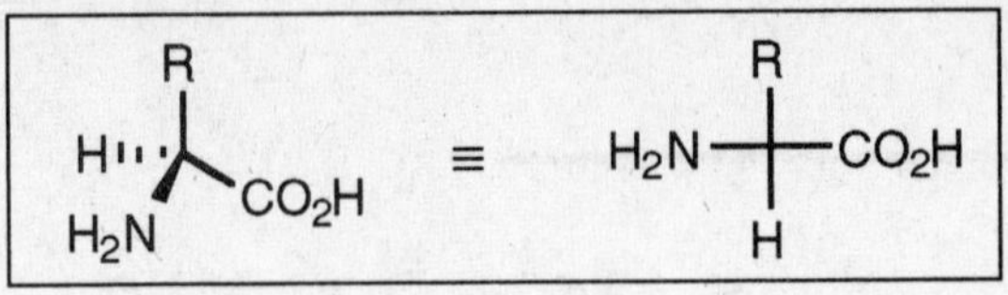

Fig. 18.1, 18.2

WHY ARE THESE AMINO ACIDS CALLED α-AMINO ACIDS?

The NH_2 group is attached to the carbon that is α- to the carboxyl group. They are 2-amino-alkanoic acids. It is important to note that there are amino acids other than α-amino acids. In a long chain carboxylic acid, the NH_2 group can appear on any carbon of the chain to give a 'non-α-amino acid'.

GIVE THE STRUCTURE OF EACH OF THE FOLLOWING: A) 4-AMINOBUTANOIC ACID B) 5-AMINOPENTANOIC ACID C) 6-AMINOHEXANOIC ACID.

Structure (a) is $H_2N-(CH_2)_3-CO_2H$. Structure (b) is $H_2N-(CH_2)_4-CO_2H$. Structure (c) is $H_2N-(CH_2)_4-CO_2H$.

ZWITTERIONIC STRUCTURE

DEFINE THE TERM AMPHOTERIC.

Amphoteric refers to a molecule that can function as both an acid and a base. At the proper pH, an amino acid can be an acid (via COOH) but changing the pH allows the amino group to function as a base.

WHY ARE AMINO ACIDS NEUTRAL AT NEUTRAL pH?

They are *zwitterions*. An internal acid-base reaction makes the structure of an amino acid an internal salt: $H_3N^+-CHR-CO_2^-$. The formal charge of this molecule is zero (electrically neutral) since the + and – charges cancel.

WHAT IS A ZWITTERION?

A zwitterion is a dipolar ion that has a positive and a negative charge in the same molecule.

GIVE THE ZWITTERIONIC STRUCTURE OF A GENERIC AMINO ACID.

$H_3N^+-CHR-CO_2^-$.

WHY DOES AN AMINO ACID EXIST AS A ZWITTERION?

At neutral pH the NH_2 group is a base and reacts with the acidic COOH group to form the zwitterion.

NEUTRAL AMINO ACIDS

WHAT IS A NEUTRAL AMINO ACID?

A neutral amino acid is an α-amino acid that at neutral pH has a side chain (R in *18.1*) that is neither acidic nor basic (no amine or carboxylic acid groups). In general, these are simple alkyl or aryl groups (methyl, ethyl, isopropyl, phenyl, *p*-methoxyphenyl, etc.).

LIST THE COMMON NEUTRAL AMINO ACIDS BY NAME (ALONG WITH THEIR 3-LETTER CODES) AND GIVE THEIR STRUCTURE.

The neural amino acids are: glycine (*Gly, 18.3*), alanine (*Ala, 18.4*), leucine (*Leu, 18.5*), isoleucine (*Ile, 18.6*), valine (*Val, 18.7*), phenylalanine (*Phe, 18.8*), serine (*Ser, 18.9*), cysteine (*Cys, 18.10*), methionine (*Met, 18.11*), threonine (*Thr, 18.12*), asparagine (*Asn, 18.13*), glutamine (*Glu, 18.14*), proline (*Pro, 18.15*), tyrosine (*Tyr, 18.16*) and tryptophan (*Trp, 18.17*). Note that the indole nitrogen in tryptophan is not very basic.

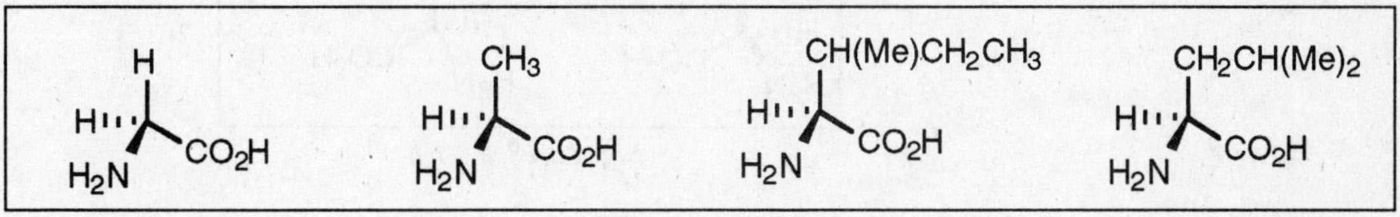

Fig. 18.3–18.6

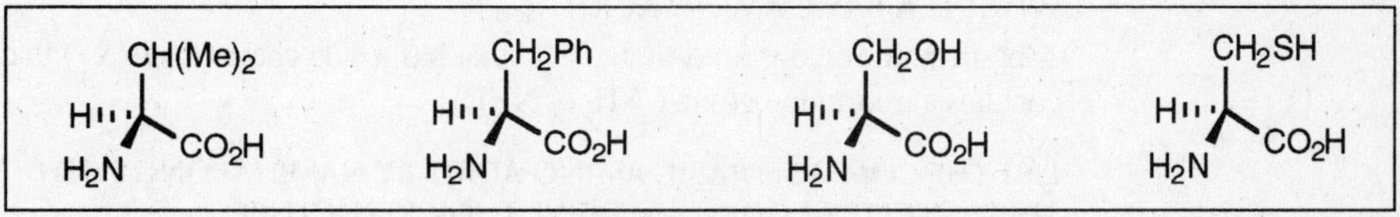

Fig. 18.7–18.10

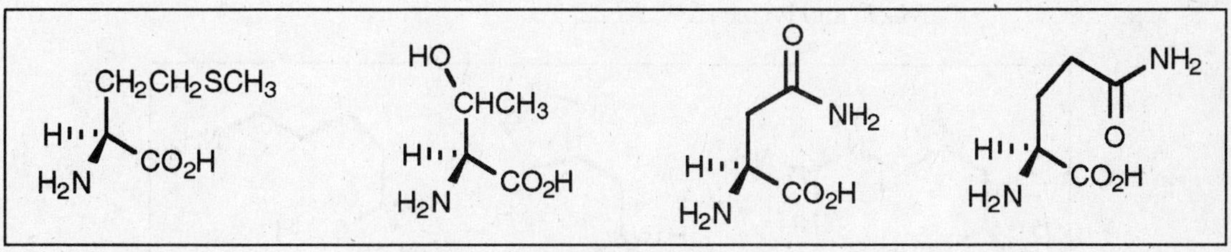

Fig. 18.11–18.14

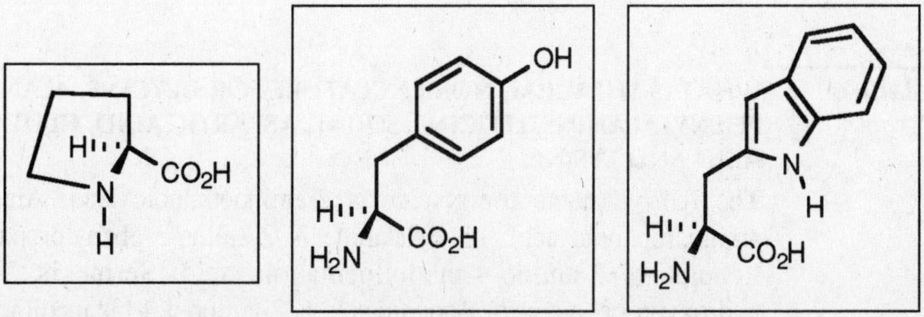

Fig. 18.15–18.17

ACIDIC AMINO ACIDS

WHAT IS AN ACIDIC AMINO ACID?

An acidic amino acid is an α-amino acid that has a side chain (R in *18.1*) that contains a carboxylic acid unit, COOH.

LIST THE COMMON ACIDIC AMINO ACIDS BY NAME (ALONG WITH THEIR 3-LETTER CODES) AND GIVE THEIR STRUCTURE.

The two common acidic amino acids are aspartic acid (*Asp, 18.18*) and glutamic acid (*Glu, 18.19*).

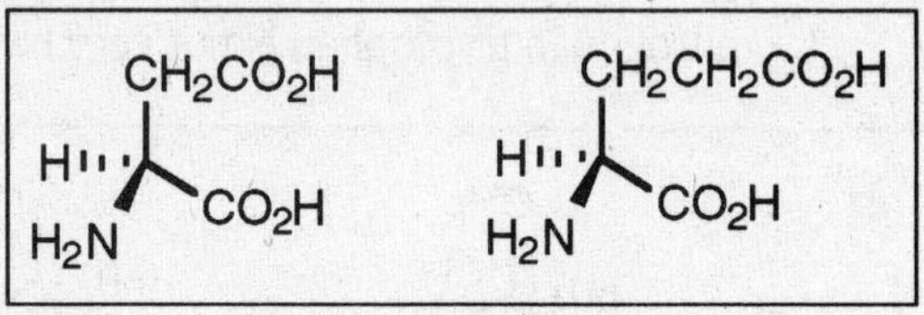

Fig. 18.18, 18.19

BASIC AMINO ACIDS

WHAT IS A BASIC AMINO ACID?

A basic amino acid is an α-amino acid that has a side chain (R in *18.1*) that contains a free amino group ($-NH_2$ or NHR).

LIST THE COMMON BASIC AMINO ACIDS BY NAME (ALONG WITH THEIR 3-LETTER CODES) AND GIVE THEIR STRUCTURE.

The most common basic amino acids are arginine (*Arg, 18.20*), histidine (*His, 18.21*) and lysine (*Lys, 18.22*).

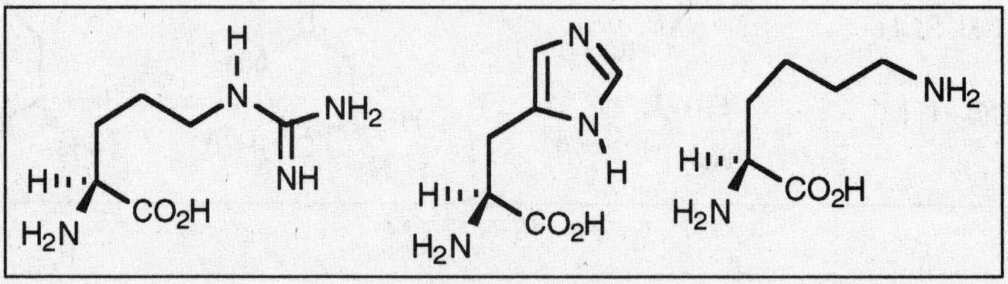

Fig. 18.20–18.22

Nomenclature

WHAT IS THE IUPAC NOMENCLATURE FOR GLYCINE, ALANINE, PHENYLALANINE, LEUCINE, SERINE, ASPARTIC ACID, GLUTAMIC ACID AND LYSINE.

The IUPAC name for glycine is 2-aminoethanoic acid. Alanine is 2-aminopropanoic acid. Phenylalanine is 2-amino-3-phenylpropanoic acid. Leucine is 2-amino-4-methylpentanoic acid. Serine is 2-amino-3-hydroxypropanoic acid. Aspartic acid is 2-amino-1,4-butanedioic acid. glutamic acid is 2-amino-1,5-pentanedioic acid and lysine is 2,5-diaminohexanoic acid.

GIVE THE 3-LETTER ABBREVIATION FOR ALL ESSENTIAL AMINO ACIDS.

The 3-letter abbreviations are shown with the structures of each amino acid (see above).

Acid-Base Properties

pK_a

THERE ARE TWO pK_a VALUES FOR NEUTRAL AMINO ACIDS. DRAW THE REACTIONS THAT ILLUSTRATE EACH ACID-BASE PROCESS.

Glycine is used to illustrate this process. In acidic solution, the NH_2 group is converted to the ammonium salt and the carboxylate is protonated as the acid (in *18.23*). Neutralization with base removes the most acidic hydrogen (from the carboxyl) to generate the zwitterion, *18.24*. Further basification removes the proton from the ammonium ion, which is also acidic. This liberates the free amine, along with the carboxylate salt, *18.25*.

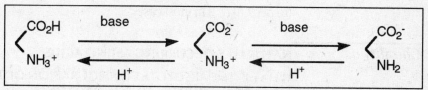

Fig. 18.23–18.25

WHY IS THE FIRST pK_a OF GLYCINE 2.34 AND THE SECOND 9.6?

The presence of an amino group of the α-carbon allows internal hydrogen bonding which makes the carboxyl proton more acidic (than acetic acid), hence the relatively low pK_a of 2.34. Removal of the proton from *18.24* is analogous to most other ammonium salts, which have pK_a values around 9-10. The 9.6 pK_a observed is, therefore, typical.

WHY IS THE pK_a OF THE CARBOXYL GROUP OF GLYCINE LOWER THAN THE pK_a OF ACETIC ACID?

The nitrogen on the α-carbon can hydrogen bond with the acidic proton (through-space interaction), weakening the O–H bond and making it a stronger acid.

IN ASPARTIC ACID, THE pK_a OF THE CARBOXYL OF THE α-AMINO ACID IS 2.09 AND THE pK_a OF THE 'SIDE CHAIN' CARBOXYL IS 3.86. WHY IS THE SIDE CHAIN CARBOXYL LESS ACIDIC?

The electron withdrawing nitrogen group is close to the COOH of the 'α-amino acid unit' and the effect is rather large. This nitrogen is much further away from the COOH on the side chain and the effects are minimal.

ISOELECTRIC POINT

WHAT IS THE ISOELECTRIC POINT FOR AN AMINO ACID?

The isoelectric point is the pH at which the amino acid is completely neutral (no longer exhibits a charge). The structure at the isoelectric point is the zwitterion form (such as *18.24*).

RELATE ISOELECTRIC POINT TO THE ACID/BASE EQUILIBRIUM SPECIES PRESENT IN GLYCINE.

At the isoelectric point, the zwitterion *18.24* (or the analogous structure for the other amino acids) represents the major species in solution.

HOW DOES THE PRESENCE OF AN ACIDIC SIDE CHAIN INFLUENCE THE ISOELECTRIC POINT OF AN AMINO ACID?

The presence of the second carboxyl group will lower the pH of the isoelectric point (to pH 3.2-3.5 typically).

HOW DOES THE PRESENCE OF A BASIC SIDE CHAIN INFLUENCE THE ISOELECTRIC POINT OF AN AMINO ACID?

The presence of the basic amino groups will raise the pH of the isoelectric point (to pH 7.6-10.8 in most cases).

Chirality

NATURALLY OCCURRING AMINO ACIDS

WHAT IS THE ABSOLUTE CONFIGURATION OF THE AMINO ACIDS MOST COMMONLY FOUND IN PROTEINS?

The major enantiomer found in most proteins is the (S) enantiomer of the amino acid.

WHAT IS A (D) AMINO ACID?

The symbol (d) is used for amino acids that have a positive (+) specific rotation.

WHAT IS AN (L) AMINO ACID?

The symbol (l) is used for amino acids that have a negative (-) specific rotation.

IS THERE ANY CORRELATION BETWEEN THE D,L DESIGNATOR AND THE R/S CONFIGURATION?

No. The R/S configuration is a name based on arbitrary (but universally accepted) rules (see section 3.3). The d,l label represents specific rotation, which is an unchangeable physical property of the molecule.

D AND L NOMENCLATURE

WHAT IS THE STRUCTURE OF GLYCERALDEHYDE?

The structure of glyceraldehyde is $HOCH_2CH(OH)CHO$.

WHAT IS THE D NOMENCLATURE?

The structure of R-(+)-glyceraldehyde is *18.26* (in Fischer projection). Fischer invented a system of nomenclature which compared amino acids to glyceraldehyde. He assigned the letter D to *18.26* (D-glyceraldehyde, where D is dextrorotatory and is a nomenclature designator). The D represents the absolute configuration when placed in the Fischer projection (OH is on the right and CHO is on the 'top'). Fischer guessed at the absolute configuration (he was later proved to be correct). The D-nomenclature system places the amino acid in a Fischer projection (see *18.27* for alanine) where the COOH of the amino acid correspond to the CHO of glyceraldehyde. The amino acid side chain is compared with the CH_2OH of glyceraldehyde and the amino group is compared with OH. If the COOH is at the 'top' and the side chain is at the 'bottom', the NH_2 group will be on the left (L) or the right (D). As drawn, *18.27* is D-alanine (R-alanine).

WHAT IS THE L NOMENCLATURE ?

As described above, the NH_2 group in the Fischer projection will appear on the left side, as in *18.28*, which is L-alanine (S-alanine).

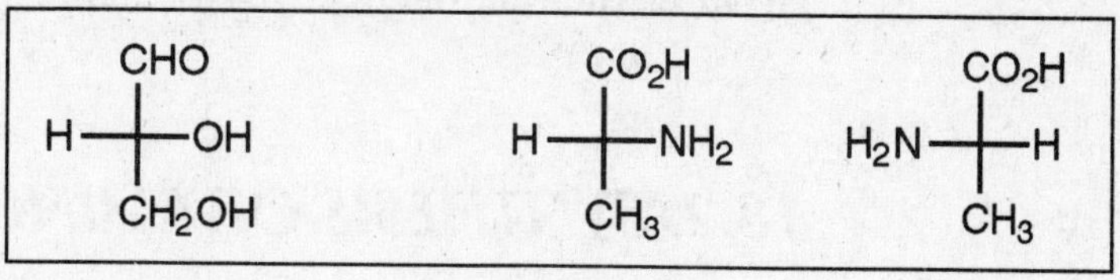

Fig. 18.26–18.28

DRAW D-(+)-GLYCERALDEHYDE IN FISCHER PROJECTION.

D-(+)-glyceraldehyde is *18.26*.

HOW DOES D-(+)-GLYCERALDEHYDE RELATIVE STRUCTURALLY TO D-ALANINE?

The CHO correlates with CO_2H and the NH_2 correlates with the OH.

DRAW THE FISCHER PROJECTION OF L-PHENYLALANINE. OF D-LEUCINE. OF L-SERINE. OF D-CYSTEINE.

The Fischer projection of L-phenylalanine is *18.29*, D-leucine is *18.30*, L-serine is *18.31* and D-cysteine is *18.32*.

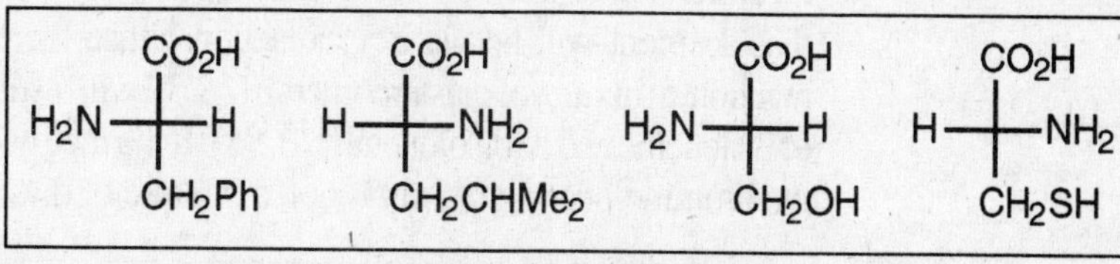

Fig. 18.29–18.32

WHAT IS ALLOTHREONINE? ALLOISOLEUCINE?

Two of the amino acids have a second chiral center in the side chain, threonine (*18.33* is L-Thr in Fischer projection) and isoleucine (*18.34* is L-Ile in Fischer projection). The diastereomer of threonine is called allothreonine (*18.35*) and the diastereomer of isoleucine is alloisoleucine (*18.36*).

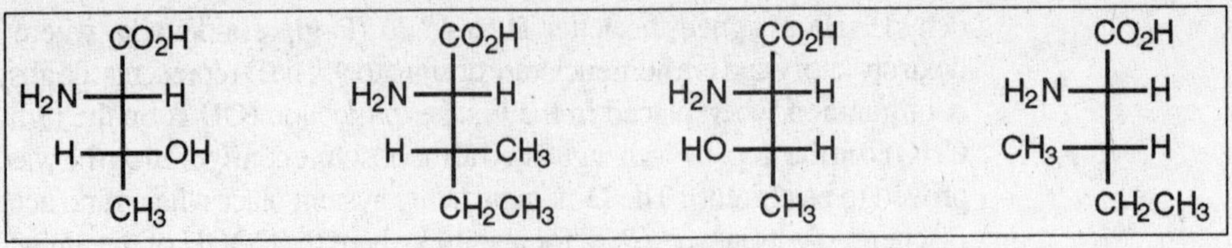

Fig. 18.33–18.36

IS THERE ANY CORRELATION BETWEEN THE d,l DESIGNATOR AND THE D,L DESIGNATORS?

No. The (d,l) nomenclature refers to specific rotation (+,-) whereas the (D,L) refers to the name of the absolute configuration (analogous to R,S).

IS THERE ANY CORRELATION BETWEEN THE D,L DESIGNATOR AND THE R,S DESIGNATORS?

Both refer to absolute configuration but (R,S) is based on the Cahn-Prelog-Ingold selection rules and (D,L) is based on a comparison with glyceraldehyde.

18.2. SYNTHESIS OF AMINO ACIDS

WHAT IS THE PRODUCT WHEN 2-BROMOETHANOIC ACID IS HEATED WITH AN EXCESS OF AMMONIA?

The product is glycine.

WHAT IS THE PRODUCT WHEN 2-BROMO-3-METHYLPENTANOIC ACID IS HEATED WITH EXCESS AMMONIA?

The product is isoleucine.

DOES THIS REACTION PRODUCE A SINGLE ENANTIOMER OR A RACEMIC MIXTURE? A SINGLE DIASTEREOMER OR A MIXTURE? EXPLAIN.

If the starting bromide (*18.37*) is racemic, the final product (*18.38*) will also be racemic. There may be some enatioselectivity if the bromide is chiral since displacement will be via a S_N^2 reaction. Since there is no stereocontrol in this reaction, a mixture of diastereomers in *18.37* will result in a diastereomeric mixture of isoleucine and alloisoleucine (*18.38*). If the methyl-bearing carbon is chiral and the bromine-bearing carbon is not, a mixture of diastereomers will result.

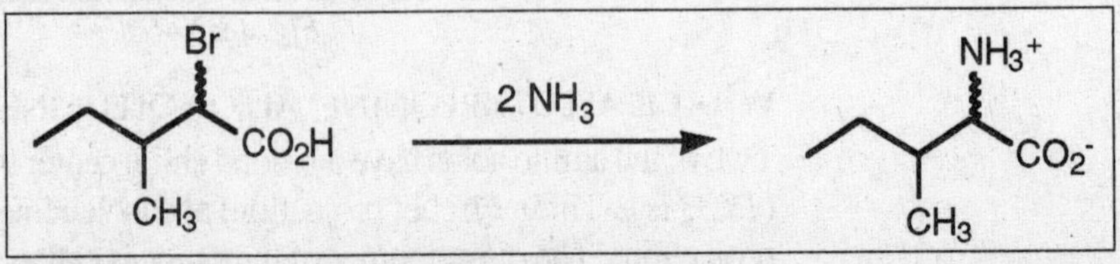

Fig. 18.37, 18.38

The Strecker Synthesis

WHAT IS THE PRODUCT WHEN PHENYLACETALDEHYDE IS REACTED WITH SODIUM CYANIDE AND AMMONIUM CHLORIDE?

The initial product of the reaction with phenylacetaldehyde (*18.39*) is the cyanoamine, *18.40*.

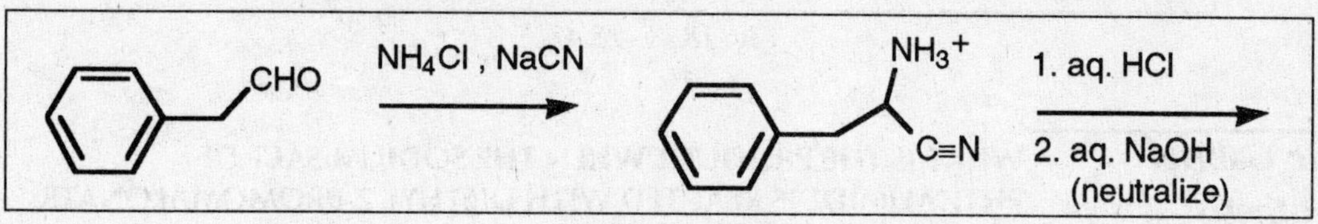

Fig. 18.39, 18.40

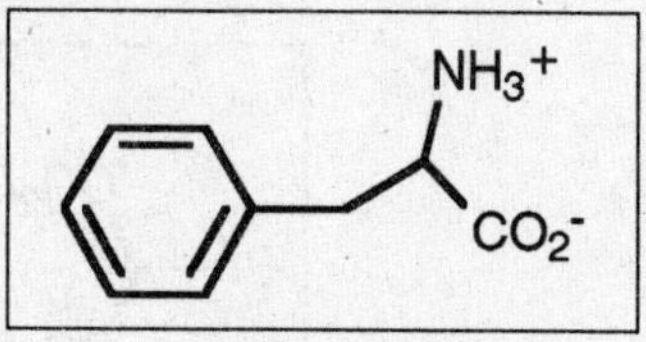

Fig. 18.41

IF THIS PRODUCT IS TREATED WITH i. AQ. HCl ii. NaOH, WHAT IS THE PRODUCT?

When *18.40* is treated with acid, the cyano group in hydrolyzed to a carboxylic acid (see section 15.3) and neutralization with base will give the zwitterionic amino acid, phenylalanine (*18.41*).

WHAT IS THE NAME OF THIS PROCESS?

This reaction sequence is called the *Strecker Synthesis*.

GIVE THE MAJOR PRODUCT FOR THE REACTIONS OF *18.42–18.44*.

In all three cases, the product is a racemic amino acid. In (a) aldehyde *18.42* is converted to *18.45*. In (b) aldehyde *18.43* is converted to *18.46* and in (c) aldehyde *18.44* is converted to *18.47*.

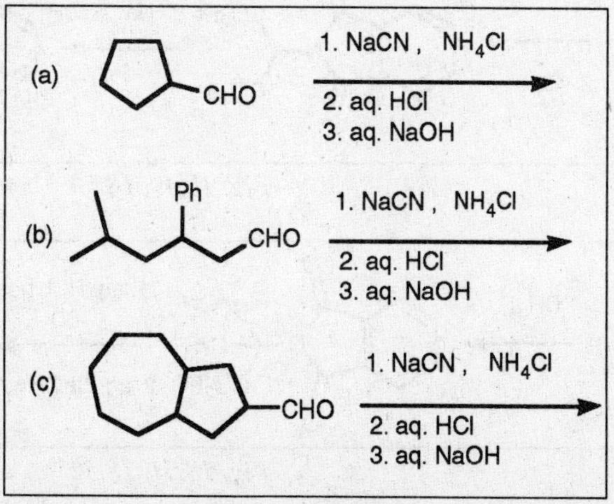

Fig. 18.42–18.44

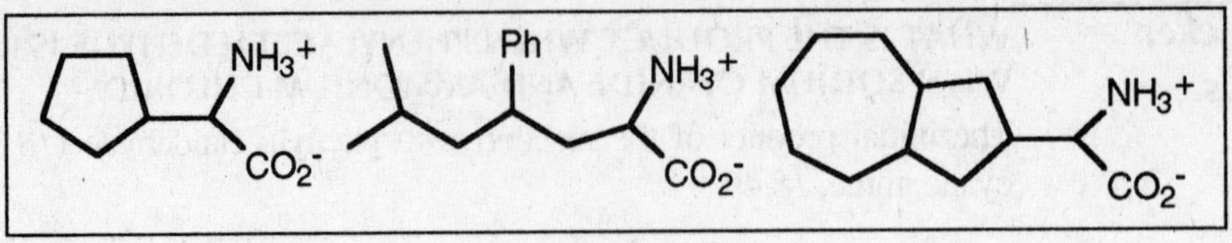

Fig. 18.45–18.47

The Gabriel Synthesis

WHAT IS THE PRODUCT WHEN THE SODIUM SALT OF PHTHALIMIDE IS REACTED WITH DIETHYL 2-BROMOMALONATE (*18.48*)?

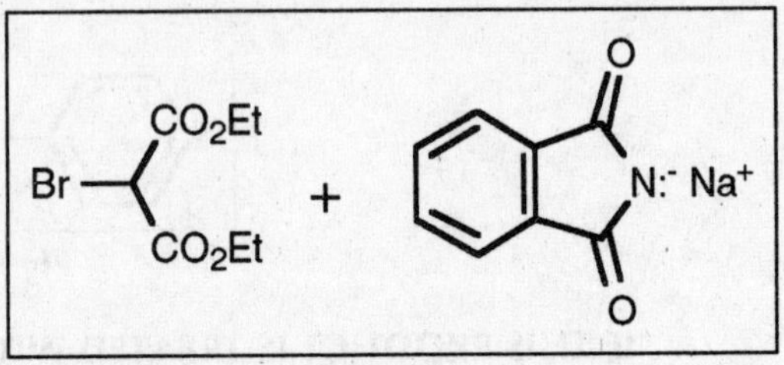

Fig. 18.48

The nucleophilic phthalimide anion displaces the bromide to give *18.49*.

IF THIS PRODUCT IS REACTED WITH Na/EtOH, WHAT IS THE RESULTING PRODUCT? IF IODOMETHANE IS ADDED, WHAT IS THE PRODUCT?

Treatment of *18.49* deprotonates the acidic α-proton to form the enolate anion (*18.50*) and subsequent reaction with iodomethane gives the alkylated product, *18.51*.

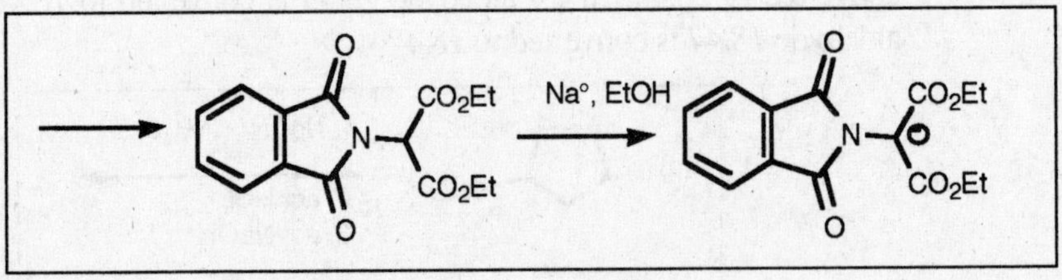

Fig. 18.49, 18.50

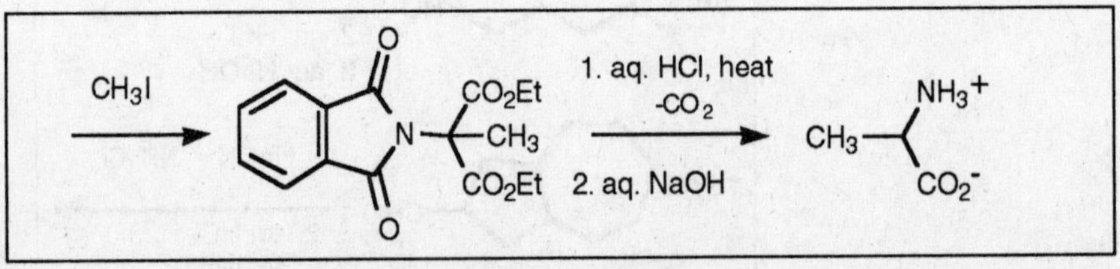

Fig. 18.51, 18.52

HYDROLYSIS OF *18.51* AND NEUTRALIZATION WITH BASE GIVES WHAT PRODUCT?

The hydrolysis sequence converts the phthalimide unit into an amino group. The ester groups are hydrolyzed to the corresponding acid and heating the 1,3-diacid leads to decarboxylation. The overall sequence generates an amino acid, alanine (*18.52*).

WHAT IS THE NAME OF THIS OVERALL PROCESS?

The name of this synthetic sequence is the *Gabriel Synthesis*.

18.3. REACTIONS OF AMINO ACIDS

Esterification of C-Terminus

WHAT PRODUCT IS FORMED WITH ALANINE IS TREATED WITH METHANOLIC HCl?

Under these conditions, the amino acid is converted to the ammonium acid $NH_3^+–CH(R)–COOH$ and in the presence of methanol, the methyl ester is formed. In this case the product is the methyl ester of alanine [$H_3N^+–CH(Me)CO_2Me$].

Amide Formation Via N-Terminus

WHAT IS THE PRODUCT WHEN ISOLEUCINE IS TREATED WITH ACETIC ANHYDRIDE?

Under these conditions, isoleucine is converted to the acetamide derivative (*18.53*).

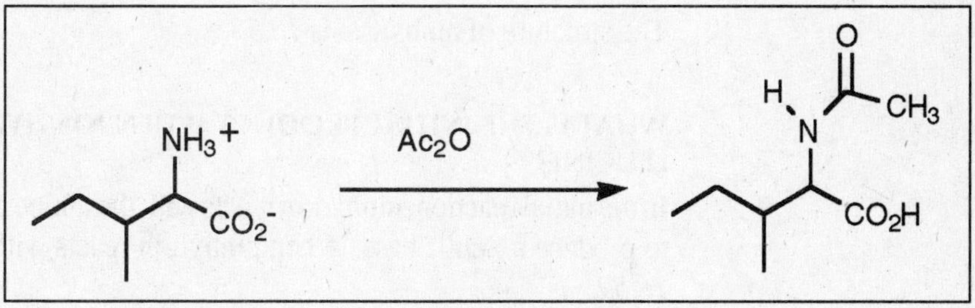

Fig. 18.53

WHAT IS THE PRODUCT WHEN ALANINE WITH TREATED WITH BENZYL CHLORIDE IN THE PRESENCE OF AN AMINE? WITH TOSYL CHLORIDE IN THE PRESENCE OF AN AMINE?

In the first reaction, the benzamide derivative (*18.54*) is formed and in the second, the N-tosyl derivative is formed (*18.55*).

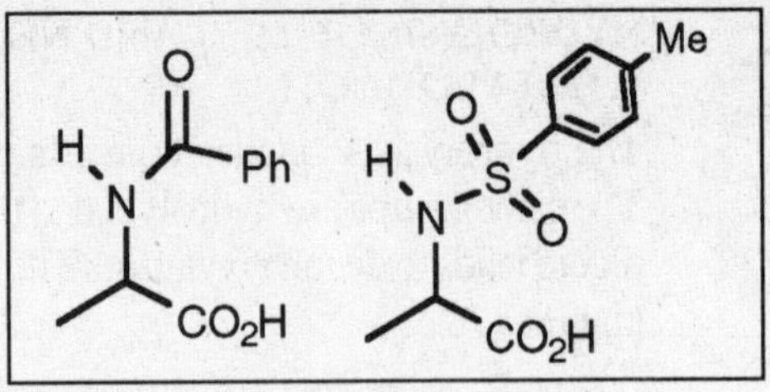

Fig. 18.54, 18.55

WHAT IS A CARBAMATE?

A carbamate has the basic functional group O–(C=O)–N=(O$_2$C–N).

WHAT IS THE PRODUCT WHEN GLYCINE IS REACTED WITH BENZYL CHLOROFORMATE (*18.56*)?

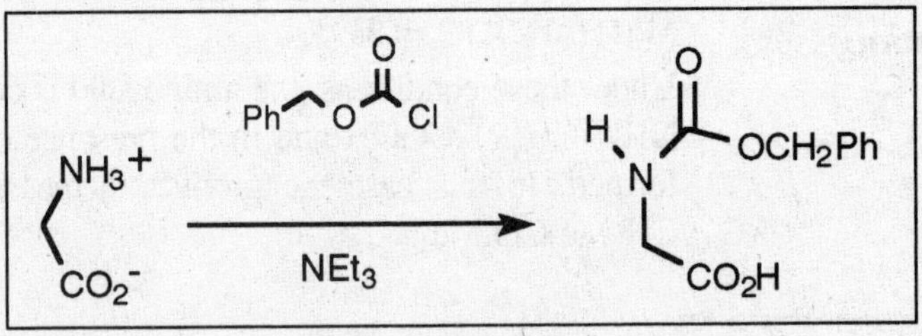

Fig. 18.56, 18.57

The product is the benzyl carbamate (CBz derivative), *18.57*.

WHAT IS THE STRUCTURE OF NINHYDRIN?

The structure of ninhydrin is *18.58*.

WHAT IS THE INITIAL PRODUCT WHEN NINHYDRIN REACTS WITH LEUCINE?

In the initial reaction, ninhydrin reacts with the amine portion of the amino acid to produce a Schiff base. When ninhydrin reacts with leucine, the product is *18.59*.

The initially formed Schiff base (*18.59*) decarboxylates under the reaction conditions to form a new Schiff base, *18.60*. This imine can react with more ninhydrin to form a new imine (*18.61*) which is known as Ruhemann's Purple (absorbs strongly at 570 nm in the visible spectrum—it has a bluish-purple color). The alkyl side chain of the amino acid is lost as an aldehyde (*18.62*). This reaction is diagnostic for amino acids that contain a primary amino function (-NH$_2$). It does not work with secondary amines. Proline, therefore, does not react in this way with ninhydrin. Proline reacts but does not give Ruhemann's Purple.

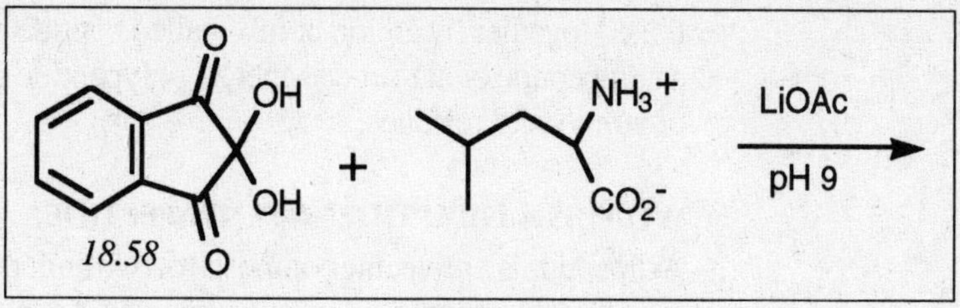

Fig. 18.58

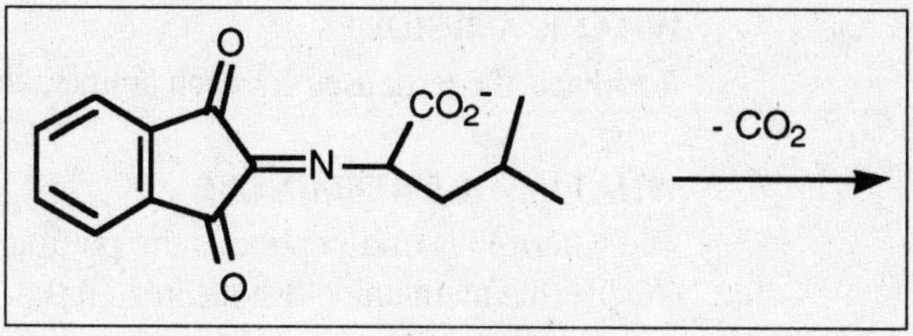

Fig. 18.59

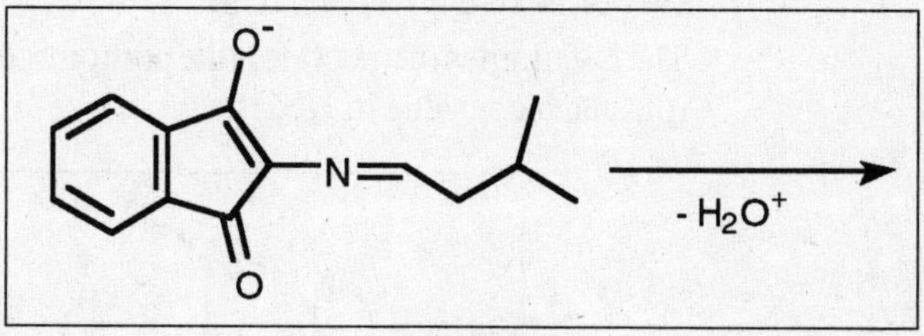

Fig. 18.60

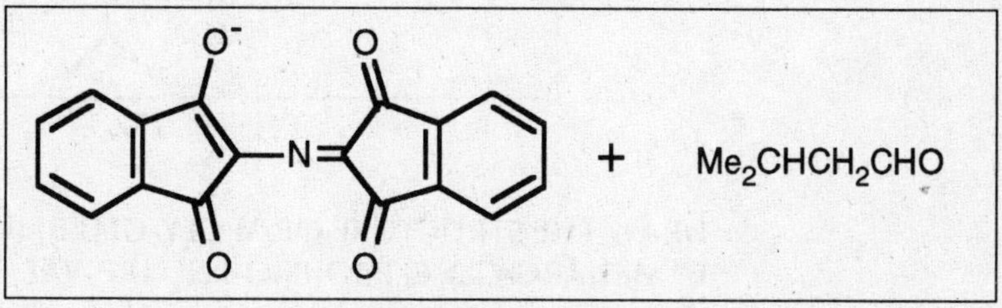

Fig. 18.61, 18.62

WHAT IS THE FINAL PRODUCT OF THE REACTION BETWEEN NINHYDRIN AND LEUCINE? OF ANY AMINO ACID?

The final product is Ruhemann's Purple (*18.61*) and an aldehyde, *if* the amino acid contained primary amino functionality.

18.4. PEPTIDES

WHAT IS A PEPTIDE?

A peptide is a biologically important polymer composed of several amino acids, linked together by amide bonds (called peptide bonds). An example is *18.63*, a tetrapeptide of ala-ser-val-met. A polypeptide can be composed of hundreds of amino acid residues.

WHAT IS A DIPEPTIDE? A PENTAPEPTIDE?

A dipeptide is a molecule composed of two amino acid residues. A pentapeptide is a molecule composed of five amino acid residues.

WHAT IS A RESIDUE?

Residue is the term used for each amino acid unit in a peptide.

WHAT IS THE C-TERMINUS?

The C-terminus of a peptide is the portion of the peptide that terminates in COOH (the methionine residue in *18.63*).

WHAT IS THE N-TERMINUS?

The N-terminus of a peptide is the portion of the peptide that terminates in -NH$_2$ (the alanine residue in *18.63*).

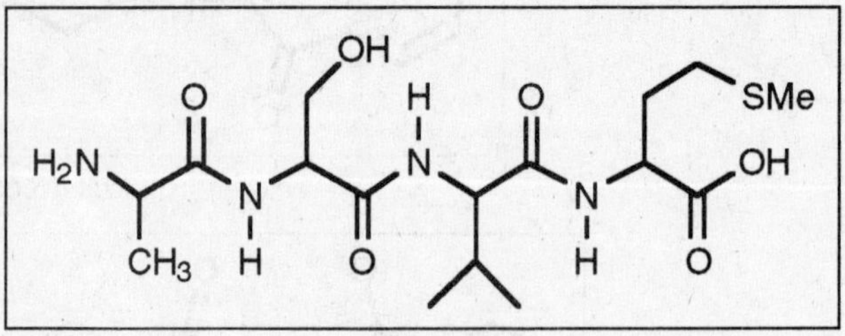

Fig. 18.63

DRAW THE STRUCTURE OF A) GLY-GLU B) ILE-ALA C) TYR-SER D) MET-ARG-GLY E) PRO-PRO-PHE-TRP-VAL

The structure of dipeptide (a) is *18.64*. The structure of dipeptide (b) is *18.65*. The structure of dipeptide (c) is *18.66*. The structure of tripeptide (d) is *18.67* and the structure of pentapeptide (e) is *18.68*.

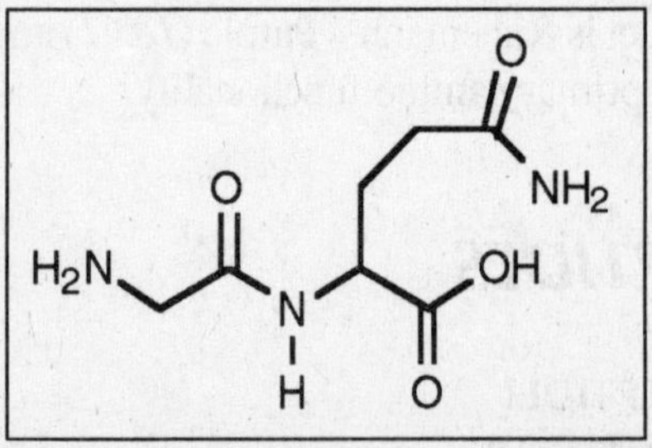

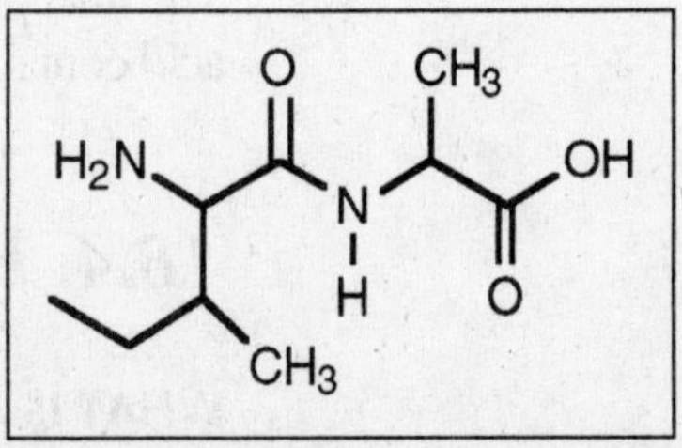

Fig. 18.64, 18.65

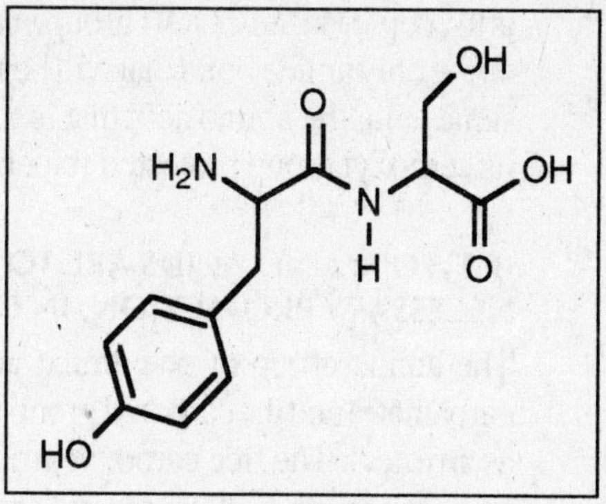

Fig. 18.66

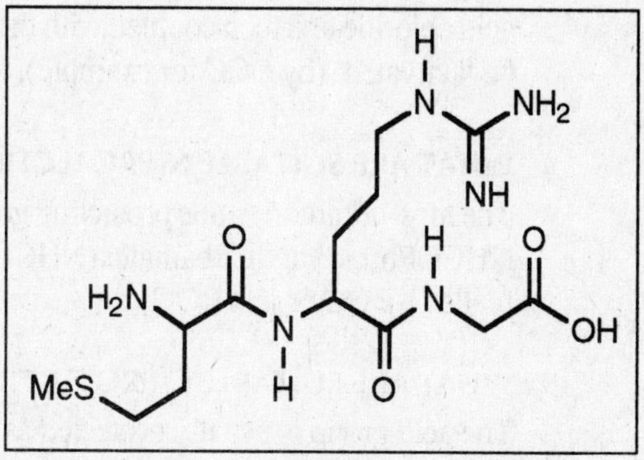

Fig. 18.67

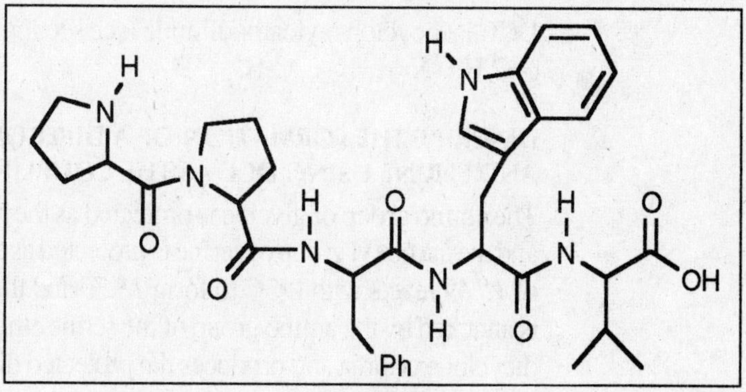

Fig. 18.68

Amino Acid Coupling Reactions

DIPEPTIDE FORMATION

WHY IS IT NECESSARY TO PROTECT THE AMINO GROUP OF AN AMINO ACID OR A PEPTIDE IF COUPLING IS TO OCCUR AT THE C-TERMINUS?

When a peptide is formed, the amino group on one amino acid is reacted with the carboxyl of a second to form the amide (peptide) bond. The amino acid that is to couple via the COOH group *must* have its amino group protected (blocked) so the only amide bond that will be formed is with the second amino acid. In the same vein, the amino acid that is to be coupled via the -NH_2 group must have its carboxyl group protected (blocked) in order to prevent unwanted coupling.

IF TWO AMINO ACIDS ARE TO BE COUPLED, DESCRIBE THE NECESSARY PROTECTION, IN GENERAL TERMS.

The amine group of one amino acid is protected (usually as an amide or a carbamate) and the carboxyl group of the second amino acid is blocked (usually as an ester). The free carboxyl group on one amino acid is then coupled to the free amino group of the second amino acid to give the amide bond. There are several methods for doing this coupling. In one, the COOH is converted to an acid chloride and then coupled with the amine. Alternatively, the carbonyl can be 'activated' (by DCC for example), allowing reaction with the amino group.

WHAT ARE SUITABLE N-PROTECTING GROUPS?

The most common amine protecting groups for this purpose are amide (NHAc, NHCOPh, etc.) and carbamates (NHCO$_2$CH$_2$Ph [called Cbz] and NHCO$_2$CMe$_3$ [called t-BOC or just BOC].

WHAT ARE SUITABLE C-PROTECTING GROUPS?

The acid group is usually protected as a methyl or ethyl ester.

WHAT IS DCC?

DCC is dicyclohexylcarbodiimide (see section 15.2):
c–C_6H_{11}–N=C=N–c–C_6H_{11}.

DESCRIBE THE FORMATION OF A DIPEPTIDE BETWEEN GLYCINE AND SERINE USING DCC AS THE COUPLING AGENT.

The amino group of glycine is protected as the benzyl carbamate to give *18.69* and the carboxyl group of serine is protected as the ethyl ester. The acid moiety of *18.69* reacts with DCC to form *18.70* and the carbonyl of this intermediate is attacked by the amino group of the serine ethyl ester. This reaction displaces dicyclohexylurea and produces the protected dipeptide, *18.71*. Saponification removes the ester group and reaction with hydrogen (Pd catalyst) removes the CBz group to give the dipeptide, *18.72*.

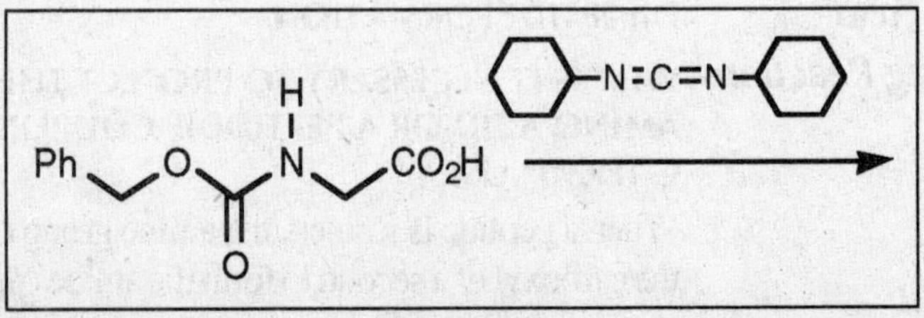

Fig. 18.69

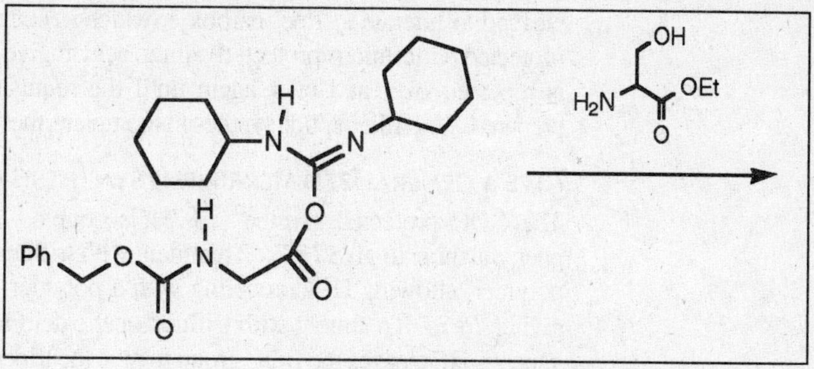

Fig. 18.70

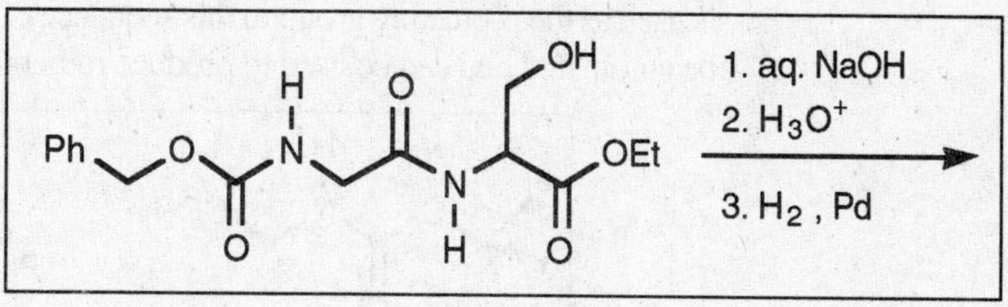

Fig. 18.71

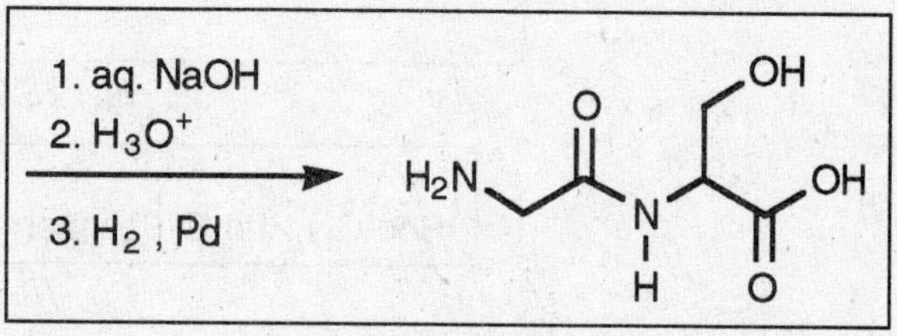

Fig. 18.72

HOW ARE C-TERMINUS PROTECTING GROUPS REMOVED?

If the C-terminus (the COOH) is protected as an ester, saponification (i. aq. OH⁻ ii. aq. H⁺) will convert the ester to the carboxylic acid.

HOW ARE N-TERMINUS PROTECTING GROUPS REMOVED?

If an amide group is used (acetamide, benzamide) basic hydrolysis followed by neutralization with acid usually removes the group. If the benzylic carbamate is used (CBz) catalytic hydrogenation with a palladium catalyst removes the protecting group.

POLYPEPTIDES

WHAT IS THE MERRIFIELD SYNTHESIS?

This is a solid-phase peptide synthesis where the growing peptide is bound to a polymer (the peptide is usually attached at the C-terminus). A C-terminus amino acid, bound to a chloro-methylated polystyrene polymer) is coupled via DCC to an amino protected amino acid to form a peptide. The polymer ester is cleaved to liberate a 'free' carboxyl, which is coupled with a new polymer protected (C-terminus protected) amino acid to give a tripeptide. This process is repeated over and over again until the requisite polypeptide has been prepared. When the peptide synthesis is complete, the N-terminus is deprotected.

GIVE A GENERALIZED MERRIFIELD SYNTHESIS OF GLY-PHE-ALA.

The BOC protected glycine (*18.73*) is coupled with the polymer-bound phenylalanine to give *18.74*. Treatment with trifluoroacetic acid removes the polymer, allowing DCC coupling with a polymer-bound alanine molecule, giving *18.75*. Treatment with trifluoroacetic acid removes the polymer and aqueous HF cleaves the BOC group to give the tripeptide (*18.76*). Very often, aqueous HF cleaves both the polymer and the BOC group (which is why BOC is used as the protecting group in this sequence). The Merrifield synthesis can be automated and can be used to produce rather large polypeptides.

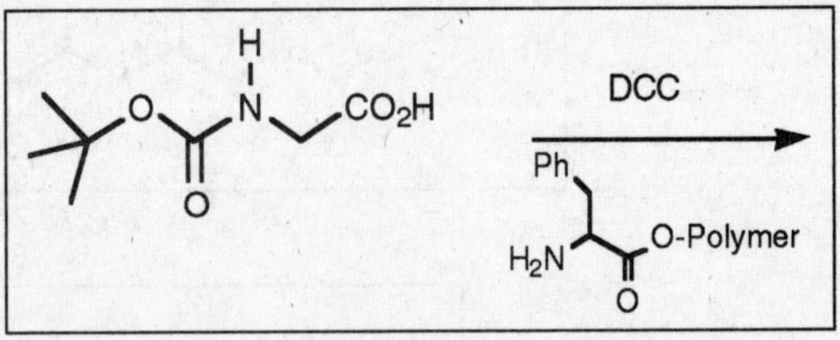

Fig. 18.73

Fig. 18.74

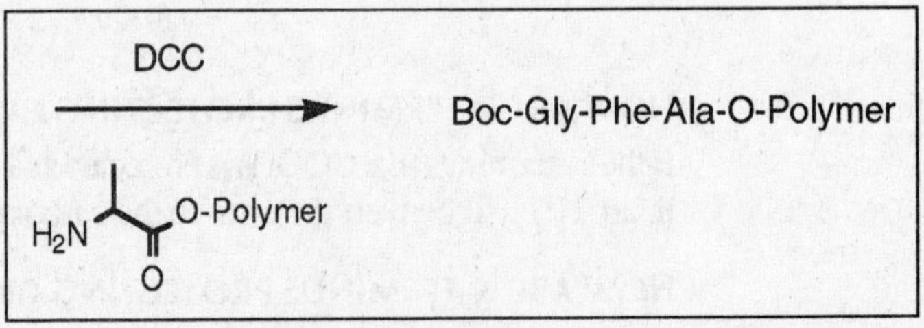

Fig. 18.75

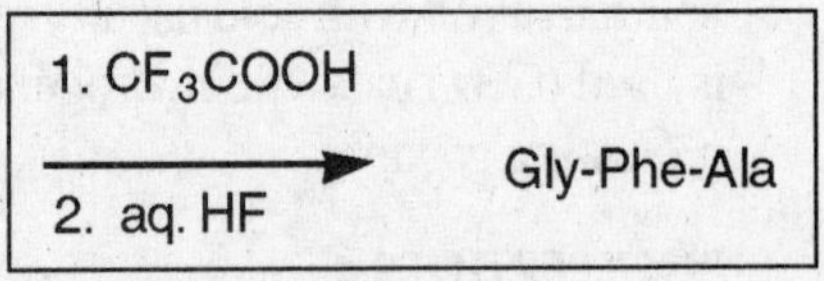

Fig. 18.76

End Group Analysis

WHAT IS END GROUP ANALYSIS?

These are chemical reactions that cleave the amino acid residues from the N-terminus or the C-terminus of the peptide, allowing them to be identified.

HYDROLYSIS

IF A POLYPEPTIDE IS HEATED WITH 6N HCL, WHAT IS THE RESULT?

If a peptide is heated in 6N aqueous HCl (usually for one day at greater than 100°C), all amide (peptide) bonds in the molecule are cleaved to give all constituent amino acid residues as discreet units. Complete degradation to the amino acids occurs with most peptides but occasionally partial degradation occurs to give a mixture of amino acids and small peptides.

ANALYSIS OF C-TERMINUS RESIDUES

WHAT IS A CARBOXYPEPTIDASE?

A carboxypeptidase is an enzyme that selectively cleaves the peptide bond to the C-terminal amino acid in a peptide. It can be used to cleave and identify what that amino acid is.

An enzyme that cleaves only terminal amino acid residues and not internal amino acid residues is called an *exopeptidase*.

WHEN A PEPTIDE IS DIGESTED WITH THE ENZYME TRYPSIN, WHAT IS THE RESULT?

Trypsin is an enzyme that cleaves peptide bonds at the carbonyl group of *arginine* or *lysine*, if these amino acids are *not* the N-terminus of the peptide and if they are *not* followed by a proline. Under these conditions, however, treatment of a peptide with trypsin will lead to cuts in the peptide chain specifically at arginine or lysine.

An enzyme that cleaves a peptide bond within the chain rather than at a terminal amino acid residue is called an *endopeptidase*.

WHEN A PEPTIDE IS DIGESTED WITH THE ENZYME CHYMOTRYPSIN, WHAT IS THE RESULT?

Chymotrypsin is an enzyme that cleaves peptides at amino acids containing aromatic side chains such as phenylalanine, tyrosine and tryptophan. This enzyme will also cleave amino acids with large aliphatic side chains such as leucine or isoleucine in some cases. Incubation of a peptide with this enzyme will, therefore, cleave the peptide at specific and predictable locations.

ANALYSIS OF N-TERMINUS RESIDUES

WHAT IS SANGER'S REAGENT?

Sanger's reagent is 2,4-dinitrofluorobenzene (*18.77*). It reacts selectively with the N-terminal amino acid residue of a peptide via nucleophilic aromatic substitution. When *18.77* reacts with the glycine residue of a peptide, *18.78* is formed. Aqueous acid hydrolysis with 6N HCl will 'release' all amino acids, but only the N-terminal amino acid will be attached to the Sanger's reagent (forming *18.79*). This N-aryl amino acid usually has a yellow color and is easily identified.

WHAT IS THE STRUCTURE OF DANSYL CHLORIDE?

Dansyl chloride is 5-dimethylamino-1-naphthalenesulfonyl chloride (*18.80*).

WHAT IS THE RESULT OF REACTING A PEPTIDE WITH SANGER'S REAGENT?

The N-terminal amino acid will displace the fluorine to form an N-aryl derivative (such as *18.78*).

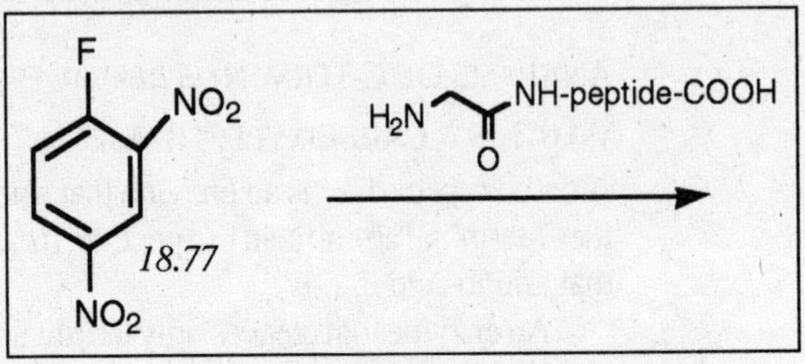

Fig. 18.77

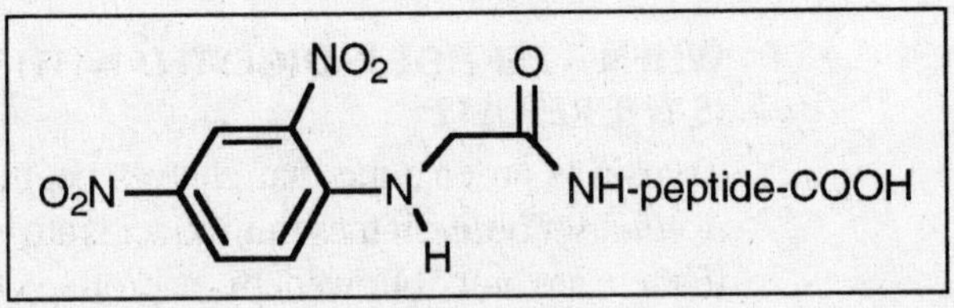

Fig. 18.78

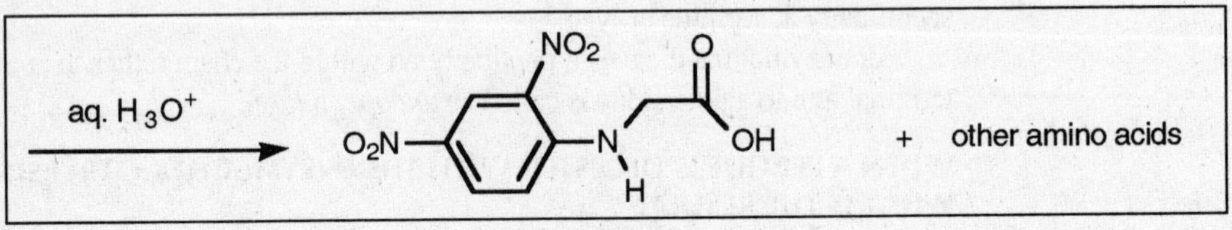

Fig. 18.79

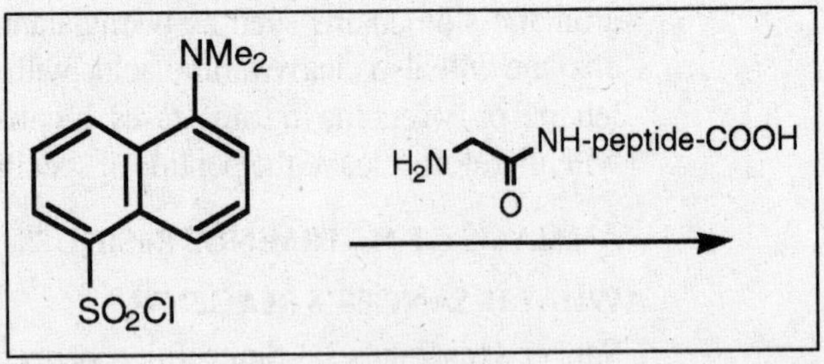

Fig. 18.80

WHAT IS THE RESULT OF TREATING A PEPTIDE WITH DANSYL CHLORIDE AND THEN HEATING THIS PRODUCT WITH AQUEOUS ACID?

The result is initial formation of sulfonamide, *18.81*. Hydrolysis leads to cleavage of the N-terminal amino acid residue from the peptide as a dansylamino acid (*18.82*), which is fluorescent and easily detected in the presence of the other amino acids liberated in the hydrolysis step.

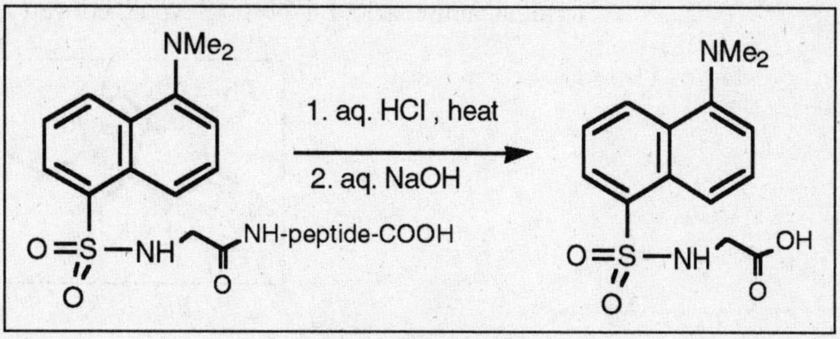

Fig. 18.81, 18.82

WHAT IS THE EDMUND DEGRADATION?

The *Edmund Degradation* is the process for derivatizing and cleaving the N-terminal amino acid of a peptide by first treating the peptide with phenyl isothiocyanate [Ph–N=C=S] and then subjecting the peptide to acid hydrolysis. The N-terminal amino acid is converted to a N-phenyl-thiohydantoin by this procedure, cleaving only the terminal amino acid from the peptide and allowing easy identification of that amino acid.

WHAT IS THE KEY REAGENT IN THE EDMUND DEGRADATION?

Phenylisothiocyanate, Ph–N=C=S.

DRAW THE PHENYLTHIOCARBAMOYL DERIVATIVE RESULTING FROM THE REACTION OF ALA-PHE AND PHENYL ISOTHIOCYANATE.

The initial product of the reaction between dipeptide *18.83* and N-phenylisothiocyanate is an N-phenylthiourea derivative, *18.84*.

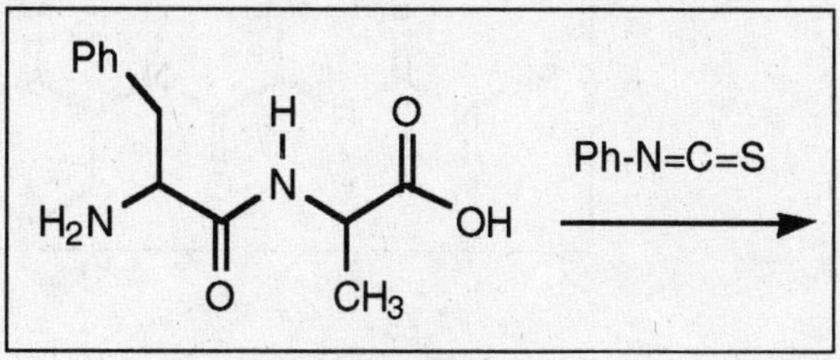

Fig. 18.83

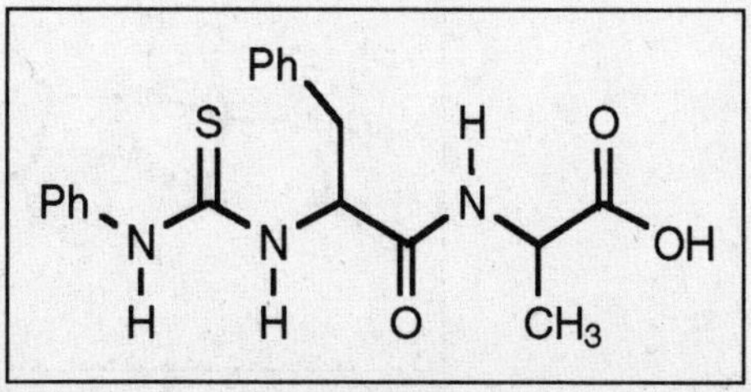

Fig. 18.84

WHAT IS THE THIAZOLONE DERIVATIVE OF ISOLEUCINE?

A thiazolone is the IUPAC name for a thiohydantoin. If isoleucine were the N-terminal amino acid, Ph–N=C=S would convert it into *18.85*.

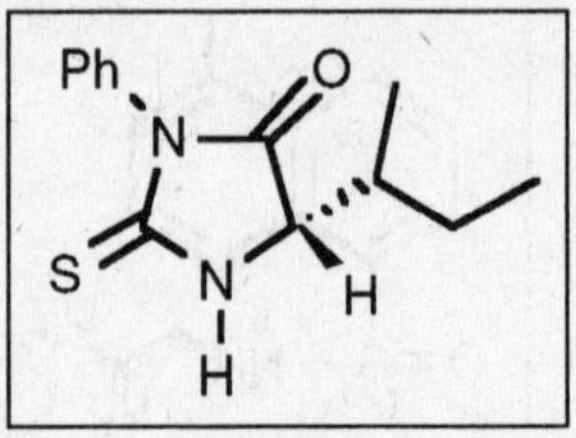

Fig. 18.85

DRAW A COMPLETE SEQUENCE FOR THE EDMUND DEGRADATION OF ALA-MET.

The dipeptide ala-met is first treated with Ph–N=C=S to form *18.86*. Upon acid hydrolysis (which cleaves only at the terminal amino acid, even in a long peptide) the nitrogen of the phenylthiourea attacks the amide carbonyl in *18.87* to form the cyclic ammonium derivative, *18.88*. When the met residue is cleaved, the N-phenylthiohydantoin of alanine is formed (*18.89*).

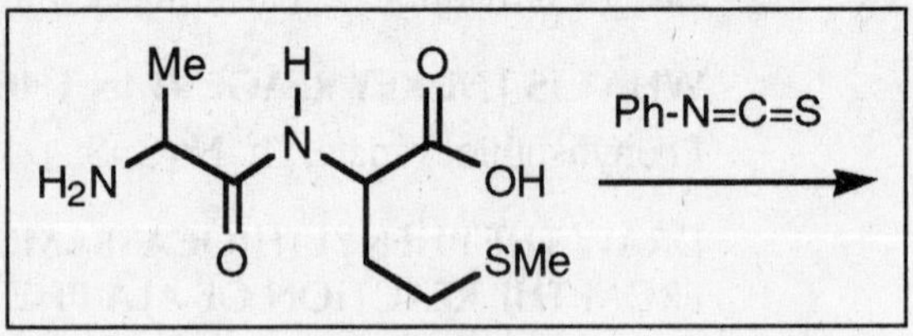

Fig. 18.86

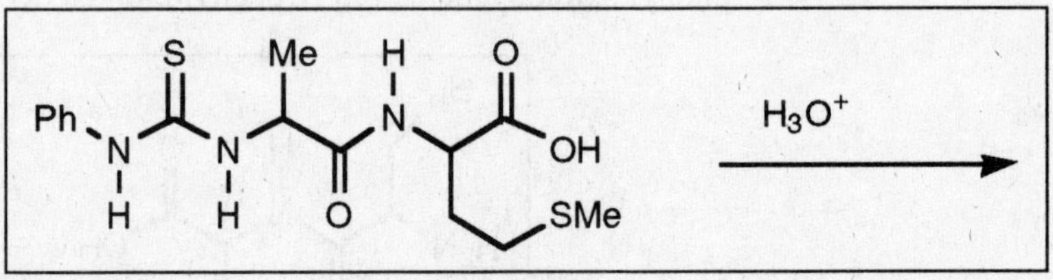

Fig. 18.87

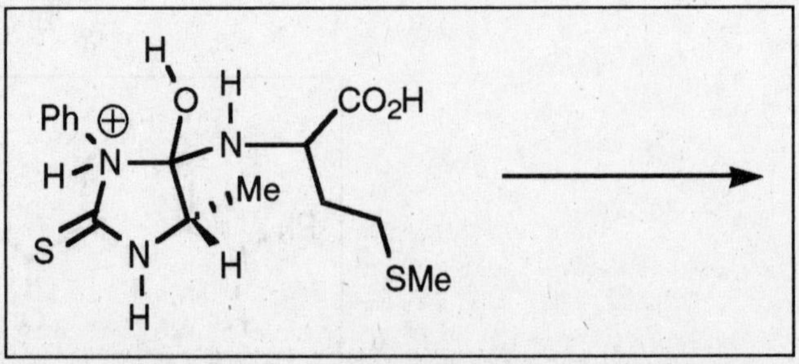

Fig. 18.88

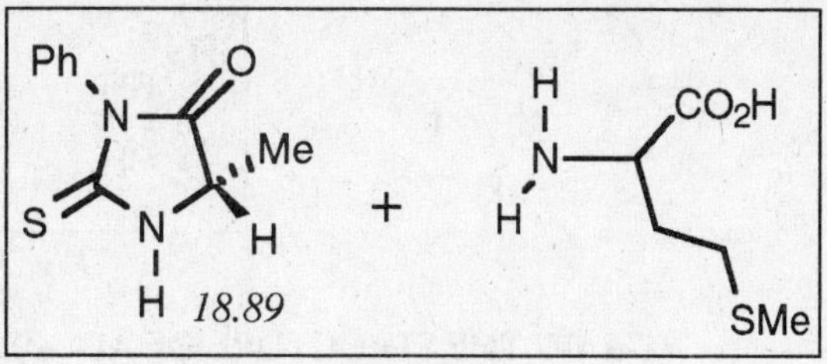

Fig. 18.89

18.5. PROTEINS

WHAT IS A PROTEIN?

A protein is a long chain biopolymer composed of amino acids joined together by amide bonds (usually called peptide bonds). There are two basic types of proteins: *simple proteins* which yield only amino acids and no other organic compounds upon hydrolysis and *conjugated proteins* which give other compounds along with amino acids upon hydrolysis.

WHAT IS AN ENZYME?

Enzymes are proteins that are the biological catalysts required to initiate chemical reactions in biological systems.

Properties of Proteins

WHAT IS THE PRIMARY STRUCTURE OF A PROTEIN OR PEPTIDE?

The primary structure of a peptide is the sequence of amino acids that comprise its basic structure.

WHAT IS THE PRIMARY STRUCTURE OF ALA-PHE-ILE-TRP?

The sequence ala-phe-ile-trp *is* the primary structure.

WHAT ARE DISULFIDE BONDS?

When cysteine is incorporated in a peptide or protein, two SH units can come together and react to form a disulfide bond (R–S–S–R).

WHAT DOES DITHIOTHREITOL DO WHEN REACTED WITH A DISULFIDE BOND?

Dithiothreitol (*18.90*) reacts with a disulfide to 'liberate' two thiol moieties and form *18.91*. Dithiothreitol is sometimes called *Cleland's* reagent.

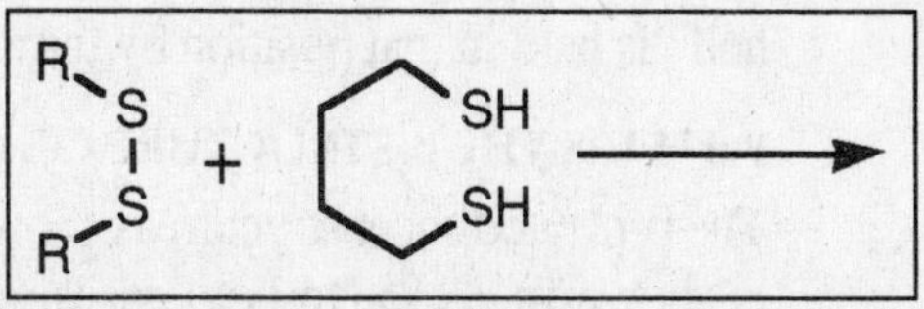

Fig. 18.90

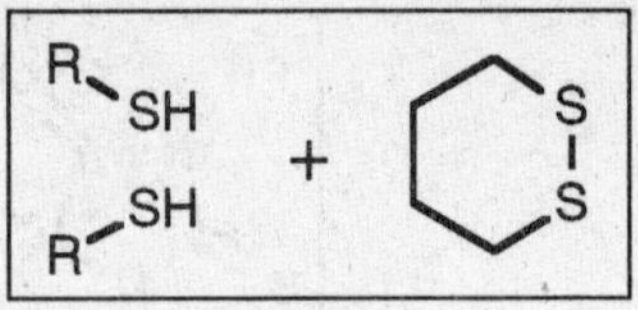

Fig. 18.91

DRAW THE STRUCTURE OF ALA-PHE, SHOWING THE RELATIVE POSITIONS OF THE CARBONYL GROUPS, AMINO GROUPS AND SIDE CHAINS.

The basic structure of a protein involves amide bonds where the alkyl side chain of one amino acid residue is effectively 'anti' to the alkyl side chain of the adjacent amino acid residue (as in *18.92*). The amide carbonyls are also 'anti' in this low energy conformation of the peptide. This alternating pattern appears throughout most proteins or peptides.

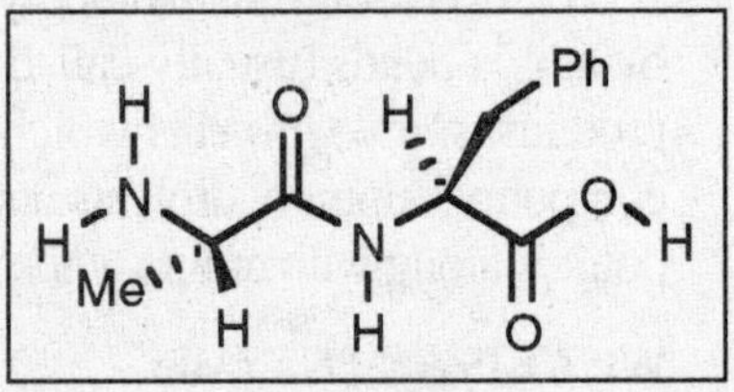

Fig. 18.92

SECONDARY STRUCTURE

WHAT IS THE SECONDARY STRUCTURE OF A PROTEIN OR PEPTIDE?

The secondary structure of a protein or peptide is the amount of structural regularity which results from intermolecular hydrogen bonding. The most common secondary structure features are formation of an α-helix or a β-pleated sheet structure.

WHAT IS AN α-HELIX?

An α-helix is the shape of peptide assumes due to the chirality of the individual amino acids, forming a spiral type structure (see *18.93*), held in that shape by hydrogen bonding between NH, OH, C=O and other heteroatom functional groups.

WHAT IS THE IMPORTANCE OF HYDROGEN BONDING IN THE SECONDARY STRUCTURE OF A PROTEIN OR PEPTIDE?

Intramolecular hydrogen bonding between various NH, OH, SH, C=O and C=N groups of the peptide stabilize the helical structure. Each 'turn' of the α-helix is held in that position by intramolecular hydrogen bonding.

WHAT IS THE β-STRUCTURE OF A PROTEIN OR PEPTIDE?

The β-pleated sheet structure is shown in *18.94*. The antiparallel pleated sheet is shown in *18.95*. In both cases, intermolecular hydrogen bonding allows 'stacking' of the peptide chains.

Fig. 18.93

In the pleated sheet the peptide chains align in a parallel manner, with all chains oriented N→C.

In the antiparallel structure the chains alternate N→C, C→N, N→C, etc., as shown.

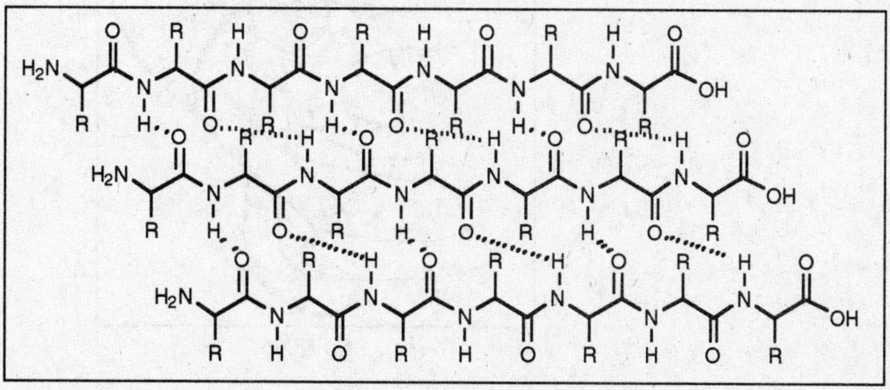

Fig. 18.94

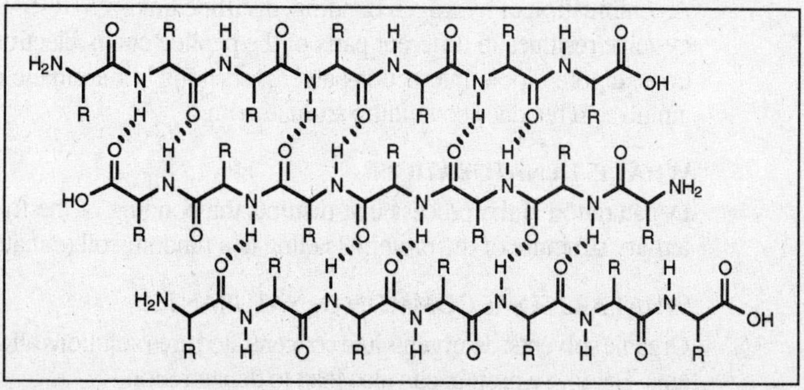

Fig. 18.95

WHAT IS A RANDOM COIL?

A random coil is a type of secondary structure that is 'random' and does not conform to a distinct structure. The peptide chains arrange in a random manner, held together by hydrogen bonding.

ARE MOST PROTEIN COMPOSED OF ONE OF THE ABOVE MENTIONED SECONDARY STRUCTURES OR MIXTURES OF SEVERAL?

Most proteins assume several different secondary structures and a typical protein is composed of various percentages of each of the structural types.

TERTIARY STRUCTURE

WHAT IS THE TERTIARY STRUCTURE OF A PROTEIN OR PEPTIDE?

The tertiary structure of a protein is its complete three-dimensional structure due to folding and coiling of the peptide chain. The tertiary structure will be the result of both the primary and secondary structure as well as 'folding' of the peptide chains, loosely illustrated by the structure *18.96*.

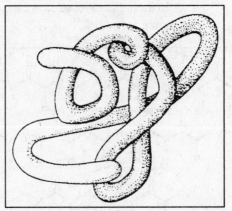

Fig. 18.96

WHAT IS PRIMARILY RESPONSIBLE FOR THE TERTIARY STRUCTURE?

A combination of hydrogen bonding, disulfide linkages (R–S–S–R) between cysteine residues in different parts of the peptide chain, electrostatic interactions, dipole-dipole interactions and "π-stacking" of aromatic rings in those amino acid residues containing aromatic rings.

WHAT IS DENATURATION?

Denaturation is the process that disrupts the bonding of the folded or coiled tertiary structure of the protein, leading to a random coil (denatured protein).

WHAT ARE SOME COMMON DENATURANTS?

Organic solvents, detergents and concentrated urea solutions all act as denaturants. Heating a protein can also lead to denaturation.

IS A DENATURED PROTEIN BIOLOGICALLY ACTIVE?

The biological activity of a protein is often a function of its tertiary structure and denaturation usually deactivates the protein.

WHAT ARE HYDROPHOBIC RESIDUES?

When two hydrocarbon fragments of different amino acids (such as the interaction of two isopropyl groups of two different valine residues) come in close proximity, the 'like-dissolves-like' rule suggests these residues will interact with each other.

QUATERNARY STRUCTURE

WHAT IS THE QUATERNARY STRUCTURE OF A PROTEIN OR PEPTIDE?

The quaternary structure of a protein or peptide is the interaction of two or more peptide chains that join together to form 'clusters' of peptides. This cluster is usually necessary for the biological activity. A schematic example is *18.97* which is composed of three separate 'units'.

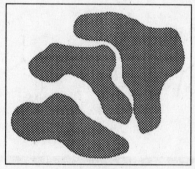

Fig. 18.97

BRIEFLY DISCUSS THE STRUCTURE OF HEMOGLOBIN.

Hemoglobin is the protein that transports oxygen in the bloodstream of mammals. It is composed of two different peptide chains (the alpha-chain and the beta-chain). It is an aggregate of four polypeptide chains (four sub-units), two alpha and two beta. These sub-units are generally held together by hydrogen bonds, van der Waals forces or electrostatic interactions.

Much of the chemistry described in this chapter is best left to a biochemistry course. It is impossible to adequately describe this complex and important chemistry in such an abbreviated fashion. The chemistry of peptides and proteins was presented primarily to show how amino acids are utilized. The main focus of this chapter was the chemistry and properties of amino acids. There are many possible combinations of different functional groups that can be used in a single molecule. the fundamental lesson of this chapter is that each functional group will bring its own characteristics to the molecule but that there are special characteristics that result from the interaction of those functional groups.

END OF CHAPTER PROBLEMS

1. Give the IUPAC name for each of the following.

(a)

CO$_2$H

NH$_2$

(b)

CO$_2$H

NMe$_2$

(c)

NEt$_2$

CO$_2$H

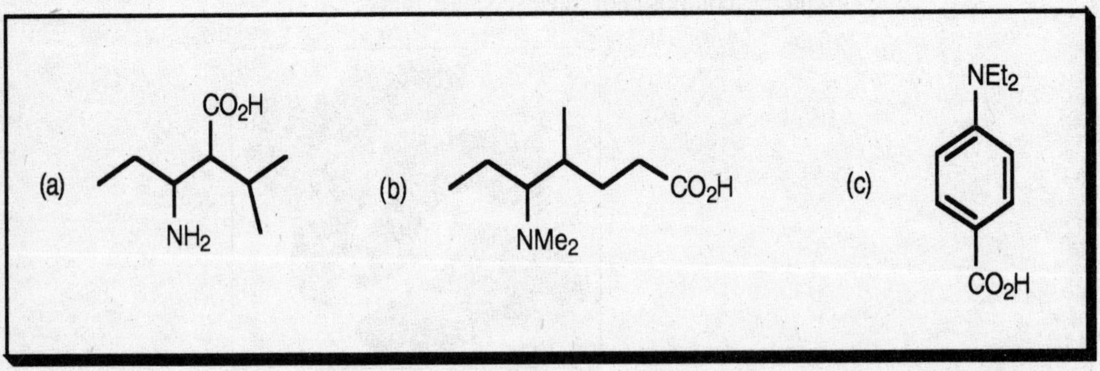

2. Give the structure for each of the following, in Fisher projection.
   (a) glu (b) val (c) ile (d) ser (e) pro (f) ala (g) asp (h) his (i) arg (j) met
3. In each case give the major product. If there is no reaction, indicate by N.R.

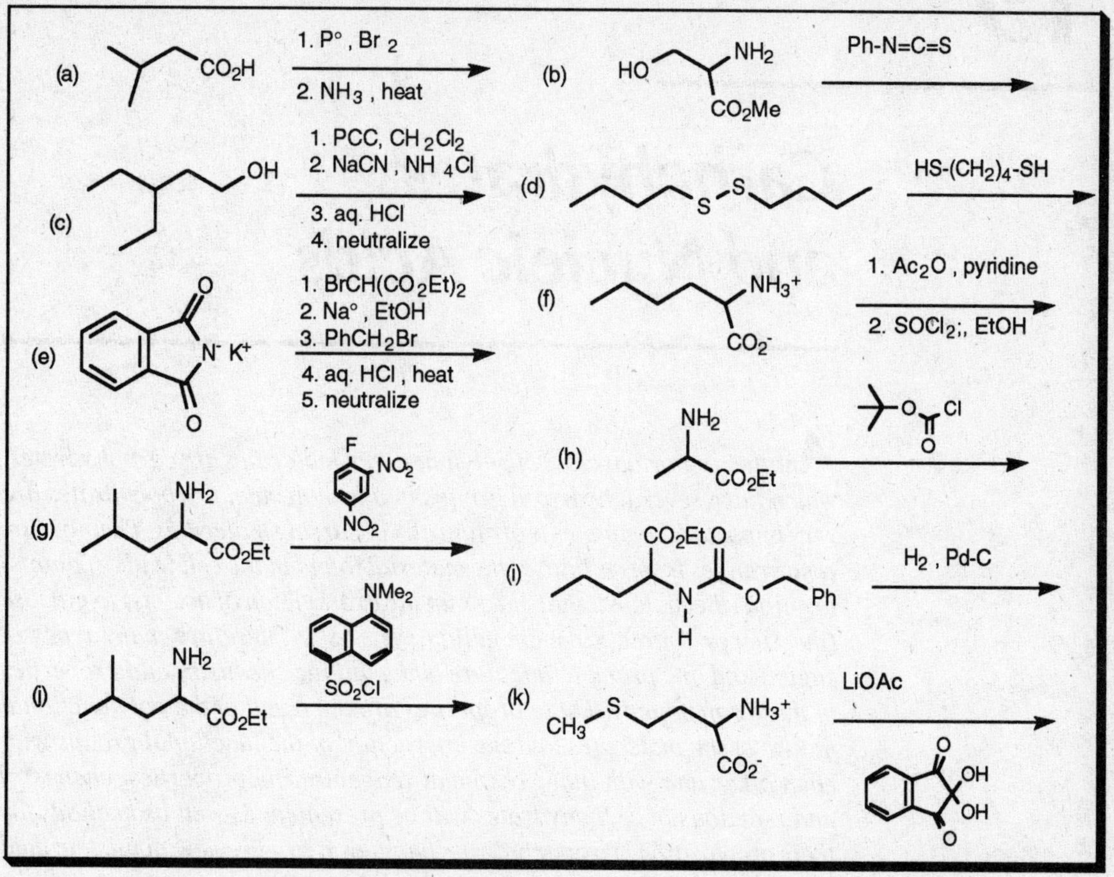
(a)
CO2H
1. P°, Br 2
2. NH3, heat
(b)
HO
NH2
CO2Me
Ph-N=C=S
(c)
OH
1. PCC, CH 2Cl2
2. NaCN, NH 4Cl
3. aq. HCl
4. neutralize
(d)
S
S
HS-(CH2)4-SH
(e)
O
N⁻ K⁺
O
1. BrCH(CO 2Et)2
2. Na°, EtOH
3. PhCH2Br
4. aq. HCl, heat
5. neutralize
(f)
NH3⁺
CO2⁻
1. Ac2O, pyridine
2. SOCl2;, EtOH
(g)
NH2
CO2Et
F
NO2
NO2
(h)
NH2
CO2Et
O
Cl
O
(i)
CO2Et O
N
H
O
Ph
H2, Pd-C
(j)
NH2
CO2Et
NMe2
SO2Cl
(k)
CH3
S
NH3⁺
CO2⁻
LiOAc
O
OH
OH
O

4. In each case provide a suitable synthesis. Show all reagents and intermediate products.

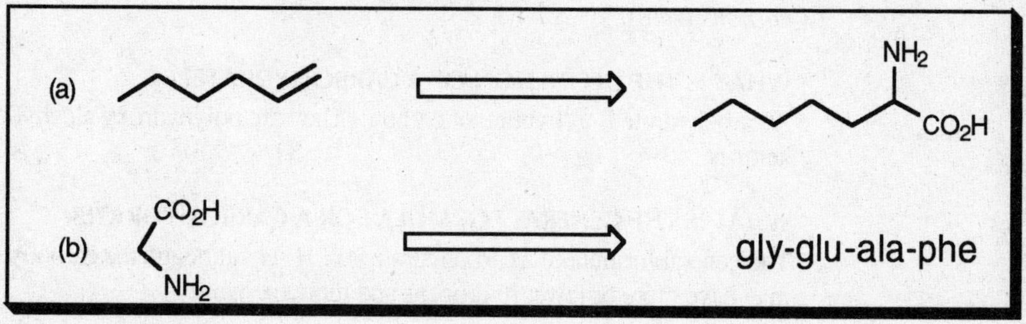
(a)
NH2
CO2H
(b)
CO2H
NH2
gly-glu-ala-phe

19

Carbohydrates and Nucleic Acids

Another important class of polyfunctional molecules are carbohydrates, which have several hydroxyl groups in one molecule. Carbohydrates are very important components of naturally occurring molecules. Their occurrence ranges from cellulose (the material found in the cell walls of plants) to chitin (the material that makes up the exoskeleton of insects) to glucose (the energy source for mammalian systems). There are many types of sugars and one prominent feature is the unique chemistry and properties of these compounds. These properties are the result of the polyfunctional nature of the molecules and the interaction of the functional groups with each other and with other chemical reagents. The properties, chemistry and reactions of carbohydrates will be presented, as well as methods for their preparation. To conclude the chapter, a brief review of nucleic acid chemistry, which contain sugars as a key structural component, will be presented. This is not intended as an in-depth review of biological chemistry or biochemistry but simply as an illustration of the importance of carbohydrates.

WHAT IS THE DEFINITION OF A CARBOHYDRATE?
A carbohydrate is a 'hydrate of carbon'. They are polyhydroxy aldehydes or ketones.

WHAT IS THE GENERAL FORMULA FOR A CARBOHYDRATE?
The general formula of a carbohydrate is $C_nH_{2n}O_n$, although the carbohydrate may have more or fewer hydrogens and more oxygens.

WHY ARE CARBOHYDRATES ALSO CALLED SUGARS?
Sucrose is common table sugar and glucose is the common sugar used as an energy source in mammalian systems. Both of these compounds are carbohydrates and typical examples of this class of compounds. For this reason carbohydrates are often referred to as 'sugars'.

WHAT IS A SACCHARIDE?

Saccharide is another term for carbohydrates or sugars.

19.1. PROPERTIES OF CARBOHYDRATES

Chirality

GIVEN THE STRUCTURE OF GLUCOSE (19.1), HOW MANY CHIRAL CENTERS ARE PRESENT? IDENTIFY EACH USING THE R/S NOMENCLATURE.

Glucose is drawn in two forms, as the cyclic hemiacetal (*19.1*) and as the open-chain aldehyde, *19.2*. Using *19.2* (drawn in Fischer projection), C_2 (attached to CHO) is R, C_3 is S, C_4 is R and C_5 is R. In the cyclic form (*19.1*), the CHOH group attached to the oxygen in the ring is also chiral but can exist as both R or S (see below).

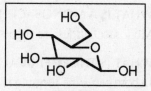

Fig. 19.1

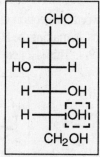

Fig. 19.2

D AND L SUGARS

DESCRIBE THE D/L SYSTEM FOR SUGARS.

As with amino acids, the D,L system is based on comparison to (+)- or (-)-glyceraldehyde. When the OH of (+)-glyceraldehyde is 'on the right' (in the box in *19.3*) of the Fischer projection, it is given the label D-glyceraldehyde. If the OH on the next to last carbon in the open chain form of the carbohydrate (C_5 in *19.2*) is on the right, it is a D-sugar. If the OH is on the left, it is an L sugar.

In *19.2*, that OH (in the box) is on the right and this molecule is called D-glucose.

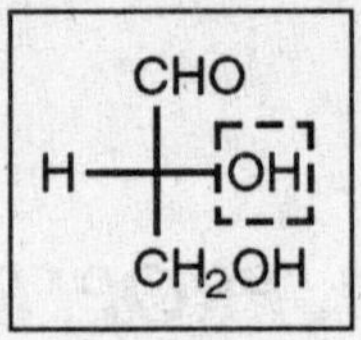

Fig. 19.3

HOW IS GLUCOSE RELATED TO D-GLYCERALDEHYDE?

The C_5 carbon in *19.2* has the H–C–OH group oriented exactly as in D-glyceraldehyde (H–C–OH) and is, therefore, assigned the label, D.

19.2 CLASSIFICATION OF CARBOHYDRATES

Monosaccharides

WHAT IS A MONOSACCHARIDE?

Monosaccharides are sugars that can *not* be hydrolyzed into simpler sugars.

WHAT IS THE EMPIRICAL FORMULA FOR GLUCOSE? FOR FRUCTOSE?

In both cases the formula is $C_6H_{12}O_6$.

WHAT IS A HAWORTH PROJECTION?

A Haworth projection takes the cyclic hemiacetal form of the sugar (*19.1*) and 'flattens' it, making the H and OH groups appear either on the 'top' or the 'bottom', as in *19.4*. This is a general way in which to present the structure of sugars.

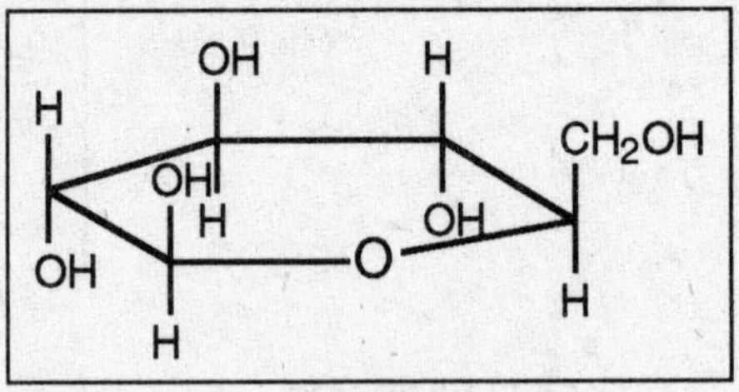

Fig. 19.4

ACYCLIC (OPEN CHAIN) FORMS

WHAT IS AN ALDOHEXOSE? A KETOHEXOSE? AN ALDOPYRANOSE? A KETOFURANOSE?

An aldose is a polyhydroxy aldehyde and a ketose is a polyhydroxy ketone. A hexose is a six-carbon sugar and a pentose is a five-carbon sugar. A furose is the cyclic hemiacetal or hemiketal form of the sugar that exists in a five-membered tetrahydrofuran ring. A pyranose is the cyclic hemiacetal or hemiketal form of the sugar that exists in a six-membered pyran ring. An example of an aldohexose is glucose (*19.2*) and an example of a ketohexose is fructose (*19.5*). An aldopyranose is the cyclic form of glucose (*19.4*) and a ketofuranose is the cyclic form of fructose (*19.6*).

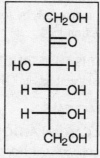

Fig. 19.5

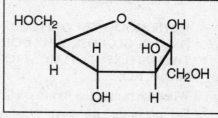

Fig. 19.6

DRAW D-GLUCOSE IN FISCHER PROJECTION AS THE OPEN CHAIN ALDEHYDE.

The Fischer projection of D-glucose is *19.2*.

DRAW L-GLUCOSE IN FISCHER PROJECTION AS THE OPEN CHAIN ALDEHYDE.

The Fischer projection of L-glucose is *19.7*.

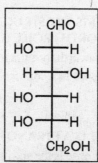

Fig. 19.7

DRAW D-FRUCTOSE IN FISCHER PROJECTION AS THE OPEN CHAIN ALDEHYDE.

The Fischer projection of D-fructose is *19.5*.

CYCLIC FORMS

WHAT IS THE USUAL REACTION OF AN ALDEHYDE AND AN ALCOHOL?

In general, aldehydes react with alcohols to form acetals (RCH[OR']$_2$) but the reaction proceeds by formation of an unstable hemiacetal [RCH(OH)OR']. See section 13.4.

WHAT IS THE STRUCTURE OF A HEMIACETAL?

A hemiacetal has an OH and an OR on the same carbon [RCH(OH)OR'].

HEMIACETALS

HOW CAN AN ALDOHEXOSE FORM A HEMIACETAL?

An aldohexose such as glucose forms a hemiacetal by cyclizing, to a pyranose (*19.4*) for D-glucose. The appropriate alcohol moiety attacks the acyl carbon of the aldehyde carbon.

IF THE ABSOLUTE CONFIGURATION OF ALL ALCOHOL GROUPS IS FIXED IN GLUCOSE, WHY DOES THE CYCLIC HEMIACETAL FORM TWO DIFFERENT CYCLIC STRUCTURES? DRAW BOTH IN HAWORTH PROJECTION.

When the hemiacetal forms, cyclization can occur from two faces to give the OH 'up' or the OH 'down' (*19.4* or *19.8*).

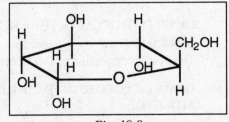

Fig. 19.8

WHAT IS THE STRUCTURE OF α-GLUCOSE AND β-GLUCOSE IN HAWORTH PROJECTION?

The Haworth formula for β-D-glucose is *19.4* and the Haworth structure of α-D-glucose is *19.8*.

Pyranoses

WHAT IS A PYRANOSE?

A pyranose is the six-membered hemiacetal structure formed by aldohexoses such as glucose. The structure *19.9* is an example of a pyranose.

WHAT IS AN ANOMER?

When the hemiacetal forms, the OH group of that carbon can be either R or S. These diastereomeric products are referred to as anomers [*19.4* and *19.8* are anomers].

WHAT IS AN ANOMERIC CARBON?

The hemiacetal (or hemiketal) carbon is the anomeric carbon.

DRAW THE EIGHT DIFFERENT D-ISOMERS OF GLUCOSE (INCLUDING GLUCOSE) IN THEIR D-PYRANOSE FORM? GIVE THE NAME OF EACH ISOMER.

The eight isomers are D-(+)-glucose (*19.9*), D-(+)-allose (*19.10*), D-(+)-mannose (*19.11*), D-(+)-altrose (*19.12*), D-(-)-gulose (*19.13*), D-(-)-idose (*19.14*), D-(+)-galactose (*19.15*) and D-(+)-talose (*19.16*).

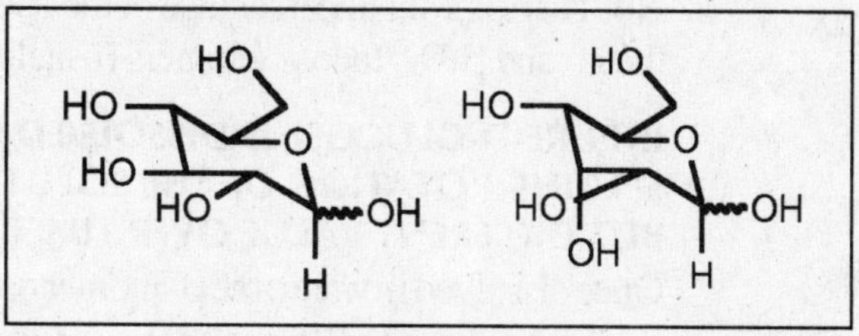

Fig. 19.9, 19.10

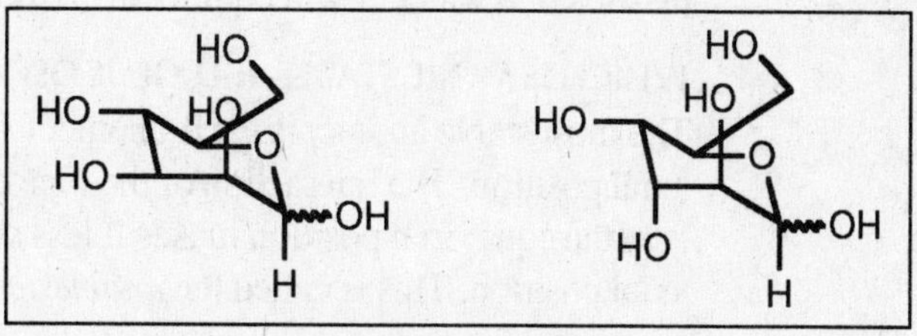

Fig. 19.11, 19.12

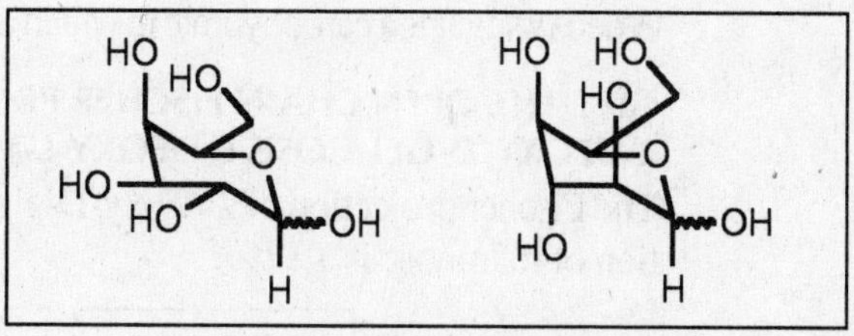

Fig. 19.13, 19.14

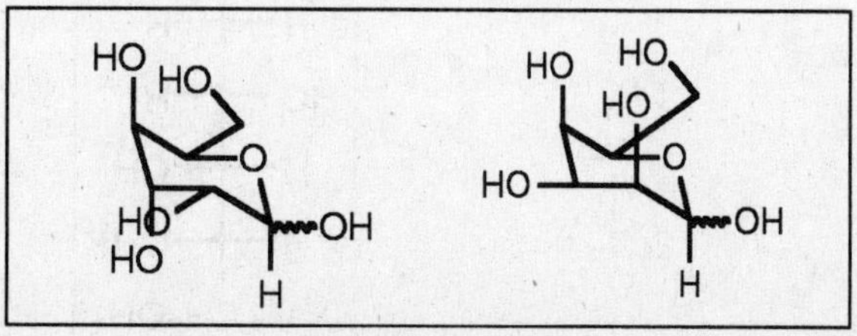

Fig. 19.15, 19.16

DOES D-GLUCOSE EXIST PRIMARILY IN THE α-FORM OR THE β-FORM? EXPLAIN.

D-glucose exists primarily as the β-anomer (*19.17*). There is actually an equilibrium mixture of 64% of *19.17* and 36% of the α-anomer, *19.9*.

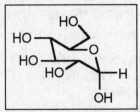

Fig. 19.17

DOES D-GLUCOSE EXIST 100% AS A PYRANOSE? EXPLAIN.

No. There is a small percentage of the open-chain aldehyde in equilibrium with the α- and β-D-glucose anomers (usually less than 1%).

IF PURE-D-GLUCOSE IS DISSOLVED IN WATER, WHY DOES THE SPECIFIC ROTATION OF THE SOLUTION CHANGE TO A CONSTANT BUT DIFFERENT VALUE OVER TIME?

Once dissolved in water, the β-anomer opens to the aldehyde and then can close again to either the β-form or the α-form. Similarly, if the pure α-anomer is dissolved in water, it will equilibrate to the same mixture of the two anomers.

WHICH IS MORE STABLE, α-D-GLUCOSE OR β-D-GLUCOSE? EXPLAIN.

The most stable anomer is the β-anomer (*19.17*), where the OH group is in the axial position. The interaction of the lone electron pair on the oxygen when it is in the equatorial position makes it less stable than having the oxygen in the axial position. This is called the *anomeric effect*.

WHAT IS A DEOXY SUGAR?

A deoxy sugar is a carbohydrate in which at least one of the OH groups is missing.

GIVE THE OPEN CHAIN FISCHER PROJECTIONS OF 2-DEOXY-D-GLUCOSE. 6-DEOXY-L-MANNOSE (RHAMNOSE).

The Fischer projection of 2-deoxy-D-glucose is *19.18* and the Fischer projection of rhamnose is *19.19*.

```
        CHO                   CHO
   H ——|—— H           H ——|—— OH
  HO ——|—— H           H ——|—— OH
   H ——|—— OH         HO ——|—— H
   H ——|—— OH         HO ——|—— H
       CH₂OH                 CH₃
```

Fig. 19.18, 19.19

**GIVE THE PYRANOSE FORM OF 2-DEOXY-D-GLUCOSE.
6-DEOXY-L-MANNOSE (RHAMNOSE).**

The pyranose form of 2-deoxy-D-glucose is *19.20* and rhamnose is *19.21*.

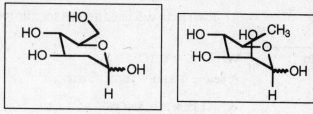

Fig. 19.20, 19.21

Mutarotation

WHAT IS MUTAROTATION?

Mutarotation is the change in specific rotation of a sugar when dissolved in water. This occurs when the hemiacetal form of a carbohydrate (such as *19.9*) changes the configuration of the O–CHOH group from C_1-R to C_1-S (or from C_1-S to C_1-R). A sample of pure C_1-R-*19.9* will equilibrate to a mixture of C_1-R + C_1-S-*19.9* in water and the specific rotation will change to reflect the equilibrium mixture.

WHAT PROPERTIES OF A SUGAR SUCH AS GLUCOSE LEAD TO MUTAROTATION?

Taking glucose as an example, the open chain form (*19.22*) will close to the hemiacetal (*19.9*) by attack of the C_5 OH on the carbonyl of the aldehyde. In this hemiacetal, the carbon bearing the C_1–OH can assume either the R or S configuration (*19.9* ⇆ *19.22* ⇆ *19.17*). The specific rotation of *19.9* (α-D-glucose) is +112.2° and the specific rotation of pure *19.17* (β-D-glucose) is +18.7°. When pure *19.9* is dissolved in water, the specific rotation changes to +52.6° and if pure *19.17* is dissolved in water the specific rotation also changes to +52.6°. Each pure glucopyranose equilibrates to a mixture of 36% of *19.9*, 64% of *19.7* and <0.2% of *19.22*.

Fig. 19.9, 19.22, 19.17

WHY DOES D-GLUCOSE HAVE MORE THAN ONE VALUE FOR SPECIFIC ROTATION?

D-Glucose exists in two anomeric forms, α-D-glucose (*19.9*) and β-D-glucose (*19.17*).

Each form will have its own specific rotation when pure.

Furanoses

WHAT IS A KETOSE?

A ketose is a polyhydroxy ketone.

WHAT IS A FURANOSE?

A furanose is a five-membered ring hemiacetal or hemiketal in which the ring contains an oxygen. It is essentially a polyhydroxy tetrahydrofuran derivative.

WHAT IS THE OPEN CHAIN STRUCTURE OF D-RIBOSE? D-RIBULOSE? L-XYLULOSE? D-FRUCTOSE?

The Fischer projection of ribose is *19.23*, D-ribulose is *19.24*, L-xylulose is *19.25* and D-fructose is *19.5*.

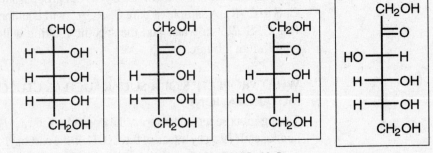

Fig. 19.23–19.25, 19.5

DRAW THE FURANOSE FORM OF β-D-RIBOSE, β-D-RIBULOSE, β-L-XYLULOSE, AND β-D-FRUCTOSE.

In each case, the β-form of these sugars is shown. The Haworth formula *19.26* is β-(D)-ribose, *19.27* is β-(D)-ribulose, *19.28* is β-(L)-xylulose and *19.29* is β-(D)-fructose.

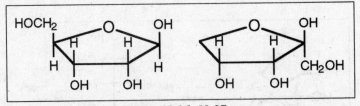

Fig. 19.26, 19.27

WHAT IS THE FURANOSE FORM OF 2-DEOXY-D-RIBOSE?

The structure of β-(D)-2-deoxyribose is *19.30*.

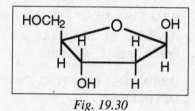

Fig. 19.28, 19.29

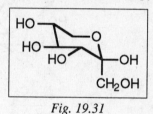

Fig. 19.30

DOES D-FRUCTOSE UNDERGO MUTAROTATION?

Yes. At equilibrium there is about 4-9% of α-D-fructofuranose and 21-31% of β-D-fructofuranose. Complicating this picture is the fact that fructose also exists in the pyranose form. At equilibrium there is 0-3% of α-D-fructopyranose and the dominant isomer is 57-75% of β-D-fructopyranose (*19.31*).

Fig. 19.31

Disaccharides

WHAT IS A DISACCHARIDE?

A disaccharide is a carbohydrate that gives two monosaccharides upon hydrolysis.

α AND β LINKAGES

DRAW TWO GLUCOSE MOLECULES AS A DISACCAHRIDE CONNECTED BY AN α-LINKAGE BETWEEN C_2 AND $C_{2'}$. A β-LINKAGE BETWEEN C_2 AND $C_{4'}$.

In *19.32* the C_2 and C_4 carbons of one glucose molecule are marked, as well as the C_2/C_4 carbons of the second glucose ($C_{2'}$ and $C_{4'}$). In *19.32*, the term 'α-linkage' refers to the C_2-$C_{2'}$ connection (the anomeric carbons) being axial (α). This 'linkage' appears to be an ether type linkage but is, in fact, a linked acetal. A second type of disaccharide connects the anomeric OH with the C_4 OH to give *19.33*, which is a β-linkage with the anomeric C_2 oxygen being equatorial. The name of *19.32* is maltose and *19.33* is cellobiose.

DRAW A D-GLUCOSE AND A D-FRUCTOSE CONNECTED BY A α-LINKAGE BETWEEN C_2 AND $C_{2'}$.

This disaccharide has the structure *19.34*. This molecule called sucrose.

WHAT IS A HEAD-TO-HEAD DISACCHARIDE?

A head-to-head disaccharide is a molecule composed of two monosaccharides linked by the C_2-$C_{2'}$ atoms.

WHAT IS A HEAD-TO-TAIL DISACCAHRIDE?

A head-to-tail disaccharide is a molecule composed of two monosaccharides linked by the C_2-$C_{4'}$ atoms.

DRAW THE STRUCTURE OF A) MALTOSE B) CELLOBIOSE C) LACTOSE D) SUCROSE.

The structure of maltose is *19.32*, cellobiose is *19.33*, lactose is *19.35* and sucrose is *19.34*. Lactose is composed of a D-galactose and a D-glucose, with a C_2-$C_{2'}$ β-linkage.

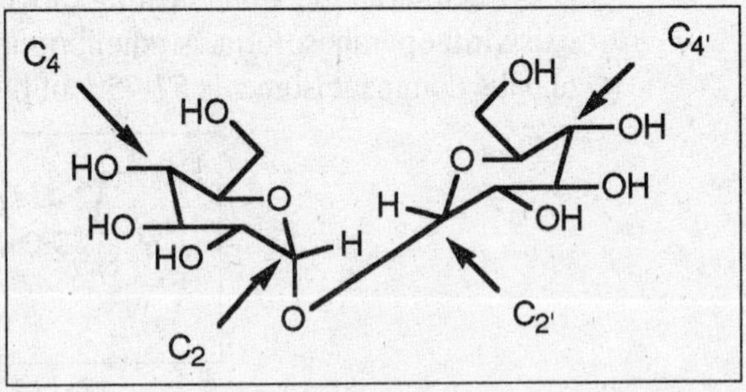

Fig. 19.32

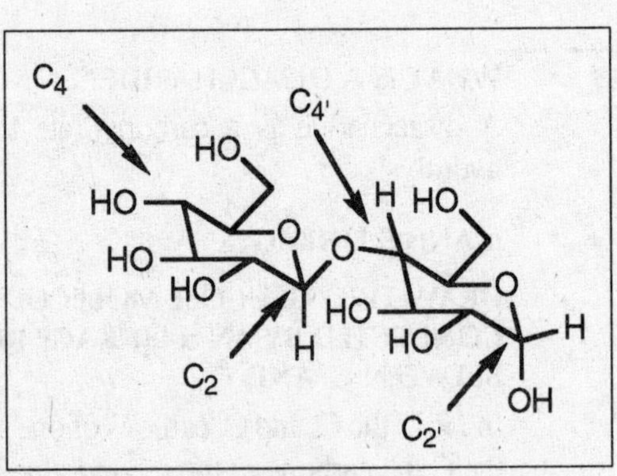

Fig. 19.33

Polysaccharides

WHAT IS A POLYSACCHARIDE?

A polysaccharide is a carbohydrate composed of many monosaccharide units. It is essentially a polymer composed of monosaccharide monomers.

WHAT IS AN OLIGOSACCHARIDE?

An oligosaccharide is a polysaccharide composed of about 3-10 monosaccharide units.

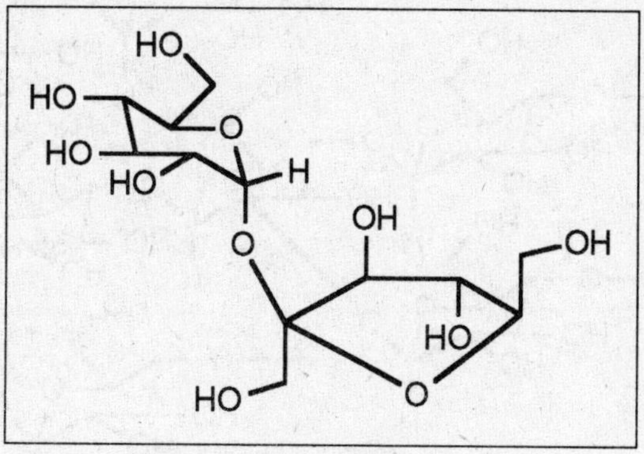

Fig. 19.34

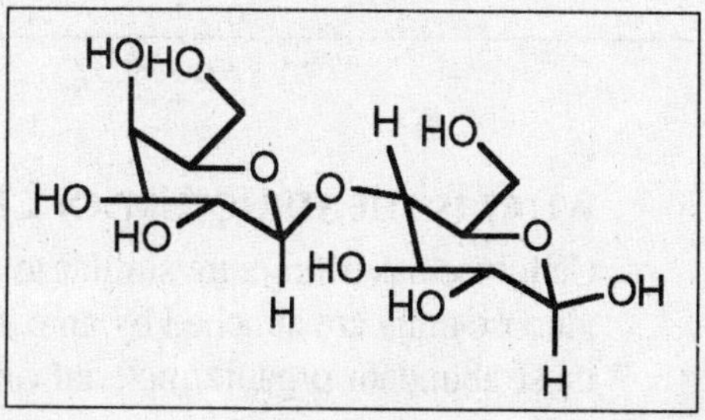

Fig. 19.35

WHAT IS THE STRUCTURE OF STARCH?

Starch is actually a mixture of two polysaccharides. One is a water soluble polysaccharide called amylose, which is a linear polymer (100-several thousand D-glucose units) attached by 1,4-β-linkages. The second polysaccharide is called amylopectin and is a branched polymer (100-several thousand D-glucose units) attached by 1,4-β-linkages.

WHAT IS THE STRUCTURE OF AMYLOSE? OF AMYLOPECTIN?

The linear polysaccharide amylose has the structure *19.36*, with repeating D-glucose molecules. The branched polymer amylopectin can be represented as *19.37*, again with repeating D-glucose units.

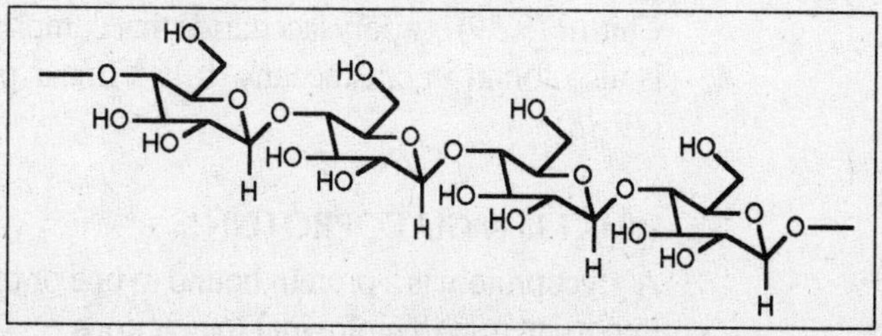

Fig. 19.36

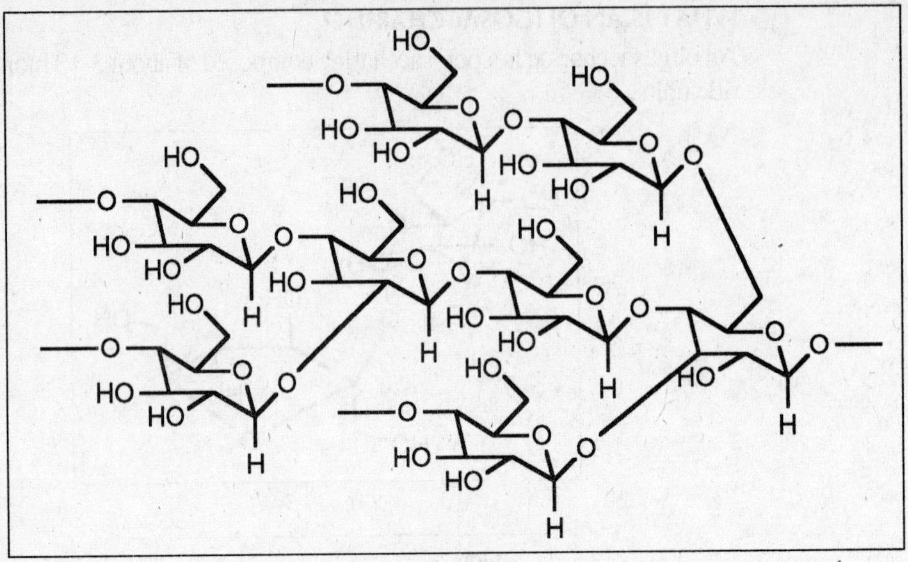

Fig. 19.37

WHAT IS THE STRUCTURE OF CELLULOSE?

Cellulose has a structure similar to amylose (*19.36*) except that the linear D-glucose units are attached by an α-linkage (see *19.32*). Cellulose may be the most abundant organic material on earth and is the structural material that composes most plants.

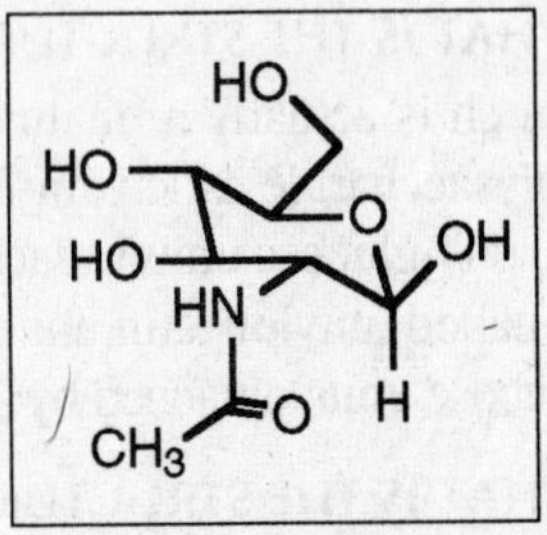

Fig. 19.38

WHAT IS THE STRUCTURE OF CHITIN?

Chitin (*19.39*) is a polysaccharide that comprises the exoskeleton of insects and is also found in crustaceans. It is a linear polymer of N-acetylglucosamine (*19.38*).

WHAT IS A GLYCOPROTEIN?

A glycoprotein is a protein bound to one or more carbohydrates. They play an important role in biological interactions.

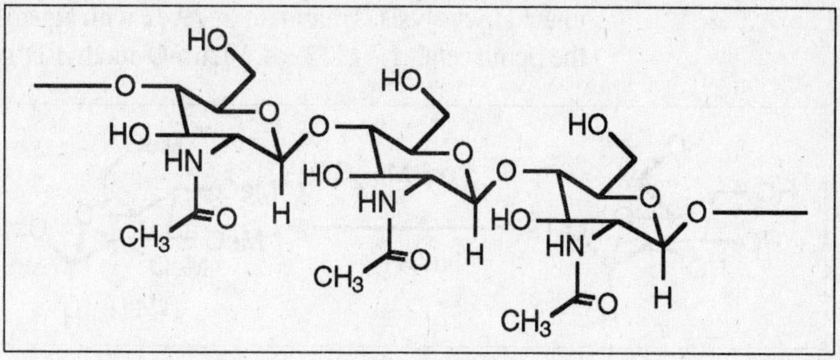

Fig. 19.39

19.3. REACTIONS OF CARBOHYDRATES

Esterification

WHAT IS THE PRODUCT WHEN β-D-GLUCOSE IS REACTED WITH EXCESS ACETIC ANHYDRIDE AND PYRIDINE?

As with any alcohol, treatment with acetic anhydride leads to an acetate ester. Since there are five OH groups, the product is 1,2,3,4,6-penta-O-acetyl-β-D-glucopyranose, *19.40*.

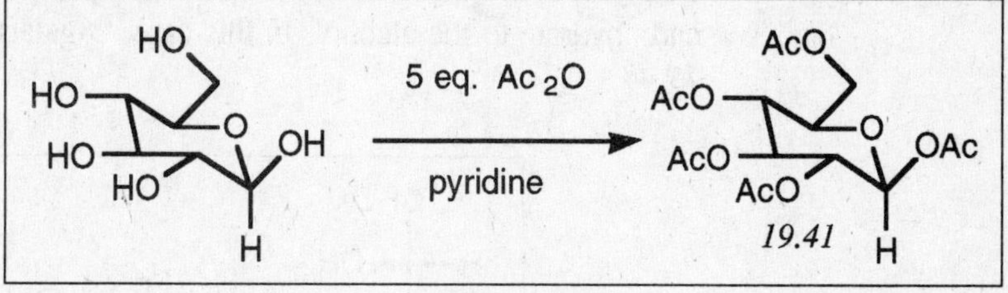

Fig. 19.40

Etherification

WHAT IS THE PRODUCT WHEN α-D-GLUCOSE IS TREATED WITH DIMETHYL SULFATE?

Dimethyl sulfate (Me_2SO_4) converts alcohols into methyl ethers (R–O–Me) and reaction of α-D-glucose with dimethyl sulfate forms 1,2,3,4,6-pentamethoxy-α-D-glucopyranose, *19.41*.

IF PENTAMETHOXY-D-GLUCOSE (*19.41*) IS REACTED WITH AQUEOUS HCl, WHAT IS THE EXPECTED REACTION PRODUCT?

In general, methyl ethers are resistant to aqueous acid hydrolysis. The OMe at the anomeric carbon, however, is part of an acetal structure and, as such, subject to acid hydrolysis. Treatment of *19.41* with aqueous HCl will, therefore, give the hemiacetal, *19.42* (2,3,4,6-tetra-O-methyl-D-glucopyranose).

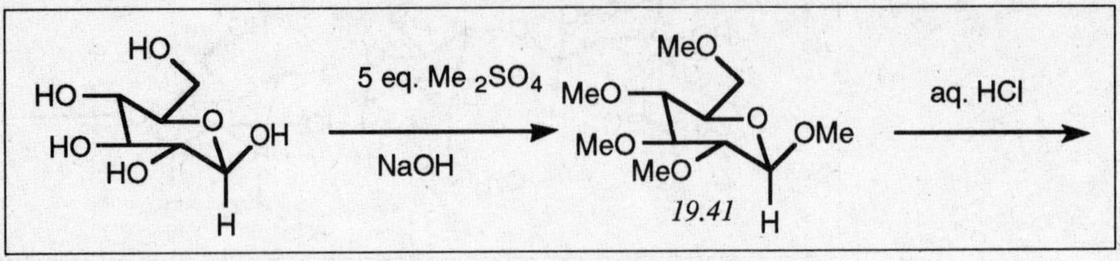

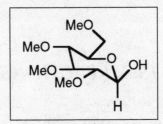

Fig. 19.41

Fig. 19.42

Reduction

WHAT IS THE PRODUCT OF THE REACTION BETWEEN D-GALACTOSE AND HYDROGEN IN THE PRESENCE OF A NICKEL CATALYST?

Catalytic hydrogenation will reduce the open-chain aldehyde form of the carbohydrate to the alcohol. In this case, D-galactose (*19.43*) is reduced to *19.44*.

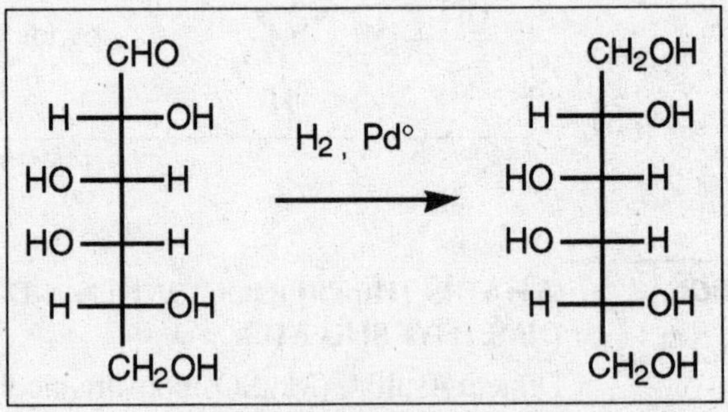

Fig. 19.43, 19.44

IF D-GLUCOSE IS TREATED WITH NABH$_4$, WHAT IS THE PRODUCT?

If D-glucose is reduced with NaBH$_4$, the aldehyde group in the open-chain aldehyde is reduced to the alcohol, giving D-glucitol (also called D-sorbitol, *19.45*) as the major product.

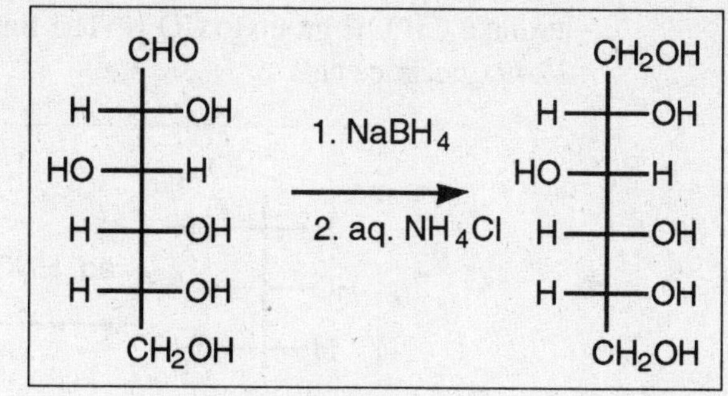

Fig. 19.45

Oxidation

WHAT IS THE PRODUCT OF D-GLUCOSE AND AQUEOUS BROMINE BUFFERED WITH CALCIUM CARBONATE?

When D-glucose is treated with bromine, the aldehyde group of the open-chain form is oxidized to a carboxylic acid (CHO → COOH), *19.46* (called gluconic acid). In the presence of the various OH groups, this acid (drawn again as *19.47*) will cyclize to form a lactone, *19.48* (there will also be a small amount of the six-membered ring lactone).

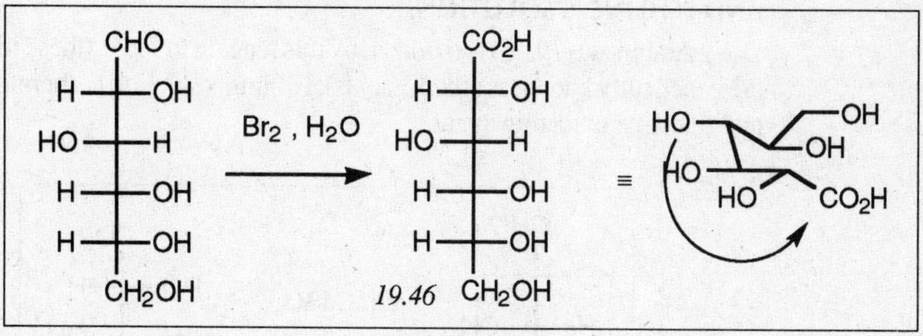

Fig. 19.46, 19.47

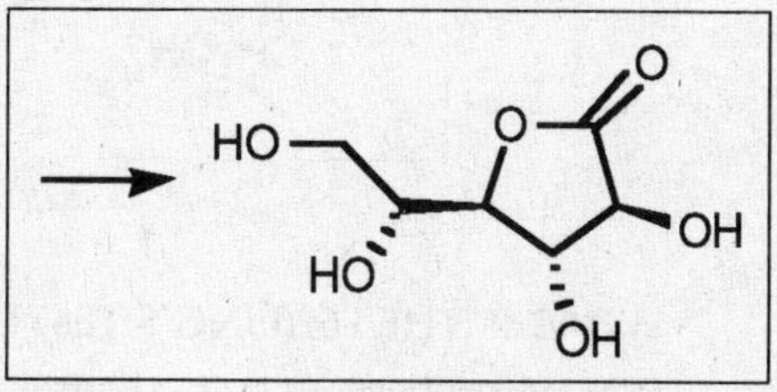

Fig. 19.48

WHAT IS THE PRODUCT OF D-ALTROSE AND DILUTE NITRIC ACID WHEN HEATED?

Under these conditions, nitric acid is a sufficiently strong oxidizing agent not only to convert the CHO group to a carboxylic acid but also to convert the terminal CH$_2$OH group to CO$_2$H. The final product is, therefore, the diacid, *19.49* (glucaric acid).

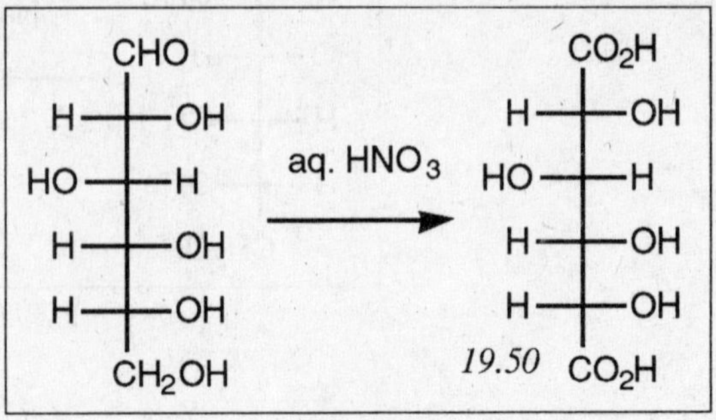

Fig. 19.49

Oxidative Tests for Carbohydrates

WHAT IS FEHLING'S SOLUTION?

Fehling's solution is an aqueous solution of copper (II) sulfate complexed with tartaric acid.

GIVE THE PRODUCT OF THE REACTION BETWEEN D-(-)-ARABINOSE AND FEHLING'S SOLUTION.

D-(-)-Arabinose (*19.50*) is oxidized by this reagent to *19.51* (these mono acids are generically known as aldonic acids). Fehling's solution is, therefore, a mild and selective oxidizing agent.

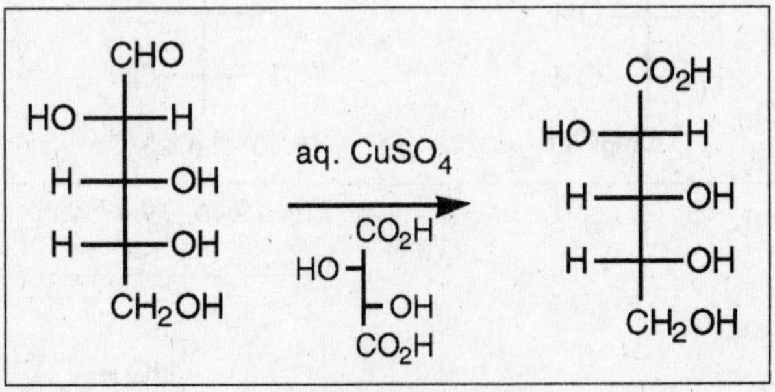

Fig. 19.50, 19.51

WHAT IS THE FEHLING'S TEST?

When an aldose or ketose [both α-hydroxy aldehydes (CHOH–(C=O)H) and ketones as well as 'normal' aldehydes react] is treated with Fehling's solution, the oxidation to the acid is accompanied by disappearance of the bluish color of the cupric solution and precipitation of a reddish-copper precipitate of cuprous oxide. This is taken as diagnostic of the presence of an aldehyde moiety (or an α-hydroxy aldehyde or ketone) in the carbohydrate. These types of sugars are called *reducing sugars*.

WHAT IS BENEDICT'S REAGENT?

Benedict's reagent is a solution of cupric sulfate using citric acid as the complexing agent rather than tartaric acid.

WHAT IS THE PRODUCT WHEN BENEDICT'S REAGENT REACTS WITH MALTOSE? WITH D-FRUCTOSE?

Benedict's reagent also oxidizes an aldose to the aldonic acid (monocarboxylic acid) and is used to detect reducing sugars. In these examples, maltose is oxidized to *19.52*. Fructose also reacts by interconversion of the hydroxyketone to an enol (*19.53*) which equilibrates to the aldehyde (*19.54*) and is then oxidized to the aldonic acid (*19.49*). Fehling's solution oxidizes α-hydroxy ketones in this manner.

Fig. 19.52

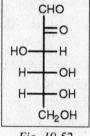

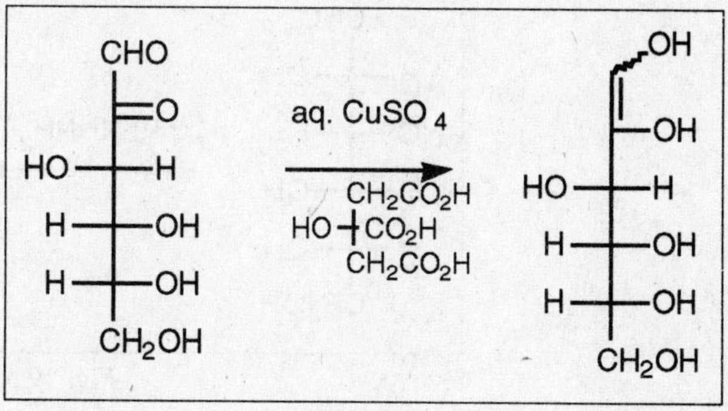

Fig. 19.53

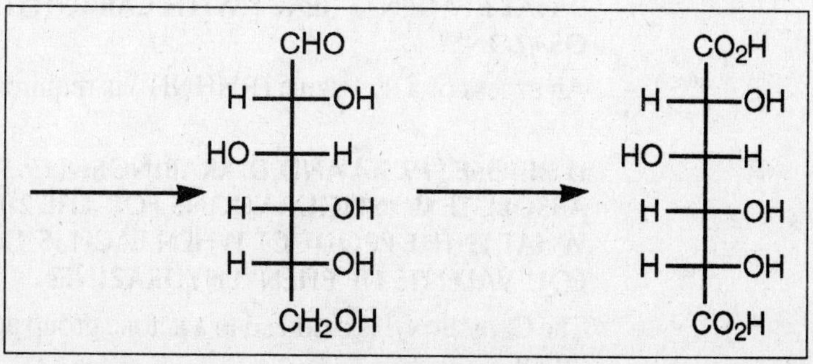

Fig. 19.54, 19.49

WHAT DOES THIS TEST INDICATE?

A positive Benedict's test (loss of the blue color and precipitation of the red-copper cuprous oxide) indicates the presence of an aldehyde group or an α-hydroxy ketone or aldehyde moiety in the carbohydrate.

WHAT IS THE TOLLEN'S TEST?

The Tollen's test oxidizes aldehydes to carboxylic acids using silver oxide (Ag_2O) in aqueous ammonium hydroxide. The Tollen's test oxidizes reducing sugars to the aldonic acid. A positive Tollen's test is accompanied by precipitation of silver on the sides of the reaction vessel (usually a test tube)—a silver mirror.

WHAT DOES THE TOLLEN'S TEST INDICATE?

As with other oxidizing tests, the Tollen's test indicates the presence of an aldehyde or an α-hydroxy ketone.

Osazone Formation

WHAT IS AN OSAZONE?

An osazone is a *bis*-hydrazone formed by reaction of carbohydrates with a hydrazine such as phenylhydrazine ($PhNHNH_2$). An example is the reaction of D-(+)-glucose with phenylhydrazine to give the osazone, *19.55*.

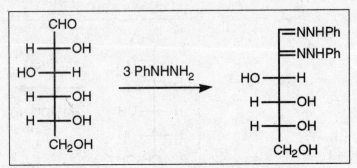

Fig. 19.55

WHAT REAGENTS REACT WITH CARBOHYDRATES TO GIVE AN OSAZONE?

An excess of a hydrazine ($RNHNH_2$) is required.

D-RIBOSE (*19.56*) AND D-ARABINOSE (*19.57*) HAVE OPPOSITE ABSOLUTE CONFIGURATIONS FOR THE 2-HYDROXYL GROUP. WHAT IS THE PRODUCT WHEN EACH IS TREATED WITH THREE EQUIVALENTS OF PHENYLHYDRAZINE?

The C_2 hydroxyl is oxidized to a ketone group and in both cases the product is *19.58*.

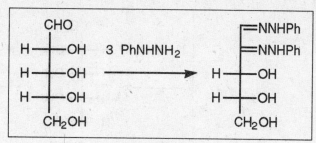

Fig. 19.56–19.58

19.4. SYNTHESIS OF CARBOHYDRATES

WHAT IS THE KILIANI-FISCHER SYNTHESIS?

The Kiliani-Fischer synthesis extends the chain length of a carbohydrate by reacting an aldose with HCN to form the cyanohydrin. Reduction of the nitrile then leads to a new aldose (with one additional carbon relative to the starting carbohydrate).

DOES THE KILIANI-FISCHER SYNTHESIS PROVIDE PURE D- OR PURE L-CARBOHYDRATES?

No. The initially formed cyanohydrin (see *19.59*) is a mixture of diastereomers. These diastereomers must be separated prior to conversion of the nitrile to the aldehyde in order to obtain pure D- or pure L-carbohydrates.

WHAT IS THE PRODUCT WHEN D-RIBOSE IS TREATED WITH i. HCN ii. AQUEOUS ACID iii. Na(Hg)?

When D-ribose (*19.56*) reacts with HCN, a cyanohydrin is formed (*19.59*). Nitriles are hydrolyzed to carboxylic acids with aqueous acid and treatment of *19.59* with acid gives the aldonic acid, *19.60*. When the acid is treated with sodium amalgam (Na[Hg]), a powerful reducing agent, the acid group is reduced to an aldehyde, *19.61* (a mixture of allose and altrose).

Fig. 19.56, 19.59

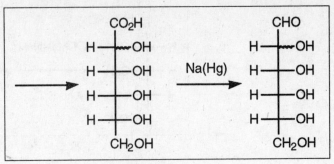

Fig. 19.60, 19.61

WHAT IS THE RUFF DEGRADATION?

The Ruff degradation involves oxidation of an aldose to an aldonic acid with bromine in water, followed by oxidative cleavage to a new aldose with hydrogen peroxide (H_2O_2) and ferric sulfate [$Fe_2(SO_4)_3$]. This procedure gives a carbohydrate with one fewer carbon than the starting carbohydrate. An example is the oxidation of D-glucose to *19.62* with bromine, followed by cleavage to D-arabinose (*19.63*) with hydrogen peroxide and ferric sulfate.

Fig. 19.62, 19.63

WHAT IS THE WOHL DEGRADATION?

The Wohl degradation is virtually the opposite process to the Kiliani-Fischer synthesis. The aldehyde group in an aldose is converted to a nitrile (via conversion to the oxime and dehydration with acetic anhydride). The nitrile is then treated with base to give an aldehyde with loss of HCN (and one carbon from the carbohydrate chain).

WHAT IS THE MAJOR PRODUCT WHEN D-XYLOSE IS TREATED WITH i. HYDROXYLAMINE ii. ACETIC ANHYDRIDE AND iii. SODIUM METHOXIDE?

Hydroxylamine (NH_2OH) reacts with the aldehyde of the aldose (D-xylose, *19.64*) to give the oxime (*19.65*). Dehydration with acetic anhydride gives the nitrile, *19.66*. When the α-hydroxy nitrile group is treated with base, HCN is lost to give the new aldose (*19.67*, D-threose). This overall process is called the Wohl Degradation.

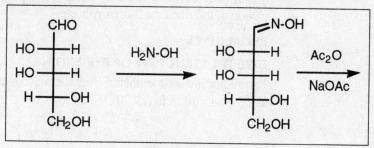

Fig. 19.64, 19.65

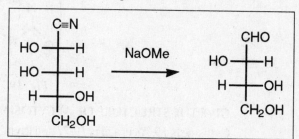

Fig. 19.66, 19.67

19.5. NUCLEIC ACIDS, NUCLEOTIDES AND NUCLEOSIDES

WHAT IS A NUCLEOSIDE?

A nucleoside is a carbohydrate, usually a cyclic furanose, that is attached to a heterocyclic amine base. The amine base is attached at the anomeric carbon of the sugar.

WHAT SUGARS ARE USUALLY INVOLVED IN THE STRUCTURE OF A NUCLEIC ACID?

The most common sugars are ribose (*19.68*) and 2-deoxyribose (*19.69*), although other sugars are often seen. Both ribose and 2-deoxyribose are shown in their cyclic forms.

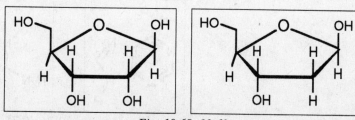

Fig. 19.68, 19.69

Bases

WHAT IS THE AMINE PART OF A NUCLEOSIDE?

The amine base is usually a pyrimidine or a purine, attached at the anomeric carbon of the ribose or 2-deoxyribose.

PYRIMIDINES

GIVE THE STRUCTURE OF PYRIMIDINE.

Pyrimidine is a six-membered aromatic ring containing two nitrogens at the 1- and 3-positions as in (*19.70*).

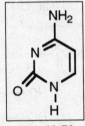

Fig. 19.70

GIVE THE STRUCTURE OF A) CYTOSINE B) URACIL C) THYMINE.

Cytosine is *19.70*, uracil is *19.71* and thymine is *19.72*. All are considered to be pyrimidine bases.

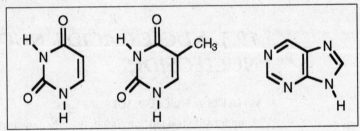

Fig. 19.71–19.73

PURINES

GIVE THE STRUCTURE OF PURINE.

Purine is a bicyclic aromatic amine, *19.73*.

WHAT IS THE STRUCTURE OF A) GUANINE B) ADENINE?

Guanine is *19.75* and adenine is *19.74*. Both are considered to be purine bases.

Fig. 19.74, 19.75

Nucleosides

WHAT ARE THE TWO BASIC TYPES OF NUCLEOSIDE?

The most common nucleosides are purine and pyrimidine nucleosides. When cytosine is attached to a ribose (a nucleoside) it is called cytidine; uracil gives uridine, thymine gives thymidine, guanine gives guanosine and adenine gives adenosine.

WHAT IS THE STRUCTURE OF A) ADENOSINE B) GUANOSINE C) URIDINE D) THYMIDINE

Adenosine is a nucleoside with structure *19.76*, guanosine has the structure *19.77*, uridine is *19.78* and thymidine is *19.79*.

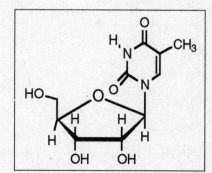

Fig. 19.76, 19.77

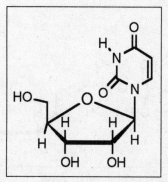

Fig. 19.78, 19.79

WHAT ARE THE SINGLE-LETTER CODES FOR THE IMPORTANT NUCLEOSIDES?

Each nucleoside has a single-letter code: *A* for adenosine, *G* for guanosine, *U* for uridine, *T* for thymidine and *C* for cytidine.

Nucleotides

WHAT IS A NUCLEOTIDE?

A nucleotide is the phosphoric acid ester of a nucleoside. The $(HO)_2P(=O)-O$ unit is attached at the C_5-CH_2OH moiety of the sugar. If two phosphoric acids are attached, the molecule is called a diphosphate, and if three phosphoric acids are attached it is a triphosphate.

WHAT IS THE STRUCTURE OF ADENOSINE MONOPHOSPHATE? WHAT IS THE ABBREVIATION FOR THIS MOLECULE?

The structure of the monophosphate nucleotide is *19.80*. It is given a three-letter abbreviation (AMP—adenosine monophosphate).

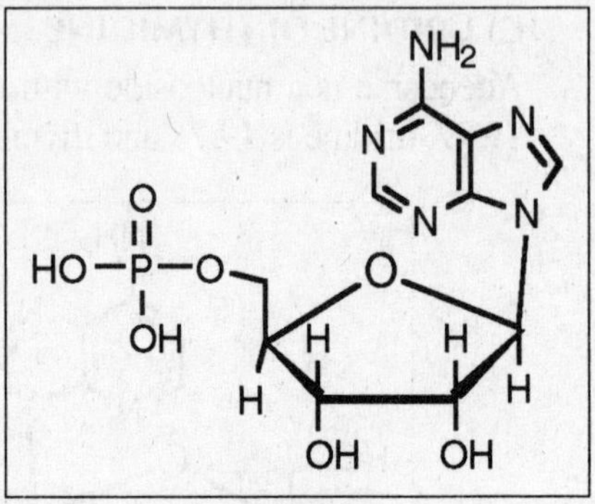

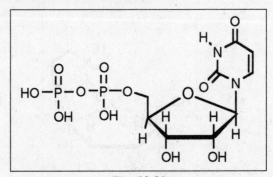

Fig. 19.80

WHAT IS THE STRUCTURE OF URIDINE DIPHOSPHATE? WHAT IS THE ABBREVIATION FOR THIS MOLECULE?

Uridine diphosphate is a nucleotide diphosphate and has the structure *19.81*. The three-letter code for this molecule is UDP.

Fig. 19.81

WHAT IS THE STRUCTURE OF THYMIDINE TRIPHOSPHATE? WHAT IS THE ABBREVIATION FOR THIS MOLECULE?

The triphosphate nucleotide thymidine triphosphate has the structure *19.82* and is given the three-letter code TTP.

WHAT ARE THE THREE-LETTER CODES FOR ALL FIVE IMPORTANT NUCLEOTIDE TRIPHOSPHATES DERIVED FROM THE IMPORTANT PURINE AND PYRIMIDINE BASES?

Adenosine triphosphate is ATP, uridine triphosphate is UTP, thymidine triphosphate is TTP, guanosine triphosphate is GTP and cytidine triphosphate is CTP.

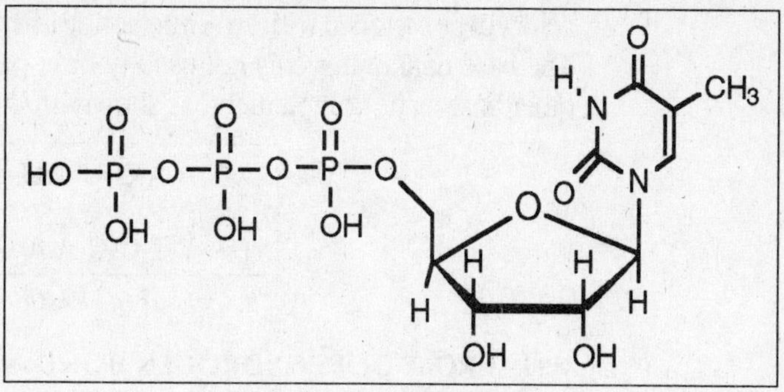

Fig. 19.82

WHAT IS A POLYNUCLEOTIDE?

A polynucleotide is a polymer of nucleosides linked together by phosphate linkages (usually monophosphate linkages). A polynucleotide of this type is called a *nucleic acid*.

WHAT IS A DEOXYRIBONUCLEOTIDE?

This is a nucleic acid that uses 2-deoxyribose as the carbohydrate portion of the nucleotide.

Base Pairing

WHAT IS BASE PAIRING?

Purine bases in a nucleic acid will form strong hydrogen bonds when in close proximity to certain pyrimidine bases in another nucleic acid or within the same nucleic acid. The two bases that form these hydrogen bonds are said to *base pair* and are referred to as *complementary bases*. The usual complementary bases are: C-G, T-A. These hydrogen bonds are shown in *19.83* for C-G and *19.84* for T-A.

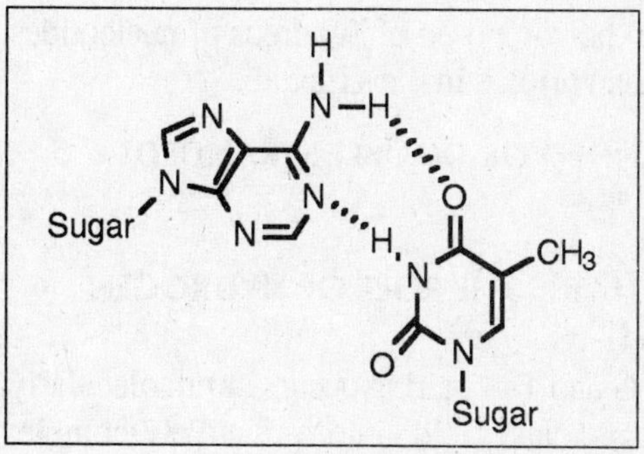

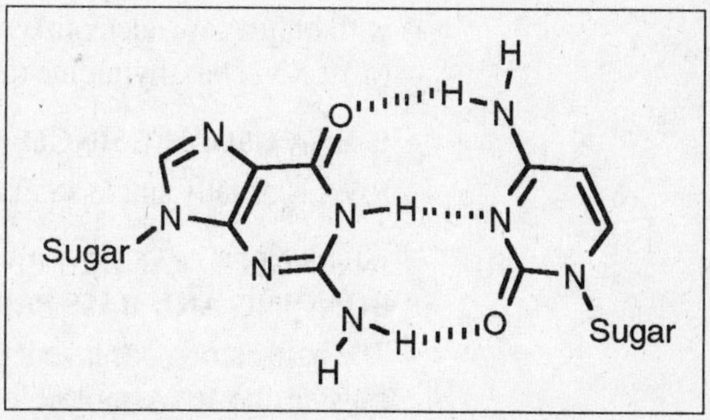

Fig. 19.83, 19.84

WHAT DOES THE TERM 'DOUBLE STRANDED' MEAN?

Two nucleic acids that join together in an antiparallel manner, as in *19.85*. Complementary bases are usually important (i.e., a T nucleotide in one nucleic acid will be matched with an A nucleotide in the second nucleic acid, as shown). The base containing U is not usually base-paired and can have virtually any other base as its complement, as shown in *19.85*.

A-T-A-A-G-U-T-U--C-T-G

T-A-T-T-C-C-A-A-G-A-C

Fig. 19.85

WHAT ROLE DOES HYDROGEN BONDING PLAY IN DOUBLE STRANDED NUCLEOTIDES?

The hydrogen bonding between the C-G and T-A base pairs is largely responsible for 'binding together' the two nucleic acid strands into the 'double strand'.

WHAT BASE PAIRS CAN HYDROGEN BOND IN A NUCLEOTIDE?

The most common hydrogen bonding pairs (complementary bases) are C-G (cytidine and guanosine) and T-A (thymidine and adenosine).

RNA

WHAT IS RNA?

RNA is a ribonucleic acid where the nucleotide backbone of the polymer is composed of ribose units.

NUCLEOTIDE FORMATION

WHAT IS THE GENERAL STRUCTURE OF RNA?

A general structure of RNA is shown in *19.86*. Each nucleotide (linked by a monophosphate unit) is usually attached at the 3'-OH and the 5'-OH. The 5' OH is the CH_2OH unit. Each sugar is a ribose unit and the 'BASE' is one of the five bases described above. This is a polymeric structure and may be relatively short with only a few nucleotides or can be composed of hundreds of nucleotides. Most RNA has thymidine rather than uridine in the structure.

IS RNA USUALLY SINGLE STRANDED OR DOUBLE STRANDED?

RNA is usually single stranded.

IN SINGLE STRANDED RNA, WHAT IS THE ROLE OF HYDROGEN BONDING AND BASE PAIRING?

The base pairing occurs but the C-G and T-A pairing occurs intramolecularly, causing the RNA molecule to 'bend' and 'fold' into a relatively complex structure.

TYPES OF RNA: TRANSFER RNA

WHAT IS THE GENERAL STRUCTURE OF A TRANSFER RNA?

The usual representation of RNA is *19.57*. The single stranded nucleic acid is folded in a relatively specific pattern (a 'cloverleaf'), allowing it to interact with messenger RNA.

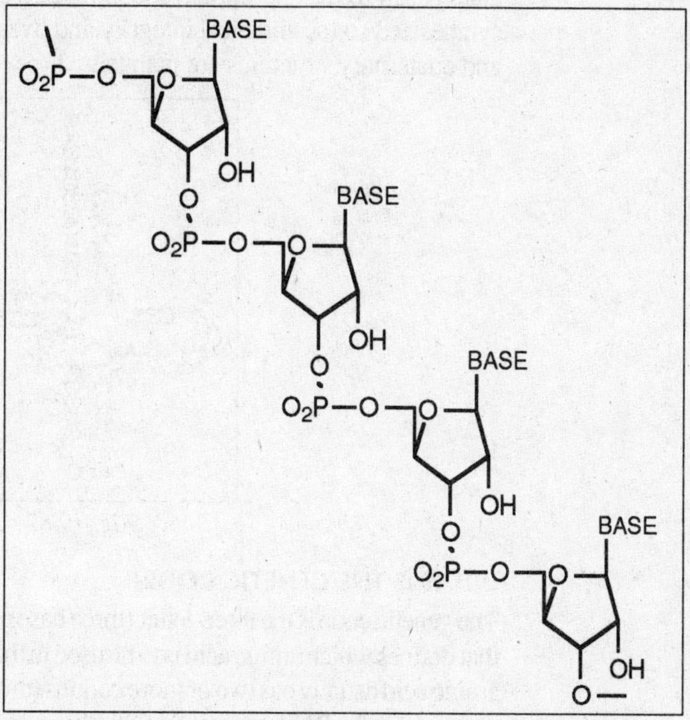

Fig. 19.86

WHAT IS THE ROLE OF TRANSFER RNA?

A molecule of transfer RNA (t-RNA) transports a molecule of an amino acid, attached as an ester at the 3' OH end. The transfer RNA contains a three base-pair anticodon (the three highlighted nucleotides at the 'bottom' of t-RNA *19.87*) which bind to the messenger RNA at a specific site. This allows transfer of only this particular amino acid in the biosynthesis of a growing peptide chain.

MESSENGER RNA

WHAT IS THE GENERAL STRUCTURE OF A MESSENGER RNA?

Messenger RNA is a nucleic acid that is generally single stranded and contains the three base-pair codons that correlate with the anticodons of the transfer RNA.

WHAT IS THE ROLE OF MESSENGER RNA?

Messenger RNA acts as a template, containing a series of three-base-pair codons, each of which correlates with a particular transfer RNA that carries a particular amino acid. The anti-codon of the transfer RNA binds to the codon of the messenger RNA and the amino acid is 'unloaded' from the transfer RNA by formation of a peptide bond to the growing peptide chain. The transfer RNA is then 'released' and the next transfer RNA (loaded with an amino acid) will attach itself to the appropriate codon. In this way, peptides, enzymes, etc. are synthesized so the chemical integrity and overall primary, secondary, tertiary and quaternary structures are maintained.

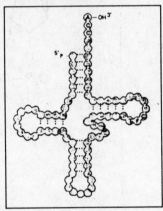

Fig. 19.87

WHAT IS THE GENETIC CODE?

The genetic code is the three-letter (three base pair) codon on a messenger RNA that defines which amino acid is to be used in the biosynthesis of a peptide. Each amino acid usually has two or more codons (three letter code) that will allow the proper transfer RNA to interact with the messenger RNA.

DNA

WHAT IS DNA?

DNA is deoxyribonucleic acid and is a double stranded pair of nucleic acids composed of nucleotides using 2-deoxyribose as the sugar portion.

WHAT IS THE GENERAL STRUCTURE OF DNA?

A fragmentary structure of DNA (single stranded) is represented by structure *19.88*. This single strand will be phase paired (complementary bases) in a double stranded array.

IS DNA USUALLY SINGLE STRANDED OR DOUBLE STRANDED?

In most cases, biologically active DNA is double stranded. In order to replicate, however, DNA must become dissociated and single stranded (partially or totally). After replication, DNA will again resume its double stranded form.

WHAT IS THE a-HELIX?

Double stranded DNA has a helical structure that resembles a spiral in its natural conformation. This spiral structure tends to "rotate" to the left, and is referred to as the α-helix.

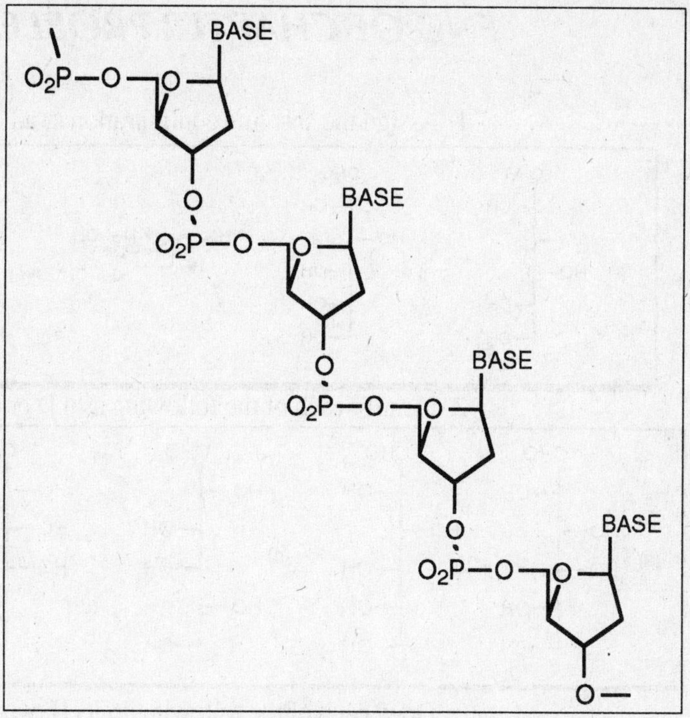

Fig. 19.88

WHAT IS THE WATSON-CRICK MODEL?
The Watson-Crick model is the double stranded, helical model of DNA.

*T*he chemistry of carbohydrates is often considered to be 'special topics' material and its inclusion near the end of this book and most organic chemistry courses should in no way be considered an indication of its relative importance. The chemistry is often unique, but the roots of all carbohydrate chemistry are the fundamental chemical reactions discussed throughout this book. That is the important lesson to take from this chapter, as it was in chapter eighteen. Several functional groups can lead to unique properties, but the fundamental chemistry is based on each individual group as well as the interactions of those groups.

END OF CHAPTER PROBLEMS

1. Assign the absolute configuration to all chiral centers.

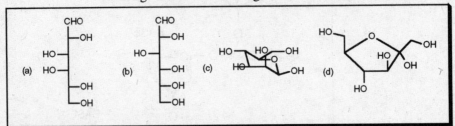

2. Identify each of the following as a D or an L sugar.

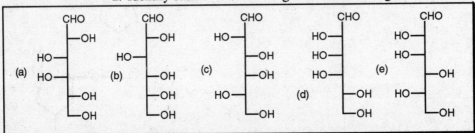

3. Draw each of the following in its Haworth formula. (a) D-glucose (b) L-mannose (c) D-gulose (d) L-altrose

4. Draw the Fischer projection of (a) 3-deoxy-D-altrose (b) 2-deoxy-L-idose (c) 6-deoxy-D-galactose (d) 5-deoxy-D-talose

5. Draw (a) α-D-fructofuranose (b) β-D-fructofuranose (c) α-D-fructopyranose (d) β-D-fructopyranose.

6. Draw the following disaccharides: (a) head-to-head α-D-gulose-L-altrose; (b) head-to-tail-a-D-talose-D-galactose; (c) head-to-tail-β-D-glucose-D-mannose.

7. Give the structures of: (a) dimethyl sulfate(b) diethyl sulfate(c) Ac$_2$O.

8. Draw the structures of (a) CDP(b) ATP(c) GMP.

9. What is the complementary strand for G-A-A-T-U-C-A-C-T-T-U-C?

10. In each case give the major product. Remember stereochemistry.

(a) α-L-mannose	5 Ac$_2$O , pyridine ⟶	(b) L-altrose	1. NaBH$_4$ / 2.aq. NH$_4$Cl ⟶
(c) β-D-gulose	5 Me$_2$SO$_4$ ⟶	(d) D-talose	aq. HNO$_3$ ⟶
(e) D-ribulose	H$_2$, Pd-C ⟶	(f) β-D-fructose	3 PhNHNH$_2$ ⟶

11. In each case provide a suitable synthesis. show all reagents and intermediate products.

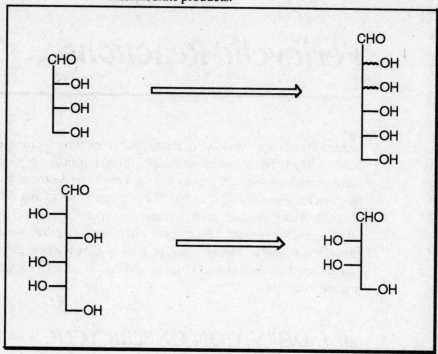

20

Pericyclic Reactions

*T*here are several types of reactions that do not involve ionic or radical intermediates. These reactions usually involve transfer of electrons and bond formation via a π-framework. A very brief introduction to such reactions is given in this chapter. The primary focus of this discussion is the Diels-Alder reaction, one of the most useful and important reactions in all of organic chemistry. This chapter will also give a cursory introduction to molecular orbital theory, with the goal of showing how this technique can be used to understand organic molecules and to explain certain organic reactions.

20.1. DEFINITION OF PERICYCLIC REACTIONS

WHAT IS THE DEFINITION OF A PERICYCLIC REACTION?

A pericyclic reaction is one in which electrons are transferred within a π-system to form new bonds. This type of reaction generally involves transfer of double bonds from one position to another within a molecule as well as formation of sp^3 hybridized carbon-carbon bonds.

WHAT DOES THE TERM [M+N] REFER TO IN A PERICYCLIC REACTION?

The *m* and *n* refer to the number of π-electrons that are transferred during the reaction. Typical examples are 2+2, 4+2, etc. The Diels-Alder reaction is an example of a 4+2 pericyclic reaction.

20.2. FRONTIER MOLECULAR ORBITAL THEORY

HOMOs

WHAT IS A HOMO?

The term HOMO stands for *H*ighest *O*ccupied *M*olecular *O*rbital. It is the highest energy π-molecular orbital that contains valence electrons.

WHAT IS THE HOMO OF 1,3-BUTADIENE?

1,3-Butadiene has four π-molecular orbitals that can react in pericyclic reactions (see *20.1*). Note the different symmetry of the orbitals. The most symmetrical orbital is the lowest in energy and the highest energy molecular orbital has the least amount of symmetry. Since 1,3-butadiene has a total of four π-electrons, the lowest energy orbital contains two electrons and the next highest energy orbital has the next two electrons. This highest energy orbital that contains electrons is the HOMO.

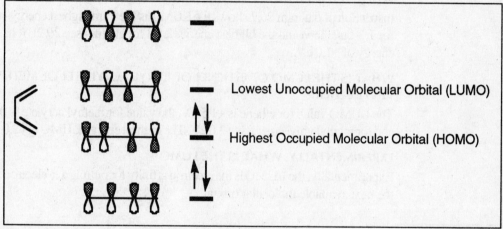

Lowest Unoccupied Molecular Orbital (LUMO)

Highest Occupied Molecular Orbital (HOMO)

Fig. 20.1

DOES A SIMPLE ALKENE HAVE A HOMO?

Yes. There are two π-electrons and two orbitals (see *20.2*). The two electrons are in the lowest, symmetrical molecular orbital, the HOMO.

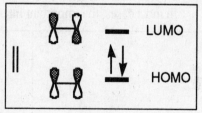

Fig. 20.2

WHAT IS THE HOMO OF ETHENE IN ELECTRON VOLTS? OF METHYL ACRYLATE? OF METHYL VINYL ETHER?

Alkenes have a HOMO that represents an energy level. Its relative energy is expressed in terms of electron volts (eV, where 1 eV ≈ 23 kcal/mol). The HOMO of ethene appears at -10.52 eV, that of methyl acrylate (CH_2=$CHCO_2Me$) is at -10.72 eV and that of methyl vinyl ether (CH_2=CHOMe) is at -9.05 eV. On this scale, -10.52 eV is lower in energy than -9.05 eV.

EXPERIMENTALLY, WHAT IS THE HOMO?

Experimentally, the HOMO is the ionization potential for the π-electron.

LUMOs

WHAT IS A LUMO?

A LUMO is the *Lowest Unoccupied Molecular Orbital*. It is the lowest energy orbital available to an electron if sufficient energy is added to the system. That orbital does not contain an electron in the ground state.

WHAT IS THE LUMO OF 1,3-BUTADIENE?

Inspection of diagram *20.1* shows the LUMO is the third highest energy level for 1,3-butadiene and the highest energy level for ethene (see *20.2*). It has an energy of +1.0 eV.

WHAT IS THE LUMO OF ETHENE? OF ETHYL ACRYLATE? OF METHYL VINYL ETHER?

The LUMO value for ethene is +1.5 eV, the value for methyl acrylate is 0 eV and for methyl vinyl ether it is +2.0 eV. The highest energy LUMO is +2.0 eV.

EXPERIMENTALLY, WHAT IS THE LUMO?

Experimentally, the LUMO is the electron affinity for putting a π-electron into the next available molecular orbital.

Conservation of Orbital Symmetry

USING 1,3-BUTADIENE AND ETHENE, WHICH ORBITALS CAN REACT?

Only those orbitals that have the proper symmetry can react. Specifically, the orbitals on C_1 and C_4 of butadiene can react with the two orbitals of ethene. In addition, the orbitals must have the correct symmetry to react. This means that only the HOMO of the diene can react with the LUMO of the alkene (ΔE^1) or the LUMO of the diene can react with the HOMO of the alkene (ΔE^2), as in *20.3*. In most cases, the important interaction is ΔE^1 (HOMO$_{diene}$ - LUMO$_{alkene}$).

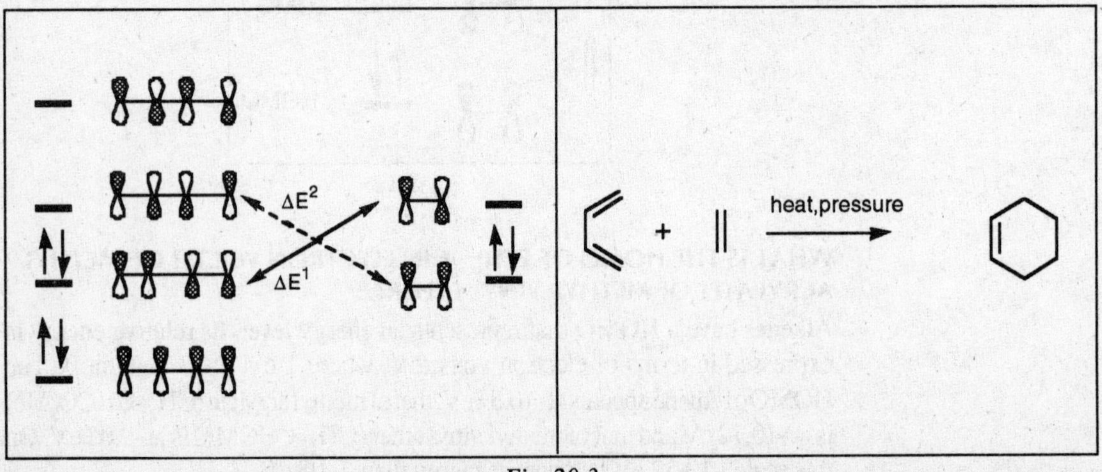

Fig. 20.3

HOW DO THESE ORBITALS REACT?

The interaction of the $HOMO_{diene}$ and the $LUMO_{alkene}$ is drawn again in *20.4*. This clearly shows the like symmetry of the C_1–C_4 orbitals of the diene HOMO and the alkene LUMO. The electron rich HOMO can be thought of as donating electrons to the electron poor LUMO, if the ΔE is sufficiently small. This initiates a reaction that transfers 6 π-electrons (as shown), forming two new sigma bonds and moving the pi-bond. As drawn, this reaction will generate cyclohexene (*20.5*).

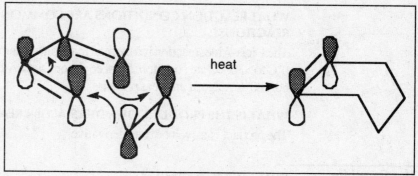

Fig. 20.4, 20.5

WHICH IS MORE REACTIVE, 1,3-BUTADIENE AND ETHENE OR 1,3-BUTADIENE AND ETHYL ACRYLATE? EXPLAIN.

The HOMO of 1,3-butadiene is at -9.07 eV. This means the ΔE^1 for $HOMO_{butadiene}$-$LUMO_{ethene}$ is 10.57 eV (+1.5-[-9.07]). Similarly, the ΔE^1 for $HOMO_{butadiene}$-$LUMO_{ethyl\ acrylate}$ is 9.07 eV (0-[-9.07]). Since ΔE^1 for ethyl acrylate is lower than for ethene, ethyl acrylate is expected to react faster (or at a lower reaction temperature) with 1,3-butadiene than is ethene.

WHICH IS MORE REACTIVE, 1,3-BUTADIENE AND ETHENE OR 1,3-BUTADIENE AND METHYL VINYL ETHER? EXPLAIN.

Using the same rationale, if ΔE^1 for $HOMO_{butadiene}$-$LUMO_{ether}$ is 10.57 eV, ΔE^1 for $HOMO_{butadiene}$-$LUMO_{methyl\ vinyl\ ether}$ is 11.07 eV (+2.0-[-9.07]). Since the ΔE^1 for methyl vinyl ether is larger than for ethene, ethene will react faster (or at a lower temperature).

20.3. THE DIELS ALDER REACTION

WHAT IS THE DEFINITION OF A DIELS-ALDER REACTION?

A Diels-Alder reaction is the 4+2 cycloaddition of a 1,3-diene and an alkene to give a cyclohexene derivative. 1,3-Butadiene will react with ethene, for example, to give cyclohexene, but only at high reaction temperatures and at high pressure (250°C and 2500 psi are typical for reaction conditions).

WHAT IS THE [M+N] DESIGNATOR FOR A DIELS-ALDER REACTION?

A Diels-Alder reaction is a 4+2 cycloaddition (4 π-electrons from the diene and 2 π-electrons from the alkene).

WHAT REACTANTS ARE REQUIRED FOR A DIELS-ALDER REACTION?

A diene (called an enophile) and an alkene (an ene, called a dieneophile).

WHAT REACTION CONDITIONS ARE COMMON IN DIELS-ALDER REACTIONS?

The Diels-Alder reaction is a thermal reaction and temperatures in the range of 0°C to >300°C are common. Most common Diels-Alder reactions occur in the 60-180°C range at ambient pressure.

WHAT IS THE PRODUCT OF A DIELS-ALDER REACTION?

The product is a cyclohexene derivative.

The Enophile

WHAT IS AN ENOPHILE?

An enophile is an 'ene lover'. Since the 'ene' is the alkene, the enophile is that molecule which reacts with the alkene, namely the diene.

WHAT ARE COMMON ENOPHILES?

Methyl acrylate, acrylonitrile, maleic acid and maleic anhydride, fumaric acid, acrolein, methyl vinyl ketone and cyclohexenone are typical alkenes that react with common dienes under relatively mild conditions.

WHAT IS A CISOID DIENE? A TRANSOID DIENE?

A cisoid diene is the rotamer of a 1,3-diene where the two C=C groups are syn (cisoid), as in *20.6*. A transoid diene is the rotamer of a 1,3-diene where the two C=C groups are anti (transoid), as in *20.7*. These two rotamers are in equilibrium and both are present in an acyclic diene.

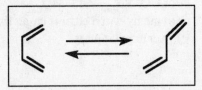

Fig. 20.6, 20.7

WHICH IS MORE REACTIVE IN A DIELS-ALDER REACTION, A CISOID DIENE OR A TRANSOID DIENE?

Since it is the C_1 and C_4 carbons of the diene that undergo reaction, those carbons must *both* be in close proximity to the alkene orbitals. Only the *cisoid* conformation brings all the reactive carbons close enough together.

WHICH OF THE DIENES (*20.8–20.12*) CAN UNDERGO A DIELS-ALDER REACTION?

Of these dienes, *20.8* is *not* a conjugated diene and will not undergo the Diels-Alder reaction as a diene. Diene *20.12* is conjugated but is 'locked' into a transoid conformation. It is, therefore, impossible for that diene to undergo the Diels-Alder reaction. In all other cases the diene reacts normally. Both cyclohexadiene (*20.9*) and furan (*20.10*) are 'locked' in the cisoid conformation and can react. Furan is relatively unreactive, however, requiring more vigorous reaction conditions. Although diene *20.11* is drawn in the transoid conformation, it is acyclic and is not locked in that rotamer. The cisoid conformation will be in equilibrium with *20.11* and the cisoid rotamer will react normally.

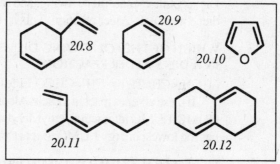

Fig. 20.8–20.12

WHICH IS MORE REACTIVE, 1,3-BUTADIENE OR CYCLOPENTADIENE?

Since cyclopentadiene (*20.13*) is locked into the cisoid conformation, it is much more reactive than 1,3-butadiene. When cyclopentadiene reacts with an appropriate alkene (such as ethyl acrylate) a mixture of two bicyclic products are formed, *20.14* and *20.15*. In *20.14* the CO_2Et group is in the *exo* position whereas CO_2Et is in the *endo* position in *20.15*. In general, the endo product (*20.15*) is preferred by about 3:1.

WHAT IS DICYCLOPENTADIENE? HOW IS IT FORMED?

Dicyclopentadiene (*20.16*) is the Diels-Alder adduct resulting from the reaction of cyclopenta-diene with itself. This reaction occurs at about 35°C.

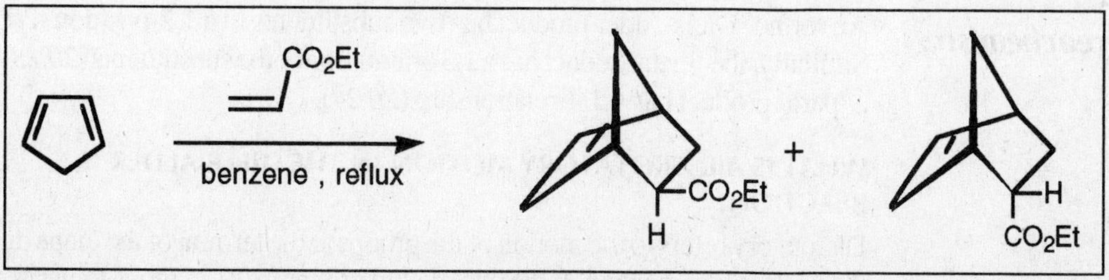

Fig. 20.13–20.15

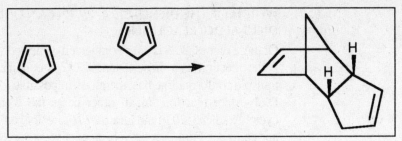

Fig. 20.13, 20.16

The Dieneophile

WHAT IS A DIENEOPHILE?

Dieneophile means 'diene loving' and refers to a molecule that reacts with the diene in a Diels-Alder reaction. This is, of course, the alkene (ene).

WHICH OF THE FOLLOWING DIENEOPHILES IS THE MOST REACTIVE IN A DIELS-ALDER REACTION?

(a) $CH_2=CHCH_3$ (b) $CH_2=CHCO_2Et$ (c) $CH_2=CHOMe$?

If these alkenes react in a Diels-Alder reaction such that ΔE^1 dominates the HOMO-LUMO interaction, ethyl acrylate (b) will be the most reactive since it has the lowest energy LUMO to react with the HOMO of the diene.

LIST SEVERAL COMMON DIENEOPHILES.

Some of the more common dieneophiles are diethyl fumarate (*20.17*), diethyl maleate (*20.18*), maleic anhydride (*20.19*), N-phenylmaleimide (*20.20*) and tetracyanoethylene (*20.21*).

Fig. 20.17–20.21

Regiochemistry and Stereochemistry

WHAT IS AN 'ORTHO' PRODUCT IN THE DIELS-ALDER REACTION? A 'META' PRODUCT? A PARA PRODUCT?

An 'ortho' Diels-Alder product has two substituents in a 1,2-position (*20.22*). Similarly, the 'meta' adduct has a 1,3 orientation of the substituents (*20.23*) and a 'para' product has a 1,4-relationship (*20.24*).

WHAT IS A DISROTATORY MOTION IN THE DIELS-ALDER REACTION?

Disrotatory refers to the motion of the groups at the termini of the diene during the Diels-Alder reaction. If the two methyl groups in *20.25* move towards each other (as shown), this motion is referred to as disrotatory (moving in opposite directions). This will lead to a *cis* relationship of the two methyl groups in the final cyclohexene product (*20.26*).

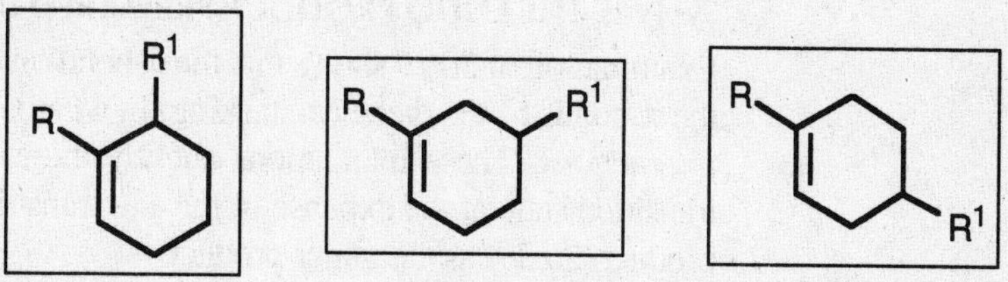

Fig. 20.22–20.24

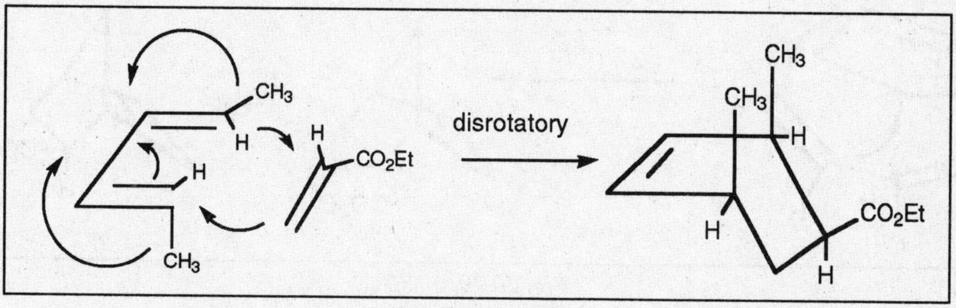

Fig. 20.25, 20.26

WHAT IS A CONROTATORY MOTION IN THE DIELS-ALDER REACTION?

Conrotatory means the groups on the diene are moving in the same direction (the opposite of disrotatory). In *20.27*, the two methyl groups are moving in the same direction, leading to a *trans* relationship in the cyclohexene product (*20.28*).

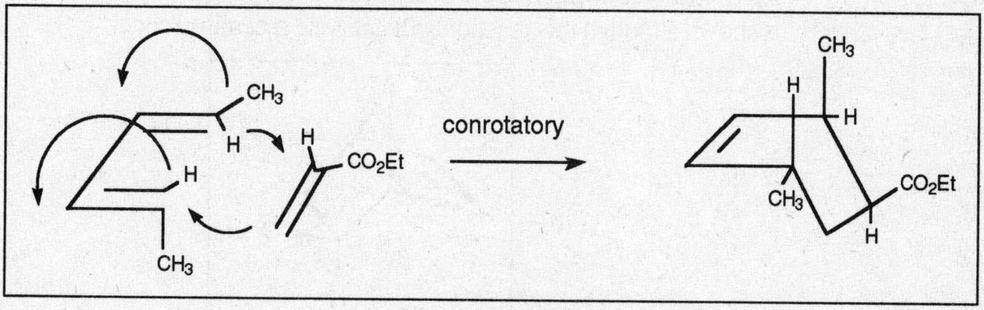

Fig. 20.27, 20.28

WHAT IS THE STEREOCHEMISTRY OF THE GROUPS IN THE FINAL PRODUCT WHEN 1,3-PENTADIENE REACTS WITH MALEIC ANHYDRIDE?

The major product is *20.30* (the endo product). About 75% of *20.30* is produced, along with about 25% of the exo product (*20.31*). The alkene portion of ethyl acrylate reacts with cyclopentadiene and the transition state with the C=O of ethyl acrylate 'tucked under' the cyclopentadiene ring leads to the endo product (*20.30*).

WHY IS THE ENDO PRODUCT PREFERRED IN THIS REACTION?

Examination of *20.29* shows that the π-bond of the carbonyl can interact with the π-bonds of the diene (π-stacking) in what is known as *secondary orbital interactions*. These interactions slightly increase the stability of the endo transition state at the expense of the exo transition state, leading to the endo product (*20.30*) as the major product.

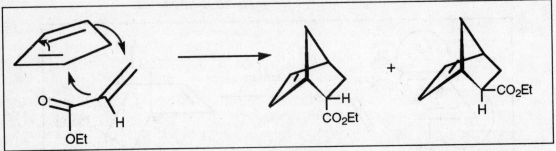

Fig. 20.29, 20.30

WHAT IS THE STEREOCHEMISTRY OF THE GROUPS IN THE FINAL PRODUCT WHEN E,Z-1,4-DIPHENYL-1,3-BUTADIENE REACTS WITH ETHYL ACRYLATE?

Reaction of *E,Z*-1,4-diphenyl-1,3-butadiene (*20.31*) with ethyl acrylate will give *20.32* (assuming the endo transition state is most favorable). The disrotatory motion of the groups on the terminal atoms leads to the *trans*- relationship of the two phenyl groups and the endo transition state fixes the relative position of the CO_2Et group with respect to the two phenyl groups. Only one enantiomer is shown although this reaction will generate racemic product.

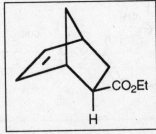

Fig. 20.31

WHAT IS THE STEREOCHEMISTRY OF THE GROUPS IN THE FINAL PRODUCT WHEN DIETHYL FUMARATE REACTS WITH 1,3-BUTADIENE?

The reaction of diethyl fumarate (*20.34*, the diethyl ester of fumaric acid) and 1,3-butadiene gives *20.35*. The *trans*- relationship of the two CO_2Et group of the dieneophile is retained during the Diels-Alder reaction and in the final cyclohexene product.

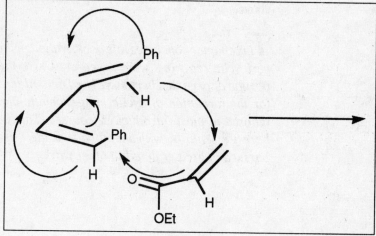

Fig. 20.32

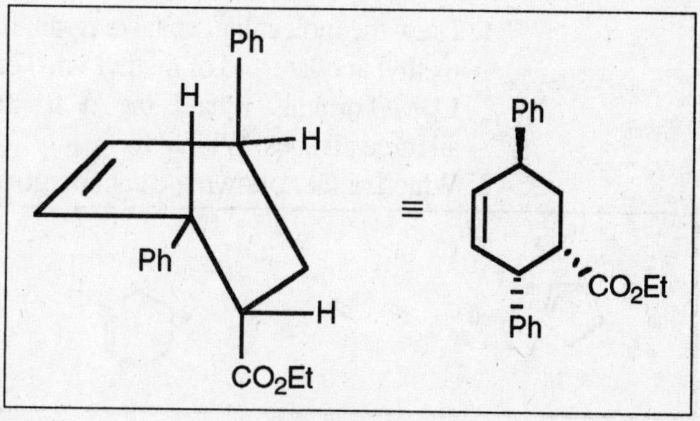

Fig. 20.33

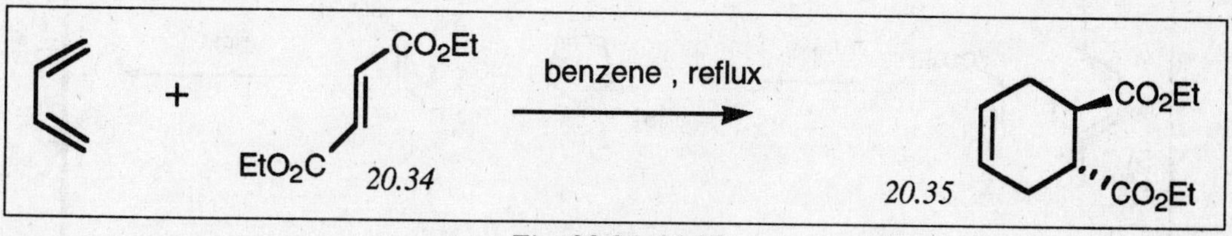

Fig. 20.34, 20.35

WHAT IS THE PRODUCT WHEN CYCLOPENTADIENE REACTS WITH ETHYL ACRYLATE?

This reaction was shown earlier. The product is *20.30* as the major product, with smaller amounts of the exo product, *20.31*.

WHAT IS THE ALDER ENDO RULE?

The preference for an endo transition state that leads to an endo product is called the *Alder endo rule*. It is the result of the secondary orbital interactions discussed above.

This chapter concludes this book. Although the Diels-Alder reaction and pericyclic reactions were saved until last, they comprise an important portion of organic chemistry. The Diels-Alder reaction is very important for the formation of cyclic, non-aromatic compounds, an area largely ignored in most introductory courses. This introduction gives only the barest essentials, with the hope that these important reactions will be pursued in greater detail in other work.

END OF CHAPTER PROBLEMS

1. Draw the molecular orbital diagram of 1,3-butadiene, of ethene, of methyl acrylate and of methyl vinyl ether. Label all HOMO and LUMO orbitals. What is the ΔE for the $HOMO_{butadiene}$-$LUMO_{alkene}$ for all three alkenes. Which one reacts faster?

2. Which of the following can undergo a Diels-Alder reaction?

3. Predict the stereochemistry of each Diels-Alder product.

4. In each case give the major product. Remember stereochemistry and if there is no reaction, indicate by N.R.

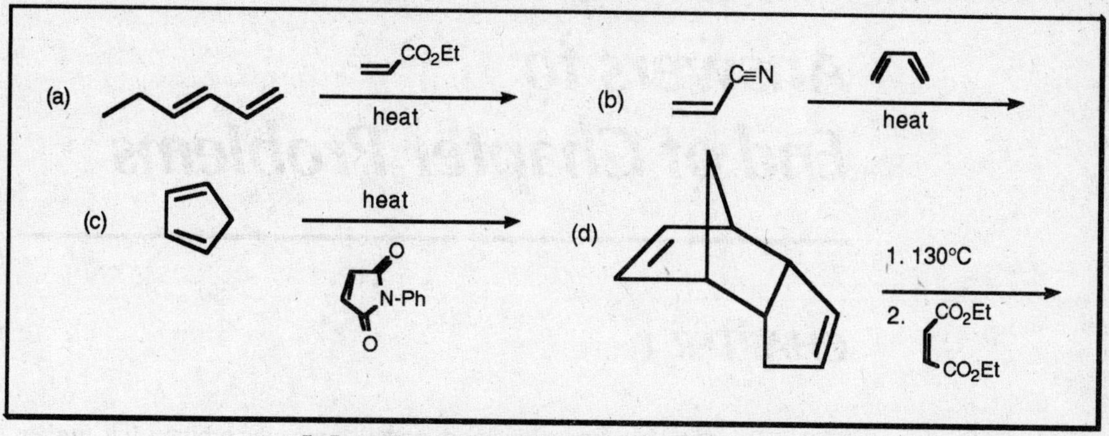

(a)

(b)

(c)

(d)

5. In each case provide a suitable synthesis. Show all reagents and intermediate products.

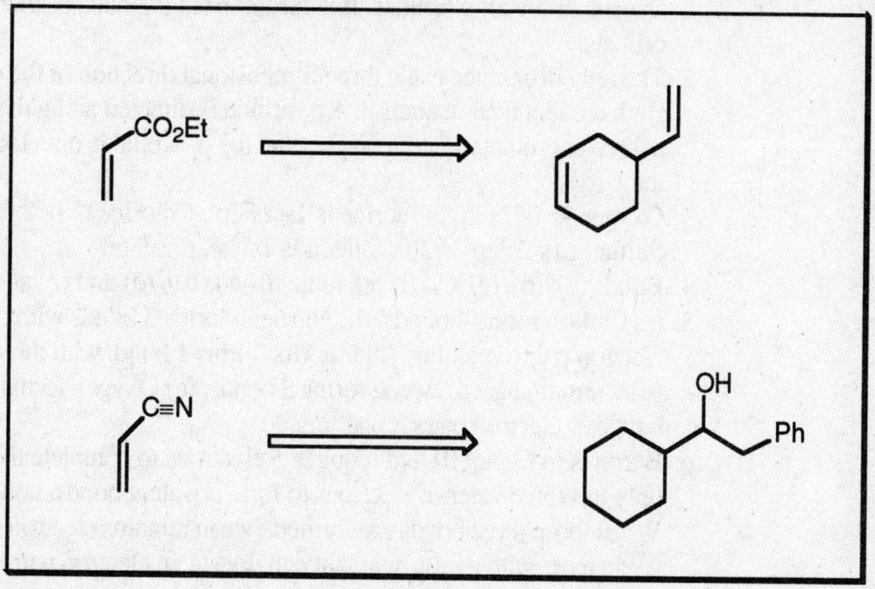

Answers to
End of Chapter Problems

CHAPTER 1

1. A 3s orbital is spherically symmetrical, as are all s orbitals. It is further from the nucleus than the 1s or 2s orbital. A 3p orbital is 'dumbbell' shaped, as are all p orbitals. It is further from the nucleus than the 2p orbitals.

2. The only difference is the three-dimensional direction of the orbital. Both are identical in energy. A p_x orbital is directed along the x-axis of a three coordinate system (x-y-z) and the p_y orbital is directed along the y-axis.

3. Oxygen is $1s^2 2s^2 2p^4$. Fluorine is $1s^2 2s^2 2p^6$. Chlorine is $1s^2 2s^2 2p^6 3s^2 3p^6$. Sulfur is $1s^2 2s^2 2p^6 3s^2 3p^3$. Silicon is $1s^2 2s^2 2p^6 3s^2 3p^2$.

4. Bonds (a), (b), (e) and (f) are ionic. Bonds (c), (d) and (g) are covalent.

5. (a) Carbon forms 4 bonds. (b) Nitrogen forms 3 bonds with one electron pair remaining. (c) Fluorine forms 1 bond, with three electron pairs remaining. (d) Boron forms 3 bonds. (e) Oxygen forms 2 bonds with two electron pairs remaining.

6. Boron is in Group III and requires 5 electrons to complete the octet. It only has three valence electrons to form covalent bonds, however. When those three bonds are formed, boron remains electron deficient. It can react with a molecule that can donate an electron pair, a Lewis base, making BF_3 a Lewis acid.

7. Since fluorine is the most electronegative, the C–F bond is the most polarized.

8. In (a), the third molecule (1-butanol) can hydrogen bond whereas the others cannot and has the highest boiling point. In (b) the first compound (butanoic acid) hydrogen bonds to a much greater extent than the other compound and has the higher boiling point. In (c) there is no hydrogen bonding or dipole-dipole interactions and the higher mass 7-carbon molecule (heptane) has the higher boiling point.

9. In (a) the 2s and 2p electrons are valence electrons and this is N. Atom (b) is Na and the 3s orbitals are the valence electrons. In (c) the 1s electrons are valence and this is He. In (d) the 3s and 3p electrons are valence and this is P.

10. Molecule (a) is angular about the oxygen (bent), as is (c). Molecule (b) is tetrahedral about the central carbon. Molecule (d) is pyramidal with N at the apex of the pyramid and the H and two carbon groups at the other corners.

11. In (a) the dipole bisects the C–O–C bond, as it does in (c). In (b) the dipole is along the C–H bond (towards H). In (d) the dipole is along the N-lone electron pair line and in (e) the dipole bisects the Br–C–Cl bond.

12. Eight isomers of (a) and (b) are:

(a)

CH_3—CH_2—CH_2—CH_2—CH_2—CH_3

CH_3—CH_2—CH_2—CH_2—CH(CH_3)—CH_3

CH_3—CH_2—CH_2—$CH($CH_3$)—$CH_2$—$CH_3$

CH_3—CH_2—$CH($CH_3$)—$CH_2$—$CH_3$

CH_3—CH_2—$CH($CH_3$)—$CH(CH_3)—CH_3

CH_3—CH_2—$C($CH_3$)($CH_3$)—$CH_3$

CH_3—$CH($CH_3$)—$CH(CH_3)—CH_2—CH_3

CH_3—$CH($CH_3$)—$CH_2$—$CH(CH_3)—CH_3

(b)

CH_3—CH_2—CH_2—CH_2—CH_2—CH_3

CH_3—CH_2—CH_2—$CH($CH_3$)—$CH_2$—$CH_3$

CH_3—CH_2—$C($CH_3$)($CH_3$)—$CH_3$

CH_3—CH_2—$CH($CH_3$)—$CH(CH_3)—CH_3

CH_3—$CH($CH_3$)—$CH_2$—$CH(CH_3)—CH_3

CH_3—$CH($CH_3$)—$CH_2$—$CH_2$—$CH_3$

CH_3—$CH($CH_3$)—$CH_2$—$CH(CH_3)—CH_3

CH_3—$C($CH_3$)($CH_3$)—$CH_2$—$CH(CH_3)—CH_3

13. The alcohol functional group is C–O–H. The ketone functional group is C=O where the carbonyl is connected to two carbon groups. The alkyne functional group is C≡C and the aldehyde functional group is

C=O, where at least one of the groups attached to the carbonyl carbon is a hydrogen.

14. For molecule (a); C^1, $C^2 = 0$; $N = +1$; H^1-$H^5 = 0$; $O^2 = 0$ and $O^1 = -1$. The formal charge for the molecule is 0 (+1-1). For (b) C^1, C^2 and $C^3 = 0$ but $C^4 = -1$. The $N = +1$ and H^1-$H^6 = 0$. The O = -1. For the molecule, the formal charge is -1 (-1+1-1 = -1).

15. In (a) the alcohol has the higher boiling point due to hydrogen bonding. In (b) the diol has the higher boiling point since two OH groups can hydrogen bond more extensively than one OH group. In (c) the carboxylic acid hydrogen bonds more than the alcohol and has the higher boiling point.

16. Of these three molecules, molecule (c) is more symmetrical and will 'pack' into a crystal lattice more efficiently. For this reason, it will have the higher melting point.

CHAPTER 2

1. Molecule (a) is 7-ethyl-3,3,5-trimethyldecane. Molecule (b) is 2,2,3,3,4,4-hexamethyl-pentane. Molecule (c) is 3,4-diethyl-9-methyltetradecane. Molecule (d) is 4-bromo-6-chloro-5-propyl-5-(1,1,2-trimethylpropyl)tridecane.

2.

3.

4.

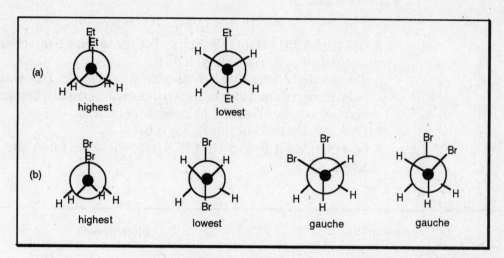

5. (a) 1,1-dimethylcyclopentane (b) 1,2,-dimethyl-3-propylcylcohexane
(c) 1,1,-dimethyl-3-(1-methylbutyl)cyclooctane.
6. Cyclopropane has the greatest angle strain and also the greatest torsion
strain. Cyclopentane, in the envelope conformation, has more angle
strain than torsion strain.
7.

(a)

(b)

(c)

CHAPTER 3

1. (a) C(Br,Me,Et) = R (b) C(Br,Et,H) = S; C(Br,Me,H) = S (c) achiral
   (d) C(OH,H) = S (e) S (f) R (g) R (h) R
2. The two alcohols that have a chiral center are unsuitable. They would rotate plane polarized light in the polarimeter and, possibly, obscure or interfere with the rotation of the molecule of interest.
3. (a) -5.23° (b) +10.95° (c) +0.12° (d) -1.67°.
4. (a) 44%R, 56%S (b) 95.5%R, 4.5%S (c) 52%R, 48%S (d) 42%R, 58%S.
5.

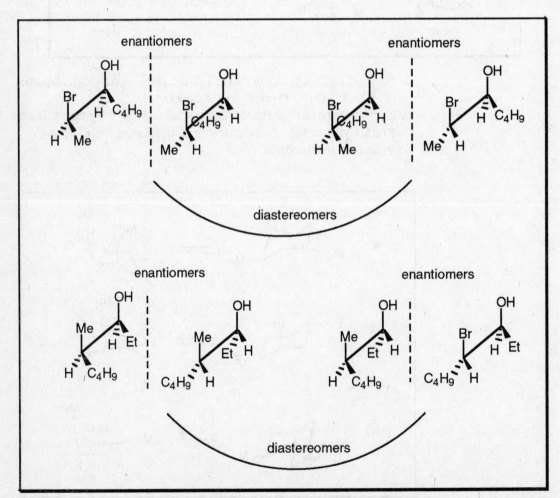

6. In both cases, there are only three stereoisomers since both compounds can form a meso compound.

CHAPTER 4

1. (a) 1,1,-dibromocyclopentane (b) 3-bromo-5-chloro-5,6-dimethyloctane (c) 9-cyclopentyl-4,4-dimethyl-8(1-iodo-1-methylpentyl)hexadecane.

2.

3.

4. Cation B has two allylic C=C groups and the positive charge can be delocalized over five carbons. Cation A is tertiary but cannot delocalize the charge by resonance. For this reason, B is more stable.

5.

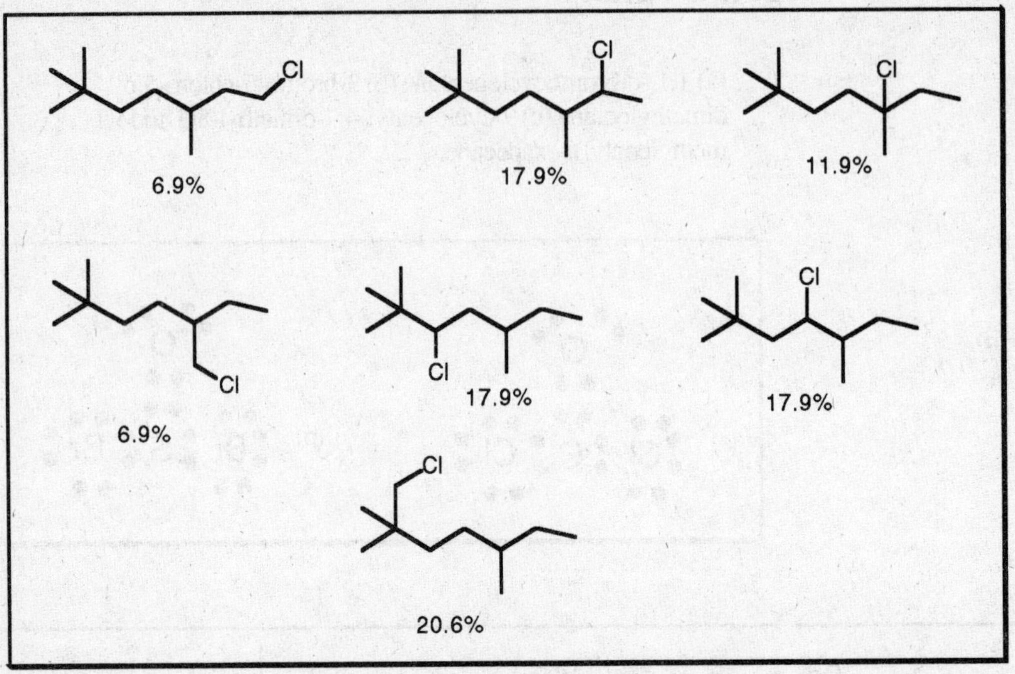

6.9%   17.9%   11.9%

6.9%   17.9%   17.9%

20.6%

6. This is an S_N^2 reaction and the rate depends on the concentration of *both* nucleophile and halide. If the concentration of KI (the nucleophile) is increased 10-fold, the rate of the reaction is expected to increase by 10.

7. Although 1-bromo-2,2-dimethylpropane is technically a primary halide, it is a neopentyl halide and the large *t*-butyl group provides enormous steric hindrance to formation of the S_N^2 transition state (therefore a very slow reaction). 1-Bromomethane is, of course, a normal methyl halide and reacts very fast.

8. In the S_N^2 transition state, the π-electrons of the carbon-carbon double bond help 'push out' the departing bromide, slightly increasing the rate of the reaction. This assist is not possible unless the π-bond is in close proximity to the carbon being attacked by the nucleophile (the allylic carbon).

9.

THF   DMF   DMSO CH_2Cl_2

10. rate = k [RX]. Since the relative ratio of nucleophile to halide has no place in the rate expression (a first order reaction), increasing the concentration has little effect. A more concentrated solution of the halide will probably react faster; however, and in this case, the reaction rate will increase by increasing the concentration of the halide. Increasing the concentration of the nucleophile will have no effect.

11. The energy required for the small hydrogen to migrate is less than for the larger methyl group. This is sufficient to make the H migrate is preference to the methyl.

12. The initially formed oxonium ion (by protonation of the OH) can either lose water to give the secondary cation (leading to a racemic mixture of chlorides) or have water displaced by chloride in an S_N2 reaction, giving the inverted chloride. The two are in competition but the cation reaction gives an equal mixture of inversion and retention and S_N2 gives only inversion. The inverted product must predominate if both process are occurring.

13. Ethanol is a strong acid in the presence of the strongly basic Grignard reagent. Ethylmagnesium bromide reacts with ethanol to form ethane and the magnesium ethoxide.

14. Butyllithium is an exceptionally strong base (pK_a of the conjugate acid, butane, is greater than 40) and an amine N–H ($pK_a = 25$) will be a strong acid in this system.

15.

In addition, (f) shows four different chloride products (1-chloro-3-methyl pentane, 1-chloro-2-ethyl butane, 2-chloro-3-methyl pentane, and 3-chloro-3methyl pentane) resulting from replacing each of the four different hydrogens. Reaction (j) gives no reaction since it is a tertiary halide under S_N^2 conditions.

CHAPTER 5

1. All of the carbon atoms are coplanar since each methyl-C=C unit is trigonal planar.
2. The endocyclic alkene (A) has three carbon groups attached to the C=C group whereas the exocyclic alkene (B) has only two. Since carbon groups release electrons into the π-bond and help to stabilize it, the more substituted alkene (A) is more stable.

3.

4. When HCl reacts with 2-methyl-2-butene, a tertiary cation is formed whereas reaction with 1-butene gives a less stable secondary cation as the intermediate.

5. (a) 4-chloromethyl-6-methyl-3Z-octene. (b) 1,2-diethylcyclohexene. (c) 3-(2-methylbutyl)-2,4,4-trimethyldec-1-ene. (d) trans-3,4-dichloro-3-hexene. (e) 5-chloro-1,5-diphenylundec-1-ene. (f) 1,5,5-tribromo-3-butyl-3-ethylcycloheptene.

6. This is a Z alkene since the priority groups are Cl and ethyl. The two like groups (Et), however, are on opposite sides of C=C, making it a trans alkene.

7. If H^+ adds to C_1, a benzyl cation is formed (the charge can be delocalized into the π-bonds of the benzene ring) whereas addition of H^+ to C_2 generates a secondary cation that is not resonance stabilized.

8. Ni, Pt, Pd, Rh, Ir, Ru.

9.

10. When a molecule such as bromine (Br–Br) comes into close proximity to a polarized molecule, the negative pole will cause the electrons in the Br–Br bond to polarize. The Br closest to the negative pole will assume a $\delta+$ pole, making the other Br a $\delta-$ pole. This is known as an induced dipole.

11. When trans-2-butene reacts with I_2, the initially formed iodonium ion can be formed on the 'top' or on the 'bottom'. Attack of the iodide ion leads to a 'trans' diiodide. This is a single diastereomer although it is racemic. This diastereomer is the meso compound, not the d,l pair. If cis-2-butene reacted with I_2, only the d,l diastereomer would be formed.

12. Once the bromonium ion is formed, the nucleophile bromide ion will attack the less sterically hindered carbon, in what is essentially an S_N^2 process.

13.

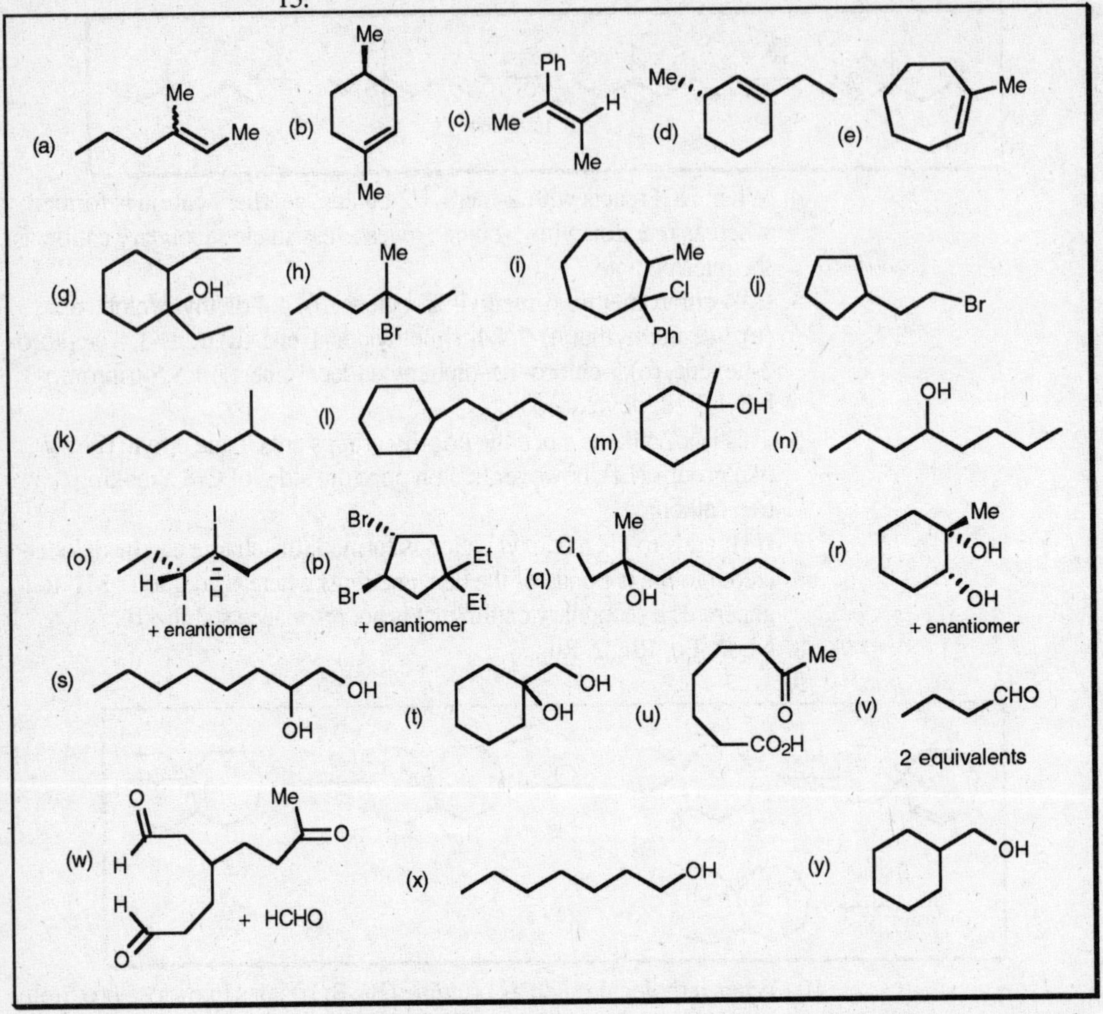

(a) — (b) — (c) — (d) — (e)

(g) — (h) — (i) — (j)

(k) — (l) — (m) — (n)

(o) + enantiomer — (p) + enantiomer — (q) — (r) + enantiomer

(s) — (t) — (u) — (v) 2 equivalents

(w) + HCHO — (x) — (y)

Reaction (f) gives no reaction since it is a tertiary sulfonate ester under S_N2 conditions.

CHAPTER 6

1. (a) 5,9,9-trimethyl-2-decyne. (b) 6-phenyl-1-hexyne. (c) undec-10-en-2-yne. (d) 7-phenyl-3-propyl-4-(1,1,-dichloropropyl)tridec-1-yne. (e) 1-cyclohexyl-1-pentyne.
2. The most acidic hydrogen is the O–H hydrogen (pK$_a$ 4.5) and that is removed much faster than the alkyne C–H (pK$_a$ 25).
3. Alkenes are better Lewis bases than alkynes and the alkene will react faster with HBr than does the alkyne.
4.

Both (c) and (d) give no reaction. In (c), there is no acidic hydrogen to be removed and in (d) there is no catalyst for the hydrogen.

CHAPTER 7

1.

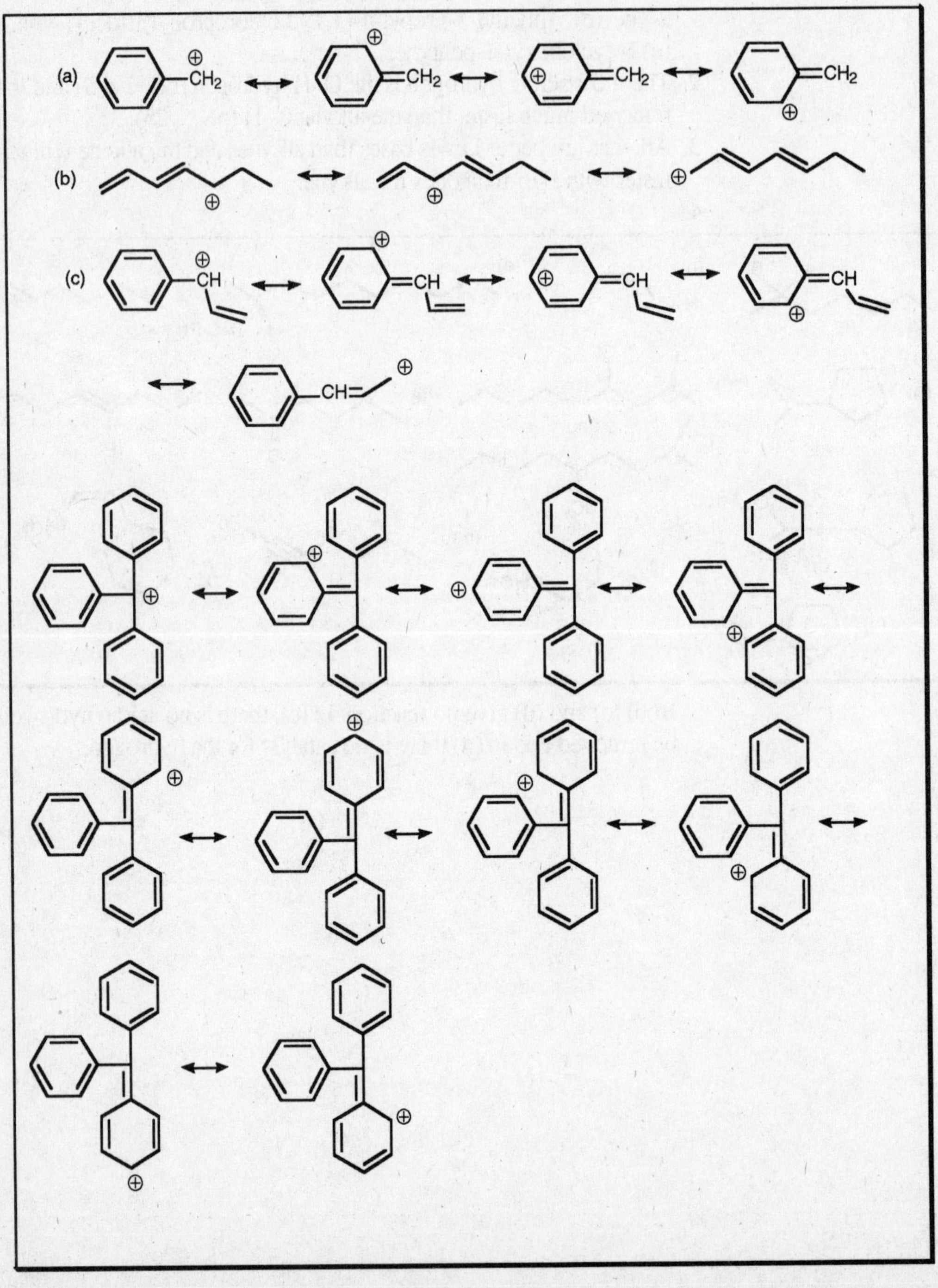

2. Molecules (b), (c), (e), (f) and (h) contain conjugated double bonds.
3. (a) 1,5-hexadiene. (b) cyclopentadiene. (c) hex-1-en-3-one. (d) 1,2,4,5-tetramethyl-1,4-cyclohexadiene. (e) penta-1,4-dien-3-one. (f) 1,4E,6-heptatriene. (g) cyclohexane (h) ethenylbenzene (styrene). The requisite structures are:

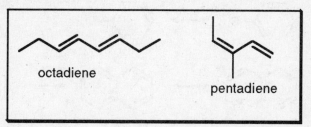

octadiene

pentadiene

4. The cisoid dienes are (a), (b) and (e). The only transoid diene is (d). Only the acyclic (a) has both cisoid and transoid rotamers in equilibrium.
5. Both the 1,2-products (E+Z 1,2-dichloro-3-pentene) and the 1,4-products (E+Z 1,4-dichloro-2-pentene) are formed. At -78°C, the kinetic product (1,2-addition) is the major product.
6. 83 kcal = 347.4 kJ = 2929.9 cm^{-1} = 2,373,800 nm.
132 kJ = 901863 nm = 9,018,633.5 Å = 31.5 kcal.
0.45 nm = 1.57x10^{-5} kcal = 5.55x10^{-3} cm^{-1}.
2.4 kcal = 68640 nm = 686400 Å = 847.2 cm^{-1}.
7. Only the conjugated double bonds will absorb strongly in the UV: (a), (b), (d), (e) and (f).
8. If A = $\varepsilon \cdot l \cdot c$, then A = 6457 x 0.3 x 5 = 9685.5 and A = 17 x 3 x .5 = 25.5
9. Since 1,4-diphenyl-1,3-butadiene is more extensively conjugated than 1,3-butadiene, it will absorb light more efficiently, leading to a larger extinction coefficient.
10.

(a) and   (b)   (c)   (d)

(e)   (f)   (g)

CHAPTER 8

1. The aromatic molecules are (a), (b), (d), (h), (i) and (j).
2.

3. (a) 3,5-dichlorophenol. (b) 1,3-dinitrobenzene. (c) 4-methylanisole. (d) 3-ethyl-5-methylbenzoic acid. (e) hexachlorobenzene. (f) 3-(2-methylbutyl)phenol. (g) N,3,5-trimethylaniline. (h) 4-bromo-3-butylbenzenesulfonic acid.

CHAPTER 9

1. (a) *para*-dichlorobenzene. (b) *meta*-diethyl benzene. (c) *ortho*-chloroanisole. (d) *meta*-ethylnitrobenzene. (e) *para*-nitrobenzoic acid.
2. (a) 1,4-dichlorobenzene. (b) 1,3-diethylbenzene. (c) 2-chloroanisole. (d) 3-ethylnitrobenzene. (e) 4-nitrobenzoic acid.
3. Since carbons can release electrons to an electron deficient center, the

presence of a carbon group adjacent to the positive charge in the Wheland intermediate will stabilize the charge and make carbon groups activating.

4.

5. The reaction will produce a mixture of both the *ortho* and the *para* products. The only way to obtain a pure sample of the *ortho* product is to separate the two products, usually via chromatography or, in some cases, fractional distillation (these products are liquids although the *para* product is a low melting solid, mp 7.2°C). Since the *para* melts at 7.2°C and the *ortho* at -72°C, it is possible that fractional crystallization might separate them.

6. (a) 3,5-dibutylbenzoic acid. (b) 4-methyl-4-phenylbutanoyl chloride. (c) 4,5,5-trimethyl-2-propylheptanoyl chloride. (d) 3-bromo-4-methylbenzoyl chloride.

7. The presence of the polar nitro group will stabilize the *ortho* attack intermediate more than the *para* attack intermediate due to dipole-dipole interactions (the *ortho* effect).

8.

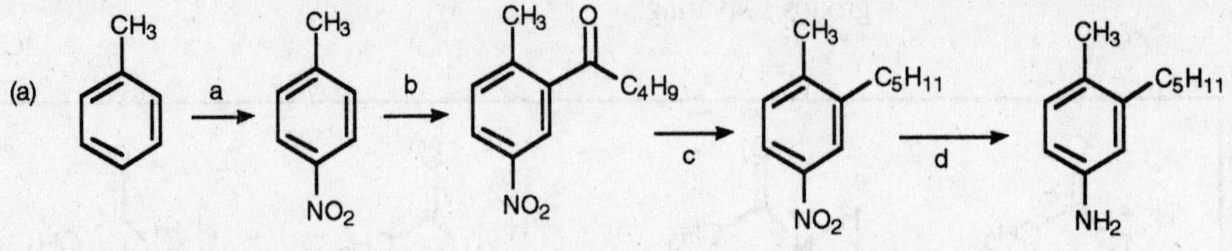

(a)

(a) HNO$_3$, H$_2$SO$_4$ (b) butanoyl chloride, AlCl$_3$ (c) N$_2$H$_4$, aq. KOH (d) H$_2$, Ni

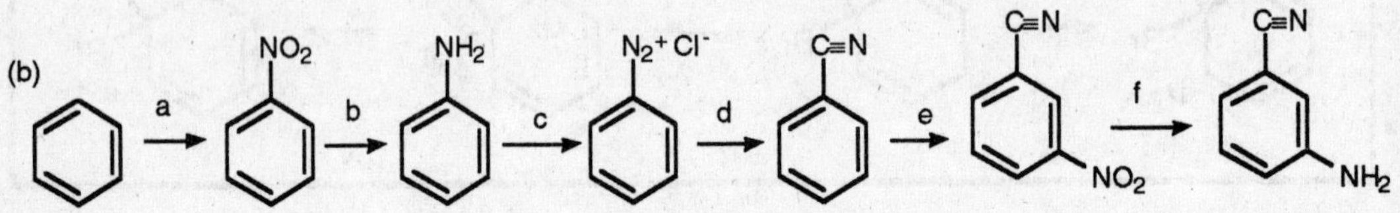

(b)

(a) HNO$_3$, H$_2$SO$_4$ (b) H$_2$, Ni (c) NaNO$_2$, HCl (d) CuCN (e) HNO$_3$, H$_2$SO$_4$ (f) H$_2$, Ni

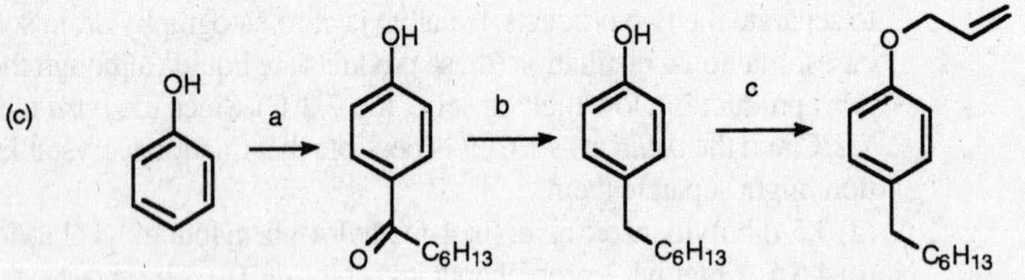

(c)

(a) heptanoyl chloride, AlCl$_3$ (b) Zn(Hg), HCl (c) allyl bromide, NaH

9. Reaction (i) gives no reaction.

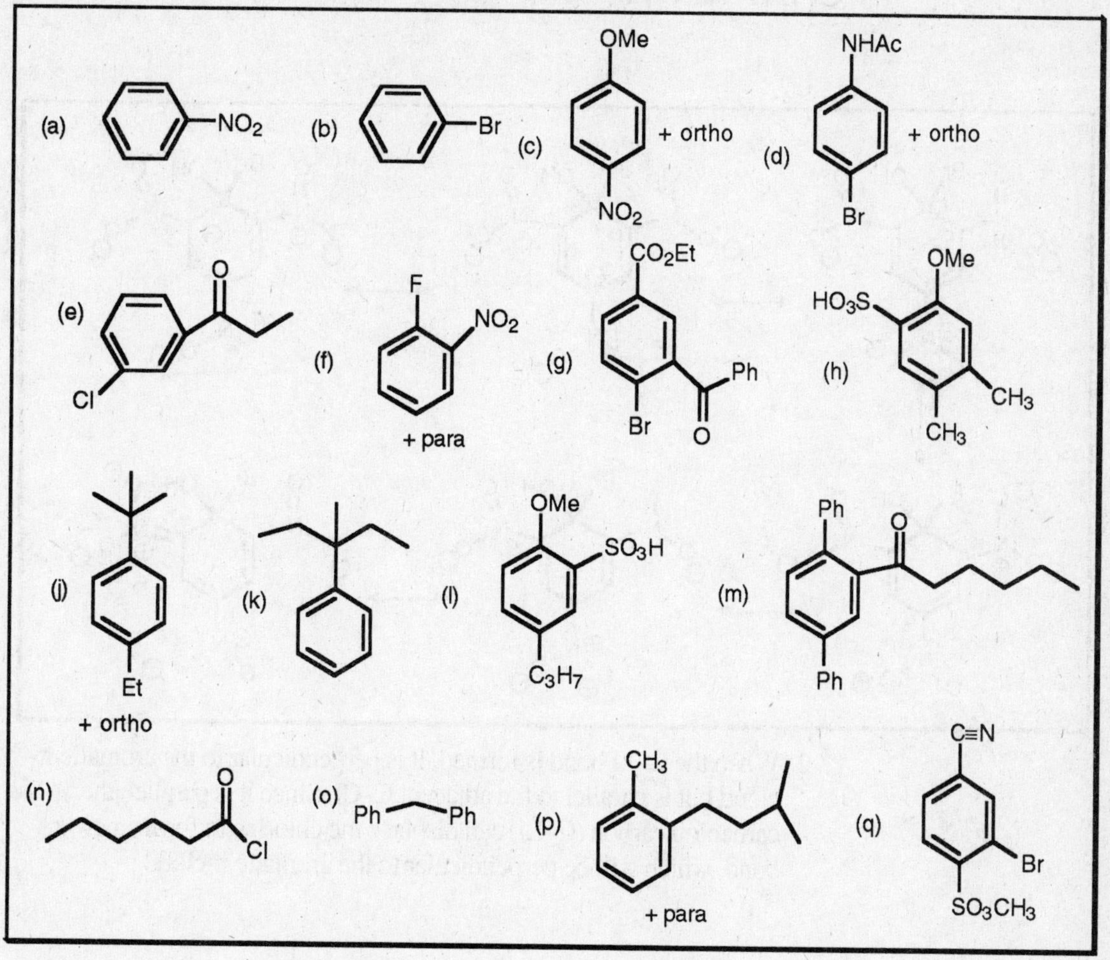
(a)
NO2
(b)
Br
(c)
OMe
+ ortho
NO2
(d)
NHAc
+ ortho
Br
(e)
O
Cl
(f)
F
NO2
+ para
(g)
CO2Et
Ph
Br
O
(h)
OMe
HO3S
CH3
CH3
(j)
Et
+ ortho
(k)
(l)
OMe
SO3H
C3H7
(m)
Ph
O
Ph
(n)
O
Cl
(o)
Ph
Ph
(p)
CH3
+ para
(q)
C≡N
Br
SO3CH3

CHAPTER 10

1.

2. When the C–Li bond is formed, it is perpendicular to the aromatic π-cloud but is parallel to the adjacent C–Cl. Since it is parallel, the carbanion carbon (C–Li) can displace the chlorine to form a new π-bond, which will be perpendicular to the aromatic π-cloud.

3.

(a) HNO$_3$, H$_2$SO$_4$ (b) H$_2$, Pd (c) Ac$_2$O, pyridine (d) HNO$_3$, H$_2$SO$_4$ (e) Br$_2$, AlCl$_3$ (f) NH$_3$, heat pressure

(a) BuLi (b) butanoyl chloride, AlCl$_3$ (c) N$_2$H$_4$, aq. KOH

4.

CHAPTER 11

1. Both (b) and (d) are alcohols and will have higher boiling points due to hydrogen bonding. Since the mass of dodecanol (d) is higher than that of pentanol (b), dodecanol is expected to have the higher boiling point.

2. Octanol has enough carbons to outweigh the 'water solubility' provided by the single OH group. Octanol is, therefore, essentially insoluble in water (0.06 g/100 g water) and an organic molecule that is insoluble in water would reasonably be expected to be soluble in octanol.

3. (a) 3-chloro-1-ethyl-3-methylcyclohexanol. (b) 3,7-dimethyl-5,9-diphenyl-4-nonanol. (c) 5,5-dimethyl-3,6-nonanediol. (d) 3-bromo-8-chlorocyclooct-3-en-1-ol. (e) 2,4,4,6,6-heptamethyl-1-octanol. (f) dec-6-yn-2-ol.

4. Disiamylborane has two sterically bulky isobutyl groups that provide steric hindrance in the four-centered transition state of hydroboration. These groups will interact with the geminal dimethyl groups of the methylenecyclopentene substrate when boron approaches the tertiary carbon. This interaction is much greater than with the hydrogens of borane. Disiamylborane will, therefore, give almost exclusively A.

5. Reactions (a), (d), (e) and (f) are reductions. (a) is -1 for both carbons of the alkene and 0 for both carbons of the alkyne (Δ is +2). (b) is -1 for both carbons of the alkene and -2 for both carbons of the alkane (Δ is -2). (c) is 0 for the carbon of the alcohol and +2 for the carbonyl carbon (Δ is +2). (d) is +2 for the carbonyl carbon and 0 for the alcohol carbon (Δ is +2). (e) is 0 for both alkyne carbons and -2 for both alkane carbons (Δ is -4). (f) is +3 for the carbon of the ester and -1 for the alcohol carbon (Δ is -4).

6.

7. Methanol (pK_a 15.5) is more acidic than *t*-butanol (pK_a 19.0). The bulky alkyl groups in *t*-butanol inhibits solvation, diminishing the acidity of the O–H.

8. No. The charge on oxygen is too far away from the C=C group ($CH_2=CHCH_2O^-$).

9. Since 2-methyl-2-iodopropane is a tertiary halide, an S_N^2 reaction (required by the Williamson ether synthesis) is not possible.

10.

11. The bulky *t*-butyl groups in A inhibit approach of a base that can remove the α-hydrogen after A is converted to the chromate ester. This steric hindrance is very small in the chromate ester of B.

12. Reaction (q) gives no reaction.

CHAPTER 12

1. (a) 4,4-dimethyl-2-phenyltetrahydrofuran. (b) 2-ethoxy-3-methylpentane. (c) 6-chloro-3-ethoxy-8-phenylnonane. (d) 4,4-dichlorotetrahydropyran. (e) 1-phenoxyhexane. (f) 4-chloro-3-ethylanisole.

2.

3. The product is a mixture of the *ortho* and *para* bromides *in the ring bearing the OR group*. The OR group is much more activating than the alkyl group and leads almost exclusively to the products shown.

4. (a) 1-ethyl-2-methyloxirane. (b) 1,2-dimethyl-1,2-epoxycyclooctene. (c) 5-chloro-3,3-dimethyl-6-phenyl-1,2-epoxynonene (d) 2-methyl-1-phenyl-1,2-epoxyoctene. (e) 5,5-dichloro-7(4-chloro-2-methoxyphenyl)-1,2-epoxyheptene.

5.

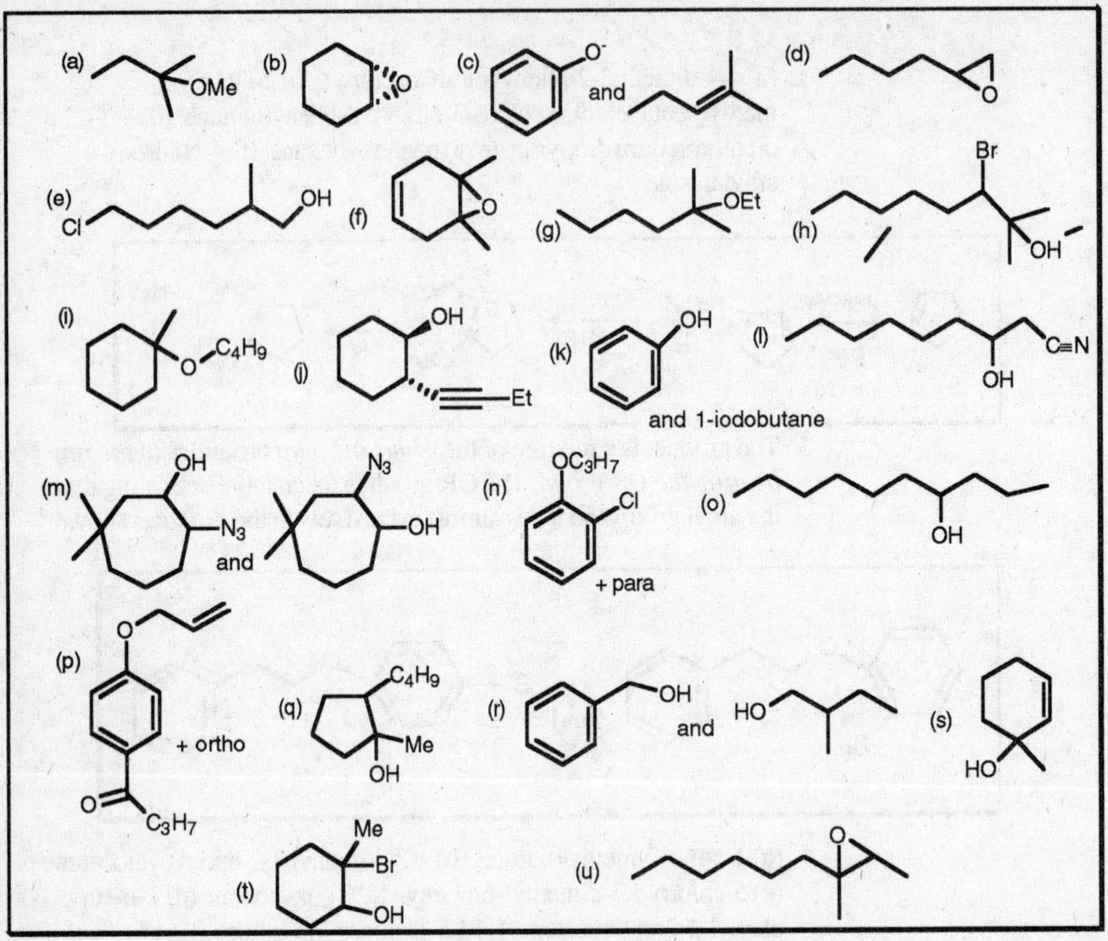

(a) ... OMe

(b) ...

(c) ... O⁻ and ...

(d) ... O

(e) Cl ... OH

(f) ...

(g) ... OEt

(h) ... Br ... OH

(i) ... O—C₄H₉

(j) ... OH ... Et

(k) ... OH and 1-iodobutane

(l) ... OH ... C≡N

(m) ... OH ... N₃ and

... N₃ ... OH

(n) OC₃H₇ ... Cl + para

(o) ... OH

(p) O—(allyl) ... + ortho ... O=C₃H₇

(q) ... C₄H₉ ... Me ... OH

(r) ... OH and HO ...

(s) ... HO

(t) Me ... Br ... OH

(u) ... O

CHAPTER 13

1. The conjugated carbonyl group in cyclohexenone will give a strong absorption band (extinction coefficient—8230) at 225 nm in the UV, whereas cyclohexanone gives a weak absorption (extinction coefficient—27) at 280 nm. This is a characteristic difference between a conjugated and unconjugated ketone.

2. (a) 3-butyl-2-heptanone. (b) 4-methyl-3-(1-methylethyl)-2-(1,2-dimethylpropyl)pentanal. (c) 2,5-dichloro-4-(1-methylpropyl)benzaldehyde. (d) 3,4-diphenylcyclopentanone. (e) 5,5-dimethyl-2,6-nonanedione. (f) cyclohexene carboxaldehyde. (g) 2-benzyl-2-ethylcyclohexanone. (h) 3-methylhex-2-enal.

3. The ketone product is also very reactive with the Grignard reagent. As it is formed, the ketone can compete with the acid chloride for reaction with butylmagnesium bromide.

4.

5.

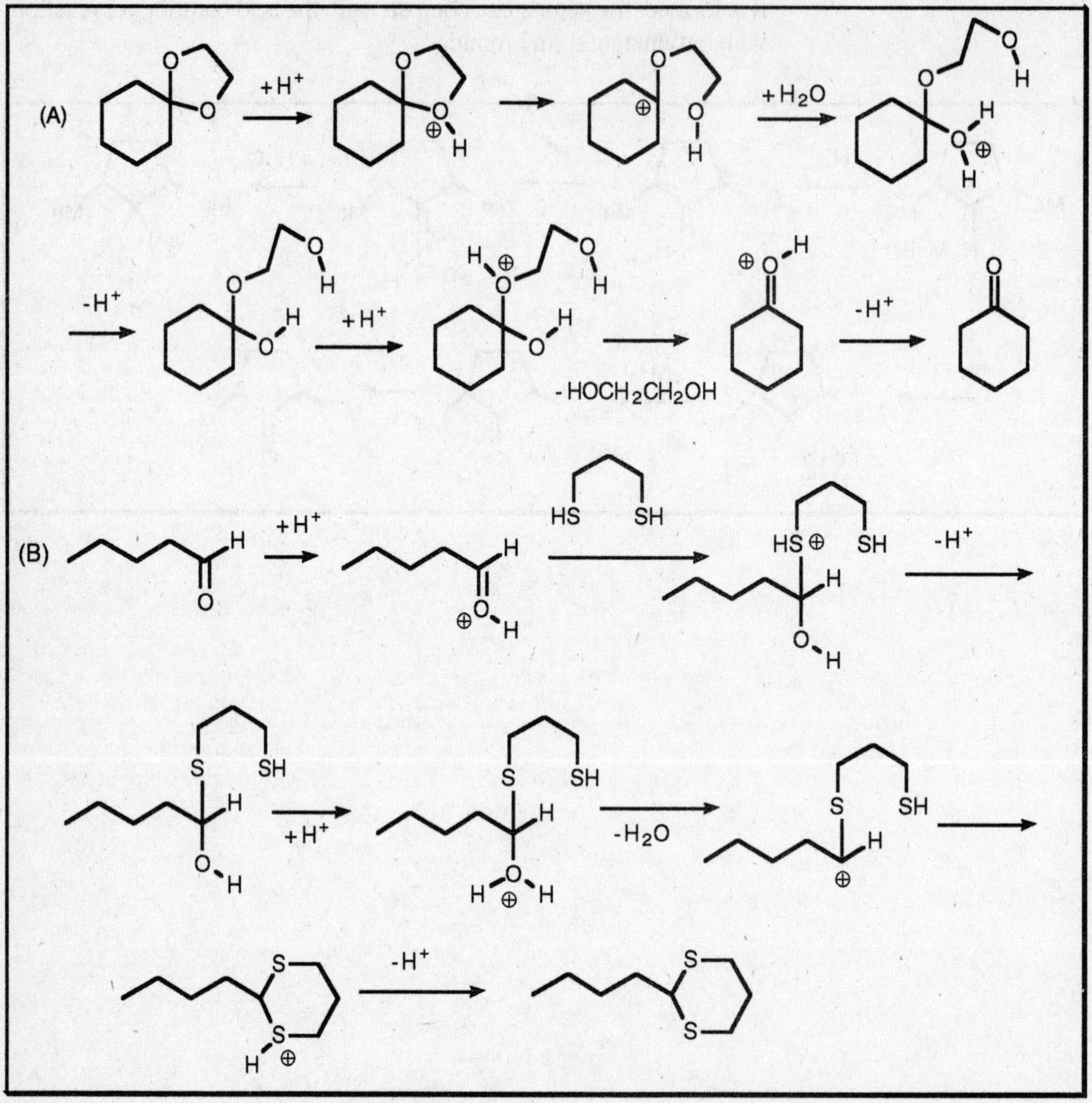

(A)

(B)

6. The initial product is an enol, which tautomerizes to the ketone, the isolated product.

7.

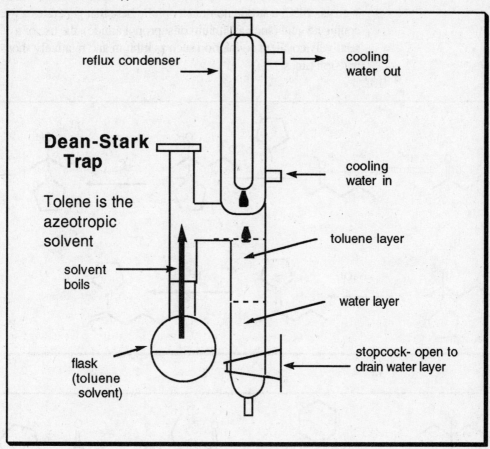

reflux condenser →

→ cooling water out

Dean-Stark Trap

Tolene is the azeotropic solvent

← cooling water in

solvent boils →

→ toluene layer

→ water layer

flask (toluene solvent)

stopcock- open to drain water layer

8.

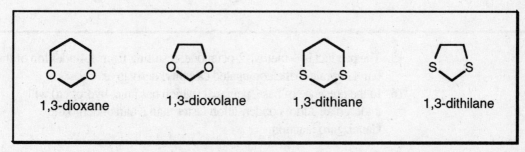

1,3-dioxane   1,3-dioxolane   1,3-dithiane   1,3-dithilane

9. (a) 3-methyl-1-pentanethiol. (b) cyclopentanethiol. (c) 4,4-dimethyl-5-phenylhexane-2-thiol. (d) 1,3-propanedithiol.

10. The most acidic hydrogens are H_b in (a), H_a in (b), H_b in (c) and H_a in (d).

11. The 1,3-carbonyl compound [compound (c), 2,4-heptanedione] will have the highest enol content.

12. An aprotic solvent such as ether or THF, low reaction temperature such as -78°C, a strong non-nucleophilic base that generates a weak conjugate acid (such as lithium diisopropyl amide), the use of a relatively covalent counterion such as lithium and relatively short reaction times.

13.

14.

15. The product is 4-methyl-2-octanone, resulting from 1,4-addition of the butyl cuprate to the conjugated carbonyl derivative.

16. In the presence of base, pentanal (which has an α-hydrogen) will undergo an Aldol condensation faster than it can undergo the Cannizzaro reaction.

17.

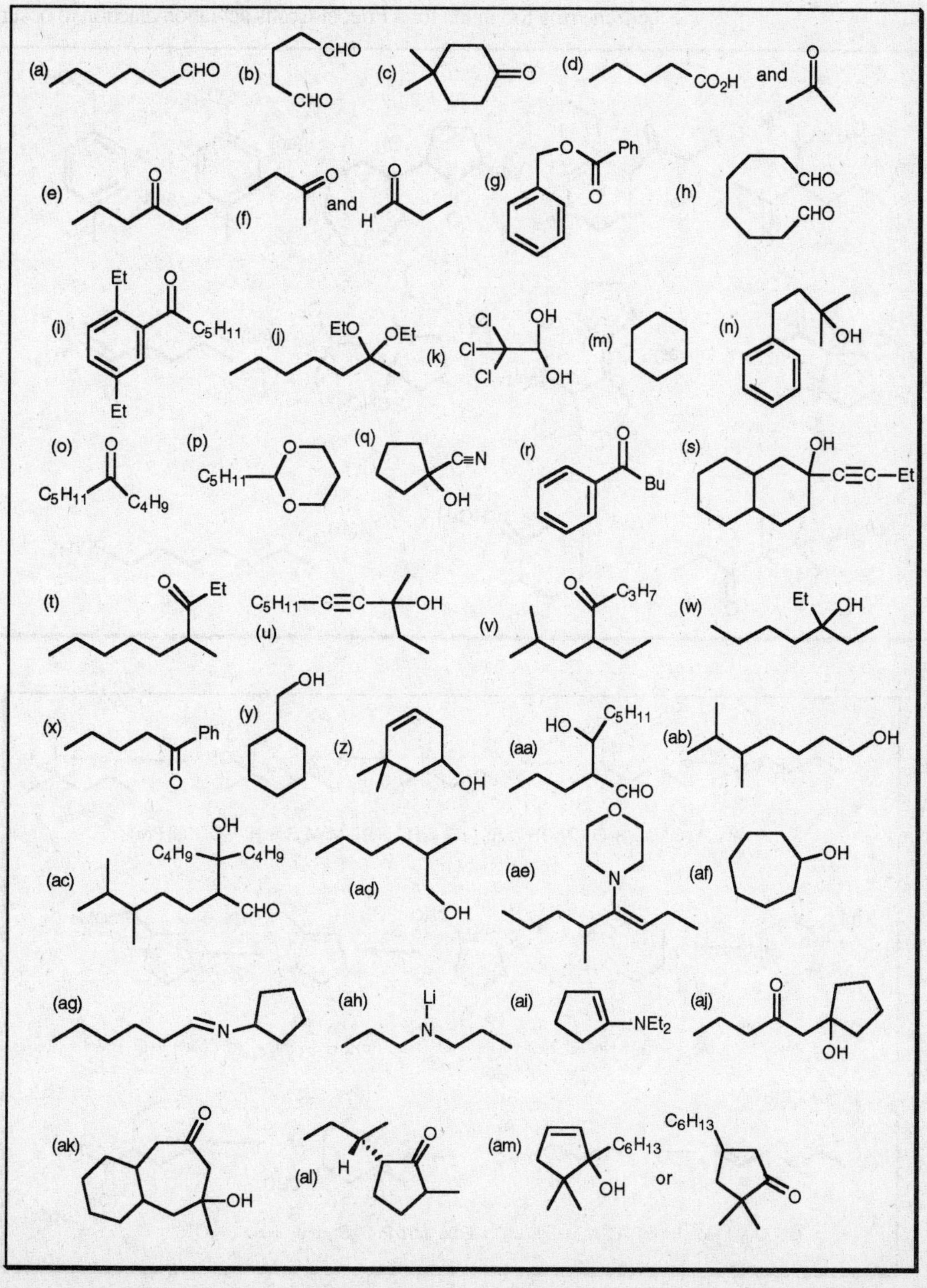

(a) CH₃(CH₂)₃CH₂CHO — pentanal chain with CHO

(b) CHO ... CHO

(c) methyl cyclohexanone with =O

(d) CO₂H and acetone

(e) ketone structure

(f) and H

(g) O—Ph benzyl benzoate

(h) cyclooctane CHO / CHO

(i) Et / C₅H₁₁ with Et

(j) EtO OEt

(k) Cl, Cl, Cl / OH, OH

(l) (m) cyclohexane

(n) Ph with OH

(o) C₅H₁₁ / C₄H₉

(p) C₅H₁₁ dioxane

(q) C≡N / OH

(r) Ph—C(=O)—Bu

(s) OH / C≡C—Et

(t) O / Et

(u) C₅H₁₁—C≡C— OH

(v) O / C₃H₇

(w) Et OH

(x) Ph / O

(y) OH

(z) OH

(aa) HO C₅H₁₁ / CHO

(ab) OH

(ac) OH / C₄H₉ C₄H₉ / CHO

(ad) OH

(ae) O / N / NEt₂ morpholine

(af) OH cyclooctanol

(ag) =N cyclopentyl

(ah) Li / N

(ai) NEt₂

(aj) O / OH cyclopentyl

(ak) O / OH methyl

(al) H / O methyl

(am) C₆H₁₃ / OH or C₆H₁₃ / O

Reaction (l) gives no reaction since the two nitro groups deactivate the benzene ring too much for a Friedel-Crafts acylation reaction to occur.

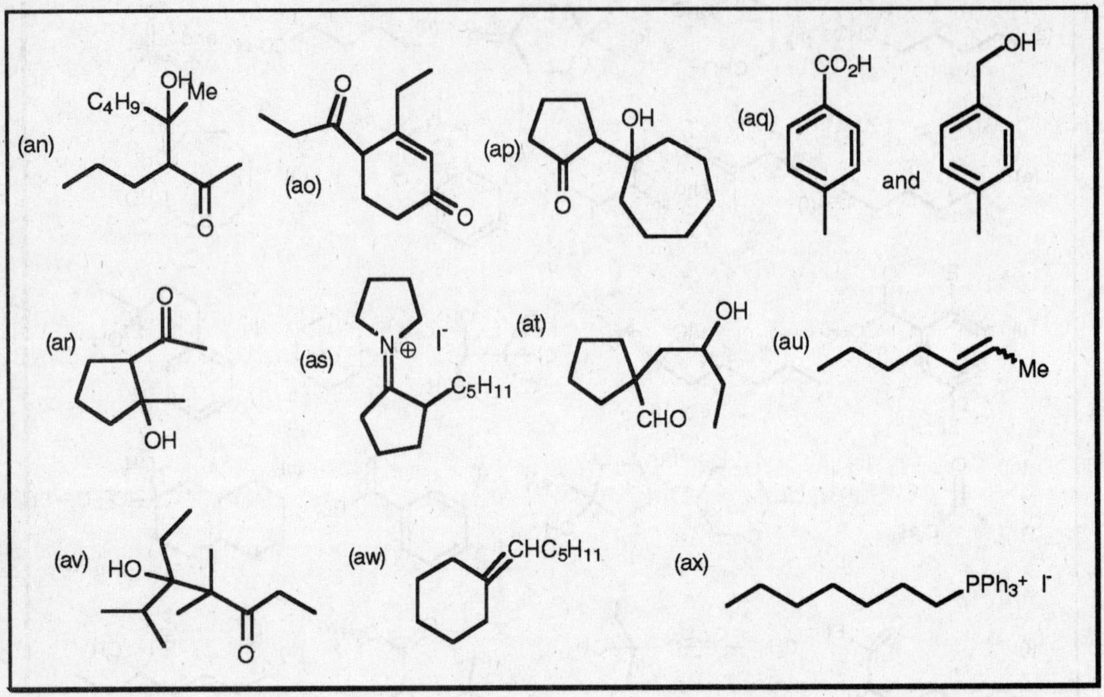

(an)

(ao)

(ap)

(aq) and

(ar)

(as)

(at)

(au)

(av)

(aw)

(ax)

18.

(a)

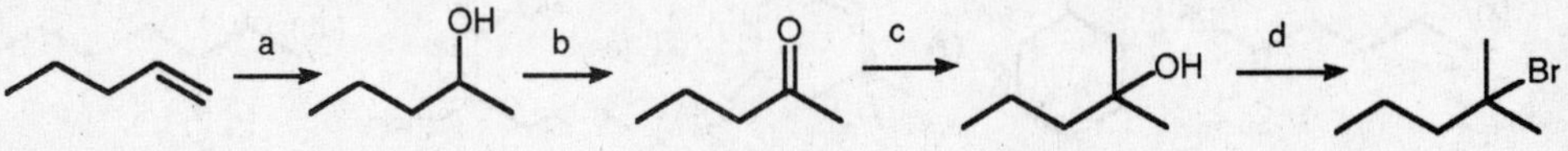

(a) i. Hg(OAc)$_2$/H$_2$O ii. NaBH$_4$ (b) CrO$_3$, H$^+$ (c) i. MeMgBr ii. H$_3$O$^+$ (d) PBr$_3$

(b)

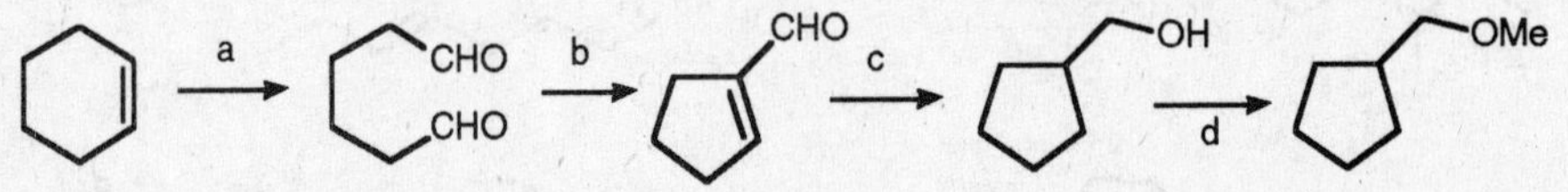

(a) i. O$_3$ ii. Me$_2$S   (b) i. NaOEt, EtOH ii. H$_3$O$^+$, heat   (c) 2 H$_2$, PtO$_2$ (d) i. NaH, THF ii. MeI

(c)

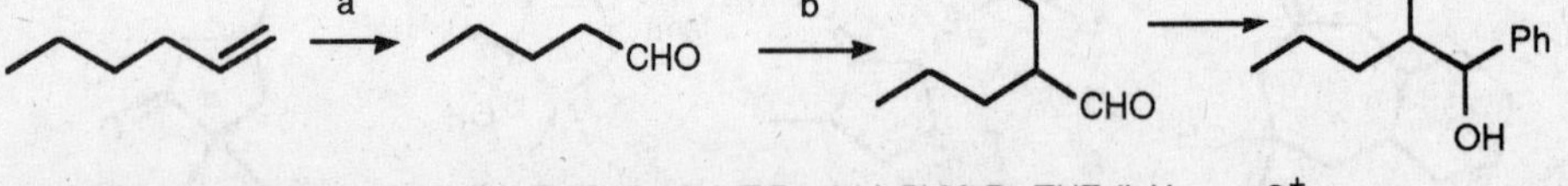

(a) i. O$_3$ i. Me$_2$S   (b) i. LDA, THF, -78°C i. EtBr   (c) i. PhMgBr, THF ii. H$_3$O$^+$

CHAPTER 14

1. (a) 4-ethyl-2-(1-methylbutyl)heptanoic acid. (b) 3,4,5-trimethylbenzoic acid. (c) 5,5-dichloro-2-methyl-7-phenylheptanoic acid. (d) hex-2-ynoic acid. (e) 4-methylhex-3E-enoic acid. (f) 2-ethylhep-6-ynoic acid. (g) 3-butyl-6-ethyl-2-pentyldecanoic acid.

2. The strongest acid is 2-chlorohexanoic acid, where the Cl is closest to the carboxyl group.

3. When the Cl is in the *ortho* position, there is a strong through-space inductive effect that strengthens the acid. This through-space effect is not possible when the Cl is in the *para* position.

4.

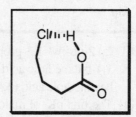

5. Water can solvate the two ions that are formed (H_3O^+ and acetate) much better than ethanol.

6. The iodoform test is specific for methyl ketones and methyl carbinols (CH[OH]Me) since a methyl group is required to eventually generate iodoform (CHI_3). A positive iodoform test (precipitation of the yellow solid, iodoform) indicates the presence of a methyl ketone unit in an unknown ketone.

7. When the OH of an acid is in the C_4 position, it can attack the carbonyl and cyclize to form a lactone. The product of this reaction is γ-butyrolactone, which does not have an acidic hydrogen.

8.

Ph—C(=O)—OEt $\xrightarrow{+H^+}$ Ph—C(=O⊕H)—OEt $\xrightarrow{+H_2O}$ Ph—C(OH)(OEt)—O⊕(H)(H) $\xrightarrow{-H^+}$ Ph—C(OH)(OEt)(OH) $\xrightarrow{+H^+}$ Ph—C(OH)(OH)—O⊕(H)—Et

$\xrightarrow{-\,EtOH}$ Ph—C(=O⊕H)—OH $\xrightarrow{-H^+}$ Ph—C(=O)—OH

9.

10. (a) 2-propyl-1,3-propanedioic acid (2-propylmalonic acid). (b) 2-ethyl-1,4-butanedioic acid (2-ethylsuccinic acid). (c) 3,4-diphenyl-1,6-hexanedioic acid (3,4-diphenylglutaric acid).

11. The first pK_a of malonic acid is lower (stronger acid) because the electron withdrawing carboxyl group is closer to the first carboxyl group.

12. (a) Phthalic acid (b) Terephthalic acid

13.

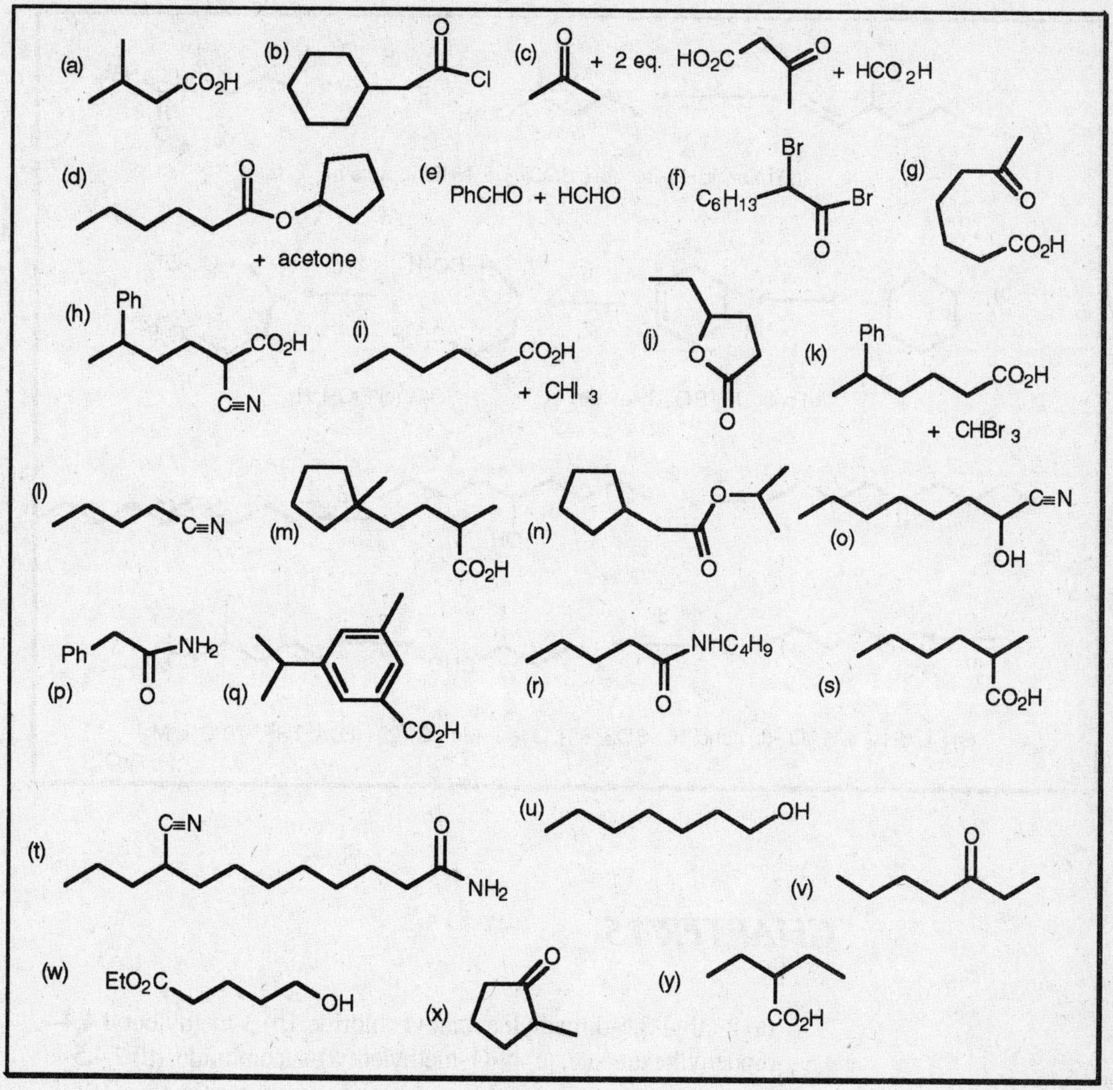

(a) CO$_2$H

(b) C(=O)Cl

(c) + 2 eq. HO$_2$C—CH$_2$—C(=O)—CH$_3$ + HCO$_2$H

(d) + acetone

(e) PhCHO + HCHO

(f) C$_6$H$_{13}$CHBr—C(=O)Br

(g) CO$_2$H

(h) Ph, CO$_2$H, C≡N

(i) CO$_2$H + CHI$_3$

(j)

(k) Ph, CO$_2$H + CHBr$_3$

(l) C≡N

(m) CO$_2$H

(n)

(o) C≡N, OH

(p) Ph—CH$_2$—C(=O)—NH$_2$

(q) CO$_2$H

(r) NHC$_4$H$_9$

(s) CO$_2$H

(t) C≡N NH$_2$

(u) OH

(v)

(w) EtO$_2$C OH

(x)

(y) CO$_2$H

14.

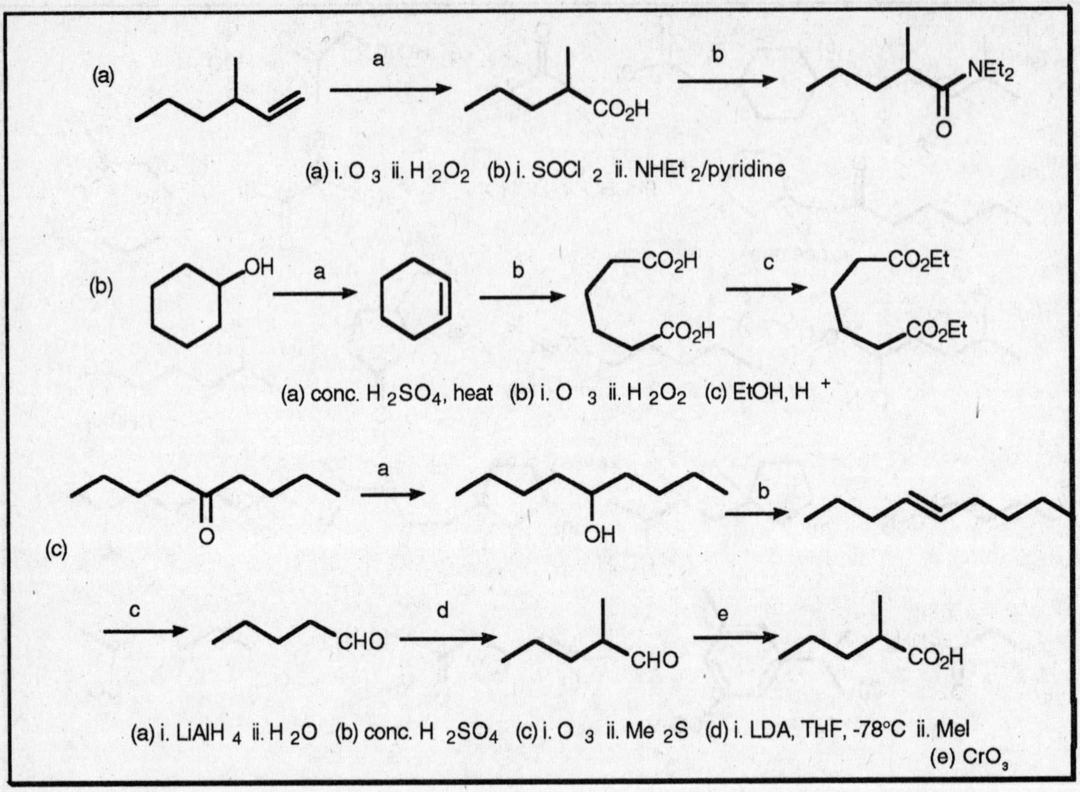

(a)

(a) i. O$_3$ ii. H$_2$O$_2$ (b) i. SOCl$_2$ ii. NHEt$_2$/pyridine

(b)

(a) conc. H$_2$SO$_4$, heat (b) i. O$_3$ ii. H$_2$O$_2$ (c) EtOH, H$^+$

(c)

(a) i. LiAlH$_4$ ii. H$_2$O (b) conc. H$_2$SO$_4$ (c) i. O$_3$ ii. Me$_2$S (d) i. LDA, THF, -78°C ii. MeI
(e) CrO$_3$

CHAPTER 15

1. (a) 2-ethyl-3,5-dimethylheptanoyl chloride. (b) 3-methylbutyl 4,4-diphenylhexanoate. (c) N-(1-methylethyl)-succinimide. (d) 2,4,5-triethylbenzamide. (e) 2-chloro-4,4-diphenylpentanolactone. (f) propanoic anhydride. (g) 2,2,4,4-tetramethylglutaric anhydride. (h) N-ethyl, N-propyl-3,4,5-trimethylhexanamide. (i) 2-methylethanoic propanoic anhydride. (j) N-butyl-5-methyl-2-pyrrolidinone.

2. Amines are more nucleophilic than alcohols and OR is a better leaving group than NR$_2$.

3.

4.

Although the mechanism is drawn with the NHEt group being neutral, in acid solution this basic amine will certainly be protonated to give the ammonium salt. It is also likely that proton transfers can occur to the amine rather than intermolecularly as shown. It is also likely that the ammonium slat is the actual acid catalyst in this reaction.

5. For ester enolates the only acidic hydrogens are on the α-carbon, and there is only one α-carbon. The kinetic and thermodynamic enolates are the same. The different conditions may be important for mixed Claisen condensations, however, in order to prevent or minimize unwanted cross coupling reactions.

6. If methanolic sodium methoxide is used as a base with an ethyl ester, transesterification can occur to give the methyl ester. This can produce a mixture of ethyl and methyl esters, which can complicate separation and identification of the products.

7. The two carbonyls in malonic esters are positioned such that the resulting enolate anion is resonance stabilized and the α-hydrogen is more acidic (two electron withdrawing groups). Since the carbonyls in succinic esters are separated by two carbons, there is no opportunity for resonance in the enolate anion and the greater distance of the second carbonyl group leads to a diminished inductive effect.

8. The enolate anion of ethyl propionate can react, under the equilibration conditions, with either ethyl propionate or methyl 2-methylbutanoate. Likewise, the enolate anion of methyl 2-methylbutanoate can react with ether ethyl propionate or methyl 2-methylbutanoate. This leads to four different Claisen condensation products.

9.

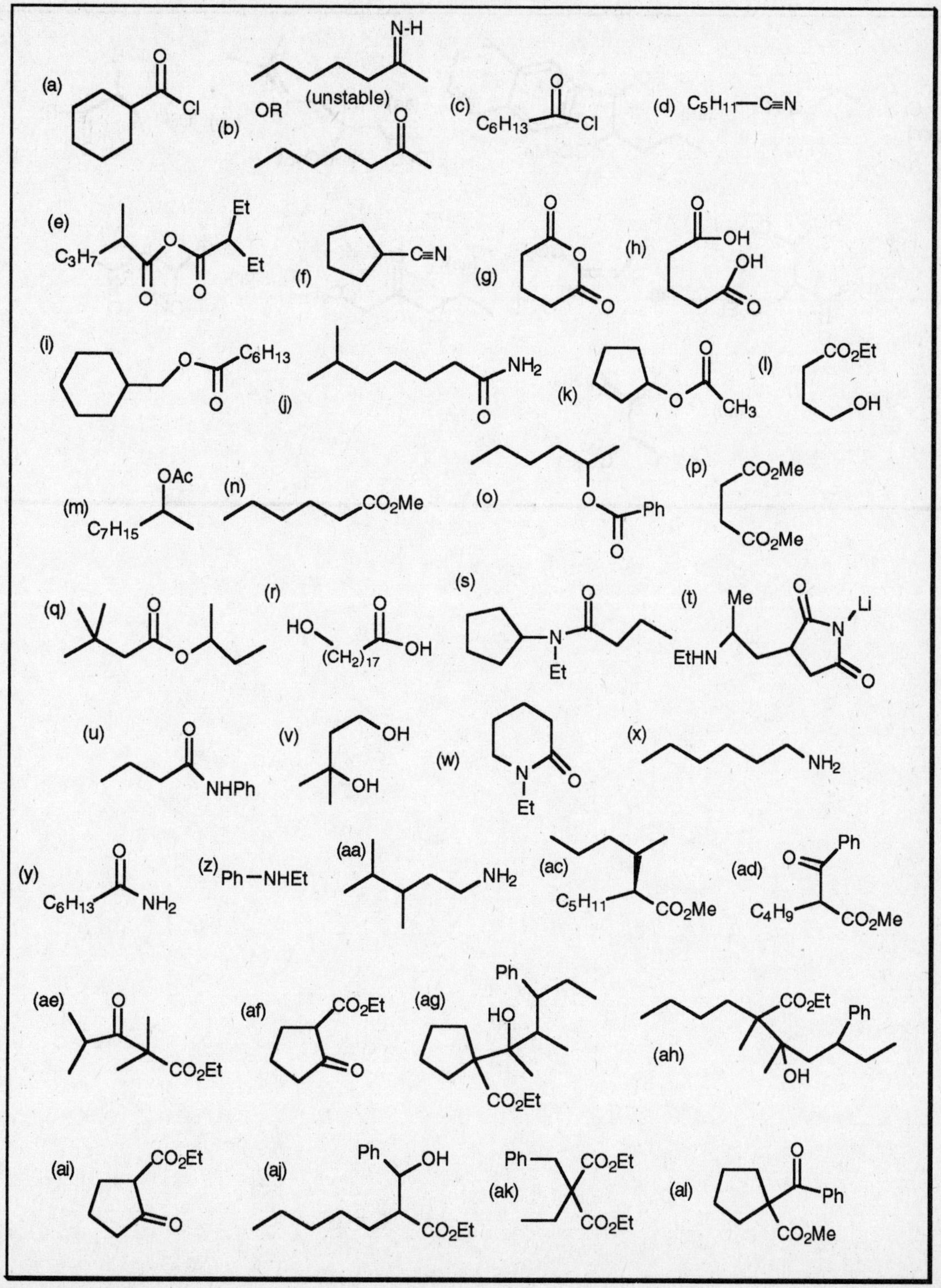

(a) [structure: cyclohexane with C(=O)Cl]

(b) OR [structure with N-H (unstable)] / [structure with C=O]

(c) C₆H₁₃–C(=O)Cl

(d) C₅H₁₁–C≡N

(e) C₃H₇ [ester structure with Et, Et]

(f) [cyclopentane–C≡N]

(g) [cyclic anhydride structure]

(h) [HOOC...COOH structure with OH]

(i) [cyclohexane–CH₂–O–C(=O)–C₆H₁₃]

(j) [structure with NH₂, C=O]

(k) [cyclopentane–O–C(=O)–CH₃]

(l) [CO₂Et ... OH structure]

(m) OAc [structure, C₇H₁₅]

(n) [structure with CO₂Me]

(o) [structure O–C(=O)–Ph]

(p) [CO₂Me ... CO₂Me structure]

(q) [ester structure]

(r) HO–(CH₂)₁₇–C(=O)–OH

(s) [cyclopentane–N(Et)–C(=O)–structure]

(t) [structure with Me, EtHN, N–Li, two C=O]

(u) [structure C(=O)–NHPh]

(v) [structure with OH, OH]

(w) [piperidinone with N–Et, C=O]

(x) [structure with NH₂]

(y) C₆H₁₃–C(=O)–NH₂

(z) Ph–NHEt

(aa) [structure with NH₂]

(ac) C₅H₁₁ [structure with CO₂Me]

(ad) [structure with Ph, C₄H₉, CO₂Me, C=O]

(ae) [structure with C=O, CO₂Et]

(af) [cyclopentanone with CO₂Et]

(ag) [structure with Ph, HO, cyclopentane, CO₂Et]

(ah) [structure with CO₂Et, Ph, OH]

(ai) [cyclopentanone with CO₂Et]

(aj) [structure with Ph, OH, CO₂Et]

(ak) [structure with Ph, CO₂Et, CO₂Et]

(al) [cyclopentane with C(=O)Ph, CO₂Me]

Reaction (ab) gives N.R. There is no α-hydrogen.

(am) C_6H_{13}—CH_2—CO_2H

(an)

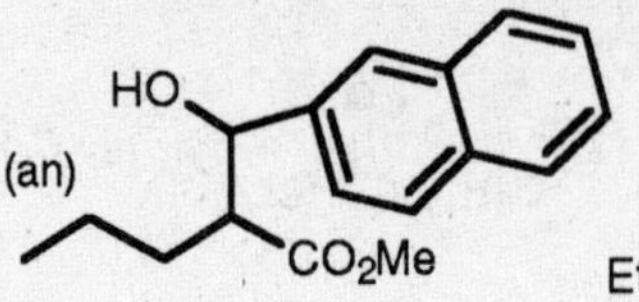

(ao)
EtO_2C CO_2Et

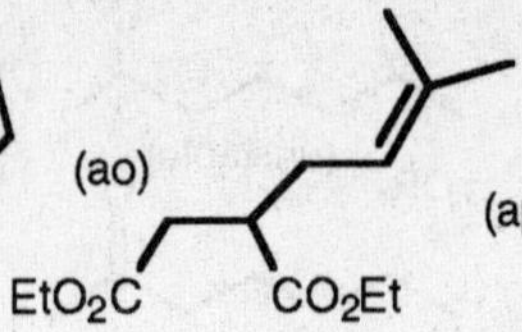

(ap) C_5H_{11} — with Br, Br, O

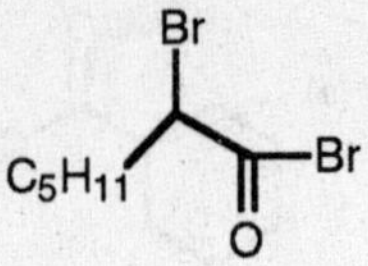

(aq) HO, C_4H_9 ; C_4H_9 — CO_2Et, O

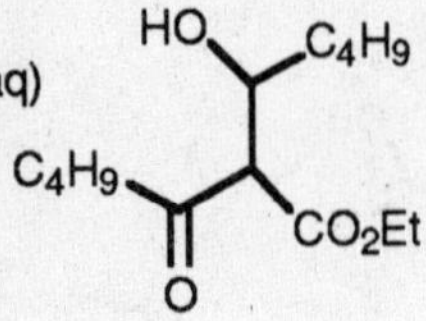

(ar) Ph — CO_2Et / CO_2Et

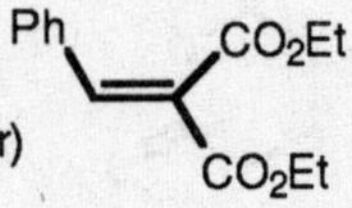

(as) O — C_9H_{19}

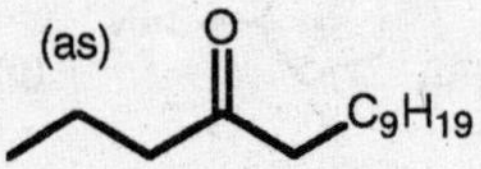

(at) Ph — OH, O

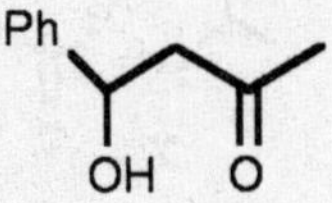

(au) O, C_6H_{13} ; C_5H_{11} — CO_2Et

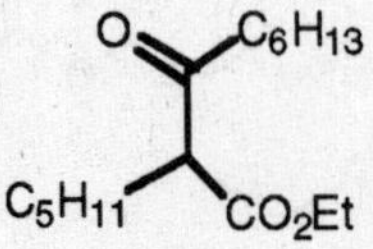

10.

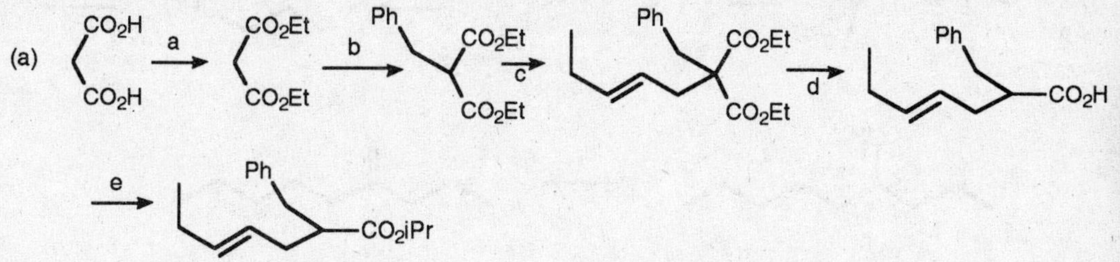

(a)

(a) EtOH, H$^+$ (b) i. NaOEt ii. PhCH$_2$Br   (c) i. NaOEt ii. 1-bromo-2E-pentene
(d) i. saponification (ii) 200°C   (e) iPrOH, cat. H$^+$

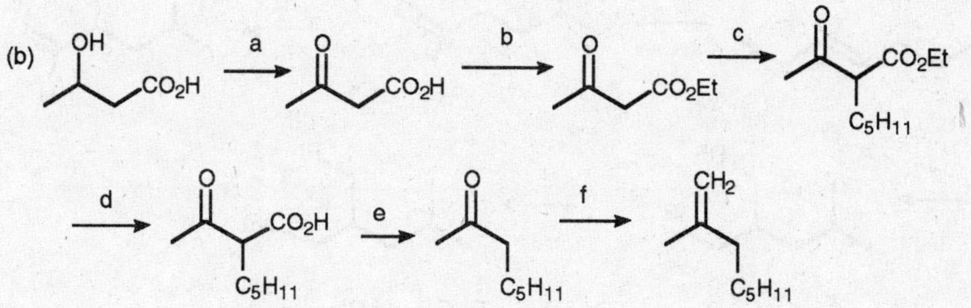

(b)

(a) CrO$_3$, H$^+$ (b) EtOH, H$^+$ (c) i. NaOEt ii. C$_5$H$_{11}$Br   (d) saponification   (e)200°C   (f) Ph$_3$P=CH$_2$

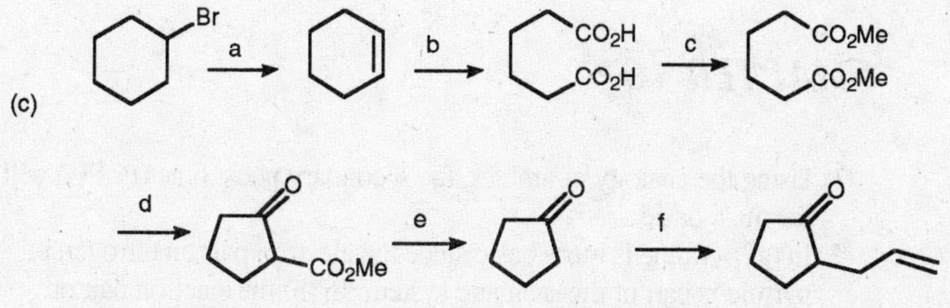

(c)

(a) KOH, EtOH   (b) i. O$_3$ ii. H$_2$O$_2$ (c) MeOH, H$^+$ (d) i. NaOMe ii. dil H$_3$O$^+$
(e) i. saponification ii. 200°C   (f) i. LDA, THF, -78°C ii. allyl bromide

(d)

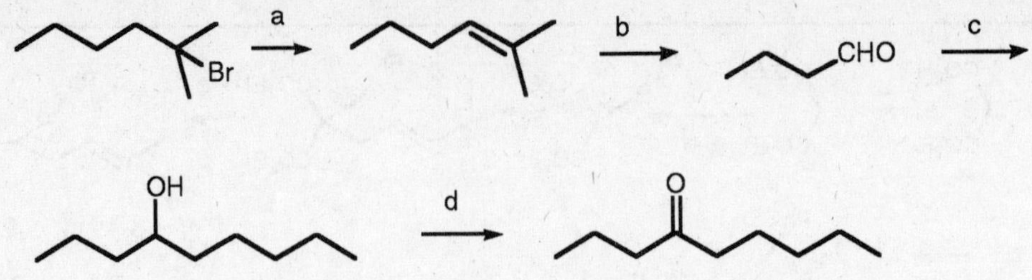

(a) KOH, EtOH (b) i. O_3 ii. Me_2S (c) i. $C_5H_{11}MgBr$ ii. H_3O^+ (d) CrO_3, H^+

(e)

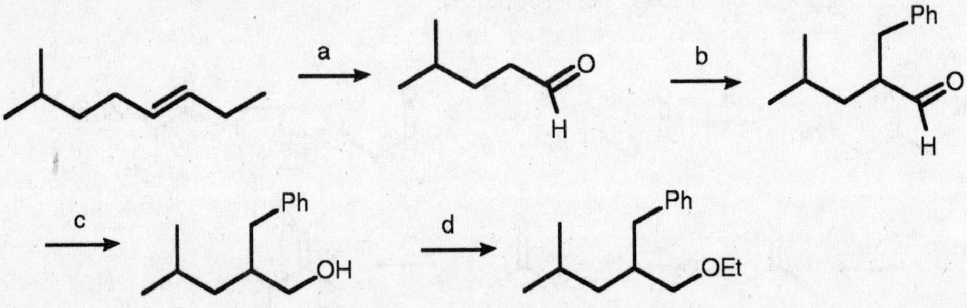

(a) i. O_3 ii. Me_2S (b) i. LDA, THF, -78°C ii. $PhCH_2Br$
(c) i. $NaBH_4$ ii. aq. NH_4Cl (d) i. NaH, THF ii. EtBr

CHAPTER 16

1. Using the analogy of amines, the secondary phosphine (Pr_2PH) will be the most basic.
2. In (a) pyridine is more basic since the electron pair on nitrogen in pyrrole is part of the aromatic system. In (b) the electron pair on nitrogen is 'tied back' in the bicyclic amine, which is more basic than triethylamine, which exists as the fluxsional isomers discussed in this chapter.
3. (a) N-ethyl-2,3-dimethylbutanamine. (b) triheptylamine. (c) 1-benzyl-2-methylpropanamine. (d) N-methyl, N-pentyl-4-bromoaniline. (e) N-benzyl-N,2-diphenylhexanamine. (f) N,2,2-trimethylpyrrolidine.
4. The Hinsberg test will distinguish this product as a secondary amine.
5. (a) 4-bromopyridine. (b) 3,4-dimethyl-N-propylpyrrole. (c) N-ethylpyridinium bromide. (d) 2,3,4-triethylpyrrole.

6. In (ac) there is no reaction since there are no aromatic hydrogens to be replaced.

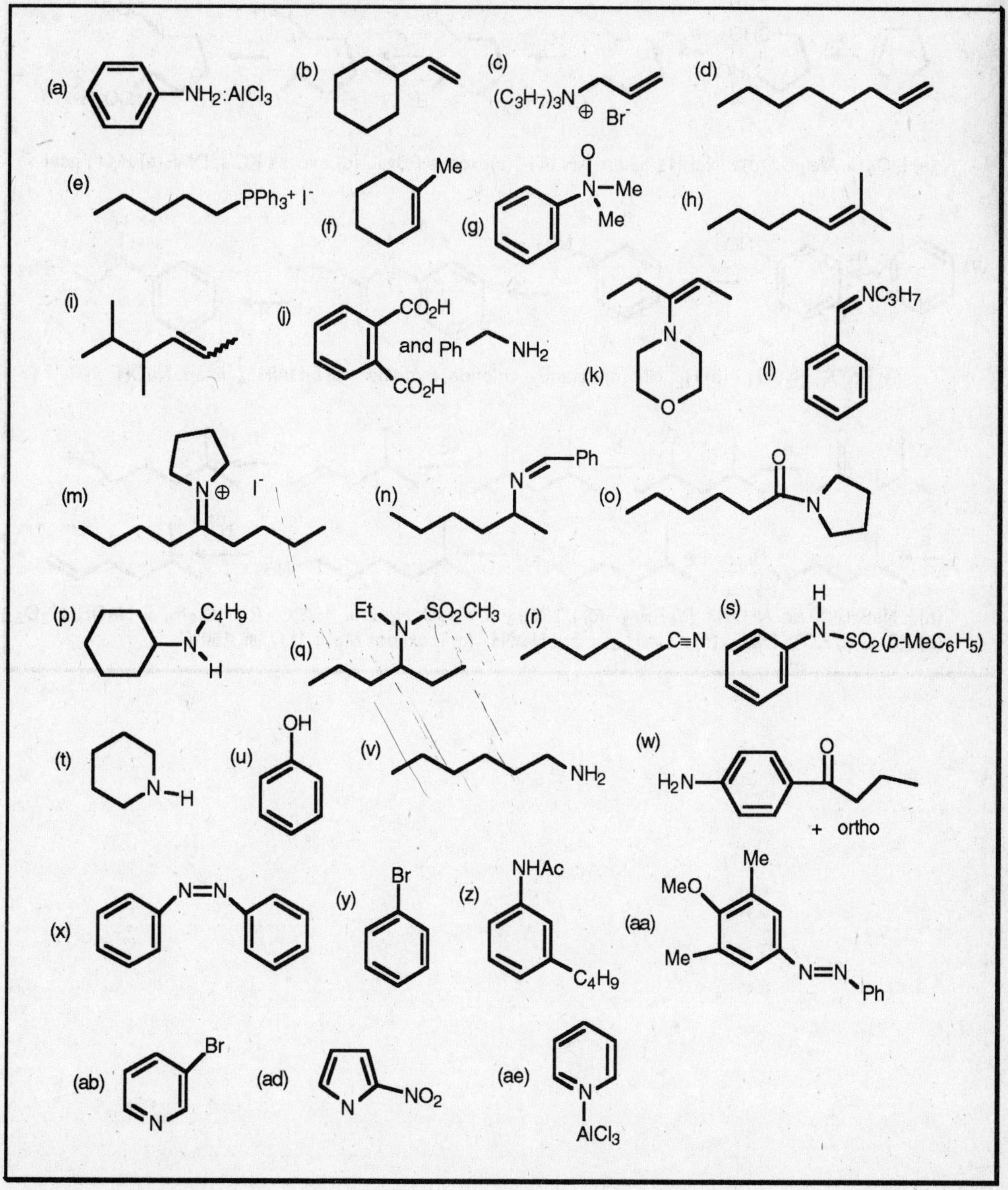

(a) —NH$_2$:AlCl$_3$

(b)

(c) (C$_3$H$_7$)$_3$N$^{\oplus}$ Br$^-$

(d)

(e) PPh$_3$$^+$ I$^-$

(f) Me

(g) N—Me, Me (N-oxide)

(h)

(i)

(j) CO$_2$H, CO$_2$H and Ph—CH$_2$—NH$_2$

(k) (morpholine enamine)

(l) NC$_3$H$_7$

(m) N$^{\oplus}$ I$^-$

(n) N=CH—Ph

(o) (pyrrolidine amide)

(p) C$_4$H$_9$, N, H

(q) Et—N—SO$_2$CH$_3$

(r) C≡N

(s) H, N—SO$_2$(p-MeC$_6$H$_5$)

(t) N—H

(u) OH

(v) NH$_2$

(w) H$_2$N— + ortho

(x) N=N

(y) Br

(z) NHAc, C$_4$H$_9$

(aa) MeO, Me, Me, N=N—Ph

(ab) Br N

(ad) N—NO$_2$

(ae) N AlCl$_3$

7.

(a) i. O$_3$ ii. Me$_2$S   (b) i. NaBH$_4$ ii. aq. NH$_4$Cl   (c)excess PBr$_3$ (d) excess KCN, DMF (e) H$_3$O$^+$, heat

(a) HNO$_3$, H$_2$SO$_4$ (b) H$_2$, Ni   (c) octanoyl chloride, pyridine   (d) i. LiAlH$_4$ ii. aq. NaOH

(a) i. NaBH$_4$ ii. aq. NH$_4$Cl   (b) PBr$_3$ (c) i. NMe$_3$ ii. Ag$_2$O, H$_2$O iii. 150°C   (d) i. B$_2$H$_6$ ii. NaOH, H$_2$O$_2$
(e) PBr$_3$ (f) KCN, DMF   (g) i. LiAlH$_4$ ii. aq. NaOH   (h) i. excess MeI ii. H$_2$O$_2$ iii. 150°C

(d)

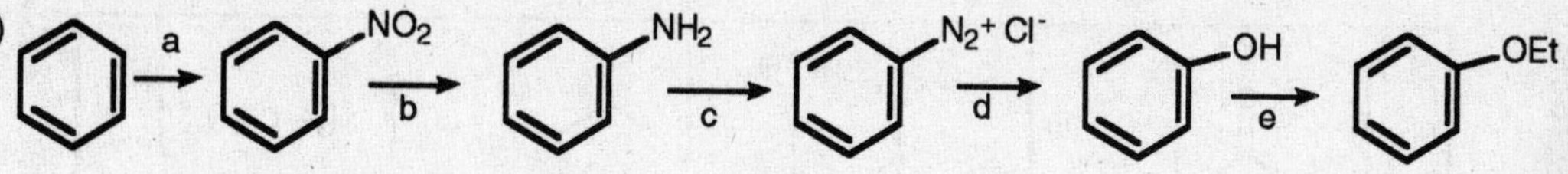

(a) HNO$_3$, H$_2$SO$_4$ (b) H$_2$, Ni (c) NaNO$_2$, HCl (d) H$_2$O, reflux (e) i. NaH, THF ii. Et-I

(e)

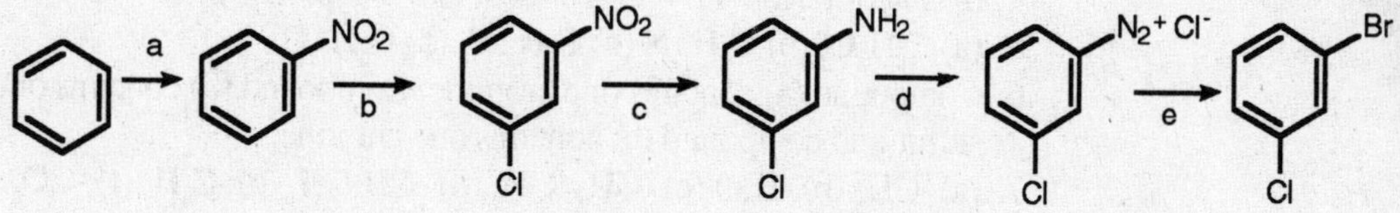

(a) HNO$_3$, H$_2$SO$_4$ (b) Cl$_2$, AlCl$_3$ (c) H$_2$, Pd (d) NaNO$_2$, HCl (e) CuBr

(f)

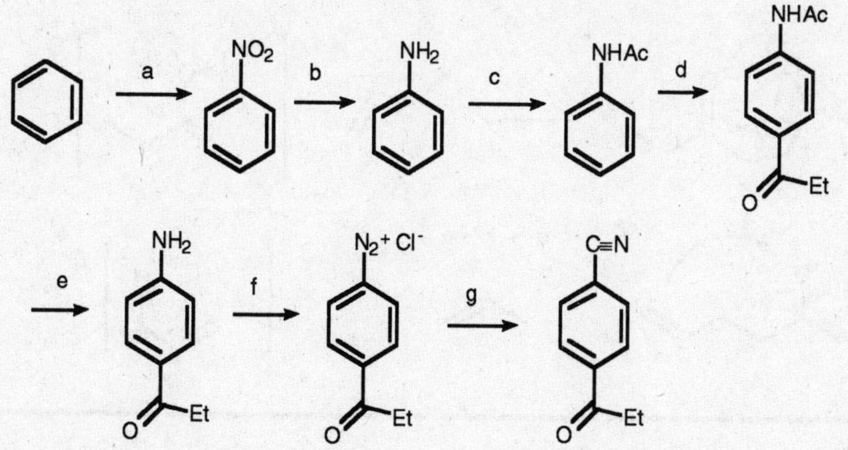

(a) HNO$_3$, H$_2$SO$_4$ (b) H$_2$, Ni (c) Ac$_2$O, pyridine (d) propanoyl chloride, AlCl$_3$ (e) saponification
(f) NaNO$_2$, HCl (g) CuCN

CHAPTER 17

1. (a) 6.16×10^{15} Hz. (b) 2.35×10^{-5} cm. (c) 4.34×10^2 nm. (d) 3.8×10^{-4} μ. (e) 4.67×10^7 Hz. (f) 6.09×10^{-2} m. (g) 1.14×10^8
2. (a) 1.61×10^3 kcal, 6.74×10^3 kJ. (b) 6.9×10^2 kcal, 2.89×10^3 kJ. (c) 52.2 eV. (d) 9.34 eV.

3.

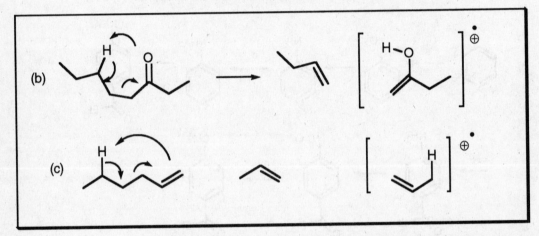

(a), (b), (c), (d) structures

4. In all cases, P = 100%. (a) P+1 = 5.55% of P, P+2 = 0.35% of P. (b) P+1 = 9.25% of P, P+2 = 0.39% of P. (c) P+1 = 5.55% of P, P+2 = 0.55% of P.(d) P+1 = 11.47% of P, P+2 = .0.82% of P.

5. (a) $C_8H_8O_2$ (b) $C_7H_{17}N$ (c) $C_5H_{12}N_2$ (d) $C_6H_{12}O$.

6. Compound (a) contains one bromine. Compound (b) contains one sulfur and compound (c) contains one chlorine.

7. (a) $-CH_3$ (b) $-H_2O$ (c) $-CH_2=CH_2$ (d) $-CH_2CH_3$ (e) $-C_3H_7$ (f) $-CO_2$.

8. Both (b) and (c) can undergo a McLafferty rearrangement.

(b)

(c)

9. Water can eventually dissolve pressed KBr. Brief exposure will 'etch' or otherwise damage the surface of the plates, interfering with the transmission of light and the quality of the infrared absorption peaks. It also drastically reduces the lifetime of the plates.

10. A bending vibration describes a bond vibration in which the two atoms connected to the bond move 'up and down' more or less in unison. A stretching vibration describes a bond vibration in which the two atoms connected to the bond move alternately away and towards each other, along the line between the two atoms (along the bond).

11. The strong $C \equiv C$ bond gives a much less intense signal. The C–O absorption band is rather strong. The C–O signal appears at lower energy since it takes less energy to make that bond vibrate.

12. (a) 1.488×10^{-23} (b) 1.073×10^{-23} (c) 0.996×10^{-23}

13. (a) The most prominent band is the carbonyl at 5.80μ (1724 cm^{-1}). In (b) The most prominent band is the O–H band at about 2.8μ (3571 cm^{-1}).

The bromine in (c) appears at about 16 μ (625 cm⁻¹) but is not diagnostic. The acid band (COOH) between 3-4 μ (3333 - 2500 cm⁻¹) is the most prominent and the carbonyl band at 5.80 μ (1724 cm⁻¹) is also diagnostic.

14. (a) 3 (b) 1 (c) 1 (d) 1 (e) 1 (f) none—this nucleus does not lead to the NMR phenomenon.

15. (a) 122.5 MHz. (b) 538.6 MHz. (c) 1273.3 MHz.

16. (a) 5.21 ppm. (b) 16.39 ppm. (c) 7.2 ppm. (d) 4.24 ppm.

17.

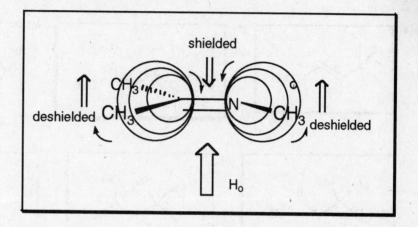

18. (a) HC–NR₂ (b) H–C–C=O (c) C=C–C–H (d) C≡C–H

19.

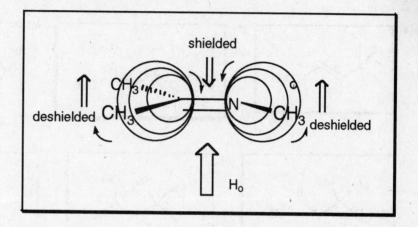

20. (a) 4 (b) 2 (c) 6 (d) 0 (e) 3.

21.

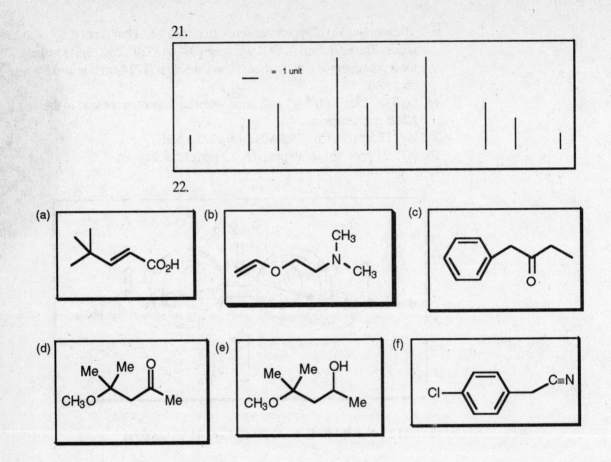

22.

(a)

(b)

(c)

(d)

(e)

(f)

CHAPTER 18

1. (a) 3-amino-2-(1-methylethyl)pentanoic acid. (b) 5-(N,N-dimethylamino)-4-methylheptanoic acid. (c) 4-(N,N-diethylamino)benzoic acid.

2.

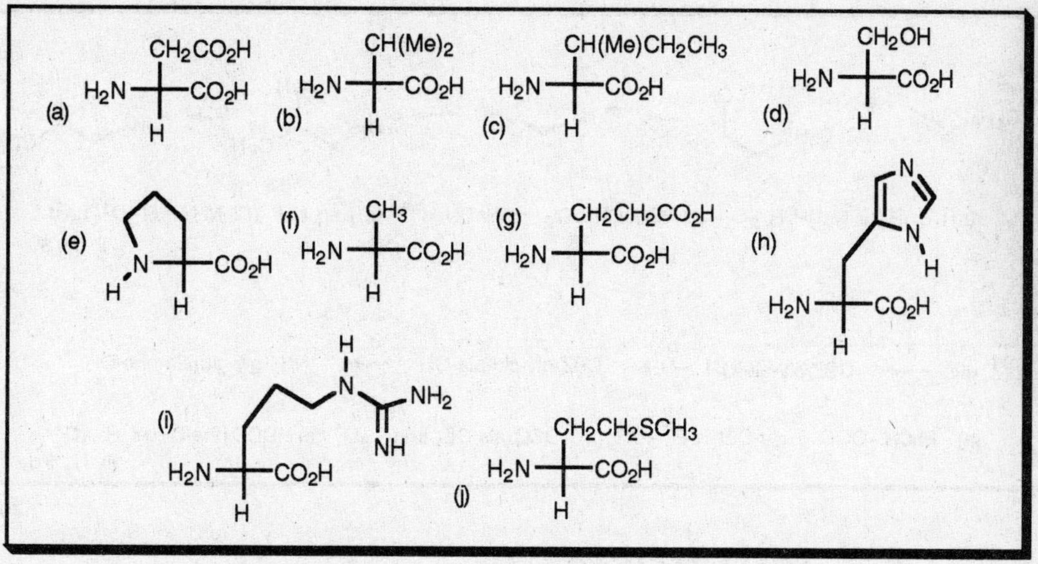

(a) H₂N—C(CH₂CO₂H)(CO₂H)—H

(b) H₂N—C(CH(Me)₂)(CO₂H)—H

(c) H₂N—C(CH(Me)CH₂CH₃)(CO₂H)—H

(d) H₂N—C(CH₂OH)(CO₂H)—H

(e) proline structure (H–N ring with CO₂H)

(f) H₂N—C(CH₃)(CO₂H)—H

(g) H₂N—C(CH₂CH₂CO₂H)(CO₂H)—H

(h) histidine structure, H₂N—C(imidazole-CH₂)(CO₂H)—H

(i) H₂N—C(CO₂H)—H with side chain to N–H, N, NH₂, NH (guanidino group)

(j) H₂N—C(CH₂CH₂SCH₃)(CO₂H)—H

3.

(a) valine amide structure with NH₂ and C(=O)NH₂

(b) thiohydantoin structure: N–H, C=S, N–Ph, C=O, with OH and CH₂

(c) ethyl-branched amino acid with NH₂ and CO₂H

(d) 2 × butyl–SH + cyclic disulfide (S–S ring)

(e) Ph—CH₂—C(NH₂)(CO₂H)

(f) chain with NHAc and CO₂Et

(g) O₂N substituted, NH—(2,4-dinitrophenyl)—NO₂, with CO₂Et

(h) H–N–C(=O)–O–tBu (Boc) with CO₂Et

(i) chain with NH₂ and CO₂Et

(j) NH·SO₂—naphthalene—NMe₂ with CO₂Et

(k) bis-indanedione imine (N linking two 1,3-indandione systems) plus MeS—CH₂CH₂CH₂—CHO

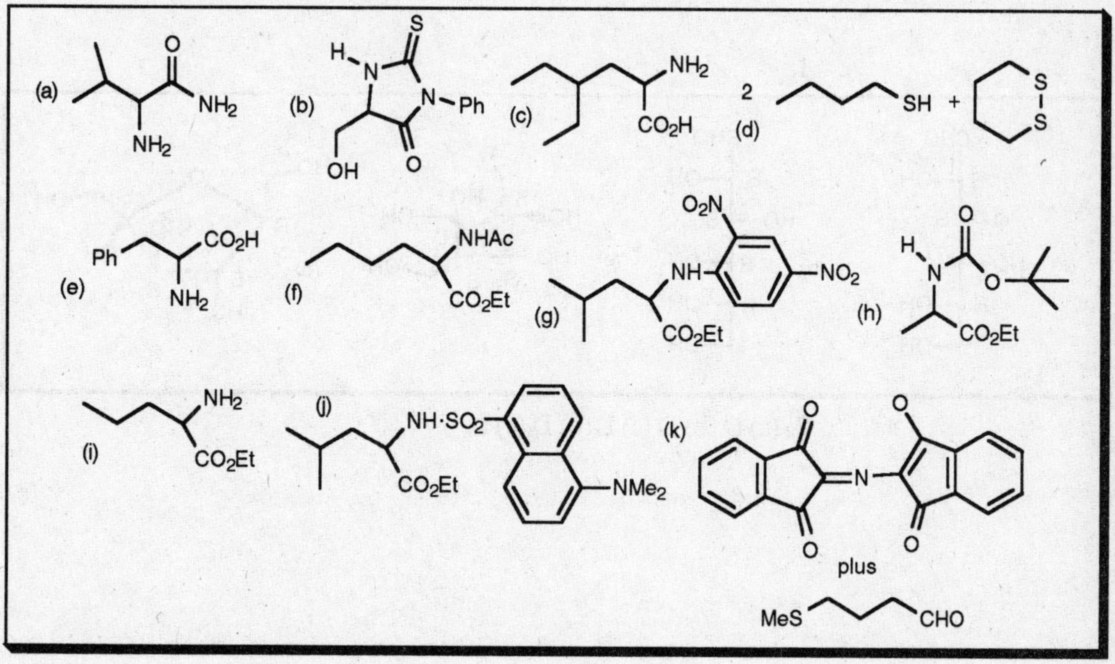

4.

(a)

(a) i. B$_2$H$_6$ ii. NaOH, H$_2$O$_2$ (b) PCC, CH$_2$Cl$_2$ (c) NaCN, H$^+$ (d) i. aq. NH$_4$Cl, NH$_3$ ii.H$_3$O$^+$, heat
ii. pH 8

(b)   gly $\xrightarrow{a}$ CBZ-gly-glu-OH $\xrightarrow{b}$ CBZ-gly-glu-ala-OH $\xrightarrow{c}$ NH$_2$-gly-glu-ala-phe-OH

(a) i. PhCH$_2$COCl ii. glu-OEt iii. H$_3$O$^+$ (b) i. DCC, ala-OEt ii. H$_3$O$^+$ (c) i. DCC,phe-OEt ii. H$_3$O$^+$
iii. H$_2$, Pd

CHAPTER 19

1.

2. (a) D (b) D (c) L (d) D (e) L.

3.

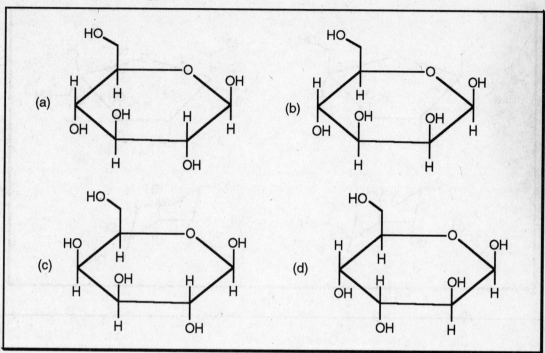

4.

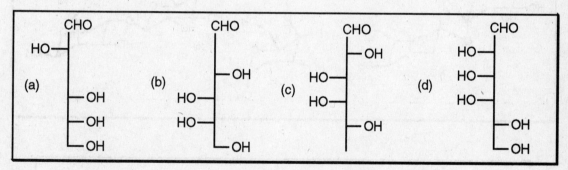

5.

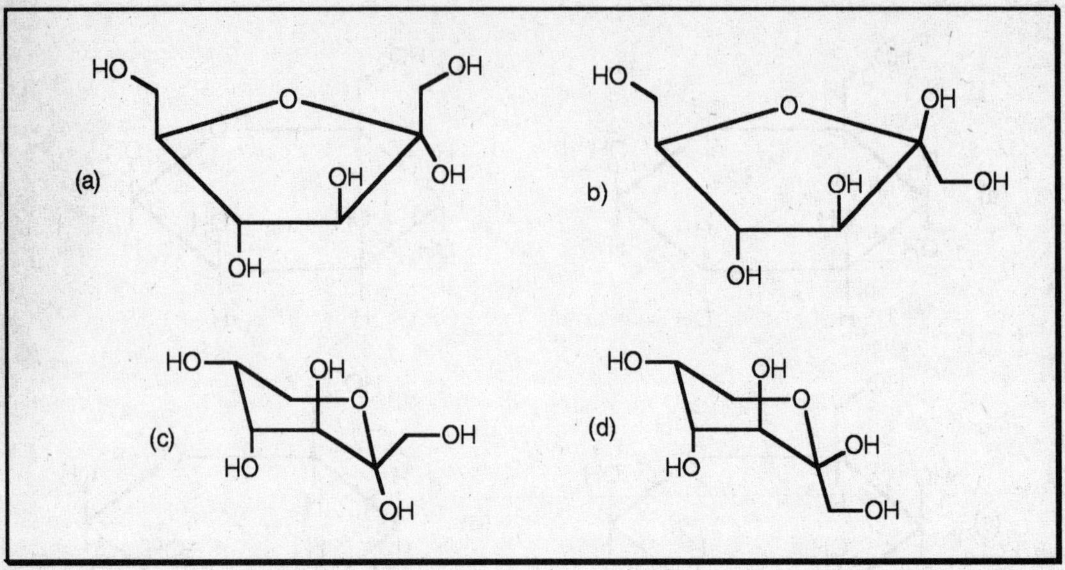

(a)

b)

(c)

(d)

6.

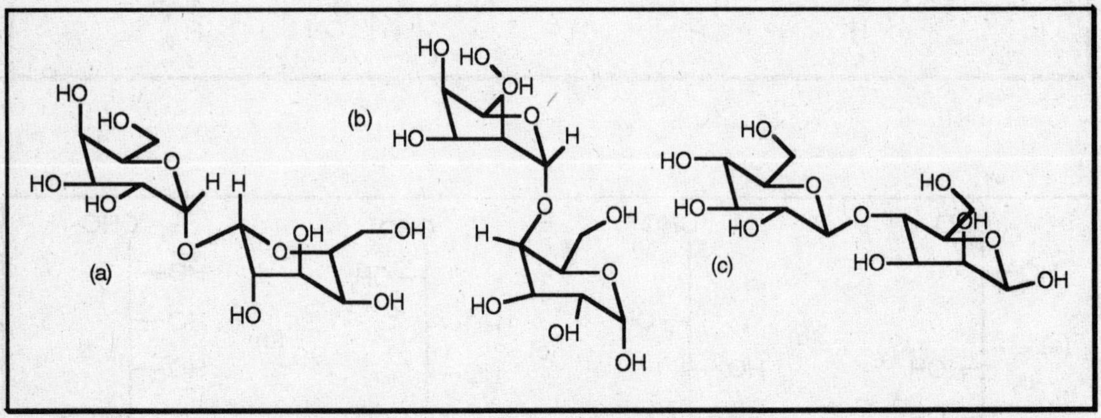

(a)

(b)

(c)

7.

(a)

(b)

(c)

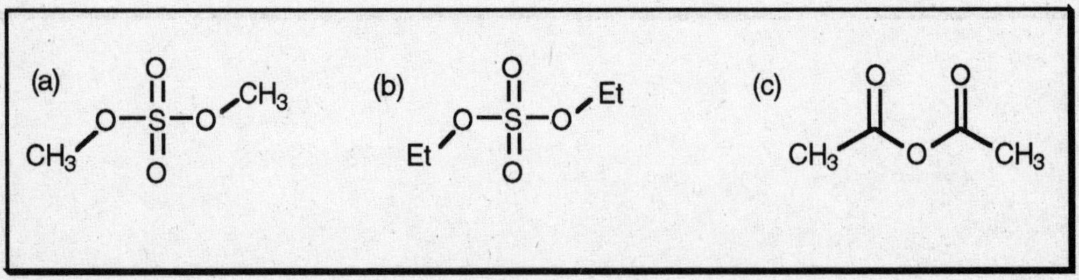

8.

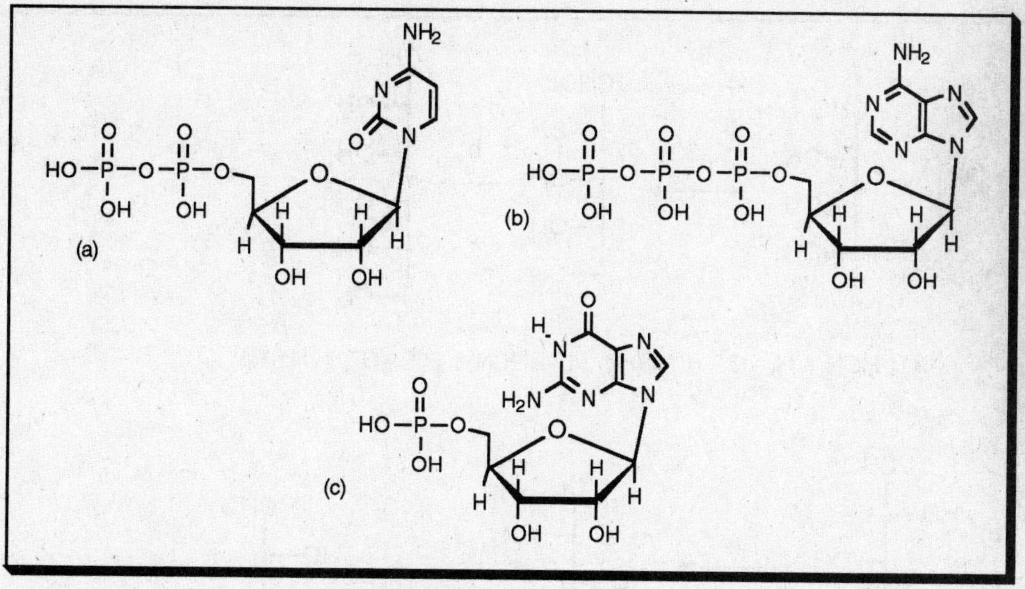

(a) (b) (c)

9. C-T-T-A-G-G-T-G-A-A-C-G

10.

(a) (b) (c) (d) (e) (f)

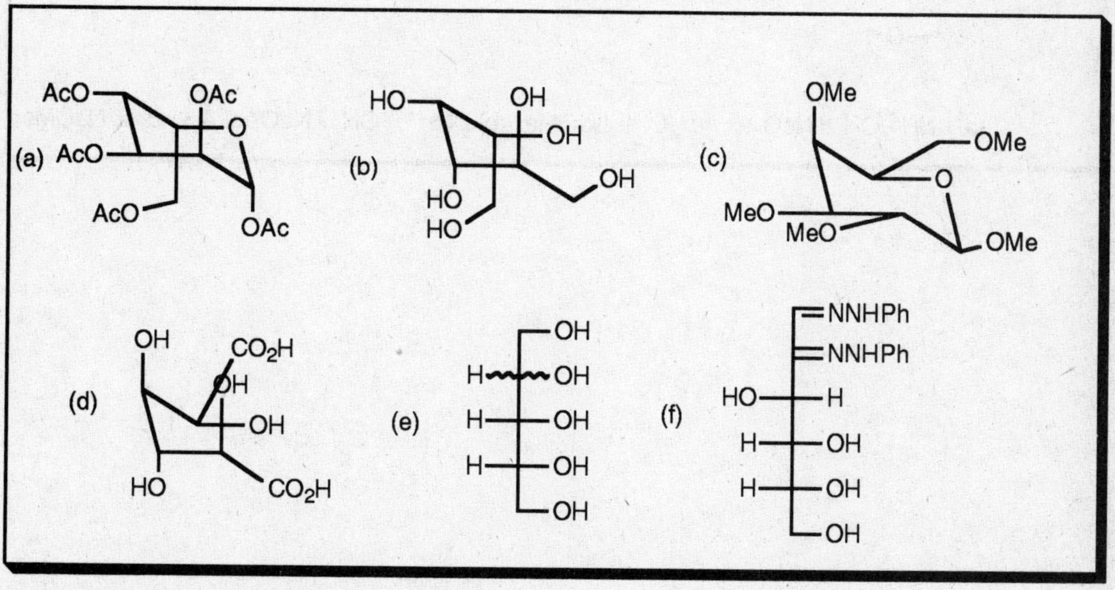

11.

(a)

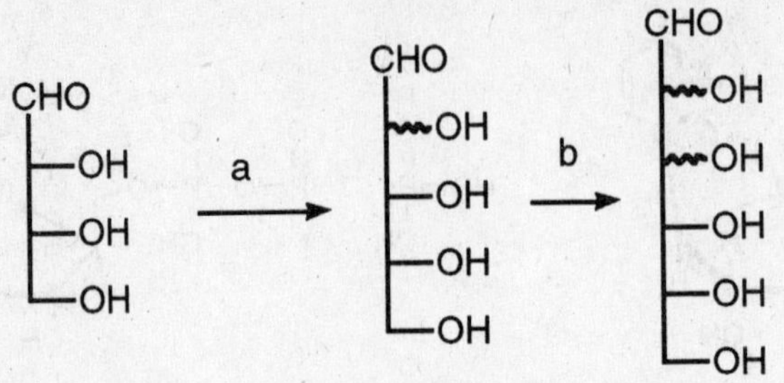

(a) i. HCN ii. H $_3$O$^+$ iii. Na(Hg) (b) i. HCN ii. H $_3$O$^+$ iii. Na(Hg)

(b)

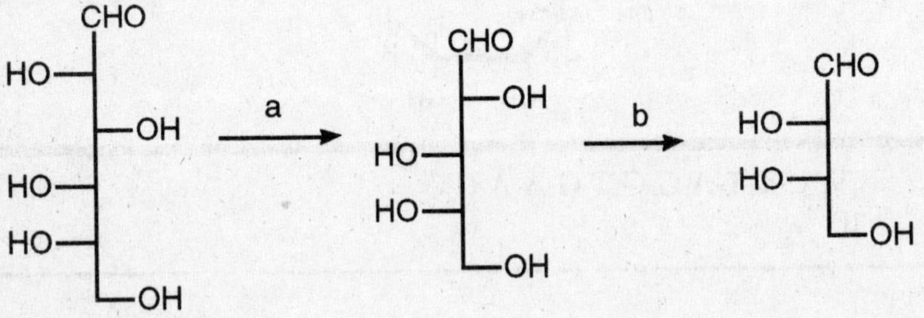

(a) i. NH $_2$OH ii. NaOAc, Ac $_2$O iii. NaOMe (b) i. NH $_2$OH ii. NaOAc, Ac $_2$O iii. NaOMe

CHAPTER 20

1.

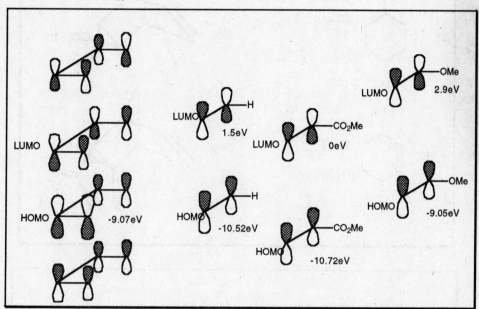

The ΔE for butadiene-ethene is 10.57 eV and is 9.07 eV for butadiene-methyl acrylate and 11.07 eV for butadiene-methyl vinyl ether. Methyl acrylate reacts faster since it has the smallest ΔE.

2. (a), (b) and (c). Triene (d) might react with a diene in a Diels-Alder reaction but it cannot react as a diene (with another alkene).

3.

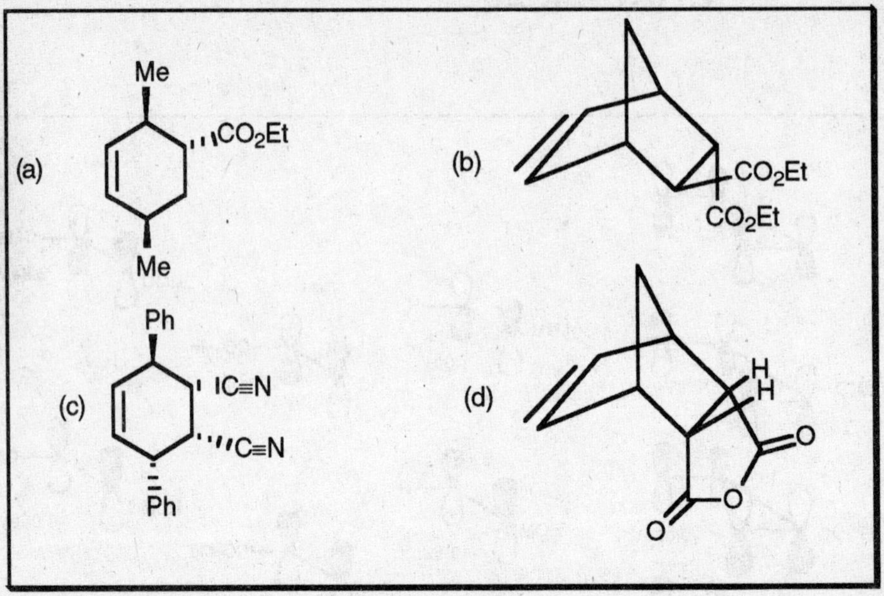

(a)

Me
CO₂Et
Me

(b)

CO₂Et
CO₂Et

(c)

Ph
IC≡N
C≡N
Ph

(d)

H
H
O
O
O

4.

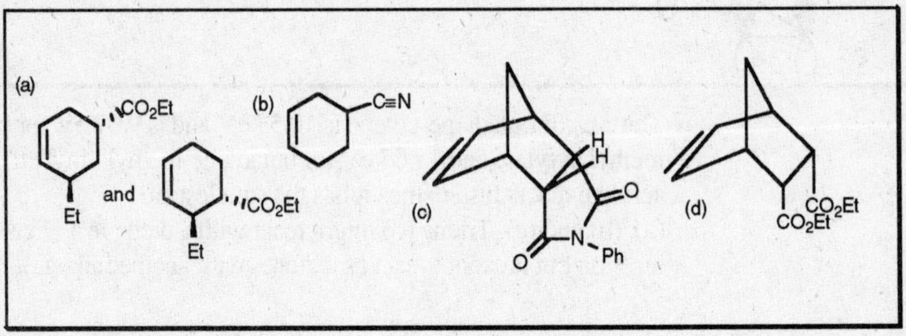

(a)

CO₂Et
Et
and
CO₂Et
Et

(b)

C≡N

(c)

H
H
O
N—Ph
O

(d)

CO₂Et
CO₂Et

5.

(a)

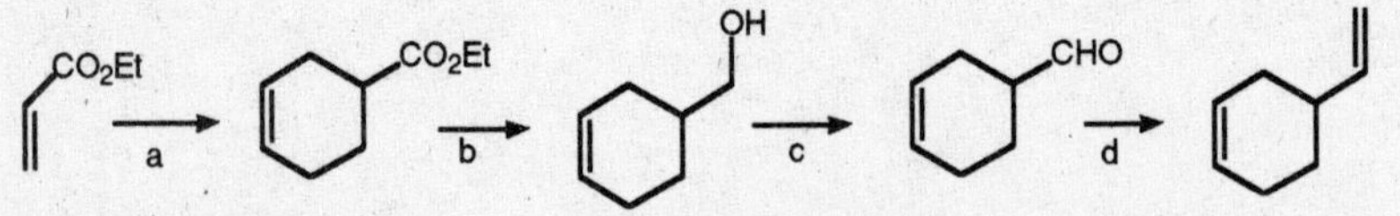

CO₂Et
→a→
CO₂Et
→b→
OH
→c→
CHO
→d→

(a) 1,3-butadiene, heat   (b) i. LiAlH₄ ii. H₃O⁺   (c) PCC, CH₂Cl₂   (d) Ph₃P=CH₂

(b)

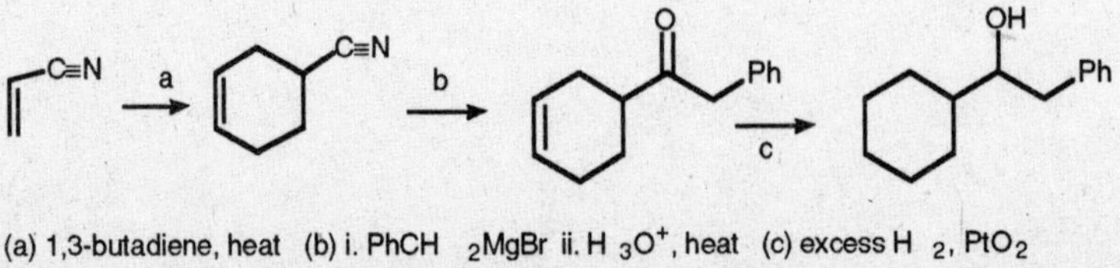

C≡N
→a→
C≡N
→b→
O
Ph
→c→
OH
Ph

(a) 1,3-butadiene, heat   (b) i. PhCH₂MgBr ii. H₃O⁺, heat   (c) excess H₂, PtO₂

Index

OTHER BOOKS IN THE HARPERCOLLINS COLLEGE OUTLINE SERIES

ART
History of Art 0-06-467131-3
Introduction to Art 0-06-467122-4

BUSINESS
Business Calculus 0-06-467136-4
Business Communications 0-06-467155-0
Introduction to Business 0-06-467104-6
Introduction to Management 0-06-467127-5
Introduction to Marketing 0-06-467130-5

CHEMISTRY
College Chemistry 0-06-467120-8
Organic Chemistry 0-06-467126-7

COMPUTERS
Computers and Information Processing 0-06-467176-3
Introduction to Computer Science and Programming
   0-06-467145-3
Understanding Computers 0-06-467163-1

ECONOMICS
Introduction to Economics 0-06-467113-5
Managerial Economics 0-06-467172-0

ENGLISH LANGUAGE AND LITERATURE
English Grammar 0-06-467109-7
English Literature From 1785 0-06-467150-X
English Literature To 1785 0-06-467114-3
Persuasive Writing 0-06-467175-5

FOREIGN LANGUAGE
French Grammar 0-06-467128-3
German Grammar 0-06-467159-3
Spanish Grammar 0-06-467129-1
Wheelock's Latin Grammar 0-06-467177-1
Workbook for Wheelock's Latin Grammar
   0-06-467171-2

HISTORY
Ancient History 0-06-467119-4
British History 0-06-467110-0
Modern European History 0-06-467112-7
Russian History 0-06-467117-8
20th Century United States History 0-06-467132-1
United States History From 1865 0-06-467100-3
United States History to 1877 0-06-467111-9
Western Civilization From 1500 0-06-467102-X

Western Civilization To 1500 0-06-467101-1
World History From 1500 0-06-467138-0
World History to 1648 0-06-467123-2

MATHEMATICS
Advanced Calculus 0-06-467139-9
Advanced Math for Engineers and Scientists
   0-06-467151-8
Applied Complex Variables 0-06-467152-6
Basic Mathematics 0-06-467143-7
Calculus with Analytic Geometry 0-06-467161-5
College Algebra 0-06-467140-2
Elementary Algebra 0-06-467118-6
Finite Mathematics with Calculus 0-06-467164-X
Intermediate Algebra 0-06-467137-2
Introduction to Calculus 0-06-467125-9
Introduction to Statistics 0-06-467134-8
Ordinary Differential Equations 0-06-467133-X
Precalculus Mathematics: Functions & Graphs
   0-06-467165-8
Survey of Mathematics 0-06-467135-6

MUSIC
Harmony and Voice Leading 0-06-467148-8
History of Western Music 0-06-467107-7
Introduction to Music 0-06-467108-9
Music Theory 0-06-467168-2

PHILOSOPHY
Ethics 0-06-467166-6
History of Philosophy 0-06-467142-9
Introduction to Philosophy 0-06-467124-0

POLITICAL SCIENCE
The Constitution of the United States 0-06-467105-4
Introduction to Government 0-06-467156-9

PSYCHOLOGY
Abnormal Psychology 0-06-467121-6
Child Development 0-06-467149-6
Introduction to Psychology 0-06-467103-8
Personality: Theories and Processes 0-06-467115-1
Social Psychology 0-06-467157-7

SOCIOLOGY
Introduction to Sociology 0-06-467106-2
Marriage and the Family 0-06-467147-X

Available at your local bookstore or directly from HarperCollins at 1-800-331-3761.